P9-AQC-167

FOR REFERENCE
Do not take from this room

# GREAT LIVES FROM HISTORY

# GREAT LIVES FROM HISTORY

## Twentieth Century Series

**Volume 5**

Rou-Z

*Edited by*

FRANK N. MAGILL

SALEM PRESS

Pasadena, California     Englewood Cliffs, New Jersey

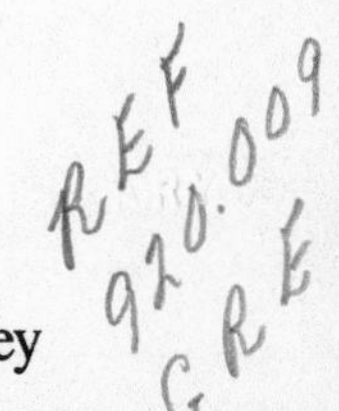

∞ The paper used in these volumes conforms to the American National Standard for Permanence of Paper for Printed Library Materials, Z39.48-1984.

**Library of Congress Cataloging-in-Publication Data**
Great lives from history. Twentieth century series / edited by Frank N. Magill.
p. cm.
Includes bibliographical references.
Includes index.
1. Biography—20th century. 2. Community leadership. 3. World history. I. Magill, Frank Northen, 1907- .
CT120.G69 1990
920′.009′04—dc20
[B]
[920] 90-8613
ISBN 0-89356-565-2 (set) CIP
ISBN 0-89356-570-9 (volume 5) AC

PRINTED IN THE UNITED STATES OF AMERICA

# LIST OF BIOGRAPHIES IN VOLUME FIVE

LIST OF BIOGRAPHIES IN VOLUME FIVE

# GREAT LIVES FROM HISTORY

# GEORGES ROUAULT

*Born:* May 27, 1871; Paris, France

*Died:* February 13, 1958; Paris, France

*Area of Achievement:* Art

*Contribution:* One of the greatest painters of the twentieth century, Rouault combined an existential philosophy and a strong Catholic faith with a prodigious artistic energy to amass a unique and distinctly identifiable body of work over fully seventy years of creativity.

## *Early Life*

Georges Rouault was born during a bombardment of Paris during the "troubled days of the Commune," his mother having taken shelter in the cellar of a house in the Belleville district. His cabinetmaker father worked at a piano factory; Rouault acquired much of his artistic taste from his maternal grandfather, Alexandre Champdavoine, a collector of the work of Honoré Daumier, Gustave Courbet, and Édouard Manet.

However oversimplified the observation may be, much of Rouault's distinct painting style can be traced to his very early apprenticeship in the stained-glass ateliers of Georges Hirsch. In his mature work, the bright colors and clearly defined shapes, separated by dark areas, are suggestive of the traditional stained-glass techniques.

Formal training came from the famous art studios at the École des Beaux-Arts, briefly under Élie Delaunay, but quickly followed by the tutelage of Gustave Moreau, whose favorite pupil he became. Rouault began his career with traditional paintings in line with the principles of the Academy painters but was encouraged by Moreau to seek his own way. His desire to find his own style can be seen as the positive outcome of his failure to win first prize in several early competitions. In 1895, encouraged by Moreau, he left the École to paint a series of sacred and profane scenes set in fantastic landscapes. A series of notebooks that the student maintained during his school years, *Souvenirs intimes* (1926; intimate memories), attest the importance on Rouault's whole aesthetic attitude of Moreau's lectures and admonitions to paint the spiritual life.

The death of Moreau in 1898 left Rouault without his best friend and spiritual adviser. Yet, in his will, Moreau arranged for Rouault to manage the archives of the Musée Gustave Moreau, thereby freeing Rouault from financial difficulties and allowing him to concentrate on his painting. Scholars have listed as Rouault's early influences the art of Daumier, Francisco de Goya, and Paul Cézanne, and the writings of Joris-Karl Huysmans, Léon Bloy, and Fyodor Dostoevski.

## *Life's Work*

Rouault's career parallels the Fauvist movement, but he was not among them; their descent into the primitive was contrary to Rouault's ascent into the spiritual, although their use of color bears definite similarities, with its richness and purity. Influenced by the Catholic writer Bloy (who befriended him but loathed his paintings), Rouault's work became more and more religious, sometimes in subject matter, as with his innumerable portraits of the Passion, but equally often in his approach to secular subjects. By 1905, figures such as clowns, prostitutes, and peasants, always shown in despair, never cartooned or ridiculed but depicted at a moment of deep philosophical grief, can be found in his paintings. This tendency to take seriously the angst of the common person has been connected with the existentialist philosophers of this and later periods, notably fellow Frenchmen Jean-Paul Sartre and Albert Camus, and also the earlier philosophers Søren Kierkegaard and Martin Heidegger.

Rouault's existential view, however, was a Christian one, in which suffering was humankind's earthly fate and temptations of the flesh a universal shortcoming. Almost never dealing with inanimate objects or landscapes, Rouault sought to capture the deep tragedy of human existence, expressed most succinctly in the faces of clowns, lower-class subjects, and Christ figures, often on the cross. His obsession with the crucifixion came from his acute sensitivity to the fact of Christ the man, capable of experiencing human pain and death.

Marrying, in 1908, Marthe Le Sidaner, who bore him four children, he began to settle into his working habits, a meticulous reworking of every painting and engraving over a period of years. A period of residence in Versailles in 1911 brought friendship with Jacques Maritain, who was to influence his religious views profoundly. The years until the beginning of World War I were filled with work in watercolors of a particularly brilliant palette, as he examined the themes of circus and prostitution equally fully. An extremely private man, especially for the glittering world of Parisian modern art, Rouault needed to be sought out by his slowly growing admirers. Exhibits of his paintings were sparse on the calendars of the leading galleries, and those that did manage to acquire his work could only get hold of a few paintings at a time. In this sense, Rouault was truly an expressionist painter (another movement of this time, but centered in Germany), more concerned with putting his personal feelings onto canvas than with satisfying a commercial market.

Even though he was a prolific painter all of his life, there was a period from about 1910 to 1918 in which Rouault concentrated on other media, working in gouache, ink, and watercolor, only to return to oil painting occasionally; some years later, he again concentrated on oil, a slower, more contemplative medium.

Almost in passing, the established world of traditional art began to acknowledge Rouault's genius. The Musée d'Unterlinden in Colmar purchased his early work *Child Jesus Among the Doctors* in 1919; other museum purchases of the kind that ensured a growing reputation followed, as Rouault was preparing for his first major show, a 1924 retrospective at Bruet's Gallery in Paris, which brought together all of his scattered works from the past twenty years.

The year 1913 marked Rouault's commercial success and his first artistic commitment to a major gallery; it was the year that Ambroise Vollard bought his entire studio's output, including rights to subsequent paintings. By investing in the relatively unknown painter (Vollard had originally been attracted to some ceramic work of the artist), he made both a wise investment and a commitment to support the painter's work for life. He had previously bought the studio of Maurice de Vlaminck, who was to become a major force in the Fauvist movement, paralleling Rouault's career but separate from it.

At the center of the Vollard-Rouault relationship were two controversies. The first was artistic: Vollard commissioned a publication of a major engraving project, one hundred works originally to be called *Miserere et guerre* but later reduced by almost half and changed to *Miserere*, consisting of fifty-eight works. The project combined the energies of the two men for a period of thirty years. The project was impeded by Rouault's insistence on reworking the smallest detail of each engraving and Vollard's insistence on perfection. A similar attention to detail by both men accounts for the overlayering of paint on the canvases, resulting from the reworking of entire canvases sometimes over a period of twenty years. Other features of Rouault's style were the intense coloration of discrete segments, the outlining of areas, a frontal presentation of the subjects accompanied by a two-dimensionality common to icons, and a pronounced elongation of forms. The stained-glass windows of his youth were more than passingly instrumental in their effect on Rouault's perceptions.

The second controversy involved the right of the artist to change his work after its purchase by another party. Upon the death of Vollard in 1939, Rouault sued the estate for the return of some eight hundred paintings in Vollard's possession, claiming that they were unfinished and that his reputation as a painter would be jeopardized by their sale in the unfinished state. He won his case in 1947 and one year later, in front of horrified witnesses whose attitude was as though a wake were taking place, destroyed more than three hundred paintings, believing that he would never have a chance in his lifetime to complete them properly.

The Paris World's Fair of 1937 finally brought to Rouault the world recognition he long deserved. Entitled "Masters of Independent Art," the exhibit came just in time, as World War II was to endanger all Paris galleries and artists alike. His popularity in the United States came rather late in life, with a traveling exhibit in 1940-1941 to Washington, Boston, and San Francisco and major exhibits at the Museum of Modern Art (a print exhibit in 1938 and a comprehensive show in 1945) and the Cleveland Art Museum, 1953.

Rouault's last works, to which he refers as the "dawn" after a lifetime of painting "twilights," were iconographic landscapes of ancient Eastern lands, with Christ and other religious figures now distantly on the horizon, receding from individuality, blending into the pastoral landscape. He died in 1958, at the age of eighty-six.

*Summary*

The megalomania and egotism of the stereotypical artist were entirely absent in Georges Rouault, replaced by an intensity of commitment to perfection in everything he did. The act of painting was for Rouault an act of prayer, an intimate cry of anguish into the ontological void. Where other painters kept one eye on their commercial value, Rouault's attention to his public image was less selfish; it came from a desire to unify his artistic voice into one symphony for the eye, a kind of supplication before his Master.

That the modern art public has accepted his work as the masterpieces they are does not automatically mean it understands the man who created them. More than one art critic has noted that Rouault's life paralleled Dante's *Inferno*, *Purgatorio*, and *Paradiso*; the artist lived long enough to find peace in his art. Rouault is too often loved as the great religious essayists are loved: for the beauty of the form rather than the zeal of the content. It is not too much to say that Rouault prayed with his brush, or that his prayers were all one prayer: the *Miserere*.

*Bibliography*

Fowlie, Wallace. *Jacob's Night: The Religious Renascence in France*. New York: Sheed & Ward, 1947. Chapter 2, "Rouault: The Art of a Painter," is a discussion of Rouault's distinctly Catholic view of Sartre's existentialism, manifested in the anguished generic portraits of prostitutes, clowns, and peasants. A study of Rouault's religion, the chapter fits into Fowlie's larger discussion of the renaissance of Catholicism in early twentieth century France, indebted to the writings of Charles Péguy and Jacques Maritain. Index of last names.

*Georges Rouault*. New York: Crown, 1983. This collection illustrates the variety and intensity of Rouault's work, with representatives of all styles and subjects. One reproduction, *Pierrot* (1920), is tipped in for optimum clarity. Text follows Rouault's life through the years of apprenticeship, "days of anger," during the "school of stoicism," and "en route to peace." Biographical chronicle, strong bibliography, and table of main exhibits.

Getlein, Dorothy, and Frank Getlein. *Georges Rouault's "Miserere."* Milwaukee: Bruce, 1964. A presentation of the final fifty-eight monochrome prints, with subjective and poetic commentaries by the Getleins. The long preface traces Rouault's life and concentrates on the techniques and the history of the production of the *Miserere* collection. This project took up a large part of the center of Rouault's career; the Getlein study is particularly valuable for an analysis of Rouault's Catholicism, the light shed on the Vollard-Rouault relationship, and the details of the multiple engraving techniques of this important print series, spanning thirty-five years from conception to birth.

Rouault, Georges. *G. Rouault, 1871-1958*. Text by Bernard Dorival. Translated by P. S. Falla. Manchester, England: Manchester City Art Galleries and the Arts Council of Great Britain, 1974. Dorival's introduction is a poetic recapitulation of Rouault's qualities. Detailed descriptions of paintings, with provenance and identifications, prove valuable to understanding his slow, meticulous processes.

Venturi, Lionelle. *Rouault: A Biographical and Critical Study.* Translated by James Emmons. New York: Skira, 1959. An appreciation by one of the first Rouault scholars, whose catalog of the 1940 exhibit still stands as the definitive Rouault biography. An introductory essay accompanies fifty-eight magnificent color reproductions, tipped in and therefore of a superior quality, but disappointingly small in size. Includes an exhaustive chronological survey with parallel artistic events, text references, bibliography, list of exhibitions, index of names, and list of color plates, all definitive and comprehensive.

*Thomas J. Taylor*

# GERD VON RUNDSTEDT

*Born:* December 12, 1875; Aschersleben, Germany
*Died:* February 24, 1953; Celle, West Germany
*Area of Achievement:* The military
*Contribution:* Rundstedt, though not an innovator, supported Manstein's revolutionary strategy, which led to victory over France in 1940. He did not participate in anti-Hitler conspiracies, though he disliked the Nazis and Hitler in particular. Prussian military honor and obedience guided his professional and personal life.

## *Early Life*

Karl Rudolf Gerd von Rundstedt's father was a Prussian general of old Brandenburg/Prussian nobility, which had provided officers for the Prussian army for centuries. Young Rundstedt became a cadet at age sixteen and was commissioned in the infantry a year later. He served as battalion and regimental adjutant and received further training at the Kriegsakademie, the army's "graduate school." In 1907, Rundstedt entered the prestigious General Staff, Germany's military elite. After serving as company commander, Rundstedt spent the war years in General Staff positions.

Rundstedt advanced rapidly in the postwar *Reichswehr.* Initially he served as divisional chief of staff and from 1923 to 1927 as commander of an infantry regiment; in 1927, he became major general and commander of the Second Cavalry Division. In 1929, Rundstedt advanced to lieutenant general and in January, 1932, became commander of the Third Division and of the Military District (*Wehrkreis*) III (Berlin). In October, 1932, three months before Adolf Hitler assumed power, Rundstedt was promoted to general of infantry and became commander of Army Group I (Berlin), one of two Army Groups within the *Reichswehr.* Rundstedt had thus reached the highest rank within the *Reichswehr.* Rundstedt's unwilling involvement in politics began in July, 1932, when Chancellor Franz von Papen was named federal commissioner for the state of Prussia, in what history has dubbed the "Rape of Prussia": the transfer of the state's executive power to the federal chancellor. (This move put Prussia's police and executive functions under Papen's authority, a position that Hitler inherited in January, 1933, upon becoming chancellor.) As commander of Military District III (Berlin), Rundstedt exercised this executive power, in keeping with constitutional provision.

## *Life's Work*

Rundstedt advocated modernization of the infantry, in both equipment and training. He called for mechanization and the increase of firepower, being convinced that the tanks' function was to support the infantry, contrary to views being developed in Germany and elsewhere. Rundstedt, however, did not oppose creation of armored (tank) divisions, as long as that development did not hinder the infantry's modernization.

Rundstedt had been unhappy with the Weimar Republic's democratic nature but also quickly developed dislike for the Nazis, the "brown dirt," as he called them. In 1934, when President Paul von Hindenburg died, Rundstedt, together with the entire army, took a new personal oath to Hitler, a fact that proved to be of great consequence later. His deeply rooted, traditional Prussian sense of honor brought him into conflict with Hitler during the Fritsch Crisis in early 1938, when he protested Fritsch's dismissal as the Army's commander in chief. Thereafter, however, he urged his fellow generals to avoid the "rash actions" contemplated by some and await the outcome of legal proceedings. Hitler, who respected Rundstedt's natural dignity and military ability, promoted him to colonel general in March, 1938. During the Sudeten Crisis of October, 1938, he commanded Army Group IV of Germany's expanded *Wehrmacht*. Rundstedt did not involve himself in the incipient conspiracy against Hitler, centered on the army's former commander in chief, General Ludwig Beck, though he was aware of it. In late October, 1938, Rundstedt accepted retirement, ostensibly at his request, actually as part of a purge that removed a number of senior officers.

Within less than a year, however, Rundstedt was recalled. Neither he nor his fellow generals opposed war with Poland to recover lost territory (Versailles Treaty, 1919), especially after Hitler's treaty with Joseph Stalin made war with the Soviets unlikely. The generals, including Rundstedt, however, realized that a Polish war might lead to a wider conflict. During the Polish campaign, Rundstedt commanded Army Group South. His forces cut off the Polish retreat across the Vistula River and played a key role in the capture of Warsaw. Rundstedt vainly urged Hitler not to bombard Warsaw and to extend humane treatment to the civilian population.

Following a brief and unwelcome tenure as commander in chief east (occupation of Poland in cooperation with Germany's civilian administration of that unhappy country), Rundstedt asked for and received reassignment as commander of Army Group A facing France. Rundstedt strongly supported the revised operational plans for the western campaign (following the need to discard the original Schlieffen-like plan). The new plan, developed by General Erich von Manstein, his chief of staff in Poland and on the Western Front, called for a daring armored thrust through the Ardennes, trapping the Allied field armies in Belgium and northern France. It was on Rundstedt's advice that Hitler accepted this controversial plan, initially rejected by the army's high command.

Following the western victory, Rundstedt and eleven others were elevated to field marshals, Rundstedt being the eldest. He was slated to play a major role in Operation Sea Lion, the invasion of Great Britain. Following its cancellation, Rundstedt commanded Army Group South during the invasion of the Soviet Union in June, 1941. His task was to capture the Ukraine and the Caucasus oil fields and to penetrate as far east as Stalingrad to cut off the Soviets' southern supply route. Army Group South had an inadequate force of 750 tanks, and Rundstedt soon recognized that this task was impossible. When Hitler rejected first his request for additional forces and then his proposal to fall back on a defensive winter line, Rundstedt asked to be replaced. In December, 1941, he retired again, as part of a larger shake-up within the high command.

Despite strong differences in opinion, Hitler again recalled Rundstedt, this time as commander in chief west, to create the "Atlantic Wall." Rundstedt's Prussian sense of duty, as well as the natural ambition of military men, caused him to return to active duty again and again, even though he no longer believed in German victory.

Little was done on anti-invasion defenses until the matter became increasingly urgent in 1943. Soon a controversy arose between Rundstedt and his subordinate, General Erwin Rommel. Rommel wanted to place all reserves, especially the armored divisions, in the immediate vicinity of the potential landing sites, while Rundstedt desired to hold the reserves back. Rommel believed that the invasion could only be defeated on the beaches, and Rundstedt, though doubtful that the invaders could be stopped at all, wanted to engage them in a war of movement in the interior. General Heinz Guderian, Germany's paramount tank expert, as well as Hitler, agreed with Rundstedt. Rundstedt compromised by strengthening the forward units but retaining the armor in strategic reserve. The question of who would control these reserves, Hitler or the field commanders, produced yet another controversy.

Following the invasion and the inability to stop the Allies in Normandy, Rundstedt requested permission to withdraw behind the Seine River. Hitler refused, and, when Field Marshal Wilhelm Keitel, chief of staff of the high command, telephoned on June 29, 1944, to inquire what could be done in such a desperate situation, Rundstedt responded acidly, "Quit, you idiots! What else do you still want to do?" On July 6, 1944, Rundstedt was retired a third time.

By 1944, a determined military resistance to Hitler had coalesced. Rundstedt was in sympathy but was unwilling to commit himself to the cause, invoking his 1934 Hitler oath. Following the failed plot of July 20, 1944, Rundstedt was once more recalled, to preside over the military "Court of Honor" that had the task of dishonorably discharging the involved officers. Under Rundstedt's presidency, fifty-five officers were discharged without the opportunity to defend themselves.

In September, 1944, while the German forces in the west were in headlong retreat across northern France, Rundstedt returned as commander in chief west. Hitler's trust was not misplaced, and Rundstedt halted the rout, temporarily stabilizing the front. The attempt to turn the tide in the unsuccessful Ardennes Offensive (Battle of the Bulge) of mid-December, 1944, however, was Hitler's own plan. Following this campaign, Rundstedt was awarded the Knight's Cross with Oak Leaf and Swords.

On March 9, 1945, following the American crossing of the Rhine River at Remagen, as the Third Reich and its *Wehrmacht* were in their final death throes, Hitler dismissed Rundstedt a fourth and final time. On May 2, 1945, Rundstedt became a prisoner of war. The British intended to try him for war crimes. Those proceedings, however, were halted because of Rundstedt's ill health, and he was released in May, 1949. It is doubtful that Rundstedt was guilty of war crimes. Rundstedt died of a heart ailment in February, 1953, in Celle near Hannover.

*Summary*

Gerd von Rundstedt was the product of a Prussian aristocratic upbringing and thorough General Staff training. His personal dignity, undisputable ability, and scrupulous devotion to duty and honor as he saw them saved him from the bitter personal criticism that Hitler heaped on other aristocratic officers. Though Rundstedt repeatedly faced Hitler early in the war and though he had a great disdain for Nazi ideology, he never forced a showdown but simply offered, or accepted, his resignation when he could no longer take responsibility for proposed actions. In July, 1944, when Rundstedt was dismissed, he told Rommel that he "was grateful not to have to experience the coming catastrophe in a position of leadership." At the Nürnberg Trial he explained that "we did our duty because Hitler had legally been made Chancellor by Hindenburg, and because, after his death, he appeared as the Führer on the basis of the [Hindenburg's] testament."

Rundstedt was a thoroughly competent military leader, though not an innovator, and is certainly counted among the war's most capable generals. General Dwight D. Eisenhower considered him the most capable German general, though that judgment might be questioned. Eisenhower never faced Manstein, Rundstedt's erstwhile chief of staff, who may well deserve that accolade. Rundstedt was always determined not to become a "political general," yet his acceptance of, and tacit support for, Hitler and his resignation from uncomfortable positions were in fact indirect support. His unwillingness to become involved in the 1938 and 1944 conspiracies constituted setbacks to these efforts precisely because his colleagues respected him. In the final analysis one cannot escape the feeling that Rundstedt was either the epitome of the honorable Prussian officer in the best sense or "an accomplished cynic, the Talleyrand of Hitler's [generals]"; maybe he was a bit of both.

*Bibliography*

Brett-Smith, Richard. *Hitler's Generals*. London: Osprey, 1976. A comprehensive treatment. Rundstedt is discussed under "The Old Guard," and there are substantial references to him throughout. Includes maps, appendices, a glossary, a bibliography, and an index.

Dziewanowski, M. K. *War at Any Price: World War II in Europe, 1939-1945*. Englewood Cliffs, N.J.: Prentice-Hall, 1987. A college-level textbook that put Rundstedt and the campaigns he was involved in into an overall framework. The author integrated military and nonmilitary developments and placed all in the broader global setting of the war. Excellent for general reading. Includes an extensive bibliography.

Horne, Alistair. *To Lose a Battle: France 1940*. New York: Little, Brown, 1969. An extensive discussion of the background to the war, military resistance to Hitler, and war plans. Considerable discussion of the Manstein plan, armored tactics, and Rundstedt's involvement in the western campaign. The book includes an extensive bibliography.

Liddell Hart, B. H. *The German Generals Talk*. New York: William Morrow, 1948. Rundstedt is discussed in the chapter 'The Old Guard'—Rundstedt," with extensive references throughout. Includes an index and a table of the German High Command.

Mellenthin, F. W. von. *German Generals of World War II: As I Saw Them*. Norman: University of Oklahoma Press, 1977. Mellenthin served in various theaters as a German General Staff officer. The book contains separate chapters on fourteen generals, though not on Rundstedt, since Mellenthin was not directly associated with him. The book, however, contains extensive references to Rundstedt and provides an excellent discussion of command decisions in World War II.

*Frederick Dumin*

# NELLY SACHS

*Born:* December 10, 1891; Berlin, Germany
*Died:* May 12, 1970; Stockholm, Sweden
*Area of Achievement:* Literature
*Contribution:* Sachs, primarily because of her focus upon the deaths of Europe's six million Jews in World War II and her anguished outcry against this ghastly event, has become known as the poet of the Holocaust. One who escaped Nazi horrors because of last-minute maneuvering on her behalf, Sachs was a witness who had to find a fitting way to commemorate the dead and engender hope despite the horror of the event; incredibly, given the difficulty of the task, Sachs succeeded brilliantly.

## *Early Life*

Nelly Sachs was the only daughter of humane, highly cultured parents. Her father, William, was a prosperous manufacturer living in Berlin; her mother, Margarethe, was a pleasant, refined woman. Sachs's Berlin was busy with trade and self-importance, being the arrogant new capital of a recently united Germany bent upon proving its worth to the world. Though certainly no stranger to anti-Semitism as a child, Sachs was spared an acquaintance with the rough side of life as a child and grew up in a household in which self-expression was esteemed. A member of the upper-middle class, she had ample time to create puppet plays and stories as well as write verse.

Sachs's parents sent her to fine schools and encouraged her interests, especially her love of music. Adept at dancing, she wanted to be a dancer in her teen years but also harbored the hope of becoming a mime. At age seventeen, Sachs wrote her first poetry, which was of a romantic, even florid type conventionally approved of in Berlin and therefore acceptable to the local newspapers to which she sent her poems. Berlin intellectuals, however, paid no attention to her newspaper poems, for they enjoyed the avant-garde poetry of the expressionists then in vogue. The tame and often mawkish poems of Sachs's teen years gave no hint of the powerful verse she would one day write.

Sachs's safe, secure, and pleasant Berlin began to change for the worse beginning in the pivotal year 1933, when Adolf Hitler assumed the office of German chancellor. Anti-Jewish feeling, on the rise throughout the post-World War I period, had grown intense, leading to the persecution of all Jews regardless of financial position. To escape the oppression and hatred she felt, Sachs turned to studies of such books as the Kabala, the Bible, and those of mystic writers such as Jakob Böhme.

## *Life's Work*

Fortunately for Sachs, she had corresponded for a long time with Swedish author Selma Lagerlöf, whose *Gösta Berlings saga* (1891; *The Story of Gösta Berling*, 1898) and other writings she passionately admired. In fact, Sachs had been writing to Lagerlöf since Sachs published her first volume of work, *Legenden und Erzählungen* (1921; legends and tales). When it became apparent that the Nazis would sent Sachs and her mother to the gas chambers, Lagerlöf used whatever influence she could muster to persuade the King of Sweden to intercede for her friends in Germany—which he did. Sachs and her mother fled to Stockholm, narrowly missing being caught by the Gestapo and sent to a concentration camp.

From 1933 to 1940, the year Lagerlöf engineered Sachs's escape, Sachs had kept to herself as much as possible, fearing that contact with the world outside her home would bring disaster. Living a hermetic existence, Sachs studied Hebrew and German literature, absorbing the rhymes and rhythms found there as well as the authors' mystical sense of the world. Thwarted in her pursuit of a writer's career because of the fact that she was Jewish, Sachs put all of her energies into honing her imagination. Also during this period she fell in love with a man, though little is known about him except for the fact that the Nazis dragged him away to his death.

When she went to Sweden in 1940, she knew only one person there—Lagerlöf; yet Lagerlöf died only two months after her arrival in Stockholm, a further source of anguish for Sachs and her mother. A stranger in a strange country, Sachs, exiled from a country gone insane with blood lust and hatred of the Jews, started to write as a survivor surveying the wreckage of lives she had known. Gone were the nature poems of her youth. In their place was a new kind of poetry, a harder, tougher poetry that spoke of the unspeakable—tortures, ashes, smoking chimneys, madness, suicide, mass death, all the realities with which she was faced as a survivor of the cruelest spectacle in mankind's cruel history. In her tiny apartment she could join with her ailing mother in lamenting the loss of friends and family. In Stockholm she was alone and unknown as a writer. Her poetry became her only way out of spiritual torpor and anguish.

Out of the wartime exile came her first notable poems, those of *In den Wohnungen des Todes* (in the dwellings of death), first published in 1946, in which she discovered her true themes and poetic voice. Here she concentrated her considerable imaginative powers upon the sufferings of the people of Israel and, for the first time, took as her own responsibility the solemn, enormous task of remembering the dead victims of Hitler's tyranny. To Sachs, there could be no division between herself and those who perished; she consciously chose to craft a poetic monument worthy of them.

Writing in German and living in Sweden meant that Sachs's audience was far smaller than if she had chosen to write in Yiddish or English or lived in New York, London, or Paris. Nevertheless, German recognition came to her because she wrote in that language and later international attention was finally given her.

Her collection of poetry entitled *Sternverdunkelung* (1949; eclipse of the stars) increased her readership and gained for her some critical attention. The biblical cadence, the magnificent themes of death, life, and rebirth, and the harrowing intensity of these poems announced that the wandering Jews of Europe, those alive and those dead, had found their poetic voice. Though heartened by the critical reception of her latest poems, Sachs and her mother endured extreme economic hardship in the early phase of their exile. After her mother's death in 1950, however, Sachs's burden began to lighten as money from her translations of Swedish writers into German came in. Moreover, she was heartened by sales of *Eli: Ein Mysterienspiel vom Leiden Israels* (*Eli: A Mystery Play of the Sufferings of Israel*, 1967), a verse play written in 1943 but published in 1951 which dealt with the death of a Jewish shepherd boy at the hands of a Nazi soldier.

In Sachs's next volume, *Und niemand weiss weiter* (1957; and no one knows where to turn), she began to universalize the torments of the Jews, seeing them as part of the larger story of human suffering throughout history; by so doing, she no longer envisioned the Holocaust as the only catastrophic event in history but as the greatest of them all. This new vision of universal suffering and the searching of all people for meaning and hope found further expression in her subsequent collection, *Flucht und Verwandlung* (1959; light and change), which brought her increased critical attention, especially in Germany.

Sachs's collected poems, *Fahrt ins Staublose* (1961; journey beyond the dust), brought her new readers intrigued by her ability to ask the difficult questions of God that naturally occur after Auschwitz. Following this volume came *Zeichen im Sand: Die szenischen Dichtungen* (1962; signs in the dust), *Späte Gedichte* (1965; later poems), and *Glühende Rätsel* (1964-1966; glowing enigmas), in which her exploration of silence and the questions God leaves unanswered deepens. Here again is the Jewish experience translated into the experience of all human beings alive in the twentieth century—and of all who have ever lived.

To Sachs, the apocalypse that was the Holocaust is contrasted with the promise held by a resurrected state of Israel, the sorrow mitigated though not erased by the joyful re-creation of the Jewish nation. Sustained by the hope for the future of not only Jewry but also mankind, Sachs increasingly appreciated her adopted homeland and grew ever more proficient in speaking and writing Swedish. Her Swedish admirers were many but so too were her East and West German ones. In fact, she was honored by many German societies in several cities and towns.

The culmination of her career, however, came in two ways: with her being awarded the 1966 Nobel Prize in Literature and with the publication of what would become her most noted work, the epic-length lyric *O the Chimneys* in 1967. With characteristic modesty, Sachs accepted the Nobel Prize on behalf of the millions of Jews who perished in the Holocaust and dedicated it to their memory. This award enabled Sachs once more to widen her reading public, yet she did not become a popular poet. Her works were thought by many to be far too painful or too difficult to read, their abstract quality and enormous themes tending to overwhelm first-time readers.

*O the Chimneys* is generally acknowledged as Sachs's finest poem. She labored on it for many years, trying to create a mighty epic of lasting significance. With the publication of this great poem, Sachs's reputation as the poet of the Holocaust was established for all time. Lyrical at a time when lyric poetry was thought archaic, long when brevity was sought in poetry, and biblical in tone and cadence when sophisticated readers looked for irony, *O the Chimneys* bewildered some critics and disappointed others. Yet most critics who wrote about it found it masterful. Sachs determined that this poem would be an unsentimentalized lament for a vanished people as well as a wellspring of hope for a desperate, confused world.

Sachs's final years were relatively happy ones spent in an adopted land she came to acknowledge as home, where her fellow Swedes saw her as a national treasure. Always the mystic, she spent her last years as she had spent previous ones—in contemplation. She died quietly in Stockholm on May 12, 1970, and her mourners were many.

### *Summary*

Nelly Sachs wrote as an outcry against horrors and evils she had known and those she had narrowly escaped knowing. In her career as a poet, she began as a romantic nature poet and ended as a portrayer of history's darkest event. Increasingly, she dealt with the biggest themes: death, life, resurrection, man's destiny, God's love, and peace, and her poetry became less and less descriptive and more abstract, even hermetic.

No other poet gave herself over so completely to the incredibly difficult task of portraying the Holocaust. Perhaps the only others who could have written about the concentration camps, gas chambers, and ovens were murdered or, if they survived, were too emotionally scarred to express their horror and outrage adequately. Postwar Europe needed a poet of Sachs's intensity to help understand the incomprehensible event that was the Holocaust. With her biblical language, Sachs gave her readers a sense of the mystery at the heart of human experience, the sense of wonder and terror one experiences when one contemplates monstrous crimes and their aftermath.

Sachs is undeservedly little known in North America, but her reputation is assured in Europe. Ironically, Germans remain her most avid readers. Her sustained vision of freedom for all people is that of a remarkable woman who never allowed hatred to dominate her life or her art. Hers is one of the twentieth century's most resonant voices, and she needs to be heard.

### *Bibliography*

Kurz, Paul K. *On Modern German Literature*. Translated by Mary Frances

McCarthy. 2 vols. University: University of Alabama Press, 1970-1971. The author emphasizes Sachs's considerable contribution to modern German poetry, citing her as a master of form and technique. Included is a valuable bibliography.

Opfell, Olga S. *Lady Laureates*. 2d ed. Metuchen, N.J.: Scarecrow Press, 1986. Opfell chooses Sachs as one of several seminal women writers who have earned lasting recognition. Her analysis of Sachs's inner qualities is fascinating as is her discussion of Sachs's achievements.

Rosenfeld, Alvin H. "The Poetry of Nelly Sachs." *Judaism* 20 (Summer, 1971): 356-364. Rosenfeld's article discusses Sachs being close to silence, even madness, asking unanswerable questions to an unfathomable God. He emphasizes how fragile are her abstract concepts in the face of the horror of the Holocaust.

Slater, Joseph. "From Death to Rebirth." *Saturday Review* 1 (November 4, 1967): 36. Slater discusses the various elements that make Sachs' poetry so powerful and makes a strong plea for her to be accepted by American readers.

Spender, Stephen. "Catastrophe and Redemption." *The New York Times Book Review*, October 8, 1967: 5, 34. One of Sachs's most ardent admirers, Spender compares Sachs to other notable writers of the twentieth century and finds her contribution unique. He also expounds upon the essential unity of her themes developed over the decades.

*John D. Raymer*

# ANWAR EL-SADAT

*Born:* December 25, 1918; Mit Abul-Kum, Egypt
*Died:* October 6, 1981; Cairo, Egypt
*Areas of Achievement:* Government and politics
*Contribution:* Sadat was awarded the Nobel Peace Prize in 1978 for his role in preparing the first permanent peace between Israel and an Arab country (Egypt). Beyond this recognition for his efforts as a statesman, however, there is no doubt that Sadat was an excellent military strategist, a fact that was clearly illustrated in the first stage of the October, 1973, Arab-Israeli War.

*Life's Work*

Anwar el-Sadat, who was destined to become President of Egypt in 1970 and to die by an assassin's hand in 1981, was born in the modest Nile delta village of Mit Abul-Kum on December 25, 1918. His father, who was then stationed with the Anglo-Egyptian army in the Sudan, had at least completed basic-level public schooling. This made it possible for him to follow his military service with an appointment as a senior clerk in the Department of Health. These modest accomplishments qualified him and his own children, all of whom also attended school, to effendi status in the eyes of Mit Abul-Kum commoners. Sadat's education began when his family moved, and he was enrolled first in the private Islamic Benevolent Society School in Cairo, then in the Sultan Hussein School. By 1930, despite the heavy weight of tuition charges for his father's modest budget, Sadat entered Fu'ād I Secondary School. It was only after considerable difficulty (and transfer to another school) that he finally earned his general certificate of education.

Sadat's first attempts to gain entry to the Royal Military Academy were unsuccessful, obliging him to fill a short interim by becoming enrolled first at the Faculty of Law and then the Faculty of Commerce. Once admitted to the military academy, and especially after being commissioned as a second lieutenant in 1938, Sadat met and conversed with a number of cadets and young officers who harbored strong nationalist political sentiments. Their aim was to rid Egypt of all remaining indirect controls that the British (foreign occupants of Egypt between 1882 and 1914, and holders of a formal protectorate from 1914 to 1922) had redefined in an Anglo-Egyptian treaty in 1936. As international conditions deteriorated and the outbreak of World War II came closer, politically active officers formed a group called the Free Officers Organization, whose members included Sadat and another officer who would become famous earliest: Gamal Abdel Nasser. This group not only believed that Egypt's vital nationalist interests demanded that it should not tie itself irrevocably to Great Britain but also that it should also deal directly with Germany, then very near to winning the North African War at

Egypt's borders. Sadat's association with political nationalism led to his arrest and imprisonment in 1942, until his escape in 1944. Continued radical political activity, this time involving plots against high-level postwar Egyptian political figures, brought another two-year prison term in 1946.

Between 1948 and 1951, when Sadat renewed ties with the underground Free Officers Organization, he was reinstated in the army, rising to the rank of lieutenant colonel. By 1952, he had become one of Nasser's confidants, participating in the coup that overthrew Egypt's corrupt monarch, King Farouk I, in July, 1952. One year later, the Egyptian monarchy was abolished by the Free Officers Organization, now transformed into the Revolutionary Command Council.

### *Life's Work*

Sadat's political career should be divided into two main periods: from 1952 to 1970, during which time he rose gradually to become one of the most important members of the Egyptian Revolutionary Command Council organized by Nasser, and from 1970 to the end of his presidency in 1981. During the first years of the first period, Sadat held a number of significant but not key policy-making posts, including that of minister of state without portfolio (1954-1955) and secretary general of Egypt's Islamic Congress (an unprecedented and largely ineffective body). By the time of Egypt's attempted "revolutionary" union with Syria (1958-1961), he had gained enough of Nasser's confidence to serve as speaker of the union's joint parliament. From that point on, Sadat's responsibilities tied him ever more closely to Egypt's real power center. His appointment as speaker of the Egyptian National Assembly (1966) was significant but was overshadowed in real political terms by other tasks he carried out personally for Nasser. These included membership in Egypt's special delegations to both the Soviet Union and the United States in 1966.

Although Sadat played no direct role in the disaster of the Arab-Israeli War of 1967, it is clear that his predictable loyalty to Nasser was a vital support for the latter during the difficult three years to 1970. Nasser made him vice president in 1969, a responsibility that became very serious when, during Nasser's "summit" meeting with the Soviets in December, 1969, and again when the president was incapacitated by illness at several points in 1970, Sadat served as acting president.

Thus, when Nasser died (September, 1970), Sadat seemed to have many of the qualifications required to succeed him, but he also had critics and even enemies. Primary among these was another former vice president of Egypt, Ali Sabri, then head of Egypt's single revolutionary party, the Arab Socialist Union. Sabri was the primary spokesman of the pro-Soviet wing of the Egyptian regime. Within less than a year, in May, 1971, Sadat was able to isolate the political and military clique headed by Sabri and remove the members from positions of prominence, even while assuring the Soviets that his actions were not aimed against them.

Part of the reason behind Sadat's success in challenging his critics was his insistence that the "Year of Decision" in Egypt's confrontation with Israel was at hand and that internal unity of purpose had to be maintained. As the new president searched for the means to prepare for a show of force against Israel, however, he discovered that Egypt's Soviet allies, by this date engaged in the spirit of détente with Washington, were unwilling to escalate their military commitment to Cairo. Sadat made history, therefore, in deciding to expel thousands of Soviet technicians and military personnel from Egypt in 1972. During more than a year, plans were laid for a carefully coordinated surprise attack on heavily fortified Israeli positions along the Suez Canal—the opening phase of the Yom Kippur War of October, 1973.

Although the October War was not entirely successful from the Arab point of view, it had enormous consequences, especially because it caused the United States to play a more active role in seeking a negotiated settlement to the Arab-Israeli conflict. From the Egyptian point of view, these consequences would make President Sadat a figure of internationally recognized importance. Within two years of the 1973 conflict, the good offices of, among others, United States Secretary of State Henry Kissinger had led to the Sinai Agreement, providing for Israeli withdrawal to strategically defensible fortifications in the interior of the Sinai Peninsula.

Most spectacular, however, were Sadat's decisions, between 1975 and 1977, first to declare a reversal of Nasserian policies of state socialism in Egypt (which was to be replaced by economic liberalization, or "opening," with foreign assistance), and then personally to open peace negotiations with Israel. His November, 1977, visit to Jerusalem, where he addressed the Israeli Knesset, represented an unprecedented action by an Arab leader to prepare the way for a lasting peace in the Middle East. It was followed in stages by United States sponsorship, through the personal offices of President Jimmy Carter, for direct negotiations between Sadat and Israeli prime minister Menachem Begin, which took place at Carter's Camp David retreat in September, 1978. The dramatic outcome of the Camp David accords was a bilateral Egyptian-Israeli peace treaty, signed at the White House on March 26, 1979. By this treaty, Israel committed itself to withdraw from the Egyptian Sinai. Both parties were to initiate full normal bilateral relations. A separate document, which proved to be quite ineffective, called for progress toward solving the Palestinian political and territorial dilemma.

Although Sadat gained worldwide recognition for his peace initiative and was awarded the Nobel Peace Prize in 1978, Egypt's political and economic situation was not a peaceful one. In his attempt to deal with various forms of unrest at home, including criticism of the Egyptian-Israeli peace and growing religious fanaticism, Sadat assumed extraordinary presidential powers in

May of 1980. In a little more than a year, following riots in June, 1981, and mass arrests in September, Sadat was assassinated by splinter elements of the extremist Islamic underground.

*Summary*

Anwar el-Sadat's career illustrates several key aspects of nationalism as it has operated in the Middle East since World War II. His early career was obviously marked by extremist positions against perceived enemies of Egypt's national destiny: Great Britain, Israel, and, by 1952, insufferable internal corruption. Although Sadat followed a revolutionary path to make gains against these obstacles, ultimately he proved to be a pragmatist, tying Egypt's destiny to the necessity to compromise. This was visible not only in his dealings with Israel but also in his attempt to bring Egypt's economy, badly displaced by twenty years of revolutionary socialism and the massive costs of war, back into a situation of internal and international equilibrium. This latter decision was not an independent one but was tied to the assumption that foreign participation in Egypt's economic future would be essential.

*Bibliography*

Blaisse, Mark. *Anwar Sadat: The Last Hundred Days*. London: Thames and Hudson, 1981. This mainly pictorial volume contains a textual narrative based on the author's own conversations with Sadat.

Hirst, David, and Irene Beeson. *Sadat*. London: Faber & Faber, 1981. Following an abbreviated summary of Sadat's earlier career under Nasser's presidency, the authors of this book offer the most detailed account of the period from the 1973 Yom Kippur War to the Egyptian-Israeli peace treaty.

Israeli, Raphael. *"I, Egypt": Aspects of President Anwar al-Sadat's Political Thought*. Jerusalem: Magnes Press, 1981. This survey of Sadat's views contains numerous citations of his speeches and writings. Commentary is organized under eight topics, including "Concepts of Leadership," "Sadat between Arabism and Africanism," and "Peace Strategy."

__________. *Man of Defiance: A Political Biography of Anwar Sadat*. Totowa, N.J.: Barnes & Noble Books, 1985. This not only is the most complete biography of Sadat in English but also is a quite scholarly analysis of both the men and political issues that affected his life, both in its earlier and later stages.

Sadat, Anwar el-. *In Search of Identity: An Autobiography.* New York: Harper & Row, 1978. Sadat's life based on his personal reflections. The narrative includes valuable descriptions, not only of Sadat's own personal ideas but also of the roles played in his career, up to 1977, by other Egyptian and foreign personalities.

Sadat, Camelia. *My Father and I*. New York: Macmillan, 1985. This is a combined biography/autobiography by Sadat's daughter, who was born in 1949. In addition to recollections concerning her father, it contains valuable views on the status of women in Egypt both before and during his presidency.

*Byron D. Cannon*

# ANDREI SAKHAROV

*Born:* May 21, 1921; Moscow, U.S.S.R.
*Died:* December 14, 1989; Moscow, U.S.S.R.
*Areas of Achievement:* Physics, civil rights, social reform, and politics
*Contribution:* Sakharov's work as a scientist and human rights activist made him an important international figure. His scientific work played a key role in the production of the first hydrogen bomb and later in the study of the structure of the universe. His calls for civil rights in the Soviet Union commanded attention and respect throughout the world and earned for him the Nobel Peace Prize in 1975.

### *Early Life*

Andrei Dmitrievich Sakharov was born in Moscow on May 21, 1921, son of Dmitri Sakharov, a professor of physics at the Lenin Pedagogical Institute and author of several classroom texts and popular science books. Beyond the fact that the family led a comfortable life in a large communal apartment, little is known about Sakharov's childhood. By his own account, the major influence on him, apart from his parents, was his grandmother, who read to him every evening from the Gospel and such English authors as Charles Dickens and Christopher Marlowe. The atmosphere at home, he was later to write, was pervaded by a strong, traditional family spirit, "a liking for work, and dedication to mastery of one's chosen profession."

In 1938, Sakharov completed high school and entered Moscow State University as a student of physics and mathematics. He was graduated in 1942 as one of the most brilliant students in the annals of the university and was exempted from military service. Instead, he was assigned to work as an engineer in a war plant, where he developed several inventions relating to ammunition quality control. With the end of World War II, Sakharov resumed his studies, entering the P. N. Lebedev Physics Institute of the Soviet Academy of Sciences to work under Igor Tamm, the leading Soviet scientist in the field of quantum mechanics and the head of the institute's theoretical division. In 1947, Sakharov was awarded the degree of candidate for doctor in science (roughly equivalent to the American Ph.D.) for his work on cosmic ray theory.

### *Life's Work*

Up to the mid-1960's, Sakharov's research focused on weapons development. In the spring of 1948, he became a member of a research team headed by Tamm, which worked under strict security on the development of a new generation of nuclear weapons. In 1950, Sakharov and Tamm achieved a breakthrough when they formulated the theoretical foundations of the hydrogen bomb. In recognition of this and other achievements in hydrogen weapons research, Sakharov was awarded the Stalin and Lenin prizes, and on three occasions he received the Order of Socialist Labor, the Soviet Union's highest civilian honor. Shortly after the first testingof the hydrogen bomb in 1953, he received the title of doctor of science and was elected to full membership in the Soviet Academy of Sciences. At the age of thirty-two, he thereby became the youngest scientist ever to have reached this prestigious position. From then to 1968, he continued his work in the secret Soviet nuclear weapons research center.

Between January and March, 1958, the Soviet Union conducted a series of atmospheric nuclear tests. When it became known that an additional series was being planned for the autumn of the same year, Sakharov wrote an article in which he warned against severe genetic damage caused by atmospheric tests; to reduce international tension and decrease the threat of nuclear war, he demanded their total cessation. The same arguments were repeated in a memorandum that Sakharov sent to the chief scientific administrator of the Soviet nuclear weapons program, and this came to the attention of the Communist Party leader Nikita S. Khrushchev. What impact if any this had on Soviet policy is unclear, but, after concluding the 1958 tests, the Soviet Union joined the United States in an informal moratorium on nuclear atmospheric tests, which lasted until the summer of 1961.

Sakharov's protest activities were soon extended beyond the issues relating to his research interests. Already in 1958 he had taken a stand against Khrushchev's proposed reforms in secondary education, which would have required all students to devote two or three years to farm or factory work before graduation. In June, 1964, he took part in a successful effort to end the politically motivated scientific research associated with Trofim Lysenko and to resist Khrushchev's demand to admit his followers to the Academy of Sciences. In so doing, he put himself squarely on the liberal side of an ideological conflict that had stunted the development of the biological and agricultural sciences in the Soviet Union since the mid-1930's.

The year 1966 constituted a watershed in the direction of Sakharov's political activity. With the fall of Khrushchev, conservative elements in the Communist Party sought to rehabilitate Joseph Stalin. On the eve of the Party's Twenty-third Congress, Sakharov, Tamm, and twenty-three other intellectuals signed an open letter opposing the move. Later in the same year, Sakharov again joined Tamm and others in signing a collective appeal to the Supreme Soviet to prevent the approval of decrees curtailing dissent that were being added to the criminal code. In February, 1967, he sent yet another appeal to Soviet president Leonid Ilich Brezhnev, protesting the arrest of four members of the group and demanding their release. This was his first attempt to intercede on behalf of individual citizens.

Sakharov's conversion to dissidence was followed by his formulation of a theory linking his hitherto divergent social and political activities. Previously he had addressed his protests to the political and scientific elites. In 1968, however, he wrote an article that he published himself and that was smuggled to the West. The article constituted the first effort to relate the issues of civil rights in the Soviet Union to global peace and human progress. Its main thesis was that a rapprochement between the Soviet Union and the West is the only alternative to thermonuclear holocaust. Moreover, only by pooling American and Soviet resources can humankind overcome the dangers of poverty, environmental pollution, and overpopulation. Without freedom of thought, Sakharov maintained, Soviet society will never attain the stage of peaceful convergence with the democratic world. Sakharov therefore advocated ending censorship and the suppression of dissidents as a first step in an ideal process that would culminate in the formation of a world government dedicated to the advancement of humankind.

Shortly after the article was published, Sakharov's security clearance was withdrawn, and he was barred from all secret work. Earlier in the decade, he had begun research in macrophysics, resulting in several papers on the expansion of the universe and on the structure of quarks. In 1969, he continued his work on gravitation and the structure of the universe as a senior researcher in the P. N. Lebedev Physics Institute. At about the same time, he suffered a personal loss with the death of his wife, Klavidia. It was in this period too that his political perspective underwent its final evolution. Up to his dismissal from the Soviet atomic weapons program, he was "isolated from the people" by his "extraordinary position of material privileges" and tended to treat world peace and human rights as theoretical problems. With the loss of these privileges, he became more acutely aware of concrete wrongs suffered by specific individuals and groups in society. This sensitivity was heightened through the work of the Moscow Human Rights Committee, which he founded with two younger physicists in the fall of 1970 to monitor and publicize human rights violations in the Soviet Union. This sense of moral obligation and urgency led Sakharov to embark on an accelerated campaign of letters, appeals, press interviews, and protestations on behalf of Jews seeking emigration, Crimean Tatars demanding repatriation, Ukrainian and Volga German nationalists, fellow dissidents, and political prisoners. During a protest vigil outside a courthouse where dissidents were standing trial, he met Elena Bonner-Alikhanova, and the two were married in 1972.

In September, 1972, Sakharov was detained by the police after participating in a demonstration protesting the murder of Israeli athletes at the Munich Olympics. This was the first episode in a campaign of harassment and intimidation that included the expulsion of his two stepchildren from the University of Moscow, press attacks on his views and activities, and summonses to appear before the Komitet Gosudarstvennoi Bezopasnosti (KGB). In August,

1973, after he had appealed to United Nations Secretary-General Kurt Waldheim to intercede on behalf of dissidents confined to mental hospitals, Sakharov was called to a meeting with the deputy procurator-general, who threatened him with prosecution on the charges of defaming the state. A week later, in defiance of such pressures, Sakharov convened a press conference in his apartment to warn against "détente without democratization." A month later, Sakharov appealed to the U.S. Congress, calling on it to support the Jackson-Vanik Amendment linking the Soviet Union's preferred trade status to the level of Soviet emigration. In December, 1973, Sakharov was awarded the Human Rights Prize by the International League for the Rights of Man. Two years later, he became the first Soviet to win the Nobel Peace Prize. On both occasions, Sakharov was denied an exit visa to attend the ceremonies. His Nobel Prize acceptance speech was read by his wife, Bonner.

Despite Sakharov's continuous defiance, he was not arrested until 1980. In January of that year, after denouncing the Soviet invasion of Afghanistan and calling on the United Nations to persuade it to withdraw, he was stripped of his honors and banished without trial to Gorki, a military-industrial city officially closed to foreigners. Confined to the city limits, he was placed under KGB supervision, his mail was scrutinized, and he was forbidden any contact with other dissidents. Nevertheless, he continued his study of cosmology and the physics of elementary particles and was elected in 1980 and 1981 as a member of the Italian and French Academies of Sciences. At first, even his political work was not totally disrupted, for his statements and appeals were communicated to the outside world by his wife, who traveled back and forth between Moscow and Gorki. In 1984, however, Bonner too was restricted to Gorki after being accused of slandering the state.

Several days before Christmas, 1986, Soviet leader Mikhail Gorbachev in person telephoned Sakharov to announce his release from exile. Back in Moscow, Sakharov resumed his scientific and political activities. A week after his return, he appeared on American television and vowed to continue the struggle for the liberation of all "prisoners of conscience." A symbol of his changed status was the transmission of his interview through the satellite facilities of the Soviet government. Toward the end of 1988, Sakharov left the Soviet Union for the first time in his life for a tour of meetings with major European and American politicians, including United States President Ronald Reagan. While continuing his advocacy of civil rights in the Soviet Union and calling for Soviet troop cutbacks and reduction of military spending, he now called on the West to support Gorbachev's reforms. In April, 1989, he was nominated by the Soviet Academy of Sciences for a seat in the new Soviet National Congress of Deputies. There he became a leader of the Interregional Deputies Group, a faction dedicated to the acceleration of reform in the Soviet Union. Sakharov continued his political dissent to the end of his life, which occurred on December 14, 1989. Only two days before his death, he engaged Gorbachev in an angry debate, demanding the abolition of the Communist Party's monopoly of political power in the Soviet Union.

*Summary*

The final assessment of Andrei Sakharov's scientific contribution must await the lifting of the veil of secrecy that still shrouds his military-related work. Nevertheless, it is clear that he played a key role in the production of the first hydrogen bomb and the industrial utilization of nuclear energy. He is also accepted as a pioneer in research into the structure of the universe and the quark phenomenon. These accomplishments were intimately related to his activities in the cause of human rights and global peace. His position at the pinnacle of Soviet society and fame as the developer of the thermonuclear bomb added weight to his arguments and enabled him, almost single-handedly, to change the dissident movement into a force that could not be ignored. He himself regarded his scientific and political endeavors as complementary aspects of a single quest for human dignity and a world in which science and technology can be harnessed for the advancement of humankind.

There is no available method by which to gauge Sakharov's impact on the policies of his government. He admitted that his struggles to remedy specific wrongs "almost always met [with a] tragic absence of positive results." Yet, perhaps his greatest achievement lies in the mere fact of his activity. He himself explained this clearly when he argued that, in a repressive society, "there is a need to create ideals even when you can't see any route by which to achieve them, because if there are no ideals then there can be no hope and then one [is left] completely in the dark. . . ." His courage, personal example, and relentless advocacy of human rights helped keep alive ideas and aspirations without which no reforms are possible. The era of *perestroika* and *glasnost*, and his election to the National Congress of Deputies, may serve as proof that his efforts were not in vain.

*Bibliography*

Babyonyshev, Alexander, ed. *On Sakharov.* New York: Alfred A. Knopf, 1982. A collection of essays, stories, and poems written by prominent Soviet dissenters and dedicated to Sakharov, offering an insider's view of the problems of the dissent movement and of Sakharov's place within it.

Bonner, Elena. *Alone Together.* Translated by Alexander Cook. New York: Alfred A. Knopf, 1986. Written during Bonner's six-month leave of absence from Gorki, this book contains important information about the activities of the Sakharovs in the 1980's as well as interesting anecdotes about and insights into their personalities and private life.

Dorman, Peter. "Andrei Sakharov: The Conscience of a Liberal Scientist." In *Dissent in the USSR*, edited by Rudolf Tökés. Baltimore, Md.: Johns

Hopkins University Press, 1975. An excellent exposition of Sakharov's social and political ideas based on his writings, statements, and activities up to 1974.

LeVert, Suzanne. *The Sakharov File: A Study in Courage*. New York: Julian Messner, 1986. Intended for young people but offers a good historical background and a clear account of Sakharov's human rights activities.

Rubenstein, Joshua. *Soviet Dissidents: Their Struggle for Human Rights*. Boston: Beacon Press, 1980. Explores the origins and development of the dissident movement in Moscow through the lives and activities of Sakharov and other prominent human rights activists.

Sakharov, Andrei. *Alarm and Hope*. Edited by Efrem Yankelevich and Alfred Friendly, Jr. New York: Alfred A. Knopf, 1978. A collection of Sakharov's short writings, correspondence, and press interviews. Includes the text of his 1975 Nobel Peace Prize lecture and an appendix offering brief sketches of some of the individuals he sought to publicize and defend.

___________. *Sakharov Speaks*. Edited by Harrison E. Salisbury. New York: Alfred A. Knopf, 1974. Contains a valuable foreword by Salisbury and some of the most important early writings of Sakharov himself, notably *Progress, Coexistence, and Intellectual Freedom* and a 1973 interview with Olle Stenholm on his view of life and the goals of his human rights activities.

*Jonathan Mendilow*

# ALBERTO SANTOS-DUMONT

*Born:* July 20, 1873; Palmira, Brazil
*Died:* July 24, 1932; Guarujá, Brazil
*Areas of Achievement:* Aeronautics, invention, and technology
*Contribution:* Santos-Dumont, a leading European aviator during the period of early development of manned flight, is recognized as an inventor and innovative designer in both major categories of flight: lighter than air (airships) and heavier than air (airplanes). Working with semirigid airships, he adapted the internal-combustion engine as a source of power for lighter-than-air vehicles, and he was the first to design, build, and fly a heavier-than-air machine in Europe. Two of the airplanes he designed and built played a major role in the development of European aviation.

## *Early Life*

Alberto Santos-Dumont was born in Brazil, the third son and the last of seven children of Francisca Santos and Henriques Dumont, known as the Brazilian "coffee king." An avid reader, especially of Jules Verne's science fiction, Alberto was enthralled by the idea that man might fly, and he was also fascinated by machinery. At an early age, he drove the huge steam-powered tractors and locomotives that transported coffee beans to the processing plant. There, the young Santos-Dumont would observe how the machines operated, and he soon became adept at making needed repairs. During a visit to the Palace of Industry in Paris, Alberto was completely captivated by a working exhibit of an internal-combustion engine, the first he had ever seen. He bought an automobile, to which he applied his mechanical talents, and he was soon able to disassemble an engine and rebuild it perfectly. He also read every book he could find on balloons and aerial navigation. Such experiences were to influence his later work much more than did his formal education, which ended with his graduation from the academy at Minas Gerais province, although he did later take some studies in physics, mechanics, electricity, and chemistry with a private tutor in France.

In 1897, the young Santos-Dumont went to France, where he became a balloon pilot for Henri Lachambre and Alexis Machuron, whom he then commissioned to build a balloon to his design: small, light, and made of Japanese silk. Although the two experts had maintained that silk would not be strong enough, tests proved Santos-Dumont correct: The silk was stronger than the material previously used. He named his tiny balloon the *Brazil* and flew it time after time, becoming a familiar sight and a popular hero to the Parisians, who reacted enthusiastically, taking him to their hearts.

## *Life's Work*

Having learned to fly, Santos-Dumont turned his back on everything else and devoted all of his energies to the goal of controlled, powered flight. This dream was scoffed at by his friends, who argued that an engine mounted under a balloon would shake itself to pieces. Undeterred, Santos-Dumont experimented with a small, motor-powered tricycle, which he suspended by ropes from tree branches, finding that it vibrated less in the air than on the ground. The success of this experiment and of his first balloon encouraged the inventor to rely increasingly on his own intuition, refusing suggestions from others.

Santos-Dumont's first controllable airship was an elongated balloon with rigging lines, from which was suspended a basket on which was mounted a modified internal-combustion engine. The vehicle incorporated two control mechanisms: one a crude but movable rudder, the other a method of controlling pitch (vertical angle) by moving weights, thus allowing the pilot to climb or descend. On September 20, 1898, the designer made the first successful flight in his airship number 1. He was able to steer the ship, but its balloon envelope collapsed in midair, and he was saved from crashing only by a group of boys who grabbed the lines and ran into the wind, allowing the balloon to settle gradually to the ground.

Santos-Dumont's airship number 2, constructed from parts of number 1, also collapsed on its first flight, dumping its pilot in a tree. Undaunted, he began plans for his first semirigid airship. Its construction was similar to that of its predecessors but with a bamboo pole added to the underside of the envelope, providing some rigidity. After his first flight in number 3, the designer was ecstatic; for the first time he believed that he was mastering control of the airship. This success hardened Santos-Dumont's resolve to pursue aviation as his life's work.

In April, 1900, a prize of 100,000 francs was offered by M. Deutsch de la Meurthe to the first person to fly from the Parc d'Aérostation of the Aéro Club de France in St. Cloud, near Paris, around the Eiffel Tower, and back to the Parc d'Aérostation without landing, in thirty minutes or less. Santos-Dumont began construction of his airship number 4 immediately, using a combination of old and new ideas. The envelope was of the same basic design as number 3, with a longitudinal bamboo spar underneath to add rigidity; attached to this was an engine, mounted now as a tractor rather than a pusher. The basket was omitted, replaced by a bicycle seat mounted aft of the engine. Horizontal steering was done with controls attached to bicycle handle bars. Pitch was again controlled by shifting weights, but with a new component, water ballast, which the pilot could dump by simply turning a tap. Although Santos-Dumont made several successful flights in this airship, it lacked the speed necessary to win the Deutsch Prize.

In his next model, Santos-Dumont made four major changes. First, he built a girderlike keel of aluminum and pine, which provided a lightweight, rigid framework on which to mount the engine and basket. Second, he braced the framework with piano wire rather than rope, greatly reducing drag. Third, he enlarged the rudder for more effective control. Finally, he installed an air-cooled fifteen horsepower Buchet engine, into which he incorporated an electric ignition system. On its maiden voyage, the engine failed, and once again Santos-Dumont landed in the trees. The damage was quickly repaired, but on his next attempt the airship lost its rigidity and deflated, crashing into the Hotel Trocadero. Rescuers found the pilot perched on a windowsill high above street level; safe on the ground again, he announced that construction of number 6 would begin immediately. It took only twenty-two days, the only design change being a modified water-cooled Buchet engine. On October 19, 1901, Santos-Dumont made the round-trip flight from the Parc d'Aérostation around the Eiffel Tower and back again. Although his flight had lasted forty seconds more than the allotted time, the people of Paris demanded that he be awarded the prize, half of which he gave to the poor of Paris and the other half to his mechanics and other workers. Santos-Dumont went on to design a total of fourteen airships, of which his number 9 is considered the most successful. This short, fat vehicle, so easy and convenient to fly that he used it as his "runabout," reflected his credo of smallness, lightness, and simplicity of design.

In 1905, Santos-Dumont entered the race for prizes offered by Ernest Archdeacon, a wealthy patron of aviation, for the first heavier-than-air flight of more than twenty-five meters, and by the French Aéro Club for a flight of more than one hundred meters. His first design was an ungainly looking "canard-type" airplane, with a rectangular, fabric-covered fuselage and tail unit forward of the main wings with its propeller in the rear. Its wings, which resembled large box kites, were attached at a pronounced dihedral angle, providing lateral stability. Attached to the leading end of the fuselage was a small boxlike device that pivoted both vertically and horizontally, the sole means of control during flight. The pilot stood in a wicker basket directly in front of the engine. The airplane's first test, which involved towing by a donkey harnessed to a pulley arrangement, occasioned a series of colorful comments by observers, which were not appreciated by the designer. He then decided to suspend it from his number 14 airship, resulting in the appellation number 14-*bis* (again, twice). On October 23, 1906, at Bagatelle, near Paris, Santos-Dumont made the first successful European airplane flight, covering some sixty meters before crashing to earth. He had won the Archdeacon Prize and was the toast of Europe. To improve control, he now added ailerons, modified from an earlier design of Robert Esnault-Pelterie. Wires from the ailerons ran to a piece of metal sewn into the back of his jacket. To activate them, he shifted his body to and fro, controlling the airplane through a sort of dance. On November 12, 1906, Santos-Dumont flew his modified number 14-*bis* a distance of 220 meters, in slightly more than twenty-one seconds, to win the Aéro Club Prize of fifteen hundred francs.

Santos-Dumont forged ahead, trying to solve the still-worrisome lack of control. In March, 1909, he surprised the aviation world by unveiling a totally new design—a tractor (front propeller) monoplane with a silk-covered wing and tail surfaces and a skeletal fuselage made of bamboo. He had returned to his original criteria of small, light, and simple. This beautiful machine, powered by a Dutheil-Chambers engine which Santos-Dumont had modified extensively to give it more horsepower, was the prototype for his number 20, the *Demoiselle* (dragonfly). Incorporated into its construction were his solutions to control problems: a rudder and an elevator for control about the longitudinal and vertical axes and wing warping for lateral control. The mechanism for the latter was a pair of metal rings worn around the pilot's arms; when he wanted to turn, he moved his arms up or down, twisting the wings. The *Demoiselle*, relatively easy to construct and an excellent flying machine, was an instant success, joining Santos-Dumont's number 9 airship and his number 14-*bis* airplane as the third jewel in his crown of achievements.

In 1910, Santos-Dumont, ill with multiple sclerosis, retired from his work in aviation and, after a period of wandering, returned to Brazil. In July, 1932, despondent because the machine to which he had devoted his life was being used to kill people in war, he took his own life.

### *Summary*

Working independently of developments in the United States, Alberto Santos-Dumont designed and built the first airplane to fly successfully in Europe. He was the third person in the world to pilot an airplane, with only Wilbur and Orville Wright having preceded him in achieving sustained heavier-than-air flight. In early 1910, Santos-Dumont was the only aeronaut qualified to fly all four types of flying machines then in existence: balloons, airships, biplanes, and monoplanes. His major technological contributions were the design of a small, light, controllable airship, powered by an internal-combustion engine, and of a small, light, reliable airplane, the *Demoiselle*, whose ease of construction and flying helped to open the field of aviation.

A pilot, mechanic, skilled craftsman, adapter, and inventor, Alberto Santos-Dumont did not engage in systematic research in the same way as did the Wright brothers and others; rather, he built, tested, modified, and rebuilt as necessary to reach his goal. His contribution to the science of aviation is considered by historians to be minimal. Nevertheless, his influence on the development of aviation remains important. His refusal to patent any of his innovations made possible the use and development of his ideas by others, furthering the advancement and popularization of aviation, and his criteria of smallness, lightness, and simplicity became the quintessential concepts of aircraft design.

Santos-Dumont's other major contribution to aviation was his impact on people's perception of flight. Moving easily through all levels of society, he did more than any other person during the early 1900's to make Europeans "air-minded." Santos-Dumont's daring aeronautical successes thrilled people and awakened in them an overwhelming curiosity about and awareness of aviation. In a period of history erupting in technological advances, Santos-Dumont fired the imagination of a continent.

*Bibliography*

Emde, Heiner. *Conquerors of the Air: The Evolution of Aircraft, 1903-1945*. New York: Viking Press, 1968. Contains a large number of detailed drawings of airplanes, with specifications and descriptions. The short section on Santos-Dumont describes his 14-*bis* and his *Demoiselle* airplanes.

Gibbs-Smith, Charles H. *The Invention of the Aeroplane, 1799-1909*. London: Faber & Faber, 1966. A definitive study of early aviation, in which are chronicled Santos-Dumont's achievements along with those of other early aviators. The book is essential for anyone interested in the early development of the airplane.

Napoleão, Aluizio. *Santos-Dumont and the Conquest of the Air*. 2 vols. Translated by Luiz Victor Le Cocq d'Oliveira. Rio de Janeiro: National Printing Office, 1945. Volume 1 contains a brief history of the Santos-Dumont family, followed by a detailed factual description of Santos-Dumont's work in the development of flying machines. Volume 2 is a compilation of untranslated documents on the aeronautical accomplishments of Santos-Dumont, with some explanatory annotations in English.

Santos-Dumont, Alberto. *My Airships: The Story of My Life*. New York: Dover, 1973. An unabridged republication of the English translation originally published in 1904 by Grant Richards in London of Santos-Dumont's *Dans l'air*. Santos-Dumont's own detailed account of how he designed, constructed, and flew each of his airships. Drawings aid the reader in understanding the problems faced by the inventor, and his descriptions of his adventures make enjoyable reading.

Villard, Henry S. *Contact!—The Story of the Early Birds*. New York: Thomas Y. Crowell, 1968. An excellent history of early aviation, its participants and events, by an author who knew many of the pioneers. Contains many anecdotes that add to the enjoyment of the reader.

Wykeham, Peter. *Santos-Dumont: A Study in Obsession*. London: Putnam, 1962. This entertaining, informative, and factual book is the definitive biography of Santos-Dumont, covering every aspect of his life. The major portion, however, is devoted to his aviation-related experiments, adventures, and triumphs. The author's respect and admiration for Santos-Dumont is evident throughout.

*P. John Carter*

# NATHALIE SARRAUTE

*Born:* July 18, 1900; Ivanovo-Voznessensk, Russia

*Area of Achievement:* Literature

*Contribution:* Sarraute is often called the mother of the French New Novel. The New Novel rejected nineteenth century novelistic concerns of character and plot and changed the face of French literature. After a thirty-year career of novel writing, Sarraute began playwriting and found new success on the Parisian stage.

## *Early Life*

The daughter of Ilya Tcherniak, a chemist and owner of a dye factory, and Pauline Chatounowski, Sarraute was born in Russia on July 18, 1900. Her parents had met in Geneva while studying at the university; they were exiled from their native Russia because Nicholas II had barred Jewish students from attending universities in Russia. When Sarraute was two, her parents were divorced, and she began an unsettled childhood, constantly on the move between Russia, France, and Switzerland. Sarraute's own mother was a writer, who, having returned to Russia with her daughter and remarried, had published a number of novels and short stories under the male pseudonym Vichrowski. At the age of eight, Sarraute was finally settled in Paris with her father in the fourteenth arrondissement, the hub of Russian émigré activity in the city.

Through the influence of her artistic mother and the vital intellectuality provided by her father and the Russian community, Sarraute came to believe that women could equal the career success enjoyed by men. Sarraute pursued her studies in English at the Sorbonne, but she also read history at Oxford, England, and sociology at the Faculty of Letters, Berlin, before entering the University of Paris law school in 1922. While Sarraute chose to lead a highly demanding academic career, she also had a family life and, in 1925, married a fellow law student, Raymond Sarraute. Sarraute was a member of the Paris bar for twelve years, during which time she became the mother of three daughters and began her career in letters.

## *Life's Work*

Sarraute's first work, *Tropismes* (1938, 1957; *Tropisms*, 1963), consists of a series of sketches that received a highly positive appraisal by Jean-Paul Sartre, but this one review comprised the only critical attention for the novel. This debut work already demonstrated the theoretical and innovative approach to writing that was to set Sarraute in the forefront of contemporary artists. The sketches are fragile moments in which an observer experiences alienation from another through gestures and tones of voice. Sarraute chose the term "tropism" from the field of biochemistry to describe a preverbal, instinctive, psychic movement, as primitive and imperceptible as that of a plant's response to light and water. Overt human acts or words—often those demanded by social convention—obscure these authentic responses according to Sarraute.

After the publication of *Tropisms*, Sarraute, a Jew, spent World War II posing as a governess to her children. Despite the lack of critical attention received for *Tropisms*, Sarraute began work on *Portrait d'un inconnu* (1948; *Portrait of a Man Unknown*, 1958). Sartre wrote an introduction to this second novel, which he described as an "anti-novel" because it rejected nineteenth century concepts of plot and character. Sarraute also rejects the position of omniscient narrator in the sense that she refuses to assume authority; her writing tends to conjure up the reader's own memories as well as creating her own imaginative world; rather than imposing her own vision through artistic manipulation, she allows room for the reader's participation in her texts.

It was not until nearly twenty years after the publication of *Tropisms*, after the publication of *Portrait of a Man Unknown* in 1948, *Martereau* (English translation, 1959) in 1953, and the popular *Le Planétarium* (1959; *The Planetarium*, 1960), that Sarraute began to receive recognition by the majority of French critics and the public. Since then, Sarraute has published a novel every four or five years: *Les Fruits d'or* (1963; *The Golden Fruits*, 1964), *Entre la vie et la mort* (1968; *Between Life and Death*, 1969), *Vous les entendez?* (1972; *Do You Hear Them?*, 1973), *"Disent les imbéciles"* (1976; *"Fools Say,"* 1977), and *L'Usage de la parole* (1980; *The Uses of Speech*, 1980).

For a relaxation between novels, Sarraute turned to playwriting in the early 1960's. She transferred the preverbal "tropisms" into dialogue, at first for the radio, then for the stage. The plays' characters use everyday, conversational language that reveals deeply hidden animosities and rivalries. In order to retain the same anonymity as her characters possess in the novels, Sarraute simply provided identifying labels such as M.1 and 2, for first and second man, for example. Among her plays are *Le Silence* (1964; *Silence*, 1981), *Le Mensonge* (1966; *The Lie*, 1981), *C'est beau* (1973; *It's Beautiful*, 1981), and *Pour un oui ou pour un non* (1982).

During the 1980's, Sarraute's work began to receive recognition by readers and critics, especially feminists, outside France. A feminist criticism tends to examine her authorial refusal to manipulate the reader as well as the autobiographical work—such as *Enfance* (1984; *Childhood*, 1984)—which she has produced. Sarraute lives a hardworking and quiet life, dividing her time between Paris and the country, although she also frequently visits the United States.

*Summary*

While Nathalie Sarraute's writing is highly experimental, she compares herself to Fyodor Dostoevski, Gustave Flaubert, Dame Ivy Compton-Burnett, and Virginia Woolf, all exceptional creators of character and all experts in the use of irony. As her career progressed, Sarraute began to distance herself from the New Novel movement. In 1963, she added a foreword to a new edition of *Tropisms* in which she denies that she wished to suggest that humans are like plants in her use of the term "tropisms": "It obviously never occurred to me to compare human beings with insects or plants, as I have sometimes been reproached with doing." In the 1970's and 1980's, feminist criticism began to explore Sarraute's writing from more useful avenues, regarding her as a major autobiographical writer, and as a novelist with particular insight into human psychology, while pursuing the twentieth century tradition of experimentation at the level of the word. Sarraute's reputation has been enhanced since she has been viewed as separate from the very school of writing she was credited with founding.

*Bibliography*

Britton, Celia. "The Self and Language in the Novels of Nathalie Sarraute." *Modern Language Review* 77 (July, 1982): 577-584. This paper argues that Sarraute's novels are about language itself and, in particular, language as used in encounters between the novels' characters.

Cismaru, Alfred. "Conversation with Nathalie Sarraute." *Telescope* 4 (Spring, 1985): 17-24. An informal interview that provides a glimpse of Sarraute's rather private life and her views on writing in general.

Henderson, Liza. "Sarraute's Silences." *Theater* 20 (Winter, 1988): 22-24. A close study of Sarraute's play *Silence*, and of the drama in general as consisting of lies and silences.

Knapp, Bettina L. "Nathalie Sarraute's Between Life and Death: Androgyny and the Creative Process." *Studies in Twentieth Century Literature* 11 (Spring, 1987): 239-252. Knapp's paper examines Sarraute's novel *Between Life and Death*, its treatment of the creative process, and its creation of an archetypal writer, who creates at the level of the word as a living thing.

Minogue, Valerie. *Nathalie Sarraute and the War of the Words: A Study of Five Novels*. Edinburgh, Scotland: University of Edinburgh Press, 1981. A straightforward, in-depth study of five of Sarraute's novels with an emphasis on language. Includes an extensive bibliography. An appendix adds a letter from Sarraute herself, whose theorizing about writing is always clear and illuminating.

Munley, Ellen W. "I'm Dying but It's Only Your Story: Sarraute's Reader on Stage." *Contemporary Literature* 24 (Summer, 1983): 233-258. Munley argues that Sarraute's novel *The Uses of Speech* is interested in the separation of self from others, at the same time as the self becomes confused with others.

Sarraute, Nathalie. *The Age of Suspicion: Essays on the Novel.* Translated by Maria Jolas. New York: George Braziller, 1963. Sarraute presents her own theories of narrative method in this clear collection of essays that analyze her own writing in comparison to that of others. These theories have influenced a generation of subsequent writers of the New Novel, including Alain Robbe-Grillet and Michel Butor.

Watson-Williams, Helen. *The Novels of Nathalie Sarraute: Towards an Aesthetic.* Amsterdam: Rodopi, 1981. A full-length study of Sarraute's writings and their concern with the artistic process and the value and appreciation of art in everyday life.

*Joanne E. Butcher*

# JEAN-PAUL SARTRE

*Born:* June 21, 1905; Paris, France
*Died:* April 15, 1980; Paris, France
*Areas of Achievement:* Philosophy, literature, and social reform
*Contribution:* A powerhouse of intellectual energy, French existentialist Sartre poured out novels, plays, screenplays, biographies, criticism, political essays, and philosophy. Journalist, teacher, and perennial activist, he served in the first rank of worldwide liberal causes.

## *Early Life*

Jean-Paul Sartre was the only child of Anne-Marie Schweitzer and Jean-Baptiste Sartre. Jean-Baptiste had been a promising naval officer, active in several engagements in China, where he contracted the enterocolitis that killed him in September, 1906. The young widow and her son, then fifteen months old, returned to her parents' home. Charles Schweitzer, Anne-Marie's father, an overbearing intellectual, undertook the education of the precocious boy, who was soon reading voraciously and writing imitations of adventure comic books. Anne-Marie kept her son in long, golden curls. When the curls were finally cut, he recognized himself as ugly, with one eye turned out and blinded by an early illness. This ugliness and his small adult stature (five feet, two inches) fueled his self-consciousness. Formal schooling was intermittent until he was enrolled in the Lycée Henri-Quatre in 1915. After a rocky start, he was academically successful and began making friends.

In 1917, Anne-Marie remarried and moved with her son and new husband to La Rochelle. The move was unhappy for Sartre, who returned to Paris in the fall of 1920 as a boarding student. Thus began a happy period of his life. He renewed and deepened his school friendships and in 1924 entered the rigorous École Normale Supérieure. He shared an interest in philosophy with several classmates and spent hours in reading and discussion, and in the fun of movies, music, jokes, and girl-watching. Sartre loved the regimented life of all-male schools with their camaraderie and emphasis on intellectual achievement. He read widely, preferring Plato or René Descartes to his living professors. He also began to develop his own philosophical attitudes.

Probably his stubborn originality lay behind his failure at the *agrégation* in 1928. Since this competitive exam was the sole entry into the national system of secondary schools and universities, failure made a would-be academic unemployable. Sartre began a year of concentrated preparation for a retake. Early in that year, he met Simone de Beauvoir, a brilliant philosophy student also preparing for the *agrégation*. Although Sartre's romantic life was already crowded, de Beauvoir soon took the central position. They became partners, each the other's first reader and critic. They openly shared all experiences, and, although each had other lovers, they never broke with each other. They took the *agrégation* in July, 1929; Sartre took first place, de Beauvoir second.

In November, 1929, Sartre was called up for military service. Trained as a meteorologist, he spent his spare time in reading and writing. Both Sartre and de Beauvoir felt driven to put everything on paper, but neither had published when he was demobilized in February, 1931. Both accepted teaching jobs, Sartre's unconventional style made him a favorite with students. He spent 1933-1934 in Berlin, studying the works of Martin Heidegger and the phenomenology of Edmund Husserl. Sartre finally gave up teaching for professional writing in 1945.

*Life's Work*

In the years before World War II, Sartre settled into a lifelong pattern of regular hours of work, often at café tables and while traveling. Very prolific, he was unconcerned with the fate of his manuscripts, losing some and leaving several works unfinished. In the years 1937-1939, he published philosophical essays on imagination, ego, and emotions. Simultaneously, he published the novel *La Nausée* (1938; *Nausea*, 1949) and a collection of short stories, *Le Mur* (1939; *The Wall and Other Stories*, 1948). These writings were well received, in spite or because of their pessimistic view of absurd human life. Albert Camus, later a close friend, was an early, enthusiastic reviewer.

Sartre was called into active service as a meteorologist on September 2, 1939, the day after German troops invaded Poland. His military duties were minimal, and he spent most of his time writing letters, a journal, and the first draft of a novel, *L'Âge de raison* (1945; *The Age of Reason*, 1947), first of the planned tetralogy, *Les Chemins de la liberté* (1945-1949; *The Roads to Freedom*, 1947-1950). Equally important was his philosophical work *L'Être et le néant* (1943; *Being and Nothingness*, 1956), begun in the same period. In June, 1940, he was captured and sent to a German prison camp. Paradoxically, Sartre felt liberated as a prisoner. He enjoyed the solidarity of inmates against their jailers. He discussed theology and philosophy with the priests who served the camp and wrote his first play, *Bariona: Ou, Le Fils de tonnere* (1962; *Bariona: Or, The Son of Thunder*, 1970), a Christmas story published much later that camouflaged a call to resistance against foreign invasion. When he escaped in March, 1941, he returned to occupied Paris and resumed teaching.

Sartre and de Beauvoir were active in the Resistance as writers and distributors of underground material, but Sartre also continued writing philosophical and literary texts. *Being and Nothingness* was completed in October, 1942. The second novel of his tetralogy, *Le Sursis* (1945; *The Reprieve*, 1947), was finished in November, 1943. In 1943, *Les Mouches* (*The Flies*,

1946), a play based on the Greek myth of Orestes' revenge on his mother Clytemnestra, appeared in Paris, using an ancient story to mask a call to violent resistance and passed the German censors. During rehearsals, Sartre met Camus. They became friends, and Sartre wrote for Camus's underground paper, *Combat*. In May of 1944, he presented a new play, *Huis clos* (1944; *No Exit*, 1946). The direct audience contact of the theater was congenial. As in his novels, Sartre used the conventions of plot and character to present his philosophical concepts to a wider public.

During the war, Sartre and de Beauvoir collected a family of former lovers, students, and friends who ate or starved together, with de Beauvoir coordinating the scanty rations. A social network of avant-garde artists and writers met for all-night parties in defiance of wartime curfews. Sartre, an accomplished jazz pianist, played and sang. A heavy drinker and smoker, he always preferred café atmosphere to academic circles. Shortages of food and goods meant little to him. He did not collect property. He idealized the solidarity of students, prisoners, and resistance fighters and, in the decades that followed, would yearn for and never quite recapture the euphoria of the war years. He remained on good terms with his mother and, after the death of his stepfather, shared an apartment with her from 1946 until 1961, when bomb threats made the arrangement dangerous for her. She died in January, 1969.

The end of the war coincided with Sartre's entry into full-time writing and celebrity. Between 1945 and 1965, he wrote eleven plays and filmscripts, set in times and places as disparate as occupied France and medieval Germany. He promised a study on ethics to follow *Being and Nothingness*; it never came, but many considerations of good and evil were transposed into his biography of the outlaw genius Jean Genet, *Saint Genet: Comédien et martyr* (1952; *Saint Genet: Actor and Martyr*, 1963). He published a major biographical essay entitled *Baudelaire* (English translation, 1950) in 1947, but his massive biography of Gustave Flaubert, *L'Idiot de la famille: Gustave Flaubert, 1821-1857* (3 vols., 1971-1972; *The Family Idiot: Gustave Flaubert, 1821-1857*, partial translation, 1981), was never finished. His own autobiography, *Les Mots* (1964; *The Words*, 1964), covers only the early years of his childhood. He published *La Mort dans l'âme* (1949; *Troubled Sleep*, 1950), the third volume of his tetralogy, but the projected fourth book never appeared. Even his *Critique de la raison dialectique, I: Théorie des ensembles pratiques* (1960; *Critique of Dialectical Reason I: Theory of Practical Ensembles*, 1976) was never finished, although some themes were transposed into other works. The sheer press of demands from all sides, coupled with the ferment of his ideas, made completion of these works unlikely, but their open-ended state gave an illusion of freedom; he still had the option of working on them. A series of essays, gathered in collections entitled *Situations* (1947-1976), dealt with specific issues, rather than philosophical generalizations. His emphasis was less on systematic consistency than on spontaneity of thought in relation to individual circumstances. His *Qu'est-ce que la littérature?* (1947; *What Is Literature?*, 1949) examines aesthetics, especially in literature, and makes the case for the "engaged writer," who aims at action in the world and rejects "art for art's sake."

Sartre was the most prominent of a group loosely defined under the label "existentialist," and his writings of the 1940's and 1950's most clearly define the terms of that movement in French literature, criticism, and philosophy. Sartre detested all labels. He argued that each man is responsible for himself, that the external definitions of history or religion conceal the chaos to which actions give shape, and that choice of those actions defines human liberty. To a France bowed down by the shame of defeat, existentialism offered a fresh start with a clean slate.

Immediately after the war, Sartre worked to found a new journal, *Les Temps modernes* (a bow to Charlie Chaplin), whose diverse editorial board encouraged freewheeling discussion of political and literary subjects. By the time of the French student uprisings of May, 1968, Sartre spoke a frank Maoist line and loaned his name to the editorial boards of radical underground journals, helping to distribute them in defiance of the law.

Sartre died of long-standing vascular illness on April 15, 1980. He had been virtually blind since 1973, able to work only with the help of patient friends such as de Beauvoir, who would talk with him and record his words. He had remained active, going to demonstrations and speaking at rallies, but gradually decaying flesh triumphed over will. He had been idolized and hated by a diverse, worldwide audience.

*Summary*

A listing of Jean-Paul Sartre's plays, articles, biographies, philosophical studies, causes he espoused, travels, talks, demonstrations, and volatile friendships is dizzying. He declined a Nobel Prize in Literature in 1964, the first person ever to do so, because he said he preferred not to be made an institution. The example of writers of the Resistance who risked their lives in their work defined his artistic position. In a sense, Sartre always believed himself to be such a Resistance writer. As he worked for liberal causes around the world, he was never deterred by fears of ridicule. His flirtation with the French Communist Party and the governments of Cuba, the Soviet Union, and China was long-standing. A frequent apologist for Marxist movements, he still opposed oppression within the Eastern Bloc, speaking out against the Soviet use of force in Hungary and Czechoslovakia.

Sartre's ideas influenced scholars, artists, and ordinary people. The novels and plays that brought his ideas directly before the public continue to be read and studied throughout the world. Situational ethics grew out of the existentialist milieu, as did the contemporary antihero, a figure whose anguish is measured by his individual reactions to life rather than eternal standards of good and evil. Although literary and critical fashion passed him by in the 1970's, some fifty thousand people followed his funeral procession through the streets of Paris.

*Bibliography*

Beauvoir, Simone de. *Adieux: A Farewell to Sartre*. Translated by Patrick O'Brian. New York: Pantheon Books, 1984. A look at Sartre by his lifelong companion, de Beauvoir. If anyone can write a meaningful reflection on Sartre's life it is de Beauvoir.

Cohen-Solal, Annie. *Sartre: A Life*. Translated by Anna Cancogni. New York: Pantheon Books, 1987. A lucid, flowing account of Sartre's life, with particular attention given to the development of his interpersonal relationships. Contains illustrations, notes, a bibliography, and an index.

Gerassi, John. *Jean-Paul Sartre: Hated Conscience of His Century.* Vol 1. Chicago: University of Chicago Press, 1989. In a personal work, encouraged by Sartre, who knew the journalist author well, Gerassi presents the bourgeois writer on his way to revolutionary politics. The first volume covers the years before Sartre's World War II Resistance work.

Hayman, Ronald. *Sartre: A Life*. New York: Simon & Schuster, 1987. An invaluable, scholarly work, this biography focuses with particular clarity on the progression of Sartre's ideas and his changing philosophical stance. Contains illustrations, notes, a bibliography, an index, and a chronological table.

Sartre, Jean-Paul. *The Words*. Translated by Bernard Frechtman. New York: George Braziller, 1964. This autobiographical work covers the childhood years of the author, giving a hypnotic, highly impressionistic picture of his relationship to his family and to the world of words and ideas. Few hard facts, no index or bibliography, but fascinating.

*Anne W. Sienkewicz*

# ERIK SATIE

*Born:* May 17, 1866; Honfleur, France
*Died:* July 1, 1925; Paris, France
*Area of Achievement:* Music
*Contribution:* Satie was a unique figure in French music at the beginning of the twentieth century. In the 1890's he played an important role in turning French music away from the influence of nineteenth century German Romanticism. During and after World War I, he was the major composer of the French avant-garde; he turned away from Impressionism, in which he never really took part, and prefigured the neoclassicism of the 1940's and 1950's.

## *Early Life*

Erik Satie was born in a coastal town in the Normandy region of France to Jules Alfred Satie, a marine broker, and Jane Leslie Anton, a Scotswoman. In 1870, at the close of the Franco-Prussian War, the family moved to Paris. When Satie's mother died two years later, he and his brother and sister returned to Honfleur to live with their grandparents, who reared them in a strict Catholic tradition. Satie attended school in Honfleur with little distinction.

In 1874, Satie's grandfather started him in piano lessons with a church organist, who introduced the boy to liturgical music, particularly Gregorian chant; this exposure influenced the full range of Satie's later work. Another notable influence at this time was an eccentric uncle, nicknamed the Sea Bird because he spent much of his time sitting in a beautifully outfitted boat that never left the dock. The Sea Bird also took young Satie to see traveling circuses and acting troupes, and the boy got a glimpse backstage while the uncle pursued various female performers.

Satie's music teacher left Honfleur in 1878, the same year his grandmother died, and shortly thereafter he returned to live with his father in Paris. At this point all aspects of his formal education languished except for music. In 1879, he entered a preparatory class at the Paris Conservatoire and began auditioning for the regular piano class. For the next seven years, he continued to take the biannual examinations with no success. In November of 1885 he finally passed the entrance exam for the intermediate class, where he spent a year working under an intolerant teacher. Throughout his conservatory experience, Satie's teachers took note of his natural talent but chastised him for laziness.

Partway through his second year of the intermediate class, Satie dropped out and volunteered for military service. This allowed him to shorten the customary five years' compulsory service to one year, but he ended his military career even earlier with a self-inflicted case of bronchitis. While convalescing he began to sketch out the *Trois Gymnopédies* and *Trois Sarabandes*, his earliest significant compositions. Later that year, 1887, Satie left his father's home and settled at the foot of Montmartre, the Bohemian section of Paris. The following year he began playing piano at the Chat Noir, a Montmartre café, and he assumed the full costume and role of a bohemian eccentric.

### *Life's Work*

While earning a living as a café pianist, Satie also began his career as a serious composer. With the *Trois Gymnopédies*, which he finished in 1888, and the *Trois Gnossiennes* of 1890, he prefigured many of the harmonic innovations of Claude Debussy and Maurice Ravel at a time when the German Romanticism of Johannes Brahms and Richard Wagner still dominated European music. These early works for piano combine exoticism and awkwardness into a simple but purely original style, and they set a pattern for Satie's career by anticipating popular taste by at least ten years. In fact the *Gymnopédies* did not achieve their full initial popularity until 1911.

Satie's early fascination with the mysticism and ritual of the Catholic church drew him to a brief affiliation with the Rosicrucian sect in 1890, and over the next two years he composed incidental music and fanfares for their elaborate ceremonies. He then disassociated himself from the group, but his affinity for religious pomp reasserted itself in the next few years in the form of the "Metropolitan Church of the Art of Jesus the Conductor," an imaginary institution under the auspices of which Satie published attacks on his perceived enemies and rivals in the Paris music scene. A small inheritance in 1892 allowed him to indulge such fantasies with increased vigor. He proposed himself three times for the Institut de France, an impossible honor for an obscure bohemian in his twenties, and he maintained a pose of complete seriousness throughout, all the while mocking the prosperous bourgeois self-importance of such established institutions. Thus Satie carried the bohemian ethos to fulfillment.

While performing in the cafés of Montmartre, Satie met many of the painters and poets of the artistic avant-garde that flourished in Paris from the 1890's through the 1920's. In later years, he acknowledged having spent more time with and learned more from painters than musicians. In 1891, however, while playing at the Auberge du Clou, Satie met Debussy and began a close friendship that would last thirty years. The two composers influenced each other, particularly at the beginning of their friendship, as they attempted to find a new direction for a more uniquely French music than was then being composed. Debussy had already achieved some renown as a composer, but his wider experience had exposed him to more of the Wagnerian influence then prevalent. Satie played an important role in Debussy's career by liberating his more famous friend from that tendency. Satie also met the young Ravel in the 1890's and exercised a similar influence on his development. These two composers went on to create Impressionism in music, drawing in part from Satie's earliest work.

Satie's stylistic development moved in a different direction. His music reached the height of its liturgical phase with the *Messe des pauvres* (1895) and then returned to the simplicity and playfulness of his earlier work with *Pièces froides* (1897). A year later, he moved across Paris from Montmartre to the obscure suburb of Arcueil-Cachan, where he lived in a second-floor flat over a bistro called The Four Chimneys. Although he still composed and performed popular songs in Montmartre to make his living—and in fact he made the six-mile walk twice a day—he essentially shut himself off from the frenzy of artistic activity in his former neighborhood and retreated into solitude. Over the next twelve years, Satie composed very little work of importance, and his grandiose public gestures ceased. The most notable composition of these years is *Trois Morceaux en forme de poire* (three pieces in the shape of a pear), his most ambitious work for piano. Debussy is said to have advised Satie to pay more attention to form in his composition; Satie supposedly responded to his friend's advice with *Trois Morceaux en forme de poire*, a formless piece having no relation to pears or to the number three. In fact the work is a twenty-minute conglomeration of short pieces spanning the previous fifteen years of Satie's career. In it he combined the style of his popular songs with the modal and harmonic characteristics of his more serious liturgical work.

Satie laid the foundation for the second half of his career when, nearing the age of forty and against Debussy's advice, he returned to school. In 1905, he entered the Schola Cantorum, a music school founded ten years earlier by Vincent d'Indy, and he studied counterpoint under Albert Roussel for the next three years. Satie was a diligent student; he worked with seriousness and deep conviction, and this time he earned the admiration of his teachers. Upon graduating in 1908, he received a diploma entitling him to pursue a life of composition, but at first Satie composed nothing at all. Rather, he devoted his energies in the winter of 1908-1909 to local affairs in his neighborhood of Arcueil. He joined the local Radical-Socialist Party, gave music lessons to his neighbors, and wrote a column in the local newspaper.

Satie put aside his civic activities in 1910 and returned to composition. Following his intense study of counterpoint, he now wrote in a spare, linear, contrapuntal style. His titles grew increasingly grotesque, as in *Embryons desséchés* (dried embryos), and his directions on interpretation began to mock those of Debussy: "Like a nightingale with a toothache," for example. He grew increasingly playful and humorous with the running commentary of text in his piano works: A musical quote from Chopin's funeral march appears in *Embryons desséchés* deliberately mislabled as "a well-known mazurka by Schubert."

At the same time, Satie began to receive recognition for the compositions of his youth. Ravel and Debussy both presented such early works as *Trois Gymnopédies* in performance in 1911, praising Satie for anticipating Impressionism. The critics began to mention him favorably, and publishers began requesting new compositions. Satie's style had changed, however, and the work he submitted in response was rejected. He found it bewildering that twenty-year-old works previously considered simplistic were now considered charming, while the works he now composed were considered too complex, too academic. Ultimately Satie ignored the fashion and continued to write what have become known as his humoristic works. This period culminated in *Sports et divertissements*, a collection of twenty fragments that combines poetry, painting, and Satie's exquisite calligraphy with his music.

In 1915, the young poet Jean Cocteau heard Satie perform *Trois Morceaux* and was moved to propose a collaboration on a ballet with Sergei Diaghilev, the producer of the Ballets Russes. Pablo Picasso designed the sets and costumes, and Satie wrote a score that included parts for typewriters, sirens, and similar effects. The result was *Parade*, a rendering of cubism in music and choreography, premiered in 1917. The first performance caused a minor uproar in the audience, and Satie is said to have joined in the whistling from his seat in the balcony. The critics responded with such hostility that Satie sent one critic an insulting postcard and wound up with a damage suit that led to a stiff fine and a week's prison sentence; he avoided prison only with the urgent intercession of his friends.

*Parade* established Satie's reputation as an opponent of Impressionism and a friend to the newer schools. When Dubussy, now an invalid and nearing the end of his life, neglected to send Satie any congratulations over *Parade*, Satie took offense. As far back as the 1890's, Satie had been known for quarreling with his friends over imagined slights, and this was no exception. He wrote Debussy a reproachful letter in 1918, the year Debussy died. The two friends were never reconciled, and Satie later regretted this last falling out.

At this point Satie began to collect a following of his own; a group of young French musicians, later dubbed "Les Six," including Francis Poulenc and Darius Milhaud, were attracted as much by Satie's personality as by his music. Satie was amazed by this; he asked their advice, quarreled with them, but refused to assume the role of master of a school.

As the critics began to recognize the importance of *Parade*, Satie turned to a new form. His next major composition, *Socrate* (1919), was a musical setting of the *Dialogues* of Plato for chamber orchestra. Often called Satie's masterpiece, *Socrate* is the culmination of his spare, linear conception of music. Satie anticipated its reception with a note in the program for its premiere: "Those who are unable to understand are requested to adopt an attitude of complete submission and inferiority." In fact, part of the audience giggled at its apparent monotony, and the critics responded with both praise and scorn.

A few months later, in March of 1920, Satie engaged in an experiment with "furniture music," an idea that originated with the artist Henri Matisse, who envisioned an art without subject matter, an art similar in function to a comfortable easy-chair. At the intermission of a play by Max Jacob being performed in an art gallery, Satie and Milhaud had musicians dispersed about the gallery start playing rhythmic but purposefully inconsequential music. The audience was instructed to ignore the music, to treat it as merely a background. Thus Satie was disappointed when the audience ignored his instructions and kept silent; he rushed about the gallery, urging them to talk, move around, make noise, but not listen.

Satie further developed this approach to music several years later with background music for a Surrealist film by René Clair, which formed the entr'acte of his Bballet *Relâche* (1924). Here the function of the music was to underline the action of the film indirectly, without drawing attention to itself. *Relâche*, subtitled *Ballet instantanéiste* (instantaneous ballet), was Satie's last work. The performance included dancers smoking cigarettes, a fireman wandering through the set, and costume changes on stage. Satie's music elicited heckling and laughter: His prelude was based on an indecent student song, and the rest was considered dull. At the end of the premiere, Satie drove on stage in a tiny automobile to take his bow. Like *Parade*, the performance was considered scandalous, and, true to form, Satie ignored the response.

Shortly thereafter Satie grew ill with cirrhosis of the liver. The illness lasted for six months, during which time he refused to see most of the old friends with whom he had quarreled, and he died in St. Joseph Hospital on July 1, 1925.

### *Summary*

Erik Satie has never been considered more than a minor composer. His collected works would make a slim volume, and most of his individual compositions are very short. Even now only a handful of his early piano works are regularly performed. Yet his contributions to the development of Western music in the early twentieth century are considerable. Tonal music over the preceding centuries had used chords to create motion, as one chord implies motion to another related chord. Satie ignored that tradition; he was one of the first to use chords as isolated sonorities, with no need to move in any given direction. Starting from this harmonic conception, Debussy developed a style of great complexity, while Satie's music always retained an apparent simplicity, ever avoiding grand, transcendent sentiment. Often his work took the form of parody, not only of Romanticism but also of Impressionism; in his more serious work he stripped his music of all pretension, revealing austere essence. Thus, while Debussy's music has been compared to the works of the Impressionist painters, the sonorities of his chords resembling their brushstrokes, critics have compared Satie's *Trois Gymnopédies*, for example, to the cubist still-life paintings of Picasso and Georges Braque, not only for the motionlessness of his harmonies but also because the three movements seem to take three different perspectives on the same theme, like the painters view their subjects from different angles and superimpose the images.

These qualities in his music combined with his eccentric social behavior, his ability to ignore current fashion and anticipate future styles, and his emphasis on graphics and textual elements to put him at the center of the Parisian avant-garde after 1910. Ultimately he outpaced the avant-garde as well: A play he wrote in 1913, *La Piège de Meduse*, anticipated the Dada movement by eight years, and it was unearthed and celebrated by the Dadaists in 1921. His later music, with its clarity, simplicity, and wit, influenced Poulenc, Milhaud, and beyond them the American neoclassical composer Virgil Thomson. The same attributes in Satie's personality set an example for the entire artistic avant-garde.

*Bibliography*

Gillmor, Alan M. *Erik Satie*. Boston: Twayne, 1988. Gillmor's biography of Satie derives mostly from Myers' (see below), but his musical analysis is excellent, providing a clear, concise, and readable discussion of technical issues. Includes a bibliography, a chronology of Satie's life, a list of works, and an excellent discography.

Harding, James. *Erik Satie*. New York: Praeger, 1975. In this biography Harding vividly portrays the spirit of Satie's times, focusing particularly on the years leading up to his collaboration with Cocteau and Diaghilev. Smoothly written and very readable, the book includes a bibliography and a catalog of Satie's published works and writings.

Myers, Rollo H. *Erik Satie*. London: Dennis Dobson, 1948. This monograph was the first biography of Satie available in the English language. Short but comprehensive, it provides a balanced portrait of his life and a general introduction to his music.

Shattuck, Roger. *The Banquet Years: The Origin of the Avant-Garde in France, 1885 to World War I*. Rev. ed. New York: Vintage Books, 1968. This social history provides a detailed analysis of the French avant-garde, focusing on four of its members: the painter Henri Rousseau, the poets Alfred Jarry and Guillaume Apollinaire, and Satie. Shattuck's approach is scholarly and incisive. Includes illustrations and a bibliography with a list of principal works and published writings.

Templier, Pierre Daniel. *Erik Satie*. Translated by Elena L. French and David S. French. Cambridge, Mass.: MIT Press, 1969. This translation of the first biography of Satie, originally published in France in 1932, provides an excellent starting point. Templier gives a sympathetic analysis of Satie's character and a general description of his music. Written mostly from primary sources, the book contains excellent documentation as well as an extensive selection of Satie's illustrations and drawings, a discography, and a few pages from his original scores in sixty pages of plates.

*John Neil Ries*

# EISAKU SATŌ

*Born:* March 27, 1901; Tabuse, Japan
*Died:* June 2, 1975; Tokyo, Japan
*Areas of Achievement:* Government and politics
*Contribution:* Satō served consecutively as Prime Minister of Japan longer than any other individual. He is the only modern Japanese politician to expand the country permanently. One of the founders of the Liberal-Democratic Party, he not only followed its traditional probusiness policy but also tripled the per capita income of the Japanese. In 1974, he became the first Asian to receive the Nobel Peace Prize.

## *Early Life*

Eisaku Satō was born to a samurai family in Tabuse, Yamaguchi Prefecture, in southwestern Japan, far from the center of power. The family, however, was one of the leaders in that area, and his two elder brothers also became famous. The eldest was Ichiro, who ultimately became a vice admiral in the Japanese navy. The second son was adopted by his wife's family and took the name of Nobusuke Kishi. He served as Prime Minister of Japan from 1957 to 1960.

Satō was born on March 27, 1901. Relatives at first considered him as the most personable of the brothers but the least intelligent, which was not a large slight in a brilliant family. He attended the Fifth Higher School in Kumamoto (essentially a combination high school and junior college). One of the other graduates was Satō's immediate predecessor as prime minister, Hayato Ikeda.

Satō then entered the Imperial University at Tokyo (Todai), the traditional school for governmental and top business leaders in Japan. He received a law degree in 1924. His classmates included six other members of the diet, one supreme court justice, three bank presidents, Fuji Iron and Steel president Nagasno, and *Sankei Shimbun* (newspaper) president Mizuno. The latter two formed half of Satō's Koba Chu quartet, giving him in effect a joint chiefs of staff relationship to the business community during his prime ministership.

Immediately upon graduation, Satō joined the Ministry of Railways (later Transportation), for which he held a number of administrative positions. In 1926, he married the niece of the president of the Manchurian Southern Railroad. It was a typical arranged marriage, and his wife said it took her ten years to understand him. They had two sons, Roataru and Shingi, the latter of whom has a close marital relationship to Michiko, Empress of Japan. From August, 1934, to April, 1936, Satō was on a study tour of the United States, learning railroad operations and business methods. In both 1938 and 1939, he was sent to China to direct railroad construction. During World

War II, he continued to operate in the ministry, trying to keep transportation going during wartime. Satō remained a part of the Asian Study Group throughout his political career.

*Life's Work*

At the end of the Pacific War, Satō was not imprisoned, as was his second brother, who had served in the Tōjō cabinet. Fortunately, Satō was still at the subdirector level, whose members mostly escaped imprisonment. In 1945, he was named director of the Osaka District Railway Bureau and then vice minister of transportation in 1947. His efficiency in dealing with the construction led him to the attention of Prime Minister Shigeru Yoshida, who named him cabinet secretary in 1948. The next year he was elected to the diet as a member of the Liberal Party. Working well with the liberal, pro-United States Yoshida (the U.S. installed prime minister), Satō also served as minister of posts and telecommunications and as minister of construction. In 1953, he became the secretary-general of the Liberal Party. By now he was displaying the ability to work well with all factions in politics, which was one of his greatest assets.

In 1954, the *zosen gigoku* scandal rocked Japanese politics. Several shipping companies were accused of giving kickbacks and bribes to government officials and party leaders in return for government contracts and subsidies. Satō was involved, and a warrant was issued for his arrest; yet Prime Minister Yoshida had his minister of justice order that Satō not be arrested. Later in the year, however, Satō was indicted on charges of violating the Public Funds Regulation Law, but the case was dropped in 1956 as a part of a general amnesty celebrating Japan's entry into the United Nations. Meanwhile, in 1955, Satō had been one of the founding members of the Liberal-Democratic Party (LDP), emerging in 1957 as the head of his own faction in the party.

In 1957, Satō's brother Kishi became prime minister, and the next year brought Satō back into the cabinet as minister of finance. Satō and Kishi both strongly supported Prime Minister Ikeda from 1960 to 1964, and Satō served as minister of international trade and industry at a time when Japan was vastly increasing its international efforts. The climactic effort of Satō's early career was the directorship of the Tokyo Olympics, which is considered to be the extravaganza that notified the world of the reemergence of Japan as a major power. Certainly it was quite successful for Satō.

On July 10, 1964, Satō challenged the incumbent Ikeda for the LDP presidency and prime ministership. Also in the race was Aiichiro Fujiyama. The election was close and hard-fought, but Ikeda was reelected. Yet the fellow graduate of the Fifth Higher School in Kumamoto was stricken with terminal cancer. In October, Ikeda announced his decision to resign. There was great concern in two areas. The LDP members in the diet feared another acrimonious election. Furthermore the *zaikai*, or leaders of the community of large businesses, were fearful of both of the other major contenders, Fujiyama and Kono. Consequently the secretary-general of the party and the vice president of the party were allowed to choose the successor through consultation. Ikeda announced on November 9, 1964, that the sole candidate for the party presidency was Satō, and he was unanimously elected to begin the longest single term of any Japanese prime minister, serving until July 6, 1972.

During his prime ministership, Satō was always closely aligned with the business community, which gave him strong support and advice. The leading business club was the Choeikai, made up of approximately fifty presidents, vice presidents, and chairmen of big corporations, including the Bank of Japan, the Fuji Bank, Mitsubishi Heavy Industry, Hitachi Shipbuilding, Sony, Tokyo Gas, and Nissan, among others. The club was coheaded by the vice president of Tokyo Gas, who was the father of Satō's daughter-in-law. Yet Satō was highly unusual in one way in his relationship to business, which was a long-term LDP policy. He had approximately twenty clubs, which included a total of 280 different members from business. Even his elder brother Kishi had been unable to maintain such a pace. In fact, older *zaikai* members were quite unhappy at times with this larger advisory group, even saying that their era had ended. It was during Satō's regime, however, that *Time* magazine named the combination of business, bureaucracy, and legislative/executive leadership in Japan "Japan, Inc." Certainly, Japanese business continued to prosper and expand under the Satō administration, but it was a Japanese business of far greater diversification.

One of Satō's main interests was in party politics. He was reelected as prime minister three more times in 1966, 1968, and 1970. Only during the first election was there serious opposition, and he beat Fujiyama by 289 to 94 with 81 other scattered votes. Quickly he became known as Satō the "personnel manager" for his ability to see that each of the factions in the party, of which his was the largest, had a stake in the jobs available in the government.

As for any politician, domestic activities were extremely important to Satō. One of his major efforts was to persuade the businesses of Japan, in exchange for continued governmental assistance, to liberalize their pay policy. The average factory worker's pay went from $500 to $1,500 annually, making this a very prosperous period for the worker in Japan. Satō also increased the governmental support for the national health insurance and the rice subsidy for the farmers. Always interested in transportation, he extended the Shinkansen (bullet train) line from Ōsaka to Okayama between 1967 and 1972. Discovering that Haneda (Tokyo International) Airport was seriously overcrowded, he originated in 1966 the new Tokyo International Airport Authority, which began construction at the farming village of Narita, Chiba Prefecture, about forty miles east of Tokyo in 1969. Serious opposition developed among both local residents and the opposition parties, which led to riots and eventual suspension of construction in 1971. Eventually, the airport was completed in 1978, after Satō's death.

Satō's policy concerning atomic weapons was extremely popular in Japan. It was named Hikaku Sangensoku, or "three nonnuclear principles," and called for nonmanufacturing of atomic weapons in Japan, nonpossession of atomic weapons by Japan, and nonintroduction into Japan of atomic weapons. The latter policy, though widely popular in Japan, led to problems with the United States at times, particularly over the reversion of Okinawa to Japan. The sponsorship of the Osaka International Exposition (World's Fair) in 1970 was also considered a great success. These policies made Satō extremely popular in Japan and allowed him to win general elections in 1967 and 1970.

Satō is best known for his foreign policies. He was always interested in Asia, and one of his first policies was to normalize relationships with South Korea, a policy that was popular in the United States also. He also made a commitment of $800 million to build up Korea's economy. In 1967, he made two visits to Southeast Asia and began assistance to several countries there. His China policy, however, was an anomaly. Though he had expressed interest in normalized relationships earlier, his original policy was support of the isolation of China, similar to that of the United States. In 1971, however, when Richard Nixon went to China, Satō and the Japanese government were not informed of the trip, and it created what was called the Nixon Shocks. This policy seemed a great affront to a loyal ally and was considered a possible hindrance in the continuation of normal relationships. Yet Satō loyally continued to support the United States.

Much of this continued support related to the policy of reversion of Okinawa and the Ryukyu Islands. First acquired by Japanese rulers in the 1600's, the Ryukyus had come under complete Japanese control in 1895. They had been occupied by U.S. forces in 1945 and not returned to Japan. Satō made it his policy from the first to obtain their reversion. At first he was unwilling to allow continued U.S. bases there but soon relented as long as atomic weapons were not allowed. In 1968, unable to effect a treaty for these islands, he obtained a reversion of the Bonin Islands, sixty miles south of Tokyo. The next year, Nixon and Satō signed a reversion agreement for the Ryukyus, which became completely Japanese on May 15, 1972.

Having obtained the desired foreign policy result that made him the only modern Japanese politician to expand the country permanently, Satō retired on July 6, 1972. One final honor, however, awaited him. In 1974, Satō was named a cowinner, with Sean MacBride of Ireland, of the Nobel Peace Prize. Several reasons were cited for his selection, the most notable being his nonnuclear policy. Also important were his Southeast Asia support, his support for the denunciation of war as set out in the 1947 constitution of

Japan, and the reversion of the Okinawa area peacefully to Japan. The honor was almost as much that of Japan as it was of Satō, since he was the first Asian to receive the Nobel Peace Prize. In his acceptance speech, Satō emphasized the ordinary people's portion in peace with their activities in art, culture, and religion, among other things, and saw himself as a practical politician who wanted to achieve policies peacefully and warned of nuclear dangers. Satō died in Tokyo on June 2, 1975.

*Summary*

Eisaku Satō was a Japanese bureaucrat from a prominent country family who served continuously as prime minister from November, 1964, to July, 1972, longer than any other man in his country's history. His greatest success was in the acquisition of the Ryukyu and Bonin islands for his country; he became the only modern Japanese politician to expand Japan permanently. He was also quite successful in expanding his country's gross national product through an alliance with business, while at the same time tripling the average worker's salary. He also normalized relationships with nearby South Korea and began the policy of assistance to less developed nations. The climax of his career was the receipt of the 1974 Nobel Peace Prize.

*Bibliography*

Eiji, Tominomori. "Satō's Legacy." *Japan Quarterly* 19, no. 2 (1972): 154-159. This is a summary article mostly interested in Satō's foreign policy, written just before his retirement.

Gray, Tony. *Champions of Peace*. New York: Paddington Press, 1976. This work has the best article on Satō and the Nobel Peace Prize.

Kim, Hong N. "The Satō Government and the Politics of Okinawa Reversion." *Asian Survey* 13, no. 11 (1973): 1021-1035. This article summarizes well the politics involved in persuading the United States to accept the reversion of the Ryukyus and the Japanese diet that it was permissible for the Americans to retain their bases.

Thayer, Nathaniel B. *How the Conservatives Rule Japan*. Princeton, N.J.: Princeton University Press, 1969. Written during Satō's administration, this book best summarizes Satō's political policies.

Yanaga, Chitoshi. *Big Business in Japanese Politics*. New Haven, Conn.: Yale University Press, 1968. This book, also written during Satō's administration, illustrates well his election by business and his policies toward business.

Yasutomo, Dennis T. "Satō's China Policy." *Asian Survey* 17, no. 6 (1977): 530-544. This article is mostly interested in the early China policy before the Nixon Shocks.

*Fred S. Rolater*

# FERDINAND DE SAUSSURE

*Born:* November 26, 1857; Geneva, Switzerland
*Died:* February 22, 1913; Vufflens, near Geneva, Switzerland
*Areas of Achievement:* Language and linguistics
*Contribution:* Primarily through a book written by colleagues after his death, Saussure established the foundations of twentieth century linguistics. His focus on the systematic structure of language is the fundamental principle of structuralism in linguistics, anthropology, and literary criticism, and he provided the theoretical basis of semiology—the study of signs.

## *Early Life*

When Ferdinand de Saussure was enrolled in chemistry and physics courses at the University of Geneva in 1875, he was following a tradition long established on his father's side of the family. Ferdinand's great-grandfather was Horace-Bénédict de Saussure, a famous scientist; his grandfather was professor of geology and mineralogy; and his father, Henri, had a doctorate in geology. Ferdinand, too, was to become a scientist, but it was the science of linguistics that captured his attention at an early age.

Adolf Pictet, a friend of the family, and Count Alexandre-Joseph de Pourtalès, Ferdinand's maternal grandfather, encouraged the young boy to study languages. By the age of twelve, Ferdinand had read chapters of Pictet's book on linguistic paleontology. He knew French, German, English, and Latin, and he began Greek at the age of thirteen. The year before entering the university, the young Saussure, on Pictet's advice, studied Sanskrit from a book by the German scholar Franz Bopp.

Saussure's career in physics and chemistry lasted for only two semesters. During that time, he continued his studies of Greek and Latin and joined the Linguistic Society of Paris. By autumn 1876, he had transferred to the University of Leipzig in Germany. For the next four semesters, Saussure attended courses in comparative grammar, history of the German language, Sanskrit, Greek, Old Persian, Celtic, Slavic languages, and Lithuanian. His teachers were the leading figures of the time in historical and comparative linguistics, including, among the younger generation, the "Neogrammarians," scholars of Indo-European who established the famous principle that sound changes in the historical development of languages operate without exception.

In the Leipzig environment of August Leskien, Hermann Osthoff, and Karl Brugmann, Saussure wrote extensively, publishing several papers through the Linguistic Society of Paris. At age twenty-one, in 1878, he produced the monograph that was to be the most famous work of his lifetime, *Mémoire sur le système primitif des voyelles dans les langues indo-européennes* (1879; memoir on the original system of the vowels in the Indo-

European languages). When it appeared, he was in Berlin studying Sanskrit. Returning to Leipzig in 1880, he received his doctoral degree with honors.

## *Life's Work*

Saussure's *Mémoire sur le système primitif des voyelles dans les langues indo-européennes* was a daring reconstruction of an aspect of proto-Indo-European which was met in Germany with little understanding, even with hostility. Yet the work was very well received in France; in the fall of 1880, Saussure moved to Paris. He attended courses in classical languages, lectures by the leading French linguist Michel Bréal, and meetings of the Linguistic Society of Paris. The next year, on October 30, 1881, with Bréal's strong support, he was unanimously named lecturer in Gothic and Old High German at the École des Hautes Études. His lifelong career as a teacher began a week later.

Saussure's courses dealt primarily with comparative grammar of the Germanic languages, but he was highly critical of the earlier nineteenth century German tradition in such studies. Comparison of individual words in different languages or over time within one language seemed to him haphazard, unfruitful, and unscientific. In his *Mémoire sur le système primitif des voyelles dans les langues indo-européennes*, he had used the notion of a language as a structured system in which all forms are interrelated, and this fundamental concept had led him to hypothesize forms in Indo-European that had disappeared in the languages for which there were historical records. It was a half century after the publication of the *Mémoire sur le système primitif des voyelles dans les langues indo-européennes* that evidence was discovered in Hittite proving him correct.

At the École des Hautes Études, Saussure's courses attracted substantial numbers of students, and, with Bréal, he set the foundation for comparative grammar in France. He taught Sanskrit, Latin, and Lithuanian as well, and some of his students and disciples became the most prominent French linguists of the early twentieth century. One of these, Antoine Meillet, was later to emphasize the intellectual excitement and commitment generated by Saussure in his classes. So engrossed was Saussure in his teaching during the Paris years that his publications became increasingly infrequent, but he was greatly admired, and when he left the École des Hautes Études for a position at the University of Geneva in the winter of 1891, his French colleagues nominated him for the Cross of the Legion of Honor.

At Geneva, too, students and colleagues were devoted to Saussure and committed to his teachings. Were it not for this dedication, there would be little more to say about Saussure. He married Marie Faesch; they had two sons. He entirely ceased to publish, rarely traveled, and attended only a few local scholarly meetings. From 1891 until 1899, he taught primarily comparative grammar and Sanskrit, adding a course on French verse in 1899; once in 1904, he taught a course on German legends.

Between 1906 and 1909, he conducted research on a topic that some scholars have called "esoteric"; others, more direct, labeled it "strange." Saussure believed that he had found "hidden texts" within Latin verse—deliberately concealed proper names, relevant to the meaning and repeated throughout the poems, whose spellings could be detected distributed among the words of the verse. He called these "anagrams," and he compiled more than a hundred notebooks of examples. He abandoned this work, without publishing a single paper on the topic, after receiving no response from a contemporary poet to whom he had written seeking confirmation of this poetic device.

The work on anagrams seems to have been an escape from Saussure's overriding preoccupation—probing the very foundations of the science of linguistics. Toward the end of his life, he confided to a former student that he had added nothing to his theory of language since the early 1890's, yet he struggled with the subject off and on for many years. At the University of Geneva, his teaching responsibilities for fifteen years in specific languages and comparative grammar precluded the incorporation of his general linguistic theory into his lectures. Then, in December, 1906, upon the retirement of another faculty member, Saussure was assigned to teach a course on general linguistics and the history and comparison of the Indo-European languages. He accepted the assignment reluctantly.

The course was offered three times, in alternate academic years. The first offering, in 1907, was actually only half a year, and Saussure focused almost entirely on the historical dimension. Five or six students were enrolled. In 1908-1909, there were eleven students, and, again, the emphasis was on the historical study of languages, although this time Saussure did begin with more general topics. For 1910-1911, Saussure spent the entire first semester on general linguistic theory. There were a dozen students in the course. Before he could teach the course again, Saussure fell ill in the summer of 1912. He died near Geneva on February 22, 1913, at the country home of his wife's family.

Two of Saussure's colleagues at the University of Geneva gathered the few lecture notes that Saussure had not destroyed and collected course notes from students who had attended his classes in general linguistics. Using the third offering of the course as a base, Charles Bally and Albert Sechehaye attempted "a reconstruction, a synthesis" of Saussure's thought on the science of linguistics. First published in 1916, Saussure's *Cours de linguistique générale* (1916; *Course in General Linguistics*, 1959) initially received mixed reviews and relatively little attention.

In Europe, Saussure's views on linguistics, as represented in *Course in General Linguistics*, were discussed and adopted, often with alterations, only among members of the Copenhagen, Moscow, and Prague Linguistic Circles. It was not until the 1930's that *Course in General Linguistics* had any significant affect on linguistics in France. In the United States, little attention was paid to Saussure's work until the 1941 arrival in New York of Roman Jakobson, a founding member of the Linguistic Circles of both Moscow and Prague. In the development of the discipline of linguistics, Saussure has been more acknowledged in retrospect than followed directly.

*Summary*

In *Course in General Linguistics*, Ferdinand de Saussure made a sharp distinction between what he termed synchronic linguistics and diachronic linguistics. The latter is the study of change in language; to a great extent, diachronic work had dominated the nineteenth century. Synchronic linguistics, however, concentrates on a static view of language, as it exists for speakers at a particular point in time, and this became the major focus of twentieth century linguistics, particularly in the United States. Saussure also maintained that the proper object of study in linguistics should be not the actual speech of individual members of a linguistic community (which he labeled *parole*) but rather the common code, the language (*langue*), that they share. This distinction became so widely recognized that Saussure's original French terms are still in international use.

Of all the concepts for which Saussure is now known, however, the most influential has been his view of a language as a system of signs, each of which is meaningful and important only in terms of its relationships to the other signs in the system. This system of relationships constitutes a structure, and it is this notion that is the foundation of twentieth century structuralism not only in linguistics but also in anthropology and literary criticism.

In his discussion of signs, Saussure proposed that linguistics was only one dimension of a broader science of the study of signs that he called "semiology." Referred to as semiotics in the United States, this field has been all but ignored by linguists, but for many nonlinguists the name of Saussure is intricately intertwined with semiology. It is interesting, therefore, to note that semiology is mentioned in less than a dozen paragraphs in the entire *Course in General Linguistics*.

*Course in General Linguistics* has been the subject of numerous commentaries, and scholars have explored the origins of Saussure's ideas and compared the work with the notes from which it was constructed. This research shows that some of the concepts often credited to Saussure may have their origins with other nineteenth century scholars, and there has been a continuing debate about the "authenticity" of the work in representing Saussure's views. Regardless of these findings, the assessment of Saussure provided in a 1924 review of *Course in General Linguistics* by the great American linguist Leonard Bloomfield has been confirmed by the twentieth century: "He has given us the theoretical basis for a science" of language.

*Bibliography*

Culler, Jonathan. *Ferdinand de Saussure*. Rev. ed. Ithaca, N.Y.: Cornell University Press, 1986. This is the most readable account of Saussure's theory and legacy in linguistics and semiotics, with suggestions for additional reading.

Gadet, Françoise. *Saussure and Contemporary Culture*. Translated by Gregory Elliott. London: Hutchinson Radius, 1989. The first part offers extended quotations from Saussure's *Course in General Linguistics* with exegesis, while part two deals with the editorial fortunes of the book and its reception and influence.

Harris, Roy. *Reading Saussure: A Critical Commentary on the "Cours de linguistique générale."* London: Gerald Duckworth, 1987. A personal reading of Saussure with chapter-by-chapter commentary and summations of general issues by the author of a controversial translation; assumes basic background in linguistics and some familiarity with Saussure's place in intellectual history.

Hawkes, Terence. *Structuralism and Semiotics*. Berkeley: University of California Press, 1977. An overview of structuralism in linguistics, anthropology, literature, and semiotics; pages 19-28 deal specifically with Saussure, but his influence is described throughout the book. Contains a good selective bibliography of works available in English.

Koerner, E. F. K. *Ferdinand de Saussure, Origin and Development of His Linguistic Thought in Western Studies of Language: A Contribution to the History and Theory of Linguistics*. Braunschweig, West Germany: Vieweg, 1973. The most extensive biographical information available in English, with considerable coverage of possible sources of Saussure's thought; includes a substantial bibliography.

Sampson, Geoffrey. "Saussure: Language as Social Fact." In *Schools of Linguistics*. Stanford, Calif.: Stanford University Press, 1980. Sampson provides a clear and engaging discussion of several of Saussure's most influential concepts, including the distinction between *langue* and *parole*. Other chapters treat a variety of twentieth century approaches to linguistics, most of which deal with issues raised by Saussure.

Saussure, Ferdinand de. *Course in General Linguistics*. Edited by Charles Bally and Albert Sechehaye in collaboration with Albert Reidlinger. Translated by Wade Baskin. New York: Philosophical Library, 1959. This is the standard English translation; also available in a number of reprintings. A book of less than 250 pages, this is the cornerstone of Saussure's influence.

Starobinski, Jean. *Words upon Words: The Anagrams of Ferdinand de Saus-*

*sure*. Translated by Olivia Emmet. New Haven, Conn.: Yale University Press, 1979. Extensive extracts from Saussure's notebooks on anagrams.

*Julia S. Falk*

# MAX SCHELER

*Born:* August 22, 1874; Munich, Germany
*Died:* May 19, 1928; Frankfurt, Germany
*Areas of Achievement:* Philosophy, sociology, and religion
*Contribution:* Scheler was one of the most brilliant and creative moral philosophers of the twentieth century. His system of ethics, in sharp disagreement with Kantian ethics as well as with positivism, attempts to give the emotional life its due as an epistemologically reliable response to objective values.

## *Early Life*

Max Scheler was born into a family with considerable domestic tension. His father, Gottfried, died before Max entered high school, his will to live devoured by his own unhappiness and that of his wife. Although his father was of Protestant extraction and his mother was a Jewess, Scheler became a convert to Catholicism at age fourteen. He was attracted to the spirit of community that he found in the Catholic religious festivities.

While on vacation during the summer after his graduation from high school, Scheler met Amelie von Dewitz. She was married, had a small child, and was eight years older than Scheler. All this notwithstanding, she soon became his mistress. Eventually Amelie divorced her husband, and she and Scheler were married in a civil ceremony on October 2, 1899, in Berlin. The marriage was not a happy one, but it lasted for thirteen years. Amelie and Max had one child, Wolfgang, born in 1905.

In 1895, Scheler moved to Jena, where he completed a doctorate in philosophy with Rudolf Eucken as his adviser. In his dissertation, Scheler argued that values are not apprehended by the intellect but by a separate nonrational faculty in human beings that perceives values.

Scheler's second work, *Die transszendentale und die psychologische Methode* (1900; the transcendental and the psychological method), showed the continuing influence of Eucken's philosophy. This work earned for Scheler a position at Jena, where he taught ethics and the history of philosophy. Scheler was, however, gradually becoming dissatisfied with the transcendental, neo-Kantian approach of Eucken. A meeting with Edmund Husserl in 1901 sparked Scheler's own search for an enlargement of the concept of philosophical intuition.

In 1906, Scheler moved from Jena to teach at the University of Munich. The move was precipitated by marital problems. Scheler's professional life flourished in Munich, but his marriage continued to deteriorate. Within a year after the move, he was separated from his wife. Amelie avenged herself on her unfaithful husband by informing the Munich socialist newspaper that Scheler had gone into debt to support his affairs with other women, leaving her and his children in poverty. In 1910, Scheler was asked to resign from the University of Munich and was deprived of the right to teach at any German university.

Scheler moved from Munich to Göttingen, the center of the phenomenological movement in Germany, in the spring of 1911. There he quickly established himself as a phenomenologist of note and as a charismatic lecturer. Yet a falling-out with Husserl occurred at this time. Tension between Husserl and Scheler became so great that Scheler moved from Göttingen back to Munich.

*Life's Work*

The personal resentment and pessimism that Scheler felt as he found himself isolated and jobless in Munich in 1911 enabled him to express the resentment and pessimism of many in Germany at the time. Wilhelmian Germany was seething with criticism of modern industrial society. It was at this time that Scheler began work on *Das Ressentiment im Aufbau der Moralen* (1912; *Ressentiment*, 1961) and other essays pointing to the need for modern society to return to precapitalistic Christian communal ideals. What the modern world was lacking, according to Scheler, was a metaphysics of community. It was only at the metaphysical level that true cooperation among human beings could take place.

Several years earlier, Scheler had met and fallen in love with Marit Furtwangler. Furtwangler's mother had forced her to separate from Scheler after the scandal of 1910, but Scheler continued to correspond with Marit, who was living in Berlin. They decided to marry as soon as Scheler could secure his divorce from Amelie. Scheler and Furtwangler were married on December 28, 1912, in the Church of St. Ludwig in Munich.

World War I had a profound impact upon Scheler's evolving political consciousness and inaugurated his years of intense literary productivity, which lasted from 1915 until his death in 1928. In *Der Genius des Krieges und der deutsche Krieg* (1915; the genius of war and the German war), Scheler praised the community-building powers of the German nation and welcomed war as a form of liberation from decadence. One year later, with the publication of *Krieg und Aufbau* (1916; war and rebuilding), he reversed both of these positions. By then he had come to see war as the evidence of decadence rather than as a means of liberation from it. He had also turned away from German nationalism to seek in the Church the community-building powers that he now failed to find in the German nation.

Most of Scheler's thought and action during the remainder of the war years was related to his reconversion to Catholicism. From 1917 until the end of the war, Scheler proclaimed the need for a universal repentance. He now saw the war as God's punishment for human greed. He lectured on such topics as "Germany's Mission and the Catholic World View," "The Contemporary Relevance of the Christian Idea of Community," and "The Renewal of European Culture."

In the postwar chaos, Germany's universities were flooded with young men returning from the army. The rector of the newly reestablished University of Cologne, Christian Eckart, found it possible to overlook the Munich indiscretions that had blocked Scheler's academic career. In January, 1919, Scheler accepted an appointment to the Sociological Institute, since the new university, supported by Cologne businessmen rather than by state funds, could not afford a chair of philosophy.

Scheler's social and political ideas suffered a drastic reorientation between 1921 and 1924. In 1919, Scheler had believed that the resolution of the conflicting religious and political ideologies in the Weimar Republic could be found in the religious sphere, specifically in the Roman Catholic faith. By 1924, Scheler had lost faith in the community-building powers of the Catholic religion. He now believed that political and ideological disunity could only be resolved by persons who had scientific knowledge of the sociological basis of ideological conflicts. Modern society had become so diversified that no religious leader, no matter how charismatic, could win the allegiance of persons from every social strata. The solution was to recognize the partial truth of every viewpoint. Political leaders must learn to develop flexible practical programs based on the conditions of the time rather than on abstract ideological principles. This was Scheler's position in 1923 when he published his pioneer work on the sociology of knowledge, *Schriften zur Soziologie und Weltanschauungslehre*. Scheler's work established sociology of knowledge as a significant field of study within German sociology for the next decade.

While he was teaching at the University of Cologne, Scheler became involved in an affair with a young, beautiful, and intelligent woman by the name of Maria Scheu. He still loved his wife but seemed powerless to break off the affair despite the fact that his marriage, his career as a Catholic philosopher, and his membership in the Catholic church were all at stake. Scheler was unable to decide between his wife and his mistress for quite a while but finally chose to divorce his second wife and marry Maria Scheu. The inner turmoil caused by this decision appears to have continued throughout the rest of his life. He continued to write to Marit and to see her until the time of his own death. After his marriage to Maria, Scheler decided that he had to leave Cologne because of difficulties with his colleagues and superiors who refused to condone his personal life-style. Catholic students, especially seminarians, were forbidden to attend his classes. Scheler, in turn, attacked the Catholic church for its crude dogmatism.

At the peril of contradicting his prewar attack on the Western scientific tradition, Scheler opposed the antirationalist tendencies of the 1920's. Before the war, Scheler had denounced the modern industrial world and idealized the community life of medieval Europe. In the 1920's, however, Scheler allied himself with the traditions of the Enlightenment. This allegiance became evident in his speech at the Lessing Institute for Adult Education in 1925 entitled *Die Formen des Wissens und die Bildung* (the forms of knowledge and culture).

In the face of the plethora of conflicting worldviews afoot in postwar Germany, Scheler adopted a relativistic approach toward truth as a sociologist, but as a philosopher he retained the insights into eternal essences offered by phenomenology. He also maintained his theory of absolute values, a product of his Catholic period. The link between his sociological and philosophical stances was provided by what he called "functionalization," the process whereby truth is splintered as it descends from its absolute realm into its concrete cultural manifestations in history. Furthermore, Scheler argued that although different people saw reality differently, it was still the same ultimate reality that they were viewing from different perspectives.

In the last years of his life, Scheler devoted himself to the construction of a metaphysics of man. Scheler died before he had a chance to put his thoughts on this topic into book form, yet some idea of his central concerns can be drawn from his articles and lectures of the mid-1920's. The human being, according to Scheler, is both a microcosm and a microtheos. The human person is a microcosm because he or she participates in all the aspects of being: physical, vital, spiritual, and personal. The human person is a microtheos, because he or she participates in the ultimate metaphysical principles of the universe, mind, and instinct. Contrary to the claims of traditional Western metaphysics, the human person is not to be viewed as merely the imitator of a world of ideas that was already present in the mind of God before creation. Rather, human persons were to be viewed as the cocreators and coexecutors of the stream of ideas that enables the Absolute to realize itself in the course of world history.

In 1928, Scheler accepted an appointment at the University of Frankfurt. He died suddenly of either a stroke or a heart attack on May 19, 1928, immediately prior to beginning his work at Frankfurt.

### *Summary*

Along with Edmund Husserl and Martin Heidegger, Max Scheler was one of the three founding fathers of the philosophical school known as "phenomenology." Scheler was the most versatile and comprehensive thinker of the three. Among the wide variety of topics treated in his writings are ethics, value theory, philosophy of religion, repentance, humility, the foundation of biology, psychology, metaphysics, the theory of cognition and perception, Buddhism, education, culture, philosophy of history, the sociology of knowledge, pragmatism, capitalism, the sense of suffering, love, death, awe, and shame. One of Scheler's most radically new contributions to philosophy was his development of a phenomenological theory of ethics. His theory of nonformal or "material" values situates the emotional experience of values as the primordium of all experiences of reality. His ethics is based upon this nonrational, intuitive grasp of values.

Scheler also made important contributions to the sociology of knowledge, in which he struggled for a middle way between idealism (a Hegelian approach) and materialism (a Marxist, or Positivist, approach); the philosophy of religion, an area in which he has attracted a steady number of commentators, especially among Roman Catholics; and philosophical anthropology.

José Ortega y Gasset, Nicolai Hartmann, Dietrich von Hildebrand, Alois Dempf, and Paul L. Landsberg are merely a few of the thinkers who have been influenced by Scheler. Scheler's writings continue to inspire philosophers and others who are interested in the perennial and humanitarian themes of community, value, love, person, and God. Scheler offers no neat and tidy systematic treatment of any of these themes. Nevertheless, he can justly be described as an inspirational and brilliant philosopher who consistently offers creative and profound insights upon these topics.

*Bibliography*

Deeken, Alfons. *Process and Permanence in Ethics: Max Scheler's Moral Philosophy.* New York: Paulist Press, 1974. A systematic exposition of Scheler's ethics. Generally thorough except for the lack of any discussion of community. Includes a bibliography and indexes.

Emad, Pravis. "The Great Themes of Scheler." *Philosophy Today* 12 (Spring, 1968): 4-12. A concise summary of Scheler's philosophy. A good place for the general reader to begin.

Frings, Manfred S. *Max Scheler: A Concise Introduction into the World of a Great Thinker.* Pittsburgh: Duquesne University Press, 1965. One of the earliest studies of Scheler to appear in English. Each chapter discusses one of the fundamental ideas of Scheler's philosophy. A good overview, but lacks consideration of the chronological development of Scheler's thought. Includes a bibliography and indexes.

Kelly, Eugene. *Max Scheler.* Boston: Twayne, 1977. Despite its title, this work is not a biography. It is an analysis and critique of Scheler as a phenomenologist.

Ranly, Ernest W. *Scheler's Phenomenology of Community.* The Hague: Martinus Nijhoff, 1966. This book is an outgrowth of the author's doctoral dissertation on Scheler's theory of community. It includes a careful discussion of Scheler's description of the emotions and their role in community. Contains a bibliography and an index.

Schutz, Alfred. "Max Scheler's Epistemology and Ethics." *The Review of Metaphysics* 11 (1957): 304-314, 486-501. A good, short explanatory article written by a fellow phenomenologist. Part 1 covers Scheler's epistemology, and the second part covers his ethics.

Staude, John Raphael. *Max Scheler, 1874-1928: An Intellectual Portrait*. New York: Free Press, 1967. The most detailed biography of Scheler in the English language. The author offers an insightful and generally sympathetic interpretation, although he can be critical when he deems it appropriate. Includes a bibliography and an index.

*Ann Marie B. Bahr*

# BERNHARD VOLDEMAR SCHMIDT

*Born:* March 30, 1879; Island of Naissaar, Estonia

*Died:* December 1, 1935; Hamburg, Germany

*Areas of Achievement:* Astronomy, invention, technology, and physics

*Contribution:* In 1930, Schmidt invented an optical system that revolutionized astronomy by significantly widening the field of vision of the largest telescopes then in use. The Schmidt photographic telescope used a spherical mirror in combination with a glass plate to capture celestial images on photographic plates. For the first time, wide areas of the sky could be photographed with sharp definition across the entire field, edge to edge.

## *Early Life*

Bernhard Voldemar Schmidt was born on Naissaar, an island in Estonia in 1879. His family was poor, and he had little formal schooling. Yet he had an early interest in science and often conducted simple experiments. One such experiment with gunpowder resulted in a disastrous explosion that cost him part of his right arm. Despite that handicap, his curiosity was undeterred, and he continued to study physical science and eventually demonstrated a strong aptitude for optical engineering, aided by an intuitive understanding of the physical nature of optical structures. While still a youth, he made his first telescope lens by cutting the bottom from a glass bottle and grinding it with sand. Schmidt was as resourceful as he was curious and conducted fairly complicated optical experiments with extremely crude instruments.

In 1900, Schmidt entered the Institute of Technology at Göteborg, Sweden, where he studied engineering. He left Göteborg, to study in Mittweida, Germany, where he became a skilled crafter of mirrors and lenses for telescopes. He remained in Mittweida after graduation and created a top-quality, fifteen-inch mirror for an observatory at Potsdam, Germany.

From the earliest days of his life, Schmidt was a loner. He was moody, difficult to approach, and often unpredictable. He worked alone at a variety of jobs until 1926 when, at the age of forty-seven, he joined the staff of the Hamburg Observatory. He was considered an eccentric by fellow astronomers. He refused to accept a conventional position with the observatory staff, preferring to continue working alone as a crafter of optical instruments. He had few, if any, friends and labored with crude equipment. Occasionally he would disappear on drinking binges that would often last for days. Despite his contrary disposition and antisocial nature, Schmidt was considered a genius in the field of optics, wherein he made the discovery that revolutionized celestial photography.

## *Life's Work*

Schmidt devoted his life to the development of mirrors and optic lenses for use in astronomical observatories. Late in life, he developed the optical system for which he became famous, one that was later modified and enhanced to improve significantly the field of observational astronomy. Ironically, the basis for that system came from an idea proposed by Sir Isaac Newton in the early eighteenth century, but which had been long abandoned by astronomers. Newton, better known for his study of the laws of gravity than for his lifelong work in the field of optics, recognized the need for a telescope lens that could take in a significantly larger field of view than was possible with the telescopes of his day. He designed such a lens using spherical curvature. Yet telescope-makers found the concept to be unworkable because different areas of lens received light-beams of varying length, thus causing aberrations in the focus of captured images. Schmidt overcame the problem by placing an error-correcting glass plate as far ahead of the focal point of the telescope as the spherical mirror lay behind it. Since the telescope was designed to function with a relatively short focus, the length of the tube required to house the optics was also relatively short. A curved film was placed in front of the mirror, and for the first time ever a clear, sharp image of an area of the sky greater than 20 degrees of arc could be photographed. This allowed scientists to study galactic star clusters in several wavelength ranges, while searching for young stars, the study of which is useful in understanding the structure of the universe. Before 1930, most telescopes were of the reflector or refractor type. Each was useful in the study of stars and star clusters in distant space but had the inherent disadvantage of being able to see only a small portion of the sky. Interestingly, in 1910, Kellner invented the optical components that became the basic technology incorporated in the Schmidt telescope, but it was Schmidt who actually constructed the first one.

The theory behind the Schmidt telescope, often referred to as a camera, relates to the physical properties of reflected light. Parallel light-rays reflected at the edge of a spherical mirror travel shorter distances to a medium placed above it than does light reflected from the center of the sphere. That causes the focus to be in one region of the medium, or film, rather than over its entire area. Schmidt's glass-correcting plate compensated for those variant distances, thus achieving sharp images over the full range of the area being viewed through the telescope. In later versions of the Schmidt telescope, the correcting plate was ground so thinly that very little chromatic distortion occurred at that point, making the image even sharper.

The largest Schmidt photographic telescope was installed on Mount Palomar in California. Its intended function was to do the first full-scale photographic sky mapping. It was equipped with a forty-eight-inch correcting lens and a seventy-two-inch reflecting mirror with a radius of curvature of twenty feet. The focal length was ten feet. Photographs were taken in both red and blue light, with all stars displaying luminescence down to a magnitude of 21.1 appearing on the blue plates and those down to a magnitude of 20 appearing on the red plate. More than seventeen hundred plates were required for each photographic image in order to accommodate both colors. The first photographs taken by the Schmidt camera were published in the 1950's.

It is important to note that the Schmidt telescope was used only as a camera. Photographically, the f/ratio, or focal length divided by the aperture, of the Schmidt telescope was similar to that of a fast photographic lens. That fact, combined with developments in photographic image processing, resulted in modifications to the Schmidt telescope that made the instrument more efficient and led to new estimates of the distances of galaxies far from Earth.

In spite of the breakthrough for astronomers that was embodied in the Schmidt telescope, one problem resulted from the curved photographic plates required to achieve wide-area coverage: They made it awkward for making precise determinations of distances among stellar objects. Nevertheless, the Schmidt photographic telescope became extremely popular, primarily because it was able to accomplish significantly more mapping at those infrequent times when weather conditions were ideal. Schmidt died in an asylum for the insane in Hamburg in 1935. His personal life was troubled, but his contribution to astronomy was great.

*Summary*

Bernhard Voldemar Schmidt was a technician, not an astronomer. He was concerned with developing the technology of astronomy rather than with studying the universe. Yet his optical system has earned for him a place among the great astrophysicists of his time. Over the centuries prior to 1930, the study of astronomy had been carried on in much the same way. While lenses and other telescopic components had been enlarged and refined over time, the techniques of astronomical observation were much the same. The Schmidt telescope represented a major step forward, providing a means for expanding the field of celestial observation. Over a seven-year period, a giant Schmidt telescope at Mount Palomar photographed the entire sky that could be viewed from that location in California. Schmidt telescopes were later installed in other regions of the world to photograph celestial objects visible only from those regions, adding significantly to the body of knowledge about the structure of the universe.

*Bibliography*

Hoyle, Fred. *Astronomy.* Garden City, N.Y.: Doubleday, 1962. Contains several good photographs of the Schmidt telescope, an index, and an appendix.

Marx, Siegfried, and Werner Pfau. *Observatories of the World.* New York:

Van Nostrand Reinhold, 1982. An excellent description of several of the important astronomical observatories of the world, including Schmidt's home observatory at Hamburg, Germany. Includes photographs and an index.

Moore, Patrick. *Men of the Stars*. New York: Gallery Books, 1986. Contains a brief biographical sketch and picture of Schmidt. This highly illustrated book is particularly useful to the young reader looking for a fine introduction to astronomy.

Richardson, Robert S. *The Star Lovers*. Toronto: Macmillan, 1967. A survey of the work of many of the best-known personalities in astronomy. Tracks the evolution of astronomy through the early 1960's and contains many useful photographs, including several of Schmidt photographic telescopes, including the one at Mount Palomar. Includes a brief passage on Schmidt's professional relationship with Walter Baade, one of the great astronomers of the early twentieth century. Includes a bibliography and an index.

Ronan, Colin A. *Changing Views of the Universe*. New York: Macmillan, 1961. An overview of developments in astronomy over the centuries as viewed from the social perspectives that prevailed at the time. Contains a passage on the significance of the Schmidt camera from a social and political context.

Rousseau, Pierre. *Man's Conquest of the Stars*. New York: W. W. Norton, 1961. A highly readable survey of the evolution of astronomy for the layperson. Contains no complicated, technical descriptions. Includes an index.

Shapley, Harlow, ed. *Source Book in Astronomy, 1900-1950*. Cambridge, Mass.: Harvard University Press, 1960. Contains a discussion of the instrumentation used during the first half of the twentieth century to study the solar system and the position and motion of stars.

Sidgwick, J. B. *Amateur Astronomer's Handbook*. London: Faber & Faber, 1961. Contains a good discussion of the technical components of astronomy: telescopic function, optics, oculars, mountings, and several modifications to the Schmidt camera, including the thick mirror Schmidt, solid Schmidt, folded solid Schmidt, off-axis Schmidt, all reflector Schmidt, Spectroscopic Schmidt, and others. Bibliography and index.

*Michael S. Ameigh*

# KARL SCHMIDT-ROTTLUFF

*Born:* December 1, 1884; Rottluff, Germany

*Died:* August 10, 1976; West Berlin, West Germany

*Area of Achievement:* Art

*Contribution:* The period 1905-1915 marked the beginning of twentieth century artistic principles. This was the decade of *Die Brücke*, an organized group of European artists and art lovers whose common interest was to encourage revolutionary methods of artistic expression. Schmidt-Rottluff, as a founding member of this influential group, maintained a lifelong dedication to its purposes.

## *Early Life*

Karl Schmidt-Rottluff was born Karl Schmidt. As a young man, he added "Rottluff" to his name, for the rural village, near Chemnitz (now Karl-Marx-Stadt), where he was born in 1884. Schmidt-Rottluff received his formal schooling between the years 1897 and 1905 at the *Gymnasium* in Chemnitz. He was virtually self-taught as an artist, though he received some formal training in the art classes that he attended twice weekly at the Chemnitz *Kunstverein*. As a student, he demonstrated interests in poetry, music, and the humanities as well as in art.

In 1905, Schmidt-Rottluff became a student of architecture at the Technical College of Dresden. It was in the same year that he and three of his fellow students, Ernst Ludwig Kirchner, Fritz Bleyl, and Erich Heckel, decided to terminate their formal studies and seek free expression in painting. They were the founding members of a group known as *Die Brücke* (the bridge), so named by Schmidt-Rottluff because he wanted their label to symbolize that membership would bring together not only artists but also collectors, connoisseurs, and writers—any and all who sought and appreciated fresh, new approaches to human expression.

The group of young artists painted, produced graphics, and occasionally sculpted wherever they could find space available at a price they could afford. *Die Brücke* produced an annual portfolio and sponsored group exhibitions of members' works. By 1910, the group had reached its peak as an artists' community. After that year, some members of the group moved to Berlin, where there was not the same degree of communal activity and cooperation. The year 1913 saw the dissolution of *Die Brücke*. Schmidt-Rottluff remained true to its goals, however, and attempted, in 1926, to start a new group, but his efforts were generally unsuccessful. The group and its spirit of community had been, for Schmidt-Rottluff, a most important part of his long, productive life as an artist.

## *Life's Work*

Schmidt-Rottluff had begun painting in oils as a high school student in

Chemnitz, but he later wrote that he considered his first works to date from 1905, the year of *Die Brücke*'s creation. Erich Heckel, however, who was Schmidt-Rottluff's lifetime friend, considered the earlier works to have been very worthwhile, especially as to the use of color. By 1904, Schmidt-Rottluff had begun experimenting with woodcuts, which proved to be, for Schmidt-Rottluff, a most appropriate means of describing the relationship of plane surfaces to one another. His first were impressionistic, but within a short time he had developed a more abstract style. It was his desire, as well as that of the entire Dresden group, to create in a manner that would be in contrast with that of the previous generation, for whom painting had virtually been abandoned in favor of what was termed "Art Noveau," the practical application of art. *Die Brücke* artists, in their youthful self-confidence, wished to preserve their naïveté and rejected the idea that in order to be an artist one must employ traditional techniques and skills.

In 1906, Schmidt-Rottluff extended, on behalf of *Die Brücke*, an invitation for membership to the artist Emil Nolde. Subsequently, Schmidt-Rottluff spent time with Nolde at his home on the North Sea island of Alsen. The wild, harsh landscape of the island had a great appeal for Schmidt-Rottluff, who loved the freedom of nature, and he began to develop a consistent need for isolated, outdoor environments in which to paint. An earlier van Gogh exhibition in Dresden had been seen by the artists of *Die Brücke*, and Schmidt-Rottluff's painting began to reflect the influence of the Dutch artist, even though he would deny that he was able to put to any use the expressionism of van Gogh in what he, himself, was attempting. Nolde hoped he could help Schmidt-Rottluff to rely less heavily on the example of van Gogh. The effects of nature notwithstanding, Schmidt-Rottluff's self-portrait of that year, with its heavy impasto brushstrokes, purposeful placement of contrasting colors—colors not necessarily descriptive of the subject—and the strong suggestion of movement in the painting, reflects a definite van Gogh influence.

Schmidt-Rottluff spent winters in Dresden, but in 1907 he made the first of what was to become an annual summer visit to the area of Oldenburg flanking the North Sea. *Windy Day*, a 1907 landscape, still reflects the van Gogh influence. It is considered a dominant work of Schmidt-Rottluff's early period. In 1908, the artist spent the period from May until October in Oldenburg. The richly textured surface of that season's *Midday on the Moor*, the intensity of color applied in broad, expressive brushstrokes, along with the resulting near absence of definition of subject continued to be reminiscent of van Gogh, though there was obviously an emerging individual style. A distinctive technique of the artist was to describe the subject in terms of its planes, sometimes emphasizing them by the use of black outlines. Schmidt-Rottluff's work in these early years focused primarily on landscape painting.

Schmidt-Rottluff was one of *Die Brücke*'s members who exhibited in 1910 with the New Secession in Berlin. The group's work received critical favor in Berlin, thus enhancing the emerging national reputation of the artists. Schmidt-Rottluff had been living in Hamburg in that year and had had a number of one-man shows in that city. The group's Dresden show of that year had been a failure. It became desirable, if the artists were to maintain their newly earned status, to move to Berlin.

In 1912, in Berlin, Schmidt-Rottluff painted *Houses at Night*. This and other paintings of that period reflected the artist's movement toward a form of expressionist abstraction. He rejected the idea, however, of totally nonrepresentational art. He began to utilize a more precise definition of subject matter. Figures and still lifes began to appear as subjects for his development of color planes, and his brief experiment with cubism is seen in *The Pharisees* of 1912. It was during the early years in Berlin that Schmidt-Rottluff's work also reflected his exposure to the work of the Fauvists and to primitive, African art. Meanwhile, Schmidt-Rottluff received wide exposure through his work published in *Der Sturm*, a Berlin weekly that promoted the new movements in art, and through his participation in several important exhibitions.

By 1914, Schmidt-Rottluff's work became more somber, perhaps in anticipation of war. Typical works of this period contain figures that have, for the first time, human expression instead of figures absorbed by nature; his landscapes of this period also are more realistic in detail. Colors are dark, emphasizing the sadness reflected in the pictures. In the final months before he entered the military, Schmidt-Rottluff painted single figures with spiritual quality; these figures filled the entire picture. *Portrait of a Girl* is typical of this brief period.

During his three years of military service, Schmidt-Rottluff produced only woodcarvings and woodcuts, many having religious themes, including a series of nine woodcuts concerning the life of Jesus. After the war, his works contained symbolism as the dominant element, reflecting the internal personal changes that his experiences as a soldier in Russia had brought about. Titles of his postwar works included *Stellar Prayer*, *Melancholy*, and *Conversations About Death*.

Schmidt-Rottluff settled in Berlin after World War I, but during the next ten years he traveled widely, leading study groups to Italy, Paris, Dalmatia, and Ticino. Between 1936 and 1939, the first American exhibitions of his work were held. In 1931, he had become a member of the Prussian Academy of Arts, but, along with many German artists, was removed from academy membership during the Nazi regime. As many as 680 of Schmidt-Rottluff's paintings were stripped from German gallery holdings during the twelve years of the Third Reich. Some were sold for cash; many were destroyed. In 1941, Adolf Hitler condemned Schmidt-Rottluff as one of the artists he considered decadent and therefore dangerous to the German culture. In that year, the artist was forbidden to create works of art in his own country.

After the close of World War II, in 1947 the artist, in order to pick up the pieces of his life, accepted a professorship at the Hochschule für Bildende, where he remained until his retirement. In 1974, the year of his ninetieth birthday, he was made an honorary member of the American Academy of Arts and Letters and the American National Institute of Arts and Letters for his pioneering work in expressionist art. He died in West Berlin in 1976. Having no immediate heirs, his entire estate became part of the Karl and Emy Schmidt-Rottluff Foundation, which is in the custodial care of the Brück Museum. He had helped to establish the small museum in 1967 at a site in the Grunewald landscape of Berlin. It houses a collection of *Die Brücke* artists' works that survived the purges of the Nazi regime.

### *Summary*

Like most *Die Brücke* artists, Karl Schmidt-Rottluff was, in the beginning, a provincial who was drawn to Dresden for professional training. He was perhaps awkward and ill-equipped as to city manners and social customs. Yet he and his colleagues brought to the world an expression and an emotion stronger than that perhaps of any other art movement. Their dependence on one another for support was in part responsible for the rapid development of each member as an accomplished artist. Audacity, originality, and emotionalism were their contribution.

The courage of these artists who survived two wars and despicable treatment by the Nazis serves as an example to all artists and patrons of the arts. Schmidt-Rottluff, as one of the survivors, left to his country and to the entire world all that he had salvaged, in order to preserve for posterity the remaining evidence of an important movement in the arts. Of his work as an individual artist, his religious woodcuts are perhaps his most important and unique contribution.

### *Bibliography*

Dube, Wolf-Dieter. *The Expressionists*. Translated by Mary Whittall. London: Thames and Hudson, 1972. Contains effective descriptions as well as plates of the artist's work.

Grosshans, Henry. *Hitler and the Artists*. New York: Holmes & Meier, 1983. Schmidt-Rottluff is only one of the sixteen artists who are the subject of this work. It is important, especially, because it provides a perspective of the artist in historical context as a contemporary and as a victim of Hitler, who considered himself the cultural leader of the German peoples.

Halasz, Piri. "German Expressionism, Explosive Art Movement in a Troubled Age." *Smithsonian* 11 (January, 1981): 88-95. This article describes German expressionism, its history, and its participants. In this article, Schmidt-Rottluff is placed within the movement.

Reidemeister, Leopold. *The Brücke Museum.* Translated by Margot Dembo and Edna McCowen. Fort Lee, N.J.: Penshurst Books, 1981. The author describes his contact with the artist and other members of *Die Brücke* and their successful establishment of a museum to house their works. With twenty-four plates of Schmidt-Rottluff's works and English-language notes.

Selz, Peter. *German Expressionist Painting.* Berkeley: University of California Press, 1957. A comprehensive study of the expressionist movement. The artist is discussed as he relates both to the group, *Die Brücke*, and to his individual work. Contains extensive notes and a bibliography as well as plates.

Willett, John. *Expressionism.* London: Weidenfeld and Nicolson, 1970. A broad overview of the movement and its history from 1900 to the date of publication. Covers the literature, music, and drama as well as the painters and graphic artists of the movement. Contains a discussion of each artist, his work, and the sociocultural context.

*P. R. Lannert*

# ARNOLD SCHOENBERG

*Born:* September 13, 1874; Vienna, Austro-Hungarian Empire
*Died:* July 13, 1951; Los Angeles, California
*Area of Achievement:* Music
*Contribution:* Schoenberg was the leading composer of the second Viennese school, a manifestation of the expressionist movement in music. By breaking from the tradition of tonality, a process he later codified in his twelve-tone method, Schoenberg introduced compositional techniques and aesthetic principles that became pervasive throughout the first half of the twentieth century.

## *Early Life*

Arnold Franz Walter Schoenberg (originally Schönberg) was born in Vienna on September 13, 1874. His parents were Jewish and reared their three children in this heritage. Samuel, his father, owned a small shoe shop. The family was never wealthy, and Samuel's death in 1890 forced Schoenberg to leave school in order to support his family. Neither Samuel nor his wife Pauline (née Nachod) was particularly musical, although Samuel had sung in amateur choirs, and the Nachod family had for generations provided cantors for synagogues in their native Prague. The main cultural influence in Schoenberg's youth was his uncle Friedrich (Fritz) Nachod, who taught the young Schoenberg poetry, drama, and French.

There was no piano in the Schoenberg home; Arnold began his musical training at age eight on the violin, later switching to viola and a homemade cello. He immediately began to compose violin duets to play with his teacher; as his circle of musical friends grew, so did his early compositional efforts, which soon included string quartets, songs, and piano pieces. While Schoenberg was essentially self-taught as a composer, his musical friendships played an important role in his early development and throughout his career. One friend, the philosopher Oskar Adler, became his first true music teacher, providing instruction in harmony and ear training. Most influential, however, was the composer/conductor Alexander von Zemlinsky, who met Schoenberg while conducting an amateur orchestra. Schoenberg's elder by two years, Zemlinsky had been trained at the Vienna Conservatory and had attracted the attention of Johannes Brahms. While later recollections as to the nature of the tutelage differ, it appears that Zemlinsky not only offered specific compositional advice but also brought to Schoenberg's attention the rich possibilities of combining the then-opposed Brahmsian and Wagnerian traditions. The two friends became brothers-in-law in 1901, when Schoenberg married Zemlinsky's sister Mathilde; Zemlinsky remained a lifelong friend and advocate of Schoenberg's music.

It was through Zemlinsky that Schoenberg's music received its first public performance; his String Quartet in D Major (1897) was presented in 1898 by the Wiener Tonkünstlerverein. The next year, however, this same organization rejected Schoenberg's first mature composition, the string sextet *Verklärte Nacht*, Op. 4 (1899; transfigured night), on the basis of a single unconventional chord. This sort of misguided rejection proved to be the first indication of the harsh and shortsighted criticism that would continue to be levied against Schoenberg throughout his career.

*Life's Work*

Schoenberg's career has often been described in terms of four stylistic periods: the tonal, late-Romantic works of 1899-1908; the expressionist, atonal works of 1909-1920; the application of the twelve-tone method in the works of 1920-1936; and a broader, more eclectic approach that evolves in the works from the mid-1930's onward. Such delineations do not merely serve to categorize Schoenberg's works; rather, they highlight the continuity of his development. The stylistic diversity of his oeuvre is paralleled by its breadth, which encompasses important operas, orchestral works, chamber music, songs, and theoretical treatises.

Schoenberg never considered his own work to be revolutionary. Rather, he viewed it as descendant from the German late-Romantic tradition of Richard Strauss and Gustav Mahler (the latter of whom, like Zemlinsky, grew to be a close friend and professional ally). While such stylistic derivation was overlooked by the critics of the time, Schoenberg's early works are now understood in this light. *Verklärte Nacht* adopts the nineteenth century genre of the tone poem, projecting imagery of transfigured love through broad melodic lines and a rich harmonic palette. Similar musical and symbolic richness characterizes the orchestral tone poem *Pelleas und Melisande*, Op. 5 (1903) and the setting of Jens Peter Jacobsen's *Gurrelieder* (1900-1911), a massive song cycle that calls for five soloists, multiple choirs, and a huge orchestra.

Schoenberg soon found such grandiose gestures to be at odds with the goal of immediate and direct expression and adopted a leaner, more transparent style, apparent in the String Quartet in D Minor, Op. 7, No. 1 (1904-1905), and particularly in the First Chamber Symphony, Op. 9 (1906), the culmination of his first period. The instrumental forces here have been trimmed to fifteen solo winds and strings, allowing for greater clarity within the highly contrapuntal texture. Melodic and harmonic aspects coalesce through the motivic manipulation of whole-tone collections and superimposed fourths. Yet the work remains ostensibly tonal, although resolutions to tonal centers are relegated to mark only the major structural divisions. While the contrapuntal complexity, the rapid rate of motivic development, and the extension of tonality all proved to be stumbling blocks for critics of the time, these traits have come to be seen as progenitors of Schoenberg's subsequent development.

It was immediately following this period, in which he was reevaluating the efficacy of various means of musical expression, that Schoenberg became increasingly active as a painter. He studied with the young Richard Gerstl (with whom Mathilde would subsequently have a devastating affair) and developed sufficiently to mount a one-man exhibition in 1910. Through these activities, Schoenberg became active in the burgeoning expressionist movement, befriending such important painters as Wassily Kandinsky and Oskar Kokoschka; Schoenberg contributed to the Blaue Reiter (Blue Rider) exhibition of 1912. While his interest in painting as his principle means of artistic expression soon waned, Schoenberg's foray into this medium helped to solidify the aesthetic principles that continued to form the basis of his musical style.

Similar to the expressionist painters who sought to convey directly the innermost essence of the human experience (as was recently being examined in the work of Sigmund Freud), Schoenberg sought to bring similar depth to musical expression, resulting in the remarkable series of works that inaugurate his second period. First apparent in the final two movements of the String Quartet, Op. 10, No. 2 (1907-1908), which incorporate a soprano singing texts by Stefan George, these musical advances coalesce in the mystifying and delicate song cycle *Das Buch der hängenden Gärten*, Op. 15 (1908-1909; the book of the hanging gardens), also on texts by George, and in the Three Piano Pieces, Op. 11 (1909). Most harrowing, however, is the synergy of Marie Pappenheim's text and Schoenberg's music in the creation of the angst-filled nightmare world of the monodrama *Erwartung*, Op. 17 (1909; expectation), where all distinction between reality and hallucination is lost. Similar effect describes the parodic dreamworld of *Pierrot Lunaire*, Op. 21 (1912; moonstruck Pierrot), a cycle of twenty-one rondels by Albert Giraud scored for *Sprechstimme* (a hybridization of speech and song) and five instruments, which remains one of Schoenberg's most popular works and epitomizes the style of his second period.

The sound of these works is quite unlike that of any other music in history, but it is born of the same artistic impulse and musical language that shaped Schoenberg's first period. Motivic manipulation has become the paramount means of direct expression, with reference to tonal centers, previously relegated to background structural functions, dispensed. Although the outmoded tonal system is no longer operative, the label "atonal," often applied pejoratively, was dismissed by Schoenberg as being nonsensical, for the purity of the tones and their interrelationship as motives remain. The music thus develops in accordance with its own inherent logic, not that of an applied hierarchical system, thereby representing direct, unencumbered artistic expression.

The ramifications of this stylistic direction were never fully explored by either Schoenberg or his growing coterie of students (the two most important of whom, Alban Berg and Anton von Webern, became known along with Schoenberg as the second Viennese school), for World War I interrupted much of the artistic activity in Europe. Schoenberg was called up twice, but was at first rejected for goiter and later released because of asthma, a problem that plagued his entire life. The interwar years were marked by other hardships as well, including continued financial difficulties; further critical rejection, which he attempted to counter through the formation in 1918 of the Verein für musikalische Privataufführungen (the Society for Private Musical Performances); and the death of Mathilde in 1923. He married Gertrud Kolisch, sister of his student Rudolf Kolisch, in 1924. The difficulties of this period continued to motivate the evolution of his religious beliefs (he had converted to Lutheranism in 1898 and would reconvert to Judaism in 1933), apparent in the influence of August Strindberg and Emanuel Swedenborg in the text of the incomplete oratorio *Die Jakobsleiter* (1917-1922; Jacob's ladder). This work also proves to be an important musical link, for in retrospect it displays the beginnings of serial compositional processes that would soon develop into Schoenberg's most widely known contribution: the twelve-tone (dodecaphonic) method of composition.

The new method brought to fruition Schoenberg's continual search for the complete integration of linear and vertical musical dimensions. The twelve notes of the chromatic scale are ordered to form a tone row, from which the melodic and harmonic materials of a composition are sequentially drawn; the continued manipulation of a single row throughout the course of a piece contributes to its structural unity. The formalization of the technique in the Five Piano Pieces, Op. 23 (1920-1923) and the Suite for Piano, Op. 25 (1921-1923) demonstrates the new structural order, for these works no longer rely upon the framework of a text as had many of the earlier, freely atonal expressionist works.

It is ironic that the twelve-tone method has often been maligned as being a stylistic determinant rather than a compositional device. In fact, the new syntactic logic that the method provided allowed Schoenberg's work to adopt neoclassical formal models in the piano pieces as well as in the Variations for Orchestra, Op. 31 (1926-1928) and the Third String Quartet, Op. 30 (1927). A broadening perspective is found in later works such as the Fourth String Quartet, Op. 37 (1936), but the method's stylistic adaptability is most readily demonstrated in the delicate pointillism of Webern's application as compared to the lush lyricism of Berg. In the opera *Moses und Aron* (1930-1932), Schoenberg draws upon the full richness of the method. While the music to the short third act was never composed, the first two acts stand both dramatically and musically complete, portraying the trials of the prophet being compelled to accept his task. Such a subject calls for great breadth in its treatment, which the vast technical and artistic resources of Schoenberg's development could supply; the resultant work remains Schoenberg's monumental profession of faith.

As with the earlier stages of stylistic evolution, the growing eclecticism apparent in the works from the mid-1930's onward reflects in part Schoenberg's reactions to the continuous upheavals of the world around him. The growing anti-Semitism in Germany caused him to flee to the United States in 1933; the three late works for speaker and ensemble, *Kol Nidre*, Op. 39 (1938), *Ode to Napoleon*, Op. 41 (1942), and particularly the chilling *A Survivor from Warsaw*, Op. 46 (1947), reflect the profound effect that the horrors of World War II had on his Jewish consciousness. Poor health prompted him to move from Boston to Los Angeles in 1934; the compelling String Trio, Op. 45 (1946), which followed a near-fatal heart attack, presents his personal reflection on mortality and death. Along with poor health, the poverty and critical misunderstanding that he had endured throughout his life plagued him to the end; he was retired at age seventy from teaching at the University of California at Los Angeles with a pension of only thirty-eight dollars a month, only to be refused in 1945 for a grant from the Guggenheim Foundation that would have allowed him to complete *Die Jakobsleiter*, *Moses und Aron*, and a series of theoretical textbooks. He died in Los Angeles on July 13, 1951; the last word that he spoke was "harmony."

### *Summary*

Since his death, recognition of the importance of Arnold Schoenberg's work has superseded the indictment of his contemporaries. He now stands regarded as one of the great innovators in the history of music who, similar to Johann Sebastian Bach, stood at the juncture of two distinct stylistic eras yet incorporated characteristics of each. Thus arises the paradox of his apparent revolutionary stature with his self-assessment of continuing the German Romantic tradition.

Similar paradoxes characterize much of Schoenberg's life and career, reflecting his intellectually curious yet fiercely independent nature. Essentially self-taught as a composer, he went on to become one of the most influential teachers of his era. Yet, as innovative as his own compositional work was, his approach to teaching was thoroughly grounded in the traditional practices of tonal harmony and counterpoint; he never taught the twelve-tone method to his students and rarely lectured or wrote about it. Yet it is precisely for this method that Schoenberg is best known; his music has unfortunately been more widely analyzed than performed.

In both his teaching and compositional practices, Schoenberg's ultimate goal was clarity of expression and a compelling sense of inevitability through structural logic and coherence. This objective outlook was balanced by his view of music as reflecting the innermost psyche, as the intensity of works such as *Erwartung* testifies. Constant self-evaluation contributed to the continual evolution of both his musical style and his personal beliefs, journeys perhaps reflected in the reluctantly prophetic stance of the protagonists of both *Die Jakobsleiter* and *Moses und Aron*. Yet, through the many disappointments that marked his life, Schoenberg held tenaciously true to the tenet that underscored his life and work: complete honesty to the integrity of one's own artistic convictions.

*Bibliography*

MacDonald, Malcolm. *Schoenberg*. London: J. M. Dent & Sons, 1976. A balanced account of Schoenberg's life, works, beliefs, and musical style. Four chapters give a biographical overview; eleven discuss his artistic ideals and describe his work by genre. The appended calendar, catalog of works, personalia, and bibliography prove useful.

Neighbour, Oliver. "Arnold Schoenberg." In *Second Viennese School: Schoenberg, Webern, Berg*. Vol. 16 in *The New Grove Dictionary of Music and Musicians*, edited by Stanley Sadie. *Second Viennese School* is part of the New Grove's Composer Biography series. This article provides a concise yet thorough survey of Schoenberg's life and work. Separate sections discuss his life, beliefs, and works in chronological order. The appended list of works and bibliography are among the most comprehensive available.

Reich, Willi. *Schoenberg: A Critical Biography.* Translated by Leo Black. New York: Praeger, 1971. Reich, a student of Berg and Webern, provides an in-depth look at Schoenberg's personality and his relationship to those around him through plentiful quotations from letters and commentaries, given in the context of a general biographical overview. Much emphasis is placed on contemporary criticism of Schoenberg's work and his reaction to it. Five long essays, a short bibliography, and a list of works are appended.

Rognoni, Luigi. *The Second Vienna School*. Translated by Robert W. Mann. London: John Calder, 1977. A study of the stylistic derivation of expressionism, and its relationship, as applied by Schoenberg, Berg, and Webern, to other artistic trends of the era. Schoenberg's works are discussed in terms of genre and period, the emphasis being stylistic description rather than biographical delineation.

Rosen, Charles. *Arnold Schoenberg*. Edited by Frank Kermode. New York: Viking Press, 1975. Part of the Modern Masters series, this is a concise discussion of the stylistic traits that characterize Schoenberg's music: expressionism, atonality, serialism, and neoclassicism. By describing these traits in artistic and historical perspective, Rosen emphasizes the inseparable relationships of musical form, function, and expression.

Schoenberg, Arnold. *Style and Idea*. Edited by Leonard Stein. Translated by Leo Black. New York: St. Martin's Press, 1975. This collection of writings and lectures, spanning forty years, provides great insight into

Schoenberg's complex and often paradoxical beliefs. The balance of technical topics, artistic discussion, critical commentary, and personal reflection presents a very human view of the multifaceted composer.

Stuckenschmidt, Hans Heinz. *Schoenberg: His Life, World, and Work*. Translated by Humphrey Searle. London: John Calder, 1977. One of the longest and most thorough, if wide-ranging, biographies available. Provides a detailed account of Schoenberg's life, personal and professional relationships, documentation, and the artistic and historical atmosphere that shaped these events. Includes numerous photographs, an analytical essay on Schoenberg's process of motivic manipulation, translations of a number of documents and lectures, a list of works, and a select bibliography.

*Paul A. Siskind*

# ERWIN SCHRÖDINGER

*Born:* August 12, 1887; Vienna, Austro-Hungarian Empire
*Died:* January 4, 1961; Alpbach, Austria
*Areas of Achievement:* Physics and philosophy
*Contribution:* Schrödinger invented wave mechanics in 1926, for which he received the Nobel Prize in Physics (along with Paul Adrien Maurice Dirac) in 1933, and he helped to develop the formal equations that are central to quantum mechanics. His pioneering work on the relationship between physics and living systems influenced the growth of molecular biology.

## *Early Life*

Erwin Schrödinger was born on August 12, 1887, the only child of a well-to-do Viennese family. The Schrödinger family was part of the intellectual life of Vienna during a period when scholarly attainment was regarded as a loftier goal than material or political well-being. Erwin's father, Rudolf Schrödinger, operated a prosperous linoleum business, but he managed to find time in his schedule to pursue studies in Italian painting, in botany, and in chemistry.

With the exception of a brief stay at a public elementary school in Innsbruck, Erwin was educated by a tutor who visited the family home twice a week. His maternal grandmother was British, and fluency in English gave his studies a considerable boost; as he matured, Schrödinger added proficiency in German, French, and Spanish to his arsenal of languages. Until the age of eleven, Erwin's primary educational influence was his father, who proved to be an invaluable sounding board on a host of subjects. At this time, Erwin entered the academic *Gymnasium* at Vienna and commenced a program of studies in the classics and in mathematics and physics.

Schrödinger entered the University of Vienna in 1906. The following year, he began to attend lectures in theoretical physics. In 1910, he received his doctorate and assumed a position as assistant to Franz Exner at the university's Second Physics Institute, where he remained until the outbreak of World War I. During this period, Schrödinger published papers on a range of subjects, including magnetism, radioactivity, X rays, and Brownian motion. Exner was heavily influenced by Ludwig Boltzmann, an influence which carried over to Schrödinger's later work. When Schrödinger was awarded the Nobel Prize in 1933, he declared that "his [Boltzmann's] line of thought may be called my first love in science. No other has ever thus enraptured me or will ever do so again."

Following an undistinguished service in the military, brief appointments at Jena, Stuttgart, and Breslau culminated with Schrödinger's appointment in 1921 to the chair of theoretical physics in Zurich, a position formerly held by Albert Einstein. Prior to his stay in Jena, he had married Annemarie Bertel of Salzburg on June 6, 1920. During this period, his papers touched on a number of subjects, including general relativity, probability theory, a lengthy review of dielectric phenomena, and a series of papers on three- and four-color theories of vision. Schrödinger's main efforts, however, were targeted on atomic theory. The papers that secured his reputation were composed in a half-year's flourish of creativity before he left Zurich. It was there in 1926 that Schrödinger, at the relatively advanced age of thirty-nine, invented wave mechanics and published what is known as the Schrödinger wave equation, the formalism which is the foundation of modern quantum mechanics.

### *Life's Work*

Schrödinger's invention of wave mechanics represented an attempt to overcome some difficulties generated by Niels Bohr's theory of the hydrogen atom. In particular, attempts to construct a theory of a stable system of more than two particles (such as the helium atom, with a nucleus and two electrons) had failed. The inspiration for Schrödinger's wave mechanics was Louis de Broglie's suggestion that particles are nothing more than a wave crest on a background of waves. De Broglie supposed that electrons display wave features, and, in order to support this thesis, he attempted to fit a whole number of wavelengths into each electron orbit, in a way which precluded the possibility of in-between orbits. He concluded that both wave and particle behavior are inextricably combined in the case of the electron. On behalf of his thesis, de Broglie predicted that matter-waves would be detected by diffracting a beam of electrons from a crystal. Even as de Broglie was formulating his ideas, this effect was observed in 1922 by Charles Kunsman and Clinton Davisson.

Schrödinger used the mathematics of waves in a way which attempted to eliminate quantum jumps, or the notion that electrons move instantaneously from one level to another. He sought to represent this quantum transition as the passage of energy from one vibrational form into another, rather than as the jumping of electrons. The transition of an electron from one energy state to another, Schrödinger believed, was akin to the change in the vibration of a violin string from one note to another. These results were announced by Schrödinger in four seminal papers published in the *Annalen der Physik* early in 1926, the first of which contains his famous wave equation.

Schrödinger's wave mechanics was eagerly embraced by numerous scientists who had been puzzled by the emerging atomic theory and regarded the model of a wave as furnishing a realistic account of microprocesses; it was also criticized on a number of counts. It was not clear, for example, how an entity such as a wave could make a Geiger counter click as though a single particle were being recorded. Furthermore, it was not evident how black-body radiation was to be explained in terms of Schrödinger's waves. A further wrinkle was added when Carl Eckart and Paul Adrien Maurice Dirac showed that Werner Heisenberg's equations (which were based on the supposition that electrons are particles) were equivalent to Schrödinger's theory that electrons are waves.

Bohr suggested that both models, particle and wave physics, were valid and complementary descriptions of the world—that there are some cases when it is appropriate to utilize the particle concept and other cases when it is better to use the wave concept. Max Born's suggestion that Schrödinger's wave function expressed the probability of finding a particle at a given point in space furnished support for Bohr's resolution to the controversy. The location of a particle cannot be ascertained with certainty, but the wave function enables one to work out the probability that the particle will be found in a certain place. Finally, Heisenberg suggested in 1926 that scientists cannot measure both the position and the momentum of an electron at the same time. The more one knows about its position, the less one knows about its momentum, and vice versa.

These developments were largely accepted by the time Schrödinger succeeded Max Planck in 1927 in the renowned chair of theoretical physics at the University of Berlin. This position allowed Schrödinger to enjoy the intellectual companionship of the greatest collection of physicists anywhere in the world, and his working environment was second to none; yet quantum mechanics was completed in other centers, primarily because the Berlin group, including Schrödinger, was opposed to the statistical and dualistic aspects of quantum theory as it was being developed in these other centers.

In Berlin, Schrödinger enjoyed a fruitful period until Adolf Hitler assumed the reins of power in 1933, the same year that Schrödinger and Dirac received the Nobel Prize. Schrödinger's background ensured that his position was secure. His opposition to the Nazi regime, however, induced him to give up his post. Schrödinger settled in Oxford for a brief and unproductive period, but in 1936 he succumbed to homesickness and accepted a position in Graz, Austria. This decision was imprudent, since his opposition to the Nazi regime was common knowledge, and he was dismissed from his position without notice in 1938. With no recourse, he fled Austria when Hitler's forces invaded later the same year.

During 1935, Schrödinger had published a paper that criticized the current state of quantum theory. In quantum mechanics, the laws of physics are governed by probability; a radioactive atom might decay and emit an electron, or it might not. Schrödinger was upset by the absurdity of this implication and framed a famous thought experiment designed to expose it. In this experiment, he envisioned a box that contains a radioactive source, a device for detecting the presence of radioactive particles, a live cat, and a container of poison. The experiment is constructed such that the detector is switched on long enough so that there is a fifty-fifty chance that one of the atoms in the radioactive material will decay and that the detector will record the presence of a particle. If the detector does record such an event, the poison container is broken and the cat dies. If the detector does not record the presence of a particle, the cat lives.

In the world of ordinary experience, there is a fifty-fifty chance that the cat will be killed. Without examining the contents of the box, it is safe to assert that the cat is either dead or alive. In the world of quantum physics, neither of these two possibilities has any reality unless it is first observed. The atomic decay has neither occurred nor not occurred. Since the fate of the feline is tied to the state of the radioactive material, one cannot say that the cat is dead or alive until the inside of the box is examined. This implication, Schrödinger declared, reveals the absurdity of quantum mechanics. It is one thing to conceive of an elementary particle such as an electron being neither here nor there but quite another to conceive of a concrete thing such as a cat in this indeterminate state.

Schrödinger was encouraged in his decision to leave Graz by a message from Eamon de Valera, the President of Ireland, who invited him to serve as the first director of the school of theoretical physics at the Dublin Institute for Advanced Studies. The intellectual atmosphere of Dublin was fruitful for Schrödinger because its mandate was to foster breadth of interest and intellectual speculation. Among the eminent mathematical physicists at the time, Schrödinger most aptly fulfilled these criteria. During this period, Schrödinger published many works on the application and statistical interpretation of wave mechanics, and on problems concerning the relationship between general relativity and wave mechanics. As senior professor, it was Schrödinger's pleasant duty to give a series of lectures from time to time. Four of his books, *What Is Life?* (1944), *Science and Humanism: Physics in Our Time* (1951), *Nature and the Greeks* (1954), and *Mind and Matter* (1958), were written for these lecture series. The most famous was his lecture series "What Is Life?" presented in 1944 to a large and enthusiastic audience. The thesis of these lectures is that quantum physics is required for understanding biological replication. Although his theme was controversial, it aroused much interest among many promising young physicists, such as Francis Crick, and encouraged them to turn to biology.

In 1956, near the end of Schrödinger's stay in Dublin, asthma and bronchitis curtailed his productivity. His friend, Hans Thirring, arranged a special chair for him as professor emeritus of theoretical physics at the University of Vienna. He wrote only two articles during this period, one on the interpretation of quantum mechanics and a second on the problem of nature and the self. Schrödinger died after a prolonged illness at the age of seventy-three.

*Summary*

Erwin Schrödinger is primarily known for inventing wave mechanics and for the equation which bears his name, but his legacy is much greater. His collected papers include important contributions to virtually every branch of physics, and he constantly encouraged physicists to examine the foundations of their discipline and its relationship to other scientific endeavors. As a philosopher, he was worried about the problems of knowers in a world governed by probabilistic laws. Schrödinger was also interested in the classics and in poetry, and he even tried his hand at sculpture.

While his interests knew no bounds, Schrödinger was somewhat narrow in his outlook on questions of physics. His conservativeness was not surprising granted that, when he made his most important contributions during the mid-1920's, he was already a senior member of the scientific community and steeped in traditional concepts and theories. Indeed, Schrödinger resisted the new innovations of indeterminacy and the instantaneous jumping of electrons from one state to another to the end of his days. His most important contribution—the wave mechanics—attempted to describe atomic structures in terms of waves, an established model in the scientific community. Schrödinger furnished scientists with invaluable tools for problem-solving, but his wave mechanics represented a return to nineteenth century ideas.

*Bibliography*

Atkins, Kenneth R. *Physics: Once Over Lightly.* New York: John Wiley & Sons, 1972. This book is a serious guide to modern physics for the casual reader or the nonscience major. It is invaluable as an aid to further study.

Born, Max. *The Restless Universe.* 2d ed. Mineola, N.Y.: Dover, 1951. One of the best contemporary accounts of the new physics by one of its central participants. This is a popular book about the birth of modern physics that can be read for profit by the nonspecialist.

Gribbon, John. *In Search of Schrödinger's Cat: Quantum Physics and Reality.* New York: Bantam Books, 1984. The author believes that Schrödinger's wave mechanics attempted to restore nineteenth century concepts, an assessment first made by some of Schrödinger's contemporaries, such as Born. This book provides a historical backdrop for the development of the central concepts of quantum mechanics, and it contains a useful bibliography.

Schrödinger, Erwin. *What Is Life? The Physical Aspect of the Living Cell.* Cambridge, England: Cambridge University Press, 1944. This book was very influential on an entire generation of scientists, including Crick, who unraveled the structure of the living molecule. It is mistaken on some key points, but it stands as a testament to the importance of quantum theory for genetic engineering.

Scott, William T. *Erwin Schrödinger: An Introduction to His Writings.* Amherst: University of Massachusetts Press, 1967. An invaluable account of Schrödinger's life and work. Many of the chapters are highly technical, but the first chapter gives a good synopsis of Schrödinger's life and work. The bibliography of Schrödinger's publications is indispensable for additional research.

*Brian S. Baigrie*

# KARL SCHWARZSCHILD

*Born:* October 9, 1873; Frankfurt am Main, Germany
*Died:* May 11, 1916; Potsdam, Germany
*Area of Achievement:* Astronomy
*Contribution:* Schwarzschild developed a new use for photography, as a tool for measuring the brightness of stars, particularly variable objects. He was the first scientist to develop a solution for Albert Einstein's general relativity field equations, dealing with gravity around a star of such intensity that it becomes a black hole, surrounded by a boundary known as the Schwarzschild radius.

## *Early Life*

Karl Schwarzschild was the eldest child of six children. His father, a prosperous businessman in Frankfurt, encouraged Karl's early interest in science, particularly astronomy. He was the first of his family to be interested in science; indeed, he wrote and published his first two astronomical papers, on the topic of double-star orbits, when he was only sixteen. While in school, he was introduced to J. Epstein, a mathematician with a private observatory. From Epstein's son, Schwarzschild learned to make and to use a telescope, and studied advanced mathematics and celestial mechanics. After education at the local level, he spent two years at the University of Strasbourg (1891), then two more at the University of Munich. He received his doctorate from that university in 1896, graduating summa cum laude. The thesis for his Ph.D. was on the application of the theory of stable configurations in rotating bodies, developed by Henri Poincaré, to investigations of tidal deformation in satellites and the validity of Pierre-Simon Laplace's theory for the origin of the solar system. He also invented a multislit interferometer for measuring separation of double stars.

## *Life's Work*

Schwarzschild was interested in observational astronomy. In the early 1890's, he developed the use of photography, later called photographic photometry, to measure the apparent magnitude of stars using a photographic plate to substitute for the human eye at the telescope. Using his new method of measuring the image densities on the plates, he was able to establish the magnitude of 367 stars; he used those results to get a teaching position at the University of Munich. In all, he worked on thirty-five hundred stellar objects of magnitude greater than 7.5, at the same time showing conclusively that there was a vast difference between visual (with the unaided eye) and photographic magnitude or brightness, a difference later known as the star's color index. His results also led him to suggest that periodic variable stars behaved as they did, going through a regular cycle of maximum and minimum brightness, because of periodic temperature changes. In turn, this hypothesis led to further work on Cepheid variables by the famous astronomer Sir Arthur Eddington.

From 1896 to 1899, Schwarzschild worked as an assistant at the Kuffner Observatory in Vienna. After some time spent lecturing and writing (his lectures conveyed the excitement of astronomy to nonastronomers to such an extent that the lectures would become famous), he received an associate professorship in 1901 from the University of Göttingen. A year later, he became a professor of astronomy there, and was also made director of its observatory. In 1909, he succeeded Hermann Vogel as the director of the Astrophysical Observatory in Potsdam.

Schwarzschild worked extensively in theoretical astronomy and also in subjects as diverse as orbital mechanics, the curvature of space throughout the known universe, stellar energy production, and the surface structures of the Sun. In 1900, he suggested that the geometry of space did not necessarily have to conform to Euclidean geometry, in which two parallel lines are forever parallel, and the sum of interior angles of a triangle is always 180 degrees. Light rays from a star hitting Earth's orbit at two widely separated points form an overextended triangle. By measuring the interior angles of such a hypothetical structure, he attempted to determine the curvature of space, since he knew that, if the angles added up to more or less than 180 degrees, he would be dealing with non-Euclidean space. He concluded, from his experimental results, that if space were curved, it had an extremely large radius of curvature, so large as to be unnoticeable in as small a region as the solar system.

In 1906, Schwarzschild worked diligently on a paper showing that a star should not be considered as a simple gas held together by its own gravity. Thermodynamical properties, particularly concerning the transfer of heat inside the stellar surface by both convection and radiation, had to be present. To deal effectively with this situation, he invented the concept of radiative equilibrium in astrophysics, a balance of the energy flowing inward and outward to help maintain the star's stability. He showed how, mathematically, radiative processes would be important in conveying heat in stellar atmospheres—how energy could be transferred at and near the Sun's surface. Many of his ideas were stimulated by his observation of the total solar eclipse in 1905, an event he photographed with a newly devised instrument, one forming spectrograms from an objective prism at the eyepiece of the telescope. This instrument allowed him to derive information on the chemical composition of various areas at differing depths in the Sun's atmosphere.

Among the topics to which he contributed was stellar statistics, how to deal with large numbers of stars and their associated data. The methods and techniques he developed are now standard in graduate stellar astronomy courses. He designed, as a new tool for analysis, a spectrographic objective that provided a reliable means of determining a star's radial velocity, the speed and direction in which it is moving. Many new contributions to geometric optics stemmed from this fertile period.

Schwarzschild volunteered for military service in 1914, at the start of World War I, spending his time first in Belgium manning a weather station, then transferring to France for the job of calculating the trajectories for long-range cannon shells. Craving action, he managed to get transferred again, to Russia. While in Russia in 1916, he heard of Albert Einstein's new general theory of relativity. As a result, Schwarzschild wrote two papers on the theory, both published that year. He provided a solution, the first to be found, to the complex partial differential equations fundamental to the theory's mathematical basis. Schwarzschild solved the Einstein equation for the exterior space time of a spherical nonrotating body. He showed that when a star is contracting under the influence of gravity, a result of the amount of mass present, if it reaches a particular radius, the gravitational potential, representing the energy needed to escape from the object, becomes infinite in quantity. This solution showed that there is an enormous redshift, virtually infinite, when a body of large mass contracts to that certain radius, a size known as the Schwarzschild radius. The value of that size is easily calculated by a simple astrophysical formula he derived, relating the radius to the universal gravitational constant, the star's mass, and the speed of light ($R = 2GM/c[2]$). Surprisingly, he showed that the general theory of relativity gave basically the same results as Isaac Newton's more common theory of gravitation, but for different reasons. When the mass of the object is measured in units of the Sun's mass, the Schwarzschild radius is neatly given by three times the ratio of the mass to the Sun's mass, the answer expressed in kilometers ($R = 3 \times M/M[\text{Sun}]$). If the Sun were contracted to a radius of 3 kilometers, it would be of the right size to be labeled a "black hole." A body becomes a black hole when it shrinks to a radius of less than the critical radius; at that point, nothing, including light, will have enough energy ever to escape from the body—hence the name "black hole," since no light escapes and anything falling in remains. Earth's mass is such that it would have to contract to a radius of approximately one centimeter to become such a glorified vacuum cleaner for the universe.

The theoretical study of black holes and the continuing search for them has become an important field in modern astronomy, particularly since they can be used to solve some of the most fundamental problems of stellar, galactic, and cosmological astronomy.

While in Russia, Schwarzschild contracted pemphigus, an incurable metabolic disease of the skin. He was an invalid at home in 1916 when he died. For his service in the war effort, he was awarded an Iron Cross. In 1960, he was honored by the Berlin Academy, which named him the greatest German astronomer of the preceding century.

*Summary*

Karl Schwarzschild, as an astronomer and theoretician, achieved many great things in his chosen field, despite his short life. As a final contribution to history, he was father to Martin Schwarzschild, born in 1912, who has done his own great work in astronomy, primarily on the theory of stellar structure and evolutionary dynamics.

Schwarzschild early developed the kind of flair for science of which many scientists only dream. His practical skill he demonstrated by the superb and innovative instruments he designed and built, including astrophotographic tools, spectral analysis instruments, and many important contributions to the theory and design of geometrical optics. With his exceptional mathematical ability, he was able to contribute greatly to theoretical astronomy, in subjects including celestial mechanics, stellar physics, solar dynamics, thermodynamics of stellar interiors, and applications of the theory of relativity, all of which are important fields of research in modern astronomy.

Schwarzschild attached great importance to lecturing and writing on popular astronomy. He attempted to make difficult subjects in physics and astronomy more lucid, presenting pictures with words that the average nonscientist could understand. He was equally at home with his scientific associates, ready to discuss and extend any conjecture or idea. As a theoretical astrophysicist, he was one of the great promoters of Niels Bohr's theory of atomic spectra, presented in 1913, a theory that he believed would solve most of the analytic problems of stellar spectral analysis. While on his deathbed, Schwarzschild finished a famous paper on that subject, in which he developed the rules of quantization, work that, developed independently by Arnold Sommerfeld, provided for the theory of the Stark effect and the quantum theory of molecular structure. Perhaps he expressed his wonderment at nature best regarding relativity and the curvature of space when he wrote: "One finds oneself here, if one will, in a geometrical fairyland, but the beauty of this fairy tale is that one does not know but that it may be true." One wonders how far he might have gone if war had not ended his brilliant career so early.

*Bibliography*

Bergman, Peter G. *The Riddle of Gravitation*. Rev. ed. New York: Charles Scribner's Sons, 1987. A detailed study of the effects of gravity in the universe, from the viewpoints of Newton and Einstein. A major portion of the book is spent on the role of gravity in the operation of stars and the formation of black holes. Excellent glossary and extensive pictures. Some mathematics; difficult reading.

Bowers, Richard, and Terry Deeming. *Astrophysics*. Vol. 1, *Stars*. Boston: Jones & Bartlett, 1984. A detailed excursion into the features and history of stellar bodies. Beginning with observational data, the work proceeds with the life history of stars, to the endpoints, including black holes, supernovas, and white dwarfs. Very detailed in mathematics; recommended for the advanced layperson. References.

Calder, Nigel. *Einstein's Universe*. New York: Viking Press, 1979. A brief but clearly written account of how the universe works under the actions of the special and general theories of relativity. Deals with the origin of the universe and the evolution of stars to the black-hole stage. Interesting discussion of the curving of space as a result of effects of large masses. Good diagrams and pictures; easy reading.

Hartmann, William K. *Cycles of Fire*. New York: Workman, 1987. An immensely enjoyable book dealing with the stars. Covers their origins and lives, to the end when they die, by using basic telescopic data to explain, in simple terms, basic astrophysics. Also deals with possible planetary systems and life-forms. Fantastic pictures and paintings. Additional references and a well-written glossary.

Kaufmann, William J., III. *Black Holes and Warped Spacetime*. San Francisco: W. H. Freeman, 1979. A book for the layperson on the general theory of relativity and its consequences, particularly in terms of star deaths. Extensive section on the Schwarzschild radius and its importance in forming black holes, altering the space around the star. Well written, with a comprehensive nonmathematical treatment.

Kippenhahn, Rudolf. *100 Billion Suns*. New York: Basic Books, 1986. A well-written overview of the development of knowledge of stellar astronomy. Using extensive drawings, Kippenhahn details the evolution of stars, from original dust clouds collapsing, through middle age, to the death throes of various-sized objects. Black-hole formation is nicely discussed. Numerous pictures and drawings, and extensive references.

*New Frontiers in Astronomy: Readings from "Scientific American."* San Francisco: W. H. Freeman, 1975. A collection of major articles from the magazine representing the major areas of research in astronomy. Excellent sections on stars, black holes, and the role of relativity in the universe. Written for the advanced layperson. Additional bibliographies for each article. Numerous pictures and explanatory diagrams.

Verschuur, G. L. *The Invisible Universe Revealed*. New York: Springer-Verlag, 1987. Using the previously unknown parts of the electromagnetic spectrum, this work traces the development of radio astronomy and its offshoots. Details the types of observations made and the nature of the data gathered on black holes, quasars, galaxies, nebulas, and stellar objects. Excellent and extensive collection of pictures; extensive references.

*Arthur L. Alt*

# ALBERT SCHWEITZER

*Born:* January 14, 1875; Kaysersberg, Germany
*Died:* September 4, 1965; Lambaréné, Gabon
*Areas of Achievement:* Theology, peace advocacy, philosophy, music, and medicine
*Contribution:* Schweitzer, a renowned organist, student of the music of Bach, and an unorthodox biblical scholar, dedicated himself as a medical missionary to the natives of Africa, a decision that led to a fifty-year career that captured the admiration of many people and led to his receiving the Nobel Peace Prize. He also actively urged the public, politicians, and statesmen to come to grips with the threat of nuclear war and work for peace.

## *Early Life*

Albert Schweitzer was born in Kaysersberg, Haute Alsace, on January 14, 1875. During that year his father, Louis Schweitzer, a liberal protestant, became pastor of the village church in Gunsbach, Alsace. There in what today is the Rhineland of France, Schweitzer grew up. Alsace has in its history been alternately governed by France and Germany. Because of this background Schweitzer spoke both French and German fluently. He studied and wrote in both languages.

Schweitzer's father began teaching him to play the piano and organ when he was five and eight years old, respectively. At nine he occasionally substituted for the regular organist in his father's church. When he was ten, he was sent to school in Mulhouse, where he lived with a great uncle and began taking music lessons from Eugene Munch. It was during the eight years he spent in Mulhouse that his creative, intellectual, and musical abilities blossomed.

In order to follow in the footsteps of his father, he was enrolled in the University of Strasbourg as a student of theology and philosophy at the Theological College of St. Thomas. He did not, however, give up his new love, music. It was music, particularly the editing of the organ works of Johann Sebastian Bach, and his organ playing, building, and restoring abilities that supported Schweitzer through much of his life and brought him international acclaim. His college career was interrupted when he was drafted into the infantry. He, however, did not leave his mind at home. He took what he had learned at St. Thomas and a copy of the Greek New Testament with him. He spent many hours thumbing through it, reading and meditating on the words of Jesus in the light of the modern historical criticism he had been taught.

Immediately after graduation, Schweitzer entered a postgraduate program in philosophy that took him to the Sorbonne in Paris, the University of

Berlin, and finally back to the University of Strasbourg, which awarded him the doctor of philosophy degree for his treatise on the religious philosophy of Immanuel Kant. He believed that he was ready to begin working toward a doctor of theology degree, which he completed one year later. In September, 1900, he was ordained at St. Nicholas Church in Strasbourg and the following spring received an appointment to the faculty of the Theological College of St. Thomas at the University of Strasbourg, a post he held for six years. During this time he continued his study of the organ and gained quite a reputation as a performer.

*Life's Work*

Schweitzer, on his thirtieth birthday, informed his friends that he had decided to devote the rest of his life to the natives of Africa as a doctor of medicine. This created quite a stir among family and friends, most of whom thought he had lost his mind. He was not to be dissuaded. While continuing his duties as a faculty member and completing a biography of Bach, Schweitzer began taking the science courses needed to enter medical school. He made contact with the Paris Missionary Society, whose newsletter containing an article on the need for medical missionaries in Africa had inspired him, volunteering his services as a medical missionary. To his surprise, he was not readily accepted, because of his unorthodox biblical views. He finally convinced the Paris Missionary Society to grant him permission to set up a medical facility for them when he promised not to preach but only to serve as a medical doctor.

From 1906 to 1912, Schweitzer studied medicine at the University of Strasbourg, all the time teaching religion at the university, preaching at St. Nicholas, giving organ concerts, working with Charles Widor on an edition of Bach's organ works, writing several books and treatises, and making plans for his work in Africa. In 1912, he resigned his positions at the University of Strasbourg and St. Nicholas Church and on June 18, 1912, married Helene Bresslau, the daughter of a Jewish colleague and professor of history. In February, 1913, he completed his internship in tropical medicine, finished his thesis on the psychiatric study of Jesus, and received his M.D. degree. On March 26, 1913, he and his wife, who had become a nurse in order to work with him, set sail from Bordeaux, France, to set up a hospital on the land of the Paris Missionary Society in Lambaréné, French Equatorial Africa, today known as Gabon. This trip was the first of his many trips between Europe and Africa and marks the end of Schweitzer's life of preparation for service and the beginning of his life of service to Africans.

Schweitzer's life in Africa can be divided into four periods, each of which was marked by three events over which he had no control: World War I, World War II, and the death of his wife. Schweitzer had barely established his hospital when he was put under house arrest in Lambaréné by the French.

He was considered an enemy alien because he was German and came from German Alsace. In 1917, he and his wife were transferred to France, where they were interred in two different prison camps for civilian aliens. It was to be ten years before he was able to return to Lambaréné. When he did so, this time without his wife, he found his hospital in ruins.

During the years from 1927 to 1947, Schweitzer built a new hospital at a new location not far from the first site. He traveled back and forth to Europe four times. One additional trip was cut short—so short, in fact, that the same boat that took him to Europe took him back to Africa. He was afraid that Hitler would attack France and somehow, perhaps because he was now considered a French citizen or perhaps because he had a Jewish wife, prevent him from returning to French Equatorial Africa. There were four reasons for these frequent trips: to visit his wife; to give concerts in order to raise the money he needed to operate his hospital and support himself; to deliver lectures to gather charitable support; and to recruit doctors and nurses to serve with him in Africa.

Schweitzer's longest sojourn in Africa took place during World War II. He was hard pressed to keep his hospital afloat. His concert tours in Europe could not be held, medical supplies were consumed by the war, and his supporters in Alsace were surrounded by the war. Fortunately, a speaking tour that his wife made in the United States brought his cause to the attention of some Americans who raised money and sent medical supplies to him when the people of Europe could not do so.

The years between 1947 and 1957 Schweitzer spent mostly in Europe. During this time he was in great demand as a lecturer and organist. Both of these activities brought him and his work into the public eye, and support for his work was no longer in question. During this time he was idolized by Europeans and Americans alike. He was courted by people seeking support for their own causes. In 1952, he was awarded the Nobel Peace Prize. Perhaps it was his experiences with war, perhaps it was his Christianity, perhaps it was both and more—in any case he gave wholehearted support to the antinuclear protests of the late 1950's. He made only four short stays in Africa. Unfortunately, it was during the last sojourn that his wife died. Shortly after Helen's death, he made one more trip to Europe when, besides the usual public appearances, he put his European house in order. Schweitzer brought his wife's ashes with him to Africa and buried them on his hospital grounds in Lambaréné. This time he returned to stay. He no longer felt the need to visit Europe. Support for his work was assured, and he wanted to see his hospital, especially his leprosarium, developed in his way. Now, more than ever before, people came to see him and his hospital at Lambaréné. The hospital they saw was not necessarily what they expected, but Schweitzer, himself, disappointed only those who had come with their own agenda. He had fought his own battles; he was now an old man too occupied with his work to take up causes other than his own.

In July, 1964, Schweitzer designated Walter Munz as chief of staff of his hospital. On August 28, 1965, Schweitzer appointed his daughter, Rhena Schweitzer-Eckert, as administrator of the hospital. On September 4, 1965, his house in order, Schweitzer died. African drums, similar to those that told the Africans that he had arrived in Lambaréné more than a half a century earlier, now told of his death. Modern forms of communication spread the news throughout Gabon to the rest of the world.

*Summary*

It is really incorrect to say, as many do, that Albert Schweitzer's life's work began with his first trip to Africa. Everything he did leading up to that time and everything he did from then until his death revolved around his work in Africa. The proceeds of his books on the life of Bach financed his personal expenses for the first years in Lambaréné. He supported himself while in Africa by writing about his work there, by writing on theology, philosophy, and music for book publishers and magazines. He kept up his skills as an organist by practicing in Africa on a piano outfitted with organ pedals so that he could give organ concerts while visiting Europe. All this made it possible for him to care for the sick, operate on the ill and injured, comfort the dying, plan and supervise the construction of his hospital, and recruit people with medical skills to his hospital.

It was Schweitzer's theology that led him to his interpretation of Jesus' command, "Follow me." He traced his ethical philosophy back to Jesus' teaching to love your neighbor. Schweitzer was a man of heroic proportions, yet he was human and had human failings. This plus the human failings of others caused him to be subjected to a fair amount of unkind and unjustified criticism. This criticism never seriously affected him or his reputation. His place in history seems secure.

*Bibliography*

Anderson, Erica. *The Schweitzer Album: A Portrait in Words and Pictures.* New York: Harper & Row, 1965. This work strives to explicate Schweitzer's thought through quotations from his conversations, speeches, and letters. Also contains many photographs of Schweitzer.

____________. *The World of Albert Schweitzer: A Book of Photographs.* New York: Harper and Bros., 1955. This book is an excellent place to start a study on the life of Schweitzer. Contains pictures taken by Anderson during the several trips she made to Lambaréné plus many others she selected in order to complete this photographic essay.

Brabazon, James. *Albert Schweitzer: A Biography.* New York: G. P. Putnam's Sons, 1975. A long, balanced, and well-written biography published ten years after Schweitzer's death. Its strength is in its discussion of the last part of Schweitzer's life. It has an epilogue about life in Lambaréné after Schweitzer. The book contains photographs, a bibliography, scholarly notes, and an index.

Cousins, Norman. *Dr. Schweitzer of Lambaréné*. New York: Harper, 1960. An account of Cousins' visit to Schweitzer's hospital in Lambaréné during January, 1957. The appendix contains Schweitzer's radio broadcast, "Peace or Atomic War." The book contains photographs of the persons and sights to be seen at the Schweitzer Hospital. It gives insight into Schweitzer's work and accomplishments during the last years of his life.

Hegedorn, Hermann. *Prophet in the Wilderness: The Story of Albert Schweitzer.* New York: Macmillan, 1947. An early, popular account of Schweitzer's life. It has bibliographic references to English works about Schweitzer and to English translations of Schweitzer's books that were published before 1947.

Marshall, George, and David Poling. *Schweitzer: A Biography.* Garden City, N.Y.: Doubleday, 1971. If only one book about Schweitzer can be read, this one should be considered. It tells the story of his life and evaluates him as a man and as a world citizen. This book contains a chronological biography, an index, a bibliography of English translations of Schweitzer's books, collections based on his works, selected biographies of Schweitzer, and recordings by and films about him. The bibliography is annotated and includes references to two books containing negative criticism.

Payne, Robert. *The Three Worlds of Albert Schweitzer.* New York: Thomas Nelson & Sons, 1957. A positive biography written for the general public at the height of Schweitzer's popularity.

Picht, Werner. *The Life and Thought of Albert Schweitzer.* Translated by Edward Fitzgerald. New York: Harper & Row, 1964. This book is less on the life and more on the thought of Schweitzer. It is an examination of Schweitzer's writings on Kant, Jesus, Paul, and Johann Wolfgang von Goethe. It discusses his music, ethics, and theological views on the "Kingdom of God."

Schweitzer, Albert. *Music in the Life of Albert Schweitzer with Selections from His Writings*. Edited by Charles R. Joy. Boston: Beacon Press, 1951. Schweitzer was renowned as a performer of music. This book, however, concentrates on his thoughts on music, organs and organ building, and his writings about Bach. While it does this, it is not just a book for musicians. It, like most books about him from the 1950's, was written to satisfy the curiosity of people who wanted to know more and more of the person about whom everyone was talking.

__________. *The Wit and Wisdom of Albert Schweitzer.* Edited by Charles R. Joy. Boston: Beacon Press, 1949. A topically arranged collection of quotations, some short, some longer, which show the wide range of Schweitzer's interests. The book contains a bibliography of Schweitzer's writings and a good chronology of Schweitzer's life up until October, 1949.

Seaver, George. *Albert Schweitzer: The Man and His Mind*. New York: Harper Brothers, 1947. This work devotes equal time to Schweitzer's biography and to a discussion of his writings. Appendix 1 and 3 feature Schweitzer's thoughts on colonization, race relations, and religion (ethics) in modern civilization, areas of thought where Schweitzer is most controversial.

*Theodore P. Aufdemberge*

# HANS VON SEECKT

*Born:* April 22, 1866; Schleswig, Prussia
*Died:* December 27, 1936; Berlin, Germany
*Area of Achievement:* The military
*Contribution:* Seeckt reshaped Germany's small post-1918 *Reichswehr* on modern lines, emphasizing the principles of mobility and combined attack later employed in the Blitzkrieg victories of 1940.

## *Early Life*

Johannes (Hans) Friedrich Leopold von Seeckt was born on April 22, 1866, the second surviving child and only surviving son of Captain (later General) Richard von Seeckt, and Auguste von Seeckt aus Greifswald. *Gymnasium*-educated and more intellectual than athletic, Hans joined the select Alexander Guards Regiment of the Prussian army as an ensign in 1885 and made second lieutenant in 1887. Hard work and intelligence earned for him a year at the War Academy in 1893, promotion to first lieutenant in 1894, General Staff assignments in 1897, and appointment to the German General Staff, with subsequent promotion to captain in 1899. Seeckt worked on the mobilization of the 1900 China Expedition and was promoted to major in 1906.

In 1893, Seeckt married Dorothea Jacobson Fabian, of German-Jewish middle-class background, in a happy though childless union. Seeckt's foreign observer assignments plus holidays provided the couple with travel experience in Europe, North Africa, the Middle East, and India. Their Berlin home became a center for a varied society with broad cultural interests. By 1914, the slim, monocled, somewhat elegant major already had much the appearance of his later years.

In the War of 1914, Lieutenant Colonel von Seeckt planned the attack at Soisson well enough to be promoted to colonel and was sent to the Eastern Front as chief of staff for the Eleventh Army and Mackensen's Army Group. Seeckt's spectacular success in the Gorlice-Tarnow breakthrough of May, 1915, earned for him a promotion to major general but also the lasting jealousy of Paul von Hindenburg and Erich Ludendorff. In 1916 and 1917, as chief of staff for Archduke Karl of Austria and later Archduke Joseph, he coordinated Austro-German operations in Southeastern Europe. In 1918, Seeckt served as a lieutenant general in, and chief of staff for, the Turkish army under Enver Pasha.

## *Life's Work*

Late in 1918, General von Seeckt returned to a Germany shaken by the November collapse of the *Kaiserreich*. He strongly urged the view that the new *Reichswehr* was the legitimate heir to the old army rather than simply a creation of President Friedrich Ebert's hastily contrived Weimar Republic. As organizer of Northeastern defenses, Seeckt successfully pushed the recapture of Riga to show that Germany still counted in Eastern Europe. As an adviser, however, on the 1919 Treaty of Versailles settlement, he found the Allies adamant on German disarmament, which included abolishing the General Staff and reducing the army to four thousand officers plus ninety-six thousand men, all on long-term enlistments.

Seeckt preserved a de facto General Staff through the *Truppenamt* (troops bureau), which he headed after the retirement of Hindenburg and General Wilhelm Gröner in 1919. General Walther Reinhardt became army commander, and with him, and under Defense Minister Gustav Noske, Seeckt shared the tumultuous domestic and *Freikorps* conflicts of 1919 and 1920.

Such a conflict brought Seeckt to national prominence in March of 1920, when the right-wing Kapp Putsch in Berlin threatened to overthrow the republic. Seeckt consistently opposed this attempt, in which General Ludendorff was a chief figure, but he refused to sanction divisive bloodshed. His persistent "*Reichswehr* do not shoot *Reichswehr*" line of argument preserved army unity, and, after civil officials and labor unions thwarted the putsch, the government promoted Seeckt to army commander in place of Reinhardt. Seeckt's subsequent leniency toward some former putschists has been criticized.

Shaping Germany's 100,000-man army into a credible military force was now the great task confronting Seeckt. The insignificance in numbers was compounded by Treaty of Versailles prohibitions on military aircraft, tracked vehicles, heavy guns, and trained reserves. What officer of ability and ambition would join an army incapable of beating any country worth calling an enemy? The situation required imaginative alternatives, political as well as military. Seeckt turned to Russia in 1921 to establish in that diplomatically isolated country some jointly owned factories for tank and airplane design. These covert projects were small, but their experimental planes and tanks loomed large in Seeckt's military thinking. Also, this not totally secret prelude to the Rapallo Pact (1922) gave the German generals a sense of direction. Any Russo-German cooperation endangered Poland, and thereby weakened the French alliance structure in Eastern Europe.

In the Silesian border plebiscite of March, 1921, Seeckt sanctioned unofficial *Freikorps* activities, and these increased in scope during the 1923 French occupation of the Ruhr and the Rhineland Republic attempt. With the skyrocketing inflation of 1923, the economic and political weakness of the Weimar Republic invited a renewal of the "putsch politics" to which the *Freikorps* leaders gravitated. Seeckt adroitly squelched the Küstrin-Spandau Officers' Putsch of September 30 and forcibly suppressed the Leipzig "Red Militia" in October. In the November, 1923, Munich Putsch, Seeckt strung out negotiations until, with emergency powers and Hindenburg's support, he persuaded the Bavarian separatist leaders and the *Reichswehr* commanders to acknowledge and uphold the authority of the republic. This did not prevent Ludendorff and Adolf Hitler from leading a November 9, 1923, "March," but its suppression by the local authorities seemed at the time a vindication of Seeckt's methods.

There was in early 1924 some press speculation that Seeckt might use his emergency powers to make a putsch of his own, but Seeckt's special powers had been conditioned on clear and public promises to support the republic. Seeckt may have intended to position himself for a presidential try in 1926, but on Ebert's unexpected death in 1925, the patriotic candidate elected to be Reich president was Field Marshal Hindenburg. Seeckt was now no longer "the coming man" in politics, or at the top of army authority, but was henceforth an unnecessary and even inconvenient figure in both fields.

In February of 1926, Seeckt gave an incautious casual agreement to Crown Princess Cecilie's request that her eldest son, Prince Wilhelm, be allowed to take part in some *Reichswehr* exercises. Seeckt's staff failed to keep this participation (September 13-21) as discreetly obscure as he had ordered, and German news stories inspired foreign fears of a Hohenzollern restoration. Worse, when War Minister Otto Gessler asked for an explanation, Seeckt penned such an unsatisfactory reply that Gessler asked for his resignation. Seeckt appealed to the president, but Hindenburg accepted Seeckt's resignation on October 8.

The last decade of Seeckt's life was active but less influential. After travel vacations with his wife, Seeckt wrote several books and articles and was from 1930 to 1932 a People's Party member of the Reichstag. The 1932 reelection of Hindenburg and the 1933 accession to power of the Nazis ended his political activities. Still nominally an "adviser" to the *Reichswehr*, from 1933 to 1935 he established the German military mission to the Chinese Nationalist Government of Chiang Kai-shek. In 1935, Seeckt returned to Germany in ill health, and the final year of his life was one of ceremonies and tributes, in great part from the Nazi leaders who now controlled the Reich. Seeckt died in Berlin on December 27, 1936.

### *Summary*

The narrative of Hans von Seeckt's political fortunes accounts for much of his career, but the task of rebuilding the army was the work for which he was, and remains, celebrated. Briefly, Seeckt rejected the World War I overemphasis on mass armies and entrenched defensive firepower and proposed a mobile offensive with new technology to win by disorganizing the enemy's power to resist. Effective general staff control of war policy was a key to success, and the preserving, organizing, and directing of this staff was an immediate priority for Seeckt. The mobile offensive involved a coordinated firepower concentration with a capacity to advance in the course of battle.

The airplanes, tanks, gun carriers, and even cavalry of the attack must be accompanied or closely followed by men, ammunition, and fuel. The mechanization, motorization, and radio command of the next war would impose a speed of action controllable only by a staff of highly trained professionals. Seeckt evidently had no exact blueprint for the practical details and technical problems involved, to the frustration of many of his staff, who had to prepare "maneuvers" with conspicuously imaginary weapons. Seeckt's general concept of the next war was not unique among contemporary military theorists, but his fellow visionaries in France and Great Britain were not in command, and their supreme commanders did not share the vision, with results made manifest in 1940.

In restoring the morale of a defeated army, Seeckt succeeded beyond all expectations, as the dispirited though dogged style of 1919 steadily improved into the energetic and purposeful confidence of 1926. This was a morale that refused to accept the defeat of 1918 as final and that defied the 1919 treaties. These sentiments were felt, or at least understood, by most Germans. The burdens of Versailles, weakness of the League of Nations, and Allied hypocrisy on "disarmament" seemed to justify Seeckt in making Germany's small army at least one that was ready to fight. The later political developments of the 1930's were not then anticipated.

Politics, indeed, were not Seeckt's métier. His ability at logical deduction from fixed principles, perhaps useful in his idea of an army-state, was ill-suited to Germany's experiment in democracy. As a monarchist and authoritarian, Seeckt could not love the republic, although he served it better than some of his critics have admitted. Like many others, Seeckt in 1932 believed that Hitler might be the leader Germany needed and learned better only when it was too late.

Seeckt was not by training or nature an innovator, and his turn of thought was contemplative rather than original or creative, a fact that limited his capacity for inventing new mobile offensive tactics for practical operations. He saw with logical clarity that the accepted objectives and principles of warfare were lost sight of in World War I's "strategy of attrition," which opposed modern technology with great human numbers until the side with more lives to spend became the winner. For soldiers to exploit the technology of war rather than to be exploited by it was the useful premise of Seeckt's thinking.

*Bibliography*

Carsten, Francis L. *The Reichswehr and Politics, 1918-1933*. Oxford, England: Clarendon Press, 1966. Best account of army politics in the Seeckt era. This is not a biography or a sympathetic look at Seeckt's politics but a detailed and scholarly work drawn from extensive research in the papers of many army leaders.

Craig, Gordon A. *The Politics of the Prussian Army, 1640-1945*. Oxford, England: Clarendon Press, 1955. A moderately critical history by an American scholar; provides a useful introduction and background.

Dupuy, T. N. *A Genius for War: The Germany Army and General Staff, 1807-1945*. Englewood Cliffs, N.J.: Prentice-Hall, 1977. This general work includes a good two-page biography of Seeckt plus a readable account of Seeckt's political career, with a practical sense of the normal military role.

Goerlitz, Walter. *History of the German General Staff, 1657-1945*. New York: Frederick A. Praeger, 1953. Standard general history by a respected German scholar; gives a good introduction and background.

Gordon, Harold J. *The Reichswehr and the German Republic, 1919-1926*. Princeton, N.J.: Princeton University Press, 1957. Best defense of Seeckt's politics by an American scholar. Well documented. Critical of the republic's antimilitary bias. Overlooks some points covered by Carsten and is too credulous of police reports but gives more inside information than most authors attempt.

Salomon, Ernst von. *The Outlaws*. Translated by Ian F. D. Morrow. London: Jonathan Cape, 1931. A *Freikorps* member's memoir. Distasteful, but generally authentic, and an essential supplement to academic studies of *Freikorps* politics.

Seeckt, Hans von. *Thoughts of a Soldier.* Translated by Gilbert Waterhouse. London: E. Benn, 1930. This is the most useful of several short works published in English. Seeckt's style does not translate easily.

Wheeler-Bennett, Sir John Wheeler. *The Nemesis of Power: The German Army in Politics, 1918-1945*. London: Macmillan, 1953. The most widely read and broadly informative version of the thesis that the German generals undermined the republic and sold out to Hitler. The chapter on Seeckt presents more interpretation than research.

*K. Fred Gillum*

# ANDRÉS SEGOVIA

*Born:* Probably February 17, 1893; Linares, Spain
*Died:* June 2, 1987; Madrid, Spain
*Area of Achievement:* Music
*Contribution:* Renowned as one of the foremost concert performers of the twentieth century, Segovia is responsible for establishing the guitar as a serious musical instrument. In addition to adapting works of Mozart, Haydn, Bach, and others for the classical guitar, Segovia stimulated modern composers to write new works for his instrument.

## *Early Life*

Andrés Segovia was born in Linares, Spain, in mid-February, 1893. A baptismal certificate suggests that the date was probably February 17, but various sources list dates ranging from February 17 to 23. His parents were Rosa Torrez Cruz and Bonifacio Segobia y Montoro, but Segovia was adopted at an early age by an aunt and uncle in Granada. (Although his father's name is spelled with a "b" on the baptismal certificate, he has been universally known as Segovia.) He was interested in music as a child and received instruction in piano, violin, and cello, but none of these inspired him. The guitar became Segovia's choice as soon as he heard a flamenco guitarist play. In fact, after the performance at a friend's home, the guitarist is said to have given Segovia his first lesson, though he could, in fact, teach the boy very little. Segovia's interest was at first clandestine, because the guitar was thought to be appropriate only for flamenco or folk music, as an accompaniment for exuberant singing and dancing. Despite opposition from family and teachers at the Granada Music Institute, young Segovia pursued his instrument. The first techniques he learned, and later had to unlearn, were those used by flamenco players. When Segovia could not find a qualified teacher, he taught himself. He applied his previous musical knowledge—particularly piano techniques—to the guitar, and his principles of fingering are said to stem from this early period. During his teenage years, Segovia became increasingly familiar with the works of Johann Sebastian Bach, Ludwig van Beethoven, Wolfgang Amadeus Mozart, and others and became aware of guitar virtuosos of the nineteenth century such as Fernando Sor, Julian Arcas, and Francisco Tárrega.

Although Segovia acknowledged the influence of these early masters, he developed a style and a technique that were essentially his own and distilled his program from various sources, transcribing and adapting lute, vihuela, and early guitar compositions. The encouragement of a young aristocrat, Rafael de Montis, based on what Segovia considered to be more cosmopolitan standards than the praise of the local people, helped convince him to attempt a concert career. In 1909, at the age of sixteen, Segovia made his public debut in Granada under the auspices of a local cultural organization, Circulo Artístico. He eventually moved to Madrid, where he heard musicians of international reputation perform, and Segovia considered that his "real debut" took place in 1916 at the Madrid Ateneo, the Spanish equivalent to Carnegie Hall. In 1919, he toured in Latin America, playing for enthusiastic Spanish-speaking audiences who were already inclined toward the guitar and, until 1923, performed only for such audiences.

*Life's Work*

The year 1924 was pivotal in Segovia's career. He performed at the home of well-known French musicologist Henri Prunières, who had invited top musicians to hear Segovia play this instrument, which was still considered unusual; the positive reception set the stage for Segovia's most important early success: his Paris debut in April, 1924. At this debut, arranged with the encouragement of fellow countryman Pablo Casals, Segovia played to a large audience that included such musical dignitaries as Paul Dukas, Joaquín Nin, Albert Roussel, Miguel de Unamuno y Jugo, Manuel de Falla, and Madame Debussy. Unveiling the brilliance of the Spanish guitar, Segovia was an immediate sensation with the general public and critics alike. In 1924, he also made successful debuts in Berlin and London, and he undertook a second Latin American tour including Argentina, Mexico, and Cuba (where he had his first recording session). In that same year, Segovia met George Krick, an American who later persuaded impresario Sol Hurok to arrange a recital tour in the United States.

By this time, Segovia's international reputation was firmly established, and he was attracting composers such as Federico Moreno Torroba, Joaquín Turina, Roussel, Manuel Ponce, Gustave Samazeuilh, Alexandre Tansman, and de Falla, who were stimulated to compose original works that liberated the guitar from the restrictions of its past. During the next four years, Segovia gave concerts in Spain, France, England, Italy, Germany, Scandinavia, and the Soviet Union. In 1926, the first editions of Schott's Segovia Guitar Archive Series were published, an important event in the guitar's history. While on tour in Germany, Segovia came across a complete edition of Bach's compositions for lute, which he transcribed for guitar and later became a familiar part of his repertoire. Several of these were published in 1928 in the Segovia Guitar Series, and, in 1934, Segovia's most important transcription of Bach was published as his edition of the "Chaconne." For some musicians, transferring this piece written for violin to the guitar amounted almost to blasphemy, but mastery of Segovia's edition eventually became a standard by which classical guitarists were measured.

In January, 1928, Segovia undertook his first performance tour in the United States. His first engagement was an intimate recital in Proctor, Massachusetts. His U.S. concert debut was at the Town Hall in New York City, with a program that included music by Bach and Joseph Haydn. Critics praised him highly, some even comparing him with Casals and Fritz Kreisler. He played five more sell-out concerts and then toured about forty other American cities in eleven weeks. For the next ten years, Segovia toured annually in the United States and developed an enthusiastic following. In 1928, he also toured in the Far East and again in Latin America. Segovia made his first trip to Japan in 1929 and subsequently performed there regularly. In the twenty years since his first public debut at age sixteen, Segovia rose from obscurity to international acclaim, and his reputation was to grow still more over the next years, as he continued to give concerts and recitals, transpose and adapt compositions for guitar, and inspire composers to compose original works for him.

In 1932, Segovia traveled to Venice with Falla and attended the International Festival of Music. While there, he met Mario Castelnuovo-Tedesco, a leading Italian composer, who became a great guitar enthusiast and composed for Segovia until he died in 1968. By the 1930's, many composers were writing for the guitar. Those such as Castelnuovo-Tedesco, Ponce, Joaquín Rodrigo, and Heitor Villa-Lobos introduced woodwind, brass, and percussion into guitar compositions, a practice that soon became popular with both guitarists and audiences. Then, Segovia's life in Spain was disrupted by the Spanish Civil War. In 1938, he left his home in Barcelona and lived away from his native land for the next sixteen years. After a brief stay in Italy, Segovia established residence in Montevideo, Uruguay, and toured extensively from there, though, during the years of World War II, Segovia did not perform in Europe. In 1943, he returned to the United States after a hiatus of five years. It seemed at first that Segovia had been almost forgotten by the public, but his popularity was soon reestablished, and he was also introduced to a wide American audience through the medium of television. During the 1940's, the guitar world experienced two important technological events, and Segovia incorporated both advances into his work. The first was Albert Augustine's introduction of nylon guitar strings, which gave the instrument a more reliable sound than gut strings. The second was the invention of the long-playing (LP) record; the LP recordings that Segovia made in the 1950's are considered some of his finest. Segovia gave about one hundred concerts each year during the 1950's and 1960's and performed in almost every non-Communist country.

By this time, through Segovia's influence, the repertoire for the guitar had become rich in depth and scope. Composers, both old and new, wrote for Segovia and his instrument. The unrivaled master of classical guitar, Segovia inspired and challenged the next generation of guitarists. He taught at Santiago de Compostela in Spain, the Academy Chigi in Siena, Italy, and the University of California, Berkeley, among other schools, and helped to establish the guitar as a respected part of the curriculum at music schools throughout the world. In addition, he made numerous recordings, including a wide range of composers and periods from classical to romantic to modern. Into his seventies and eighties, Segovia continued to perform internationally. Even into his nineties, he was still playing up to sixty concerts each year—though in his later years he decided to forego concert tours to faraway places—and he conducted master classes into the final months of his life. Segovia's commitment to the guitar as the central focus in his life never wavered; in recognition of his service to music, he received many honors, including two dozen Grand Crosses and Medals and many honorary doctorate degrees. He was also made an honorary citizen of several cities.

Segovia preferred to discuss his instrument rather than himself, and thus many details about his personal life are not well documented. Segovia married three times. His final marriage was to a former student in 1960, and he and his wife Emilie had a son, Carlos, in 1970. Segovia's autobiography indicates that one previous marriage was to pianist Paquita Mardiguera, and he also had a son Andres and a daughter Beatrice. Throughout his long and celebrated career, Segovia was nourished by his music. He said that he belonged to "that small minority of artists that toil in good faith. Around these the world of phenomenal vanishes, and happens to mystics when they give themselves to prayer." On June 2, 1987, Segovia died in Madrid at age ninety-four. His musical tradition lives on, especially through celebrated guitarists such as Julian Bream, John Williams, and Alirio Diaz, who themselves continued to perform Segovia's masterpieces and inspire composers to write for classical guitar.

### *Summary*

Andrés Segovia has been called the founding father of the modern guitar movement. Almost singlehandedly, he elevated the guitar to the status of solo concert instrument, achieving a brighter sound by plucking with his fingernails rather than playing with his fingertips in the traditional manner. He established a wide repertoire, arranging works for the classical guitar himself, encouraging others to do so, and inspiring composers to compose original works. Segovia dedicated himself to the creation of beauty, even though he lived through times of great international unrest; his music reflects order in the midst of chaos. In recitals that delighted audiences and critics, Segovia filled huge concert halls with the intimate sounds of the guitar, which he called an orchestra in miniature, and classical guitar study became widely available through the efforts of this tireless master who generously encouraged young artists.

Segovia stated in *Guitar Review* that he had five ambitions in life:

> To extract the guitar from the noisy and disreputable folkloric amusements . . . to create a wonderful repertoire for my instrument . . . to make the guitar known by

> the philharmonic public all over the world . . . to provide a unifying medium for those interested in the development of the guitar . . . [and] to place the guitar in the most important conservatories of the world for teaching the young lovers of it, and thus securing its future.

During his lifetime, Segovia achieved his goals. In later years, he was pleased by the instrument's expanding popularity but remained steadfastly opposed to electronic amplification of the guitar. "The real music lover wants to hear the small instrument speaking straight to the heart of the people," he said. Fortunately, numerous recordings are available so that Segovia will continue to speak to the hearts of people for generations to come.

*Bibliography*

Chotzinoff, Samuel. *A Little Nightmusic*. New York: Harper & Row, 1964. This volume presents seven interviews with distinguished musicians. The thirteen-page chapter on Segovia, written in an informal style, describes a lunch with Segovia in 1961 and offers a glimpse of Segovia's charming personality and wit as he discusses his early influences and recollections.

Clinton, George, ed. *Andrés Segovia: An Appreciation*. London: Musical News Services, 1978. This collection of facts, opinions, and anecdotes contains articles and reviews published in *Guitar* as well as previously unpublished interviews, essays, and reminiscences from Julian Bream, Alirio Diaz, John Duarte, Christopher Nupen, Alice Artzt, John Williams, Vladimir Bobri, Akinabu Matsuda, and Ivor Mairants.

Gavoty, Bernard. *Andrés Segovia*. Geneva: Rene Kister, 1955. Written by the then music critic of *Figaro*, this pamphlet presents an intimate portrait of Segovia illustrated with twenty-three photographs by Roger Hauert and three drawings. Part of the Great Concert Artists series, it includes a selected list of Segovia's Decca recordings as well as a copy of a handwritten letter from Segovia to Gavoty and its English translation.

Gelatt, Roland. *Music Makers*. New York: Alfred A. Knopf, 1953. Reprint. New York: Da Capo Press, 1972. This volume includes twenty-one entries on musicians who interested the author. The chapter on Segovia gives a brief account of his life to 1950, which includes interesting detail as well as thoughtful commentary by Gelatt.

Purcell, Ronald C. *Andrés Segovia, Contributions to the World of Guitar*. 2d ed. Melville, N.Y.: Belwin Mills, 1975. This is a compilation of Segovia's many contributions to the world of music. Its forty pages include listings of articles by Segovia, books and articles about Segovia, his music editions, and his discography. It is illustrated with five photographs and an unusual line drawing of Segovia by Bobri.

Segovia, Andrés. *Andrés Sevogia: An Autobiography of the Years 1893-*

*1920*. Translated by W. F. O'Brien. New York: Macmillan, 1976. Segovia intended to publish several volumes of memoirs, but this indexed first volume is the only one he completed. Written without a ghostwriter, its two hundred pages present a fascinating picture of Segovia's life, and the reader comes away realizing that it is the guitar that is really the main character.

Wade, Graham. *Segovia: A Celebration of the Man and His Music*. London: Allison and Busby, 1983. Although it does offer some biographical details, the volume focuses on aspects of Segovia's development that had previously been unexplored, such as Segovia's relationship with flamenco and the influence of Spanish literary and artistic figures on his life. Illustrated with photographs, it includes lists of Segovia's honors, his principal recordings, and composers' works recorded by him. It also includes a listing of his music editions, a representative selection of his recital programs from 1936 to 1982, and a bibliography.

*Jean C. Fulton*

# LÉOPOLD SENGHOR

*Born:* October 9, 1906; Joal, Senegal

*Areas of Achievement:* Literature, government, and politics

*Contribution:* Senghor, one of Africa's leading poets and intellectuals, is best known for having helped create and having greatly contributed to the *négritude* movement begun in the 1930's. A writer of rich, complex poems illuminating his love for his native Senegal as well as that for his beloved France, Senghor was also both a diplomat representing colonial Senegal in the French National Assembly and the President of Senegal after its independence in 1960. He has been a forceful, intelligent, influential pro-African leader respected throughout the world.

## *Early Life*

Léopold Sédar Senghor was born in Joal, a Senegalese town on the Atlantic Coast of Africa to a well-to-do Christian merchant from a minority tribe. Much of his youth was spent at various schools, the first of which was a Roman Catholic mission school, where he was given the standard fare of French colonial education. In such schools, French rather than African culture was highlighted, and one learned about French geography, politics, and history. A devout Catholic, Senghor was a bright, avid pupil, though his teachers failed to comprehend how special were his talents.

Senghor spent four years at a seminary in Dakar, yet left after he found he had no calling to the priesthood. Thereafter, he was allowed to attend the Dakar *lycée*, a secondary school administered by French people, which he entered in 1928. There he studied the standard French course offerings. His command of the French language combined with scholarly prowess led to his being sent to Paris, first to the Lycée Louis-le-Grand and then to the famous École Normale Supérieure of the University of Paris. At the latter, he received the sought after *agrégation* designation, which made him the first West African to be so honored.

His Parisian studies were the most formative of his career, but simply being in Paris, and therefore in contact with brilliant thinkers from around the world, was just as important for Senghor. At the university were other colonial intellectuals who did much to encourage his mental restlessness and his burgeoning interest in African life and culture. To this young outsider, Paris was not only the center of the France that exploited Africans but also an alluring, often enchanting city. Senghor participated in the life of the city as teacher, writer, and seminal thinker whose ideas about African culture and black identity became part of the *négritude* movement that flourished in the 1930's.

In Paris, Senghor, together with such fellow intellectuals as Aimé Césaire from Martinique, boldly postulated that black people the world over were not merely equal to whites but in some ways their superiors. In an influential review they helped establish, *L'Étudiant noir*, Senghor and Césaire came to believe that, in fact, blacks would offer the world an alternative to the destructive whites who, in Europe during World War I, created a truly fallen world of hatred and despair. Unlike the death-dealing, mechanical culture of whites, black culture was, in their estimation, happy, spontaneous, alive to possibilities, and invigorating—a true life force in a world ruled by death and destruction.

### *Life's Work*

The 1930's was a decade of dissatisfaction for black members of the French intelligentsia like Senghor, a time when colonialism with its assumptions of European superiority over nonwhite cultures became increasingly resented and even hated by African, Caribbean, and American black people. Senghor's feelings about France were pained and decidedly mixed: He appreciated the cultural offerings and opportunities in his adopted country, yet felt disparaged and belittled by French condescension toward anything African. To his despair, Senghor realized that white Europeans would continue to scorn African history and culture unless someone could boldly and graphically assert the power and beauty of African literature, art, and tribal existence.

Out of Senghor's association with writers Césaire and Léon Dumas came the concept of *négritude*, which became a major force behind revolutionary worldwide developments such as the independence movement in Africa and the Caribbean and the Black Pride movement in the United States. Nevertheless, Senghor, for all of his bitterness toward France for its racism and despoilation of part of the African continent, still continued to have a profound respect for French civilization and the positive things that French civilization had wrought in Senegal.

It became Senghor's passion to fuse his Senegalese experience with that of his French life into a meaningful synthesis wherein French themes and motifs were interwoven with those of Africa. In Senghor's poetry of the 1930's, African masks and ancestor worship make their appearance, especially in his first volume of poetry, *Chants d'ombre* (1945), in which he contrasts his pastoral childhood village life with the harsh, mechanized reality of Parisian life and the alienation he sometimes feels there. In trying to fuse Senegal and France into a coherent vision of life, Senghor deviated from what his black contemporaries were doing in their verse. Césaire and Dumas, for example, found little or nothing worth writing about in European culture and were unhappy with Senghor's "colonialist" values.

After his student days ended, Senghor served in the French army during World War II, an experience that disturbed him greatly; yet, as always, he found his reactions mixed. On one hand, he felt vaguely hopeful that France's taste of German occupation would lead to its freeing the African colonies, yet intuitively he realized that it would take more than the Occupation to free the Africans from their oppression. Senghor, horrified by the widespread destruction of the war, looked even more longingly to Africa and black people the world over for answers to European soul-sickness.

As *négritude* gathered momentum after the war and the desire of French colonies to free themselves from colonial rule became keen, Senghor became Senegal's delegate in the French parliament, wherein he received considerable praise for giving graceful, powerful, authoritative speeches. This marked the beginning of a political career as distinguished as Senghor's career as a writer. He found to his joy that he could not only influence people with his considerable literary gift but also exhort them in oratory to recognize black Africa's need for recognition and freedom. Senghor's demands for change were among the most eloquent heard in the National Assembly.

Increasingly in the years between 1945 and 1958, Senghor's reputation as a forceful advocate of the rights of Senegalese grew to the point where he eclipsed such rivals as Lamine Guèye. Elected in 1951 and 1956, he also was appointed to Edgar Fauré's cabinet in 1955. Out of this period of maturation, Senghor produced some of his more noted poems, including those in the collections entitled *Hosties noires* (1948), *Chants pour Naëtt* (1949), and *Éthiopiques* (1956). In *Hosties noires*, he contrasts his growing love for France with his fading memories of a Senegal only seen upon rare occasions, a problem of allegiance created by his having to live in France in order to serve as a delegate. Senghor, because he could not repudiate France, remained a man caught between worlds; his poetry reflects the tensions of his predicament.

After 1958, Senghor's attentions turned toward Senegal. He returned home after a long absence and rediscovered his home and people. He gained political support, first becoming president of the legislative assembly in the Mali Federation of which Senegal was a part, then President of Senegal Republic when Senegal broke away from the federation in 1960. Always working for African unity, Senghor was popular within and without Senegal, particularly in many West African countries. He was reelected president in 1963, 1968, and 1973.

Beginning with his rivalry with Mamadou Dia, who, as the original cabinet minister of Senegal, shared power with Senghor, a rivalry that created a 1962 *coup d'état* attempt, Senghor has not been universally admired: considerable countergovernment activity resulted from his concentrating all power in Progressive Union Party hands, and he had to worry constantly about being ousted from office. In 1967, his fears proved justified when there was an attempt on his life. Senghor's best poetry was behind him at this point in his life. Perhaps the fecundity of his imagination had been diminished by the strain of political life as some critics maintain.

### *Summary*

Léopold Senghor will continue to be remembered as the spokesman of the *négritude* movement who did some of his best, most moving work in the form of verse. His strong, sensual, vibrant early poetry is his best, and in it resonates the life of Senegal and, by extension, that of Africa itself. Without Senghor's unique ability to deal with French people on their own soil, it is questionable whether Césaire and other intellectuals caught up in the notion of *négritude* would have been as successful in drawing attention to their beliefs. With Senghor as spokesman, the movement had a strong voice to proclaim the importance of the African experience and African culture and the need for Africans to pursue their own destinies.

Senghor's verse, appreciated around the world, teems with African masks and the scents and sounds of African rivers and savannahs, bold African tribal women of powerful sexual presence, a paean to Africa, the mysterious mother and necessary restorer of the human race, the force for peace, justice, and harmony in the world. Yet his France, if not equally compelling as his Africa, is certainly a kind of homeland of the heart, a mother of culture and a teacher of the Christian religion to those lacking spiritual guidance. Thus Senghor will always be seen as one of the intermediaries between Europe and Africa, explaining each to each. In this role, Senghor records the creative tensions existing between these two worlds in a way no other French-speaking colonial poet has done. By not limiting his cultural horizon to Senegal, Senghor has served as a bridge connecting European writing with that of Africans and, as such, has interested the world outside Africa in its poetry.

Senghor did more for *négritude* than did most other writers, for he refused to address himself to an exclusively black audience but rather chose to write for all people interested in serious poetry. As a Senegalese politician of considerable presence and ability, he was able to lead his country into nationhood and out of colonialism, a complex and difficult process. His life story is one of remarkable achievement.

### *Bibliography*

Allen, Samuel. "Négritude, Africa, and the Meaning of Literature: Two Writers, Senghor and Soyinka." *Negro Digest*, June, 1967: 54-67. Allen offers readers one of the finest essays on the subject of how the ideas arising from the *négritude* movement influenced the writing of Senghor's poetry. His discussion of theme is particularly useful.

Bâ, Sylvia Washington. *The Concept of Négritude in the Poetry of Léopold Sédar Senghor.* Princeton, N.J.: Princeton University Press, 1973. Bâ's account is an enriching, engaging study of the tensions within Senghor because of his divided allegiance. She delves into the origins of *négritude* and proves it to be a powerful influence upon Senghor's poetry.

Cartey, Wilfred. *Whispers from a Continent: The Literature of Contemporary Black Africa*. New York: Random House, 1969. A classic study of African literature, this book deals with, among other things, the *négritude* movement as it pertains to the poetry of Senghor and others earmarked as key African writers.

Hymans, Jacques L. *Léopold Sédar Senghor: An Intellectual Biography.* Edinburgh, Scotland: Edinburgh University Press, 1971. Hyman's superb study does give Senghor proper credit for being a leading poet who is also a fine statesman. Here Senghor is portrayed as a complex, often troubled human being who had a vision of what black Africa could become.

Peters, Jonathan A. *A Dance of Masks: Senghor, Achebe, Soyinka*. Washington, D.C.: Three Continents Press, 1978. A West African himself, Peters offers a lively study (complete with useful bibliography) of Senghor's development as an artist. His discussion of the *négritude* movement is enlightening and includes a discussion of Senghor's cultural context.

Spleth, Janice. *Léopold Sédar Senghor.* Boston: Twayne, 1985. Part of the Twayne World Authors series, this book is a good introduction to Senghor's life and works. Contains a fairly in-depth biographical essay, basic discussion of his major writings and influences, a selected bibliography, notes, and an index.

*John D. Raymer*

# DMITRI SHOSTAKOVICH

*Born:* September 25, 1906; St. Petersburg, Russia
*Died:* August 9, 1975; Moscow, U.S.S.R.
*Area of Achievement:* Music
*Contribution:* Shostakovich was a first-rank composer in the Soviet Union for a full five decades. He adroitly balanced the insistent requirements of totalitarian political dictatorship over artistic culture with his own irrepressible inspiration for superb creativity to win worldwide acclaim.

## *Early Life*

Dmitri Dmitrievich Shostakovich grew up in a musical family, adopting a musical vocation quite naturally. His mother, a product of the St. Petersburg Conservatory, was a piano teacher. Amateur musical evenings in the family home were a regular part of Shostakovich's childhood. At the age of fourteen, Shostakovich himself entered the conservatory, where he studied piano and composition. Already he had displayed a talent for composition with pieces, as their titles suggest (*Soldier* and *In Memory of the Heroes Who Fell in the October Revolution*), that manifested another of his natural inclinations, namely the reflection of contemporary political conditions in his creative productions.

Shostakovich acquired international fame early with his symphony (1925), written as his graduation composition when he was only nineteen. After Bruno Walter introduced it in Berlin in 1927, performance of the symphony soon spread around the world and contributed to a positive view of artistic creativity in Soviet music during the New Economic Policy (1921-1928). The government showed its recognition of Shostakovich's potential value to it by subsidizing a European tour in 1927, during which he received an award in the International Chopin Competition as a pianist. Presently he made the decision to concentrate his talents upon composition at the expense of piano performance.

## *Life's Work*

The 1920's in the Soviet Union was a period of experimentation in all aspects of human social existence. Shostakovich celebrated the new society in his compositions. His second (1927) and third (1929) symphonies carried explicitly political titles, *October* and *May Day*, respectively, and expressed the optimistic triumphalism of the revolutionary milieu with bold instrumental and grandiose choral movements. Shostakovich ventured into the arena of social criticism with modernist ballets—*The Golden Age* (1928), *The Bolt* (1930), and *The Limpid Stream* (1935)—and operas—*The Nose* (1928) and *Lady Macbeth of Mtsensk* (1932)—that satirized bourgeois values, some of which he found surviving in Soviet Russia.

Of his ballets and operas, only *Lady Macbeth of Mtsensk* earned sustained critical praise, but it was also the work that brought him into collision with the Stalinist regime that put an end to the opportunity for artistic experimentation that the 1920's had afforded. After the opera enjoyed numerous successful performances for two years in both the Soviet Union and abroad, Joseph Stalin attended a performance in January, 1936. The Communist Party daily *Pravda* published a vicious attack upon it under the rubric "chaos instead of music." The work was condemned as discordant, incomprehensible, and pornographic, whose true meaning was revealed by the approval it won among capitalist enemies. The shock of the *Pravda* attack changed Shostakovich's behavior, and his composing became cautious. He withdrew his fourth symphony (1936) from rehearsal, and it waited until the cultural thaw of 1961 for its premiere. With his fifth symphony (1937), Shostakovich adopted a new, more straightforward and traditional compositional style. The success of the symphony established his position as the preeminent Soviet composer.

After the German invasion in 1941, Shostakovich wrote two patriotic symphonies (seventh, 1942, and eighth, 1943) in which the world heard the inspirational celebration of the heroism and courage of the Soviet people. Shostakovich's world fame reached its greatest height. Western appreciation of Shostakovich waned after the war. One reason for the fading of his luster was the recognition that the wartime symphonies were not great compositions by modern aesthetic standards. Another reason was the imposition of stifling artistic restrictions in the Soviet Union by Stalin's cultural dictator, Andrei Zhdanov.

In January, 1948, Zhdanov staged an event that actually amounted to a trial of Shostakovich, at which he was accused, in effect, of possessing musical talent that was appreciated in the rest of the world. Zhdanov assembled a conference of composers at which, in the guise of an exchange of opinions about Soviet music, he set the example for a parade of speakers who attacked Shostakovich for his failure to "reform" in the years since 1936. Other composers also were attacked, but Shostakovich was the principal target. Although he was defended by the courageous intervention of such talented musicians as Aram Khachaturian and Visarion Shebalin, Shostakovich meekly requested that the Party explain what he must do. That explanation came on February 10, 1948, in the form of a resolution of the Party Central Committee that condemned the "formalism" and obedience to Western artistic standards of Shostakovich and the composers who defended him. The resolution declared socialist realism the only style that could be tolerated in the country, and that meant that music must be simple and straightforward enough to be enjoyed by unsophisticated laborers, that it must be tuneful, harmonious, and elevating.

The resolution's effect was like that of the *Pravda* article in 1936. Other musicians spoke against Shostakovich's "formalistic" work, especially his sixth (1939), eighth, and ninth (1945) symphonies, and Shostakovich recanted. In a public statement, he acknowledged that the Party had criticized him justly because his music had failed to speak the idiom of the people. He offered as propitiation civic music—*Song of the Forests* (1949)—and patriotic film scores—*The Fall of Berlin* (1949) and *The Unforgettable Nineteen-Nineteen* (1951)—all of which heaped exaggerated praise upon Stalin, who did not fail to show his appreciation. Shostakovich not only was permitted to retain his privileged living conditions in Moscow but also could travel to Western countries and was awarded the Stalin prize. Yet in the period between the resolution and Stalin's death, the musical compositions that Shostakovich published were artistically inferior.

Only after Stalin's death did Shostakovich unfetter his talent. The tenth symphony, which premiered in December, 1953, proved its worth in both the acclaim it won at home and abroad and the controversy it stirred. For it, Shostakovich won the highest honor that the Soviet Union bestows on an artist, the title "People's Artist of the Soviet Union." The 1948 resolution that had cast a shadow over Shostakovich was substantially rescinded by formal action of the Central Committee in 1958.

In the circumstances of the post-Stalin cultural "thaw," Shostakovich regained his artistic footing to become the moral leader of Soviet music. His best years were the ten between 1954 and 1964. In February, 1954, Shostakovich published an article condemning the Party's dogmatic and brutal imposition of ideological strictures on artistic creativity. This article served as a manifesto upon which Shostakovich based his repeated advocacy of the right of the Soviet composer to experiment with modern techniques. At the same time, Shostakovich balanced his appeals for freedom of the creative spirit with forthright recognition of the artist's social responsibility, which meant, for Shostakovich, that the musician was morally obligated to promote the just society toward which the Communist Party aspired. He confirmed this recognition by his successful application for membership in the Communist Party in 1960.

Shostakovich excelled in creative production in this period with artistically successful grand works. These included his eleventh (1957) and twelfth (1961) symphonies (the latter dedicated to Lenin's memory), the second concerto for piano, and a magnificent concerto for cello (1959). He added to the body of his successful quartets by writing the worthy seventh and eighth (1960) quartets. He made an especially bold statement with his thirteenth symphony (1962), which carried the title "Babi Yar," the name of a palace in the Ukraine where Germans had conducted a mass slaughter of Jews. Shostakovich teamed with the anti-Stalinist poet Yevgeny Yevtushenko to produce this patriotic piece, which also directed a clear attack upon anti-Semitic manifestations that remained vigorous within Soviet society even at the time of the composition. Further evidence of Shostakovich's rehabilitation was the production of the very opera that had occasioned his first brutal censure in 1936. In 1963, *Lady Macbeth of Mtsensk* returned to the Soviet theater, renamed *Katerina Izmailova*. Yet soon the reality that he was not entirely free manifested itself. Khrushchev banned the thirteenth symphony after only two performances, and it was withdrawn from the repertoire.

About one year before his death, as the maestro Mstislav Rostropovich (for whom Shostakovich wrote two cello concertos) was in the process of emigrating from the Soviet Union because of restrictions on his artistic expression, Shostakovich addressed the fifth congress of the Union of Composers (April, 1974) with words that repeated his formal adherence to the Soviet artistic standard. It is immoral, he declared, for music to satisfy the tastes of the elite or merely to entertain. The composer is ethically bound to direct his art to the construction of Communism and to the creation of hope and happiness for humankind. When he died of heart disease in the Kremlin hospital on August 9, 1975, Shostakovich was honored officially as a "true son of the Communist Party" and a "civic-minded artist." After a week of official mourning, Shostakovich was buried at the Novodevichy Cemetery.

*Summary*

The date of Dmitri Shostakovich's death marked the end of an era of Russian music history. Shostakovich was a composer very much in tune with his own time and his native society. Shostakovich provided resounding refutation of a widely held belief that a great artist could not prosper publicly in a society dominated by a Communist Party that aspired to totalitarian control and that great art could not be produced by someone who sincerely supported the social vision that Party promoted. Although he was rebuffed repeatedly because of the directions in which his creative genius drove him, he consistently sought to restore harmony between himself and the revolutionary transformations that surrounded him. He was a man of his own people, even while he reserved to himself the right to protest against society, with its vulgarity, anti-Semitism, and bloody suppression of human value.

Shostakovich's fifth symphony (1937) can be taken as a touchstone of interpretation of his significance as a composer. He himself named it a "response to just criticism" of the *Pravda* article on *Lady Macbeth of Mtsensk*. Widely acknowledged as a superb technical masterpiece of the symphonic form, it also has been criticized as an unfortunate abandonment of the avant-garde directions implied in works immediately preceding it. Political convictions appear to bias unavoidably the evaluations of even the most sophisticated critics. While most acknowledge the work as a masterpiece, some see in it a maturing of the talent of an artistic genius informed by patriotism, while others excoriate a craven submission to politically inspired cultural terrorism. In its grandiose and precise dimensions, it mirrors the new society toward which the Stalinist regime aspired, yet this frankly political statement was achieved without compromise of aesthetic excellence. Such was Shostakovich's distinct achievement throughout his life.

*Bibliography*

Kay, Norman. *Shostakovich*. London: Oxford University Press, 1971. A brief but useful biography of Shostakovich, in the Oxford series of composers, which will serve satisfactorily until the definitive scholarly treatment of Shostakovich is prepared.

Norris, Christopher, ed. *Shostakovich: The Man and His Music*. Boston: Marion Boyars, 1982. A collection of scholarly essays evaluating Shostakovich's compositions, with separate treatments of the various forms in which he wrote.

Schwarz, Boris. *Music and Musical Life in Soviet Russia*. Rev. ed. Bloomington: Indiana University Press, 1983. A detailed treatment of Soviet musical history in which the figure of Shostakovich looms large.

Seroff, Victor Ilyich, with Nadejda Galli-Shohat. *Dmitri Shostakovich: The Life and Background of a Soviet Composer*. New York: Alfred A. Knopf, 1943. This book, written in collaboration with Shostakovich's aunt, is a detailed biography up to the year of its publication. Includes appendices, an index, and photographs.

Sollertinsky, Dmitri, and Ludmilla Sollertinsky. *Pages from the Life of Dmitri Shostakovich*. Translated by Graham Hobbs and Charles Midgley. New York: Harcourt Brace Jovanovich, 1980. A highly laudatory yet complete biography. Includes several photographs and an index.

*Paul D. Steeves*

# JEAN SIBELIUS

*Born:* December 8, 1865; Tavastehus, Finland
*Died:* September 20, 1957; Järvenpää, Finland
*Area of Achievement:* Music
*Contribution:* Closely identified with Finnish nationalism, Sibelius not only is a national hero in his own country but also is considered by many to have been the greatest symphonic composer of the twentieth century.

## *Early Life*

Johan "Jean" Julius Christian Sibelius was born in the house of his father, a surgeon of the Tavastehus territorial army battalion, on December 8, 1865. His family was of mixed Swedish and Finnish ancestry, and like most middle- and upper-class Finns, he grew up speaking Swedish as his first language. When Johan was less than three years old, his father died during a cholera epidemic, and the boy was reared by his mother and grandmother. As a youth, he took the first name of an uncle who had been a sea captain and was ever after known as "Jean."

Like many great composers, Sibelius displayed a precocious talent: He was playing the violin and had composed his first piece (a duet for violin and cello) by age ten. He began formal studies in violin and composition at fourteen, hoping, at least for at time, to become a great violin virtuoso. During his teens, he wrote numerous chamber works and also developed a deep interest in the *Kalevala*, the Finnish national epic collected from traditional ballads in the 1860's. This was later a great inspiration to him, as was his passionate love of nature.

Though his family enjoyed his music, his mother wanted him to have a more secure profession, and he acceded to her wishes by entering the law school of the University of Helsinki in 1885. Somewhat covertly, however, he also took courses in the school of music, and, after a year, gave up the law for full-time training on the violin and in music theory. His teacher, Martin Wegelius, was a versatile and widely experienced composer, pianist, and conductor, who recognized Sibelius' talents and took the young musician under his wing. Sibelius was also befriended by the Italian composer Ferruccio Busoni, who was teaching at the time in Helsinki.

After three years of Wegelius' patient encouragement, Sibelius left for Berlin to study with the famous theorist Albert Becker, a thorough and demanding teacher. He also indulged a taste for high living, hard drinking, and financial extravagance. Apparently, this life-style led to problems, and, after only a year, he left for Vienna to study with Karl Goldmark, a popular Romantic composer. Under Goldmark's tutelage, he expanded his studies from solo and chamber music and began to work toward composing for the orchestra.

In 1891, Sibelius returned to Finland, possibly because his high-society life-style had exhausted his resources. He made his living by teaching, but most of his energies were directed toward the composition of his first orchestral work, *Kullervo*, based on the *Kalevala*. In view of the fact that Sibelius had only recently had any training in writing for the orchestra, *Kullervo* seems little short of miraculous. Not only is it a work of very large proportions—more than an hour long—but also it includes a highly dramatic central movement with vocalists. Once *Kullervo* had received its first performance, in April, 1892, Sibelius' position as the leading Finnish composer was never again seriously questioned.

*Life's Work*

A few months after the premiere of *Kullervo*, Sibelius was married to Aino Järnefelt, the daughter of a prominent Finnish nationalist. Since 1809, Finland had been an autonomous grand duchy, with its own popular assembly, under the sovereignty of the Russian Empire. A movement for independence had started in the 1870's, gaining momentum toward the end of the century because of the czarist government's attempt to impose the Russian language and culture on the Finns. Sibelius had always been strongly patriotic, and, following the success of *Kullervo*, he expressed these feelings in a series of powerful orchestral works based on Finnish legends. Among these were the well-known *En saga* and a group of four tone poems called the *Lemminkäinen*. In 1899, he composed *Finlandia*, a short tone poem that remains his most famous and popular work. It has been claimed that this piece did more to promote Finnish independence than a thousand speeches and pamphlets. Many Americans, in fact, have mistakenly assumed that it is the national anthem of Finland.

By the 1890's, Sibelius had developed a very personal style of composition. Most composers are affected, at least to some extent, by models from the past, and Sibelius was no exception. His early works reveal the influence of his studies of Peter Ilich Tchaikovsky, Edvard Grieg, Joseph Haydn, and even Richard Wagner, though he rejected Wagner's dense, grandiose orchestral textures by the turn of the century. The most important factor in the evolution of Sibelius' musical style, however, was his fascination with the natural landscapes and folk culture of his country. In 1892, he had visited Karelia, a somewhat primitive area of eastern Finland, where he absorbed the rhythms and harmonies of native folk singing. Though Sibelius always insisted that he had never used any actual folk tunes in his works, their spirit, at any rate, can be clearly discerned. Most of his later music evokes images from the myths of the ancient Finns, as well as the mystery and power of Finland's primeval forests and lakes.

In 1897, in acknowledgment of his achievements, the Finnish assembly granted Sibelius a state pension. Though this was not a large amount, and certainly not enough to support the composer's expensive tastes, it did free him to begin work on his greatest compositions, the seven symphonies. The first of these was created in 1899, after Sibelius returned from a tour of Italy and Germany. Though both his first and second symphonies are relatively conventional works in the late Romantic idiom, already Sibelius was moving toward a sparseness of texture and condensation of form that would later be referred to as "neoclassicism." It has been said that Sibelius had a natural affinity for the processes of musical logic and development, which is demonstrated by his ability to weld coherently short, even fragmentary, motives into great organic structures full of dramatic tension and momentum.

Around the turn of the century, Sibelius began to achieve international fame. When the Helsinki Philharmonic Orchestra toured Europe in 1900, several of Sibelius' tone poems were on its program, and concert audiences loved them. Over the next few years, Sibelius himself was invited to conduct performances in cities throughout the Continent. By 1903, however, his insouciant life-style began to catch up with him, and his mounting debts and episodes of drunkenness seem to have provoked changes in both his personal life and his method of composition. In 1904, he bought a plot of land at Järvenpää, in the forests outside Helsinki, and he had a villa built there. Though he continued to travel until the beginning of World War I, much of the rest of his life was spent in seclusion in this new home.

In his next major works, the Violin Concerto (1903) and Symphony No. 3 (begun in 1904, but not completed until 1907), Sibelius turned away from the exuberant nationalism of his earlier music, and both of these pieces create instead a moody, somber sense of loneliness and dissonant energy. Such feelings are fully realized in Symphony No. 4, finished in 1911. Highly dissonant, even savage, harmonies dominate, and, of all Sibelius' symphonies, the fourth comes closest to the atonal and twelve-tone systems that would soon characterize much of European serious music. Yet, in this symphony, as in everything he wrote, Sibelius clearly demonstrated total independence from any "school" or movement: His style was uniquely his own.

Throughout the period before the beginning of World War I, Sibelius' international reputation continued to grow, and he was honored in England, France, and Austria. In 1914, he made a triumphant visit to the United States, where he was amazed by his popularity. This was his last major tour for many years; the beginning of the war disrupted international travel, and, by its end, Sibelius had largely retired from the world.

Seclusion did not, however, end his artistic activity. His expansive, uncomplicated Fifth Symphony was finished in time for his fiftieth birthday celebration in December, 1915; this was treated in Finland as a national holiday. Sibelius continued to revise this symphony, though, as he did many of his works, and it did not reach its final form until three years later, by which time his world had been completely disrupted.

The Russian Revolution of October, 1917, led Finland to declare its independence, but, early in the following year, Communist Red Guards invaded the country and provoked a civil war. Sibelius, whose sympathies were not only nationalist but also anticommunist, was forced to flee Järvenpää when the Red Army invaded his home. He did not return until after the war, and, from that time onward, he composed less and less. The Sixth Symphony, not completed until 1923, may reveal his feelings in this era, for in it Sibelius again eschews any nationalist exuberance or heroism; its themes are bleak and full of anguish. Though it is the least popular of his major works, many music critics regard the Sixth Symphony as Sibelius' greatest achievement, the most complete demonstration of his mastery of orchestral technique.

Both the Sixth and Seventh symphonies have been characterized as being "religious" in spirit, and Sibelius himself has been said to have had the sensibilities of religion but not the faith. The Seventh Symphony (1924), especially, seems to have left Finland—and perhaps even the earth itself—behind, for it suggests a kind of final cosmic vision of the reaffirmation of life. In fact, the seventh symphony seems also to signal the end of Sibelius' creative inspiration, for he wrote only one other major work, *Tapiola*, a tone poem for orchestra, in 1926. Tapio was the ancient forest god of Finland, and *Tapiola*, like some of Sibelius'earlier pieces, portrays the awesome mystery of the Finnish forests and the power of the spirits said to inhabit them. Unlike his earlier images, however, the world depicted in *Tapiola* is one of desolate isolation, an appropriate, but nevertheless devastating, portrait of life in the twentieth century.

After the completion of *Tapiola*, Sibelius' musical voice was stilled, and his last published work, a group of relatively insignificant pieces for piano, appeared in 1929. Though his sixtieth and seventieth birthdays were, like his fiftieth, celebrated in Finland as national holidays, Sibelius seldom ventured from the seclusion of his country villa. His last concert tour occurred in 1921; after conducting several of his symphonies in London, Rome, and Göteborg, Sweden, he returned permanently to Järvenpää, where he died of a cerebral hemorrhage on September 20, 1957, only three months short of his ninety-second birthday.

### *Summary*

Though for many years, especially in England and the United States, Jean Sibelius' music enjoyed great critical acclaim, an apparently inevitable reaction set in among critics on the Continent. In Germany and France, particularly, music was now dominated by the cerebral, acrid dissonances of composers such as Arnold Schoenberg, Igor Stravinsky, and the French group known as "Les Six." Though he expressed an affinity with a few of the "modernists," among them Béla Bartók, Sibelius generally rejected the avante-garde movements. They, in turn, rejected him as representing an obsolete tradition of tonality and emotionalism. Perhaps most damning, Sibelius' music remained popular with concert audiences, a sure sign that he was not "in tune" with the latest trends in serious music.

Throughout his productive life, Sibelius had pursued what may be seen as two creative paths. One of these is expressed in his "lesser works," the nationalistic tone poems and other popular pieces such as the *Valse triste*, a beautifully lyrical work composed in 1904. His first and second symphonies might also be considered as following this more accessible, popular style. His other approach may be seen in the Fourth, Sixth, and Seventh symphonies, as well as certain tone poems, such as *Barden* (1913) and *Tapiola*. These pieces demonstrate both Sibelius' mastery of classical technique and his success in concentrating melodic and harmonic development into austere, unaffected motives of great clarity and classical purity.

Yet to attempt to classify or categorize Sibelius' works into any kind of consistent "system" would have repelled him, for, as many critics have noted, with particular reference to his symphonies, each is unique, a theoretical and creative unity unto itself, expressing a deeply personal concept of symphonic structure. As a result, no other twentieth century composer has excited such deep and enduring controversy. Writers of the "modernist" schools have often viciously attacked Sibelius as trite, sentimental, and old-fashioned, and his retention of the tonal system—despite the highly innovative ways in which he used it—has been regarded as showing his lack of originality. Some have relegated him to the nineteenth century as a "late Romantic" or purely "nationalist" composer, or have even chosen to dismiss him altogether. On the other hand, to many critics, especially in England and the United States, Sibelius remains the finest symphonic composer of the twentieth century and one whose individuality stands above the transient fads and intellectualism of much of today's serious music. In any case, his works remain extremely popular with audiences, and their many recordings assure Sibelius of a prominent and permanent place in the history of great music.

*Bibliography*

Abraham, Gerald, ed. *The Music of Sibelius*. New York: W. W. Norton, 1947. A compilation of eight essays. Only the first, by Ralph Hill, is biographical. The others analyze Sibelius' music, classifying it by type. Therefore, much of this volume may be beyond those without musical training. It does include, however, a very useful bibliography, a chronology, and an indexed list of compositions.

Ekman, Karl. *Jean Sibelius: His Life and Personality.* Translated by Edward Birse. New York: Tudor, 1946. Ekman is Sibelius' principal biographer. Since he was a close friend of Sibelius, and because this work was written before the composer's death, it can hardly be called "objective." Sibelius was often given to somewhat melodramatic and less-than-accurate claims about himself and his music, all of which Ekman faithfully recorded as truth. Nevertheless, this is a valuable and entertaining account of Sibelius' creative life.

Lambert, Constant. *Music Ho! A Study of Music in Decline*. London: Faber & Faber, 1934. Lambert, himself a prominent British composer before his premature death in 1951, offers a challenging view that dissents from the critical bombast, gnosticism, and pedantry that has often characterized discussions of "revolutionary" twentieth century music. Lambert was one of Sibelius' most enthusiastic critics, and he suggests that it is Sibelius, rather than Schoenberg or other "modernists," who should offer a model for the music of the future.

Layton, Robert. "Jean Sibelius." In *Schuetz to Spinto*, vol. 17 in *The New Grove Dictionary of Music and Musicians*, edited by Stanley Sadie. London: Macmillan, 1980. Though articles in this set are often too technical for those without musical training, this essay on Sibelius is among the best brief sources available. While some sections will be difficult for general readers, the wealth of biographical information, as well as the clarity and balance with which it is presented, make this article well worth the effort. Contains an extensive bibliography.

Machlis, Joseph. *Introduction to Contemporary Music*. New York: W. W. Norton, 1961. Esssential for general readers interested in twentieth century music. Introduces modern music through comparison with earlier periods, providing a painless introduction to music theory. European and American composers are grouped by types; each receives a concise biographical treatment and analysis of important works. Includes an excellent bibliography, discography, and texts and translations of vocal works.

Mellers, Wilfrid. *Romanticism and the Twentieth Century, from 1800*. Fair Lawn, N.J.: Essential Books, 1957. An excellent analysis of romantic music in the late nineteenth century and its relationship to twentieth century music. Useful comparisons and contrasts of twentieth century composers, especially those considered to be inheritors of the Romantic tradition. Sibelius is discussed in this framework as a nationalist and "naturist" composer.

*Thomas C. Schunk*

# NORODOM SIHANOUK

*Born:* October 31, 1922; Pnompenh, Cambodia

*Areas of Achievement:* Government and politics

*Contribution:* King of Cambodia from 1941 to 1955, then alternately prime minister, head of state, and leader of various opposition movements, Sihanouk could for many years be found at the center of Cambodia's fractious and highly controversial politics.

## *Early Life*

Norodom Sambeth Preah Sihanouk's privileged position in Cambodian politics came in part because his parents were direct descendants of modern Cambodia's two main royal lines. Sihanouk's father, Prince Norodom Suramarit, was the grandson of King Norodom (reigned 1860-1904), the man who first welcomed the French colonization of his country but then became bitterly disillusioned and hence a popular symbol of Cambodian nationalism. His mother, Princess Kossamak Neariréath, was the granddaughter of two kings named Sisowath who ruled between 1904 and 1927, and 1927 and 1941, respectively. Sihanouk's parents separated, and his childhood was apparently not a happy one. While still a student at the exclusive Lycée Chausseloup Laubat in Saigon (now Ho Chi Minh City), Vietnam, Sihanouk was unexpectedly chosen by the French resident general to succeed his uncle as king, apparently in hopes that he would be easy to control. Sihanouk instead made efforts to rule well, refusing, among other things, the annual French gift of opium. He also took advantage of the Japanese takeover of the French colonial administration between March and October, 1945, to press for independence. Sihanouk angered more radical nationalists by compromising when French troops returned in 1946, but he again pressed his case when the French were doing badly in their war against Ho Chi Minh in neighboring Vietnam. Full independence was finally granted in the multination Geneva Conference of July, 1954.

## *Life's Work*

Sihanouk's major concern over the next decade and a half appeared to be to keep Cambodia out of the rapidly escalating conflict in neighboring Vietnam between the American-backed South Vietnamese government on the one hand and the National Liberation Front (often crudely called "Viet Cong") and North Vietnamese Communist forces led by Ho Chi Minh on the other. Abdicating the throne to his father in 1955, Sihanouk soon founded the Sangkum Reastre Niyum, or "People's Socialist Community" organization, that was designed to spread his own mix of capitalist and Marxist elements in what he liked to call a unique form of "Buddhist Socialism."

Energetically touring the country distributing gifts and giving long-winded and apparently quite earthy speeches in his rather unique high-pitched voice, Sihanouk had much appeal in the countryside. Even in the cities he remained powerful, however, both because he could be ruthless toward his enemies and because few of Cambodia's constantly squabbling politicians could agree on who should take his place.

Sihanouk initially tried to be neutral toward the United States, refusing both as king and prime minister to join the Southeast Asia Treaty Organization (SEATO), yet accepting United States military aid and advisers. In 1963, he veered sharply to the left, nationalizing the import-export trade and Cambodia's banks, while also cutting off all U.S. aid and, indeed, breaking relations with the United States in 1965. Sihanouk took these actions in part because he blamed the United States Central Intelligence Agency (CIA) for supporting Son Ngoc Thanh's Khmer Serei ("Free Khmer," or "Free Kampuchean People") movement, in part because he was horrified by the apparent U.S. involvement in the overthrow and subsequent assassination of the South Vietnamese prime minister Ngo Dinh Diem and his brother Nhu, and in part, some argued, because he simply was convinced that the North Vietnamese and National Liberation Front troops were going to win. Fully aware that only French colonial rule had previously kept the traditional Vietnamese enemy at bay, Sihanouk in this period was now busy emphasizing his Socialist credentials.

In 1966, Sihanouk was forced to move back toward a more conservative position, in part because of the fact that Cambodia's more wealthy urban elite, and particularly the military, resented the loss of U.S. aid and because the protests reflected anger at the new opportunities for corruption that Sihanouk's nationalization schemes provided. Sihanouk himself also appears to have been bothered by a revolt against high taxes that took place in Battambang Province in 1967, and he may also have concluded that the arrival of U.S. troops in Vietnam in 1965 and the U.S. policy of bombing North Vietnam made it advisable for Cambodia to move a bit away from the Left. For complex reasons, then, Sihanouk did not prevent the conservative general Lon Nol and many of his supporters from winning seats in the National Assembly in 1966, nor did he object to Lon Nol's brutal suppression of the Battambang Revolt the following year. He apparently agreed to allow the North Vietnamese and National Liberation Forces to send supplies through Cambodia to their troops in return for guarantees of Cambodia's borders, yet he also allegedly sanctioned the United States' secret bombing raids against those forces as long as these were not brought to his official attention. Intensive U.S. bombing soon began.

Try as he might, then, Sihanouk was unable to prevent Cambodia from becoming sucked into the increasingly violent war in Vietnam. On the one hand, leftists such as Khieu Samphan, Hou Youn, and Hu Nim no longer believed that they could work safely with Sihanouk, and they therefore fled to the jungles, where they joined a revolt of certain Cambodian Communists (called by Sihanouk himself the Khmer Rouge, or "Red Khmers") led by a radical leader named Pol Pot. Rightists, on the other hand, objected to what they believed was increasingly erratic and even bizarre behavior by their longtime leader. The last straw in this process may well have been the opening of a gigantic gambling casino in Pnompenh in 1969, most of the profits of which appeared to be somehow connected to previous corruption schemes by Sihanouk's Eurasian wife, Monique. As the Cambodian economy deteriorated, the corruption and maneuvering that appeared to surround Sihanouk's rule became all the more alarming.

In 1970, therefore, Lon Nol took advantage of Sihanouk's visit to France to proclaim a new and more conservative government. The U.S. government apparently had advanced notice of the coup, may have supported it, and certainly did little to work out a compromise between the more actively anticommuist Lon Nol and their nemesis Sihanouk. Sihanouk, therefore, repaired to the Chinese capital of Peking, where the Chinese foreign minister Chou En-lai quickly gave him enthusiastic support. Swinging again leftward, Sihanouk now embraced the Khmer Rouge cause and hence gave the leftists far more support among the peasants and moderates within Cambodia. Fighting between the Lon Nol and Khmer Rouge forces continued to be bitter for the next five years, with little quarter asked or given. Finally Lon Nol was defeated, and a new government headed by Pol Pot and Khieu Samphan took over the country in 1975.

During the next three years, Sihanouk first briefly toured a number of foreign countries to proclaim the worthy social purposes of the new regime and then returned to Pnompenh to announce a new constitution that ended his role as head of state and placed him under virtual house arrest. During this time, the Khmer Rouge emptied the cities of almost all of their residents, executed thousands of "class enemies," and forced most of the people to work exhausting hours on ambitious but cruelly misplanned agricultural collectivization schemes. The historically deep hatred of the Vietnamese was used to rally support for the new regime, and border incidents were gradually increased until a full-scale war erupted between Vietnam and Cambodia in 1978. Only after the Pol Pot regime had been quickly defeated and forced back into the craggy jungles on the border with Thailand was Sihanouk finally released by the Khmer Rouge. His job now was to be at the United Nations to make sure that the new government installed by the Vietnamese invaders did not get Kampuchea's seat in the United Nations.

Throughout the 1980's, Sihanouk tried hard to find an acceptable political future for Cambodia. During this time, the People's Republic of Kampuchea ("Kampuchea" being the name originally given Cambodia by the Communist regime), led by Hun Sen and backed by the Vietnamese, made slow but steady progress in restoring a more normal economy and providing a reasonable amount of security in all but the more rural areas near Thailand. Vietnamese occupying forces, meanwhile, began a plan of total withdrawal that was to be completed by the end of 1989. Against them, Sihanouk's Coalition Government of Democratic Kampuchea consisted of an uneasy coalition of Sihanouk's own forces, Son Sann's Khmer People's National Liberation Front, and the slightly modified Khmer Rouge. Each of these groups had its own army, and each accused the others of ruthlessness, corruption, or betrayal. United in their hatred of the Vietnamese-backed Hun Sen government, yet quite distinct in their ideas about what should replace it, each had different major powers on its side. A country that had once been a symbol of apparent pastoral bliss was now a perfect example of the cruelties to which human beings can sink.

*Summary*

Norodom Sihanouk appears to have been at the center of most every major event in Cambodia since 1941 and hence to be indistinguishable from the modern history of Cambodia. His detractors would deplore this history and point a major finger of blame at Sihanouk. The sometime-king was enormously vain and erratic, they would say. He dabbled in films, played the saxophone, and boasted of his successes with women when he should have been running the country. The father of many children by several wives and mistresses—including his mother's half sister—he was not considered to be a very good parent. Fond of giving moral lectures, he nevertheless tolerated an extraordinary amount of corruption, particularly by his mother, Kossamak, and by his Eurasian wife, Monique. Sihanouk could be ruthless to the point of foolishness, as, for example, when his police humiliated the future Khmer Rouge leader Khieu Samphan by leaving him naked in the street. Not surprisingly, one of Sihanouk's last Western advisers found him an erratic man who was alternately a "Prince Charming" and a "Prince of Darkness."

Supporters of Sihanouk could find much to respect in Sihanouk's boundless energy and his repeated attempts to preserve the security of a very small nation surrounded by extremely hostile neighbors. Dismissing Sihanouk's personal foibles as either typical of Cambodian males or of little consequence in the life of the nation, supporters of Sihanouk instead saw the Cambodian tragedy as part of a "proxy war" in which the United States both inflicted terrible damage by bombing an enraged Khmer Rouge and supported unsatisfactory right-wing regimes that would help its cause in Vietnam, in which China inspired radical reforms and kept the Khmer Rouge supplied with arms so as to hurt the Vietnamese, and in which the Russians supported Vietnamese efforts to establish a friendly regime. Since Cambodia was caught in the middle of a major struggle between the great powers of the world, the wonder is that Sihanouk was able to do as much as he did to preserve the fragile nation's independence. Sihanouk perhaps put it best himself when he said that the "great misfortune" of the Cambodian people "is that they always have terrible leaders who make them suffer. I am not sure that I was much better myself, but perhaps I was the least bad."

*Bibliography*

Kiernan, Ben. *How Pol Pot Came to Power.* London: Verso, 1985. Though primarily a history of Cambodian Communism, this book does deal with Sihanouk's rule.

Kissinger, Henry. *The White House Years.* Boston: Little, Brown, 1979. Kissinger's eloquent defense of his dealings with Sihanouk should be read in conjunction with the William Shawcross book listed below to understand the complex relations between United States policy and Sihanouk's rule.

Lacouture, Jean. *The Demigods: Charismatic Leadership in the Third World.* Translated by Patricia Wolf. New York: Alfred A. Knopf, 1970. Lacouture's work emphasizes Sihanouk's appeal to peasants rather than his use of power and his corruption.

Lancaster, Donald. "The Decline of Prince Sihanouk's Regime." In *Indochina in Conflict*, edited by Joseph J. Zasloff and Allan E. Goodman. Lexington, Mass.: Lexington Books, 1972. An attempt by one of Sihanouk's last Western advisers to convey the complexity of Sihanouk's personality.

Osborne, Milton. *Before Kampuchea: Preludes to Tragedy.* Boston: G. Allen & Unwin, 1979. This useful recounting of the author's experiences and observations helps explain the later tragedy.

___________. *Politics and Power in Cambodia: The Sihanouk Years.* Camberwell, Australia: Longman, 1973. A more formal history than the 1979 book, hence a useful supplement full of valuable information.

Shawcross, William. *Sideshow: Kissinger, Nixon, and the Destruction of Cambodia.* London: Hogarth, 1986. This controversial book blaming U.S. policy for the Khmer Rouge has much information on Sihanouk's role. The new edition responds to Secretary of State Henry Kissinger's comments.

Sihanouk, Norodom, as related to Wilfred Burchett. *My War with the CIA: The Memoirs of Prince Norodom Sihanouk.* New York: Pantheon Books, 1973. Written between the 1970 coup and the Khmer Rouge victory in 1975, this work reflects one of Sihanouk's anti-American periods and makes a number of disturbing charges about U.S. policy.

*Peter K. Frost*

# NATHAN SÖDERBLOM

*Born:* January 15, 1866; Trönö, Sweden
*Died:* July 12, 1931; Uppsala, Sweden
*Areas of Achievement:* Religion and peace advocacy
*Contribution:* Söderblom, as Archbishop of Uppsala, was a principal promoter of the Universal Christian Conference on Life and Work. He was awarded the Nobel Peace Prize for his work in promoting international understanding through the ecumenical movement. He is also noted for his work on behalf of war prisoners and displaced persons following World War I. A prolific writer, he emphasized the need to reunite Christianity and make it a practical, humanitarian movement.

## *Early Life*

Lars Olaf Jonathan Söderblom was born on January 15, 1866, at Trönö, Gävleborg's Län, Sweden. At an early age, he determined to pursue the same calling as his father, a Lutheran pastor. He also chose to shorten his name and became known as Nathan for the rest of his life. Söderblom earned his licentiate of theology at the University of Uppsala. Consecrated a Lutheran minister in 1893, he served briefly as chaplain of the Uppsala Mental Hospital. In 1894, he began graduate studies at the famed Sorbonne in Paris, where he earned the highest academic honor granted by the Protestant theological faculty. He was the only Swede ever to be so honored. His specialties were comparative religions with emphasis on the Persian Zoroastrianism. At the Sorbonne he was influenced by the liberal Protestants, especially by Auguste Sabatier, under whom he studied. Because of this influence, he became interested in the ecumenical movement and a reunification of the Christian denominations.

Söderblom was able to pursue his studies by serving as pastor of the Swedish legation in Paris from 1894 to 1901. Among those who consistently supported the Swedish church in Paris was Alfred Nobel, the inventor-philanthropist, who was often referred to as an atheist. The two men became close friends, and Nobel donated generously to the Swedish congregation. When Nobel died in 1896 at his villa in San Remo, the youthful Söderblom officiated at the funeral services.

## *Life's Work*

Upon receiving his doctorate of theology in 1901, Söderblom returned to Sweden to become a professor of the history of religions at the University of Uppsala. From 1912 to 1914, he was an instructor at the University of Leipzig. In 1914, he was nominated to become Archbishop of Uppsala and primate of the Church of Sweden, the most prestigious ecclesiastical position in Lutheranism. As archbishop he transformed the archdiocese at Uppsala into a center of world ecumenism. Together with the Archdiocese of Canterbury, England, the Archdiocese of Uppsala was the ecclesiastical center of world Protestantism.

The terrors of World War I occupied the first four years after Söderblom became archbishop. Because of the years spent in France and Germany, Söderblom was intimately acquainted with many of the battle sites, and he grieved over the loss of lives. An outspoken pacifist and proponent of Christian unity, he intervened on behalf of war prisoners and displaced persons. This was the beginning of his many efforts to unite Christianity for the purpose of saving lives and promoting social justice.

Even before the war began, Söderblom actively helped form a "General World Union of Churches for International Understanding." It closed with the outbreak of war. Undaunted, he tried to continue by working with a Norwegian and Danish bishop. A planned conference for 1917 failed to materialize, however, so a purely Nordic Conference was held at Uppsala from September 14 to 16, 1917. At this conference, a manifesto, clearly inspired by Söderblom, was drafted and issued. The churches, it declared, must work to remove the causes of war, and each religion must strive to understand the differences of other beliefs. In 1920, he managed to convoke an international meeting in Geneva, where the foundations were laid for an ecumenical conference in Stockholm. After five years of very careful preparation, the Universal Christian Conference on Life and Work was convened. Nearly six hundred delegates from thirty-one Protestant and Orthodox church communities in thirty-seven different nations attended. The Roman Catholic church did not attend.

Although interested in the ecumenical "Faith and Order Movement" begun in Scotland in 1910, Söderblom insisted that the Stockholm Conference be separate from the World Conference held at Lausanne in 1927. "Doctrine divides—Service unites," he wrote, and he intended the churches to provide the necessary leadership to encourage social justice, not to squabble over doctrinal traditions. After the Stockholm Conference, a continuation committee was named to pursue the objectives of the conference and plan for later meetings. Söderblom was its first president. It was this committee that in 1930 became a permanent organization with the title, the Universal Christian Council for Life and Work.

Despite his demanding tasks as archbishop, Söderblom found time to write in the fields of theology, church history, the history of religions, and the reinterpretations of the life and thought of Martin Luther. His numerous publications included *Religionproblemst inom Katolicism och Protestantism* (1910; the religious problem of Catholicism and Protestantism) and *Humor och melankoli och andra Lutherstudier* (1919; humor and melancholy with other studies of Luther). Although he was definitely high church, his writings show considerable liberal influence. He firmly espoused ecumenism, or the reunion of all Christianity to meet the social justice, economic, and civil rights needs of the world as well as to establish international peace. All religion depended on revelation, he wrote, but the "reality of revelation," as he perceived it, was the manifestation of godliness through the genius and leadership abilities of extraordinary people in all civilizations. Finally, he saw the practical application of Christianity to the needs of modern man as the "social justice" for which he worked.

Because of his unfailing determination to promote international understanding through the church, Söderblom was awarded the Nobel Peace Prize in 1930. He was also invited to deliver the famous Gifford lectures on natural theology at Edinburgh, Scotland, in 1931. A brief illness led to his death on July 12, 1931, only a few weeks after those lectures.

*Summary*

Nathan Söderblom was honored with the highest academic honors at the Sorbonne, and, when he returned to Sweden, he became the first to occupy the chair of chief professor in the religious history department. As archbishop, he also served as vice chancellor of the University of Uppsala. Söderblom's influence was not restricted to Sweden or Scandinavia. The 1925 Stockholm Conference was a seminal conference for the international ecumenical movement, and he was a dominant figure at that meeting. As one of the founding fathers and pioneers, he sought cooperation of all Christian denominations in solving social problems and in serving society without consideration of doctrinal differences. Largely because of his work, the Universal Christian Council on Life and Work came into being. This movement was one of two that in 1948 merged in the World Council of Churches.

Söderblom did not perceive himself as merely archbishop of Uppsala; his parish was the world. He envisioned a united Christendom providing social justice and international peace. For these efforts, he was the first Swedish churchman to receive the Nobel Peace Prize. The reason for his being so honored was his promotion of international understanding through the church. His prominent role in the spiritual and intellectual life of Sweden was given recognition by his election to the Swedish Academy of Sciences in 1921. Ironically, this academy was one of those prescribed by Nobel as the selectors of the Nobel Prize recipients. The contributions of the archbishop were recognized before the Nobel Prize was awarded, for he was accorded honorary doctorates from eleven universities and membership in numerous learned societies.

*Bibliography*

Curtis, C. J. *Contemporary Protestant Thought*. New York: Bruce Publishing, 1970. This work presents an excellent definition of Söderblom's ecumenical theology. It presents a foundation for the so-called Life and

Work Movement of practical Christianity that became Söderblom's preoccupation. The work includes a brief biographical sketch.

Duff, Edward. *The Social Thought of the World Council of Churches*. London: Longmans, Green, 1954. This is an excellent source of the history, development, and goals of the World Council of Churches. Söderblom's stellar role as a pioneer in establishing the Conference of Life and Work is put in context with the larger World Council, or ecumenical movement.

Kaplan, Flora, comp. *Nobel Prize Winners: Charts, Indexes, Sketches*. Chicago: Nobelle, 1941. This collection of short biographies includes a brief sketch of Söderblom and the reasons for which he was awarded a Nobel Peace Prize. It includes a complete (through 1938) listing of all prizewinners.

Nobelstiftelsen. *Nobel: The Man and His Prizes*, edited by H. Schuck et al. Norman: University of Oklahoma Press, 1951. This book presents a history of Nobel, his bequests, and the selection process of recipients of this coveted award. It includes the brief relationship of the priest Söderblom and the philanthropist Nobel. Both men desired world peace, Nobel through the encouragement of peacemakers, Söderblom through the Church. Details the actions and contributions that earned the archbishop the nomination for the Peace Prize.

Pfisterer, K. Dietrich. "Soderblom." *The McGraw-Hill Encyclopedia of World Biography*, vol. 10. New York: McGraw-Hill, 1973. A brief biographical essay on Söderblom that relates the major events of his life and encapsulates his ideas. Includes a list of further reading.

*H. Christian Thorup*

# ALEKSANDR SOLZHENITSYN

*Born:* December 11, 1918; Kislovodsk, U.S.S.R.

*Areas of Achievement:* Literature, government, politics, and social reform
*Contribution:* One of three persons to hold honorary U.S. citizenship, Solzhenitsyn has produced a striking body of literature and has led a long, heroic life, working for freedom in the Soviet Union. His nomination for the Lenin Prize affected de-Stalinization, and his Nobel Prize has positively influenced East-West relations.

*Early Life*

Aleksandr Isayevich Solzhenitsyn scarcely had a childhood. He was born during the Russian Civil War as White and Red armies raced back and forth across the Caucasus, where his family had long resided. His understanding of family history and of the father who died in a freak hunting accident six months before Solzhenitsyn was born are detailed in *Avgust chetyrnadtsatogo* (1971, 1983; *August 1914*, 1971, 1989). His earliest memory (1921) is of Soviet soldiers looting a church. Growing up fatherless and with a mother (born Taissa Zakharovna Shcherbak) struggling to hold any kind of a job—her family's wealth, although confiscated, made her "a social alien"—encouraged in Solzhenitsyn precocity, self-reliance, and incredible self-discipline. Living in harsh circumstances was valuable preparation for the rigors of war and the camps. Private penury merged with public penury after termination of the New Economic Policy in 1928, giving Solzhenitsyn another reason to feel sorry for the Soviet Union (the reason his father had enlisted) and to be attracted to the vision of Leninism.

Solzhenitsyn labored harder on household chores than most boys, read voraciously, always made top marks in school in Rostov-on-Don, and wrote tales and journals regularly from age ten. He read Leo Tolstoy's *Voyna i mir* (1865-1869; *War and Peace*, 1886) ten times and drank in Vladimir Dahl's collection of Russian proverbs. Other of his favorites were William Shakespeare, Friedrich Schiller, Charles Dickens, Jack London, and the Russian poet Sergei Yesenin. Though Solzhenitsyn idolized Tolstoy, he termed Maxim Gorky Russia's greatest writer. In 1936, Solzhenitsyn began to research World War I in preparation for a history of the Russian Revolution, his main task in life, as he had known from early childhood.

Top marks earned for Solzhenitsyn admittance to the University of Rostov on scholarship and without entrance examinations or inquiry into his social origins, and continued top marks along with his activities in Komosol (youth wing of the Communist Party) earned for him a Stalin scholarship paying two and a half times as much. In the summer of 1939, he was enrolled in the Moscow Institute of Literature, Philosophy, and History (MILFI), and he was moved by his first visit to that city. On April 27, 1940, he married Natalia Reshetovskaya after a relationship centered on their studies. He was graduated from the University of Rostov in June, 1941, and applied for a position as a village schoolmaster instead of for one of the prestigious positions that his top marks warranted. On June 22, 1941, war was declared. Solzhenitsyn was not permitted to enlist, because of an old groin injury, but total mobilization on October 16, 1941, made him a private soldier.

### *Life's Work*

Solzhenitsyn's military career began as a farce and ended as a tragedy, but he regarded it as a central part of his life's work. He was defending the Soviet Union and Leninism, and he studied and wrote, not knowing his letters were being intercepted. Assigned to the Seventy-fourth Horse-Drawn Transport Battalion of the Stalingrad Command, Solzhenitsyn spent the winter mostly mucking stables. On March 22, 1942, he learned through an old friend of the need of a courier to Stalingrad. Solzhenitsyn volunteered and managed to get assigned to artillery school. Commissioned as a lieutenant in October, 1942, Solzhenitsyn served in several locations through the winter and in April, 1943, was assigned to Orel, about midway between Rostov and Moscow. Now a battery commander, he was always on the front lines, because his mission was to locate enemy gun positions by measuring their sounds. He served in the decisive Battle of Orel in July, 1943, was decorated with the Order of the Patriotic War, and pursued the Germans toward Poland. The Soviets crossed the Dnieper River in February, 1944. Solzhenitsyn was wounded and promoted to captain, and the advance continued. "The Last Offensive," aimed at Berlin, began in January, 1945. Solzhenitsyn, disobeying Stalin's orders to loot everything in just revenge, felt sympathy for conquered peoples and restrained his battery, although he did liberate some rare Russian books from a house and appropriated stacks of white, blank paper from a Prussian post office. Solzhenitsyn was stunned by the sight of liberated Soviet prisoners of war and was totally shocked on February 9, 1945, to be summoned to his commanding general's office, where he was arrested by Smersh agents and stripped of his insignia.

Solzhenitsyn arrived at the famous Lubyanka Prison in Moscow on February 20, 1945, where procedures for receiving prisoners had been crafted into a fine art over twenty-five years. The process is described in the arrest of Volodin at the end of *V kruge pervom* (1968; *The First Circle*, 1968). Solzhenitsyn was charged with creating anti-Soviet propaganda (disparaging remarks about Joseph Stalin had been found in his letters) and of founding a hostile organization. On July 27, 1945, he was sentenced to eight years by the Special Court.

Solzhenitsyn served eight years in various prison camps, which are immortalized in *The First Circle*, the three volumes of *Arkhipelag GULag*,

*1918-1956: Opyt Khudozhestvennogo issledovaniya* (1973-1975; *The Gulag Archipelago, 1918-1956: An Experiment in Literary Investigation*, 1974-1978), and other writings. Like Gleb Nerzhin in *The First Circle*, he accommodated himself to camp society. Seen from outside, Nerzhin's life was unhappy—nearly hopeless—but he was secretly happy in that unhappiness. In the camps he got to know people and events he could have learned nowhere else. Solzhenitsyn's sentence was officially ended February 9, 1953, and he was exiled in perpetuity to Kok Terek, Kazakhstan, 250 miles from China. He slept in ecstasy in the open on March 5, 1953, heard of Stalin's death the next day, and wrote the poem "The Fifth of March." After administrative technicalities, in May, 1953, he began teaching math, physics, and astronomy in the high school at Kok Terek, population four thousand, about equally divided between natives and exiles. His teaching was interrupted at the end of 1953 by the diagnosis of his cancer and by his two treatments in Tashkent, a thousand miles to the west, in 1954. It is not known how literally autobiographical the case of Oleg Kostogolotov in *Rakovy Korpus* (1968; *Cancer Ward*, 1968) is, but his own tumor was most serious (one had been removed in the camps) and treatment and recovery were most difficult.

The political climate changed in 1956, beginning with the secret speech of First Secretary Nikita S. Khrushchev admitting crimes of Stalin and announcing the end of Gulag and exile. In April, 1956, Solzhenitsyn's sentence and exile were ended. He went to Moscow and was amazed to find bureaucrats almost friendly and to be able to see his file in Lubyanka Prison and to see a prosecutor laugh at it. Solzhenitsyn found a teaching job in Torfoproduct on the rail line a hundred miles east of Moscow. Natalia joined him there, and they were remarried February 2, 1957. In 1958, Boris Pasternak was awarded the Nobel Prize, and there was a furor in the Soviet Union. While polishing *The First Circle*, Solzhenitsyn began a tale entitled "One Day in the Life of a School Teacher"—Solzhenitsyn was then an excellent and happy teacher—but in May, 1959, he changed the title to *Shch-854* and the scene to a labor camp in Ekibastuz. He completed it in six weeks, burned the drafts, and hid the finished copy. His first published writing "Post Office Curiosities," on the failings of the Soviet postal service, appeared in *Priokskaya Pravda* in Ryazan in March, 1959, and a year later the newspaper *Gulok* published his article on rail service. Times were changing, yet *Literaturnaya Gazeta*, the organ of the Union of Soviet Writers, and other periodicals rejected his work. Solzhenitsyn had read the journal *Novy mir* since December, 1953, when an article entitled "On Sincerity in Literature" had appeared in it and on November 4, 1961, he took *Shch-854* to *Novy mir* in Moscow. The editor of *Novy mir* loved the story. How it became *Odin den' Ivana Denisovicha* (1962; *One Day in the Life of Ivan Denisovich*, 1963) and got on Khrushchev's desk is legendary and embellished, but it was printed in

*Novy mir* in November, 1962, and was nominated for the Lenin Prize in 1964. The vote was close, but conservatives, fearing that de-Stalinization was proceeding too rapidly, struck it from the list. Even so, Solzhenitsyn was now famous, and publishers scrambled for his works. Publication of his works in the Soviet Union, however, was denied.

Solzhenitsyn's works circulated in *samizdat* (underground literary network), *The First Circle* and *Cancer Ward* were published in the West without authorization, and he was expelled from the Union of Soviet Writers in 1969. He refused to go to Sweden in 1970 to receive his Nobel Prize in fear of not being readmitted to the Soviet Union. In 1974, he was arrested and exiled. After a brief time in West Germany, he moved to Zurich, Switzerland. In 1976, he settled in a rural retreat in Vermont, where he made his home in closely guarded privacy with his second wife, Natalia Svetlova (they had met in 1967), and their three sons.

In exile, Solzhenitsyn began working on a project that he first conceived in 1937, when he was still in his teens: a multivolume fictional chronicle of Russian history in the years leading up to the Revolution of 1917. To write this massive work, collectively entitled *Krasnoe koleso* (*The Red Wheel*), he has assembled a historical archive that includes documents of all kinds from that period. The first installment, or "knot" (*uzel*), to use Solzhenitsyn's own term, is the revised version of *August 1914*, which is more than half again the length of the original. The second knot, *Oktiabr shestnadtsatogo* (1984; October, 1916), was actually published after the third, *Mart semnadtsatogo* (1983; March, 1917); at least one more volume is projected. In general, critical reaction to this ambitious work, which the author regards as his most important, has been very negative. In response, Solzhenitsyn has said that he is writing for readers fifty or a hundred years in the future.

### *Summary*

It is difficult to place in historical perspective an established giant of literature who, in his seventies, is only in the middle of what he calls his life's work. He is also a part of each of the world's two superpowers, a friend and a critic of each. Aleksandr Solzhenitsyn could be an important influence on each superpower's better understanding and improving itself and improving relations with each other and in working toward world peace. Some of Solzhenitsyn's eventual reputation may lie with Mikhail Gorbachev's success with *glasnost* and *perestroika* and with George Bush's success in leading a more open United States. Many will find in Solzhenitsyn's works hope for the positive benefits of suffering and inspiration for spiritual values over material success.

Students and critics will be sorting out Solzhenitsyn's distinctive contributions for some time to come. The volume of his works, the copies sold, and the different languages into which his works have been translated are enormous and growing. Solzhenitsyn is a poet and a prophet; he is a master storyteller with an incredible capacity for details; he is accomplished in many genres; and he has a mission to tell the truth about what happened in the Soviet Union in his lifetime. Solzhenitsyn believes that his experiences and knowledge of eyewitness sources justify the placing of *August 1914* and subsequent volumes in a category beyond historical fiction. Perhaps critics will invent a genre or perhaps Solzhenitsyn will remain his own genre.

*Bibliography*

Allaback, Steven. *Alexander Solzhenitsyn*. New York: Taplinger, 1978. A short discussion of Solzhenitsyn's four best-known works, this work provides an easy way to become acquainted with the basics of these stories by Solzhenitsyn.

Berman, Ronald, ed. *Solzhenitsyn at Harvard: The Address, Twelve Early Responses, and Six Later Reflections*. Washington, D.C.: Ethics and Public Policy Center, 1980. This work is important to any student of world affairs. Most Americans were hurt that the famous victim of Soviet dictatorship did not love the United States as much as he hated dictatorship. Most of Solzhenitsyn's points are probably more valid than they were ten years ago; much of the criticism is less relevant.

Brown, Edward J. *Russian Literature Since the Revolution*. Rev. ed. Cambridge, Mass.: Harvard University Press, 1982. Describes the literary environment in which Solzhenitsyn wrote and provides helpful background and context. Solzhenitsyn's prose is discussed. Contains a selected bibliography.

Burg, David, and George Feifer. *Solzhenitsyn*. Briarcliff Manor, N.Y.: Stein & Day, 1972. The best early biography, clearly written and easy to read. Written while Solzhenitsyn was still in Russia, so it is incomplete in several respects. Includes a short bibliography, eight pages of illustrations, and a very helpful chronology.

Clément, Olivier. *The Spirit of Solzhenitsyn*. Translated by Sarah Fawcett and Paul Burns. New York: Barnes & Noble Books, 1976. A thought-provoking thesis on the universality of Solzhenitsyn seeing him as speaking for every man, for everyone's freedom to speak the truth.

Dunlop, John B., Richard S. Haugh, and Alexis Klimoff, eds. *Aleksandr Solzhenitsyn: Critical Essays and Documentary Materials*. Belmont, Mass.: Nordland, 1973.

Dunlop, John B., Richard S. Haugh, and Michael Nicholson, eds. *Solzhenitsyn in Exile: Critical Essays and Documentary Materials*. Stanford, Calif.: Hoover Institution Press, 1985. These works constitute an excellent source for the serious student. Contains a select bibliography.

Scammell, Michael. *Solzhenitsyn: A Biography.* New York: W. W. Norton, 1984. As close to a definitive biography as can be done of a living and working writer in only a thousand pages. Thoroughly researched, including interviews with Solzhenitsyn, and remarkably dispassionate in treating controversies. Very helpful in translating and explaining terms and things Russian. Includes an excellent bibliography and an excellent index.

*Frederic M. Crawford*

# GEORGES SOREL

*Born:* November 2, 1847; Cherbourg, France
*Died:* August 30, 1922; Boulogne-sur-Seine, France
*Areas of Achievement:* Social reform and philosophy
*Contribution:* Sorel was the leading spokesman for revolutionary syndicalism in the first two decades of the twentieth century.

## *Early Life*

Georges-Eugène Sorel was born in Cherbourg, Normandy, in the coastal region of western France, on November 2, 1847. His parents were Catholic and middle-class; his father was the director of a business concern, and his mother was the daughter of an army officer. Georges, the second of three sons, had a traditional education with an emphasis on the utilitarian rather than the philosophical. School records indicate that he did especially well in mathematics. The capstone of this was his graduation from the École Technique in 1867. He then worked as a civil engineer for the government for the next twenty-five years in the Department of Roads and Bridges. Most of these years were spent outside Paris in Corsica, Algeria, and in Perpignan.

As was the case with most young men of his generation in France, Sorel was deeply disturbed by the French defeat in the Franco-Prussian War of 1870-1871. The crisis was compounded by the bloodshed and violence of the civil war that followed; the suppression of the Paris Commune had a lasting effect on Sorel's concept of politics and society.

Sorel took early retirement from his government job in 1892, rejected his pension, and devoted the remainder of his life to writing at his home in Boulogne-sur-Seine near Paris. The ideas expressed by Sorel in the next thirty years were shaped by his own background in engineering, by his twenty-year association with Marie David, and by his reading of the works of Alexis de Tocqueville, Pierre Proudhon, and Karl Marx. Sorel, the student of the proletariat, got to know the proletariat intimately from 1875 until 1897 in the person of Marie David. She was, he once said, part of his existence as a socialist writer. His first work, published before his retirement, *Le Procès de Socrate* (1889; the trial of Socrates) was closer to the Tocqueville tradition, but in his second publication, *D'Aristote à Marx* (1894; from Aristotle to Marx), Sorel was moving toward socialism.

## *Life's Work*

The major crisis of French politics that attracted the interest of all writers in the 1890's was the Dreyfus affair. Sorel joined with other radicals and socialists to defend Alfred Dreyfus, who was unjustly accused of selling military secrets to the Germans. After a ten-year struggle in the courts and in the press, Dreyfus was exonerated and his defenders triumphant. Sorel, however, did not see this victory in the same light as did Jean Jaurès and many other socialists. Socialist politicians were, Sorel believed, as corrupt and deceitful as bourgeois politicians. What was needed was a complete transformation of society through class war and the general strike. The working class was now ready to seize power for itself.

By the turn of the century, Sorel was a well-known Parisian, usually seen in the Bibliothèque Nationale, at the Sorbonne, or around the office of the *Cahiers de la quinzaine*, whose editor and founder was his friend, Charles Péguy. The major theme in his own writings had become the decadence of bourgeois society. Sorel considered himself a Marxist but found himself at odds with both the orthodox Marxists and the revisionists. For Sorel, Marxism, though a useful analytical tool, was not a science. It was social poetry, a body of imprecise meanings couched in symbolic forms. The cure for modern society would not come from middle-class intellectuals such as Marx but from the *syndicats*, or trade unions. These themes are the basis of his two major works: *Les Illusions du progrès* (1908; the illusions of progress) and *Réflexions sur la violence* (1908; *Reflections on Violence*, 1912). Violence for Sorel was not simply method but morality. It was not to be confused with brute force that trampled liberty. Sorel saw violence as a creative force that rejected the immoral concessions made by most politicians.

*Reflections on Violence* remains the one successful Sorelian work out of some dozen publications. It went through several editions and printings before World War I and had considerable influence. This book stresses the importance of the "social myth"—legends of the 1789 revolution, for example, which contain the strongest inclination of a people to act. This he believed was now summed up in revolutionary syndicalism, a heroic struggle in the best interests of civilization. In this book, Sorel also labels his method of analysis, *diremption*, which is best translated as abstraction. *Diremption* was used to describe the relationship of institutions and society, keeping in mind that both are continually changing. This allows the investigator to isolate and examine an institution, but the distinctiveness discovered is somewhat artificial since one has to ignore temporarily the institution's interaction with its social environment to do this. Sorel's work was closely related to the origins of modern sociology as an independent discipline. He attended Émile Durkheim's defense of his doctoral dissertation in 1893, and he published critiques of Durkheim, Jean-Gabriel de Tarde, Gustave Le Bon, and Cesare Lombroso.

Sorel's call for a true social war went unanswered despite the general turmoil in the unions in France and other European countries in the decade before World War I. Instead of a social war among the classes, Europe was plunged into a war between the nations. The internationalism of socialism broke down in the face of a new fanatic wave of patriotism, which took Jaurès' life and ruined Sorel's revolutionary syndicalism. The revolution that

Sorel had hoped for seemed shattered by the war, but he was enthusiastic about events in Russia and applauded the overthrow of the Romanovs in 1917. A new edition of *Reflections on Violence* was published in 1919 and dedicated to Vladimir Ilich Lenin. In approving Lenin's Bolshevik Russia (Sorel called Lenin the new Peter the Great), he was going against much of what he had said earlier about working-class leadership. Lenin's vanguard of the proletariat was not Sorelian, not even good Marxism perhaps, but Sorel was an old man desperate for some kind of change in a bourgeois, chauvinistic Europe, and so he gave the new revolution his wholehearted support.

This kind of support was never tendered to Benito Mussolini. Sorel had followed Mussolini's career both as a Marxist and as a syndicalist. He had as early as 1912 predicted victory for Mussolini's faction, but Mussolini's subsequent identification with Italian nationalism and the war saw their paths diverge. Nevertheless Sorel did not oppose Mussolini in the same sense that his friend and longtime correspondent, Benedetto Croce, did. Sorel did not share Croce's admiration for the old Italian liberal government and believed that Mussolini, like Lenin, was an extraordinary man. Mussolini claimed at one time that he was a disciple of Sorel, but Sorel never acknowledged this. Whether Sorel would ever have approved the new Fascist Italy is impossible to say, since he died two months before Mussolini actually came to power in October, 1922. The considered opinion of most commentators today is that Sorel would not have supported Fascism. He may have been a critic of democracy, but he loved liberty and he was careful to make a distinction between the two. Liberty would best be preserved by the *syndicats* that he had proposed in his earlier writings. The *syndicats* were designed to help the worker realize his potential in the political and socioeconomic spheres. The *syndicat* was at the heart of Sorel's concept of proletarian socialism; he sometimes compared the role of the *syndicats* to the role of the monasteries in the early history of the Church. Mussolini's *syndicats* were controlled by the middle-class capitalists in union with the Fascist state and did not further liberty.

Sorel's reputation has suffered partly from these suspicions about his link to Communism and to Fascism but mainly from his attacks on elitists and intellectuals. Unfortunately for Sorel, it was the intellectuals, not the proletariat, who would pass judgment in print on his career and his contribution to society. They were bound to have their revenge. So the legend of the guru of terrorism and totalitarianism was born; the *Reflections on Violence* was posited as their bible.

### *Summary*

Interpretations of *Reflections on Violence* and of Georges Sorel's ideas in general have ranged widely from outright condemnation by many who have been quick to label and to classify, to praise from others who valued Sorel's insights into the nature of revolution and the relationship between thought and action. Closely related to this is the question of Sorel's place in the history of political thought. He was certainly closer to the Left than the Right, despite his lukewarm support of the Third French Republic and a brief flirtation with Charles Maurras's movement called Action Française. Sorel was above all else an independent thinker, a kind of "wild Marxist" who never fully agreed with anyone else. There were two basic themes in all he wrote: first, a rejection of bourgeois society and bourgeois values, and second, a rejection of the supreme role of reason and of the intellect. The anti-intellectualism of Sorel was first developed in his book on Socrates. Socrates was not a hero for the people but a man like John Calvin, who tried to force his ideas on others. Sorel carried this argument over to apply to most of the politicians and the writers of his day. Government by the totality of its citizens was the ideal, not government by the few members of the intelligentsia.

*Bibliography*

Curtis, Michael. *Three Against the Third Republic: Sorel, Barrès and Maurras*. Princeton, N.J.: Princeton University Press, 1959. Contrasting the leaders of the Left and the Right, Curtis provides insights into the complexities of Sorel's views and concludes that Sorel was inconsistent, moving from Marxism to finally ally himself with nationalists and monarchists.

Horowitz, Irving L. *Radicalism and the Revolt Against Reason: The Social Theories of Georges Sorel*. New York: Humanities Press, 1961. A penetrating analysis of Sorel's basic ideas, but the book is difficult to read owing to the profusion of names. The inclusion of the author's translation of Sorel's *La Décomposition du Marxisme* (1908; *The Decomposition of Marxism*) is helpful.

Humphrey, Richard. *Georges Sorel: Prophet Without Honour.* Cambridge, Mass: Harvard University Press, 1951. The author makes a convincing case that Sorel should not be viewed as an advocate of violence or as the ideological source of Bolshevism or Fascism. He does an excellent job of presenting the essential Sorel, the "metaphysician of syndicalism," who searched all of his life for a humane social morality.

Jennings, J. R. *Georges Sorel: The Character and Development of His Thought*. New York: St. Martin's Press, 1985. Most recent assessment of Sorel's ideas and influence. Scholarly study that tries to explain the many transitions in Sorel's life and work. Sorel, he concludes, had a tendency to pluralize rather than to simplify or unify.

Meisel, James. *The Genesis of George Sorel*. Ann Arbor, Mich.: George Wahr, 1951. This doctoral thesis turned into a book by an obscure publisher has value if one overlooks the pretentiousness of the author. Especially good on the correspondence of Sorel with Croce, Robert Michels, and other intellectuals of the day.

Portis, Larry. *Georges Sorel*. London: Pluto Press, 1980. This book was written for a Marxist audience and places Sorel clearly in that tradition. He sees Sorel and Sartre as the most profound French Marxists and calls Sorel's revolutionary syndicalism the most legitimate realization of a Marxist revolutionary strategy.

Roth, Jack J. *The Cult of Violence: Sorel and the Sorelians*. Berkeley: University of California Press, 1980. Best single volume on the Sorelians—syndicalists, integral nationalists, Fascists—all advocates of violence and direct action, who claimed Sorel as their master.

Vernon, Richard. *Commitment and Change: Georges Sorel and the Idea of Revolution*. Toronto: University of Toronto Press, 1978. One of the best discussions of Sorel's ideas and the influence of Henri Bergson and Proudhon on Sorel. The author fails to examine fully Sorel's concept of revolution. Camus is seen as Sorel's successor.

*Norbert J. Gossman*

# WOLE SOYINKA

*Born:* July 13, 1934; Abeokuta, Nigeria

*Area of Achievement:* Literature

*Contribution:* The first African ever to win the Nobel Prize in Literature, Soyinka is generally held to be Nigeria's foremost contemporary dramatist and possibly the most influential of all black African playwrights. Although he has earned high praise equally for his poetry, fiction, and literary criticism, it is as a playwright that Soyinka has distinguished himself.

## *Early Life*

Akinwande Oluwole Soyinka (pronounced Shoy-ink-a) was born July 13, 1934, in Abeokuta in Western Nigeria, to Ayo and Eniola Soyinka. His mother was a successful businesswoman, his father the headmaster of the local missionary school, which Soyinka attended as a child. Describing his earliest memories in an autobiographical work, *Aké: The Years of Childhood* (1981), Soyinka remembers that his father seemed to be on a first-name basis with God; he recalls that his mother was nicknamed "the Wild Christian," for her flamboyant faith.

The young Soyinka was exposed early to Christian ideas and English language and culture. He attended St. Peter's School and Abeokuta Grammar School in his hometown before transferring to Government College in Ibadan. His undergraduate education began at University College, Ibadan (later to become the University of Ibadan), where he studied from 1952 to 1954. Interestingly his classmates number among them such future literary giants as Chinua Achebe and Christopher Okigbo. Soyinka traveled abroad to England to complete his undergraduate degree, graduating from the University of Leeds in 1957 with a B.A. in English. It was at Leeds that he met G. Wilson Knight, a noted scholar, whose influence started Soyinka on a lifelong interest in the metaphysical and the imagistic.

After graduation, Soyinka spent two years working as a play reader at the Royal Court Theatre, where he was exposed to the experimental and innovative of some of Great Britain's best young playwrights, among them Harold Pinter, John Osborne, Samuel Beckett, and John Arden. His experience at the Royal Court rounded out his academic and professional training in drama and theater. During these years, Soyinka wrote his first plays: *The Swamp Dwellers* (1958), about one community's history; *The Invention* (1959), a one-act satire comparing the leaders of South Africa's apartheid system to mad scientists conducting horrible experiments; and *The Lion and the Jewel* (1959), a comedy. *The Invention* was performed at the Royal Court Theatre in November, 1959, as part of a program which also featured excerpts from *A Dance of the Forests* (1960). That same year, *The Swamp Dwellers* was produced in London and in Ibadan, where *The Lion and the Jewel* was also performed.

Even as a child Soyinka had felt drawn to his Yoruba roots despite the Christian environment in which he was reared and educated. His grandfather had initiated him into adulthood through the traditional ritual incisions on the wrists and ankles to prepare him to face the world. As an adult, Soyinka realized that his dream of a thriving black African theater tradition required his immersion in traditional African culture, and in 1960 he returned to Nigeria with the support of a Rockefeller Research Fellowship. Although the fellowship attached him to the University of Ibadan, he spent much of his year as a fellow in an intensive study of Nigerian culture. He traveled widely throughout the country to participate in community rituals and traditional festivals, and he experimented with ways to combine native traditions with Western culture. At the end of his fellowship year, Soyinka accepted a position as lecturer at the University of Ife in Ibadan. Since that time, he has held various faculty positions at universities all over the world.

*Life's Work*

Soyinka returned home to a Nigeria which had no native dramatic tradition in English. Theatrical productions were limited to William Shakespeare's plays and other English classics, or to European plays in English translation. Nothing on stage had any bearing on the average playgoer's life; the only extant Nigerian play in English was written in Elizabethan speech. In 1960, Soyinka created "The 1960 Masks," a theater company composed of professionals and civil servants who were interested—if untrained—amateurs. Formed in Lagos primarily to perform in Soyinka's *A Dance of the Forests* for Nigerians' independence year celebrations, The 1960 Masks was that country's first English-language theater company—although its amateur composition kept it from being the theater group that Soyinka had dreamed of forming. The year 1960 also saw the production of two more Soyinka plays: *The Trials of Brother Jero* and *Camwood on the Leaves*, a radio script.

Because the actors involved in The 1960 Masks were dependent for their livelihoods on their positions in the civil service and in the schools, Soyinka was hesitant about involving them in political drama for fear that their participation would cost them their careers. Consequently, in 1964, he formed the Orisun Theatre group, composed of theater professionals who could present his political revues as well as his longer plays.

For Soyinka, the decade or so from the mid-1960's to the mid-1970's proved to be a period of intense and fruitful playwriting during which he wrote many of his most important and most strongly political works for theater: *The Strong Breed* (1964), his most frequently anthologized play, is a portrayal of the individual sacrifices necessary for the atonement of communal guilt, a dramatization of the ancient scapegoat ritual; *Kongi's Harvest* (1964) is a scathing indictment of Africa's new politicians who are driven by their passion for authority; *The Road* (1965) depicts a society moving inexorably toward death and destruction; *Madmen and Specialists* (1970) focuses on the gradual deterioration of humanity, which is subjected to the rigid control of an authoritative society; *Jero's Metamorphosis* (1973) is a cynical satire on the excesses of right-wing military dictatorships; and *Death and the King's Horseman* (1976) returns to the same symbiosis of rhetoric with ritual that informs the earlier *The Strong Breed*. Two plays from this period are interesting for their fusion of Western dramatic forms with Yoruba concepts and performance elements: *The Bacchae* (1973), an adaptation of the Euripides play, changes the original ending to allow for a positive interpretation inspired by Yoruba folk ritual, and *Opera Wonyosi* (1977), which caricatures modern African despots, is taken from Bertolt Brecht's *Die Dreigroschenoper* (1928; *The Threepenny Opera*, 1949).

Although Soyinka believes—as do many of his admirers—that his Nobel Prize commemorates his dramatic work, he has also earned praise for his poetry and fiction, for his autobiographical work, as well as for his essays on literary criticism. His first collection of poetry, published early in his career, featured the long poem "Idanre" (1967), which celebrates the Yoruba god Ogun, who figures prominently in a number of Soyinka's other works, including another long poem, "Ogun Abibiman" (1977). Imprisoned for two years for his outspokenness about human rights violations, Soyinka detailed the trauma of his solitary confinement in two more collections of poetry, *Poems from Prison* (1969) and *A Shuttle in the Crypt* (1972), and in his prison diary, published in 1972 as *The Man Died*. Also a product of his own experience is *Aké: The Years of Childhood*, a warm but unsentimental memoir of his childhood.

Soyinka's two novels—unlike the rest of his literary output—have elicited strongly contradictory commentary from serious students of African literature. *The Interpreters* (1965), a hilarious exposé of decadent modern African society, is the focus of much of the controversy; while some readers believe the novel to be nothing less than a masterpiece, others point out that both the language and the structure are so convoluted and dense that whole sections of the book succeed only in confusing the reader. *Season of Anomy* (1973) is a much grimmer and more artistically successful novel that deals with the horrible consequences of the lust for power displayed by dictatorial rulers.

In the field of literary criticism, Soyinka has proven himself to be a formidable theorist and thinker with his *Myth, Literature, and the African World* (1976), a collection of essays originally delivered as lectures at the University of Cambridge, and with various individual pieces, most notably "The Fourth Stage," in which he outlines a theory of Yoruba tragedy based on Yoruba theology and concepts of existence.

Soyinka's later work is more focused on the modern world and its evils, and somehow less pervaded by traditional Yoruba cultural motifs. Nevertheless, Soyinka still displays a concern with the human race's capacity for both creation and destruction. *A Play of Giants* (1984) explores the notion of power and how it is wielded for good or evil; the play is a satire on Africa's self-appointed "presidents-for-life"—men such as Idi Amin and Jean-Bedel Bokassa—who used their power to destroy anyone who dared question their authority. A more humorous piece, *Requiem for a Futurologist* (1986), takes on television charlatans and their gullible public and proves that human beings are the potential victims of their own cleverness.

### *Summary*

Whatever the focus of any specific piece of his writing, Wole Soyinka manifests a passionate concern for his society and for the fate of the human race. Much of his work is political, arising from his own outspokenness against human rights violations and from his own experience—several incarcerations in Nigerian prisons, exile, and denunciation by the corrupt powers-that-be in his own country. Out of the crucible of his own life, Soyinka has distilled his most pervasive and powerful themes: the struggle for selfhood and national identity, the cost of that struggle, the need for sacrifice and purging of collective guilt in the quest for progress, the duty of the artist, and the relationship between the health of the state and individual liberties.

Awarded the Nobel Prize in Literature in 1986, Soyinka was praised by the Nobel Committee for a body of work that is "vivid, often harrowing, but also marked by an evocative, poetically intensified diction." Soyinka's work is the artistic contribution of a man who courageously shares his vision of salvation for humanity and his denunciation of oppression in spite of harassment and persecution from the very society he seeks to serve. Characteristically, he sees the Nobel Prize not as an award for his own artistry but as a recognition of the African cultural traditions that have made his work possible.

### *Bibliography*

Coger, Greta M. K. *Index of Subjects, Proverbs, and Themes in the Writings of Wole Soyinka*. Westport, Conn.: Greenwood Press, 1988. A valuable key to references and allusions in much of Soyinka's work. The introduction is particularly useful for its brief discussion of connections between works, for its descriptions of topics of interest to Soyinka, and for its commentary on Soyinka's use of Yoruba proverbs and rituals.

Gibbs, James. *Wole Soyinka*. London: Macmillan, 1986. Part of the Macmillan Modern Dramatists series, this is a very detailed source that follows Soyinka's career from his earliest plays. Contains some good biographical information, illustrations, a bibliography, and an index.

__________, ed. *Critical Perspectives on Wole Soyinka*. Washington, D.C.: Three Continents Press, 1980. A collection of essays by various scholars on different aspects on Soyinka's work. The introduction provides a concise overview of Soyinka's life and career.

Graham-White, Anthony. *The Drama of Black Africa*. New York: Samuel French, 1974. A chronological survey of the development of a dramatic tradition in black Africa. Beginning with a chapter on "The Origins of Drama in Africa," the author points out that drama as a literary genre in Africa has its roots in the period of European colonization and that Soyinka alone of black African playwrights claims to write a new kind of drama drawn from native culture.

Jones, Eldred Durosimi. *Wole Soyinka*. New York: Twayne, 1971. An introductory critical-analytical study of Soyinka's career, including biographical, cultural, and historical material essential to an appreciation and understanding of Soyinka's work.

Katrak, Ketu H. *Wole Soyinka and Modern Tragedy: A Study of Dramatic Theory and Practice*. Westport, Conn.: Greenwood Press, 1986. An analysis of the principles of Yoruba tragedy as articulated and applied by Soyinka. Katrak focuses on the major themes of Yoruba tragedy and on the influences—Yoruba and Western—on Soyinka's tragic plays.

Palmer, Eustace. *The Growth of the African Novel*. London: Heinemann, 1979. Includes an excellent chapter on two of Soyinka's novels—the humorous early work, *The Interpreters*, and the darker *Season of Anomy*.

*E. D. Huntley*

# PAUL-HENRI SPAAK

*Born:* January 25, 1899; Schaerbeek, Belgium
*Died:* July 31, 1972; Brussels, Belgium
*Areas of Achievement:* Government and politics
*Contribution:* A Socialist member of the Belgian Chamber of Deputies, Spaak was prime minister on three occasions and foreign minister in many cabinets. He successfully opposed the return of King Leopold III to the Belgian throne following World War II. The implementor of Belgium's policy of voluntary neutrality before the war, Spaak subsequently advocated European integration and international cooperation. He shaped treaties and served in multiple international posts in service to this goal.

## *Early Life*

Paul-Henri Charles Spaak's legal and political career reflected family tradition. His father, Paul Spaak, was a lawyer who turned to literature and drama and became director of the Brussels opera. His mother, Marie (Janson) Spaak, was a Socialist who in 1921 became the first woman member of the Belgian parliament. His maternal grandfather, Paul Janson, was a leader of the Belgian Liberal Party; his uncle, Paul-Émile Janson, served as prime minister for the Liberals on several occasions. Reared in a free-thinking anticlerical tradition and educated in French-language schools, as a resident of the capital city region Spaak was less involved in the linguistic divisions of his country than were the militant Flemings and Walloons of other regions. His patriotism was strong. At the age of seventeen, during World War I, he attempted to escape from German-occupied Belgium to join the remnants of the nation's army. Detained by the Germans, he was placed in a prison camp for two years.

Spaak studied law at the Free University of Brussels and was admitted to the Brussels bar, serving for some time as counselor for the commune of Forest. More athletic than his later stout figure would suggest, Spaak was a member of the 1922 Belgian Davis Cup tennis team. In 1922, he married Marguerite Malevy, the daughter of a Liberal senator. They were to have one son and two daughters. A year following Marguerite's death in 1964, Spaak married Simonne Deal.

## *Life's Work*

In 1921, Spaak made the crucial decision to become active in the Socialist rather than the Liberal Party. The Socialist demand for justice for all was appealing. The chance to assume a leadership position quickly also lay more with the Socialists than with the aging Liberals. By 1925, Spaak was *chef de cabinet* for a Socialist minister. A year later, however, Spaak resigned rather than serve under a Catholic Party prime minister in a cabinet of national union. He founded a small paper, the *Bataille socialiste*, and became the spokesperson of the left wing of the Socialist Party. In November, 1932, he was elected to the Belgian Chamber of Deputies from Brussels. His former paper now defunct, he and friends founded the weekly *Action socialiste*. Spaak's radical views offended moderate members of his party, and in 1934 he barely escaped expulsion from the party.

Spaak's socialism was inspired more by his own sense of justice and concern for the common person than by any deep conviction concerning Marxism. He was later to admit that his extremism was in part a tactical move to break into politics. It therefore was not difficult for Spaak to come under the partial influence of Belgian socialist theorist Henri de Man. Accepting that "integral socialism" was only a distant hope, Spaak followed Man's espousal of Keynesian economics and the view that capitalism, instead of being overthrown, should be transformed into an instrument for service to the working class. Spaak decided his left-wing predilections were not so strong as to prevent him from taking in 1935 the post of minister of transport and communications in a cabinet headed by the Catholic Paul van Zeeland. He soon was recognized for his moderation and collegial collaboration.

In 1936, in his mid-thirties, Spaak became foreign minister in a cabinet led by his uncle, Paul-Émile Janson. With the chambers and populace so riven by the Flemish-Walloon language disputes that passage of a military bill was impossible as long as the Flemings believed Belgium to be linked to French foreign policy, the cabinet opted for a policy of independent neutrality. Spaak carried out the negotiations associated with this course. In May, 1938, he became the youngest prime minister in the history of his country. He left the post in February, 1939, but again became foreign minister in November. His sharp interruption of the German ambassador's announcement of the Nazi invasion on May 10, 1940, reflected his passionate nature and became a rallying point for Belgian pride in the dark years of World War II.

Spaak and other members of the government fled to France before the German onslaught. Spaak and the prime minister, Hubert Pierlot, disapproved of King Leopold's personal decision to remain in occupied Belgium. The Germans later moved Leopold to Austria. With a few compatriots, Spaak and Pierlot escaped to form a government-in-exile in London. Reflection there confirmed Spaak's sense of the need for international cooperation. The first step was to defeat the Axis powers. When approached by the British and Americans, desperate for uranium in their effort to construct an atomic bomb, he granted them first option for ten years on the world's prime source of uranium in the Belgian Congo.

A man of action, Spaak did what he could to support both his own country and the concept of internationalism in practical terms. During the war, he held preliminary negotiations with The Netherlands, which led to the Belgium-Netherlands-Luxembourg Economic Union (Benelux) Treaty of 1947. He was chief of the Belgian delegation to the conference at San Francisco that drafted the charter for the United Nations Organization. In 1946, Spaak was elected the first president of the United Nations General Assembly. Spaak declined the position for the assembly's 1947 session, for he had again become Belgian prime minister. He had also occupied that post briefly in March, 1946; this time he would remain in office into June, 1949.

In the months after he left the government, the Belgian royal question reached its climax. Spaak opposed bitterly any return of the monarch to the Belgian throne and led a massive street demonstration. Among his several objections to Leopold was the manner in which the king took crucial actions as commander in chief of the army in the crucial days before and after the outbreak of war without consulting fully with the civilian government. On July 16, 1951, Leopold relinquished the royal prerogative to his son Baudouin I.

When British foreign minister Ernest Bevin in January, 1948, called for a consolidation of Western Europe, his Belgian counterpart responded quickly. Spaak's influence speeded creation in March, 1948, of a Western European Union that entailed more political and economic cooperation, as well as military cooperation, than the British and the French had initially contemplated. Spaak also signed on behalf of Belgium the 1949 Treaty of Washington, forming the North Atlantic Treaty Organization (NATO). He took pride in Article 9 of that treaty; the permanent council it authorized provided for more continuing political and economic consultation among the members of the organization than did traditional military alliances. Spaak returned to the Belgian foreign ministry in 1954 but left the office to serve as secretary-general of NATO from 1957 to 1961. Spaak did yeoman service there by restoring confidence in the alliance shaken by the Suez crisis of 1956.

Spaak's interest in European political and economic collaboration is also reflected in the other posts that he held. He chaired from 1948 to 1950 the Council of the Organization for European Economic Cooperation, the European arm of the United States European Recovery Program (Marshall Plan). At the end of 1949, he was elected first president of the Consultative Assembly of the newly formed council of Europe. Disheartened by the failure of the council to press firmly toward economic and political integration, Spaak resigned the position in December, 1951. His efforts then turned to encouraging the integration of a smaller grouping of six nations in the nascent European Coal and Steel Community (ECSC), serving as president of its common assembly from May, 1953, to April, 1954. In 1955, Spaak was selected by his colleagues in the ECSC to chair a committee that would recommend steps to bring about a common economic market among the six. The recommendations of the "Spaak Report" became the foundation for the

1957 Treaties of Rome creating the European Economic Community and the European Atomic Energy Community.

Spaak's skill as foreign minister was once more called upon in April, 1961. The newly independent Congo had broken relations with Belgium, the province of Katanga was in secession, U.N. troops were intervening, and Belgian nationals in the Congo appeared in danger. After many difficulties, Spaak improved relations with both the Congo and the United Nations, saw the secession ended, and encouraged restoration of order in the former colony. In February, 1966, the coalition cabinet in which Spaak was serving was overthrown. That June, in the midst of a political scene dominated by the linguistic question, the Socialist Party refused to back Spaak when he urged that it support the government, which sought to host the Supreme Headquarters of the Allied Powers in Europe. Discouraged by this lack of vision by his party, Spaak retired from politics.

*Summary*

Paul-Henri Spaak served in the Belgian government for more than twenty-two years, holding the foreign ministry portfolio for most of that time. His influence was great, for the paths he set were usually followed by those who briefly relieved him at the post. His energy in promoting a united Europe was indefatigable. Spaak's skill as a diplomat lay in finding those points that brought people together. His vision was wide and ambitious, but he was willing to work patiently and determinedly to reach his goals through cumulative small steps. His sense of timing was good, and in both domestic and international politics he was not afraid to propose bold moves when he thought the moment right. His ability to extract the best from his collaborators, his straightforwardness, his clarity of expression, and even his emotional personality all contributed to his success. Frequently he led others to make efforts that they had not originally contemplated. He suffered in reappraising his prewar policy and his relations with Leopold, yet learned from his experience and did not shrink from the consequences of his conclusions. The nature of post-World War II Europe was permanently altered by his efforts. While he believed that European unity and economic and political integration had not proceeded fast or far enough by the time of his retirement, he had earned the sobriquet by which he was then widely known: Mr. Europe.

*Bibliography*

Arango, E. Ramón. *Leopold III and the Belgian Royal Question*. Baltimore: Johns Hopkins University Press, 1961. The best-balanced account of this affair in English, it describes well the view of the Socialists and Spaak.

Helmreich, Jonathan E. *Belgium and Europe: A Study in Small Power Diplomacy*. The Hague: Mouton, 1976. The last chapters provide a general review of Belgian foreign policy and Spaak's role from 1936 to 1964.

__________. *Gathering Rare Ores: The Diplomacy of Uranium Acquisition, 1943-1954*. Princeton, N.J.: Princeton University Press, 1986. Though written from the viewpoint of U.S. policy, the book tells much about Spaak's role in the uranium negotiations of this period.

Huizinga, James H. *Mr. Europe: A Political Biography of Paul Henri Spaak*. New York: Praeger, 1961. The greatest portion of this book by a Dutch journalist focuses on the evolution of Spaak's views on socialism and his breach with Leopold. The development of both Spaak's character and internationalism is well illuminated.

Spaak, Paul-Henri. *The Continuing Battle: Memoirs of a European, 1936-1966*. Translated by Henry Fox. Boston: Little, Brown, 1971. The English version slightly abridges the French text. The focus is on Spaak's work for European unity; no references are made to personal or family events or to those preceding 1936. The period of neutralism and the royal controversy are covered succinctly. Spaak demonstrates his priorities, includes quotations from significant documents and speeches, and presents incisive descriptions of international figures.

*Jonathan E. Helmreich*

# JOSEPH STALIN
## Joseph Vissarionovich Dzhugashvili

*Born:* December 21, 1879; Gori, Georgia, Russian Empire
*Died:* March 5, 1953; Moscow, U.S.S.R.
*Areas of Achievement:* Government and politics
*Contribution:* Stalin succeeded Lenin as leader of the Soviet Union. During Stalin's twenty-five years in power, the Soviet Union was transformed from a backward agricultural society into one of the world's superpowers. This was achieved through a combination of Marxist-Leninist ideology, police terror, and sheer political will.

### *Early Life*

Joseph Vissarionovich Dzhugashvili, known by his revolutionary name of "Stalin," was born in Gori in the Russian province of Georgia on December 21, 1879. His father worked in a shoe factory, expecting his son to follow in his footsteps. His mother, Ekaterina Geladze, pious and hardworking, was determined that her only surviving child should escape the family's cycle of poverty, labor, and ignorance. Since education was to her the key to success, she enrolled Joseph in a Russian Orthodox church elementary school, hoping that he would become a priest. Upon graduation in 1894 he was enrolled in a theological seminary located in the Georgian capital of Tiflis. There he was converted to Marxism, leading a Marxist study group among the local railway workers when he was only eighteen years old. His revolutionary activities caused growing friction with the clerical staff of the seminary and led to his expulsion in May, 1899.

Stalin then found employment as a clerk at the Tiflis Geophysical Observatory, continuing revolutionary agitation among the workers, which led to his arrest in 1902. During his first imprisonment, the historic split in the Russian Social Democratic Workers' Party occurred, and Stalin found his sympathies with the Bolshevik (later "Communist") radicalism of Vladimir Ilich Lenin.

Between 1902 and 1917, Stalin spent almost nine years in either czarist prisons or internal exile. When not incarcerated, he helped organize bank robberies in his native Caucasus to secure money for the Bolsheviks and continued his underground activities as a Marxist propagandist. By 1912 his loyalty came to the attention of Lenin, and Stalin began his steady rise in the Party hierarchy. In 1913, Lenin asked him to compose an article on the problems of national minorities in the Russian Empire. The resulting essay, *Marksizm i natsional'nyi vopros* (1914; *Marxism and the National and Colonial Question*, 1934), while it represents the longest piece of writing he ever did, actually reflects Lenin's ideas on the subject. Stalin argued the right of nationalities occupying contiguous territory to their own language but condemned too much decentralization as unsuited for a modern industrial state. This view foreshadowed future Communist policy: the promise of cultural autonomy behind which was political centralization and rule by the Party. By the time the essay was published, however, Stalin was again under arrest and remained in Siberian exile until the overthrow of the czar in March, 1917.

*Life's Work*

Stalin's considerable organizational skills and willingness to take on seemingly onerous desk jobs resulted in his appointment to a number of important Party offices. Between 1917 and 1922, he served as a member of the Bolshevik General Staff and Central Committee Politburo, and as Commissar of Nationalities, Commissar of the Army, director of the Workers' and Peasants' Inspectorate, and member of the government's organizational bureau. Yet his most important office was to be general secretary of the Communist Party, a post to which he was appointed in 1922 and from which he would eventually control the Party and the nation.

By the time of Lenin's death in 1924, Stalin had emerged as a major rival for power. Using his numerous political skills through his Party and government offices, he was by 1929 the undisputed leader of the Soviet Union. This power struggle was hidden behind numerous policy debates concerning the future of the socialist state. Stalin supported the concept of "socialism in one country," arguing that the Soviet Union, surrounded by hostile capitalist nations, needed to defend the revolutionary base and become the model for future socialist societies. This was his most important contribution to Marxist-Leninist theory and provided the ideological framework for his future transformation of the Soviet Union. Beginning in 1929, he began the struggle to create a socialist society in a backward agrarian country and carried it out in the face of massive popular opposition, forcibly changing the lives of millions of people, and thrusting the Soviet Union into the forefront in international leadership.

First, Stalin called for collectivization of agriculture in order for the state to gain control of the grain supply, the Soviet Union's major export item. When the peasantry resisted, Stalin unleashed the full coercive apparatus of the state, resulting in open warfare in the countryside. Party members, city workers, and police and army units were all mobilized. Faced with the loss of their homes and land, the peasants fought back by burning their crops and slaughtering their livestock, but in the end Stalin won. Those peasants who survived were banished to Siberia or dispatched to the numerous forced labor camps. By 1936 more than 90 percent of Soviet peasant households were forced to live and work on closely supervised collective or state farms.

The destruction wrought by the peasants in their struggle with the Soviet state had lasting repercussions for the rural economy. One of the main justifications for collectivization was replacement of the old-fashioned, unmechanized, individually managed peasant farm with a centralized, highly mechanized agricultural system worked by a collectivized peasantry. This new system was to produce the grain necessary to finance the purchase abroad of the heavy machinery needed for the massive industrialization effort going on at the same time. Because of the tragic nature of the collectivization process, this goal was never achieved. Instead, the Soviet people paid for industrialization through personal sacrifice, increasing regimentation, and a lower standard of living.

Collectivization was a part of the First Five-Year Plan, which called for a massive drive that would increase overall industrial production by some 250 percent, with heavy industry increasing by 330 percent. Such figures implied a social change of unimaginable scope. In actuality the plan was meant to outline and control massive changes in all aspects of the economy and society, and Stalin and his supporters in the Party could not foresee the ramifications of such a plan. Between 1928 and 1932, heavy industry more than doubled. Still, Stalin kept urging an ever more accelerated tempo. Under this kind of prodding, fulfillment of quotas became more important than quality of product. Those enterprises achieving their targets were given new and higher ones. In such an environment, force and compulsion became the rule of both industry and agriculture as the entire society was whipped forward by the general secretary.

Such a social transformation created enormous pressures. From 1929 to 1933, the urban population increased from some twenty-seven million to more than forty million, straining city services to the breaking point. The harshness of life in the city, coupled with the forced collectivization of the countryside, gave rise to various kinds of opposition. To combat this, the coercive arm of the state expanded, both through the power of the police and through Party control over all social institutions. When opposition appeared within the Party itself, the ever-suspicious Stalin unleashed the terror of the mid- and late-1930's.

While collectivization and industrialization changed the economic base of the Soviet Union, the terror transformed society. Party members associated with Lenin were purged from the ranks, and many were later executed. The terror struck the ordinary Soviet citizen as well, however, as it did all institutions of society. More than eight million people were arrested, tortured, and sentenced to hard labor as they were terrorized into sullen submission to the will of the leader.

While the 1930's witnessed the transformation of the Soviet Union from a weak, agrarian, underdeveloped state into an industrialized, collectivized, socialist giant, the 1940's would make the Soviet Union into a world power. First, however, it had to withstand military invasion by Nazi Germany. The ensuing struggle was of titanic proportions within the larger framework of World War II. By May, 1945, however, Soviet troops were in Berlin, and the Red Army had liberated most of the German-occupied countries of Eastern Europe.

With the end of the war, the Soviet Union faced a massive rebuilding effort. Now an increasingly irrational and suspicious man, Stalin reinstituted the five-year plans and recollectivized agriculture in those areas that had been under German control, all accompanied by the omniscient terror. By the end of his life, Stalin ruled over a massive socialist empire that extended beyond its European frontier into the satellite states of Poland, Romania, Bulgaria, Czechoslovakia, Hungary, and East Germany. The Soviet Union had become the main actor with the United States in a bipolar world. When Stalin died on March 5, 1953, he left a powerful but morally and physically exhausted state.

*Summary*

The language used by Joseph Stalin was, as that of Lenin before him, the language of Karl Marx. They were after the same goal, a communist society in which the basic goods and services would be available to all without exploitation by one dominant class. Marx talked about achieving this through the working out of economic laws. Yet Stalin inherited from Lenin a Soviet Union still in the first stages of industrialization and surrounded by much more advanced economic societies. Therefore, Stalin accelerated the pace of industrial development in the Soviet Union via a series of five-year plans forced upon a reluctant society through the use of police terror. In agriculture he forced the peasants onto collective farms, which, like the urban factories, were controlled and run by the Party leadership in far-off Moscow. Where Marx emphasized the forces of history to construct communism, Stalin emphasized the political will of the Party.

While Stalin's industrialization effort in the building of socialism did make the Soviet Union a major superpower in the wake of World War II, it was accomplished at incredible sacrifice on the part of the Soviet people. In one generation, despite a devastating war, the Soviet Union increased its overall production fourfold and heavy industry ninefold. The methods used, however, were those that echoed Russia's autocratic past from Ivan the Terrible to Peter the Great.

*Bibliography*

Adams, Arthur E. *Stalin and His Times*. New York: Holt, Rinehart and Winston, 1972. A readable history of the Soviet Union during the time of Stalin, meant for the general reader already familiar with the basic outlines of twentieth century history. Helps in understanding why Stalin was successful in achieving his objectives.

Conquest, Robert. *The Great Terror: Stalin's Purges of the Thirties*. London: Macmillan, 1968. A thorough and very detailed analysis of the purges and terror through which Stalin came to dominate and mold the Communist Party and Soviet society. Discusses the means by which the terror was accomplished and the reasons Stalin believed it was necessary.

Deutscher, Isaac. *Stalin: A Political Biography.* 2d ed. New York: Oxford University Press, 1967. This has become a classic biography, although dated. Emphasis is on Stalin's political skills in rising to the top of the Communist Party, especially the reasons behind his victory in the power struggle after Lenin's death.

McNeal, Robert H. *Stalin: Man and Ruler.* New York: New York University Press, 1988. A solid and well-written biography by a longtime specialist in the field. By examining the known available source material, McNeal attempts to evaluate Stalin's contribution to Soviet history from the perspective of the late twentieth century.

Tucker, Robert C. *Stalin as Revolutionary, 1879-1929.* New York: W. W. Norton, 1973. The first of a projected two-volume biography by a well-known expert in the field. This volume, spanning the first fifty years of Stalin's life, attempts to analyze those ingredients in his formative years that eventually created a dictator.

Ulam, Adam B. *Stalin: The Man and His Era.* New York: Viking Press, 1973. A thorough, well-written biographical study by a noted Sovietologist, this work examines Stalin's life against a larger world background. Includes an excellent treatment of the development of the terror as a technique of government.

Wolfe, Bertram D. *Three Who Made a Revolution.* 4th rev. ed. New York: Dial, 1964. This is a classic study of the lives of Lenin, Leon Trotsky, and Stalin, and an excellent introduction to the subject of Soviet history. Its emphasis is on the formative years of Russian Marxism up to the 1917 Revolution.

*Jack M. Lauber*

# KONSTANTIN STANISLAVSKY
## Konstantin Sergeyevich Alekseyev

*Born:* January 17, 1863; Moscow, Russia
*Died:* August 7, 1938; Moscow, U.S.S.R.
*Areas of Achievement:* Theater and acting
*Contribution:* The founder (with Vladimir Nemirovich-Danchenko) of the Moscow Art Theater, director of the plays of Anton Chekhov, and writer of the most influential acting lessons in modern times, Stanislavsky is the father of modern acting techniques; all modern actors, directors, and acting schools owe a great debt to Stanislavsky's methods, which revolutionized the theater in the early twentieth century.

### *Early Life*

Born Konstantin Sergeyevich Alekseyev, into an affluent and cultured Russian family, Stanislavsky participated in amateur dramatic entertainments at his family's estate from a very early age, putting on small plays and musical pieces with his brothers and sisters, for family guests. The Alekseyev Circle, a group of amateur players largely recruited from Stanislavsky's immediate family, provided not only the entertainments for his parents and friends but also the first school of dramatic theory for young Stanislavsky. As visiting actors from Moscow and from foreign companies visited the country estate and participated in the productions (sometimes only as audience members), Stanislavsky gleaned more and more about their techniques for creating and sustaining stage characters. Their criticism after performance, whether positive or negative, helped Stanislavsky gradually form an idea about how to approach the actor's art.

This combination of experiences was to feed him as he moved from family entertainment to amateur acting in other parts of Russia. His merchant "aristocracy" prevented his turning professional, but the amateur status did not deter him from playing important roles in major professional productions in his early life. It was necessary for Stanislavsky to assume a stage name to avoid embarrassment to his family; the profession of actor was held in low esteem in this period, especially in contrast to the prestige his father enjoyed as owner of a gold- and silver-thread manufacturing company.

A unique combination of happenstances and personal traits was to lead to the wide-ranging and even more widely accepted "method" of acting that Stanislavsky left as his heritage. His impressionable temperament, together with his absolutely ruthless ability to examine his own imperfections, caused him to examine in close study every actor he saw on stage or in society. He copied the external features of their acting styles and at the same time struggled with his external discipline to achieve the characterizations he saw and admired on stage. Rather than compromising his standards or causing him to give up, each frustrated attempt prodded Stanislavsky to try harder and harder to reconcile all the disparate influences bombarding him. Further, being of independent means, he did not have the economic burden of self-sustenance that plagues so many theater figures.

Stanislavsky's first experiments with acting styles, as well as the forming and running of his first acting companies, have been well documented, especially in his own autobiography, *My Life in Art* (1924), more an explanation of his theater philosophies than a personal memoir. Subsequent biographers have traced every detail of Stanislavsky's early roles, the development of his talent and skills, and the reaction of audiences (often friends and family members) who saw him emerge as one of Moscow's finest actors, amateur or professional.

One of the most influential factors in his development was the Meiningen Players (whose 1890 tour Stanislavsky saw), a German acting company, from whom Stanislavsky learned the power of crowd scenes, the importance of overall mood, and the value of a rigid discipline among the actors. He quickly was to refine his own ideas, however, past the militaristic limitations of the company's regisseur, Ludwig Kronegk.

*Life's Work*

Stanislavsky's work truly began with the formation of the Moscow Art Theater in 1898, with Vladimir Nemirovich-Danchenko, a literary figure and regisseur already enjoying Moscow success. That partnership began on June 22, 1897, after a now-famous eighteen-hour marathon discussion of the principles of the ideal theater. The division of labor was interesting—Stanislavsky was to deal with the artistic considerations while Nemirovich-Danchenko would be the businessman and the literary adviser (the term "dramaturge" expresses his contributions well). More accurately, each man had veto power in his particular area, but their work was a cooperative collaboration from the start. For Stanislavsky, it was the culmination of several earlier attempts at producing and honing his skills as "director," a term not fully in use at that time.

The Moscow Art Theater was propelled by the combined efforts of these two men of the theater and one great Russian writer. The playwright whose name was to be permanently linked with the Moscow Art Theater was Anton Chekhov, already a successful short-story writer and medical doctor. His plays, only five in number but central to modern drama from his time on, were produced at the Moscow Art Theater in a way that demonstrated Stanislavsky's approach to theater production and the new realistic acting style that was to become his trademark.

It was the Moscow Art Theater's production in 1898 of Chekhov's *Chayka* (1896; *The Sea Gull*, 1909) that marked the beginning of its successful relationship with the playwright. This production was the second one for the play; it had failed in St. Petersburg when a talented but misguided group of professionals tried to find its essence without understanding that this new kind of writing called for a new kind of acting. The Moscow Art Theater's production, which did in fact combine the realistic acting style with the new play script, was moderately successful, but the marriage of literary idea and theatrical realization was so ideal that the theater took the seagull as its insignia. To this day, the stylized seagull figure from the first production flies on the flag over the theater. Subsequent productions of Chekhov's plays, notably *Dyadya Vanya* (1897; *Uncle Vanya*, 1914) in 1899, *Tri Sestry* (*Three Sisters*, 1920) in 1901, and *Vishnyovy sad* (*The Cherry Orchard*, 1908) in 1904, were unqualified critical successes.

Stanislavsky's international popularity was determined by the many visitors to Moscow who saw and were astounded by his theater accomplishments. When the company toured (to Germany in 1906, and to the United States in 1922), an even larger audience appreciated the care, attention to detail, absolute discipline, and intelligence of the productions.

Stanislavsky's accomplishments with the Moscow Art Theater and Chekhov would have ensured him an international reputation all by themselves, even without his subsequent accomplishments with acting style, developed and practiced on stage, in rehearsals, and in the studios and classrooms of the theater. This style, actually a system of preparation, development, and performance, is usually referred to simply as The System (not to be confused with its American offshoot, "The Method"). It was designed gradually over the full length of Stanislavsky's career; he constantly rethought, revised, and upgraded his ideas, working in notebooks.

His complete works, published in many volumes in Russian, have come to English-speaking audiences in bits and pieces, not necessarily in the order of their composition but roughly in the order of their intended application by the individual actor. In their first English edition, they are *An Actor Prepares* (1936), *Building a Character* (1949), *Stanislavski's Legacy* (1958), and *Creating a Role* (1961). This series of theoretical speculations, illustrated and demonstrated out of Stanislavsky's own theater experiences, is considered a must-read for all modern actors. The books deal with each distinct step in the actor's art: preparing one's body, voice, and mind for roles in general, constructing a characterization from the clues of the text, and working in an actual production. Together with his analytical mid-life autobiography, *My Life in Art*, these books constitute the "bible" of acting the Stanislavsky System.

The American tour marked a major schism in the Moscow Art Theater that was not so much artistic as it was geographic. Some of Stanislavsky's best actors chose to stay behind and open schools of acting and directing in New York. As a result, a second and third generation of Stanislavsky's ideas were spread by his own students, who naturally altered the basic principles with refinements of their own, sometimes adding a vocabulary that clarified for some and obfuscated for others the original intent of the acting system Stanislavsky propounded.

Stanislavsky ended his own acting career in 1928 but actively continued to revise his theories right up to his death in 1938. Near his death, he had been discussing ideas with one of his students, Vsevolod Meyerhold, whose earlier experiments with expressionist stage techniques had temporarily estranged him from his teacher. On the day Stanislavsky died, his thoughts were on Nemirovich-Danchenko, also estranged from him over aesthetic differences. Despite these differences, Stanislavsky was deeply respected by all of his peers for his monumental contributions to and love of his art and his uncompromising zeal for truth in the theater.

*Summary*

Today's acting teachers can trace a direct line through the American acting schools and companies such as the Actor's Studio and the Group Theatre, through the Russian students of Konstantin Stanislavsky such as Michael Chekhov (Anton Chekhov's nephew) and Richard Boleslavsky, back to the Moscow Art Theater's American and European tours of that period. N. M. Gorchakov took elaborate notes of Stanislavsky's directing methods at the height of his powers; these, too, are studied by today's student directors and teachers, whose mentors in turn, such as Elia Kazan and Lee Strasberg, owe a great debt to their exposure to the Moscow Art Theater.

The Stanislavsky heritage, as Christine Edwards describes it in her book of that name, is the belief "that the actor must experience real emotion, that he must identify with the character he is portraying, that he may use his own past emotional experiences, and above all, that he must learn to speak and behave naturally, as a human being in life." The fact that it is inconceivable to challenge such a statement today is convincing testament to the ubiquitous influence of Stanislavsky on modern theater.

*Bibliography*

Benedetti, Jean. *Stanislavski: A Biography.* New York: Routledge, Chapman & Hall, 1988. An updated version of the standard biography by David Magarshack (see below), this study offers new translations of new letters and documents. It follows Magarshack's work a little too closely, reworking his anecdotes in several places. Contains twenty-nine illustrations (mostly production stills and portraits in character), a select bibliography, a chronology of roles and productions, and an index.

__________. *Stanislavski: An Introduction.* New York: Theatre Arts Books, 1982. A slim, handy introduction to "The System," weaving biographical material into an explanation of how the system functions. Of value to the actor looking for an entry into the complexities of the multivolume work of Stanislavsky himself. Includes a chronology, an index, and a list of topics discussed in the text.

Edwards, Christine. *The Stanislavsky Heritage: Its Contribution to the Russian and American Theatre*. New York: New York University Press, 1965. Puts Stanislavsky's work in the context of two important movements: traditional Russian stage practice and the emerging and developing American theater in the first half of the twentieth century. The very considerable influence of The System on the American "method" is well chronicled here. Includes a bibliography, an appendix, and an index.

Magarshack, David. *Stanislavsky: A Life*. London: Macgibbon & Kee, 1950. Still the authoritative study, not only of Stanislavsky but also of the theater itself; contains a good balance of personal and professional information and is careful in the details of production. Particularly valuable is the discussion of how Stanislavsky gradually found the vocabulary to express and teach his acting system. Includes twenty illustrations and an index.

Nemirovich-Danchenko, Vladimir. *My Life in the Russian Theatre*. Translated by John Cournos. New York: Theatre Arts Books, 1968. Stanislavsky always insisted that the Moscow Art Theater was founded by both him and Nemirovich-Danchenko. This autobiography puts the dramaturge's experiences in the context of a longer, more varied career. Literary and sophisticated compared to Stanislavsky's autobiography.

Sayler, Oliver M. *Inside the Moscow Art Theater*. Reprint. Westport, Conn.: Greenwood Press, 1970. This study was conducted during the height of Stanislavsky's success and after two American tours. Following a preliminary chapter on the effect of these tours on the temperament of the company, Sayler offers the most complete and respectful record in print of the theater's accomplishments. Full informative photographs and illustrations throughout, including marvelous portraits of leading actors, valuable production stills, a flow chart of the management, and an index.

Senelick, Laurence. *Gordon Craig's Moscow Hamlet: A Reconstruction*. Westport, Conn.: Greenwood Press, 1982. A book-length examination of the monumental production at the Moscow Art Theater in 1912, in which Stanislavsky and Edward Gordon Craig, two geniuses of the modern theater, met and worked together in what should have been but could never be the ideal collaboration. An excellent way to understand Stanislavsky's way of working on classics. Includes illustrations, two appendices, notes, a bibliography, and an index.

Wiles, Timothy J. *The Theater Event: Modern Theories of Performance*. Chicago: University of Chicago Press, 1980. One-third of this important study of modern performance theories is dedicated to Stanislavsky, especially his work on Chekhov's *The Three Sisters*. Examines the common ground between Stanislavsky's system and Chekhov's intentions; Wiles believes Chekhov may have feared that the Moscow Art Theater and

Stanislavsky "constantly misinterpreted" his plays, turning his comedies into tragedies.

*Thomas J. Taylor*

# JOHANNES STARK

*Born:* April 15, 1874; Schickenhof, Germany
*Died:* June 21, 1957; Traunstein, West Germany
*Area of Achievement:* Physics
*Contribution:* Stark's detection of the Doppler effect in a terrestrially generated light source led to his discovery that a strong electric field will split the spectral lines of chemical elements. Stark's experiments provided confirmation of Albert Einstein's special theory of relativity and evidence for the controversial quantum theories of Max Planck.

## *Early Life*

Johannes Stark was born in Schickenhof on April 15, 1874. His father was a landed proprietor, as was his maternal grandfather. The young Stark demonstrated early scholarly promise and eventually attended the *Gymnasiums* of Bayreuth and Regensburg before entering the University of Munich in 1894. After studying chemistry, crystallography, mathematics, and physics courses for three years, he received his doctorate for a dissertation entitled *Untersuchung über Russ* (1897; investigations into lampblack). Stark successfully completed the state examinations required for teaching higher mathematics in 1897 and assumed the post of assistant to Eugen Lommel of the Physical Institute at the University of Munich in October of that year. Shortly thereafter, he married Luise Uepler, who eventually bore him five children.

In 1900, Stark became a privatdocent at the University of Göttingen, the beginning of a tumultuous career in higher education that lasted until 1922. Stark never got on well with his coworkers or superiors, which led to frequent moves from one university to another. In 1906, he received an appointment as professor extraordinary at the Technical High School in Hannover, where he incurred the enmity of his immediate superior, Julens Precht, who eventually managed to have Stark transferred to Griefswald in 1907 and to Aachen in 1909. In 1917, Stark returned to Griefswald as a full professor. Two years later, he took a similar position at the University of Würzburg, where he remained until 1922, when he resigned and left academia permanently.

## *Life's Work*

Stark's productive career spanned approximately the years 1902-1928. After 1920, he became increasingly involved in what might be called the racial politics of German science, a matter in which he had already become bitterly embroiled during his earlier years.

Stark's most important work involved the electrical conduction in gases, which was the subject of his first published book, *Die Elektrizität in Gasen* (1902). Stark's discoveries were based on the Doppler effect. Johann

Doppler predicted as early as 1842 that a luminous object moving toward a stationary observer would appear to be a different color than the color the same object would appear to be if it were moving away from the observer. Doppler theorized that all stars emit neutral or white light and that their apparent colors to an earthly observer are caused by their relative velocities toward or away from the earth. Doppler's theory was modified in 1845 and again in 1848 by other physicists and finally confirmed in 1870 with advances in spectroscopy.

It was not possible to detect the Doppler effect with any sources of light generated on Earth until the twentieth century, because no earthly light source could attain sufficient velocity. In his 1902 book, Stark correctly predicted that the Doppler effect might be observed in canal rays. Eugen Goldstein discovered in 1896 that, by placing the cathode in a cathode ray tube in such a way that it divides the tube into two equal parts and then piercing the cathode with a number of holes, one can observe many bright-colored rays traveling in straight lines and entering the space behind the cathode through the holes. Goldstein named these rays *Kanalstrahlen*, or canal rays.

A number of physicists subjected these canal rays to intense investigation in the early part of the twentieth century, but it fell to Stark to demonstrate the Doppler effect in canal rays in an ingenious experiment which showed it in the hydrogen lines. Stark immediately proposed his experiment as a proof of Einstein's then-new (1906) theory of special relativity and a year later as evidence for quantum theory. In 1904, Stark had founded the *Jahrbuch der Radioaktivität und Elektronik*, a scientific journal which he edited until 1913. In 1907, he became the first editor to request an article from Albert Einstein concerning relativity. In 1907, he also proposed that his experiments furnished proof of Planck's quantum theories. He was thus in the forefront of what he later contemptuously dismissed as "Jewish physics," where he remained a champion of the new hypotheses until 1913. In that year, his animosity toward Jews increased to grotesque proportions, a result in part of personal rivalries and professional jealousy.

From 1913 until his death, Stark opposed what he perceived to be the pernicious Jewish influence in science which perverted and debilitated the discoveries and course of so-called Germanic science. After 1913, he vitriolically denounced quantum theory, the special theory of relativity, and the Jewish champions of those theories from every forum to which he had access. His reactionary position regarding the new physics and his open Judeophobia combined to make for him many enemies in German academia and ultimately led to denial of his becoming a member of the two most prestigious scientific organizations in Germany and to his first retirement in 1922.

Despite his racial philosophy, Stark was accorded many honors in the international scientific community. He was awarded the Baumgartner Prize by the Vienna Academy of Sciences in 1910, and in 1914 won both the Vahlbruch Prize of the Göttingen Academy of Sciences and the Matteucci Medal of the Rome Academy. In 1919, he was honored with the Nobel Prize in Physics. Of all the recipients of the Nobel Prize, Stark was undoubtedly the most ignored by the world media and the international scientific community, which only confirmed him in his growing Judeophobia. In 1922, he resigned his university post in disgust at what he perceived to be the growing Jewish dominance in German academic life and retired to the area in which he was born to pursue private research.

His last important scientific work, *Atomstruktur und Atombindung*, appeared in 1928. The book confirmed the Judeophobic stand that had made him unpopular with many of his colleagues and had forced his retirement. Stark would almost certainly have remained in an obscure retirement and would have had no more impact on German science after 1922 had circumstances not brought Adolf Hitler to power in 1933.

The Nazis brought Stark out of retirement and appointed him president of the Physikalisch-Technische Reichsanwalt on April 1, 1933. This position gave him considerable influence over appointments to academic positions in German universities and the allocation of research funds. His enemies within the academy nevertheless prevented his election as president of the German Physics Association that year and prevented his gaining membership in the prestigious Prussian Academy the next. In June, 1934, however, the Nazis appointed Stark president of the German Research Association. His two presidencies and the concurrent passage of the so-called Nuremberg Laws allowed Stark to exercise enormous influence on the course of physics research and teaching in Germany. The Nuremburg Laws established that only "Aryans" were citizens of the Reich, and that a noncitizen could not hold a government post. Since professors were government employees, the laws gave Stark legal authority to purge the German universities of most Jewish professors. A few "non-Aryans" were able to keep their jobs because of stipulations in the laws that those noncitizen government employees who had served honorably on the front lines during the war or whose fathers had died in that war could retain their posts.

After the outbreak of widespread anti-Jewish violence in Germany on the *Kristallnacht* in 1938, Stark was able to retire the remaining Jewish professors supposedly for their own protection. In 1938-1939, he waged a heated campaign against what he called the "viceroys of the Einsteinian spirit," the "white Jews of science," and their continued championing of the new physics. Stark's definition of Jewish physics was an "un-German" predilection for theory over experiment. He was never able to remove all of his opponents from their positions, but he did much to retard the acceptance of theories which contained within them the seeds of the atom bomb.

Stark was instrumental in the exodus to the United States of the German physicists, both gentile and Jewish, who provided invaluable aid to the Allies during World War II toward the development of the first atom bomb in 1945. Concurrently, he was more than somewhat responsible for the failure of German physicists to supply that same weapon to Hitler, although that surely was not his intention.

Several influential German physicists opposed Stark's attacks against other scientists to the point that he was obliged to retire again from public life in 1939. In 1947, Stark stood trial before a denazification court for his activities on behalf of the Third Reich and his attacks on Jewish academics. The court found him guilty and sentenced him to four years in a labor camp. Stark served the entire term despite his advanced years. He died at his home in Traunstein on June 21, 1957.

### *Summary*

Johannes Stark's formidable accomplishments as a scientist have been greatly overshadowed by the ignominy attached to his name by his affiliations with the Nazis. He exerted a considerable positive influence on physics during his early years but an even greater negative influence later in his life. From 1900 to 1913, he was in the vanguard of the new physics. His championing of the theories of Einstein, Planck, and others was a powerful force in the international acceptance of those ideas. His own experiments provided much of the practical underpinnings which validated the theoretical work of the men who laid the foundations for modern physics. Even though the Stark effect is considered of comparatively little practical value by contemporary physicists in the analyses of complex spectra or atomic structure, it nevertheless represents a milestone in atomic research. Unfortunately, he is best remembered not for these accomplishments but for his political activities.

Stark will be remembered most vividly as the Nazis' "tame physicist," as a victim or a harbinger of the ideology that swept his country and the world into a holocaust of previously unimaginable proportions.

### *Bibliography*

Beyerchen, Alan D. *Scientists Under Hitler: Politics and the Physics Community in the Third Reich.* New Haven, Conn.: Yale University Press, 1977. Beyerchen's book virtually ignores Stark's early contributions to science, concentrating instead on his support for Hitler and the Nazi movement and his attacks on non-Aryan physics. Beyerchen's accounts of Stark's feud with Einstein, of his efforts to cleanse German physics of Jewish influence, and of the consequences of those efforts are the most complete available in English.

Cohen, I. Bernard. *Revolution in Science.* Cambridge, Mass.: Harvard University Press, 1985. Cohen's book is a literate and compelling history of science centered on the theme of scientific revolutions that have often mirrored political and social revolution. Cohen evaluates Stark's contribution to modern physics and places him squarely in the camp of scientific reactionaries.

Hartshorne, Edward Yarnall, Jr. *The German Universities and National Socialism*. London: Allen & Unwin, 1937. This book, written during the period when Stark was attempting to purge German physics of Jewish influence, is of interest because it contains an English translation of parts of an address delivered by Stark at the University of Heidelberg in 1935. The address includes an attack on the Jewish Einsteinian influence in German physics, which was still being championed by some German scientists, notably Max von Laue, Max Planck, and Werner Heisenberg, all Nobel laureates in their own right and old enemies of Stark.

Heathcote, Niels Hugh de Vaudrey. *Nobel Prize Winners in Physics, 1901-1950*. Reprint. Freeport, N.Y.: Books for Libraries Press, 1971. Heathcote accords Stark only seven pages in his account of the first fifty Nobel laureates in physics, one of the shortest entries. In the biographical sketch that introduces each laureate, there is no mention of Stark's Nazi affiliations, nor is there any reference to the books Stark wrote defining and contrasting German and Jewish physics.

Hermann, Armin. "Johannes Stark." In *Dictionary of Scientific Biography*, edited by Charles Coulston Gillispie, vol. 11. New York: Charles Scribner's Sons, 1975. Hermann's brief sketch of Stark's career includes a considerable amount of information concerning the many feuds between Stark and his contemporaries in the scientific community, both in Germany and around the world. He explains Stark's complete reversal of position concerning the theory of relativity, not as a result of his Judeophobia but of his compulsion always to oppose the accepted point of view.

MacDonald, James Keene Lorne. *Stark-Effect in Molecular Hydrogen in the Range of 4100-4700 A*. Montreal: McGill University Publications, 1931. MacDonald's discussion of the Stark effect is much too technical for all but those with an advanced knowledge of physics. It does contain some biographical details about Stark and the research that led to his discovery of the Stark effect.

*Paul Madden*

# HERMANN STAUDINGER

*Born:* March 23, 1881; Worms, Germany
*Died:* September 8, 1965; Freiburg im Breisgau, West Germany
*Area of Achievement:* Chemistry
*Contribution:* Staudinger became the father of a novel branch of chemistry when he conceived of and proved the existence of macromolecules. This work laid the foundation for the technological achievements in the plastics and high polymer synthetics industries. In addition, Staudinger contributed to the fields of organic chemistry and molecular biology.

## *Early Life*

Hermann Staudinger, the winner of the 1953 Nobel Prize in Chemistry, was born in Worms, Germany (modern West Germany) in 1881. He was the son of Auguste Staudinger and Franz Staudinger, a neo-Kantian philosopher. Staudinger's primary education took place at a local *Gymnasium* in Worms from which he was graduated in 1899. When he began his secondary education at the University of Halle, he was interested in botany; however, he switched his major to chemistry upon the advice of his father, who had been told that his son must first master the basic principles of science to understand plant life adequately. This interest in botany remained throughout his life and surfaced in his later work. Almost immediately, he transferred to Darmstadt after his father was appointed to a teaching position there. Staudinger pursued advanced studies at Munich (briefly) and at Halle, where he wrote his dissertation on the malonic esters of unsaturated compounds under the direction of Daniel Vorlander. He received his Ph.D. in organic chemistry on August 3, 1903.

Staudinger continued his research at the University of Strasbourg to obtain his teaching qualification, which he received in 1907. It was at Strasbourg, working under Johannes Thiele, that Staudinger made his first important discovery, the ketene, a highly reactive unsaturated form of ketone. Having earned his teaching qualification, he became an assistant professor at the Technische Hochschule in Karlsruhe, where he remained until 1912, when he succeeded Nobel laureate Richard Willstätter at the Eidgenossische Technische Hochschule in Zurich. Because of the shortages of World War I, Staudinger's work at Karlsruhe and Zurich kept very much in touch with the needs of industry and Germany. Staudinger worked on the synthesis of rubber and, with his student, Leopold Ružička, studied the composition of the insecticide pyrethrin and developed an artificial pepper. With the help of another student, Tadeusz Reichstein, Staudinger succeeded in synthesizing the aroma of coffee, a commodity cut off from wartime Germany. Yet Staudinger's main thrust of research during these early years remained the study of ketenes, about which he published *Die Ketene* (1912), a book which is still considered a standard. In 1926, Staudinger left Zurich to accept a position as a lecturer of chemistry at the University of Freiburg im Breisgau, where he remained until his retirement in 1951.

In 1927, Staudinger married Magda Woit, a Latvian plant physiologist, with whom he coauthored many papers. They had no children.

*Life's Work*

Staudinger, educator, author, inventor, and researcher, made his greatest contribution to science by enunciating and proving the macromolecular theory, which states that rubber, plastics, and similar substances (polymers) are composed of long chain molecules having hundreds of repeating units connected by primary covalent bonds. For these molecules, which can have indefinitely large molecular weights, Staudinger coined the term "macromolecule."

Prior to 1920, the relatively insoluble, uncharacterizable resinous substances which organic chemists frequently found on the bottom of their reaction flasks were an enigma, although they were suspected to be polymeric (having chains composed of repeating units) in nature. This group of substances, of which rubber is a member, displays a nonlinear relationship between viscosity and concentration, nonstoichiometry, an inability to crystallize and in general a failure to adhere to the same physical laws as conventional molecules.

There were two prevailing theories at the time, the most popular of which was the micellar theory of the German chemist Carl Harries, who believed that these substances were physical aggregates of low-molecular-weight polymers held together by weak residual forces, and the theory of Samuel Pickles, who believed that the substances were composed of long chain molecules held together by primary chemical bonds. In 1910, while working under Carl Engler at Karlsruhe, Staudinger discovered a new way to synthesize isoprene, the structural unit of synthetic rubber, and was thereby introduced to this controversy. Harries thought that the weak secondary forces which held the isoprene rings of rubber together arose from their unsaturated double bonds, so Staudinger devised an experiment to test this theory. Harries predicted that removal of the double bonds by hydrogenation would restore the native, conventional properties of these molecules, causing them to form liquid hydrocarbons, but a series of experiments carried out in 1922 by Staudinger gave no such results. Staudinger's saturated synthetic hydrorubbers were nondistillable, colloidal, and differed little from natural rubber. It was this experiment which caused him to embark on an ambitious new area of research to prove his macromolecular theory.

In an attempt to avoid the experimental difficulties associated with natural polymers, Staudinger, in the early 1920's, chose to extend his studies to the polymers of styrene and oxymethylene (the solid form of the preservative formalin), synthetic models of rubber and cellulose, respectively. The physical properties of the homologous series of paraffin waxes, long chain hydrocarbons having the general formula $C_nH_{2n+2}$, vary with chain length. Staudinger, recognizing that styrene behaves in a similar manner to these paraffins, came to the conclusion that polystyrene is also one member of a homologous series, the properties of which depend on the average chain length.

This inspiration led Staudinger to engage in a series of experiments to measure the viscosity of polymers, a technique well established as being sensitive to the molecular weight of small molecules. In this work, Staudinger indeed found a direct correlation between the viscosity and the length of the polystyrene samples from which he was able to calculate the molecular weight of the polymer molecule. The results indicated an extremely large chain, which was presented as strong evidence for his macromolecular concept. This work, as well as his hydrogenation experiments, were published in his classic book *Die hochmolekularen organischen Verbindungen, Kautschuk und Cellulose* (1932; the high-molecular organic compounds, rubber and cellulose).

Staudinger presented his results on three important occasions from 1924 to 1926, but they were not well received. Especially the last two times, at the meeting of the Zurich Chemical Society and the Düsseldorf meeting of the Association of German Natural Scientists and Physicians, Staudinger encountered vigorous opposition from the proponents of the micellar aggregate theory. In fact, Staudinger once stated that he only convinced one person at the Düsseldorf meeting, Richard Willstätter. They did not believe that Staudinger's viscosity measurements were a reliable indicator of molecular weight but thought rather that his results reflected a state of aggregation of numerous molecules. Furthermore, the well-respected mineralogist Paul Niggli insisted that a molecule with dimensions larger than the unit cell obtained by X-ray diffraction could not exist. The scientific community would not be convinced of the existence of macromolecules unless they could be sure that Staudinger was looking at a pure sample instead of an aggregate of many molecules.

At this point, some events began to turn in Staudinger's favor. Toward the end of the 1920's, Theodor Svedberg and Robin Fåhraeus conducted experiments to measure the equilibrium sedimentation of oxyhemoglobin and carbonylhemoglobin using an ultracentrifuge, a powerful new tool for determining molecular weights. From these experiments, hemoglobin was found to have a very high molecular weight of about sixty-five thousand, four times higher than that given from elementary analysis. Furthermore, this was a sharply defined molecular weight, without the spread that would be expected if hemoglobin were an aggregate. The recognition of a high-molecular-weight compound in protein chemistry by an independent method lent welcome support to Staudinger's macromolecular theory.

Staudinger hoped to measure the molecular weight of synthetic and natural polymers by this method, so he applied for a grant to purchase an ultracentrifuge for Freiburg. His grant was turned down, however, a reminder of the skepticism Staudinger and his concepts endured. In a fit of depression over this event, Staudinger turned again to viscosity measurements and in 1929, working with two students, R. Nodzu and E. Ochiai, he showed that for linear molecules the viscosity of their solutions is proportional to the number of residues in the chain. This relationship between the specific viscosity and the molecular weight is known as Staudinger's law and is widely used in industry wherever there is polymer research in progress.

Finally, other evidence emerged to support the existence of macromolecules. Flow birefringence experiments conducted by R. Signer showed that polymers in solution had very large length to breadth ratios; the American chemist W. H. Carothers succeeded in synthesizing nylon by a condensation polymerization reaction which liberated an amount of water equal to the number of residues in the product; and X-ray crystallographers at last realized that a molecule could be larger than the unit cell. With this work accomplished, Staudinger was finally able to concentrate on his first love, biology, for which he had been preparing himself for thirty years.

Staudinger's youthful interest in biology emerged in 1926, when he began studies on the structure and function of macromolecular compounds in living systems. At a lecture delivered in Munich in 1936, Staudinger stated, "Every gene macromolecule possesses a quite definite structural plan, which determines its function in life." This statement was perceptive in the light of the fact that the genetic code was not understood until 1953. Some of Staudinger's ideas in biology were simplistic, however, and he clearly lacked a strong understanding of biological concepts. For example, he took the macromolecular concept to an extreme when he calculated the molecular weight of a bacterium. In 1947, Staudinger published *Makromolekulare Chemie und Biologie*, which gives his view of future developments in molecular biology.

With the help of his wife, Magda, Staudinger spent the last part of his career working on biologically related topics and using the phase-contrast microscope to visualize macromolecules. This work ended when Freiburg was bombed in 1944 during World War II. Staudinger's energies had been spent by this time and he retired in 1951. Staudinger died of a heart condition at the age of eighty-four.

### *Summary*

By the time Hermann Staudinger began his work on macromolecules, he was already forty and had a considerable reputation as an organic chemist. Indeed, his colleagues could not understand why a man of his stature would want to do research in an area they called "grease chemistry." It is fortunate, however, that Staudinger did take up the challenge, for a less persistent, less eloquent, or less respected chemist could not have endured the attacks and controversy surrounding the macromolecular theory. Unfortunately, there was even conflict among the supporters of the macromolecular theory. Herman Mark and Frederick Eirich believed that polymers could be flexible chains and form micellelike bundles while still being macromolecules, a view which proved to be correct, but Staudinger rejected the micellar theory so completely that he believed that macromolecules could be nothing but rigid rods. Because of this controversy, Staudinger was not awarded the Nobel Prize until 1953.

Staudinger was a prolific writer, having published more than five hundred papers and books. He also founded and became the editor of the journal *Die Makromolekulare Chemie* in 1947. Staudinger was the founder of macromolecular chemistry, and his work laid the foundation for a tremendous polymer industry. In addition, his students and disciples formed the core of this area of research. Besides the Nobel Prize, Staudinger won many other prizes for scientific achievement as well as two honorary degrees.

Although best remembered for his pioneering work in polymer chemistry, Staudinger was also a first-rate teacher and administrator. Students came from all over the world to work under him; he was so successful at inspiring in others his talent for creative thinking that two of his students, L. Ružička and T. Reichstein, each won the Nobel Prize. His students remember him as a quiet man who was fond of explosions.

*Bibliography*

Furukawa, Yasu. *Staudinger, Carothers, and the Emergence of Macromolecular Chemistry.* Ann Arbor: University Microfilms International, 1983. A dissertation by Furukawa for his doctorate in the history of science. This book describes in detail Staudinger's education and work and puts them into their proper historical perspective. References are included.

Morawetz, Herbert. *Polymers: The Origins and Growth of a Science*. New York: Wiley-Interscience, 1985. The publication of this book was suggested by Staudinger's wife, Magda. The chapter "Staudinger's Struggle for Macromolecules" gives the best step-by-step account of the battle to prove the macromolecular theory.

Olby, Robert. "The Macromolecular Concept and the Origins of Molecular Biology." *Journal of Chemical Education* 47 (1970): 168-174. A lucid account of the intellectual battles fought in the effort to establish the macromolecular concept in the field of molecular biology.

Quarles, Willem. "Hermann Staudinger: Thirty Years of Macromolecules." *Journal of Chemical Education* 28 (1951): 120-122. A summary of Staudinger's life's work, written in honor of his seventieth birthday. The article emphasizes Staudinger's early years. It describes his manner, teaching accomplishments, and his relationship with his students, some of whom became Nobel laureates. A portrait is included.

Staudinger, Hermann. *From Organic Chemistry to Macromolecules*. New York: Wiley-Interscience, 1970. An autobiography based heavily on Staudinger's scientific publications. This book has the best account of Staudinger's early work and explains the motivations for his choice of research projects. Explains Staudinger's line of reasoning and why he was convinced that his macromolecular concept was correct. Contains almost all the references to Staudinger's scientific publications as well as portraits of him and of some of the men he admired.

*Kenneth S. Spector*

# EDITH STEIN

*Born:* October 12, 1891; Breslau, Germany (now Wrocław, Poland)
*Died:* August 9, 1942; Auschwitz, Poland
*Areas of Achievement:* Philosophy, theology, religion, and women's rights
*Contribution:* Stein, a disciple of the phenomenologist Edmund Husserl, became herself a leading proponent of his method of philosophy. Alongside her spiritual evolution from Judaism to atheism to Catholicism, she tried, in her writings, to relate phenomenology to personalism, Thomism, the Catholic tradition on women, and the mystical theology of Saint John of the Cross.

## *Early Life*

On the Day of Atonement, the tenth day of the seventh month (Tishri) in the Jewish calendar (October 12, 1891, in the Christian calendar), Edith Stein was born in Breslau. She was the youngest of eleven children, and Auguste Stein, her intelligent and devout mother, thanked the God of Israel in her synagogue for this sign of the special election of her last child. The Steins were merchants who had come to Breslau from Silesia in central Europe (now in southwestern Poland) when the family's lumber business failed. Soon after he had settled in Breslau, Edith Stein's father, who was only forty-eight, died of a stroke. Edith was only a year old, and her mother was left with the management of a debt-ridden lumber business and the care of seven children (four had died before Edith arrived).

With Auguste Stein's energies absorbed by her duties as principal provider, Else, her eldest daughter, assisted with the children's upbringing. Edith was a gifted but high-strung young girl, difficult to control. She possessed an agile mind and an independent spirit, which she enjoyed exhibiting by reciting poems and making witty remarks. Around the age of seven, however, she isolated herself from her family, perhaps because they treated her as "Edith, the smart one." This characterization hurt her feelings, since she recognized, even then, that being good was much more important than being smart. She did not reveal these emotional undercurrents of her interior world to her sisters or mother, and her great firmness of will allowed her to construct a placid temperament for the exterior world.

Her formal education began at the Viktoriaschule ("Victoria School") in Breslau, where, at her own insistence, she was admitted early. She quickly established herself as the best student in the class, a position she maintained throughout her schooling. She once said that she felt more at home in school than in her own family. In fact, in her need to nourish her hungry mind, she turned her home into a school by her voracious reading. Her academic success made it all the more shocking to her family when, at thirteen, she announced that she was leaving school. Unknown to her mother, Edith was passing through an adolescent religious crisis. Though remaining publicly observant, she no longer believed in God and had abandoned private prayer. The family attributed her change in personality to frail health, and she was sent to recuperate to the home of her sister Else in Hamburg (Else had married a doctor and already had three children).

After an eight-month hiatus, Edith returned to the Victoria School to recommence a college-preparatory program, for she had decided to become a teacher and dedicate herself to the discovery and communication of truth. In choosing teaching as a career, she was being faithful to the evolution of her personality as she experienced it in her thoughts, feelings, and abilities. Despite her youth, she manifested a remarkable insight into her own intellectual development and a daring independence from her family, religion, and society.

*Life's Work*

Stein entered the University of Breslau in 1911, and not long after, she came into contact with phenomenology, the philosophy that was to dominate her intellectual life. Her path to phenomenology began when she attended lectures in psychology. She hoped to discover through this "science of the soul" the undergirding coherence of human existence, but the course, which emphasized experimental psychology, disappointed her because the teacher completely ignored the soul. Amid this disillusionment, she read *Logische Untersuchungen* (1900; logical investigations), by Edmund Husserl, phenomenology's founder, and this experience revolutionized her thinking. While attending classes at the university, Stein lived at home, but her enthusiasm for phenomenology grew so keen that she soon expressed her strong desire to leave Breslau and to study with Husserl at the University of Göttingen. By this time her mother had become aware of her daughter's apostasy from Judaic beliefs and her recent conversion to a modern philosophy, and she was deeply disappointed, but she did not prevent her daughter from transferring to Göttingen.

As one of the first women admitted to Göttingen, Stein stood out at the university, but she found a comfortable philosophical home with the phenomenologists. She had come to Husserl searching for truth, and he convinced her that phenomenology, when practiced rigorously, would lead to the truth. In her early days as a phenomenologist, Stein found that empathy was her key to the truth.

Although Stein became friendly with several Catholics at Göttingen, her main entrée into Catholicism came through Max Scheler, one of Husserl's Jewish pupils who would later convert to Catholicism. His lectures on religious philosophy, which were attended by Stein, made her an admirer of the spiritual beauty of Catholicism. She was sympathetic with Scheler's attempt to rank values hierarchically, ascending from sensory through life to spiritual values. Scheler held that religious values make a person fully human, and the empathic heart of Stein responded to the message of Christianity, even though it led her to acknowledge her own spiritual poverty. Adolf Reinach, another phenomenologist who would later convert to Christianity, also helped her to start the internal transformation that would bring her to the Christian faith.

When World War I began in the summer of 1914, Stein, who had absorbed an intense patriotism from her family, felt a sense of duty to her country. She volunteered her services and was assigned to a hospital for infectious diseases in Austria, where she cared for soldiers suffering from typhus, dysentery, and cholera. After the hospital closed in 1915, she returned to Göttingen and resumed her doctoral studies. Building on her concrete wartime experiences, she was able to probe the subject of empathy more pointedly as a special kind of knowing involving the entire human person. Husserl was very impressed by her work and called her the best doctoral student he had ever had (which was high praise, indeed, since Martin Heidegger was also his student at the time). When Husserl was offered a professorship at the University of Freiburg in 1916, he asked Stein to come with him as his graduate assistant. During her first summer in Freiburg, she completed her dissertation, "The Problem of Empathy," and after its successful defense, she was awarded her doctoral degree summa cum laude. She then became a member of Freiburg's faculty and quickly gained a reputation as one of the university's leading philosophers. Her main duties were to initiate new students into the strange world of phenomenology and to edit Husserl's manuscripts.

At the end of 1917, she received the sad news that Reinach had been killed on the battlefield of Flanders, and, while attending his funeral, Stein was approached by Frau Reinach to put her husband's papers in order. Stein discovered that many of Reinach's writings were concerned with the person of Jesus Christ, and this caused her to read the New Testament. The experience of Frau Reinach's faith at the funeral and of Jesus Christ's message in the Gospels led her to abandon her atheism, and she began to wonder whether she would eventually convert to Lutheranism or Catholicism. Although intellectually convinced of God's existence and the Incarnation, she nevertheless found herself unable to take the practical step of conversion.

Upon her return to Freiburg, she applied to the University of Göttingen, where she wanted to work on her *Habilitationsschrift* (a second dissertation that would qualify her as a university lecturer), but, despite a laudatory recommendation from Husserl, Göttingen's reluctance to hire a woman professor proved to be unconquerable. Thus, in 1919, Stein returned to Breslau, where she gave lessons and continued her philosophical research. A turning point in her life occurred during the summer of 1921, when she was visiting friends at Bergzabern in southeastern Germany. She happened to pick up the autobiography of Saint Teresa of Avila, which so fascinated her that she continued reading it all night. On completing it in the morning, she had an overwhelming sense that the Catholic Christianity that guided Teresa was the truth for which she had been searching. She immediately bought a catechism and went to her first Mass. She wanted to be baptized, but the local priest informed her that a preparation period was required. She returned to Breslau and continued her teaching and research, but she returned to Bergzabern to be baptized on January 1, 1922. Prior to her conversion to Catholicism, she had always assumed that she would eventually marry, but with faith had come a call to consecrate herself to God as a nun. Realizing that her mother would have serious problems accepting her conversion, she postponed her entrance into the religious life. She continued to attend synagogue services with her mother, who was surprised that the Psalms in her daughter's breviary were the same as the Jewish Psalms.

Having abandoned her past plans for an academic career, Stein accepted a position as a German teacher at a girls' school run by Dominican sisters at Speyer in the Rhineland. Her life became a blend of teaching and prayer, and she enjoyed sharing the life of a religious community. Though not a Dominican, she lived as one, refusing to accept any salary beyond what she needed for room, board, and clothing. In 1925, Erich Przywara, a Jesuit priest and philosopher, encouraged her to resume her research, and she began to translate from Latin into German a treatise by Saint Thomas Aquinas on truth. Through Aquinas, she became familiar with Scholasticism, a philosophical approach developed in the Middle Ages to help Christians obtain a deeper understanding of revealed truth. Przywara and Aquinas helped her realize that God could be served through scholarship. Aquinas, like Teresa of Avila, effectively communicated his personal experience of God in his writings, and his example facilitated Stein's own spiritual development through her writings on phenomenology and Aquinas.

Stein's philosophical writings and translations attracted the attention of many groups, especially associations of Catholic women, and she received numerous invitations to speak on women's issues in Germany, Switzerland, and Austria. So popular did she become as a lecturer that Przywara set up periodic tours for her. Stein's success as a lecturer convinced her that she had outgrown the small school at Speyer, which she left in March, 1931, to devote herself to the writing of her *Habilitationsschrift* on phenomenology and Scholasticism. Unable, because of male chauvinism and anti-Semitism, to obtain a position at Freiburg or Breslau, she became, in 1932, a lecturer at the Educational Institute in Münster. Before moving there, she again investigated the possibility of entering a contemplative religious order, but her spiritual advisers counseled her that she could best serve the Catholic church as a teacher and lecturer. Yet after a decade's hiatus from university work and secular life, she found it difficult to reroot herself into a modern world that increasingly horrified her. She witnessed Jews being attacked, and she worried about her family in Breslau. She was a vehement opponent of Nazism, and when Adolf Hitler came to power in 1933, she, like many others of Jewish descent, lost her position.

Anti-Semitic persecution contributed to Stein's realization of her unique vocation—the reconciliation of Judaism and Christianity. She began writing *Aus dem Leben einer jüdischen Familie* (1965; *Life in a Jewish Family*, 1986), in which she tried to show young Germans that Jewish families shared the same joys and frustrations in their daily lives as their Christian neighbors. She finally decided that the time had come for her to carry out her long-held wish to enter the Carmelite Order. After applying to the convent in Cologne, she worried that, at age forty-two, she might be judged too old, but the sisters were impressed with her, and the notification of her acceptance came in June, 1933. She finally faced the soul-shattering task of telling her mother that she would be leaving her forever for a life that she knew her mother would never understand.

Many friends and relatives predicted that she would become discontented in a cloistered life with nuns of constricted intellectual interests, but she adjusted surprisingly quickly to her new environment. She found the Carmel community full of solicitous love, and, although her fellow novices were much younger than she was, she was stimulated by their sense of spiritual adventure. Stein took Teresa Benedicta a Cruce as her religious name to express her gratitude for the spiritual patronage of Saint Benedict and Saint Teresa of Avila and also to reflect her special devotion to the Passion of Christ.

At the request of her superiors, she returned to her philosophical research and writing. Most of her efforts centered on her synthesis of the major ideas of Husserl and Aquinas in a study begun several years before and now called *Endliches und ewiges Sein* (1950; finite and eternal being). Her religious experiences had changed her, however, and she no longer shared the aversion of most phenomenologists to metaphysical assertions. Consequently, she incorporated theological truths into her discussions without supporting phenomenological analysis. Despite problems of lack of an adequate library and of opportunities to consult with other philosophers, she completed her account in the summer of 1936. While awaiting news from a German publisher, she learned that her mother had died, unreconciled to her daughter's vocation, on September 14, 1936, the Feast of the Holy Cross. More bad news arrived soon after, when she was told that anti-Jewish laws prevented the publication of her book.

In the winter following her mother's death, Stein's spirits revived on hearing that her sister Rosa had entered the Catholic church, but the situation in Europe was so distressful that her happiness was short-lived. She saw the sufferings of the Carmelites in Spain during the Civil War as a harbinger of what the German Carmelites could expect. These upheavals made her eager to pronounce her solemn vows as quickly as possible. On November 8, the so-called Kristallnacht occurred, when many windows of synagogues and Jewish businesses were smashed and many Jews were beaten. Stein was aghast at the abyss of sinfulness revealed by these attacks on her fellow Jews. Many of her relatives applied to emigrate to America, and some of them were fortunate enough to escape, but others had their applications turned down. Stein herself, who had explored the possibility of emigrating to a Carmelite convent in Palestine, left Cologne on December 31, 1938, for the Carmelite convent in Echt in The Netherlands. Leaving the Cologne Carmel was difficult, since she felt so much a part of the community, but she knew that her presence there would endanger her fellow nuns. She had no illusion that she was escaping to safety, however, for in a final testament that she wrote in 1939 she stated her acceptance of the death that she believed God was preparing for her.

In 1940, Stein's sister Rosa, fleeing from the Nazis, joined her in Echt, where she became portress at the convent. Their joy of reunion soon turned to anxiety when the Nazis overran The Netherlands. Edith and Rosa again faced the threat of anti-Semitic persecution. Under the constant danger of being taken from her convent, Stein tried to continue with her life. A new superior assigned her to teach the postulants Latin, and Edith began instructing Rosa in the basics of the Carmelite life. Stein's superior also asked her to write a book on Saint John of the Cross, the great Carmelite mystic, in commemoration of the four hundredth anniversary of his birth. She devoted much time and thought to *Kreuzewissenschaft: Studie über Joannes a Cruce* (1950; *The Science of the Cross: A Study of Saint John of the Cross*, 1960), a phenomenological study of the saint's life and work.

During the summer of 1942, the Nazis began to deport Jews from The Netherlands. Throughout 1942, Stein had been desperately trying to get a Swiss visa to transfer to a Carmelite convent in Switzerland, but she was unable to make arrangements for her sister, and she refused to go without her. In July, as the deportations increased, the situation of the Stein sisters grew more critical. On August 2, Gestapo officials came to the Carmel cloister of Echt and arrested Edith and Rosa Stein. From Echt, the sisters were driven to local police headquarters for questioning and then taken to a concentration camp at Amersfoort, several miles northeast of Utrecht. While at Amersfoort, Stein gathered with other religious people to pray and to care for the sick. She was soon transported with twelve hundred fellow Jews to Westerbork, the central detention camp in the north of The Netherlands. Meanwhile, the efforts of the Carmelites at Echt and Catholic officials to obtain permission for Edith and Rosa to emigrate to Switzerland proved fruitless. By August 7, Stein and her sister were deported to Auschwitz in Nazi-occupied Poland. Stein's long-nourished sense that she would be asked to sacrifice her life intensified during these last days. Despite her fear, she approached death with serenity and in the spirit of atonement. Not much is known of her final hours, except that she was probably killed in an Auschwitz gas chamber on August 9, 1942, along with her sister and hundreds of other Jews. Her body, like the others, was initially thrown into a mass grave, but later in the year, to obliterate evidence of their crimes, the Nazis exhumed and cremated the remains.

Stein was beatified by Pope John Paul II at a ceremony in Cologne on May 1, 1987. She was proclaimed a martyr for her Catholic faith, an action that deeply disturbed those Jews who considered her an apostate as well as others who were convinced that she was murdered because she was Jewish and not out of hatred for her Catholic faith. The pope, who was an admirer of phenomenology and of Stein's personalism, wanted to make her a modern saint, but he also wanted to soothe bruised Jewish feelings. He emphasized that she had shared the fate of the Jewish people.

### *Summary*

Edith Stein's life was an intellectual and spiritual odyssey toward the truth. A highly intelligent and sensitive woman, she first became thoroughly familiar with scientific truth, but she soon discovered that this truth did not deserve her absolute devotion. Furthermore, it did not coincide with her experience of truth incarnated in persons. She once compared philosophy to a walk along the edge of an abyss, and she saw her philosophical and spiritual commitments as matters of life and death. Although she always maintained a scholar's appreciation for the value of scientific and philosophical findings, she increasingly centered her quest on spiritual truth, even when this cost her dearly. She identified herself with Jesus Christ, a deeply spiritual Jew, and she became a prayerful woman—some say a mystic—who continued to be an active and influential philosopher.

In the period following World War II, Stein's importance as a phenomenologist was overshadowed by the circumstances of her death. Many of the German Catholic women's organizations for whom she once lectured made her martyrdom into a symbol of Christian solidarity with Jews murdered in the Holocaust. Some Catholic scholars thought that her lack of theological training weakened the import of her writings, and to secular philosophers, many of whom had moved away from the phenomenological approach to a concern with language analysis, her attempt to link phenomenology and a philosophy of being seemed to be religious apologetics, with little to say to the modern world. Stein, who believed that she was living in a spiritually impoverished age, would have understood this neglect of her ideas. More recently, some scholars have begun to see her importance in the light of her work rather than in terms of her death. In this reevaluation, she emerges as a superb scholar and translator as well as a woman of penetrating moral acumen.

*Bibliography*

Graef, Hilda C. *The Scholar and the Cross: The Life and Work of Edith Stein*. Westminster, Md.: Newman Press, 1955. Graef, a British writer, based her account of Stein's life on a German biography written by the prioress of the Cologne Carmel and on new material gathered from several sources, including collections of manuscripts at Louvain and the personal reminiscences of Stein's friends and colleagues. The biography is strongest on the period after Stein's conversion to Catholicism.

Herbstrith, Waltraud. *Edith Stein: A Biography.* Translated by Bernard Bonowitz. San Francisco: Harper & Row, 1985. Herbstrith, a Carmelite nun who knew Stein, presents an affectionate portrait of her as a Jew, a phenomenologist, and a Carmelite. She intersperses her largely chronological account with ample quotations from Stein's letters and writings as well as with analyses of her philosophy, theology, and interior development. The book contains notes to primary and secondary sources, a selected bibliography, and an index.

Nota, John H. "Misunderstanding and Insight About Edith Stein's Philosophy." *Human Studies* 10 (1987): 205-212. Attempts to correct a widespread misunderstanding about Stein's use of phenomenology after she became a Catholic (several philosophers have remarked that she was lost to the phenomenological movement after her conversion). The author's thesis is that Stein remained faithful to phenomenology throughout her life and that her Catholicism made her a better phenomenologist than she had been before her conversion.

Oben, Freda Mary. *Edith Stein: Scholar, Feminist, Saint*. New York: Alba House, 1988. Oben, like Stein, is a convert from Judaism to Catholicism. Her biography, the first written since Edith Stein was beatified by John Paul II in 1987, seeks to answer the question of why Stein is more famous now than during her lifetime. Oben's work gives a balanced treatment of Stein as a Jew, philosopher, Catholic convert, educator, feminist, Carmelite nun, and martyr.

Posselt, Sister Teresia Renata de Spiritu Sancto. *Edith Stein*. Translated by Cecily Hastings and Donald Nicholl. New York: Sheed & Ward, 1952. During the years after World War II, Teresia Renata, the prioress of the Carmelite convent in Cologne, collected the biographical data then available about Stein. She published this biography—mostly a collection of reminiscences and testimonies—in Nürnberg in 1948. It proved successful, and it had gone into a fifth printing and four translations by 1950, when Cecily Hastings and Donald Nicholl made this English translation for an American audience.

*Robert J. Paradowski*

# KARLHEINZ STOCKHAUSEN

*Born:* August 22, 1928; Mödrath, near Cologne, Germany

*Area of Achievement:* Music

*Contribution:* Stockhausen is one of the most innovative and influential composers of his time, successfully bridging the gap between technology and creative endeavor and integrating a wide spectrum of musical and nonmusical concepts into his work.

## *Early Life*

Karlheinz Stockhausen was born on August 22, 1928, in the village of Mödrath, near Cologne in northwestern Germany. He was the first of three children born to Simon Stockhausen, a schoolteacher, and his wife Gertrud. When Karlheinz was only four years old, his mother, who suffered from depression, entered a sanatorium. Soon after, Simon was forced to become an active member of the Nazi Party because of his status as a teacher, and Karlheinz was occasionally pressed into service as a party messenger for his father.

Upon starting primary school in the village of Altenberg, Stockhausen began the study of the piano with the organist of the village church. Since he was gifted musically and seemed also to have inherited from his father a capacity for study, he soon was recommended for study at a secondary school in a nearby town, from which he progressed in 1941 to a teacher training college at Xanten, which lay downstream on the Rhine River from his native region.

The college in Xanten was a somewhat harsh environment where military rigor was imposed upon the students' lives. Fortunately, music was not proscribed, and Stockhausen began lessons on the violin as well as the oboe, which he played in the college wind band. His earliest contact with jazz music also dates from his three years at Xanten. During these years, Stockhausen was largely cut off from his family. His father had entered the army, and in 1942 Stockhausen learned that his mother had been put to death under the terms of a government policy to create more space for military hospitalization.

Leaving Xanten in October, 1944, Stockhausen became a stretcher-bearer in a military hospital, where he came into contact with wounded and dying American and English soldiers as well as those of the German army. He saw his father for the last time shortly before the end of the war; Simon Stockhausen is believed to have died in service on the Hungarian front.

After the war, Stockhausen found work on a farm, and soon his evenings were occupied in assisting a local operetta society in preparing performances. Qualifying in February, 1946, for entrance as a senior student at a school in Bergisch Gladbach, he supported himself with miscellaneous musical jobs until his graduation the following year. Now nineteen years old, Stockhausen was enrolled in the four-year course of the State Academy of Music in Cologne and simultaneously took courses in musicology and philosophy at the University of Cologne. At the academy, his principal areas of study were piano and school music, but in 1950 he had several lessons in composition from the Swiss composer Frank Martin, who had joined the faculty at the academy. Several short works by Stockhausen survive from these years, including *Chore für Doris* (1950; chorus for Doris), for unaccompanied chorus, and *Drei Lieder* (1950; three songs), for alto voice and orchestra. In his final year at the academy, Stockhausen was engaged largely in composing and in preparing his final examination thesis. In the midst of this demanding academic activity, the young musician continued to work nights as a jazz pianist in local bars.

In 1951, Stockhausen met the Cologne music critic Herbert Eimert, who was in charge of a series of evening broadcasts of contemporary music on North-West German Radio. Finding in the young composer both musical talent and a strong personality, Eimert arranged the first radio performance of a Stockhausen work and invited the composer to become a regular contributor to his program. Eimert also introduced Stockhausen to the Darmstadt New Music Courses, which in 1951 included a seminar by Eimert and others on music and technology. That same year at Darmstadt, the French composer Pierre Schaeffer contributed a lecture-demonstration on the activities of a Paris group pursuing the concept of *musique concrète*, electronic music employing manipulated tape-recorded sounds of the everyday, "concrete" world.

Following the Darmstadt course in the summer of 1951, Stockhausen returned to Cologne to prepare for state examinations to qualify as a secondary school music teacher, which he passed with distinction. In November, he completed his first major composition, *Kreuzspiel* (crossplay), which he dedicated to Doris Andreae, a fellow student at the academy. On December 29, Stockhausen and Doris were married (four children were born to the couple between 1953 and 1961), and in January, 1952, he went to Paris for further study.

### *Life's Work*

In the early 1950's, Parisian musical life, like that of many European centers, was dominated by the example of the composer Anton Webern, whose radically distilled works were based upon the concept of "serialism." Serialism, an evolution of developments initiated earlier in the century by Arnold Schoenberg, dictated that unity in musical composition was to be sought by rigorously and systematically interrelating musical elements such as pitch, harmony, rhythm, and instrumental tone-color. After Webern's premature death, the serialist banner was carried into the postwar period by the influential French composer Olivier Messiaen, whose music Stockhausen heard at Darmstadt in 1951. Already influenced by Messiaen's *Mode de valeurs et d'intensités* (1949; mode of values and intensities), which Stockhausen likened to "star music," the young German determined to attend Messiaen's course in analysis and aesthetics during 1952-1953.

Paris offered more to Stockhausen than just the stimulus of Messiaen's powerful musical thinking. He also worked with the *musique concrète* group, producing his first tape composition, *Étude* (1952; study), and investigated the synthesis of sound spectra by the combination of pure sounds produced electronically, thus laying the foundation for his early electronic compositions. The best-known work of Stockhausen's Parisian year is *Kontra-Punkte* (1952-1953; counterpoints), a composition of a type called "pointillist." This term, loosely derived from the technique of painting in small dots of color, is intended to evoke the sense of the free distribution of notes across a continuum of pitch and time. Pointillist form was intended as a rejection of many of the compositional ideas of European music, such as theme, contrast, and rhythmic sequence. Accordingly, Stockhausen's early compositions, like those of many of his contemporaries, were not well received by the general public, which had difficulty perceiving the constructive artistic intent behind the wholesale transformation of musical language.

In 1953, Stockhausen returned to Germany and became a collaborator at the studio for electronic music at West German Radio in Cologne, where he began work on *Electronishe Studien I and II* (1953 and 1954; electronic studies I and II), his first exclusively electronic compositions. The first of these is made up of combinations of pure sine-wave tones in fixed proportions; the second is derived from sine tones acoustically manipulated to create an element of indeterminate pitch, or "noise." The second study is historically significant in that it was the first electronic composition to be published as a score, and it was one of the first to be brought out on record. Both compositions display a nearly total "serialization" of the process of composition, in which a set of rules determines the musical content. In works such as this, a blurring of distinctions between "form" and "material" is brought about that, in theory, might render the music wholly abstract and mechanical, but Stockhausen's inventiveness and his grasp of the psychology of perception allowed him to maintain the vividness of musical experience.

While at work on the second study, Stockhausen undertook further academic study under Werner Meyer-Eppler of the University of Bonn. Lecturing on communication theory and phonetics, Meyer-Eppler provided Stockhausen with new perspectives on the physical and structural potential of sound. The result of Stockhausen's study can be heard in his *Gesang der Jünglinde* (1956; songs of the youths), which is widely regarded as one of the major early achievements of electronic music.

Stockhausen's activities outside the realm of composition continued with his participation in the journal *Die Reihe*, which first appeared in 1955 under his joint editorship with Eimert, who had also founded the Cologne Electronic Studio. Still only in his late twenties, Stockhausen was already widely recognized as a leading figure in contemporary music, and the influence of this musical thinking had begun to spread. In 1953, he began collaborating in the "International Vacation Courses for New Music" in Darmstadt, and in the 1960's, he was to lecture at universities in the United States, where his articulate and compelling exposition of his own work brought him to the attention of a widening audience.

The composition *Zeitmasze* (1956; tempi) began a new period of instrumental composition for Stockhausen. This dense, many-layered work, scored for flute, oboe, English horn, clarinet, and bassoon, represents a reassessment of the pointillist style that had been the mainstay of European avant-garde music in the early 1950's. *Zeitmasze* maintains the composer's characteristic formal rigor while allowing the physical and psychological vitality of live musical performance to take on new importance. A fundamental conception of the work is that independently varying measures of time can be made to interact in a manner that necessitates a "distributive" and "statistical," rather than a thematic and metrical, perception of musical material. To a degree, *Zeitmasze* represents the adaptation of abstract theory to an appreciation of the perception of music; its jazzlike flux of instrumental sound-events lends it a quality distinct from intellectualized, conventional serialism.

In the late 1950's, Stockhausen sought out new avenues of musical organization that often led to larger-scale works, though piano composition remained an important element in his overall development. *Gruppen* (1957; groups), employing three spatially separated orchestras directed by three conductors, signals a shift toward what has been called "group form," in which sound events can be resolved into identifiable microstructures with collective properties capable of either logical or imaginative organization. *Gruppen* seems to embody musical analogues of natural phenomena, and the composer has likened audible structures in this work to the outlines of mountains he observed in Switzerland during its composition.

Stockhausen's increasing confidence in composing large-scale works is shown by *Carré* (1960; square), written for four orchestras and four choirs, *Kontakte* (1960; contacts), for electronic sounds, piano, and percussion, and *Momente* (1964; moments), for solo soprano, four choral groups, and thirteen instrumentalists. The composer has written that *Carré* arose out of a new experience of time gained while flying for hours at a time while on tour in the United States. With his ear to the window, Stockhausen studied the vibrations coming from the engines of the propeller-driven airplanes and later composed the work as an exploration of fluctuations of continuous sounds. A notable development of *Kontakte* is the "contact" and interaction of electronic and instrumental sounds. As in *Carré*, the distribution of sound in space is a cardinal feature of the work.

In many of the compositions of the late 1950's and early 1960's, Stockhausen considered the problem of the audience's involvement in the often sterile concert environment of modern music. Surrounding the audience with moving sound, as in *Carré*, was a technical and aesthetic venture of great consequence, but he explored other ways of breaking down barriers between composer, performer, and audience. *Momente*, a work ultimately of some popularity, goes to the extreme of providing instructions to the choir to supply some of the heckling often associated with performances of contemporary music. Yet, characteristically, this somewhat ironic gesture fits seamlessly into the purely musical fabric of the composition.

*Momente* embodies in its title one of Stockhausen's most important aesthetic principles, that of "moment form." Although distinctions between pointillist form, group form, and moment form are often difficult, the composer's own explanation is that each "moment" is an individual and self-regulated state or process that neither depends on a previous musical form nor dictates a subsequent one but has an integrity in the present transcending the everyday experience of sequential time. "Moment form" is clearly a concept with a philosophical as well as a technical grounding, and it has underlain most of Stockhausen's later work.

Stockhausen was as unceasingly productive in the 1960's as in the previous decade. One of the most significant developments of these years was his turning toward Asian culture for inspiration. The year 1966 brought commissions from the national broadcasting corporation of Japan, including *Telemusik*. In 1970, Stockhausen was commissioned by the West German government to produce a work for a spherical auditorium at the World's Fair in Osaka. During a period of 183 days, more than one million visitors heard the composer and his ensemble perform his compositions in an environment designed especially for them.

Increasingly, Stockhausen's compositions have embraced intuition, performer interaction, and open forms of organization in an effort to refine the humanistic goals of his music. *Hymnen* (1967; hymns), a composition of electronic and concrete music, is a tapestry of electronically transformed national anthems that embodies, in a general way, a message of universal toleration and diversity. *Stimmung*, completed in 1968 (the composer notes that the title may be translated in various ways, including "spiritual harmony" in addition to the conventional "tuning"), is an appealing work in which precise, demanding vocal technique is used to create a meditative atmosphere.

In 1967, Stockhausen married the painter Mary Bauermeister, with whom he subsequently had two children. Several of the composer's children became involved in the composer's artistic projects, particularly Marcus Stockhausen, a talented trumpeter.

Stockhausen's "intuitive music" reached its greatest intensity in the work entitled *Aus den sieben Tagen* (1968; from the seven days), which seems to embody the resolution of a spiritual crisis that the composer experienced in 1968. *Aus den sieben Tagen* is not composed in musical notation but exists instead as a set of fifteen texts written by Stockhausen that communicate states of mind and spiritual aspirations. These have titles such as "Right Duration," "Intensity," and "Set Sail for the Sun," which essentially direct the performer toward his own musical and spiritual resources. When played by musicians attuned to its demands, *Aus den Sieben Tagen* can result in improvisation of substance and beauty, but few performing artists have the courage to proceed on the instruction "Play in the rhythm of the Universe," as one of the pieces suggests.

During the next decade, Stockhausen continued his research and speculation in the structuring and presentation of music. From this period, *Mantra* (1970) is widely regarded as a masterpiece that unites technological sophistication and creative inspiration. Much of the composer's work immediately following was on a smaller scale and had more specific objectives than his work of the 1960's, but in 1977 he began an ambitious series of compositions that would continue to occupy him for many years. The projected cycle is called *Licht, die sieben Tagen der Woche* (light, the seven days of the week), and when completed it will contain seven components, designated as operas, one corresponding to each day of the week. The first section of the work to be completed was *Donnerstag aus Licht* (Thursday from light); it was composed between 1978 and 1980 and was first performed at La Scala in Milan, Italy, in 1981. The next two years were taken up with the composition of *Samstag aus Licht* (Saturday from light), which was produced with Stockhausen's active participation in 1984 by the La Scala organization at a sports stadium in Milan. These works have proven very elaborate and demanding as stage productions; in them the composer continues to be the same uncompromising executant of his own works that he has been throughout his career.

### *Summary*

Karlheinz Stockhausen's compositional output is remarkable by any measure of creative endeavor, and, though questions of quality in twentieth century musical culture are as difficult to formulate as they are to answer, the status of many of his works is unquestioned with respect to musical integrity, inventiveness, and influence. A true burden of creative innovation in music after World War II has fallen on relatively few shoulders. Among Stockhausen's contemporaries perhaps only his friend and colleague Pierre Boulez bears comparison with him in these terms.

The complex evolution of Stockhausen's music has encompassed the analysis and electronic creation of sounds, the electronic shaping of musical material and its integration into the more familiar world of live musical performance, the reshaping of the concept as well as the experience of time in music, and the revision of the relation of the composer to performer and audience. In broad terms he has developed from an artist following intellectual models to one capable of a powerful synthesis of objective and subjective materials and processes. An appearance of calculated impersonality noted in his earlier career by some critics has yielded to a willingness to engage openly issues of deep significance, and in his advocacy of personal and social transformation he sometimes seems almost to be an elder statesman of pluralist, humanist culture. Without question, Stockhausen has attempted to restore the image of the artist as culture-hero but only by first establishing a solid foundation in musical practice.

*Bibliography*

Brindle, Reginald Smith. *The New Music: The Avant-Garde Since 1945*. London: Oxford University Press, 1975. This survey, in which Stockhausen figures very prominently, draws refreshing distinctions between the claims made by composers for their music and its actual expressive achievements. The author, himself a composer, treats technical matters with clarity and common sense.

Cott, Jonathan. *Stockhausen: Conversations with the Composer.* New York: Simon & Schuster, 1973. The author is a poet and veteran journalist who knows how to elicit a colorful response from Stockhausen, who is here an almost ideal interview subject. This book is one of the best documents of the postwar musical avant-garde.

Harvey, Jonathan. *The Music of Stockhausen*. London: Faber & Faber, 1975. This book presents Stockhausen's work with insight but with only intermittent sympathy for the nontechnical reader. Alone among books on the composer and his works, this one features an attractive design.

Heikinheimo, Seppo. *The Electronic Music of Karlheinz Stockhausen: Studies on the Esthetical and Formal Problems of Its First Phase*. Helsinki: Suomen Musiikkitieteellinen Seura, 1972. Although this is a highly technical examination of a narrow range of the composer's works, many of the central issues in Stockhausen's earlier music are lucidly presented. The translation from Finnish is excellent.

Maconie, Robin. *The Works of Karlheinz Stockhausen*. London: Oxford University Press, 1976. The author greatly admires Stockhausen's music, and this book embodies committed study of individual works and their complex interrelationships. A high degree of technical detail is enhanced by excerpts of scores and graphic notation of the works, and the book is made especially useful by the inclusion of exhaustive performance and recording data accompanying each entry.

Stuckenschmidt, H. H. *Germany and Central Europe*. Vol 2 in *Twentieth Century Composers*. New York: Holt, Rinehart and Winston, 1971. Stuckenschmidt here devotes a reliable chapter of his survey to Stockhausen's career to about 1963, but he is unable to convey the complexity of the composer's work because of limitations of space. A sense of Stockhausen's status as a German cultural figure may be gained by comparing him with other composers represented.

__________. *Twentieth Century Music*. Translated from the German by Richard Deveson. New York: McGraw-Hill, 1969. This excellent survey of the field has a particular value in detailing the thought of the Russian-born musicologist Joseph Schillinger, whose advanced theories on the relation between mathematics and music seem to have greatly influenced Stockhausen.

Tannenbaum, Mya. *Conversations with Stockhausen*. Oxford: Clarendon Press, 1987. Translated by David Butchart. Consisting of texts of interviews conducted from 1979 to 1981, this is an often amusing look at both the mundane and exalted concerns of the composer as he struggles to arrange performances of his opera *Donnerstag aus Licht*.

Wörner, Karl Heinrich. *Stockhausen*. Rev. ed. London: Faber & Faber, 1973. Translated and edited by Bill Hopkins. This book consists of a 1963 text that was updated by the author in the late 1960's, combined with descriptions by Stockhausen of most of his early works. The book is a mine of information but is loosely organized. Like most authors listed here, Wörner enjoyed the composer's cooperation in the preparation of the book.

*C. S. McConnell*

# RICHARD STRAUSS

*Born:* June 11, 1864; Munich, Bavaria, Germany
*Died:* September 8, 1949; Garmisch-Partenkirchen, West Germany
*Area of Achievement:* Music
*Contribution:* The symphonic poems composed by Strauss in the last years of the nineteenth century won for him early fame and fortune. He was widely regarded by the music community as one of the brilliant young men destined to lead music into the twentieth century.

## *Early Life*

Richard Strauss was born in Munich, Bavaria, on June 11, 1864. He was the elder and only son of two children born to Franz Strauss, a professional horn player, and Josephine Pschorr, whose family owned and operated the Pschorr Brewery. From the beginning, there was little doubt about Richard's future. The combination of the Pschorr family wealth and Franz Strauss's position as a virtuoso performer afforded Richard every opportunity to pursue a career in music. Franz, who was the principal hornist of the Munich Court Orchestra, carefully supervised the early music training of his son. He arranged for Richard to study with various members of the Munich Orchestra. Richard studied piano with August Tombo, violin with Benno Walter, and music theory with F. W. Meyer. Since Franz Strauss disliked the music of the late Romantics, it is no surprise that his son was solidly grounded in the classics, studying the music of such composers as Joseph Haydn, Wolfgang Amadeus Mozart, and Ludwig van Beethoven. His earliest composition was a Christmas song composed when he was only six years old.

Strauss studied at the *Gymnasium* in Munich until he was eighteen years old. He did not take specialized training in music at the Munich Conservatory upon his graduation from the *Gymnasium*. Instead, he was enrolled at the University of Munich, where he took courses in the humanities. In fact, Strauss's performance skills at the keyboard were regarded as respectable, but not exceptional. Strauss's father had been more intent upon encouraging and developing the compositional talents of his son rather than performance skills.

Strauss's first composition for orchestra, entitled *Festival March*, was composed in 1876 when he was only twelve years old and was actually published by Breitkopf and Härtel, attributable more to the influence of his mother's family than the merit of the piece. Another early work, the *Serenade for Wind Instruments in Eb*, was more important because it attracted the attention of Hans von Bülow, one of the more colorful figures in the history of music, who was a virtuoso pianist and a respected conductor. He was the conductor of the Meiningen Orchestra when Strauss's piece came to his attention. Bülow became one of Strauss's earliest and strongest supporters and, when the position of assistant conductor at Meiningen became vacant, Bülow recommended the twenty-one-year-old Strauss for the position, thus embarking him upon a dual career as a composer and conductor that was to continue throughout his life.

*Life's Work*

When Strauss accepted the position of assistant conductor at Meiningen in 1885, he was a conservative composer who knew next to nothing about conducting. Upon arrival at Meiningen, Strauss entered an intensive apprenticeship under the tutelage of Bülow, and, when Bülow resigned his position as conductor a few months later, he was appointed Bülow's successor. His appointment as first conductor at Meiningen may have been ill-timed in respect of his experience as a conductor, and he resigned that position several months later, early in 1886, to accept another position as third conductor at Munich. During the remaining years of the nineteenth century, Strauss was to hold the position of conductor at Weimar, a second term at Munich, and at Berlin, all the while steadily growing in confidence and stature as a conductor and as a composer.

While at Meiningen, Strauss had become good friends with and had fallen under the influence of a violinist named Alexander Ritter, who was an ardent Wagnerite. It was during this time that Strauss began to move away from the conservative camp and became interested in the music of Wagner and his followers. His first composition in the new style was a symphonic fantasy entitled *Aus Italien*, first performed in Munich in 1887, and was an outgrowth of a vacation he had taken in Italy prior to the assumption of his duties at Munich. This work was followed by a series of symphonic poems, or tone poems, as he preferred to call them, all composed in the last years of the nineteenth century, that rocked the music community and catapulted him to international fame as a composer. These works established his reputation as a radical modern composer.

Strauss was unsurpassed in his day for the creative and imaginative way he skillfully wrote for the orchestra, placing unprecedented technical demands upon the performers, creating sensitive and subtle nuances of color, and always striving to depict musically the subject content in a realistic manner. Numbering among his finest works in this genre are *Don Juan, Till Eulenspiegels lustige Streiche*, and *Ein Heldenleben*.

Strauss's output in the area of choral music remains generally neglected today, possibly because of the great difficulty in the performance of most of these works. Of the roughly two hundred songs that he composed, many were for soprano voice and written for Pauline de Ahna, who was a graduate of the Munich Conservatory. Strauss had met Ahna, a member of a respected and titled family, in the summer of 1887. A courtship ensued that extended over a period of years, and they eventually married in 1894. Some of Strauss's best efforts in this genre, such as *Standchen* and *Morgen*, were composed during the years of courtship and early marriage. Early in their relationship, Ahna actually sang roles in some of the operas that Strauss conducted, and, over the years, she would often sing his songs in recitals with him accompanying her on the piano. Their only child, Franz Alexander Strauss, was born in 1897.

Strauss's creative focus changed in the early twentieth century. He moved away from compositions for orchestra and began to concentrate on opera. The change was not as drastic as it would appear on the surface in view of the highly poetic and dramatic content of his symphonic poems, his familiarity and understanding of the voice, and his, by now, extensive experience as a conductor of opera. His earliest attempt was *Guntram*, first performed in Weimar in 1894; it was poorly received by the public and the critics, a fact he never understood or forgot.

Strauss's first major success, and one of his most powerful works, was *Salome*, which was first performed in Dresden in 1905. It was a one-act opera based on the Oscar Wilde play of the same name. The subject of the opera, which dealt with Salome's obsession with John the Baptist, proved to be quite controversial and was regarded as scandalous in some circles. The subject pushed Strauss to new artistic heights as he strived to portray musically the characters and to capture the intensity of their feelings in the music. The music can be characterized by the extreme demands placed upon the singers and the extensive use of the orchestra for coloristic effects. The high point of the opera came at the end with Salome's dance of the veils and then her kissing of the head of John the Baptist.

Strauss's next opera, *Elektra*, first performed in Dresden in 1909, marks the beginning of his collaboration with Hugo von Hofmannsthal. Hofmannsthal remained Strauss's librettist until his death in 1929. *Elektra*, which dealt with a woman's obsession with revenge, paralleled *Salome* in that it was also a very intense psychological drama. Again, Strauss placed great demands upon the singers and utilized a very large orchestra. With this work, Strauss had moved to the brink of atonality, thus maintaining a reputation as one of the more radical composers of his day.

*Der Rosenkavalier*, on a libretto by Hofmannsthal, was first performed in 1911 and marks a strong break with *Salome* and *Elektra*. The subject, which deals with the aristocracy of eighteenth century Vienna, has nothing of the brooding darkness and violence of the earlier works. In this work, Strauss returns the voice to its normal position of prominence, making use of duets and trios and using the orchestra in a more traditional role. *Ariadne auf Naxos*, which followed in 1912, confirmed the change in style. Strauss was to maintain this style, as reflected in *Rosenkavalier* and *Ariadne auf Naxos*, with little change for the rest of his career. Other operas deserving of mention with Hofmannsthal as librettist are *Die Frau ohne Schatten*, *Intermezzo*, and *Arabella*.

Strauss enjoyed an international reputation as one of the great German composers of his time. It is for this reason that the Third Reich, wanting to receive approval and support from some sectors of the German intellectual and creative community, appointed Strauss as president of the Reich Chamber of Music in 1933. Strauss was forced to resign that position in 1935 over a dispute involving his Jewish librettist, Stefan Zweig, but the damage had been done. World opinion had shifted against him, and, when the war ended in 1945, he was, for a period of time, before being cleared of all charges, regarded as a Nazi supporter. He spent his final years in his villa in Garmisch-Partenkirchen. His last composition was four songs for soprano and orchestra entitled *Vier letzte Lieder* (four last songs). Strauss died at his villa in Garmisch-Partenkirchen, Bavaria, on September 8, 1949, survived by his wife, who was to die a year later, and his son, Franz.

### *Summary*

The twentieth century has not been an easy time in which to live for many artists, including Richard Strauss. He was reared in an environment of wealth, security, and opportunity. The early years were exciting and promising ones that saw him achieve national and even international prominence as a conductor and as the composer of the tone poems and the early operas. These were the good times for Strauss.

As did so many composers, he flirted with atonality, one of the major controversies for composers and audiences in the early 1900's, and rejected it, preferring to work within a tonal framework. Thus, Strauss, who was one of the radical young leaders of the new music at the turn of the century, became one of the conservatives over a period of time, a defender of the status quo. Those who were disappointed with that decision have claimed that he abandoned his artistic principles for fame and fortune. His reputation has suffered for this in past years, but, in the long term, history will judge him most favorably, not only for his many orchestral masterpieces but also as one of the major composers of opera in the twentieth century. He found and rightfully understood that his strength of musical expression lay in the tonal language of the post-Wagnerian era, and, in this idiom, he was the undisputed master.

### *Bibliography*

Del Mar, Norman. *Richard Strauss: A Critical Commentary on His Life and Works*. 3 vols. Philadelphia: Chilton, 1969-1973. Remains the best general study. This work discusses Strauss's compositions in some detail. Accessible to the general reader, it is recommended only to those interested in an in-depth study of Strauss.

Griffiths, Paul. "The Turn of the Century." *Music Guide: An Introduction*. Edited by Stanley Sadie with Alison Latham. Englewood Cliffs, N.J.: Prentice-Hall, 1986. This chapter by Griffiths provides an excellent overview of music in the late nineteenth and early twentieth centuries. Strauss and other composers contemporary with him are covered. Highly recommended to the general reader.

Kennedy, Michael. "Richard Strauss." In *New Grove Dictionary of Music and Musicians*, edited by Stanley Sadie, vol. 18, 6th ed. New York: Macmillan, 1980. The author provides a thorough discussion of Strauss's life and works. The works are discussed by genre. A list of his compositions is provided at the end of the article along with an excellent bibliography.

Marek, George. *Richard Strauss: The Life of a Non-Hero*. New York: Simon & Schuster, 1967. This is a good account of Strauss's life. It is rich in factual material but does not make any attempt at analysis of Strauss's style or any of his works. An excellent source for the general reader.

Rolland, Romain. *Richard Strauss and Romain Rolland: Correspondence*. Edited by Rollo Meyers. Berkeley: University of California Press, 1968. Contains a translation of letters exchanged between Strauss and Rolland, a professor at the Sorbonne and a French musicologist. Also included are excerpted fragments from Rolland's diary that are of some interest in respect to Strauss.

Strauss, Richard, *Recollections and Reflections*. Edited by Willi Schuh. Translated by L. J. Lawrence. Reprint. Westport, Conn.: Greenwood Press, 1974. Often very short comments written in response to a wide variety of issues and concerns, these writings allow the reader a very special private insight into Strauss, the artist and the man. Excellent source for the general reader.

*Michael Hernon*

# GUSTAV STRESEMANN

*Born:* May 10, 1878; Berlin, Germany
*Died:* October 3, 1929; Berlin, Germany
*Areas of Achievement:* Government and politics
*Contribution:* Although unenthusiastic in his support for a German republic, Stresemann nevertheless served the Weimar Republican government as chancellor and foreign minister during the 1920's. As foreign minister, he was able to revise portions of the Treaty of Versailles and help to bring Germany into the mainstream of European diplomacy.

## *Early Life*

Gustav Stresemann was born on May 10, 1878, in Berlin. He was the youngest child of Ernst Stresemann, an innkeeper and beer distributor in the southern section of Berlin. His mother died while he was a teenager. Gustav attended the Andreas Realgymnasium in Berlin, where the headmaster placed a heavy emphasis on humanistic scholarship. Records indicate that Stresemann developed an interest in mathematics and literature. He read the great works in Latin, German, French, and English, and seemed especially impressed with the style of Thomas Macaulay. His greatest fascination as a young student was modern history. He was intrigued by the origin and consequences of great events and with the lives of people who stood above everyday routine. He put Johann Wolfgang von Goethe and Napoleon I in this category. As both of his headmasters in the Realgymnasium were trained as pastors, it is not surprising that while a schoolboy Stresemann had strong religious convictions.

In 1897, Stresemann began his advanced studies at the University of Berlin, where he escaped the solitude that had marked his younger years. At first, he concentrated on literature and history, but later, hoping to improve his business prospects, he devoted more time to economics. To pursue this interest, he moved to the University of Leipzig. He took an active part in student life by writing lighthearted articles for the *University Gazette* and by joining the Reform Burschenschaften, an offshoot of the original national liberal organization founded in the early nineteenth century. Within a short time, Stresemann was elected by the association to be chairman of its general conference. In this position, he was introduced to parliamentary style debate and to the give and take of politics. He also began to write some serious articles.

It had been Stresemann's plan to earn a doctoral degree with a dissertation heavy on economic theory. By this time, Stresemann had come under the influence of Karl Bucher, who urged him to tackle a "practical" topic for his dissertation. Accordingly, Stresemann produced a thesis entitled "The Development of the Bottled Beer Industry in Berlin, an Economic Investigation." Based on his knowledge of his father's business, the thesis describes with bitterness the decline of Berlin's independent middle class in the face of large commercial concerns. The dissertation, with its underlying call for social justice, was later used against him by right-wing elements.

After earning his doctorate in 1900, Stresemann moved to Dresden and quickly established himself in the business world. From 1901 to 1904, he was a minor administrator in the German Chocolate Maker's Association. In 1902, he founded the Saxon Manufacturer's Association and remained its chief representative until 1911. In 1903, he married Kathe Kleefeld, the daughter of Berlin industrialist Adolf Kleefeld. They had two sons, Wolfgang and Joachim. Kathe was highly visible in Berlin society of the 1920's. It was also in 1903 that Stresemann joined the National Liberal Party, in which he frequently found his support for social measures out of step with the party's right wing. In 1906, he became a Dresden city councillor, and this experience whetted his appetite for a more important career in national politics. It led to his candidacy for a seat in the Reichstag (parliament) in 1907.

*Life's Work*

In January, 1907, Stresemann began his career in the Reichstag as a National Liberal delegate from Annenberg, a district in the mining region. He argued that Germany should be strong militarily while taking care of the poor at home. At age twenty-eight he became the youngest member of the Reichstag. In his first five years in the Reichstag, Stresemann gave most of his attention to advanced economic questions: how to reform taxation, how to apportion taxation equitably, and how to create an awareness that all classes in Germany were interdependent. His first parliamentary speech (April 12, 1907) dealt with the need for the state to provide effective national social legislation for German workers. Outside the Reichstag, Stresemann wrote many articles for newspapers and periodicals dealing with economic policy. In addition, he edited a journal he had founded, *Saxon Industry,* in which he published essays regarding the relationship between workers and industry.

Stresemann's staunch support for commercial interests alienated the right-wing of his party as well as conservative supporters in Annenberg. As a result, he lost his seat in the Reichstag elections of 1912. He then visited the United States to learn something of commerce and industry there. His journey took him to such industrial and commercial centers as Boston, Detroit, Chicago, and Pittsburgh. On this trip he met the future president, Woodrow Wilson, for whom Stresemann developed great admiration.

In these years just prior to World War I, Stresemann gave support to the government's military spending. He believed that Germany must prepare for a defensive war, and he was not alarmed when the war began. In December,

1914, he was returned to the Reichstag in a by-election for the district of Aurich. He was, during the war years, an eloquent spokesman for the annexationists—those who wished to claim for Germany territory in Poland, Russia, France, and Belgium. By 1916, Stresemann had become an advocate for the views of Field Marshal Paul von Hindenburg and General Erich Ludendorff in the Reichstag. He was, as well, a proponent of the disastrous unrestricted submarine warfare policy pushed by Admiral Alfred von Tirpitz.

Appalled that conservative Chancellor Theobald von Bethmann Hollweg could not prevent the Reichstag from considering a resolution for peace offered by Matthias Erzberger in July, 1917, Stresemann played a major role in forcing Bethmann Hollweg from office. Stresemann did not comprehend Germany's weakened military circumstances until a month before the November, 1918, armistice. He was further shocked by the collapse of the monarchy and Emperor William II's abdication on November 9. It was difficult for Stresemann to adjust to a republican Germany under the Social Democratic Party. In February, 1919, he founded the German People's Party, a right-wing elite organization aimed at blunting the Social Democrats' plan for economic reconstruction. Stresemann engaged in a heated debate with Walther Rathenau over how to revive Germany's economy, with Stresemann emphasizing the role of the individual and Rathenau arguing that the state had to take the lead.

It was not until after the failure of the right-wing Kapp Putsch in March, 1920, that Stresemann was fully reconciled to a republican government. In 1920, Stresemann was returned to the Reichstag. He became chancellor in August, 1923, as a result of a coalition of deputies from the Social Democratic, Center, German Democratic, and People's parties. Stresemann remained chancellor for only four months, but it was a time of great crisis for Germany as ruinous inflation brought misery and social disorder. Although historians generally give Stresemann high marks for his brief tenure as chancellor (especially for the way in which he stabilized the currency), he was not able to hold the coalition together and resigned after a vote of no confidence.

In the new government, Stresemann stayed on as foreign minister, a post he held through various administrations until he died in 1929. In this office he had his greatest achievements. He dedicated himself to revising the Treaty of Versailles, a treaty he despised. He wished to achieve reconciliation with the Western powers. In return, he thought it was time to reduce Germany's reparation payments and allow his country to join the League of Nations. His successes began in 1924 when the Dawes Plan was signed reducing the reparations payment. The Pact of Locarno followed in 1925. This guaranteed the French-German borders and prevented the Allies from making further demands upon Germany. On September 10, 1926, Germany was admitted to the League of Nations, a proud day for Stresemann's strategy of reconciliation. After the League meeting, Stresemann and the French foreign officer, Aristide Briand, held discussions at Thoiry about the need to continue to establish goodwill between France and Germany. Both men were now extremely popular, and they shared the 1926 Nobel Peace Prize. Although nothing of substance came from the Thoiry meeting, they continued a spirit of optimism about the future. In 1928, the peak of this optimism was reached when Germany signed the Kellogg-Briand Pact, an agreement to outlaw war approved by more than fifty nations. Stresemann's health was in decline for most of 1928, and he died the next year on October 3, 1929.

### *Summary*

Gustav Stresemann's most effective years as a politician came while he served as foreign minister during the 1920's. His successful efforts to return Germany to the community of European nations stands as his single greatest achievement. With French statesman Aristide Briand, he helped to create a period of hope about the future of French-German cooperation and, indeed, about the prospects of avoiding European wars of any kind. On the other hand, as historian Henry Turner observes, in giving all of his attention to revising the Treaty of Versailles, Stresemann failed to be attentive to domestic politics. Whereas he, as a conservative leader, could have helped to strengthen the middle in German politics, he chose to stand aloof. Hence, by the time of his death in 1929, the right-wing stood ready to dominate German politics.

Although Stresemann devoted the last six years of his life to international concerns, he was not transformed into an internationalist. He remained a defender of Germany's goals in Europe, including rearmament and the recovery of Danzig, the Polish Corridor, and Upper Silesia. Germany could no longer gain these ends by force, but could do so, he believed, through finesse. Rearmament was illegal by the terms of Versailles, but Stresemann was involved in the rearming that occurred during the Weimar era. His statecraft, in the end, bore a resemblance to that of the German politician he most admired: Otto von Bismarck. Like Bismarck, Stresemann was a wholly pragmatic politician who believed that Germany was destined to be the arbiter of Central and Eastern European politics.

### *Bibliography*

Bretton, Henry L. *Stresemann and the Revision of Versailles*. Stanford, Calif.: Stanford University Press, 1953. This study brought renewed scholarly interest in Stresemann's career. It is well worth reading.

Dorpalen, Andreas. *Hindenburg and the Weimar Republic*. Princeton, N.J.: Princeton University Press, 1964. Hindenburg was President of the Weimar Republic from 1925, and Dorpalen discusses the very restrained support that Stresemann received from the president between 1925 and

1929. This is a highly readable and respected account of the collapse of the republic.

Gatzke, Hans. *Stresemann and the Rearmament of Germany.* Baltimore: Johns Hopkins University Press, 1954. In this excellent monograph, Gatzke gives a critical account of Stresemann's years as foreign minister. He provides substantial information regarding Stresemann's role in the illegal rearming of Germany in the 1920's.

Rheinbaben, Rochus, Baron von. *Stresemann: The Man and the Statesman.* Translated by Cyrus Brooks and Hans Herzl. New York: D. Appleton, 1929. This is an uncritical account written in cooperation with Stresemann shortly before his death. The book does provide much information about Stresemann's early life and influences that is not available elsewhere.

Turner, Henry Ashby, Jr. *Stresemann and the Politics of the Weimar Republic.* Princeton, N.J.: Princeton University Press, 1963. This is the best overall account of Stresemann's service to the Weimar Republic. Turner generally gives Stresemann high marks for his tenure as chancellor and foreign minister. He questions, however, Stresemann's handling of domestic politics after 1925.

*Ron Huch*

# AUGUST STRINDBERG

*Born:* January 22, 1849; Stockholm, Sweden
*Died:* May 14, 1912; Stockholm, Sweden
*Area of Achievement:* Literature
*Contribution*: Sweden's Strindberg stands, with the Norwegian Henrik Ibsen, as Scandinavia's greatest dramatist. He introduced both naturalism and expressionism to the modern European stage; considered to be the father of Swedish literature, with dozens of novels, essays, and scientific treatises as well as more than fifty plays to his credit, he never received that country's Nobel Prize but permanently influenced the shape of twentieth century world theater.

## *Early Life*

Born into a successful merchant family, the third son of Carl Oscar Strindberg and Ulrika Eleonora Norling, Johan August Strindberg enjoyed an orderly, if emotionally undemonstrative, childhood, until his mother's death when he was only thirteen. His father's coldness and hasty marriage to Strindberg's governess were, according to some biographers, the precipitating factors in Strindberg's lifelong anxieties about his place in society and his ambivalent relationships with the women in his life. His teen years became a series of explorations into literature, the occult, and science, always motivated by the emptiness he felt from the loss of his mother. He attended several schools, finally seeking a medical education at the university at Uppsala, but dropped out suddenly in 1872.

A prolific letter-writer, Strindberg chronicled his own early life in correspondence to his brothers and friends and wrote a fictionalized autobiography entitled *Tjänstekvinnans son: En själs utvecklingshistoria* (4 volumes, 1886; *The Son of a Servant: The Story of the Evolution of a Human Being,* 1966, first volume only), from which many of the details of his youth are taken. Contact with the Royal Theater of Stockholm, first as a bit-part actor and then as a playwright, began his interest in drama; his first production was of his play, *I Rom* (1870). His early writing included journalistic essays on contemporary political topics, a combative habit that was to continue throughout his life.

## *Life's Work*

Although not his first commercial work, Strindberg's play *Fröken Julie* (1888; *Miss Julie*, 1912), first brought him international recognition as a playwright in the new naturalistic vein, a trend in theater owing its popularity in large part to the independent theater movement advocated in France by André Antoine, in Germany by Otto Brahm, and in England by Jacob Thomas Grein. This one-act play (with a balletic interlude), not only a model of naturalistic pyschological characterization but also a miniature portrait of Strindberg's subsequent thematic preoccupations, was performed throughout Europe whenever the independent theater's repertory needed a new play. In this first wave of mature creativity, Strindberg fed the new theater (again alongside Ibsen) with *Fadren* (1887; *The Father*, 1899) and, after a period of instability (his "Inferno"), two other plays on the battle of marriage, *Dödsdansen första delen* (1901; *The Dance of Death I*), and *Dödsdansen, andra delen* (1901; *The Dance of Death II*, 1912), while at the same time publishing several novels, most notably the autobiographical *Inferno* (1897; English translation, 1912), in which he describes this most tumultuous period of his life.

The explosive and egoistic personality of Strindberg was often combined with his exaggerated sense of self-righteousness to produce a public image of a fiery, tyrannical man of letters; in private life he was shy, insecure, and constantly enthralled by his affection for others, first fantasizing about love affairs, next perceiving slights to his honor, and finally living in a dream construction made of his own psychological delusions. His behavior, typically artistic in that he always walked a fine line between creativity and madness, became erratic enough in the years from 1892 to 1898, especially 1895-1896, that scholars divide his life work at that point, referring to pre- and post-Inferno outlooks and styles. These years, often called the "Inferno Crisis," marked a change in Strindberg's dramatic style; whether his new attitude reflected a conversion or a regression is a matter of contention, but he clearly altered his view of stage language, if not his major themes.

He emerged from that period with even greater creative powers, turning out the three-part play *Till Damaskus* (1898-1904; *To Damascus*, 1913), *Ett drömspel* (1902; *A Dream Play*, 1912), and several other works in the first few years of the twentieth century. His dramatic style during this outburst was markedly different from the earlier naturalism: Now Strindberg moved almost cinematically from scene to scene, dealing with personal and universal symbols in great sweeps of ideas, depicting historical and archetypal characters, trying out a fragmented, internalized communication of character, theme, and plot that eventually earned the name "expressionism" and became the major framework of German drama between the world wars.

In addition to his literary contributions to the theater, Strindberg established the "intimate" theatrical style, in which a small audience experienced plays in "chamber"-sized settings. Strindberg, along with August Falck, an actor and producer who had toured *Miss Julie* to great acclaim in 1906, founded the Intimate Theater in Stockholm, contributing play after play to its repertory. In its first few seasons, Maurice Maeterlinck's *L'Intruse* (1890; *The Intruder*, 1891) was the only non-Strindberg play in the repertory.

Part of Strindberg's fascination with the theater included his love of actresses, three of whom he married: Siri von Essen (married to Strindberg from 1877 to 1892), Frida Uhl (1893-1897), and Harriet Bosse (1901-1904). His major female roles (usually in combat with a Strindbergian alter-ego) were invariably written with one or another actress specifically in mind, and today modern actresses are challenged to bring these characters to life in Strindberg's conception.

Strindberg retired to apartments in Stockholm, which he referred to as "The Blue Tower," during the last years of his life (1908-1912), and he was cared for in an ambiguous relationship with Fanny Falkner, also a young actress. There, too, his output was prodigious, but none of these works, possibly excepting one of his last plays, *Stora landsvägen* (1909; *The Great Highway*, 1954), enjoyed the same notoriety as his earlier work. The disappointment of being rejected for the Nobel Prize (probably political in motivation) was greatly relieved by the spontaneous homage paid to him on his sixtieth birthday by the workers of Stockholm, who saw Strindberg as a champion of the working class. Strindberg referred to this acclamation as the "anti-Nobel" prize.

After one last politically explosive series of his journal articles was published in Stockholm, Strindberg succumbed to stomach cancer in 1912, leaving behind a vast canon of fiction, drama, and essays as well as private correspondence that would become multivolume editions after his death. In his obsessive, almost paranoiac behavior, his unrealistic view of the secret power of women against men, and his tyrannical condescension to his peers, Strindberg never gained during his lifetime the respect afforded him after his death.

### *Summary*

Among the great names in modern theater, August Strindberg is known for his psychological insight into the workings not only of women but also of the men they dominate in his dramas. While his naturalistic plays are still performed with regularity, the more expressionistic plays are neglected, partly because of the financially exhausting demands of the multiple stage sets and large casts and partly because the matrices of symbols the plays present have lost their universality and stageability in the light of modern aesthetic sensibilities. Strindberg has become more interesting to critics and scholars employing a psychological approach to literature than he has to theater practitioners, and his unequivocal condemnation of the feminine mystique has weakened his contemporary currency. Nevertheless, theater and drama from World War I to the present day have taken shape largely through the influence of Strindberg on his followers, in the areas of naturalistic characterization and in the free-form, subjectively presented, "theatrical" styles of contemporary auteur directors. Anticipating the filmic language of cuts, zooms, segues, and similar cinematic syntax, Strindberg broke the mold he himself had helped to create. Subsequent playwrights have seen in Strindberg's life itself the raw material for dramatic presentation—Friedrich Dürrenmatt, with *Play Strindberg: Totentanz nach August Strindberg* (1969; *Play Strindberg: The Dance of Death*, 1971), and Michael Meyer (a Strindberg scholar), with *Lunatic and Lover* (1981), are examples.

*Bibliography*

Brandell, Gunnar. *Strindberg in Inferno*. Translated by Barry Jacobs. Cambridge, Mass.: Harvard University Press, 1974. A psychoanalytical study of Strindberg's turbulent middle life, illuminating the substance and power of his later writing. Brandell, considered Sweden's leading Strindberg expert, traces the playwright's path both into and out of the crisis, adding a valuable description of the works generated from 1893 to 1898. Includes notes, a bibliography, and an index of names.

Johannesson, Eric O. *The Novels of August Strindberg: A Study in Theme and Structure*. Berkeley: University of California Press, 1968. A good introduction to the prose work, which in turn informs the plays. Discusses fourteen novels available in English, examining the metaphoric language and the techniques of the novels' construction, noting Strindberg's difficulties with muddling "illusion and reality." Includes a bibliography and index of proper names.

Johnson, Walter. *Strindberg and the Historical Drama*. Seattle: University of Washington Press, 1963. Literary analysis of Strindberg's neglected (in the United States) history plays, especially those written after the Inferno period, that casts light on Strindberg's erudition, craft, and nationalistic zeal. Johnson finds lasting literary merit in at least twelve of the "dynamic" historical plays. Includes bibliographic and other notes and an index.

Lagercrantz, Olof. *August Strindberg*. Translated by Anselm Hollo. New York: Farrar, Straus and Giroux, 1984. Strindberg's life described as a series of psychological explanations for his creative output. Oddly sparse, even cavalier, regarding the details of Strindberg's theatrical and dramatic activity. Includes sixty-three illustrations throughout the text, biographical notes on figures mentioned in the text, a select bibliography of Strindberg editions, and an index.

Lamm, Martin. *August Strindberg*. Translated and edited by Harry G. Carlson. New York: Benjamin Blom, 1971. Written in the classic literary biography form, the two parts of this thorough study—"Before the Inferno Crisis" and "After the Conversion"—anticipate the major division of all subsequent Strindberg scholarship. Lamm analyzes the work from a literary rather than a theatrical viewpoint but adds some interesting details concerning the Scandinavian Experimental Theater of Denmark (Strindberg lived in Copenhagen from 1887 to 1889) and the Intimate Theater of his later years. Includes notes, a bibliography, and an index.

Morgan, Margery. *August Strindberg*. New York: Grove Press, 1985. Part of the Modern Dramatists series. A brief biography followed by a thorough critical overview of Strindberg's work as theatrical script, not merely as literature. A full description of the canon (concentrating on the dramas), with contemporary interpretation, plus a valuable section on Strindberg as director of the Intimate Theater. Contains fifteen illustrations, including a photographic self-portrait with his daughters, an appendix, notes and reference, a valuable bibliography, and an index.

Mortensen, Brita M. E., and Brian Downs. *Strindberg: An Introduction to His Life and Work*. Cambridge, England: Cambridge University Press, 1949. A centenary introduction to the man and his work, divided into four periods and four genres—plays, novels, short stories, and autobiographical writings—with an added chapter on miscellaneous works. Includes a good conclusion, a select bibliography, and an index.

Ollén, Gunnar. *August Strindberg*. Translated by Peter Tirner. New York: Frederick Ungar, 1972. Part of the World Dramatists series. Bracketed by a brief biography and an overview of Strindberg's stage work, a capsule description of each of the plays in almost encyclopedic form, in the order of their composition, is presented. This is a useful quick reference to specific titles. Includes a chronology, a bibliography, and an index.

Reinert, Otto, ed. *Strindberg: A Collection of Critical Essays*. Englewood Cliffs, N.J.: Prentice-Hall, 1971. An introduction by the editor, followed by twelve articles in three sections: "The Divided Self," "A New Theater," and "Some Major Plays." A good overview of how scholars discuss Strindberg's work, ranging from Robert Brustein's study of *The Father* to Brian Rothwell's essay on the chamber plays. Includes a chronology of important dates, notes on the editor and contributors, and a selected bibliography.

Steene, Birgitta. *The Greatest Fire: A Study of August Strindberg*. Carbondale: Southern Illinois University Press, 1973. This study moves away from the common psychological (and therefore "sour") approach to Strindberg, concentrating instead on the innovations and craft in his work and its importance in studying modern playwrights such as Edward Albee, Harold Pinter, even Tennessee Williams. Includes notes, a selected bibliography, and an index.

Strindberg, August. *Inferno, Alone, and Other Writings*. Edited by Evert Sprinchorn. Garden City, N.Y.: Doubleday, 1968. An accessible selection of Strindberg's autobiographical work, which alters facts into a fiction more true than the original. A substantial introduction defends Strindberg's genius.

___________. *Letters of Strindberg to Harriet Bosse*. Edited and translated by Arvid Paulson. New York: Grosset & Dunlap, 1959. A collection of letters to his third wife, written from 1900 (before their marriage in 1901) to 1908, when she remarried. Her personal comments and ten letters to Strindberg, are included. A frighteningly personal entry into Strindberg's mentality. Includes a brief introduction, a biographical note on Harriet Bosse, notes, and an index.

Valency, Maurice. *The Flower and the Castle: An Introduction to Modern Drama*. New York: Macmillan, 1963. On Ibsen and Strindberg, this important critical discussion of the sweeping changes in theater history from Eugène Scribe's "well-made play" to realism is a central study for both authors and for the period. Of Strindberg's neurotic predilections he remarks, "At bottom the subject matter of his plays is almost invariably the same." Of his style, it "is at the opposite pole from that of Ibsen." Includes notes, an extensive bibliography, and an index.

*Thomas J. Taylor*

# SUKARNO

*Born:* June 6, 1901; Surabaja, East Java
*Died:* June 21, 1970; Djakarta, Indonesia
*Areas of Achievement:* Government and politics
*Contribution:* A superb orator and a charismatic leader, Sukarno raised Indonesian national consciousness while providing a rudimentary administrative infrastructure under Dutch colonial and Japanese occupational forces. After the Japanese defeat in 1945, he declared his nation's independence and served as president and strongman until 1965, when involvement in a Communist-inspired coup undermined his authority.

## *Early Life*

According to his autobiography, Amhad Sukarno was the child of a Balinese mother of the House of Singaradja and a Javanese father who was a descendant of the Sultan of Kediri. Other accounts regard him variously as the illegitimate son of a Dutch coffee planter and a native peasant girl, the offspring of a Eurasian plantation overseer, and the son of Sunan Pakubuwono X of Surakarta, spirited away from the palace to escape death. The circumstances of Sukarno's birth are obscured by these and similar contradictory stories. There is no question, however, that Sukarno grew up in abject poverty. The Sukarno family of four—he had a sister two years his senior—lived on a monthly income of the Dutch equivalent of twenty-five rupiahs. Sukarno's father, Sukemi, a strict schoolteacher and a Muslim, made sure that his son received a good education at his own school in reading, writing, and mathematics, as well as being trained in the Islamic faith, the Indonesian culture, and the Western sciences. Sukarno was graduated from his father's school in 1914.

While instruction in Islamics and *gotong royong* (the Indonesian principle of mutual assistance) was readily available, access to Western thought was not. Dutch regulations allowed only a few native students to attend the Dutch schools that were a stepping stone to higher education in The Netherlands. In spite of financial difficulties, Sukemi sent Ahmad to the Dutch-language elementary school and after two years enrolled him in the Hogere Burger School in Surabaja. Umar Sayed Tjokroaminoto, who had helped Sukemi enroll his son, provided room and board for young Sukarno. Entrance difficulties paled in comparison with the ordeal of a brown Indonesian youth coping with white Dutch schoolboys. Sukarno managed, but he developed a distinct abhorrence for the culture that Dutch education at Surabaja projected. His abhorrence was enhanced by his surroundings at Tjokroaminoto's, which were suffused with discussions of colonial exploitation of ignorant masses. He was graduated from the Hogere Burger School in 1921.

Following China, India, and the Philippines, Indonesia began its movement for independence in 1908 with the *Budi Umoto* (pure endeavor) leading to Sarekat Islam (islamic union) in 1912. Headed by Tjokroaminoto, Sarekat attracted a wide spectrum of rural and urban Indonesians. Its membership included the union's founding merchant class, urban workers, and religious personages. At the time Sukarno arrived in Surabaja, the union claimed eighty branches throughout the archipelago with close to two million members. The contending factions for the union's leadership were the scripturalists and the Marxists. The former, descendants of Muslim sea merchants who had brought Islam to Indonesia in the fourteenth century, defended the feudal system encompassing Java, Sumatra, Malaya, and Borneo. The latter wished to internationalize the party, educate Indonesia's peasants, and help them arrive at self-rule. The Marxists' bid for leadership resulted in the expulsion of Communists from the party in 1920. The party's subsequent policy of refusing membership to Communists depleted Sarekat's ranks so that it was clearly on the decline by the time Sukarno left Surabaja.

In 1921, Sukarno moved to Bandung to study engineering at its newly established technical college. The city teemed with political activity, especially among Indonesian youth who had graduated from Dutch universities and who were back home, anxious to effect change. Drawing on this body, and equipped with a wealth of political savvy from Tjokroaminoto's cookshop of nationalism, Sukarno founded a Study Club in 1925 and transformed it into a political forum, the Nationalist Party of Indonesia (NPI), in 1927. The NPI platform advocated intense struggle for national independence through noncooperation with the Dutch Indies government. Sukarno was elected the party's chairman.

Initially, the Dutch exercised a policy of permissiveness. This allowed the NPI to become the hub of a still larger national coalition, the Association of Political Organizations of Indonesian People. Later, however, to put an end to Sukarno's bold activities, the Dutch government changed its stance so that, in 1929, governmental troops surrounded the house where Sukarno was a guest, arrested him, and, following a public trial, put him in prison for the next two years. Soon after his release from prison, Sukarno resumed his previous activities as the leader of the NPI. Arrested again in 1933, he was exiled without trial to Flores; he remained there until 1942, when Japanese forces invading the islands freed him.

### *Life's Work*

Sukarno emerged from exile a distinguished politician. Capitalizing on the Japanese need to reach his masses, he negotiated his way into Indonesian politics by agreeing to cooperate with the Japanese as long as they regarded him as the leader of his country's nationalists. He also received high-level assurances that he could promote his political aims, which culminated in an independent Indonesia. Satisfied that the Japanese would provide necessary means of communication to educate and unify the Indonesian masses, Sukarno began the distasteful task of placing his people as *romushas* (male laborers) at the service of the Japanese. Soon after, he founded an advisory council and established the Indonesian military force, Peta. While engaged in administering Japanese affairs, he strengthened his own position as well by placing longtime associates like Mohammad Hatta in important positions throughout the nationalist administrative hierarchy.

By early 1945, it became reasonably clear that Japan could not win the war. To prevent Indonesia's reversion to its past colonial status, the Japanese established a committee, chaired by Sukarno, to study the implications of making Indonesia independent. The committee recommended Sukarno's *pantja sila*—nationalism, internationalism, democracy, social democracy and belief in God—as the operative principles for Indonesian *merdeka* (independence). Soon after, Sukarno and Hatta jointly proclaimed Indonesia's independence.

The entrance of the Allied armies into the Pacific theater strengthened the Dutch position enough to try to reestablish colonial rule in the archipelago. Sukarno and the nationalists resisted this in the face of Western-inspired embargoes and held steadfastly to their revolutionary capital of Jogjakarta. Furthermore, with world public opinion on their side, they forced the Dutch to accept the United States of Indonesia in 1949 and the Republic of Indonesia in 1950. Sukarno moved to Djakarta and became president of the republic. Sukarno preferred an executive presidency, but, considering that Hatta and others had won the negotiations in The Hague, he conceded most of the power to them. Hatta became the vice president, governing a rather large parliament and interacting with a burgeoning system of parties. Hatta's task was difficult: He and the president had long-standing differences of opinion on the course that Indonesia should take.

In 1960, Sukarno's disagreements with Hatta culminated in the latter's dismissal and the abolition of the one-hundred-member cabinet and the parties. Sukarno then instituted his guided democracy. Based on *gotong royong*, guided democracy allowed all interested political factions to contribute their views. Unlike Western democracies, however, it did not call for a vote and a resolution. Rather a strongman, in this case Sukarno, weighed those views in private and issued a decree.

Once established as the ultimate authority in domestic affairs, Sukarno directed his attention to international politics. Even though since 1956 the United States had contributed close to one billion dollars to the Indonesian economy, Sukarno all but broke with the United States, saying, "to hell with their dollars!" By siding with Communist China in the Sino-Soviet split, he also affronted Moscow, which had poured close to a billion dollars in armaments into Indonesia. Finally, he recalled his ambassador from the United Nations, claiming that in the dispute between Indonesia and Malaysia the

United Nations had sided with Malaysia to appease the capitalists and strengthen their encirclement of the Archipelago.

Although he was neglectful of the results, Sukarno's activities on the international scene impacted his decisions at home. He could no longer administer *gotong royong* impartially and properly. He consistently found himself at odds with the army, which resented the president's attitude toward the Communists. For their part, the Communists supported Sukarno's policies, even his senseless wars, and applauded his decisions. Furthermore, freed from contending with the president, the Communists used their energies in penetrating all levels of the civil and military administration that Sukarno had painstakingly put in place over forty years.

The Communist Party of Indonesia (PKI) was founded in 1914 as a block within the Sarekat Islam on which it drew for membership as well. In spite of factionalism and many setbacks, it successfully fought nationalism and Islam so that by the 1950's it was already a force with which to be reckoned. The movement came fully into its own under Dipa Nusantara Aidit, a pro-Moscow member who adopted and promoted Sukarno's philosophy and politics. Within five years of Aidit involvement, the PKI had mustered enough strength in the army alone to attempt a coup in 1965. Ostensibly its purpose was to strengthen Sukarno's position, but the PKI's real goal was to bring Indonesia under Communist rule before the ailing president's death. The coup was not successful. Implicated in the overthrow attempt, Sukarno reverted to the figurehead that he had been before the introduction of guided democracy. Over the next months, the Communist Party was subjected to a systematic bloodbath. Sukarno's pleas to stop the bloodshed fell on deaf ears, while in Java and Bali between 250,000 and 300,000 Indonesians lost their lives. General Suharto became the acting president in 1967 and the president of Indonesia in 1968. Sukarno sank into disgrace and dotage.

Sukarno died of acute kidney poisoning at the age of sixty-nine. Rather than being buried in the garden of his Batu Tulin home as he had wished, he was interred next to his mother at Biltar, perhaps to prevent the institution of a pilgrimage place close to Djakarta. Nevertheless, Indonesians attended his funeral in droves and a magnificent mausoleum was dedicated to his efforts. Sukarno wore dark glasses, the black cap of the peasant, and the uniform of the military. His countrymen never questioned his revolutionary zeal. To them he was affectionately known as Bung Karno, Bapak, and the lifetime president of the republic. His personal life was as colorful as his public life. His love for women was proverbial. He married seven times, four of the marriages allowed by Islam. He was survived by his only son and several daughters.

### *Summary*

Sukaro and Indonesia grew up together from poverty to presidency and independence respectively. The colorful and charismatic Sukarno, who claimed he was at once Christian, Muslim, Hindu, and Marxist, made it possible. As a child Sukarno was attracted to the world of the *wayang* (shadow play). In that world the *dalang* (showman) always found a common denominator and made the diversity of the real blend and blend until it assumed the uniformity of the unreal or the shadow. The *dalang* created harmony among opposing factors. Sukarno's approach to politics included elements of the *wayang*. As a Muslim, he exercised *mushavirat* (discussion and deliberation) and *ittifaq* (consensus); as an Indonesian, he practiced *gotong royong*, and as a Marxist he interpreted the outcome as would a socialist. He then expected his people to agree with his views and, more important, to implement them.

*Gotong royong*, however, belonged to the polity of traditional Java. It could not find its proper place in the 1960's international arena when Indonesian nationalism was no longer a monolithic opposition of the oppressed against colonialism. Concrete, diverse, and diametrically opposing forces were at work both within and outside Indonesia. Internally, the country cried for economic reform and military discipline. Internationally it needed a ruler who could harness and utilize the potential benefits of Islam, Western technology, marketing, and Communism, all contending fiercely for attention in the archipelago. The 1965 coup was Indonesia's first encounter with international politics.

*Bibliography*

Benda, Harry J. *The Crescent and the Rising Sun: Indonesian Islam Under the Japanese Occupation, 1942-45*. The Hague: W. van Hoeve, 1958. A well-documented account of Indonesian Islam under Japanese rule, this book combines careful historical research with sociological insight. The chapters on "The Colonial Legacy" are especially important for understanding Sarekat Islam and its role in Sukarno's life. Includes copious notes, a comprehensive bibliography, and an index.

Brackman, Arnold C. *The Communist Collapse in Indonesia*. New York: W. W. Norton, 1969. Brackman concentrates on the dynamics of power in Southeast Asia during the Vietnam War. The book also includes a comprehensive account of the rise of Aidit and of his role in the 1965 coup. Contains notes, an annotated bibliography, and a map.

__________. *Indonesian Communism: A History*. New York: Frederick A. Praeger, 1963. The first full-length history of the Communist Party of Indonesia, this book deals with the genesis of the movement and analyzes its turbulent course between 1920 and 1963. Must reading for understanding how the political parties reacted to the Dutch, the Japanese, and Sukarno.

Crouch, Harold. *The Army and Politics in Indonesia*. Ithaca, N.Y.: Cornell

University Press, 1978. Crouch provides an in-depth examination of the role of the army in Indonesian politics and discusses the various ways whereby the army expanded its civil interests under Sukarno's guided democracy before 1965. After the coup, Crouch says, the army furthered its socioeconomic gains. Includes a comprehensive bibliography and an index.

Dahm, Bernhard. *Sukarno and the Struggle for Indonesian Independence.* Ithaca, N.Y.: Cornell University Press, 1969. Dahm studies Sukarno's complex character in the context of the Indonesian concept of *Ratu Adil* (just savior). His book is a scholarly account of the development of young Sukarno's career and of his thought before Indonesian independence. Includes a glossary, a bibliography, and an index.

Fischer, Louis. *The Story of Indonesia.* Westport, Conn.: Greenwood Press, 1959. A journalist with exclusive access to Sukarno, Fischer provides a balanced view of Indonesia's past and its revolutionary present through interviews with the country's leaders. Copiously illustrated with a bibliography and an index.

Geertz, Clifford. *Islam Observed.* Chicago: University of Chicago Press, 1968. Geertz views Islam in Indonesia as an understanding of Islamic principles rather than as a set of accepted dogma. In this context, his discussion of Sukarno differs from those of most other writers. Includes two maps, an annotated bibliography, and an index.

Hughes, John. *Indonesian Upheaval.* New York: David McKay, 1967. This firsthand report deals exclusively with the students' campaign against Sukarno after the 1965 coup and with the slaughter that ensued. Contains an index.

Legge, John D. *Sukarno: A Political Biography.* New York: Praeger, 1972. A complete biography of Sukarno, this book first surveys Sukarno's actions and words in a general context and then follows with an in-depth analysis of specific questions and issues. This work is necessary reading for understanding Sukarno's motives, accuracy of his judgment, and leadership capability. Includes an annotated bibliography and an index.

Penders, C. L. M. *The Life and Times of Sukarno.* London: Sidgwick & Jackson, 1974. Penders based his biography of Sukarno on statements made by Sukarno's associates, especially Abu Hanifa and Hatta, and on the president's autobiography and speeches. Illustrated, with notes, a bibliography, and an index.

Sukarno, Ahmad. *Sukarno: An Autobiography as Told to Cindy Adams.* Indianapolis: Bobbs-Merrill, 1965. This is a standard autobiography, written in the president's casual style. It includes a wealth of information on Indonesian culture, politics, and Islam. Factual, readable, but not always accurate and reliable. Contains a glossary and an index.

Wilhelm, Donald. *Emerging Indonesia.* New York: Macmillan, 1980. This book includes four chapters on the rise and fall of Sukarno. Chapter 4, "The Grand Conspiracy," deals with Sukarno's involvement in the 1965 Communist coup, leading to his dismissal from office. Illustrated with a good index and map.

*Iraj Bashiri*

# SUN YAT-SEN

*Born:* November 12, 1866; Choyhung, Kwangtung, China
*Died:* March 12, 1925; Peking, China
*Areas of Achievement:* Government and politics
*Contribution:* Sun founded the Kuomintang (Chinese Nationalist Party) and led the Republican Revolution of 1911. He is honored by both the Communists and the Nationalists as the founding father of the Chinese republic.

## *Early Life*

Sun Yat-sen was born on November 12, 1866, in the village of Choyhung, some eighty miles from Canton. His family was highly respectable, conservative, and ordinary. His father, a thin, ascetic man with a reputation for honesty, was a small landowner who also worked as a tailor. Sun's mother was conservative, observing ancestral rites, enduring bound feet, and teaching filial piety to her six children (Sun Yat-sen was the fifth). She was, however, literate, which was rare among Chinese women of the time. Sun apparently displayed a rebellious spirit from his early youth. He began attending his village school at the age of eight but also worked in the fields after school and during harvest season. By the age of ten, he had protested footbinding and criticized the traditional teaching methods of his school. A good student, Sun studied the Chinese language and the Confucian classics.

Sun's village was in the area of China most affected by Western influence. Two of his uncles had gone to the United States during the California Gold Rush and never returned, his grandmother told him stories about Westerners, and his elder brother, Ah-mei, emigrated in 1872 to Hawaii, where he became successful as a shopkeeper and as a rice and sugarcane grower. Sun joined his brother in Honolulu in 1879, working in his shop. He soon became bored, however, and went to the Church of England boarding school at Iolani in 1880. There he quickly learned English and became one of the first Chinese to obtain a Western education, studying geography, mathematics, science, and the Bible. He apparently became a convert of Christianity in 1882 and thereafter was an enthusiastic admirer of Western ways. All of this alarmed his elder brother, who sent him home in 1883.

Sun did not fit into village life, however, as he had learned to despise the old ways. He earned the enmity of the villagers by attacking the worship of idols. His father therefore sent him to another Christian school in Hong Kong to forestall further embarrassment. Between 1884 and 1892, Sun attended Queen's College, married a girl chosen by his parents, and earned a medical degree. His patron in medical school was the English dean of the college, James Cantlie. As the Western powers began to shear away China's peripheral territories, Sun turned to politics, hatching plots to reform or overturn the Ch'ing (Manchu) Dynasty. By 1894, he had decided to give up the practice of medicine and devote his life to revolutionary activities.

### *Life's Work*

During the Sino-Japanese War of 1894-1895, which the Chinese unexpectedly lost, Sun launched his first overt attempts at revolution. He founded his first revolutionary party, the Hsing Chung Hui ("Revive China Society"), in 1894 among overseas Chinese and plotted an uprising against the dynasty in October, 1895. Before the revolt could be launched, however, the plot was discovered, the Ch'ing officials crushed the organization, and Sun fled the country, a price on his head. He spent most of the next sixteen years outside China, traveling around the world to raise money and popular support for his revolutionary activities from overseas Chinese.

Sun arrived in London in September, 1896, to visit his former mentor, Cantlie, and to raise support for his cause. On October 11, while walking near the Chinese embassy, he was abducted by the Chinese and held prisoner in the embassy. He was to be shipped back to China and executed. Eventually, he got word to Cantlie that he was being held prisoner, and Cantlie obtained his release by taking his case to the London newspapers. Overnight, Sun became famous. He spent the next two years in Europe, reading and studying Western political theory, including the writings of Karl Marx and Friedrich Engels. In 1898, he traveled to Japan, where he continued to build his revolutionary party and to argue against Chinese moderates who believed that the Ch'ing monarchy could be reformed. His organization launched an abortive attack on the dynasty after the Boxer Rebellion in 1900. Undaunted, he traveled around the world again, from 1903 to 1905, raising more support for his plans.

By 1905, Sun was back in Japan, where he founded a new revolutionary party, the T'ung Meng Hui ("Revolutionary Alliance"), with the goals of destroying the Ch'ing Dynasty, creating a republic, establishing full diplomatic relations with the world, and carrying out a social revolution. This was a significant political party, with branches in China and among overseas Chinese. Between 1906 and 1909, the party launched six revolutionary attempts, all of which failed. Sun's attempts at violent revolution made him unwelcome in most of Asia. He therefore went to the West again in 1909. In his absence, his party launched two more abortive attempts at revolution before finally succeeding in October, 1911. Sun returned to China in December, 1911, and assumed the office of president of a provisional Chinese republic on January 1, 1912.

Yet Sun's revolution was far from complete. The Ch'ing emperor still occupied the throne, and the foreign powers continued to recognize the Ch'ing as the legitimate government of China. Moreover, Sun's armies were small and poorly organized. His problem, then, was to develop a power base sufficient to overthrow the Ch'ing. In order to accomplish this overthrow, he made an alliance with a powerful Ch'ing general, Yuan Shih-k'ai, who agreed to support the republic in return for being made the provisional president. Sun hoped that Yuan could be converted to republicanism and that genuine representative institutions could be instituted. To further this end, Sun and his associates founded the Kuomintang ("Nationalist Party") in August, 1912. It soon became clear, however, that Yuan had no loyalty to republicanism and that he aspired to become a new emperor. Consequently, in the summer of 1913 the Kuomintang launched a so-called second revolution. It quickly failed, and Sun once again fled the country, arriving in Tokyo in early December, 1913.

Between 1913 and 1920, Sun struggled to find a formula for successful revolution. His attempts to gain control of the republican government by parliamentary means after Yuan's death in June, 1916, failed, and he concluded that his only recourse was to establish a rival government in south China. This was accomplished by April, 1921. Sun hoped to launch a "northern expedition" to unify the country, but this required a strong party organization built around Sun's ideology (the "Three Principles of the People") and outside military support. On January 26, 1923, Sun signed an agreement with the Soviet Union, whereby the Soviets agreed to help unify China. Sun was apparently not attracted by Communist doctrines but by the opportunity to obtain military and political assistance. The Soviets hoped to gain control of the Chinese revolution by working within the Kuomintang.

By 1924, the Kuomintang had been reorganized into a tightly disciplined party along the lines of the Soviet Communist Party, and the Chinese Communist Party had allied with the Kuomintang. The Soviets also supplied significant military assistance. Thus strengthened, Sun traveled to Peking in 1925 to consult with the Peking government leaders about potential unification of China. While there, in March, 1925, he fell seriously ill and died.

After his death, Kuomintang leaders took steps to ensure that his memory would be preserved. Eventually, he was honored as the father of the republic by both the Nationalists and the Communists. His thought, particularly the Three Principles of the People (San-min chu-i), was canonized. In the Three Principles of the People (nationalism, democracy, people's livelihood), Sun attempted to formulate a plan for China's national development. Nationalism initially demanded the overthrow of the Ch'ing Dynasty and then the ousting of the imperialist powers from China. Democracy called for the institution of a republican form of government through three stages of military government, political tutelage, and constitutional government. The people's livelihood was a quasi-socialist program that explicitly rejected Marxism while advocating such concepts as state ownership of industries. The Three Principles of the People were adopted as the official ideology of the Kuomintang and became the national ideology of the Republic of China on the mainland of China (1927-1949) and on the island of Taiwan after 1949.

*Summary*

Sun Yat-sen was one of the most important political figures of twentieth century China. A short but strongly built man, with a broad face, wide-set eyes, and a high forehead, he had great personal magnetism and a commanding oratorical style. He was courageous, idealistic, and selfless. Yet his career as a revolutionary was marked by a continuous series of debacles and defeats. Many of his failures were attributable to his own limitations as a leader. Too often, he relied upon subordinates who flattered him but did not serve him well. His headstrong, impulsive nature led him into many foolhardy, unprofitable adventures. Nevertheless, most Chinese believe him to be the greatest man of China's twentieth century. He symbolizes honesty, sincerity, and idealism. His writings have exerted enormous influence in China. In spite of his personal and political shortcomings, he epitomizes China's long struggle to become a modern nation.

*Bibliography*

Bruce, Robert. *Sun Yat-sen.* New York: Oxford University Press, 1969. A short, popular biography, this thin volume encapsulates the major events of Sun's life and provides a reliable introduction. Contains several pages of photographs.

Chen, Stephen, and Robert Payne. *Sun Yat-sen, A Portrait.* New York: John Day, 1946. This book is an early attempt to record the essential outline of Sun's life and to place it within the context of twentieth century China. The authors received the assistance of Sun's family and the nationalist government, so it has the flavor of an authorized biography.

Leng, Shao Chuan, and Norman D. Palmer. *Sun Yat-sen and Communism.* New York: Frederick A. Praeger, 1960. The authors explore the relationship between Sun and Communism, reviewing Sun's contacts with Western thought and the process of his ideological development. It compares the similarities and differences between his thought and Chinese Communism.

Schiffrin, Harold Z. *Sun Yat-sen: Reluctant Revolutionary.* Boston: Little, Brown, 1980. Schiffrin provides a balanced appraisal of Sun's life and career in this well-written biography designed for general audiences. He presents Sun both as a man and as a symbol of China's national regeneration.

__________. *Sun Yat-sen and the Origins of the Chinese Revolution.* Berkeley: University of California Press, 1968. This brilliant, scholarly book explores Sun's early career, particularly his exposure to Western thought and institutions, and his travels among the overseas Chinese communities. It is an indispensable source for understanding Sun's early years and his relationship to the larger Chinese revolution.

Sharman, Lyon. *Sun Yat-sen: His Life and Its Meaning*. New York: John Day, 1934. Sharman witnessed the process by which Sun was turned into a national symbol and determined to write a biography that would penetrate beyond the ideological shibboleths to the man himself. As such, this is a "critical" biography that annoyed many Chinese nationalists. It is an early attempt to present a balanced image of the man.

Wilbur, C. Martin. *Sun Yat-sen: Frustrated Patriot*. New York: Columbia University Press, 1976. Wilbur focuses on the last years of Sun's career, particularly his efforts to find funding for his revolutionary activities, his search for foreign support, and his relationship with the Soviet Union. He demonstrates how Sun's hopes were frustrated by the intractable realities within China and by foreign manipulation.

Wong, J. Y. *The Origins of an Heroic Image: Sun Yat-sen in London, 1896-1897*. New York: Oxford University Press, 1986. Wong reexamines the events of Sun's abduction by the Chinese in London, attempting to clarify some of the mysteries surrounding the situation. It is a fascinating exploration of the events themselves and of the way they have entered into the popular image of Sun Yat-sen.

*Loren W. Crabtree*

# RABINDRANATH TAGORE

*Born:* May 7, 1861; Calcutta, India
*Died:* August 7, 1941; Calcutta, India
*Area of Achievement:* Literature
*Contribution:* The prolific author of more than one hundred books of verse, fifty dramas, forty works of fiction, and fifteen books of essays, Nobel laureate Tagore is recognized as a pioneer in Bengali literature, particularly the short story, and is internationally acclaimed as one of the world's finest lyric poets. The foundation for Tagore's literary achievements is his vision of the universal man, based on his unique integration of Eastern and Western thought.

## *Early Life*

Rabindranath Tagore was born on May 7, 1861, into a prosperous Bengali family in Calcutta, India. The fourteenth child and eighth son of Debendranath Tagore and Sarada Devi, he grew up surrounded by the artistic and intellectual pursuits of his elders. Agricultural landholdings in East Bengal supported the family's leisurely life-style, and their Calcutta mansion was a center for Bengalis who, like the Tagores, sought to integrate Western influences in literature, philosophy, arts, and sciences into their own culture. Young Tagore was a sensitive and interested child who, like his siblings, lived in awe of his father, a pillar of the Hindu reform group Brahmo Samaj. Cared for mainly by servants because of his mother's ill health, he lived a relatively confined existence, watching the life of crowded Calcutta from the windows and courtyards of his protected home.

From an early age, Tagore's literary talents were encouraged. Like the other Tagore children, he was thoroughly schooled in Bengali language and literature as a foundation for integrating culturally diverse influences, and, throughout his long career, Tagore composed most of his work in Bengali. In 1868, he was enrolled in the Oriental Seminary, where he quickly rebelled against formal education. Unhappy, transferring to different schools, Tagore nevertheless became appreciated as a budding poet during this time both in school and at home. In 1873, he was withdrawn from school to accompany his father on a tour of northern India and the Himalayas. This journey served as a rite of passage for the boy, who was deeply influenced by his father's presence and by the grandeur of nature. It also provided his first opportunity to roam in open countryside.

Returning to Calcutta, Tagore boycotted school and, from 1873 on, was educated at home by tutors and his brothers. In 1874, he began to recite publicly his poetry, and his first long poem was published in the monthly journal *Bhārati*. For the next four years, he gave recitations and published stories, essays, and experiments in drama. In 1878, Tagore went to England to prepare for a career in law at University College, London, but withdrew in 1880 and returned to India. Tagore's stay in England was not a happy one, but during those fourteen months, his intellectual horizons broadened as he read English literature with Henry Morley and became acquainted with European music and drama.

### *Life's Work*

Returning to India, Tagore resumed his writing amid the intellectual family life in Calcutta, especially influenced by his talented elder brothers Jyotirindranath (writer, translator, playwright, and musician) and the scholarly Satyendranath. Tagore's view of life at this time was melancholy; yet, with the metrical liberty of his poems in *Sandhya Sangit* (1882; evening songs), it became clear that he was already establishing new artistic and literary standards. Tagore then had a transcendental experience that abruptly changed his work. His gloomy introspection expanded in bliss and insight into the outer world, and Tagore once again perceived the innocent communion with nature that he had known as a child. This vision was reflected in *Prabhat Sangit* (1883; morning songs), and his new style was immediately popular. By his mid-twenties, Tagore had published devotional songs, poetry, drama, and literary criticism and was established as a lyric poet, primarily influenced by the early Vaishnava lyricists of Bengal and by the English Romantics. In 1883, he married Mrinalini Devi and continued to reflect his optimism in a burst of creativity that lasted for the next twenty years. During this period, he began to write nonsymbolic drama, and his verse *Kari O Komal* (1887; sharps and flats) is considered a high point in his early lyrical achievement.

In 1890, Tagore's father sent him to Shelaidaha, the family home in eastern Bengal, to oversee the family estates, and thus began the most productive period of Tagore's prolific career. His sympathetic observation of the daily activity of the Bengali peasant, as well as an intimacy with the seasons and moods of the rural countryside, sharpened Tagore's literary sensitivity and provided him with subject matter for his poems and essays during the 1890's. Tagore also wrote short stories—developing the genre in Bengali literature—and in 1891 started the monthly journal *Sadhana*, in which he published some of his work. In addition to literary output, Tagore began to lecture and write on his educational theories and the politics of Bengal, and he came more and more into public life. In 1898, he took his family to live in Shelaidaha, planning to spare his children the schooling against which he rebelled by educating them himself. The family soon moved to Santiniketan at Bolpur, where Tagore founded his experimental school, which became a lifelong commitment. He continued to write ceaselessly during this time: stories, poems, essays, textbooks, and a history of India. In 1901, he became editor of *The Bengal Review* and also launched into a period as a novelist, reflecting the political situation of the time in his work. Tagore's *Gora* (1910; English translation, 1924) is considered by many to be the greatest Bengali novel.

The year 1902 saw the school in serious financial condition and also brought the death of Tagore's wife. Others close to him passed away—his daughter in 1903, his favorite pupil in 1904, and his father in 1905—and Tagore experienced a time of withdrawal. In 1905, he was pulled back into public life by the division of Bengal. Tagore served as a highly visible leader in the antipartition nationalist movement and composed patriotic prose and songs popular with the people. In 1907, however, concerned about growing violence in the movement and its lack of social reform, Tagore suddenly withdrew from politics and retired to Santiniketan, where he resumed a life of educational and literary activity and meditation. Tagore's intuitive belief in the spirituality of life and the inherent divinity of all things was reflected in his work during this time: educational addresses at his school, a series of symbolic dramas that criticized monarchy, and an outpouring of religious poetry expressing his extremely intimate realization of God. A collection of such poems was published as *Gitanjali* (1910; English translation of *Gitanjali* and other poems, 1912). During this time in relative seclusion, Tagore the individual poet became, more and more, Tagore the universal man. When next he emerged, it would be to international acclaim.

Tagore became known outside India through the influence of the English painter William Rothstein, the organizer of the India Society in London. Rothstein arranged to publish a private edition of *Gitanjali* for India Society members, and, in 1912, Tagore's English translation appeared with an introduction by William Butler Yeats. Tagore and his poetry were introduced to influential critics and writers such as George Bernard Shaw, H. G. Wells, John Galsworthy, John Masefield, Ernest Rhys, and Ezra Pound. His reputation spread to Europe and to the United States, where, in 1912, his work appeared in the journal *Poetry* and a public edition of *Gitanjali* was published in 1913. In 1912, and again in 1913, Tagore lectured in the United States on religious and social themes, bringing the wisdom of the East to the West in his desire to move the world toward a true humanity. In November, 1913, he was awarded the Nobel Prize in Literature. In December, the University of Calcutta conferred upon him an honorary doctorate of letters, and he was knighted by the British government in 1915. Underlying Tagore's success at this time was his apprehension about the future. Essentially a nonconformist and solitary soul, Tagore believed that he would have no peace from that time on; this, indeed, did prove to be true. Sudden international recognition brought Tagore intense public response, ranging from adulation to disenchantment, and he was an often misunderstood public figure for the rest of his life. At the height of his popularity, Tagore published *Balaka* (1916; *A Flight of Swans*, 1955), which enhanced his reputation as a mystical poet and is considered by many to be his greatest book of lyrics. He also toured Japan and the United States, giving a series of successful lectures later published as *Nationalism* (1919) and *Personality* (1917). Yet Tagore's reputation began to diminish almost as soon as it reached its peak. Some critics have proposed that the materialistic West was not able to appreciate the spiritual depth of the East, while others suggest that the poet and his publishers were themselves to blame for inept translation and unsystematic presentation. Forced to abandon his lecture tour in 1917 because of ill health, Tagore returned to India to a period of tragedy. Although he was greatly disturbed by World War I and denounced it in his writings, Tagore was also unable to endorse wholeheartedly the activities of his own culture. In 1918, with the money received from his writing, lectures, and the Nobel Prize, Tagore founded an international university—Visva-Bharati—at Santiniketan. Yet in 1919, as he was forming the nucleus of the faculty, political turmoil in India caused Tagore to resign his knighthood in protest against the British massacre of Indians at Amritsar. As Tagore sought to unify humanity in a world that seemed at odds with his philosophy, he began to find himself less and less popular.

In 1920, Tagore undertook another international lecture tour to raise funds for the school, but the receptions in England and the United States were particularly disappointing. During the last two decades of his life, despite increasing ill health, which often forced him to cancel lectures, and problems with public relations, Tagore traveled widely in support of his ideals of a universal humanity and world peace. He also continued to write until the end of his life, mainly poetry—which critics perceive as uneven—and essays. In addition, Tagore began painting as a hobby in his later years and pursued it with increasing seriousness. In 1930, Tagore delivered the Hibbert Lectures at Oxford University, which were published in 1931 as the *Religion of Man*, and, in 1940, Oxford awarded him an honorary doctorate of letters. Because of frail health, Tagore received this honor at Santiniketan, which had become a permanent residence in his later years. On August 7, 1941, Tagore died at his family home in Calcutta.

*Summary*

Internationally known as a humanist who sought to reconcile such apparent opposites as man and nature, materialism and spiritualism, and nationalism and internationalism, Rabindranath Tagore expressed a philosophy that was uniquely his own. His vision of the underlying wholeness of life was based on intuitive synthesis of classic Eastern religious texts and the works of early Indian poets and philosophers with Western thought and modern European literature. Although critics sometimes find it difficult to separate his distinguished literary career from his considerable role in transforming the Indian culture from the nineteenth to twentieth centuries, Tagore's place in history is nevertheless a literary one. In the East, he is known as a great poet and thinker; in the West, he is best known as the author of *Gitanjali*, which is characteristic of his work and considered to be his masterpiece. Recognized as a prolific and accomplished writer in all genres, Tagore is internationally acclaimed as one of the world's greatest lyric poets.

Tagore, a man of great courage and gentleness, of nobility and grace, is generally viewed as a symbol of the integration of East and West. Yet, many critics believe that the West has known him only superficially. They suggest that much of Tagore's best work remains accessible only in Bengali, and reading Tagore in translation—even his own translation—offers no real appreciation of his scope or the depth of his genius. Tagore's biographer, Kripalani, stated that "he lived as he wrote, not for pleasure or profit but out of joy, not as a brilliant egoist but as a dedicated spirit, conscious that his genius was a gift from the divine, to be used in the service of man." Although his writing is deeply rooted in Indian social history, Tagore's gift for expressing the unity of life and the grandeur of man gives it universal appeal.

*Bibliography*

Banerjee, Hiranmay. *Rabindranath Tagore*. 2d ed. New Delhi: Government of India, 1976. One of a series about eminent leaders of India, this biographical narrative presents the depth and diversity of Tagore's character and his contributions to the heritage of India. It includes genealogical tables and a chronological list of his important works.

Ghose, Sisirkumar. *Rabindranath Tagore*. New Delhi: Sahitya Adademi, 1986. This short, interesting survey focuses on Tagore's life and his poetry, drama, short stories, and novels. It also includes chapters on Tagore's thoughts about religion, beauty, art, and education.

Henn, Katherine. *Rabindranath Tagore: A Bibliography.* Metuchen, N.J.: Scarecrow Press, 1985. This impressive, comprehensive bibliography will be useful both for general readers and for serious Tagore scholars. With short annotations, it includes Tagore's works—classified into nineteen categories—and works written in English about him up to the early 1980's.

Kripalani, Krishna. *Rabindranath Tagore*. 2d ed. Calcutta: Visva-Bharati, 1980. Written by a scholar well acquainted with the Tagore family, this interesting, 450-page work is considered the best English biography of Tagore. Includes twenty-three photographic illustrations as well as a detailed bibliography of Tagore's fiction, nonfiction, and musical compositions.

Lago, Mary M. *Rabindranath Tagore*. Boston: Twayne, 1976. This literary study concentrates on representative works by Tagore as a lyric poet and writer of short fiction. It suggests a perspective from which to view national and international response to Tagore's distinguished career and includes a chronology and selected bibliography.

Mukherjee, Kedar Nath. *Political Philosophy of Rabindranath Tagore*. New Delhi: S. Chand, 1982. In this volume, Mukherjee presents an analysis of Tagore's political philosophy—in order to fill what he perceives as a gap in the literature on Tagore—and emphasizes the value of Tagore's philosophy in contemporary political situations, both in India and the world.

Singh, Ajai. *Rabindranath Tagore: His Imagery and Ideas*. Ghaziabad, India: Vimal Prakashan, 1984. One of the few comprehensive considerations of Tagore's imagery available in English, this study relates Tagore's images to his thoughts on life, love, beauty, joy, and infinity. It also includes a selected bibliography.

Thompson, Edward. *Rabindranath Tagore: His Life and Work*. 2d ed. New York: Haskell House, 1974. A reprint of an earlier edition, this brief survey of Tagore's writing prior to 1921 includes commentary based on Thompson's own translations of Tagore's work.

__________. *Rabindranath Tagore: Poet and Dramatist*. London: Oxford University Press, 1926. This was among the first detailed literary studies of Tagore's work as poet and dramatist and is still considered to be one of the best.

*Jean C. Fulton*

# JUN'ICHIRŌ TANIZAKI

*Born:* July 24, 1886; Tokyo, Japan
*Died:* July 30, 1965; Yugawara, Japan
*Area of Achievement:* Literature
*Contribution:* Tanizaki admired Western literature early in his career but was drawn increasingly to traditional values and forms with the passage of time. His work is characterized by both intricate narratives and stylistic elegance.

## *Early Life*

Jun'ichirō Tanizaki was born in Tokyo, Japan, on July 24, 1886. His father, Sogoro Tanizaki, was a rice merchant by virtue of his marriage into the Tanizaki family, whose name he subsequently adopted. It was Jun'ichirō's grandfather, Hisaemon, who had built the business. Sogoro could not appropriate the Tanizaki business acumen as he had the name. When his father-in-law's fortune came into his hands, he grossly mismanaged it. As a result, the performance of the business fluctuated wildly, the long-term effect being a steady decline in the family fortune. The death of an elder brother left Jun'ichirō heir to the dissipated Tanizaki wealth. Although he was a brilliant student, there was at one point a serious problem regarding his tuition fee at the Tokyo Metropolitan First Middle School. Later, he would observe, in his typically paradoxical fashion, that his rearing in Tokyo's merchant class had left him with both a distaste for materialism and a strong sense of nostalgia.

Tanizaki studied classical Japanese literature at Tokyo Imperial University after first sampling English law and English literature. Very early, he had exhibited a talent for literary composition, and he published several pieces in small magazines during his years at the university. He was not graduated and, again, the lack of money was quite probably a contributing factor. In the autumn of 1910, he published two plays and two short stories in *Shinshicho*, a magazine that he and university friends were editing. The short story "Shisei" (1909; "The Tattooer," 1956) introduced one of Tanizaki's enduring themes—the erotic power of feminine beauty. Seikichi, a tattooer, becomes obsessed with a young geisha. He drugs the girl and tattoos an enormous spider sprawling across her back. When she awakens, however, she announces to Seikichi that he has become her victim.

## *Life's Work*

In January, 1911, Tanizaki's first paid piece, *Shinzei*, a play, was published in *Subaru*. In June and September, two of his stories appeared in the same periodical. The earlier of these, "Shōnen" (youth), attracted the attention of several prominent literary figures. In October, his first novel, *Taifū* (typhoon), appeared in *Mita-Bungaku*. He was married in 1915 to Chiyoko Ishikawa. The first decade of Tanizaki's career was an exciting period in Japanese literature. Japan, by virtue of its victory in the Russo-Japanese War, was now a force to be reckoned with internationally. Western literary influences had been growing since the previous century, and the hold of ancient conventions had been loosening. A controversy was in progress between the naturalist writers, who had commanded the literary field, and their opponents. Tanizaki embraced Westernism and fell under the spell of Edgar Allan Poe, Oscar Wilde, and Charles Baudelaire, especially the mixture of sensuousness and morbidity in their fiction. The critic Gwenn Boardman Petersen argues, on the other hand, that Tanizaki's Westernization has been overstated, that Japan's long tradition of ghost and horror tales is sufficient to account for the bizarre elements in his early work. These elements had by 1920 caused some critics to label him a "Satanist."

In 1923, a great earthquake struck Tokyo, and Tanizaki subsequently relocated to Okamoto, near Osaka. This move has been characterized as the turning point in Tanizaki's career. His simpler way of life, as he left the great metropolis behind, brought with it a reexamination of traditional Japanese customs and a disenchantment with industrialization and Western values. Some critics suggest that at this point Tanizaki ceased to be merely a good writer and became a great one. Again, Petersen sounds a cautionary note, pointing out that Tanizaki's residence in the Kansai area was not so very lengthy and that the writer, according to his own testimony, made no conscious break with Tokyo. Still, for whatever reasons, his writing underwent a noticeable change in the early 1920's. His themes were more surely developed. His narratives became more realistic. His style became more descriptive, less sensuously suggestive (he had been accused of disguising a lack of content with a complex and urbane style). *Chijin no ai* (1924; a fool's love), serialized in *Osaka*, reflects Tanizaki's gradual disillusionment with Western culture.

*Tade kuu mushi* (1928-1929; *Some Prefer Nettles*, 1955), set in Osaka, dramatizes the clash of East and West through a failing marriage. The husband, whose position the narrative seems to favor, has become a traditionalist, while the wife is chic and Westernized. As a result, the two are drifting further and further apart. The novel also contains a strong autobiographical element. Tanizaki's own marriage was failing. A choice bit of Tokyo literary gossip in 1928 had Tanizaki seeking to act as go-between in a proposed affair between his wife and the novelist Sato Haruo. In 1930, the marriage ended in divorce, and, in April, 1931, Tanizaki married Furukawa Tomiko. Within the next five years, he would be divorced and remarried again. Also by 1930, he had gained such distinction that his complete works were published.

An emphasis on physical mutilation and a strain of sadomasochism run through Tanizaki's work. Blindness is featured in "Momoku monogatari" (1931; "A Blind Man's Tale," 1963) and "Shunkin shō" (1933; "A Portrait of Shunkin," 1936). In the latter, a blind musician has such a profound effect upon her student that he blinds himself in order to share her suffering. Their relationship, however, despite its intensity, is very ambiguous (another quality that is characteristic of Tanizaki's fiction). Tanizaki's repeated use of unreliable narrators, multiple points of view, and peculiarly Japanese symbols often give to his narratives—especially for the Western reader—an oblique and problematical tone.

In 1937, Tanizaki was elected to membership in Japan's Imperial Academy of Arts. The coming of war had an effect upon Tanizaki, as it did upon all Japanese writers. Out of mixed feelings of nostalgia and despair, he began to re-create in *Sasame-yuki* (1943-1948; *The Makioka Sisters*, 1957) the world that after the war would never exist again. The progress of the serialized version was long and difficult and involved more than one periodical. The first installment appeared in January, 1943, the last in October, 1948. In between, Tanizaki even published a part of the novel himself, in July, 1944, after it was censured. It appeared in book form in December, 1948. *The Makioka Sisters* is set in the Kyōto-Osaka region. The regional differences that supposedly affected Tanizaki so deeply are dramatized in the novel when one sister is forced to move from her beloved Osaka to Tokyo. The novel contains a wealth of detail about daily life in Japan. Tanizaki received two prestigious awards for *The Makioka Sisters*: the Mainichi Prize for Publication and Culture in 1947 and the Asahi Culture Prize in 1949. In the latter year, he was awarded the Imperial Cultural Medal.

In 1962, more than fifty years after the appearance of "Tattoo," Tanizaki was still exploring the phenomenon of the self-willed victim of erotic desire in *Fūten rojin nikki (Diary of a Mad Old Man*, 1965). The diary of seventy-seven-year-old Utsugi Tokusuke makes up the bulk of the novel, but it is supplemented by his nurse's report, his physician's clinical record, and his daughter-in-law's note. These multiple points of view ambiguously interpret the old man's relationship with his ex-chorus girl daughter-in-law.

Tanizaki was elected to honorary membership in the American Academy and National Institute of Arts and Letters in 1964. He died on July 30, 1965, and two months later his last piece of writing appeared in the journal *Chuo Koron*.

### *Summary*

Several themes recur in the work of Jun'ichirō Tanizaki throughout his long literary career: the artist's search for beauty, the fascinating quality—both erotic and aesthetic—of womanhood, and the clash of cultures—traditional and modern, Eastern and Western. Yet, often as Tanizaki has treated these themes in stories, novels, and plays, the reader must be careful in drawing generalizations from them. Tanizaki's narrative technique is habitually ambiguous, oblique, and ironic. He may use narrators who are dishonest or naïve. He may use multiple narrators. The narrator sometimes uses the authorial voice but without comment, forcing the reader to interpret for himself the actions, words, expressions, and gestures of the characters. Tanizaki has been called the chronicler of modern Japan, but for a long period he devoted himself to retelling the tales of ancient Japan. The view from ten centuries past gave him yet another perspective for his fiction. His scenes of perversity, especially in the early stories, have led some to include him in the "Satanist," or "demonic," school of writers. The autobiographical elements in his work have linked him to the "I-novelists," the confessional school of writers. His emphasis upon the erotic and his supposed worship of women have associated him with the "love-talk" school of writers. Yet Tanizaki cannot be fitted comfortably into any school or movement. The differences are always more striking than the similarities.

In his later years, Tanizaki was considered a strong and deserving candidate for the Nobel Prize. The rumor coming out of the Swedish Academy was that he was passed over because it was believed that too little of his work was available in translation. Still, he had succeeded in accomplishing what only the greatest writers can accomplish: He had converted his homeland, with all its cultural singularity, into a universal stage. Many agreed with the Asian scholar Donald Keene when he wrote in 1955 that *The Makioka Sisters* is "the most important Japanese novel published in the years following the war."

*Bibliography*

Keene, Donald. *Dawn to the West: Japanese Literature of the Modern Era, Fiction*. New York: Holt, Rinehart and Winston, 1984. A massive study of the fiction produced since the Japanese "Enlightenment" in the nineteenth century. Chapter 20, pages 720-785, is devoted exclusively to Tanizaki, and he is mentioned in the introduction and in several other chapters in association with other writers and literary movements.

__________. *Dawn to the West: Japanese Literature of the Modern Era, Poetry, Drama, Criticism*. New York: Holt, Rinehart and Winston, 1984. A companion volume to the entry cited above. Tanizaki's writing for the stage is discussed in "Part Three: The Modern Drama," and he is also mentioned in passing in "Part Two: Poetry in New Forms" and "Part Four: Modern Criticism."

__________. *Japanese Literature: An Introduction for Western Readers*. New York: Grove Press, 1955. Unlike the comprehensive treatments cited above, this is a brief introduction to Japanese literature, designed for the neophyte reader. Tanizaki is only touched upon in the introduction and chapter 4, "The Japanese Novel," but is discussed throughout chapter 5,

"Japanese Literature Under Western Influence."

Petersen, Gwenn Boardman. *The Moon in the Water: Understanding Tanizaki, Kawabata, and Mishima.* Honolulu: University Press of Hawaii, 1979. The first section of Petersen's book, "Contexts," is a brief summary of the rich literary tradition of Japan. The second section is a practical guide to the work of Tanizaki. A partial chronology and a general bibliography are provided.

Rimer, J. Thomas. *Modern Japanese Fiction and Its Traditions: An Introduction.* Princeton, N.J.: Princeton University Press, 1978. Indicates certain structural principles important in the tradition of Japanese narrative fiction and also discusses in detail works for which the author has a profound admiration. Treatment of Tanizaki occurs throughout the entire text, and copious excerpts from his *Seven Japanese Tales* are given a close analysis.

Ueda, Makoto. *Modern Japanese Writers and the Nature of Literature.* Stanford, Calif.: Stanford University Press, 1976. A study of eight major writers of modern Japan, those writers whose work constitutes the bulk of modern Japanese fiction available in English. Chapter 3 is devoted to Tanizaki. The work is indexed, contains a selected bibliography, and furnishes extensive source notes for those who read Japanese.

Yamanouchi, Hisaaki. *The Search for Authenticity in Modern Japanese Literature.* Cambridge, England: Cambridge University Press, 1978. Tanizaki's much discussed attitude toward women is examined in chapter 5, "The Eternal Womanhood: Tanizaki Jun'ichirō and Kawabata Yasunari."

*Patrick Adcock*

# PIERRE TEILHARD DE CHARDIN

*Born:* May 1, 1881; Sarcenat, France
*Died:* April 10, 1955; New York, New York
*Areas of Achievement:* Theology, philosophy, geology, and anthropology
*Contribution:* Through his work as a geologist on the evolution of the earth and as a paleontologist on the evolution of life, Teilhard, a devout Jesuit priest, came to see human beings progressing toward a new consciousness and spiritual unity called the "Omega Point," which he identified with Jesus Christ.

## *Early Life*

From the perspective of his mature vision of the universe, Marie-Joseph-Pierre Teilhard de Chardin interpreted his own life in the light of his evolutionary doctrine. He saw as providential his birth in 1881 in a Sarcenat château amid the foothills of the Monts Dore in central France. Teilhard was the fourth child in a family that would eventually number eleven children, and on his mother's side he was distantly related to Voltaire and on his father's side to Blaise Pascal. His mother was a deeply religious Roman Catholic who ignited a spiritual fire in young Teilhard. His father was a gentleman farmer with interests in natural history, and he introduced his children to the delights of rocks, minerals, wildflowers, and animals. Thus, from an early age, Teilhard was able to combine two spheres of life—the material and the spiritual—commonly considered incompatible.

In 1892, a month before his eleventh birthday, Teilhard became a boarder at the Jesuit school of Nôtre-Dame de Mongré at Villefranche-sur-Saône, near Lyons. He was a good student, especially in science and literature, and in his free time he continued his interest in geology by collecting minerals. He eventually concluded that he had a vocation to the Jesuit life. On March 20, 1899, he entered the Jesuit novitiate in Aix-en-Provence, about twenty miles north of Marseilles, to begin a long period of spiritual and intellectual formation.

On March 25, 1901, Teilhard took his first vows of poverty, chastity, and obedience, and then began, at Laval, his studies in the Greek and Latin classics (the juniorate). These studies were interrupted when anticlerical legislation in France forced the Jesuits to transfer their juniorate to Jersey, one of the English Channel islands, in the summer of 1901. As a second-year junior in Jersey, Teilhard seriously considered abandoning the study of geology to devote himself completely to spiritual activities. One of his religious superiors wisely helped him put his spiritual evolution in perspective and guided him in a direction in which he could combine his love of matter, energy, and life (his cosmic sense) with his love of Christ and the supernatural (his Christic sense). From 1902 to 1905, he studied Scholastic philosophy at the Jesuit house on the Isle of Jersey, where he spent his free hours, geologist's hammer in hand, in scientific surveys, resulting in a paper on the island's mineralogy and geology.

In September, 1905, Teilhard was sent to teach chemistry and physics at the Jesuit College of the Holy Family in Cairo, Egypt. Although the science he taught was elementary, this experience of the chemical substances and physical forces of the universe helped him refine his still-crude understanding of the world. After three years as a teacher in Egypt, during which he published works on the Eocene period, he returned to England to complete his Jesuit training. He spent four years, from 1908 to 1912, studying theology at Hastings in southern England. While continuing his geological and paleontological research and writing, he also devoted time to the synthesis of his scientific and spiritual views.

During his theological studies at Hastings, Teilhard began to understand matter from the perspective of spirit, and this forced him to develop a new way of thinking and speaking about what he saw happening in the universe. He began to use the words of science (energy, force, radiation) to describe the previously unseen evolution of spirit that was taking shape in nature. This spiritual energy, already familiar to him in the evolution of his own consciousness, he now grasped as active in the universe, itself in the process of self-creation. Matter, as an evolutionary fact, had given birth to spirit; therefore, matter and spirit are not two separate substances but two aspects of a single evolving cosmos. Physical energy therefore contains something of the spiritual, since energy's upward trend is an observable fact in the increasing complexity of evolving organisms. By the time he was ordained, on August 14, 1911, he had discovered a vision by which he could understand scientific phenomena spiritually and spiritual phenomena scientifically. It therefore became the core of his vocation as a priest to show that evolutionism does not entail a rejection of Christianity, because Christ represented the crucial point in the universe's history at which matter and spirit met.

### *Life's Work*

Throughout the rest of his career, as priest and scientist, Teilhard devoted himself to the evolution of the universe (what he called cosmogenesis), whose ever-richening spirituality constantly became for him more real and resplendent. For him, salvation no longer meant abandoning the world but building it up. His scientific work therefore became something holy, to be undertaken not for its own sake but for the liberation of more spirit from matter.

After completing his theological studies in 1912, Teilhard went to Paris to study under Marcellin Boule, a professor at the Institute of Human Paleontology in the Natural History Museum. Boule was one of the leading experts on Neanderthal man, but Teilhard's work was mainly in the paleontology of

Tertiary mammals in Europe. His scientific studies were interrupted by his tertianship (the final year of his Jesuit formation, a period of intense prayer, meditation, and ascetical training), and then by World War I. Although he could have chosen to be a chaplain, he joined the Eighth Regiment of the Moroccan Tirailleurs as a stretcher-bearer. Teilhard, whose bravery under fire and whose generosity of spirit throughout his military service were honored by medals both during and after the war, did not allow his experiences of the war's horrors to destroy the vision of human history he was constructing. Indeed, he found that his patriotic service on behalf of a great ideal had invigorated his life. Even in the trenches he believed that he was participating in the grand work of sanctifying humanity. In his personal writings during this time, his constant theme was spiritual evolution: When everything of value in the material world has passed into the souls of men, he believed that souls will pass into a new level. In 1917, he began describing this level as the mystic milieu.

After his demobilization, Teilhard returned to his scientific studies. He completed his academic requirements at the Sorbonne and then began work on a thesis about the mammals of the lower Eocene in France. In 1922, he successfully defended his thesis and was awarded his doctorate in paleontology. During the early 1920's, he served as an assistant professor of geology at the Catholic Institute of Paris, but his position there became untenable when he taught that evolution required a revision in the Church's doctrine of original sin. The discoveries of geologists, paleontologists, and paleoanthropologists had convinced Teilhard that no evidence existed for Adam, Eve, or Eden, and consequently the Fall was an event that could not be verified. Before Charles Darwin, Christians could believe that one man's sin (Adam's) had ruined everything and that another man's suffering (Christ's) had saved everything. After Darwin, Teilhard believed that Christians must realize that original sin is not a malady specific to the earth but an inevitable consequence of the limitations of evolving matter and spirit. Because of Teilhard's heterodox views on original sin, his Jesuit superiors asked him to leave the institute and take a research post in Tientsin, China, with Father Émile Licent, a Jesuit pioneer in paleontology. For the next twenty-three years, from 1923 to 1946, Teilhard's career would center on China. He would return to France periodically, but he led what he called a vagabond existence that would continue for the rest of his life.

During his first decade as a peripatetic priest, Teilhard worked mainly in the north of China. He participated in a French paleontological mission to the Ordos and Gobi deserts directed by Father Licent. On a visit to central Mongolia in the summer of 1923, the two priests found the first evidence for paleolithic man in China. After these research expeditions, Teilhard returned to Paris, hoping to continue teaching at the Catholic Institute while making occasional field trips to China, but his superiors continued to be bothered by his evolutionary views of original sin, and he was told to restrict himself to his scientific work (his position at the Catholic Institute was terminated at the end of 1926).

Returning to China in the spring of 1926, Teilhard obeyed the orders of his superiors not to disseminate publicly his theological speculations, and for the rest of his life, he confined himself to publishing his scientific work while privately developing his evolutionary vision (which he shared with friends and fellow Jesuits). During the late 1920's, he began using the term "noosphere" to describe the earth's sphere of thinking substances. The world of matter (the geosphere) had been the source of life (the biosphere), but now the human species was taking conscious control of evolution and science, technology, and socialization were changing the earth more rapidly than natural selection ever had.

Teilhard's ideas about man's role in the universe found spiritual resonance in his manuscript of *Le Milieu divin* (1957; *The Divine Milieu*, 1960), which he wrote in 1926 and 1927 (but which was not published until after his death). In this book, which many scholars see as a spiritual portrait of Teilhard himself, he tried to set down as simply as possible the religious life that he had been living. Through his scientific work, he had become convinced that man was at the spiritual center of the cosmos, and he wanted to show how Christianity was at the center of human history and should be the center of every person's spiritual life.

During this period of intense spiritual probing, Teilhard shifted the base of his operations from Tientsin to Cho-k'ou-tien, about thirty miles southwest of Peking. There, Davidson Black, a Canadian who was a professor of anatomy at the Peking Medical College, was engaged in an organized search for prehistoric man. In the decade from 1927 to 1937, many fossils of animals and man were found in the calcareous deposits of Cho-k'ou-tien. The human fossils were first called *Sinanthropus pekinensis*, then *Pithecanthropus pekinensis*, and now *Homo erectus*. Teilhard helped to date the fossils, to show that Peking man was a toolmaker, and to publicize the importance of the finds. Although he gained wide recognition for his account of the discovery, his principal paleontological work continued to be on nonhuman fossils—for example, on fossil carnivores.

During the late 1920's and through the 1930's, Teilhard went on several expeditions into northern and central China, made periodic trips to Europe and America, and continued to refine his synthesis of evolution and Christianity. He built up a network of friends and disciples in Paris and at the American Museum of Natural History in New York. In China, he had collaborators of many nationalities, and this contributed to his strongly cosmopolitan and internationalist views. His participation in various research trips to Africa, America, and especially China deepened his understanding of evolution.

In 1938, while he was in Peking, Teilhard began writing *Le Phénomène humain* (1955; *The Phenomenon of Man*, 1959), in which he tried to show how evolutionary data pointed to a Christian interpretation of the world. His approach was phenomenological; that is, he tried to bring out the meaning of phenomena by describing them as precisely as possible. By analyzing the problem of man in terms of evolution, he hoped to bridge the gap between Christians and non-Christians, for he believed that Jesus Christ, as God Incarnate, revealed himself not only in the New Testament but also in the evolution of man. In his book, Teilhard argued that consciousness evolves, and he located the origins of consciousness in preliving as well as living matter. Thresholds, such as the origin of life and of consciousness, are important examples of emergence, where something entirely new enters the universe. Traditional science, according to Teilhard, has not well served these threshold phenomena, and modern science has almost completely ignored what he calls "the within" of the world. This spiritual energy can be studied just as scientists study "the without," matter's external face, in terms of space and time. As the capstone of his evolutionary synthesis, Teilhard believed that, through an increase in knowledge and love, human consciousness can evolve to a new level. Noögenesis, the evolution of mind, is a stage on the way to Christogenesis, the evolution of the universe toward the Omega Point, Teilhard's term for the cosmic Christ.

Teilhard was composing this optimistic vision of the world against a background of world events that would have made pessimism a more natural response. The Japanese occupation of China interfered with his work at Chok'ou-tien and his attempt to establish a laboratory for advanced studies in human paleontology in Peking. When World War II began, he was trapped in China, a situation which continued for the war's duration. He abhorred both German Nazism and Japanese Fascism, both of which he interpreted as crudely and unjustifiably transferring the laws of natural selection (the survival of the fittest) from the biological to the human level, whereas, in his vision, mankind was clearly passing to a new level of existence in which a future of love and cooperation was being built. Nevertheless, beneath the human and national tragedies of this war, he believed that something spiritual was evolving. This vision of human evolution found expression in *The Phenomenon of Man*, which he completed in 1940 and sent to Rome in 1941 for approval by his superiors. Since his approach was phenomenological, he hoped that his book would pass the censors, but in 1944 he learned that it had been rejected.

After the war's end, he was able to return to Europe in 1946. He went to Paris, where, during the late 1940's, he was frustrated in his desire to teach at the Collège de France. A visit to Rome to seek permission to publish various works on his evolutionary synthesis was unsuccessful. In 1947, he was appointed director of research in the National Scientific Research Center, which subsidized his scientific work, but he was eager to communicate his evolutionary vision, for he found the existentialism that was spreading throughout France, with its pessimistic ideas of man and matter, dangerously anachronistic in a universe that was evolving toward Christ. On June 1, 1947, he suffered a sudden heart attack, and, though he recovered, his health remained precarious for the remainder of his life. These physical sufferings were followed by psychological ones, for in September his religious superiors forbade him again to write on philosophical or theological issues, thus squelching any hope that *The Phenomenon of Man* or any of his works on anthropogenesis would be published.

Refusing to be discouraged and undertaking no action that could be seen as disobedient, Teilhard nevertheless did everything he could to circulate his ideas privately. He was enthusiastic about the new United Nations, and he worked for some of its organizations that were concerned about the future of the human race. Through contacts made in these labors, for example, with Julian Huxley, he continued to develop his cosmogenetic vision. These efforts were further stimulated by his return to field work in the 1950's. With the financial support of the Viking Fund (soon to become the Wenner Gren Foundation for Anthropological Research), Teilhard made expeditions to various excavation sites in South Africa, where important prehuman fossils, especially the Australopithecines, had been discovered.

During the last period of Teilhard's life, from 1951 to 1955, his center of operations became New York City, where, as a fellow of the Wenner Gren Foundation, he concentrated on anthropogenesis (the evolution of the human species). In the summer of 1954, he made his last trip to France, and, though the visit aroused warm feelings for his native country, he was back in New York by September. He was denied permission by a superior to travel to a meeting at the Sorbonne in April, 1955, but he accepted this without bitterness, resolving to continue fighting to increase love in the world. Teilhard died on Easter Sunday, April 10, 1955.

### *Summary*

Pierre Teilhard de Chardin did more than any other thinker to help people understand evolution in the context of Christianity. Although he wrote nearly two hundred articles and technical papers in geology and paleontology, mainly on the early Cenozoic period in Europe and the late Cenozoic period in China, his name is most likely to be remembered for his radical view that evolution has a spiritual orientation. For him, the earth, which he so lovingly studied, was profoundly linked to Jesus Christ, since every created thing will find its fulfillment in him. In Teilhard's view, evolution is a purposeful process in which matter and energy progressively evolve in the direction of increasing complexity, consciousness, and spirituality. He so tightly identified Christ and the universe that many critics have interpreted his vision as a

Christian pantheism. Although Teilhard often spoke of the universe as God's cosmic body, he also carefully distinguished pantheistic evolution, which destroys personalities in its union with matter, from Christian evolution, which culminates in a union with God that preserves personalities.

In the initial enthusiasm generated by the publication of many of Teilhard's works in the years after his death, some commentators compared the significance of his synthesis of evolutionism and Christianity with Thomas Aquinas' synthesis of Aristotelianism and Christianity. Now that most of Teilhard's writings and letters are in print, it is easier to see him as part of the intellectual development composed of such thinkers as Henri Bergson. These evolutionary philosophers were dissatisfied with the positivism and scientism of the twentieth century and attempted to provide an understanding of man's total experience, of the material as well as the spiritual, of the past and the future, of variety and unity. In this sense, Teilhard has much to teach both scientists and theologians. For scientists, his mystical temperament and loving grasp of positive values have given the world an interpretation of the universe that encourages love, progress, and unity. For theologians, his evolutionary view has necessitated a transposition of Christian revelation into a new key, where religion can profit from scientific insights.

Despite criticisms of his work, many of them justified, Teilhard did offer an alternative to the materialist vision of mankind as an accidental phenomenon, a random collection of molecules on an unimportant planet. In his view, mankind represented the culmination of the complex evolution of matter and life. It is doubtful that in the future Teilhard's evolutionary synthesis of Christianity and evolution will be completely accepted by Christians or by scientists, but as a product of a luminous mind and a loving heart, his conception of the universe as a unity in which all things work together for a final consummation in Christ has already found numerous followers, because this vision, which allows people to remain true to themselves while building union with God, reveals the deeply spiritual values in the innermost heart of mankind and the universe.

*Bibliography*

Browning, Geraldine O., Joseph L. Alioto, and Seymour M. Farber, eds. *Teilhard de Chardin: In Quest of the Perfection of Man*. Rutherford, N.J.: Farleigh Dickinson University Press, 1973. This book is the result of an international symposium held in San Francisco's Palace of Fine Arts in May of 1971. An international group of scholars analyzed the life and work of Teilhard from several perspectives—religious, scientific, psychological, and educational. This volume also contains a biographical sketch of Teilhard and a brief analysis of his philosophical beliefs.

Cuénot, Claude. *Teilhard de Chardin: A Biographical Study*. Edited by René Hague. Translated by Vincent Colimore. Baltimore: Helicon Press, 1965.

Cuénot, who was a close friend of Teilhard, has carefully documented his many travels. The evolution of Teilhard's ideas, in Cuénot's view, becomes clearer when seen against the background of his life as a Jesuit and a scientist. Contains an annotated bibliography.

Grenet, Paul. *Teilhard de Chardin: The Man and His Theories*. Translated by R. A. Rudorff. New York: Paul S. Eriksson, 1966. Contains sections on Teilhard's life, personality, and scientific career, as well as on his philosophical and theological thought. A final section of selected writings from Teilhard is followed by a brief bibliography and an index. Scholars already familiar with Teilhard's ideas will find little new here, but Grenet's book is a good primer for novices.

Lubac, Henri de. *Teilhard de Chardin: The Man and His Meaning*. Translated by René Hague. London: Hawthorn Books, 1965. One of the most enlightening studies of Teilhard's ideas. Lubac is a fellow Jesuit who bases his analysis on personal knowledge of Teilhard as well as on his mastery of the published and unpublished material by and about him. He presents both a spiritual portrait, in which he elucidates the interior life that animated Teilhard's work, and a modern apologetic, in which he shows how Teilhard tried to reinterpret Christianity for twentieth century man. Contains a bibliography, footnotes, and an index.

Mooney, Christopher F. *Teilhard de Chardin and the Mystery of Christ*. New York: Harper & Row, 1966. Mooney's basic theme is that what unifies the many facets of Teilhard's thought is the relationship between the evolving cosmos and the mystery of Christ. A Jesuit himself, Mooney is able to explicate with sensitivity and understanding the theological implications of Teilhard's ideas. Contains an extensive bibliography and a detailed index.

Speaight, Robert. *The Life of Teilhard de Chardin*. New York: Harper & Row, 1967. Speaight, a British Catholic writer, presents a straightforward chronological account of Teilhard's life. He intended his work not to compete with Cuénot's definitive biography, but to make Teilhard's thought accessible and comprehensible to a wide readership. Contains a glossary, bibliography, and index.

*Robert J. Paradowski*

# TENG HSIAO-P'ING

*Born:* August 22, 1904; Szechwan Province, China

*Areas of Achievement:* The military, government, and politics
*Contribution:* Long a member of the Chinese Communist Party, Teng has been China's most important leader since the death of Mao Tse-tung in 1976. Technological modernization under strict political control has been the main theme of his policies.

*Early Life*

Born at the end of the Ch'ing Dynasty (1640-1911), Teng Hsiao-p'ing spent the first forty-five years of his life dealing with the weak republican governments, conniving warlords, foreign imperialists, and Nationalist (Kuomintang) enemies who so dominated Chinese politics prior to the Chinese Communist victory in 1949. Profoundly affected by the so-called May Fourth Movement (an intellectual movement that began on May 4, 1919, when news of China's humiliation at the Paris Peace Conference reached Peking), Teng soon joined the future Communist leader Chou En-lai in France (1921), became a member of the Communist Party (1924), and then moved to the Soviet Union for more specialized training (1924-1926). Returning to China in 1926, Teng worked briefly for the northern warlord and Nationalist ally Feng Yü-hsiang before fleeing to Shanghai to escape a Nationalist crackdown in 1927. Joining Mao in the countryside in 1931, Teng's power grew steadily as Mao's strategy of "People's War" in the countryside gradually won out over more orthodox revolutionary approaches. Teng participated in the famous "Long March" of 1934-1936, an epic feat that guaranteed him a special place among later Chinese leaders. He then became a political leader in the Communist Eighth Route army, playing important roles in the war against the Japanese (1937-1945) and the Nationalists (1946-1949). Given this record, it is hardly surprising that Mao and Chou brought Teng to Peking in 1952 to help build the new Communist state. They knew that in doing so they were bringing to the capital a man who, while noticeably short and feisty and a heavy smoker and blunt talker, was also exceptionally bright, good at organizing people, and fully tested in battle.

*Life's Work*

By serving as a minister of finance (1953-1954), the secretary-general of the Communist Party (after 1954), a member of the Politburo (1955), a member of the six-person Politburo Standing Committee (1956), and then the general secretary of the Party Secretariat, Teng gained a tremendous amount of power during the early years of the new Chinese Communist government. He was praised for his work in building a modern bureaucracy, as well as for his general efforts to restore China's war-shattered economy while also moving steadily toward a Communist economic system and a close alliance with the Soviet Union. Yet Teng also angered Mao by rejecting the techniques of mass mobilization and ideological struggle against both the United States and the Soviet Union so favored by Mao and his followers. Particularly after the failure of Mao's "Great Leap Forward" campaign of the mid-1950's, Teng appeared to disagree with some of Mao's most deeply felt theories of development. The dispute between the two was enormously complex, as it involved personal and regional tensions as well as the aging Mao's own personal sense of frustration. Yet it was commonly described as a dispute between the "Reds," who advocated ideological purity, mass mobilization, and self-sufficiency, on the one hand, and the "Experts," such as Teng, who placed more emphasis upon technology, a few key investments, and a relationship with at least one of the two major superpowers, the United States and the Soviet Union.

Teng and many of his fellow "Experts" suffered badly when Mao finally unleashed the so-called "Great Proletarian Cultural Revolution" between 1966 and 1976. During this time, young Maoists ridiculed Teng's alleged statement that he did not care "if the cat was black or white, only if the cat caught mice," that is, that ideology was not as important as practical results in building socialism. Forced to make a public "self-criticism"—a humiliating event in a country where the dignity of officials was still considered important—Teng was also forced to leave the capital and work at the so-called May Seventh Cadre School between 1969 and 1972. Teng's son was crippled in the violence that seemed to sweep the country in this period. Never an advocate of free speech or open political debate, Teng's bitter experiences in these years seem to have left him with an even deeper sense that China was too fragmented and politically immature to have anything even remotely resembling Western conceptions of political democracy. These perceptions were only reinforced by Teng's perception that China's economy badly needed to be modernized. To Teng, economic progress, and through this the final realization of socialism, could only come to China when political order was restored and an alliance with at least one of the two superpowers was struck so that China could get the modern technology that the desperately backward nation needed.

Teng's recall in 1972 reflected in part Mao's own disappointment with the chaos of the Great Proletarian Cultural Revolution, and the aging chairman's realization that an alliance with a superpower—this time the United States rather than the increasingly belligerent Soviet Union—was necessary. By 1975, Teng had thus been promoted to Party vice-chairman, senior vice-premier, and chief of staff of the People's Liberation Army. By August of that year, Teng had also ordered attacks on the "three poisonous weeds," or alleged defects in the Communist Party, the Academy of Sciences, and the general economy. These attacks would soon become the so-called "Four Modernizations" of the Party, the economy, the sciences, and the army. They were coupled with attempts to rehabilitate various victims of the Cultural Revolution, and to place supporters of Teng in key administrative posts. This was also the time when Secretary of State Henry Kissinger and then-President Richard Nixon were invited to China to restore long-broken relations. These moves were bitterly resented by the Vietnamese Communists, who were then engaged in a fierce struggle with the United States.

Teng's fortunes suffered a second stunning reversal in 1976, when his longtime patron, Chou En-lai, died of cancer and students used genuine mourning for his death to protest the lack of political freedom in China; upset by the protests, the "Reds," whose policies were threatened by Teng's changes, used the occasion to remove Teng from office. Mao's own death in September, 1976, changed the chaotic situation once again, however, and Teng quickly found himself brought back to power to help suppress the so-called "Gang of Four," or Mao's wife and her chief "Red" advisers. By 1980, Teng was easily the most important person in the Chinese government. Though he often preferred to rule behind the scenes, in part because of his advancing age, he was the one who supervised the all-important appointment process, and it was his "Four Modernizations" that formed the main theme in China's development efforts. Teng was certainly also the person who most strongly advocated supporting the so-called "Khmer Rouge," or Cambodian Communists, in their struggles against the pro-Soviet Vietnamese. Though hardly a supporter of the Khmer Rouge's brutal domestic policies, Teng valued their stand against the Soviet Union and the Vietnamese. Teng thus ordered Chinese troops to attack the Vietnamese in 1979. The Chinese damaged their former ally before withdrawing as planned after about a month from the territory that they had occupied. The Chinese military effort was not very impressive, however, and Teng thus realized that further efforts would have to be made before China could be considered a major military power.

It was within this tangled context that Teng faced his third major challenge, that of the so-called "Pro-Democracy Movement" of the 1980's. This movement sprang from a number of earlier attempts to have a "Fifth Modernization" in basic political liberties. It was compounded by intense beliefs that Party members had become arrogant, corrupt, and inclined to place their family and friends in especially privileged positions. There was also great resentment at the spiraling inflation that took place as Teng tried to move China from a centrally organized "command economy" to a more decentralized "market socialism," in which material incentives could be used and slogans could announce that "to get rich is glorious." Dislocations, frustrated ambitions, and anger, which were compounded by comparisons between China's relatively impoverished state and the higher standard of living in other states, all combined to create a strong movement in China—as, indeed, there was in almost all the other Communist nations—to bring greater democracy. By the spring of 1989, a massive student movement had occupied the central Tiananmen Square in Peking and issued ringing calls for a sharing of political power. Several of Teng's closest advisers sympathized with the students and were willing to consider concessions. Teng, on the other hand, continued to see little value in greater personal freedom and no relationship between his modernization goals and what he considered to be the students' lack of discipline. As a horrified world watched, Teng's troops and tanks crushed the student revolt, killing many and arresting all of those whom they considered to be enemies of the state.

*Summary*

Teng Hsiao-p'ing's close involvement with many of the most turbulent events in China's long history has thus left him a controversial figure. No one could deny his abilities, his survival skills, his deeply held vision of an industrialized China, and his obvious accomplishments in repairing some of the damage done by the most radical "Red" supporters of Mao. Yet few Americans could support Teng's central concern with maintaining the Chinese Communist Party as the sole legitimate political force in the country. Teng based his refusal to share power on the belief that only a unified Communist Party could supervise orderly economic growth. Time would soon tell whether this sturdy veteran of Communism's fierce struggles was correct.

*Bibliography*

Burns, John P. "China's Governance: Political Reform in a Turbulent Environment." *China Quarterly* 119 (September, 1989): 481-518. This article in this special issue of *China Quarterly* covers China's current leadership with particular attention to Teng. It is well researched and heavily foot-noted.

Chang, David Wen-Wei. *China Under Deng Xiaoping: Political and Economic Reform*. New York: Saint Martin's Press, 1988. Contains a foreword by Robert Scalapino. This standard source is a good ideological counterbalance to the official Chinese position.

Falkenheim, Victor C., ed. *Chinese Politics from Mao to Deng*. New York: Paragon House, 1989. This is one of several possible texts that help to put Deng's positions into a broader context.

Lubetkin, Wendy. *Deng Xiaoping*. Introductions by Arthur M. Schlesinger, Jr. New York: Chelsea House, 1988. This is a part of a larger series designed for young readers.

Wallace, James. "China: What Price Peace." *U.S. News and World Report*

106 (June 19, 1989): 20-26. A rather in-depth article that explores the People's Liberation Army, Teng's control of it, and where it will go next. There is also substantial discussion of the political structure and of Teng's place within that structure.

*Peter K. Frost*

# MOTHER TERESA
## Agnes Gonxha Bojaxhiu

*Born:* August 27, 1910; Skopje, Ottoman Empire (now Yugoslavia)

*Areas of Achievement:* Religion and social reform

*Contribution:* Mother Teresa has spent most of her life caring for the "poorest of the poor." Her Missionaries of Charity have expanded their scope from the humblest beginnings on the streets of Calcutta to locations on every continent, including, in the United States, New York's South Bronx. By 1987, the International Association of Co-Workers of Mother Teresa, formally established eighteen years before, numbered more than three million people. Mother Teresa was awarded the Nobel Prize in 1979.

*Early Life*

The third child and second daughter of Nicholas and Rosa Bojaxhiu, wealthy parents of Albanian peasant stock, was christened Agnes Gonxha Bojaxhiu on August 27, 1910. In a town in what is now southern Yugoslavia, the Albanians were a minority, but the area, a historical meeting-place of East and West, was one that successfully blended many cultures. The Muslim influence was strong, as was that of the Eastern Orthodox church. Agnes' parents were devout Roman Catholics and saw to it that the children were given a strong background in that faith. The family prayed together each night. Rosa was particularly devout. It was she who prepared all three children, who attended the public school, to receive the sacrament of First Holy Communion. Nicholas Bojaxhiu was a well-educated man who owned a construction business. Agnes' parents were devoted to each other. Mother Teresa was later to recall that she and her brother and sister often teased their mother about her feelings for their father. Sadly, Nicholas died at age forty-two, a tragic blow to the family, who, in addition to the emotional loss, experienced a loss of income that drastically changed their circumstances but that brought them even closer.

As a young child, Agnes has been described as joyful and playful, not at all a "goody-goody." Her childhood home was for the most part a happy one. She was educated in Croatian at the state high school and was a soprano soloist in the parish choir. At a very early age, Agnes felt the call of a religious vocation. She was twelve years old when she began seriously to meditate on her decision. Through her membership in the Sodality of Our Lady, she became aware of the missionary work being done in India by a group of Jesuit priests. After six years of soul-searching, she finally made her decision at eighteen while praying at the sanctuary of Our Lady of Letnice. She wanted to work with the Loretto Sisters in India.

Her mother was at first against Agnes' decision to enter the religious life but eventually gave her daughter her blessing with the admonition to remember to be true to God and Christ. Agnes applied to be admitted to the Loretto Order and left home on September 26, 1928, for Rathfarnam, Ireland, to learn English in preparation for her assignment to India. She spent six weeks as a postulant of the Institute of the Blessed Virgin Mary. Agnes took the name Teresa, for the "little Teresa," St. Teresa of Lisieux, who had led a painful and brief but pious life in France in the late nineteenth century. Sister Teresa arrived in India in January, 1929, and was sent to a novitiate in Darjeeling. She took her vows two years later and spent the next twenty years teaching geography to the daughters of middle-class Indians at St. Mary's High School, where she also became the principal.

*Life's Work*

It was on a train to Darjeeling on September 10, 1946, that Sister Teresa received her second call from God. She called it a "call within a call," and it asked her to serve only the poorest of God's creatures, the destitute, the dying, the lonely, for the rest of her life. She accepted this summons without question, applying immediately for freedom from the Loretto Sisters to pursue her new duties. This was very difficult for her, as the convent and school had long been her home. She also loved teaching and was well loved by her students. With some difficulty, Teresa received permission to leave the order and work as a free nun in late 1948. She walked from the convent with only the clothes she wore. Her only real preparation was an elementary course in medicine with the American Medical Missionary sisters in Patna, India.

On December 21, 1948, Sister Teresa opened her first slum school in Moti Jheel in Calcutta. There, with absolutely no financial backing or supplies, she began to teach poor Bengali children to read and write. She wrote with a stick in the dust and begged a place to stay among another order of sisters. The following March, Subhasini Das, a nineteen-year-old former student from St. Mary's joined Sister Teresa, taking the name Sister Agnes. Slowly Sister Teresa's group grew, living in the home of a wealthy Indian citizen, begging for food, and giving love and rudimentary medical care to Calcutta's sick and dying poor.

The Missionaries of Charity, with a membership of twelve, was approved and formally instituted by the Archdiocese of Calcutta on October 7, 1950. Sister Teresa became Mother Teresa. She and her novices took vows of poverty, chastity, obedience, charity, and an additional, special vow to serve the truly destitute. This vow proscribes any member of the order from working for the rich or from accepting money for services. All material resources are donated. Mother Teresa insisted on only four preconditions to becoming a sister in her order. Applicants must be healthy of mind and body, be able to learn, have plenty of common sense, and have a cheerful disposition. A novice can be no younger than seventeen. Once accepted into the order, a woman spends six months as an aspirant, six months as a postulant, two years as a novice, and six years under temporary vows. One year before temporary vows expire, the sister is sent back to the novitiate for an additional year of contemplation before taking her final, lifelong vows.

On March 25, 1963, the Archbishop of Calcutta formally blessed the new order of the Missionary Brothers of Charity. Six years and one day later, the International Association of Co-Workers of Mother Teresa, a secular group of volunteers active since 1954, received the blessing of Pope Paul VI. The Co-Workers were started by a wealthy Englishwoman named Ann Blaikie, who had begun helping Mother Teresa by gathering donated goods for Mother Teresa's poor. By 1987, the Co-Workers included a staggering three million people in seventy countries.

The Missionaries of Charity is the only religious order of its time that is actually growing in membership. By 1987, the group numbered three thousand sisters and four hundred brothers. These selfless people have treated tens of thousands of destitute sick and given the hopelessly dying the opportunity to die with dignity. In 1952, the Nirmal Hriday ("Place of the Pure Heart") Home for Dying Destitutes was opened at 1 Magazine Road in what was formerly a Kali temple, donated by the city of Calcutta. Nirmal Hriday is a last refuge for the dying. In 1957, the missionaries began treating India's large population of contagious lepers, first establishing a colony for lepers in West Bengal. As the order grew, they were also able to open an orphanage for abandoned children. Most of the children are adopted out to homes in Europe. In 1959, the first house of the Missionaries of Charity outside Calcutta was opened in Delhi. Since then, twenty-two other cities in India have become recipients of Mother Teresa's special brand of aid.

The decision to open houses outside India was a difficult one for Mother Teresa, who had become an Indian citizen in 1948. The first foreign country to welcome her help was Venezuela. Soon after, a house was established in Rome. Ceylon, Tanzania, and Australia followed. Perhaps most surprisingly, the missionaries found it necessary to establish the Queen of Peace Home in an area popularly known as Fort Apache in the South Bronx of New York. According to Mother Teresa, the spiritual poverty in the United States is greater than anywhere else on earth. Later the sisters expanded their efforts to Harlem. On December 24, 1985, a few short months after Mayor Ed Koch gave her his wholehearted permission, Mother Teresa opened a hospice for victims of acquired immune deficiency syndrome (AIDS) in Greenwich Village called Gift of Love. By 1987, the houses of the Missionaries of Charity numbered twenty-one in the United States alone. Other modern cities have not been forgotten. Houses of the Missionaries of Charity can be found in both London and Amman, Jordan. In Dacca, India, a home was opened to care for women from Bangladesh who had been raped by Pakistani soldiers.

All the houses follow the same rigid schedule. The sisters or brothers rise at 4:40 A.M. and have prayers from 5:00 until 6:00, when Mass is celebrated. At 6:45, the religious inmates are fed a light breakfast of unleavened bread and banana. The sisters are true to their vow of poverty. Each sister owns only two or three cotton saris, underclothes, bedding, a tin bucket (for laundry), prayer books, a pen, a pencil, and paper.

Mother Teresa has been the recipient of many humanitarian prizes and honors. She was awarded the Pope John XXIII Peace Prize and the Joseph Kennedy, Jr., Foundation Award in 1971 and the Nobel Peace Prize in 1979. She has also received awards from her own government, notably the Jawaharlal Nehru Award in 1969 for International Understanding and the Shiromani Award, which was presented to her personally by Indian President Giani Zail Singh. In April, 1990, Mother Teresa stepped down from the leadership of her order because of severe illness.

*Summary*

Mother Teresa has been characterized as surprisingly humble. She insists that the work she does is all for Jesus, that she merely serves Christ in the poor. Attempts to write her personal biography have been thwarted or replaced by the story of the Missionaries of Charity and their works. What she and her workers, sisters and brothers alike, give to the poor is much more than medical care. They give unconditional love to those who are shunned by the rest of the world. Mother teaches that one may find Jesus in all persons, but he is especially present in the poor and grotesque. Recipients of the missionaries' aid are not proselytized, nor are they limited to the Catholic populaton. Unlike most missionaries, the Missionaries of Charity do not preach religion but teach by example.

The immense success that Mother Teresa has enjoyed must, despite her objections, be credited to the woman herself. Mother Teresa is an extremely practical woman with one goal in life: to serve the poor. While in charge of her order, she fed her sisters well, on the advice of the medical sisters who gave her her early training, so that they can resist contagion as they dress the sores of lepers or treat other sick people. Perhaps the most impressive phenomenon associated with Mother Teresa is the small social revolution that she has instigated in her adopted homeland. In India, girls of very old and well-to-do castes are becoming sisters to give succor to the so-called Untouchables. They have said that they were first brought to the order by a desire to work beside Mother Teresa.

Physically, Mother Teresa is tiny, but she has a toughness that reveals an indomitable personality. She has been described as unforgettable and charismatic, with mesmerizing eyes. A true believer in turning the other cheek, she has none of the righteous indignation common in others of her profession. In her, there is only the desire to serve God by loving her fellow man.

*Bibliography*

Doig, Desmond, *Mother Teresa: Her People and Her Work*. New York: Harper & Row, 1976. Mother Teresa insisted that this book, originally intended to be a biography, be written instead about the Missionaries of Charity. The book does contain a useful chronological table of events relative to Mother Teresa. Illustrated with both color and black-and-white photographs.

Gonzalez-Balado, José-Luis, and Janet N. Playfoot, eds. *My Life for the Poor: Mother Teresa of Calcutta*. New York: Harper & Row, 1985. Mother Teresa's personality comes through in this book, because it is written in the words of Mother herself. She is shown to be a highly practical person with infinite faith in God. Readers will find her concise speech refreshing.

Le Joly, Edward. *Mother Teresa of Calcutta*. New York: Harper & Row, 1985. Written by a priest and close colleague of Mother Teresa, this book does not offer as much biographical information as its title promises. It does give detailed information on the Missionaries of Charity, along with much religious editorializing. Illustrated with black-and-white photographs.

Rae, Daphne. *Love Until It Hurts*. New York: Harper & Row, 1980. This is primarily a pictorial tribute to the Missionaries of Charity. The book is aptly named; readers may find some photographs disturbing.

Tower, Courtney. "Mother Teresa's Work of Grace." *Reader's Digest* 131 (December, 1987): 163-75. Packed with information on Mother Teresa's work in India and around the world. Gives a clear picture of the organizational structure of the Missionaries of Charity. Pleasurable reading for a general audience.

*Joyce M. Parks*

# U THANT

*Born:* January 22, 1909; Pantanaw, Burma
*Died:* November 25, 1974; New York, New York
*Area of Achievement:* Diplomacy
*Contribution:* Thant took over as acting secretary-general of the United Nations when Dag Hammarskjöld was killed in an airplane crash in 1961 and served until 1971. Thant therefore was the speaker for the United Nations during the many crises of the 1960's and early 1970's, including the Cuban Missile Crisis, the Arab-Israeli conflict, the crisis in the Congo and other parts of Africa, and the U.S. involvement in Vietnam, providing the U.N. with a strong neutral voice.

## *Early Life*

Thant ("U" is an honorific, and most Burmese do not use surnames) was born in the town of Pantanaw, Burma, which was then part of the British Indian Empire, the first of four sons. His home province is probably best known for the difficult traveling conditions within the area, for the many streams forming a delta in the almost totally flat area flood easily. Thant's family was one of the moderately wealthy ones in the town, since his paternal grandfather and great uncle were the owners of a prosperous rice mill and his maternal grandfather exported woven mats. The real wealth was held by other family members, however, rather than by Thant's father.

Thant's father had, however, been educated in Calcutta and is believed to have been the only person in town then able to read and speak English. He passed on his love of learning, as well as his knowledge of English, to his eldest son, and Thant started at the regional school at age six. At the age of fifteen, Thant impressed his family by having an article printed in the Burmese boy scout magazine *Burma Scout*, and he hoped to turn that small start into a career as a journalist.

Thant's father died in 1923, and much of the family's wealth was spent on a legal dispute between various members of the extended family. Thant therefore decided that he would be unable to spend the four years at the University of Rangoon he had planned on. Instead, he would stay two years and get a teaching certificate, which he did from 1926 to 1928. He returned to his hometown and taught in the high school, rising to the headmastership. He would later marry a distant relative, Thein Tin, in 1934.

In the tense political situation of Burma during the 1930's (nationalism and anticolonialism were both growing), Thant stood between the extremes of ardent nationalism and those who favored British policy. While this gained for him enemies, it also impressed a former university friend and short-term colleague at the Pantanaw High School. U Nu would always remember his friend when an intelligent moderate outlook was needed. As

Nu rose through the ranks of the Burmese Nationalists, finally becoming prime minister of independent Burma in 1948, his need for Thant's opinions grew as well.

During the 1930's, Thant's influence grew within education circles as he became involved in various national committees. He also became a moderately well-known individual, as he started having articles published outside education journals. When the crisis of the Japanese invasion came in 1941, Thant was a respected, although not a very important, leader in Burmese society.

### *Life's Work*

The Burmese found themselves between Japanese and British imperialism during World War II. While a few still favored the British and some believed the Japanese propaganda of "Asia for the Asiatics," most Burmese nationalists joined or supported the Burmese Independence Army, led by one of Thant's former pupils, Aung San. Although it primarily fought against the British in 1942, a reorganized version would be instrumental in fighting the Japanese as well. In 1942, Thant left Pantanaw to help reorganize Burmese education under the Japanese occupation at the suggestion of San and Nu. This work, although ignored at the time, allowed the other leading nationalists to take a good look at the educator/journalist, even though Thant returned home after a few months' work.

When the British Indian Empire was dissolved in 1947, Burma was scheduled to become an independent nation. Thant moved his family to Rangoon, hoping to set up an independent magazine that would give the new nation a native literary forum. Instead, Thant first became press director of the nationalistic Anti-Fascist People's Freedom League (AFPF) and then held the same position in the Directorate of Information. During the new few troubled years, Thant became in turn the deputy to the information secretary, director of broadcasting, and then secretary of the information ministry and chair of the Burma film board. At the same time, he drew closer to his old friend Nu: accompanying him on a goodwill mission to India in 1950; leading missions to Indonesia, Thailand, and Great Britain in 1951; and then leading the Burmese mission to the United Nations in 1952. Returning in 1953, Thant became secretary of projects, secretary to the prime minister, and then secretary of the economic and social board. Finally, in 1957, he was sent to the United Nations as Burma's permanent representative, where he quickly made a reputation as a hardworking and impartial member of the General Assembly as well as for working in many of the committees and behind the scenes.

In September, 1961, the secretary-general of the United Nations, Dag Hammarskjöld, was killed in an airplane crash in Central Africa. The United States and the Soviet Union were unable to agree on any candidate put up by the other members of the Security Council, the Soviets going so far as to propose splitting the top position into three positions: one Communist, one from the West, and one from the third world, with each one having a veto. Over the next few weeks, the United Nations saw one of its greatest periods of political negotiation, as representatives from the smaller nations tried to mediate between the two superpowers and at the same time find somebody acceptable to the majority of the U.N. member nations.

Thant was one of the hardest workers in this process. Because of this, as well as all of his previous hard work, representatives started talking about having Thant fill out Hammarskjöld's term of office. Although there were some objections, based on a number of political reasons, few people had any personal objections to Thant. When the United States decided to back Thant as well, the Soviets joined in, and Thant was unanimously elected acting secretary-general of the United Nations in November, 1961. He was re-elected in 1962 and 1966, serving until December 31, 1971.

Thant faced a number of problems during his tenure as secretary-general. Decolonialization was at its height during the early 1960's, and there were a number of violent and disruptive problems, both internal and external, associated with the process, particularly in the Congo, the area to which Hammarskjöld was on his way when his plane crashed. It was up to the secretary-general to keep as many of the disputants talking as possible.

Despite his many successes, such as helping to keep the United States and the Soviet Union talking during the Cuban Missile Crisis, Thant was not always seen in a favorable light by many of the world's national leaders. He was publicly critical of U.S. military policy in Vietnam, and he was also privately opposed to the U.S. armed intervention in the Dominican Republic in 1965. The American press responded with criticism of the secretary-general. Thant was also opposed to the Soviet invasion of Czechoslovakia in 1968, although as usual he kept his criticism private. Still, it was enough to upset the Soviets.

At all times, Thant was a defender of peace, trying to get various disputants to agree to arbitration of their problems. Quite often, however, at least one (and at times all) of those involved would refuse, gaining the secretary-general criticism for not actively taking the "correct" side. Besides the international disputes mentioned above, Thant's tenure also saw the 1967 Arab-Israeli Six-Day War, fighting between Pakistan and India over two different border areas and then the start of the war that resulted in the birth of Bangladesh, and numerous other, internal and smaller international disputes. Unable to serve as more than either an impartial adviser or uninvited observer despite the many demands that he take sides in controversial situations, Thant managed in general to maintain his position despite his critics and many temptations.

After his retirement, Thant was appointed senior fellow of the Adlai

Stevenson Institute of International Affairs. He spent the last years of his life writing and speaking on the general themes he had tried to promote while he was secretary-general. He believed in the development of a true global community, which would mean not only the ending of armed conflict but also a true sharing of resources and technology as well.

Thant died of cancer in November, 1974. His body was returned to Rangoon for burial. A group of students seized the body on December 5, in order to bury it on the grounds of the university. When the police took the body back on December 11, it sparked days of riots.

*Summary*

While U Thant contributed to maintaining the precarious balance of peace during the 1962 Cuban Missile Crisis, and much of the public portion of the confrontation was played out at the United Nations, he also helped turn the United Nations from what had been primarily a forum for the East/West Cold War conflict into an arena where the emerging less developed nations could express themselves on the world stage. His strong Buddhist beliefs, along with his own moral character, helped him defend his position as a leader of the global community, rather than a mere national figure speaking in an international setting. It was Thant's hope that the United Nations would continue to grow into that sort of an organization, a place in which the world would come together, rather than a forum to air disputes.

*Bibliography*

The Asia Society. *Asia Peacemaker from Pantanaw*. New York: The Asia Society, 1977. A memorial tribute to Thant, this supplement to the journal *Asia* contains several articles assessing the historical importance of Thant to the history of Burma, the United Nations, and the world.

Bingham, June. *U Thant: The Search for Peace*. New York: Alfred A. Knopf, 1966. An early but extremely good biography of the U.N. leader, concentrating on his pre-United Nations life. Bingham had the benefit of a number of interviews with Thant, which gives this work extra importance. It also includes a chronology and a reprint of a pre-World War II article that Thant wrote on the Burmese.

Butwell, Richard. *U Nu of Burma*. Stanford, Calif.: Stanford University Press, 1963. An in-depth study and biography of the main Burmese political leader during the 1940's through the early 1960's. Nu was a longtime friend and patron of Thant, and this work describes the effort made to establish an independent Burma and the home political situation with which Thant had to deal while he was Burma's representative at the United Nations.

Cordier, Andrew, and Max Harrelson, eds. *Public Papers of the Secretaries-General of the United Nations*. Vols. 6, 7, and 8. New York: Columbia

University Press, 1976. These U.N. documents include not only official reports and speeches but also some of the behind-the-scenes memos and letters that formed Thant's positions, transcripts of press conferences, and public speeches during his tenure as secretary-general.

Johnstone, William C. *Burma's Foreign Policy: A Study in Neutralism*. Cambridge, Mass.: Harvard University Press, 1963. This work describes the political background that Thant brought with him to the United Nations and the neutralist policies that he espoused while he was working at the United Nations during the 1950's and early 1960's, which led to his being chosen secretary-general.

Nu, U. *U Nu, Saturday's Son: Memoirs of the Former Prime Minister of Burma*. Translated by Edward M. Law Yone. New Haven, Conn.: Yale University Press, 1975. Modern Burmese history as seen through the eyes of one of its nationalistic founders.

Thant, U. *Toward World Peace*. Edited by Jacob Baal Teshuva. New York: Thomas Yoseloff, 1964. This is a compilation of Thant's speeches and other public statements between 1957 and 1963, and therefore includes his opinions on the Cuban Missile Crises.

———. *View from the UN*. Garden City, N.Y.: Doubleday, 1978. Thant's memoirs of his tenure as secretary-general of the United Nations, dealing in detail with the major crises of his tenure in office.

*Terrance L. Lewis*

# AXEL HUGO TEODOR THEORELL

*Born:* July 6, 1903; Linköping, Sweden
*Died:* August 15, 1982; Stockholm, Sweden
*Area of Achievement:* Biochemistry
*Contribution:* Theorell received the 1955 Nobel Prize in Physiology or Medicine for his work on the nature and action of oxidation enzymes. He was the first to produce a pure enzyme in the laboratory and the first to produce myoglobin in a pure form.

## *Early Life*

Axel Hugo Teodor Theorell was born on July 6, 1903, in Linköping, Sweden, the son of the local military regiment's medical officer. Little has been written of the younger Theorell's early life. Like his father, he chose medicine as his vocation. He entered the Caroline Institute in Stockholm in 1921 and studied under Walther Nernst, who had won the Nobel Prize in 1920. Theorell was awarded his bachelor of medicine degree in 1924. He also studied at the Pasteur Institute in Paris.

Most of his academic work consisted of research into the chemistry of plasma lipids and their influence on red blood cells. He did this research under the direction of Einar Hammarstein at the Royal Caroline Medico-Surgical Institute. He was awarded his doctor of medicine degree by the Caroline Institute in 1930 and was preparing to embark on the career of medical practitioner when an attack of poliomyelitis left him crippled in both legs. Undaunted by this unfortunate turn of events, Theorell took up research and teaching.

Theorell was a short, stocky man, modest and reticent; for relaxation he enjoyed sailing. In 1931, he married a music teacher, Margit Alenius, who later became a professional musician. Theorell was himself a violinist and he appeared with the Academic Orchestra Society. He chaired the Stockholm Philharmonic Society. The Theorells had three sons.

## *Life's Work*

After receiving his doctorate, Theorell was appointed docent at the Caroline Institute. Using a new ultracentrifuge at the Svedberg in Uppsala, he investigated the molecular weight of myoglobin, an iron-containing protein of muscle tissue that has oxygen-carrying functions related to those of hemoglobin in the blood. Myoglobin is the pigment which makes muscles red. Theorell was an assistant professor of chemistry at Uppsala from 1932 to 1933 and from 1935 to 1936, taking leave to work in Berlin and Stockholm.

In 1933, Theorell was given a Rockefeller Fellowship to work at the Kaiser Wilhelm Institute in Berlin with Nobel Prize winner (1931) Otto

Warburg. There, using electrophoretic methods which he had worked out himself, he purified a yellow enzyme, a feat Warburg had been attempting for years without success. Other enzymes had been isolated and crystallized by American Nobel Prize winner James Sumner, but the yellow enzyme, found in yeast, heart muscle, and milk, had remained problematic.

By dialysis of an acidified solution, Theorell separated the yellow enzyme into two fragments: the nonprotein coenzyme, which acts as a catalyst, and the apoenzyme, a colorless, pure protein, and determined that the yellow enzyme's essential ingredient is albumin. The coenzyme, a substance of low molecular weight, was identified as a monophosphate of vitamin $B_2$. The substance is now known as flavin mononucleotide and is believed responsible for the yellow coloration of the enzyme. The coenzyme and apoenzyme must exist together for enzyme activity to occur. In fact, Theorell found that the separation process was reversible. Theorell also discovered the chemical chain reaction by which enzymes enable living cells to breathe (oxidation).

From 1937 to 1970, Hugo Theorell was head of the biochemistry department of the Nobel Institute. The department had been established in 1936 by the Caroline Institute in Stockholm in order to give Theorell an opportunity to continue his research. Under Theorell's direction, the department became world-renowned as a "Mecca of biochemistry."

Upon returning from Berlin, Theorell began his research on the cytochrome C molecule, a heme-containing protein associated with cellular respiration. By 1936, he had been able to produce an 80 percent pure molecule, and by 1939 he succeeded in purifying cytochrome C 100 percent. His sometime associate and colleague Linus Pauling had discovered the "Alpha" spiral, or twisted atom chains of protein molecules. Theorell's work confirmed Pauling's findings. With Anders Ehrenberg, he constructed models of hemin peptides and was able to determine the precise nature of the chemical linkage between the iron-bearing, nonprotein porphyrin portion and the apoenzyme.

At the biochemistry department of the Nobel Institute, he directed studies of ADH enzymes, which break down alcohol in the kidneys. From this research, he was able to develop a new method of determining ethyl alcohol content in the bloodstream. These techniques were later adopted by the Swedish and West German governments for use in tests for drunkenness. Theorell's research resulted in the isolation of bacteria strains which were used in the treatment of tuberculosis. He also discovered an antibiotic called proaptin.

Articles by Theorell have appeared in many scientific journals, including *Biochemische Zeitschrift*, *Arkiv för Kemi*, *Journal of the American Chemical Society*, *Bulletin de la Société de Chimie Biologique*, *Acta Chemica Scandinavica*, and *Rendiconti Istituto di Sanità Publíca*. Theorell died on August 15, 1982.

*Summary*

Axel Hugo Teodor Theorell's work helped create a modern understanding of enzyme action. His research shed light on the basic unit of life, the cell. Much of this work laid the groundwork for the creation of artificial life in the laboratory. His discoveries found wide scientific application in the study of cancer and tuberculosis, among other diseases.

Theorell was active in many professional organizations. He was secretary of the Swedish Society of Physicians and Surgeons from 1940 to 1946 and of the Swedish Society for Medical Research from 1942 to 1950, and he chaired the Swedish Chemists' Association from 1947 to 1949. He was a member of the Swedish Royal Academy of Sciences, the Scientific Council of the Swedish Board of Health, and the Swedish Academy of Engineering Science. He was a foreign associate of the United States National Academy of Sciences and a foreign member of Great Britain's Royal Society. He received honorary degrees from Belgium, Brazil, the United States, and France, including an honorary doctor's degree from the Sorbonne.

*Bibliography*

Aaseng, Nathan. *The Disease Fighters: The Nobel Prize in Medicine*. Minneapolis: Lerner, 1987. In this brief book, Aaseng details the discoveries of several Nobel Prize-winning scientists. Written for high school or younger readers.

Candee, Marjorie Dent, ed. *Current Biography Yearbook, 1956*. New York: H. W. Wilson, 1957. Published annually, this book provides biographies of people in the news. Written in clear language for the lay reader.

Ludovici, Laurence James, ed. *Nobel Prize Winners*. Westport, Conn.: Associated Booksellers, 1957. This book details the lives of fourteen well-known Nobel Prize winners, including many contemporaries of Theorell. Gives the student a perspective on the golden age of science of the late nineteenth and early twentieth centuries. For high school or beyond.

Schück, H., et al. *Nobel: The Man and His Prizes*. 2d rev. ed. New York: Elsevier, 1962. A comprehensive account of the five major Nobel Prizes. Contains the life of Alfred Nobel as well as the rationale behind the establishment of the Nobel Foundation. A page-long description of the prize-winning work by Theorell on enzymes is included. Indexed. College-level material.

Schwert, George W., and Alfred D. Winer, eds. *The Mechanism and Action of Dehydrogenases: A Symposium in Honor of Hugo Theorell*. Lexington: University Press of Kentucky, 1970. Papers read at a conference held March 16-19, 1965, at the University of Kentucky. The foreword is by Theorell, who was visiting centennial professor in the biological sciences at the time. Includes bibliographies. College-level material.

Sourkes, Theodore L. *Nobel Prize Winners in Medicine and Physiology,*

*1901-1965*. New York: Abelard-Schuman, 1966. A compilation of short biographies of Nobel Prize winners in medicine and physiology and detailed descriptions of the scientific work which won for them the prize. Much of the section on Theorell is directly quoted from the scientist. This is a revision of an earlier work by Lloyd G. Stevenson. For advanced readers.

*Maureen Connolly*

# BAL GANGADHAR TILAK

*Born:* July 23, 1856; Chikalgaon, India
*Died:* August 1, 1920; Bombay, India
*Areas of Achievement:* Government and politics
*Contribution:* Through his oratorical skill, political savvy, and editorship of several newspapers, Tilak showed the Hindu masses a connection between ancient tradition and twentieth century nationalism. His politics also were considerably more radical than those of other contemporary Indian leaders, giving the *swaraj* (self-government) movement a strong push forward.

### *Early Life*

Like two other well-known Indian nationalist leaders, Mahadev Govind Ranade and Gopāl Krishna Gokhale, Bal Gangadhar Tilak hailed from Maharashtra. This province boasted a poignant legacy: Its small army had defeated the powerful Muslim empire and, later, was the last Indian force to succumb to the British raj. Tilak also inherited the Chitpavan Brahman tradition, including caste-dictated leadership in religious and communal matters. Although his father's income remained modest, these priestly rights guaranteed the family some financial benefits, too.

Gangadharpant Tilak was a largely self-educated man who left school when his mother died. Eventually choosing a teaching career, he placed great value on learning and sent his son to class at the age of six. Bal proved to have a facile mind. Though not given to studying, he conducted intellectual debates with his teachers and supposedly even called on headmasters to settle these controversies. The Tilak family departed from village life in 1865 and moved to Poona, then considered an intellectual center of Maharashtra, where Gangadharpant became assistant deputy education inspector. His wife died the following year.

Bal continued his education and took a ten-year-old Chitpavan Brahman girl, Tapibai, to be his bride; the groom, himself, was fifteen. Neither the couple's ages nor the years between them proved at all unusual given the customs of the day. Yet, Bal soon was to experience an unexpected event—his father's death. Some scholars suggest that being orphaned at the age of sixteen may have sapped emotions from Tilak. While he possessed the passion to inspire masses of people, for example, he seemingly lacked a more personal empathy. Similarly, political solutions moved him in a way that social reform could not.

Following his graduation from high school in 1872, Tilak was enrolled in Deccan College. Sanskrit and mathematics came most naturally to him. Sometimes at the expense of his studies, however, he followed a rigorous daily exercise plan, which helped transform his formerly frail constitution into a vigorous one. Tilak appeared short and sturdy, with a broad, full mustache. In the traditional Brahman mode, he shaved his head, except for a central lock of hair. He wore orthodox garb, a beret-like *dhoti* cap perched on his head. This is the appearance he would maintain throughout his life.

While adhering to Hindu traditions, Tilak allowed himself to be shaped by other forces; indigenous political movements were starting to shake Maharashtra. Educated reformers, many admiring the advancements promised by Western civilization, formed the Poona Sarvajanik Sabha (public society) on April 2, 1870. Its leaders sought to enlighten the masses, while using the colonial system as a vehicle for social change. The brilliant jurist Ranade was at the forefront of this movement. A famine also ravaged the Deccan plateau during the late 1870's, propelling an insurrection by one Vasudeo Balwant Phadke. Though the British apprehended its leader, this rebellion proved inspirational to certain segments of the population who questioned various political aspects of colonialism.

Meanwhile, Tilak received his bachelor's degree with first-class honors and, as a senior, started to pursue legal studies. Though he never sought permanent, full-time law practice, he ably used the courtroom to further political causes. Tilak also appeared adept at integrating source material into his arguments and was forceful in presenting his viewpoint. During his law school days at Deccan College, Tilak befriended Gopal Ganesh Agarkar, another student motivated by progressive politics. The two men viewed education as a means of promoting change and sought to create a school that would conform to this ideal. While unable to secure the necessary funding for their venture, both ultimately were engaged to teach and help develop the fledgling New English School. Its founder, Vishnu Krishna Chiplunkar, favored broad learning but within a Hindu, rather than Christian or Western, cultural context.

## *Life's Work*

Both skilled educators, Tilak and Agarkar aided Chiplunkar in boosting the reputation of the New English School. The institute opened its doors with some thirty pupils in 1890 and, according to one source, boasted approximately five hundred two years later. This success spawned the Deccan Education Society (1894), dedicated to advancing the New English School model. Wealthy Indian families and royalty contributed heavily to this organization, as it reflected pride in the local heritage of which they were a part. Chiplunkar and his colleagues then founded Fergusson College, named for the retiring British governor of Bombay.

The New English School offered a collegial atmosphere, at least during its earliest days. A veteran publisher, Chiplunkar enlisted his two protégés in a new endeavor: providing political education to the older generation via weekly newspapers. Tilak became editor of the English-language *Mahratta* and Agarkar took charge of the Marathi *Kesari*. The next year, 1882, the neophyte journalists found themselves embroiled in a lawsuit. Their papers had criticized an Indian-born British official for unduly aggravating and subsequently trying to remove from power a rather unstable local prince. Convicted of slander, Agarkar and Tilak served brief prison sentences. Their bold, patriotic action, however, catapulted them into the public eye.

A new controversy, the Age of Consent debate, soon caused a rift between the young editors; it also gave Tilak his own political platform. In 1884, the reformer Behramji Merwanji Malabari called on British legislators to raise the age of marital consent for girls from the current age of ten to twelve. Reformers had long decried early marriage, citing premature death from childbirth, overpopulation, and poverty as social maladies which could be reduced, if not altogether alleviated. At around the same time, progressives debated education for women and changing the law to allow widows to remarry. Tilak vehemently opposed these measures. He believed that the imposition of British law unjustifiably tampered with Hindu culture, religion, and society; after all, Indians should govern their own lives. His editorials and speeches consequently were written to activate the religious masses. Tilak also argued that women should maintain their traditional roles in the home; education and Western, reformist ideas could turn them away from these values. While orthodox himself, however, Tilak occasionally indicated that social change would be acceptable, if publicly approved. Some scholars also cite his support of voluntary measures to raise the age of consent. Furthermore, he later sent his daughter to the Poona girls' school.

Tilak's nationalistic fervor was firmly rooted in his Brahman background. The inconsistencies that he demonstrated owed to personal dynamism, plus the ability to accept various political tactics as long as they led to the desired result: self-governance. Meanwhile, public debate manifested itself at the Deccan Education Society. Tilak left the organization in 1890, ostensibly over internal policy matters. Yet, by this time, a formal political schism had divided him from his erstwhile friend Agarkar and another faculty member, Gokhale. The latter would become a reformist leader, Indian National Congress president, and Tilak's foremost political adversary.

Having relinquished his formal teaching duties, Tilak spent more time influencing popular opinion. He became increasingly involved with Congress and helped to organize its 1895 Poona session. Tilak objected to the fact that this meeting coincided and shared facilities with the National Social Conference. His editorials blared: "Whose is the Congress? Of the people of the Classes or of the Masses?" The Congress and Conference subsequently met in separate tents, a permanent split instituted between the two groups. Seeking new methods of rallying the masses behind his platform, Tilak had revived the Ganapti Festival, honoring a Hindu deity. Its success inspired a more politically focused activity: celebration of Shivaji, the Maharashtran who led his people to victory over the powerful Muslim empire. Combined with potent newspaper editorials (Tilak now managed *Kesari*, too), these events provided constantly growing forums for revolutionary agitation.

Right after the premier Shivaji Festival (1896), plague struck India. Walter Charles Rand, a British official, used strong-arm tactics and generally showed great insensitivity during this crisis. When he was assassinated, the government put Tilak on trial for sedition, citing his incendiary editorials as an agitating force. The gentle, reform-minded Gokhale and other Indian leaders had criticized Rand's administrative methods, but they typically apologized under pressure from British officials. Tilak, on the other hand, refused to amend his statements. In fact, one of his trial arguments was that the European-dominated jury had no business interpreting subtle nuances of a language they could not speak, read, or write. Although the defendant would serve a prison sentence, his case inspired the masses. He subsequently became known as the *Lokamanya*, or "Revered of the People."

The next major controversy to embroil India was the partition of Bengal, a British administrative action taken without consulting local leaders. This measure also diluted Hindu political power, carving out for the Muslim minority a territory in which they could prevail. Bengali Hindus then called for a boycott of British goods, and Tilak broadened the appeal to his native Maharashtra. He also would advocate for the development of Indian commerce and industry, plus a more nationalist-oriented education system that would reduce the emphasis on the English language and Western culture. Gokhale and those who favored constitutional methods of reform lobbied against the boycott and other measures that they believed might cause provocation. Emotions ran high; the 1907 Indian National Congress thus ended in the "Surat split" between nationalists (Tilak) and reformers (Gokhale).

The following year, a bomb intended for District Judge Douglas Kingsford accidentally killed a British barrister's wife and daughter. Tilak and other Indian leaders lamented the death, but a *Kesari* article stated: "The bomb party has come into existence as a result of the oppression practised by the official class, the harassment inflicted by them and their obstinacy in treating public opinion with recklessness. . . ." Tilak was arrested for sedition, his apartment searched. Police turned up one damaging piece of evidence: a postcard, written in the *Lokamanya*'s hand, listing four books on explosives.

The trial again questioned the ability of a primarily European jury to judge foreign language works. Tilak also raised freedom of press issues during his twenty-two hour closing speech. A guilty verdict was rendered: The *Lokamanya* would be confined to the Mandalay prison, Burma. Eighty textile mills in Bombay subsequently struck and some violence resulted; Tilak indeed had attained a hero's status.

Tilak finally emerged from prison in 1914, by most accounts a more subdued activist. Another legal complaint was lodged against him two years later, but this time, he won. Tilak proved to be a unifying force during the 1916 Lucknow Congress; there, nationalists and reformers coalesced, opening political representation to Muslims. Unfortunately, cross-culture agreement was only temporary and Hindu-Muslim friction continued to plague the *swaraj* movement.

Tilak's last legal battle took place on his own terms,. when he went to England to prosecute Sir Valentine Chirol for slanderous remarks. Granted a passport on the condition that he refrain from political agitation, Tilak nevertheless lobbied Labor Party officials sympathetic to India's cause. He even invited some British political leaders to dinner. Although Tilak lost the lawsuit, his life continued—and concluded—in a poignant way. A new leader, Mahatma Gandhi, had chosen August 1, 1920, as the inaugural of a noncooperative movement for independence. Bal Gangadhar Tilak died on that day at the age of sixty-four.

*Summary*

Bal Gangadhar Tilak consistently evoked Shivaji as a nationalistic metaphor. Yet, this analogy presented ethnical dilemmas. Shivaji allegedly met his Muslim adversary to discuss peace terms, then surprised him with a concealed weapon. Tilak, too, held that the ends justified the means: Western-style reform could not substitute for Indian self-rule, and the latter must override all other goals. Tilak's Shivaji revival inspired young people, but it also incited them to heckle reformist leaders whom they often unjustly perceived to be colluding with the British. Similarly, his proto-Hindu agitation at times exacerbated rifts between his coreligionists and the Muslims. When Tilak saw that the two peoples could unite for their common cause, however, he urged the concessions accepted at Lucknow. He also referred to the Indians as black and to the British as white. Indeed, an outspoken nature and political flexibility proved to be Tilak's trademarks. He considered all options, and scholars debate his links to a number of subversive activities. He attempted to develop ties with Nepal, for example, either to encourage that country's armed intervention or to establish a munitions factory there. Others point to his association with the men who murdered Walter Rand.

Many things have been said about or for Tilak, but his greatest contribution was a truly steadfast, pioneering devotion to Indian self-rule. He motivated his peers, and, though his political rhetoric could be harsh, he encouraged nationalistic involvement at all levels. Speaking on the 1915 death of his adversary, Gokhale, he said: "This diamond of India, this jewel of Maharashtra, this prince of workers, is taking eternal rest on the funeral grounds. Look at him and try to emulate him." Similarly, Tilak and Ghandhi differed tremendously in personality and outlook, yet on August 2, 1920, Gandhi eloquently eulogized his colleague: "For us, he will go down to the generations yet unborn as a maker of modern India."

*Bibliography*

Brown, D. Mackenzie. *The Nationalist Movement: Indian Political Thought from Ranade to Bhave*. Berkeley: University of California Press, 1961. Chapters are devoted to the individual lives and writings of leading Indian nationalists. A twenty-page section on Tilak offers a good, concise biographical sketch, plus chronological excerpts from his articles urging *swaraj*.

Cashman, Richard I. *The Myth of the Lokamanya*. Berkeley: University of California Press, 1975. According to the author, Tilak proved an astute activist whose broad, popular appeal nevertheless was exaggerated by his followers for the purpose of defining consensus. Cashman argues that Tilak's legacy remains limited more to his caste and region than to India's larger nationalist movement. Several maps, a chart, tables, and appendices support this view.

Keer, Dhananjay. *Lokamanya Tilak: Father of the Indian Freedom Struggle*. 2d ed. Bombay: Popular Prakashan, 1969. This work depicts Tilak as one who politically roused the masses and brilliantly advocated workable revolutionary tactics, without helping to change social conditions. Debates among Indian leaders are vividly described. Here, Tilak usually appears to be more dynamic, committed, and effective than most of his peers.

Takmankar, D. V. *Lokamanya Tilak: Father of Indian Unrest and Maker of Modern India*. London: J. Murray, 1956. Commemorating Tilak's centenary and written by one of his newspaper staff, this official biography stands loyal to its subject. Tilak, stresses Takmankar, was the first to defy boldly the British imperial presence in India. His personal powers charged the masses and inspired Asian emancipation movements for years to come.

Wolpert, Stanley A. *Tilak and Gokhale: Revolution and Reform in the Making of Modern India*. Berkeley: University of California Press, 1962. Wolpert theorizes that Indian nationalism reflects the often opposing views of Tilak, the revolutionary, and Gokhale, the reformer. By coming into contact with each other, the adversaries also refined their own strong philosophies. The book draws heavily on correspondence, articles, and Marathi sources. It also contains an excellent bibliography.

*Lynn C. Kronzek*

# ALFRED VON TIRPITZ

*Born:* March 19, 1849; Küstrin, Brandenburg, Prussia
*Died:* March 6, 1930; Ebenhausen, Germany
*Area of Achievement:* The military
*Contribution:* Tirpitz, one of the ablest naval administrators in modern history, was the architect of the German High Seas Fleet that fought in World War I.

## *Early Life*

Alfred von Tirpitz was born March 19, 1849, of middle-class background. His father was a jurist and later county court judge in Brandenburg; his mother was the daughter of a physician. He joined the navy in 1865 when it was hardly a popular Prussian institution (the Prussian Navy in fact became a career for many ambitious young men of middle-class background who were barred from advancement in the army) and was commissioned four years later. Tirpitz rose rapidly in the navy. His leadership abilities were amply demonstrated when, in the 1880's, he headed the torpedo section of the German navy. Torpedoes were then coming into their own at sea, and Tirpitz worked to ensure their reliability. He was appointed captain in 1888 and gained practical experience at sea. From 1892 to 1896, he was chief of staff of the Naval High Command and was given responsibility for developing and codifying fleet tactics. He was promoted to rear admiral in 1895. His last assignment at sea was in 1896 to 1897, when he was chief of the cruiser squadron in East Asia. He was not a great success, as one of his vessels, the *Iltis*, sunk on a misson near Kiaochow, generating unfavorable publicity. Ironically, Tirpitz never commanded a modern battleship, much less a squadron of capital ships.

Tirpitz was a large man who had a strong personality. A trademark, and later a cartoonist's delight, was his great two-pronged beard. He radiated competence and leadership. A devoted family man, he liked to dress elegantly and had a polish lacking in many of his class. Patriotic and energetic, he could also be overbearing, ruthless, and domineering. Certainly he was an adroit politician and manipulator of men. He was also ambitious and very confident of his own abilities and came into office with a fully developed plan for naval expansion.

## *Life's Work*

On June 18, 1897, William II appointed Tirpitz as state secretary of the navy office, a post that he retained until he resigned all of his offices on March 15, 1916. In 1898, he became a voting member of the Prussian Ministry of State and two years later was raised to the hereditary Prussian nobility. In 1911, he was made admiral of the fleet. Tirpitz made his place in naval history on land, as the architect of the navy. Ironically, although Tirpitz built the German navy, in World War I he was not allowed to use it as he wished.

Tirpitz was appointed specifically to build up the size of the navy, which had languished under Chancellor Otto von Bismarck. In 1888, William II became kaiser. His mother, the Empress Frederick, wrote, "Wilhelm's one idea is to have a Navy which shall be larger and stronger than the Royal Navy." William was determined to pursue a more aggressive foreign policy (a chief reason for his break with Bismarck), and a strong navy was seen as a principal element in this *Weltpolitik*. The army had given Germany hegemony in Europe; the kaiser and Tirpitz saw the navy securing the same result for Germany in the world, elevating the nation to world power (*Weltmacht*) status. Justification for this view was provided by the timely publication of Alfred Thayer Mahan's *The Influence of Sea Power upon History, 1660-1783* in 1890. Mahan contended that history did not offer a single example of a world commercial power that was not also a sea power. Tirpitz agreed with the kaiser on the need for a strong fleet but disagreed that the emphasis should be on a *guerre de course* with commerce-raiding, cruiser-type vessels. Mahan had argued for the absolute primacy of the battleship, and Tirpitz won the kaiser to this viewpoint.

Tirpitz saw to it that the navy, unlike the army, came under the personal control of the Supreme War Lord. He assured the kaiser in February, 1898, that he would "remove the disturbing influence of the Reichstag upon Your Majesty's intentions concerning the development of the Navy," and he did precisely that. The Reichstag had no control over naval construction or organization. The Second Navy Bill of 1900 provided that a set number of vessels would be authorized, then built regardless of cost. Funds for personnel, maintenance, and training were all to be made available automatically, based on the number of ships in service.

Tirpitz was able to take advantage of growing support in Germany for a strong navy, especially from the small but influential German Colonial League and the Pan-German League. Still, winning approval for a strong navy was in large part the result of Tirpitz' own extraordinary abilities as promoter and publicist. In March, 1897, the Reichstag rejected the modest naval building program advocated by his predecessor, Friedrich Hollmann. In April, 1898, the same body passed the much more ambitious Tirpitz program by a vote of two to one.

Tirpitz cultivated an alliance with the Rhineland industrialists, who embraced the navy as their vehicle to rival the old Prussian-Junker combination centered in the army. He supported the creation of the Navy League, which had its own publication and speakers who traveled throughout Germany. Although the Navy League had only about 100,000 members, it was quite influential. Tirpitz also did not hesitate to appeal to German nationalism, and he took advantage of foreign policy crises to push for additional naval construction.

Tirpitz relied on a program of steady expansion (*Etappenplan*) of the navy, or the "patient laying of brick upon brick." In part this was designed to deceive the Reichstag and German public as to his true aims. For public consumption Tirpitz announced only modest goals; Germany wanted a fleet capable of keeping the North Sea and Baltic shipping lanes open in time of war; a strong navy was also justified as necessary to protect steadily expanding German commerce and her overseas empire. By 1895, Germany was second in the world in the value of her foreign trade, but her navy was only the fifth largest.

For public consumption also, Tirpitz argued that the navy was to be a "risk" fleet, that is, only large enough that another major naval power would not "risk" doing battle with the German navy for fear that its strength might be crippled to the point at which it would be vulnerable to the fleet of another major naval power.

Tirpitz also argued that Germany did not need a fleet as large as that of Great Britain; her warships could be concentrated, whereas the Royal Navy had to dissipate its strength in worldwide commitments. Tirpitz also advanced the belief that the fleet would be a useful diplomatic tool, making Germany a more attractive ally. In private, Tirpitz spoke of a panic-stricken British government willing to surrender up to half of her colonial empire to Germany in return for an alliance.

Such arguments were, in fact, a smoke screen designed to mask Tirpitz' real intent of creating a fleet strong enough to challenge Great Britain for control of the seas and world mastery. Tirpitz saw Great Britain as the enemy. He stated in 1897 that the navy had become "a question of survival" for Germany. He believed that the navy, supported by the middle-class industrial German state, was the future, to which eventually the army would have to give place. He opined in 1899 that if Germany could not, with her battle fleet, take advantage of shifts in world power, she "would sink back to the status of a poor farming country." In his view, Germany had to prepare for a showdown with the Anglo-Saxon powers. This would probably be in one great naval battle in the North Sea or Atlantic Ocean between Germany on the one side and either Great Britain or Great Britain and the United States on the other. Ironically, this was precisely the scenario anticipated by English navalists, and it almost came to pass at Jutland in World War I. Such a battle, Tirpitz believed, should take place only after 1920, when Germany would stand a good chance of winning it. His greatest concern was that the British might opt for a preemptive strike before that time, to "Copenhagen" his new creation before it was ready.

The first Tirpitz naval bill passed the Reichstag in April, 1898. It called for the construction, by April, 1904, of nineteen battleships, eight armored cruisers, and twelve large and thirty small cruisers. Taking advantage of the international situation (the impact of the Spanish-American War, sentiment against Great Britain aroused during the Boer War, and the Boxer Rebellion in China), Tirpitz introduced a second naval bill, which passed the Reichstag in June, 1900. It doubled the size of the projected navy to a total of thirty-eight battleships, twenty armored cruisers, and thirty-eight light cruisers—all to be built within twenty years. This was a direct challenge to the British Home Fleet, then about thirty-two battleships.

A naval building race between Great Britain and Germany ensued. In 1906, the British answered with the new super-battleship, *Dreadnought*, the first all big-gun ship, driven by steam turbines. Later they introduced the battle cruiser class as well. Tirpitz followed suit. Although the pace of construction subsequently slowed somewhat, Tirpitz used two crises over Morocco to secure the passage of supplementary German naval construction laws (*Novellen*) in 1906, 1908, and 1912. Six dreadnoughts were to be built by 1918; six large cruisers were also to be built, and additional funds were granted to expand dock facilities and widen existing canals so as to enable the warships to pass from the Baltic Sea to the North Sea. Battleship replacement was also to occur every twenty years instead of twenty-five as previously agreed. This meant, in effect, that new dreadnoughts would reach the fleet at a faster rate (four were to be built yearly from 1908 to 1911, and two per year from 1912 to 1917). The third *Novelle* of 1912 increased the projected size of the fleet to forty-one battleships (in five squadrons), twenty large cruisers, and forty light cruisers. It is by no means clear that Tirpitz intended to stop there. He was absolutely opposed to any reductions in the naval sphere and helped scuttle British war minister Richard Burdon Haldane's 1912 mission to Germany wherein he attempted to reduce the naval race between the two countries.

The quality of German construction was quite high. Naval historians generally concede that German range-finding optics were better than those of the British, and their armor-piercing shells were also superior. Although less heavily gunned than their British counterparts, German capital ships had excellent internal subdivision by watertight compartments, which at sea meant survivability. They also had better armor protection, and they were broader of beam and hence more stable as gun platforms.

With his attention fixed on battleships, Tirpitz was a late convert to submarines. The first German *Unterseeboot*, *U1*, was not completed until the end of 1906, and it was several years before its potential was realized. The budget of 1912 projected a total of seventy-two U-boats, but Germany entered World War I with only twenty-eight, compared with seventy-seven for France, fifty-five for Great Britain, and thirty-eight for the United States. There was no plan to employ them against commerce. By 1913, Tirpitz had also been won over to the use of naval airships.

At the beginning of World War I, Tirpitz offered to assume operational control over the navy, but this was rejected. He opposed keeping the fleet in port, where it spent most of World War I. He recognized the importance of the new U-boats in the war at sea but opposed their employment too early, judging 1916 as the right time. His advice was for the most part ignored, and he resigned his offices in 1916.

After leaving the Navy, Tirpitz went into politics. He was one of the founders of the Fatherland Party (*Vaterlandspartei*), and from 1924 to 1928 he was a nationalist deputy in the Reichstag. He supported the Dawes Plan but opposed the Locarno Pact and the reconciliation with France, as he believed that they would jeopardize cooperation with Great Britain and the United States. Tirpitz died on March 6, 1930.

*Summary*

As the father of the German navy that fought World War I, Alfred von Tirpitz played a pivotal role in German history. The Tirpitz plan was, however, in the words of one historian, a "gruesome error" and a "monstrous error in judgment." Far from driving Great Britain to panic, the construction of German vessels simply goaded the British into action. Great Britain was dependent for its survival on imports of food and raw materials; British political leaders and the public long believed that the German fleet was a "luxury" designed to satisfy the kaiser's ego, whereas the Royal Navy was seen as a "necessity." The British government adopted the "two-power naval standard," which required a fleet as large as the next two naval powers combined. Although facing serious fiscal problems, the British outspent the Germans in the naval sphere; one reason this was possible was that the British Army was so small.

As Bismarck predicted, the construction of a powerful German fleet drove Great Britain away from Germany and into alliance with France. Far from making Germany an attractive ally, the plan had the effect of further isolating Germany in Europe. The Entente Cordiale of 1904 was a direct result of German naval construction, as was the agreement in 1912 whereby the French agreed to take primary responsibility for the Mediterranean and concentrate their naval units there while the British did the same for the north Atlantic.

A treaty with Japan and the elimination of the Russian Navy in the Russo-Japanese War enabled the British to strengthen their position in Europe. As a result, the Home Fleet was able to overshadow the High Seas Fleet. Although by 1914 the German Navy was second in size only to that of Great Britain, the Royal Navy had in fact widened its advantage over Germany in most classes of ships (the capital ship ratio was thirty-two to eighteen), making the Tirpitz quest more illusory than ever.

There were limits to what Germany could do financially, particularly as it was at the same time maintaining the largest standing army in the world. By 1907-1908, the army was again getting priority in armaments expenditure. Seen in retrospect, had the bulk of assets spent on the navy gone to the army instead, Germany would have had a better chance at a land victory over France in 1914.

*Bibliography*

Herwig, Holger. *"Luxury" Fleet: The Imperial German Navy, 1888-1918*. London: Allen & Unwin, 1980. This is a well-balanced, lucid, dispassionate, short, and thoroughly researched study of the Tirpitz era. It is particularly strong in discussion of ship characteristics. Herwig also provides much useful information on Tirpitz.

Marder, Arthur J. *From the Dreadnought to Scapa Flow: The Royal Navy in the Fisher Era, 1904-1919*. 5 vols. London: Oxford University Press, 1961-1970. This is a comprehensive, often highly detailed, study of the Royal Navy of the period. There is much material here on Tirpitz' counterpart, Admiral John Arbuthnot Fisher, and his efforts to meet the German challenge.

Padfield, Peter. *The Great Naval Race: Anglo-German Naval Rivalry, 1900-1914*. New York: David McKay, 1974. While utilizing mostly secondary sources, Padfield nevertheless provides an introduction to the broader area of the development of German and British naval policies and the effects of their ensuing rivalry.

Scheer, Reinhard. *Germany's High Sea Fleet in the World War*. New York: Peter Smith, 1934. Although egocentric and often unreliable, this memoir by the admiral who commanded the High Seas Fleet at Jutland is useful for its discussion of the decision-making regarding tactical employment of the Tirpitz fleet in World War I.

Steinberg, Jonathan. *Yesterday's Deterrent: Tirpitz and the Birth of the German Battle Fleet*. London: Macmillan, 1965. There is much useful material here on Tirpitz, especially on his early career. It lacks the documentation of Herwig's study but is particularly helpful in understanding the politics involved in the higher echelons of the German navy.

Tirpitz, Alfred von. *My Memoirs*. 2 vols. London: Hurst and Blackett, 1919. Tirpitz' own defense of his policies. Although these recollections are entirely self-satisfied and self-righteous, they are indispensable in understanding his point of view.

*Spencer C. Tucker*

# TITO
## Josip Broz

*Born:* May 7, 1892; Kumroveć, Croatia, Austro-Hungarian Empire
*Died:* May 4, 1980; Ljubljana, Yugoslavia
*Areas of Achievement:* The military, government, and politics
*Contribution:* Tito built and led the Yugoslav Communist Partisan army, which was the most successful guerrilla resistance force against the Nazis and Fascists in World War II. After the war, he broke away from Joseph Stalin and until his death led the country on an independent Communist path.

### *Early Life*

Josip Broz (Tito) was born of mixed Croatian-Slovenian ancestry in 1892 in Kumroveć, a Croatian village, which then was part of the Hungarian kingdom. He was the seventh child in a family of fifteen. His earliest political memories were of the peasant revolts against the Hungarian landlords in 1902. At seven he went to the new elementary school in Kumrovec, which had one teacher for three hundred and fifty pupils. At first he was a poor student but as time went on he improved. At twelve, as was customary, he stopped school and went to work for his uncle as a herder. At fifteen, although his father had hoped to send him to the United States, he went to work as a waiter. Shortly, however, he became an apprentice locksmith and learned about Marxism from a coworker.

At eighteen, Broz went to Zagreb, found work, and joined the Social Democratic Party of Croatia and Slavonia. In 1913, at twenty-one, he was drafted into the Austro-Hungarian army. At the beginning of World War I, he was briefly jailed for antiwar agitation but was acquitted and served with his regiment as an officer in the Carpathians on the Russian front. In 1915, Broz was wounded and captured by Russian troops and sent to a prisoner of war camp in the Ural Mountains, where he came in contact with the Bolsheviks. He escaped in May, 1917, during the Russian Revolution and made his way to Petrograd (now Leningrad), where he stayed briefly but was soon recaptured and returned to Siberia. After the October Revolution, he joined the international Red Guard and fought against the White forces of Admiral Aleksandr Kolchak. It was in Siberia that he married his first wife, Pelaghia Belousnova, the daughter of a Russian worker.

### *Life's Work*

In 1921, after the Russian Civil War, Broz returned to Croatia, where he joined the newly formed Communist Party of the Kingdom of the Serbs, Croats, and Slovenes. At this time, the Party was under the leadership of the old Serbian Social Democrats, and the young Croatian worker despite his experience in Soviet Russia was consigned to minor rules of propaganda and participation in demonstrations and strikes. The Party was declared illegal in 1921, and Broz was arrested in 1928 and spent five years in prison. There he came into contact with one of the most important influences in his life, the theoretical Marxist Moshe Pijade. Pijade helped Broz form his conception of Marxism. After his release from prison, Broz took the pseudonym "Tito" and went to the Soviet Union, where he witnessed the Stalinist purges of the 1930's that brought down the Serbian leadership of the Yugoslav Communist Party. Tito was now elevated to the supreme Party leadership. Tito returned to Yugoslavia and at a secret Party meeting in October, 1940, he was elected general secretary of the Party. When Nazi Germany invaded the Soviet Union in June, 1941, Tito organized the resistance that up to that time was chiefly led by the Serbian royalist nationalist Draža Mihajlović. It was as the commander in chief of the Yugoslav resistance army, the most successful in Europe, that Tito came into public renown.

As the leader of the Yugoslav forces, he built up a movement of 250,000 from all over the country including all nationalities. This gave him an advantage over his chief rival, the Serbian anti-Communist Mihajlović, and Stalin was able to convince his Western allies in 1942 to throw all support behind Tito. The guerrilla war against German, Italian, and Bulgarian occupation forces was complex and multifaceted, but it degenerated into a civil war between the partisans, as Tito's group was called, and the chetniks of Mihajlović. Both sides often made alliances with the occupiers, especially as a Fascist defeat seemed imminent and the struggle became more and more a fight for control of Yugoslavia after World War II. Although in December, 1945, Red Army troops moved into the country to fight the retreating German army, Tito won largely on his own efforts.

Thus after the conflict Tito was able to establish independent political authority over the country. Soviet leaders were anxious that they regain control of the international Communist movement and began to recruit Yugoslav agents to oppose Tito's independence. For his part, Tito not only wanted to establish independent Communist rule in Yugoslavia but also hoped to enlarge his own influence in an all-Balkan Communist federation and exerted pressure on Albanian Communist leaders, negotiated with the Communist leadership of Bulgaria, and armed the Communist insurgents in Greece. To the West, Tito appeared to be the most uncompromising of the new Eastern European Communist leaders. Therefore, it was a great surprise when the Soviets expelled Yugoslavia from the Communist Information Bureau in 1948.

Tito then decided to go his own way. He followed separate foreign and economic policies from the Soviet Union. At the time of the Cold War in the 1950's before the rupture of relations between China and the Soviet Union, Tito stood as the only Communist leader in power not allied to Moscow. He was able to use his position to gain aid from the West, and in November, 1950, the United States Congress passed the Yugoslav Emergency Relief Act. Along with Jawaharlal Nehru of India and Gamal Abdel Nasser of Egypt, he started the nonaligned nations movement in the international arena. In domestic policies, Tito advocated his own way toward socialism by emphasizing workers' control of factories. This permitted more economic liberalization in Yugoslavia than existed in other Communist-controlled countries. Although in the late 1940's Mihajlović was tried and executed as a war criminal and leading critics such as Milovan Djilas were imprisoned, more liberalism appeared in political and social life as well. As time went on, Yugoslavia enjoyed access to Western literature and freedom of travel long before the other socialist countries of Eastern Europe.

Tito could not solve all of Yugoslavia's problems. He was never able truly to unite the country, and hostility among the nationalities remained, although he was able to keep them under control while he lived. When he died, however, these burst forward with a new fury. The concept of workers' control of factories has also led to many economic problems—inflation as well as unemployment. The differences in the country from rich industrialized republics in the north to the agrarian ones in the south, combined with the national confrontations, has been one of Yugoslavia's critical issues since World War II.

Tito's dictatorial methods caused some of his closest allies to fall away. Djilas became a critic whom Tito threw in jail. Aleksander Rankovic, his chosen successor, also was jailed for abuse of power. Ironically, although Tito is best known for his clash with Stalin, he himself carried out his own "cult of personality" in Yugoslavia and became the glue to hold his fractious land together. When he died in 1980, there was no suitable successor. Under Tito's direction the League of Communists had established a system of rotating presidents to take into account the national differences—a method that was bound to fail and the consequences of which have not yet been resolved.

When asked by Vladimir Dedijer, his comrade and sympathetic biographer, to explain the differences between his system, what the West called "Titoism," and the Soviet system, Tito replied that Yugoslavia was building "genuine socialism" while the economic policies of the Soviet Union have "degenerated into state capitalism under the leadership of a dictatorial bureaucratic caste." Secondly, Yugoslavia was developing socialist democracy impeded only by the lack of technology. In the Soviet Union, there was not democracy, only a reign of terror and no freedom of thought or creative work in literature. Thirdly, Yugoslavia was a true federation of equal republics, while the Soviet Union was an equal federation on paper only. The Russian republic, through its Moscow bureaucrats, dominated everything. Critics of Tito, however, assert that the same charges could be leveled at him.

*Summary*

Tito is one of the major political leaders of the twentieth century. His military and political accomplishments enabled him to defy both Adolf Hitler and Stalin. He had the rare gift of carrying out a revolution and leading a government. As a military commander Tito was able to organize a vast guerrilla army. While it is true that he was supplied by the Allies, the effort was still monumental. He took on one of the most successful war machines of the twentieth century and was able to maneuver through an extremely complex and multifaceted array of forces fighting both foreign enemies and domestic opponents.

As the leader of a small country he was in danger of being swallowed by the superpowers during the time of the Cold War. Yet he was most successful in playing one off the other. He was the first Communist leader after World War II to become diplomatically an ally of the West. Although a European and Communist head of state, he became a leader of the Third World. The force of his personality alone held his fragile government together. Using a combination of tyranny and liberalization, he established Yugoslavia as a country to be reckoned with in international and European politics. Because of his success, he also established himself as a major contributor to the field of socialist ideology. Maintaining that his was the true Marxism, he put into practice the economic principle of workers' control of factories. He was the first Communist leader to introduce a policy of openness into a Communist-led government since the 1930's.

Tito's faults cannot be overlooked. In many ways he was as egotistical in assuming personal command as his great opponent Stalin. His cult of personality rivaled that of the Georgian dictator. His intolerance of criticism, even from persons such as Djilas who were ideologically close to him, has tarnished his claim to have been a proponent of egalitarian democracy. His unwillingness to share power or introduce genuine multiopinion councils has led to chaotic national and political problems that linger in Yugoslavia today. Furthermore his economic policies have not all proved successful. While trying to implement the benefits of socialism, Yugoslavia has experienced both unemployment and inflation. Yugoslavia's postwar development under Tito was impressive, but in the 1970's it ran into economic snags and since then has been left behind. Tito's place in modern history rests with his war effort against Hitler and his defiance of Stalin. Perhaps he owes much to the fortunes of time and place, but no one can deny the magnitude of his achievement.

*Bibliography*

Adamic, Louis. *The Eagle and His Roots*. Garden City, N.Y.: Doubleday, 1952. An early biography written by an American-Yugoslav collaborator with Tito. Partly propaganda, partly a friendly appraisal by an important historical figure himself, the president of the American Slavic Committee.

Auty, Phyllis. *Tito*. New York: Ballantine Books, 1972. An excellent short biography by one of the leading scholars of Yugoslav history. Includes maps, notes, an index, and illustrations.

Campbell, John C. *Tito's Separate Road: America and Yugoslavia in World Politics*. New York: Harper & Row, 1967. Part of the Policy Book series of the Council on Foreign Relations. A brief scholarly analysis of Tito's economics and politics especially in relation to its effect on international affairs. Contains bibliographical notes.

Clissold, Stephen. *Whirlwind: An Account of Marshal Tito's Rise to Power*. New York: Philosophical Library, 1947. A history of Tito's activities in World War II by a British officer who served alongside his partisans.

Dedijer, Vladimir. *Tito*. New York: Simon & Schuster, 1953. The semiofficial biography of Tito written by his comrade in arms and including extensive interviews with the man. A invaluable source. Contains an index.

Djilas, Milovan. *Tito: The Story from Inside*. Translated by Vasilije Kojić and Richard Hayes. New York: Harcourt Brace Jovanovich, 1980. An evaluation of Tito by a former ally and now Yugoslavia's most famous dissident. Contains a biographical appendix and illustrations.

Maclean, Fitzroy. *Eastern Approaches*. Reprint. New York: Time-Life Books, 1964. Originally published in 1949, these memoirs are written by one of the British officers who served with Tito's partisans and are an important source of information about the man and his abilities. Includes an index, maps, and illustrations.

Rusinow, Dennison. *The Yugoslav Experiment, 1948-1974*. Berkeley: University of California Press, 1977. Published for the Royal Institute of International Affairs in London. Although dealing with the history of Yugoslavia after World War II, this work by a leading scholar gives an excellent survey and appraisal of Tito's contribution to the country. Includes an index and a bibliography.

Ulam, Adam B. *Titoism and the Cominform*. Westport, Conn.: Greenwood Press, 1952. An important scholarly monograph by a respected political scientist and critic of Marxism. This work analyzes the split between Stalin and Tito and examines its theoretical basis. Includes an index and a bibliographical note.

*Frederick B. Chary*

# FERDINAND JULIUS TÖNNIES

*Born:* July 26, 1855; Oldenswort, Schleswig, Denmark
*Died:* April 9, 1936; Kiel, Germany
*Area of Achievement:* Sociology
*Contribution:* Tönnies was one of the founders of sociology as a field of scientific study. His major contribution lay in the distinction that he drew between two fundamentally different types of social orders—the realm of *Gemeinschaft* contrasted with that of *Gesellschaft*, or, in what has become the standard English translation, "community" versus "society." The continuing influence of this dichotomy upon sociological thought is shown in contemporary development theory with its distinction between traditional and modern societies.

## *Early Life*

Ferdinand Julius Tönnies was born July 26, 1855, on a farm in the parish of Oldenswort, district of Eiderstedt, Schleswig, then part of Denmark but incorporated into Germany during his boyhood. His father, of Frisian stock, was a prosperous farmer and cattle-raiser; his mother came from a family noted for its Lutheran ministers. Tönnies spent his boyhood first on the family farm and then, after his father retired in 1864, in the North Sea town of Husum. After graduating from the local *Gymnasium* in 1872, he entered the University of Strasbourg. Taking advantage of German students' freedom to travel, he spent time at the Universities of Jena, Bonn, Leipzig, and Tübingen. He received a doctorate in classical philology from Tübingen in 1877. By this time, however, the major focus of his interest had shifted to political theory and social problems. After postdoctoral work at the University of Berlin, he went on to London to continue his research on the seventeenth century English political thinker Thomas Hobbes. Tönnies gained his *venia legendi* (license to lecture) by submitting in 1881 a draft of what would become his major work, *Gemeinschaft und Gesellschaft*, as his *Habilitationsschrift* and became a *Privatdozent* in philosophy at the University of Kiel.

Tönnies had sufficient private means that he could devote the bulk of his time and energy to his own research and writing rather than to teaching. His most famous work, *Gemeinschaft und Gesellschaft*, was published in 1887. The revised and expanded definitive edition came out in 1912. An English translation by Charles P. Loomis first appeared in 1940 as *Fundamental Concepts of Sociology*; a new edition came out in 1955 under what has become the generally accepted English title, *Community and Association*. *Community and Association* is a work of immense erudition that reflects Tönnies' extensive reading in social and economic history, the political and social philosophers of the seventeenth through the nineteenth centuries, and nineteenth century anthropological writings. Two themes found in nineteenth century German thought were—along with his study of the philosophy of Hobbes—of crucial importance in shaping Tönnies' ideas. One was the distinction—inherited from the philosopher Georg Wilhelm Friedrich Hegel—between *Gesellschaft* ("society") and *Staat* ("state"): the first an organic reality, the second a mere artificial creation. The second was the concept of the *Volkgeist* ("spirit of a people"), with its corollary, the existence of a *Völkerpsychologie* (or collective psychology of a people) that was manifested in such social phenomena as customs, language, myths, and religion.

*Life's Work*

In his mature work, Tönnies distinguished between broad and narrow conceptions of sociology. The broad conception included ancillary disciplines such as demography, physical anthropology, and social psychology. The narrow conception, which Tönnies took as his own primary interest, was limited to the study of social relationships and groups, their values, and their norms of conduct. He delineated three methodologically distinct levels of inquiry in this area. One was theoretical or pure sociology aimed at the formulation of an integrated system of basic concepts or ideal types. The second, which he termed applied sociology, applied the concepts of theoretical sociology to understand the development of concrete historical societies and explain the processes of social evolution, particularly the emergence of modern society. The third, empirical sociology, involved the description and analysis of contemporary human relationships and social phenomena.

The most complete available bibliography of Tönnies' writings lists more than six hundred items. His research on Hobbes resulted in the publication from previously unprinted manuscripts of the English political theorist's *Behemoth: Or, The Long Parliament* (1889) and *The Elements of Law, Natural and Politic* (1889) followed by a full-scale intellectual biography, *Hobbes Leben und Lehre* (1896), which would remain for many years the standard account. He undertook empirical studies dealing with population, the impact of business and seasonal cycles upon society, and such examples of deviant behavior as suicide, crime, and illegitimacy, partly because of his personal humanitarian sympathies and partly because of his conviction that sociological theory must rest upon a solid foundation of empirical research. He was a champion of the application of statistics for the illumination of contemporary social phenomena and processes; he even invented a new method of correlation, which he discussed in the article "Eine neue Methode der Vergleichung statistischer Reihen," which appeared in the journal *Jarbuch für Gesetzgebung, Verwaltung, und Volkswirtschaft im Deutschen Reich* in 1909.

Tönnies' major interest, however, lay in the elucidation and amplification of the concepts set forth in *Community and Association*. The more important of his writings along this line were: *Die Sitte* (1909; *Custom: An Essay on Social Codes*, 1961), *Kritik der öffentlichen Meinung* (1922; critique of public opinion); two collections of articles and papers, *Soziologische Studien and Kritiken* (1925-1929; sociological studies and reviews) and *Fortschritt und soziale Entwicklung: Geschichtsphilosophische Ansichten* (1926; progress and social evolution: views on the philosophy of history); and *Einführung in die Soziologie* (1931; introduction to sociology).

Tönnies regarded all social interactions and groups—what he called social entities (*soziale Wesenheiten*)—as the products of human thought or will. He distinguished three levels of social entities: social relationships (*soziale Verhältnisse*); social corporations (*soziale Körperschaften*), that is, groups that were able to act through representative organs or officers; and social corporations (*Samtschaften*), that is, unorganized groups such as social classes or nations that are large enough to be independent of specific individuals. Although he acknowledged that social relationships may have their source in biological relationships, or psychological relationships, or both (such as the relationship between parent and child), he emphasized the "voluntaristic" basis of all social relationships. A parent, for example, could disown his child. Marriage similarly could be terminated by divorce or, alternately, survive in name long after the psychological relationship had died. Social relationships thus exist because they are recognized, acknowledged, and willed by the participants via the acceptance of and adherence to certain norms or rules of conduct. A social entity, in other words, is the creation of the will of its members and, in turn, imposes upon them certain obligations and grants them certain rights.

Tönnies went on to distinguish between two different kinds of "will" involved in establishing a social entity. One was *Wesenwille* (variously translated by commentators as "natural will," "organic will," or "essential will"), wherein an action is willed for its own sake, or because of primarily unconscious drives or inclinations, or out of habit, or because of its own intrinsic value. The second kind he called *Kürwille* (translated as "rational will," "reflective will," or "arbitrary will"), a term from the old Germanic word for "choosing," because the actor chooses or wills a course of action from among possible alternatives to achieve a certain end or purpose.

The kind of will involved results in two fundamentally different types of social entity. *Gemeinschaft* is the type of social entity that is the project of *Wesenwille*; *Gesellschaft* is the type that results from *Kürwille*. Examples of the first include kin, neighborhood, and village networks social clubs, and religious sects, that is, relationships whose bonds grow out of mutual sympathy, habits, or common beliefs. Examples of the second include contractual arrangements, business associations, and special-interest organizations based upon the deliberate calculation of advantage and disadvantage and weighing ends against means. Although Tönnies took pains to deny that he was writing an "ethical or political treatise," the thrust of his analysis appeared to exalt "community" over "society." Community, he suggested, answered the "need of real and organic life" and was characterized by trust and intimacy. Society, in contrast, was "a mechanical and artificial aggregate" in which every person lived for himself "in a state of tension towards all the others."

Tönnies acknowledged that *Gemeinschaft* and *Gesellschaft* were ideal types that did not exist in pure form in the real world. Even *Gemeinschaften* had their rational aspect. Men's social conduct also could not be determined exclusively by intellect or reason. A given social entity must be ranked on a scale of more or less *Gemeinschaft*-like or more or less *Gesellschaft*-like. Yet Tönnies did see a long-term historical trend. It was his ambition to trace the evolution of human society from primitive agrarian communism through the individualistic society of modern capitalism to an ultimate socialistic-type order, which he envisaged as a higher-quality version of *Gemeinschaft*. Although he published only fragments of this planned universal history in his *Geist der Neuzeit* (1935; spirit of modern times), his article and papers show that he viewed the transition from a predominantly *Gemeinschaft*-like to a predominantly *Gesellschaft*-like social order as largely the result of three major forces: growing commercialization with its attendant corollaries of competition, the market, trade, and credit; the rise of the modern state; and the advance of science.

Tönnies was a German patriot who defended the German side during and after World War I. By the standard of his time and milieu, however, he was politically a liberal, even a radical. An active participant in the Verein für Sozialpolitik (Association for Social Politics) and the Gesellschaft für Soziale Reform (Society for Social Reform), Tönnies took a sympathetic interest in the trade union and socialist movements, workers' education, consumer cooperatives, and national independence movements in such places as Finland and Ireland. In 1932, he joined the Social Democratic Party in protest against the rising National Socialist strength. Hopeful about the possibility of a nondogmatic universal religion that would unite all mankind, he was a leading figure in the Ethical Culture Society.

His pro-labor, pro-reform sympathies brought Tönnies into disfavor with the Prussian educational authorities and retarded his academic advancement. His growing international reputation, however, finally led to his appointment to a full professorship in political economy at the University of Kiel in 1913. He retired in 1916 but five years later resumed teaching as professor emeritus of sociology. His public denunciation of Nazism and anti-Semitism led to his dismissal from his professorship emeritus after Adolf Hitler came to power. He was with Max Weber, Werner Sombart, and George Simmel as one of the founders of the German Sociological Society in 1909, and he served as president from its founding to 1933. He died on April 9, 1936, at the age of nearly eighty-one, at Kiel.

*Summary*

Ferdinand Julius Tönnies was one of the founding fathers of the modern discipline of sociology. Perhaps his major intellectual significance lay in how he offered a new way of looking at the relationship of the individual to society that could resolve the long-standing conflict between the mechanical and rationalistic view of the social contract theorists, on the one hand, and the organistic conception of the romantic and historical schools, on the other. Tönnies' point was that both positions were correct and complemented each other: Man was both a social and an asocial being, and there were both preexisting social relationships into which individuals were born and others that were the result of conscious agreement among formerly independent individuals. Tönnies, one of the leading students of the history of sociology, concludes,

> formulated and even inaugurated a typology of social relations which no sociologist can henceforth ignore, if he does not wish to pass for an amateur. . . . Indeed, all discussions on the opposition between competition and accommodation, conflict and association, cooperation and hostility, fusion and tension, integration and dissolution, solidarity and rivalry, communion and revolt, and all the other forms of social concord and discord, bring us back, directly or indirectly, to the work of Tönnies.

Although Tönnies' work attracted attention and controversy in scholarly circles from its first publication, he had not much influence outside the academic world until after World War I. A disillusioned post-World War I generation romanticized the supposed virtues of the close-knit rural and small-town community in contrast to the impersonality and anonymity of modern industrial, urban society. A more recent variant upon this same theme has been the popularity of the concept of "mass society" and its resulting "alienated man." Tönnies' work was first exploited to legitimize hostility to liberal capitalism and bourgeois society by the communitarian romantics of the German political right and had via this route an indirect influence on aspects of National Socialist ideology. In the 1960's and since, Tönnies has been drawn upon to justify the communitarian nostalgia of the so-called New Left.

*Bibliography*

Cahnman, Werner, ed. *Ferdinand Tönnies: A New Evaluation, Essays and Documents*. Leiden: E. J. Brill, 1973. A valuable collection of writings about and commentaries upon Tönnies—many of which could be found previously only in not always easily accessible scholarly journals.

Freund, Julien. "German Sociology in the Time of Max Weber." In *A History of Sociological Analysis*, edited by Tom Bottomore and Robert Nisbet. New York: Basic Books, 1978. A brief but perceptive analysis that sketches the basic parameters of Tönnies' *Community and Association* distinction, places his work into the larger context of late nineteenth and early twentieth century social and philosophical thought, and offers a sympathetic appreciation of his contributions to the field of sociology.

Heberle, Rudolf. "Ferdinand Tönnies." In *International Encyclopedia of the Social Sciences*, edited by David L. Sills, 17 vols. New York: Macmillan, 1968. Despite (or perhaps because of) its brevity, Heberle's sketch is the most lucid and comprehensible introduction of Tönnies' ideas for the beginning student available.

Jacoby, E. G. "Tönnies." In *The McGraw-Hill Encyclopedia of World Biography*, vol. 10. New York: McGraw-Hill, 1973. A brief but good biographical source on Tönnies. Relates events from both his life and career and includes a bibliography.

Mitzman, Arthur. *Sociology and Estrangement: Three Sociologists of Imperial Germany.* New York: Alfred A. Knopf, 1973. A brilliant exercise in comparative intellectual biography focusing on Tönnies, Sombart, and Robert Michels. Mitzman's account is the fullest available exploration in English of the influences shaping Tönnies' thinking, the sources of his major concepts, and the evolution over time of his views.

Tönnies, Ferdinand. *Ferdinand Tönnies on Sociology: Pure, Applied, and Empirical.* Edited with an introduction by Werner J. Cahnman and Rudolf Heberle. Chicago: University of Chicago Press, 1971. The brief introduction by editors presupposes more background than the average undergraduate student is likely to have. The volume is invaluable, however, for its English translation of selections from Tönnies' previously untranslated writings. For students wishing to go further, there is a handy bibliography listing Tönnies' more important publications.

*John Braeman*

# AHMED SÉKOU TOURÉ

*Born:* January 9, 1922; Faranah, Guinea
*Died:* March 26, 1984; Cleveland, Ohio
*Areas of Achievement:* Government and politics
*Contribution:* A lifelong revolutionary nationalist, Touré led Guinea in 1958 to independence from French colonial rule by securing, in all of Francophone Africa, the only no vote against affiliation with the French Community. Guinea's president from independence in 1958 until his death twenty-six years later, he implemented radical sociopolitical transformations. A leading revolutionary African ideologue, Touré left the imprint of his socialist vision on all aspects of Guinean life.

## *Early Life*

Ahmed Sékou Touré was born on January 9, 1922, in the village of Faranah, situated on the bank of the Niger River, deep in the interior of Guinea. One of seven children born to Alpha and Aminata Touré, Malinke peasant farmers, Touré claimed to be the grandson of Samori Touré, the legendary Muslim state builder who waged a protracted resistance against French conquest until his capture in 1898. Reared a Muslim, the dominant religion in Guinea, Touré attended the École Coranique (Koranic school) and a French primary school in Kankan. In 1936, he was enrolled in the Georges Poiret Technical College in Conakry but was expelled at age fifteen for participation in a student food strike. Thereafter, Touré continued his education through correspondence courses and independent study. He became fluent in French and Soussou in addition to his native Malinké and a spellbinding orator in all three languages.

In 1940, Touré obtained a clerk's position with the Compagnie du Niger, a Unilever subsidiary, where he quickly became involved in labor union activities. The following year, after passing the qualifying exam for work with the Post, Telegraph and Telecommunications (PTT) service, he entered the colonial civil service as a postal clerk. While working in this capacity, he made his first remarkable impression as a constructive agitator by organizing the postal workers into a union. His talent and efficient work earned for him the admiration of his countrymen and the vigilance of the colonial authorities. At that time he formed connections with the Conféderation Générale de Travail (CGT), a Communist-dominated French labor organization.

By 1945 Touré was elected general secretary of the postal workers' union, the Syndicat du Personnel des PTT. A quick succession of upward moves in the trade union movement in both Guinea and French West Africa was to follow, establishing him between 1947 and 1956 as a leading West African trade unionist. In 1946 he became involved with intracolonial politics through the Rassemblement Démocratique Africain (RDA). By 1948, Touré was elected general secretary of the Territorial Union of the CGT, and two years later he was named general secretary of the coordinating committee of the CGT for French West Africa and Togoland. Touré's close relationship with the CGT was a significant influence upon the development of his skill as a mass organizer and political tactician and assisted in no small way in his mastery of Marxist-Leninist thought and practice.

### *Life's Work*

Revolutionary political and socioeconomic change is the central theme of Touré's life. From his earliest years as a labor union organizer, through the decades he labored for independence and as President of Guinea and leader of the Parti Démocratique de Guinée (PDG), he sought to effect fundamental change in his country and create a model for other African nations to follow.

The first two decades of his work life centered on labor issues and the struggle for political independence. Although clearly a radical in the 1940's, he fought within the French colonial system to advance the causes of social justice and Guinean independence. During World War II, African nationalism developed rapidly, and in 1944, at Brazzaville (French Congo) General Charles de Gaulle, president of the French Committee of National Liberation, recognized that France's postwar relationship with French Africa must be revised. The Brazzaville recommendations, accepted by the Fourth French Republic formed in 1946, scrapped the French Empire and substituted the French Union, which allowed the African "overseas territories" administrative freedom, the right to form political parties, the creation of local assemblies composed of both Africans and Europeans, and the formation of regional assemblies for French West (AOF) and French Equatorial Africa (AEF).

In Guinea three parties arose, including the PDG in 1947; by 1952 Touré had become secretary general, and the party had become dominant. That same year he became secretary general of the RDA and helped organize in September, 1953, the CGT-initiated, territory-wide strike that secured a significant increase in the minimum wage for workers in the AOF. Later that year Touré won a seat in the Territorial Assembly as the councilor for Beyla, Guinea. In 1955 he was elected mayor of Conakry, and in 1956, to a seat in the French National Assembly.

With the French government's promulgation of the *loi-cadre* for Francophone Africa in 1956, parties with a mass base such as the PDG-RDA obtained an ideal opportunity for greater support at the polls. The *loi-cadre* provided universal suffrage and home rule, with France retaining control over foreign affairs, defense, monetary affairs, justice, and higher education. Touré was elected vice president of the first Government Council of Guinea, the equivalent of prime minister and a position he used to eliminate the tribal chieftaincies, which he considered corrupt.

When the Fourth Republic collapsed and de Gaulle came to Africa in search of support for his Fifth Republic with a referendum on the French Community (an updating of the French Union), Touré urged a vote of no, asserting that the draft constitution provided neither liberty nor equality with France. A no vote meant automatic independence and the forfeiture of French economic and technical assistance. Ninety-five percent of the Guinean electorate complied; thus formal ties to France ended, and on October 2, 1958, the Republic of Guinea was proclaimed. Guinea was the only French African territory where a no vote was urged and overwhelmingly supported by the populace. Touré and the PDG had demonstrated that they enjoyed virtually undisputed support of the Guinean people, and the future of Guinea fell squarely on their shoulders.

Under the new constitution, Guinea became a democratic and secular republic. Popular rule was to prevail through election of representatives to the National Assembly and the president who was to serve a seven-year term. Economic development, Touré's prime objective, appeared brighter for Guinea than the other states of the AOF-AEF, for it was endowed with immense deposits of bauxite and iron ore, both already being exploited. For Touré the quandary was how to pursue development and fundamental social change while securing foreign investment and maintaining a foreign policy of positive neutralism. His strategies for realizing these goals were shaped by the dramatic rupture with France and Touré's own past in the CGT and PDG.

Economic decolonization, Touré quickly asserted, would be pursued by a planned economy and a noncapitalist path to development. This resulted in the nationalization of the export trade sector in 1959 and of internal trade in 1960. State agencies were created to control all aspects of marketing, and the civil service was completely Africanized. In March, 1960, he also announced that Guinea had created its own currency, which gave the state control over banking and insurance. Touré then designed an economic Triennial Plan, which was adopted at the PDG Congress in April, 1960, and which stressed developing public and social services while expanding mineral exploitation. Cooperation with foreign capital, however, was supported, and the mixed economic sector, in bauxite mining especially, became the most important source of revenue and foreign exchange.

Touré's political thinking, and hence the structure of the PDG, changed during the first decade of independence. Initially the party was conceived as a mass organization and thus voluntary associations were incorporated into it, such as the women's organizations, youth associations, and trade unions. He defined the party as the unity of Guinean people and rejected the concept of class struggle. By 1964, Touré claimed the revolution was threatened by corruption, inefficiency, smuggling, waste, and low morale. The 1964 *loi-cadre* was passed to correct this. It created standards for party membership and stiff party discipline and extended the party's reach into all factories, large businesses, the army, and the civil service, turning the PDG into a cadre party. Touré began to speak of class struggle and align himself ideologically more clearly with Marxism-Leninism. By the 1967 PDG Congress, he spoke of socialism as the official goal of the PDG and Guinea as divided into two opposing classes, the people (peasants and workers) and anti-people (their opponents).

Touré's political development placed him squarely in not only the camp of African Socialists but also the lead. Like Kwame Nkrumah, Julius Nyerere, and others who defined African Socialism, he redefined class struggle. His institutionalization of mass support through the one-party system went further than elsewhere in Africa, culminating in his declaration of a one-party state in 1978. His opponents have stressed that the evolution of the PDG as the focal institution engendering one-man, one-party rule was achieved through the creation of a permanent "state of plots" and the arrest, imprisonment, or execution of all opponents. Touré exposed nine major plots against the government between 1960 and 1976, which in each case were followed by suppression of the dissenters or protesters (that is, traditional chiefs and unionists in 1960, teachers in 1961, traders in 1965, and civil servants in 1967, 1969, and 1971). The largest crackdown occurred in 1971 after a Portuguese-backed mercenary force attacked Conakry and thousands were arrested and dozens hanged, including several former government ministers.

That invasion related to Touré's foreign policy, which emphasized African unity, support for national liberation struggles, anti-imperialism, and nonalignment. Touré extended support and refuge to the party waging a war for independence from Portuguese rule in neighboring Guinea-Bissau. Africa was the pivot of his foreign policy, but his international relations were characterized by militant rhetoric and flexible diplomacy. Thus, he sought good relations and aid from China, the Soviet Union, and the United States, receiving aid from all in the early years of independence. He nurtured strong relations with his ideological counterparts in Angola, Mozambique, Benin, Congo, and Algeria but failed to achieve good relations with his ideological opposites in the Ivory Coast, Sierra Leone, and Senegal until the late 1970's. His pan-African commitment was expressed two months after independence when Touré and Nkrumah, President of Ghana, signed a treaty of union—the Ghana-Guinea Union—as a nucleus for a union of West Africa. Mali joined two years later, uniting West Africa's most radical states, but it was a paper union and was disbanded in 1963 when the Organization of African Unity (OAU) was created.

### *Summary*

Throughout his life Ahmed Sékou Touré sought genuine independence and social transformation for Guinea. He will be forever remembered for his success in achieving Guinean independence and rejecting French neocolonialism. Although the imprint of his revolutionary vision was left in every area of Guinean life, his efforts at transforming Guinea may not be eventually judged as so successful. Within weeks of his death, there was a military coup led by Colonel Lansana Conte and the Military Committee for National Redress, which embarked on a course of liberalization and dismantling of the state sector of the economy; yet altering Touré's legacy will take a long time. When Touré died in a Cleveland hospital, flown there in the care of doctors sent by King Hassan of Morocco, much was made of his "opening to the West." In reality, during the last decade of his life he brought Guinea out of diplomatic isolation, improved Guinean and West African regional cooperation, advanced interstate mediation through his work as a peacemaker, and enticed foreign investors to Guinea with attractive financial terms.

Programmatic consistency was not always his forte, but genuine independence and economic development remained his goals. Touré's ideological shifts are spelled out in more than twenty books published between 1958 and 1977, works which clearly demonstrate his focus on radical social change, anti-imperialism, African unity, and national development. Even his many poems were politically charged paeans to the PDG, party militants, anticolonial resistance, and hard work in the service of national development. His greatest achievement was, no doubt, in forging through a protracted process of national sacrifice an independent African Socialist path; African unity and development proved more elusive.

*Bibliography*

Geiss, Imanuel. *The Pan-African Movement*. London: Methuen, 1974. An important and accessible work for understanding the development of pan-Africanism within African nationalism. Thus, Touré is seen as a representative of his generation in his pan-African concern.

Hanna, William J. *Independent Black Africa: The Politics of Freedom*. Chicago: Rand McNally, 1964. A helpful examination of independent African states in their early years, especially one-party systems such as that of Guinea.

Hargreaves, J. D. *Decolonization in Africa*. New York: Longman, 1988. A readily available work for the general reader to understand decolonization in Guinea and Africa in general.

Kaba, Lansine. "Guinean Politics: A Critical Historical Overview." *Journal of Modern African Studies* 15, no. 1 (1977): 25-45. The political evolution of Guinea and Touré is traced since World War II. A critical analysis of Touré, this article demonstrates that he created a tyranny in which he was the sole interpreter of correct politics and culture.

__________. "A New Era Dawns in Guinea." *Current History* 84 (1985):

174-178. This article provides a succinct summary of the legacy of Touré in restructuring Guinea's society and economy. It also discusses the initial policies of his successors.

Langley, J. Ayo. *Ideologies of Liberation in Black Africa, 1856-1970*. London: Rex Collings, 1979. A documentary study of African nationalism, this work places in context the revolutionary ideas of Touré as well as detailing the antecedents.

Touré, Sekou. "Speech to the Congress." *Black Scholar* 5, no. 10 (1974): 23-29. The President of Guinea's speech to the Sixth Pan-African Congress in Tanzania in June, 1974. An ode to African civilization and resistance to colonialism, it is a good example of his rhetorical style and his deep belief in African unity.

*Kathleen O'Mara*

# EIJI TOYODA

*Born:* September 12, 1913; Nagoya, Japan

*Areas of Achievement:* Business and industry
*Contribution:* For more than a half century, Toyoda has been a central management figure and a driving force in the development of a small family enterprise into one of the world's most successful corporate empires.

*Early Life*

Eiji Toyoda was born in Nagoya, Japan, on September 12, 1913. Although the family name was eventually to gain international recognition and respect for automobile manufacturing, it was already a well-known name in Japan thanks to Eiji's uncle, Sakichi Toyoda, known as the "King of Inventors." Sakichi was a skilled carpenter, and most of the 150 domestic and international patents he eventually obtained were related to the weaving industry. In early 1895, he established in Nagoya the first of a series of successful ventures in the weaving and textile machinery industry. He was an aggressive entrepreneur with a blustery self-confidence and an early vision of doing commercial battle in order to project Japan's economic might into the world market. In his autobiography, Eiji warmly acknowledged his uncle's shaping influence on his early years. When Eiji was a second-grader, Sakichi took him to visit one of his weaving works in Shanghai and used the occasion of the trip abroad to acquaint the young Eiji with the intricacies of foreign exchange rates.

Shortly before his death in 1930, Sakichi enjoined his eldest son, Kiichirō Toyoda, Eiji's cousin, to explore the possibility of expanding the Toyoda Automatic Loom Works, Ltd., by that time the main firm in the family's growing textile complex, into automobiles. It was a risky venture. Japanese companies had manufactured autos—as early as 1914 a forerunner of the Nissan Company had turned out a DAT Model 1, a precursor to the Datsun—but so thoroughly did foreign motor car companies, notably Japan-Ford and Japan-General Motors, dominate the Japanese market that none of the corporate giants of Japan was willing to commit investments. Yet, since it was his father's last wish, Kiichirō ordered the Toyoda Automatic Loom Works to begin on automobile engines. An "automotive department" was established in 1931.

It was there, while studying as a mechanical engineering student at the prestigious Tokyo Imperial University in the mid-1930's, that Eiji began to spend his summer vacations tinkering with small engines. By the time Eiji was graduated in 1937, Toyoda Automatic Loom had produced three passenger cars with economical engines of Chevrolet design and the stylish lines of a DeSoto body. Eiji's father had plans for the young graduate at his own weaving mill, but Kiichirō, Eiji's strong-willed cousin, prevailed, and it was decided that Eiji would begin work in Toyoda's automotive facility. At about this same time, in August, 1937, the Toyota Motor Company was established. ("Toyota" is an alternate reading of the two ideographs that make up the family name; it was chosen for its phonetic clarity and potential advertising appeal.)

*Life's Work*

The new company was barely on its feet when the eight-year-long Sino-Japanese War (1937-1945) began. Toyoda, who was in charge of product inspection and improvement, later conceded the poor quality of the company's early vehicles and candidly allowed that it was military procurements for the war effort that saved the company in its early years. Despite wartime procurement and production problems and an air raid that leveled a quarter of Toyoda's plant in the closing days of the war, the company tallied profits in every fiscal period during the war except for the first year. These wartime earnings were used to spin off several related companies. In 1940, for example, the Toyota Steel Corporation was founded in response to a need for locally produced, high-quality speciality steel. Toyoda eventually became director of this company after its name was changed to the Aichi Steel Works.

The immediate postwar years, 1945-1950, brought brutally harsh conditions to both industry and daily life for all Japanese. The initial policy of the U.S. occupation authorities was to "deconcentrate" Japanese industry (break up large industrial conglomerates such as Toyota), to ensure that they would remain forever weak and unable to contribute to any kind of revival of the expansionist drive that led to war. As production declined, management ordered layoffs and wage and benefit reductions without consulting the workers, and this touched off a wave of labor unrest and strikes that further damaged the country. In 1950, Toyota was close to bankruptcy.

By this time, however, the occupation authorities had come to reconsider their initial deconcentration policy. The onset of the Cold War had convinced the supreme commander, General Douglas MacArthur, of the merit in encouraging the revival of a strong industrial base that would in turn contribute to a rebuilding of a prosperous Japan that would be closely tied to U.S. strategic purposes in the Far East. One of the earliest beneficiaries of this new policy was Toyota. In the summer of 1950, at a time when few Japanese were allowed to travel abroad, U.S. occupation officials granted Toyoda permission to travel to the United States for three months to study production methods; half of this time he spent at the Ford Motor Company. The daily output of the various Ford plants was about eight thousand units, while Toyota's was a piddling forty.

As it turned out, the summer of 1950 was a watershed period for the

Toyota Motor Company. By the time Toyoda returned to Japan in October, 1950, and was made the company's managing director, a "procurement boom" was under way as orders to supply U.S. forces in Korea with everything from gunny sacks to trucks flooded the offices of Japanese factories large and small. During the first year of the war, for example, the U.S. military ordered more than three thousand trucks from Toyota—equivalent to about one-fourth of the entire Toyota production in that year. By the end of the Korean War in 1953, the Japanese auto industry had surpassed the production record of the peak year of 1941, and Toyota had pulled ahead of Nissan in sales of both cars and trucks. Once again, a war had given the company a much-needed boost.

Another major turning point in the history of Toyota came in 1957 with the decision to establish Toyota Motor Sales, U.S.A. Volkswagen was demonstrating that foreign-made small cars could command a growing share of the U.S. market, and, while other Japanese manufacturers debated, Toyota acted. The first two Crown passenger cars arrived in California in September, 1957. They turned out to be a disaster. They were cars built for short hauls on crowded city streets, not for American high-speed roads, and for function rather than comfort. They lacked acceleration and strong brakes. Sales were so poor that the American franchise nearly collapsed, and it fell upon Toyoda, who was appointed as executive vice president of Toyota Motor Company in 1960, to travel to the United States in that year to handle the staff dismissals and reduce the scale of operations. The setback did not destroy the company's determination to break into the U.S. market, but rather it conveyed a "do or die" urgency to the need for radical improvement in the quality of Toyota's product. The urgency was heightened as American automakers introduced compact cars into their 1960 lines.

It would not be until 1964 that Toyota was ready to compete again in the United States. Two years later, the company introduced a new model, the Corolla, which met international standards of excellence for the mass market; exports began to climb rapidly. In the meantime, Japan's so-called economic miracle was rapidly increasing the purchasing power of the Japanese consumer, and, by the time Toyoda became president of Toyota in 1967, the era of private passenger car ownership, when an ordinary citizen could think about buying a car, had begun. One set of figures illustrates the dramatic growth of the auto industry in Japan in the decade of the 1960's. In 1960, the total output was 165,000 vehicles; by 1969 that figure had grown to 2,611,000 vehicles, and Toyota's share of the market had expanded from 25 percent to 37 percent. By 1982, when Toyoda retired from the presidency and became chairman of the board, Japan's automobile production had surpassed that of the United States, and Toyota remained well ahead of its eight domestic rivals in output. In 1984, Keidanren, the powerful federation of Japanese business organizations, elected Toyoda as its vice chairman.

*Summary*

Eiji Toyoda's career in the industrial empire founded by his uncle and cousin spanned five decades that were as turbulent for Toyota as they were for Japan. The wartime years brought opportunity for a struggling new company, but Japan's defeat brought company and country to the brink of total economic collapse. The Korean War represented another opportunity for Toyota, but it was the drive for efficiency and quality control and improved labor-management relations that brought Toyota—and other automotive giants such as Nissan and Honda—to their world standing. By 1980, Japan's automobile industry had reached an annual production level of 11 million vehicles; Toyota had a third of that market, well ahead of Nissan, its nearest competitor. As the 1980's progressed, Toyota retained its premier position in the Japanese auto industry year after year.

Although personally very wealthy, neither Toyoda nor any other member of his family owns much of the company's assets anymore. The family's share of the holdings amounts to no more than 2 percent; banks and insurance companies own most of the company. The Japanese passion for anonymity and their belief that success is most likely to occur as a result of group rather than individual effort make it difficult to isolate the exact contribution that Toyoda personally made to the striking performance record of his company. Certainly, many of the management and production styles associated with Toyota were perfected while Eiji Toyoda was at the helm. The "just-in-time" system in which parts arrive from suppliers just in time to be part of the final assembly, thus reducing inventory costs, is an example. "There is no secret to how we learned to do what we do," Toyoda once confessed. "We learned it at the Rouge," he said, referring to the Ford plant he had visited in 1950. Toyoda deserves a large measure of the credit for the fact that the company has had no strikes since 1955. He thus illustrates the exemplary Japanese business executive who leads by building harmony and consensus among employees and instilling strong company loyalty.

*Bibliography*

Allinson, Gary D. *Japanese Urbanism: Industry and Politics in Kariya, 1872-1972*. Berkeley: University of California Press, 1975. A highly respected scholarly study of the relationship between the Toyota enterprises and the communities, in and around Nagoya, Japan, where they are located. It includes a good analytical discussion of the growth of the Toyota empire and the role of various family members including Eiji.

Cho, Yukio. "Keeping Step with the Military: The Beginning of the Automobile Age." *The Japan Interpreter* 7 (Spring, 1971): 168-178. A fascinating account of the early years of the automobile industry in Japan.

Cusumano, Michael A. *The Japanese Automobile Industry: Technology and Management at Nissan and Toyota*. Cambridge, Mass.: Harvard University Press, 1985. A scholarly examination of the history of the two companies and the personalities who helped to transform them into world-class auto manufacturers. Contains an immense amount of statistical data.

Kamata, Satoshi. *Japan in the Passing Lane: An Insider's Account of Life in a Japanese Auto Factory.* Translated by Tatsuru Akimoto. New York: Pantheon Books, 1982. A controversial account of the Toyota Company by a free-lance journalist who hired on at the company as a laborer. Kamata challenges the generally favorable view of Toyota's contented workers by depicting them as being driven as if they were machines under ferocious working conditions.

Kamiya, Shōtarō. *My Life with Toyota.* Translated by Thomas I. Elliott. Tokyo: Toyota Motor Sales Company, 1976. Although there is little mention of Toyoda in this book, it is a valuable study of the company by one of the founding members of the company and a president in the 1950's.

Toyoda, Eiji. *Toyota: Fifty Years in Motion.* New York: Kodansha International, 1987. Originally published in Japanese in 1985. A rambling autobiography with many interesting anecdotes and numerous photographs from the early years of the company. Valuable for discussion of Toyoda's relationships with other leaders of the company.

*John H. Boyle*

# ERNST TROELTSCH

*Born:* February 17, 1865; Haunstetten, near Augsburg, Bavaria
*Died:* February 1, 1923; Berlin, Germany
*Areas of Achievement:* Theology, philosophy, historiography, and sociology
*Contribution:* Troeltsch pioneered in making the study of religion a phenomenon amenable to social and scientific analysis in contrast to the standard theological approach. His sociological method stimulated in turn the comparative study of religions and helped gain acceptance for sociology as an academic discipline. His reflections on the philosophy of religion also helped establish the credibility of that field of inquiry.

## *Early Life*

Ernst Peter Wilhelm Troeltsch was the eldest son of a physician of Augsburg, where the family was prominent among the local Lutheran burgher community. Through his father, young Ernst acquired early a fascination with scientific method and observation. He later recalled his ready access in the family home to botanical and geological specimens, anatomical charts, skeletons, and a library amply endowed with scientific books. Darwinism by the 1870's had found a welcome reception among the educated classes of Germany.

Nevertheless, after a solid grounding in the classical languages and literatures at local preparatory schools, Troeltsch gravitated toward the study of theology and particularly the relationship between Christian faith and human reason, a theme that would occupy most of his scholarly career.

Between 1884 and 1888, Troeltsch studied theology at three German universities. At Erlangen he pursued, in addition to courses in Lutheran theology, a general liberal arts curriculum that included studies in history, art history, psychology, and philosophy. The breadth and variety of this program, coupled with his enduring interest in the scientific method, led him to increasing dissatisfaction with what he regarded as the narrow, dogmatic Lutheranism of the Erlangen theology faculty.

Troeltsch therefore transferred to the more cosmopolitan University of Berlin and, within a year, to the University of Göttingen. There, after three further years of study, he received in 1888 the licentiate in theology. It was at Göttingen under the tutelage of the renowned liberal Lutheran theologian Albrecht Ritschl that Troeltsch's scholarly interests came into focus. Yet, while he learned much from Ritschl's neo-Kantian perspectives and his insights regarding Christian values as essentially independent of scientific verification, Troeltsch eventually broke with his mentor.

What Troeltsch could not accept was Ritschl's fully transcendent, ahistorical approach to the history of Christianity. Troeltsch had become convinced that theological study could no longer be based only on dogmatic authority.

If theology were to be intellectually respectable it must, in his judgment, be subjected to the rigors of the scientific and historical methods. Troeltsch envisioned nothing less than a rational theory of religion rooted in concrete historical investigations. Since in his view religion had, like mankind, evolved across time, the Christian religion in particular should be studied within the framework of the comparative history of religions.

This was the message that the still obscure young scholar Troeltsch proclaimed at a meeting of German theologians in 1896. When his dramatic assertion that the old ways of theological study were tottering was sharply rebuked by a senior theologian present, Troeltsch angrily departed the assembly, slamming the door behind him. He was ready to carry forward the broad program of theological renewal that he had contemplated.

After a year as a Lutheran pastor, Troeltsch had in 1891 accepted his first academic position as a lecturer in theology at the University of Göttingen. The following year, he became associate professor of theology at the University of Bonn, where he remained until his elevation in 1904 to a full professorship in systematic theology at the University of Heidelberg. His final move came in 1915, when the now-renowned scholar became professor of philosophy at the University of Berlin. He developed his ideas within the framework of his teaching responsibilities at these institutions.

*Life's Work*

Troeltsch identified the great spiritual dilemma of his time as the "dissolution of all norms and values under the endless turbulence of the currents of historical life." He related this crisis in coherence and meaning in large measure to the decline of religion as a vital force in society. A multifaceted intellectual movement called historicism had since the latter nineteenth century stressed the relentless relativity of things, both in nature and in history. Although Troeltsch shared many of the premises and conclusions of historicism, as a committed Christian he took it as his urgent scholarly task to confront the historicist challenge in order to provide a tenable new coherence to religion and to history.

Troeltsch's problem from the outset remained the great rift between the skepticism generated by what he called "the ceaseless flow and manifold contradictions within the sphere of history, and the demand of the religious consciousness for certainty, for unity and for peace." To bridge this gap and meet the challenge of historicism, Troeltsch determined to lay the foundations of a general theory of religion. He sought above all an extrahistorical basis for what he called "the morality of conscience . . . amid the flux and confusion of the life of the instincts."

In a series of essays beginning in 1895, Troeltsch tried to establish religion as a natural human phenomenon with its roots in the structure of the human mind, parallel to the various realms of reason affirmed in the famous critiques of Immanuel Kant. Troeltsch attempted to formulate a law that would, above any historical experience, attest the a priori existence of religious ideas such as a "morality of conscience" in human beings. If he could confirm the existence of a mental structure where religious ideas originated, he believed that he could demonstrate the actuality of the absolute in finite consciousness, a point at which the infinite and the finite would meet, thereby neutralizing permanently the acids of relativism on moral values. A "science of religion" could then be philosophically validated to protect objective norms of the religious consciousness. Yet because Troeltsch was ultimately unable to define convincingly the lines of the a priori connection of the finite with the infinite, he was forced to conclude that the human mind was capable of grasping only particular historical circumstances. In short, Troeltsch found his old historicist apprehensions reaffirmed.

Troeltsch was also compelled in the process to reject all arguments for the absoluteness and uniqueness of Christianity among the world's religions. While Troeltsch's early essays affirmed Christianity as the supreme faith, further study and reflection led him to quite another verdict. In his *Die Absolutheit des Christentums und die Religionsgeschichte* (1902; *The Absoluteness of Christianity and the History of Religions*, 1971), he surmised that "it is impossible to construct a theory of Christianity as an absolute religion on the basis of any historical way of thinking, or by the use of historical means." He had already rejected arguments for the primacy of Christianity based on dogma or on miracles: "Divine activity cannot be assumed to fill gaps in the causal sequence." For Troeltsch the baffling complexity of the problem lay precisely in the sheer interconnectedness of all that exists, what he described as "the relation of individual historical facts to standards of value within the entire domain of history" in his late work *Der Historismus und seine Probleme* (1922; *Historicism and Its Problems*, 1922).

Convinced in theory of the intrinsically conditional character of human experience, Troeltsch resolved increasingly after 1905 to test his abstract reflections on the philosophy of religion in a series of concrete historical investigations. In the process, he would generate significant new insights and methods for the scholarly study of religion. Inspired in part by the sociological studies of his celebrated friend Max Weber, Troeltsch began to examine in their historical contexts a number of questions previously raised solely from a theological vantage.

These investigations culminated in his massive *Die Soziallehren der christlichen Kirchen und Gruppen* (1912; *The Social Teaching of the Christian Churches*, 1931). Troeltsch here applied the new sociological perspective and method to the whole of Christian history over the first seventeen centuries of its existence to the age of the Enlightenment. He proposed to determine the extent to which the Christian religion had been influenced by the web of secular forces in its environment.

Drawing his evidence primarily from the ethical and social teachings of the Christian churches and sects within the context of each age, Troeltsch concluded that the religious teachings, beliefs, and organization of the premodern Christian past were demonstrably affected by the social milieu of their origins. The central moral and social doctrines of Christianity did not reflect either an absolute ethic or a pure religious spirit but simply various Christian social communities coming to terms with the world around them.

Troeltsch illustrated this interaction through a set of ideal types derived in large measure from Weber but modified to account for specific historical situations. Troeltsch found three main social expressions of Christianity's relationship with the world: a church type that encompassed the majority of Christians, a minority sect type that developed largely in reaction to the mainline church type structures, and, finally, a highly personal mystical type. For Troeltsch, the story of Christianity was essentially a series of responses or reactions that ranged across a continuum that included the various compromises made by the church-type communities through the outright rejection of the world's values as in the extreme sectarian type to the even more individualistic mystical form. Troeltsch's theory of church types has remained among the most influential of his ideas.

Although greatly discouraged by the failure of his historical research to provide a firmer foundation for his metaphysical conjectures, Troeltsch continued to seek clearer answers to the urgent question as to what one can know for certain in a situation whose subjective and contingent character remained insurmountable. He would remain disappointed. By the time of his death in early 1923, Christianity had become for him "a purely historical, individual, relative phenomenon," bound up inseparably with European culture. The concept of a pluralism of religions and of religious values became a dominant theme in his last writings.

If neither an a priori "science of religion" nor the absolute status of Christianity could be sustained by the methods of theology, philosophy, or history, what instruction or solace might Troeltsch offer to one adrift in the sea of relativism? To avert what he saw as the debacle of "absolute relativism," he devised a rationale based on the subjective value of Chistianity to the individual. Troeltsch, unable to achieve scientific verification for his investigations, related the validity of Christianity directly to the subjective judgment of each Christian: "No physics . . . biology . . . psychology or theory of evolution can take from us our belief in the living, creative purpose of God."

While Christianity remained for Troeltsch a relative phenomenon when considered in its purely historical dimensions, he insisted that there were still moral values to be derived from it, norms of conduct that are "true for us [in] the religion through which we have been formed, a part of our being." Each Christian encounters the truth of Christianity for himself within the context of the local cult or church community, or in his heart.

In short, the objective and universal validity of Christian ethics was mediated to individuals only in a subjective mode. The validity of Christianity as an ethical religion lies therefore in an ever-renewed commitment of each Christian, an act of will, based on faith. As he wrote in his last work: "In every cycle of cultural values it is faith that ultimately decides and here too it is faith that justifies." Troeltsch thus found the general validity he sought neither in philosophy nor in history but through his religious belief, a version of the justification by faith precept from the Lutheran heritage of his youth.

*Summary*

Ernst Troeltsch was an extraordinarily prolific writer. His fourteen books and more than five hundred additional publications reflect the wide range of his scholarly interests, particularly in the philosophy and sociology of religion and in the historiography of Christianity. To the degree that he was never able to find a firm basis within history for the absolute values he sought, his life's work clearly fell short of his original aspirations. Yet the boldness and the magnitude of the issues that he raised and the continuing influence of his sociological approach to religious studies lend an enduring interest and merit to his major writings. He wrestled above all with a question that had long baffled theologians and philosophers alike, namely how to bridge the great chasm between the contingent realm of history and the domain of the absolute.

Compelled by his rigorous scientific methodology to remove the absolute from history, Troeltsch had to face the intellectual and spiritual consequences of his human predicament. Personally a man of deep religious convictions, he found himself caught between the need to believe and the pressing demands of the scientific method that he had imbibed from childhood. His friend Friedrich Meinecke ruefully described Troeltsch's plight as that of the ancient sages Heraclitus and Archimedes combined: "All is flux; give me a place to stand." It was in seeking a place to stand amid the historicist winds that appeared to have swept away all certainty in human affairs that Troeltsch identified the broad contours of the problem and the methods of scholarly inquiry through which to approach it. Subsequent generations have taken up the search where he left it.

*Bibliography*

Antoni, Carlo. *From History to Sociology: The Transition in German Historical Thinking*. Translated by Hayden V. White. London: Merlin Press, 1962. This work, originally published in 1939, contains an extensive pioneering essay on the dilemma of Troeltsch as theologian and as historian caught between the theologian's yearning for absolutes and the insistent counterclaims of historicism and the new sociology.

Clayton, John P., ed. *Ernst Troeltsch and the Future of Theology.* London: Cambridge University Press, 1976. Contains six essays by Troeltsch scholars that focus primarily on the relevance of his thought to current theological concerns. A noteworthy feature of the bibliography is an extensive listing of Troeltsch's works that are available in English translation.

Pauck, Wilhelm. *Harneck and Troeltsch: Two Historical Theologians.* New York: Oxford University Press, 1968. Pauck's essay remains the best single introduction to Troeltsch's career. Having studied under Troeltsch at the University of Berlin, Pauck provides a balanced but sympathetic portrait of the man as well as the thinker. He stresses Troeltsch's abiding conviction that modern theology cannot survive without availing itself of the historical and sociological perspectives.

Reist, Benjamin A. *Toward a Theology of Involvement: The Thought of Ernst Troeltsch.* Philadelphia: Westminster Press, 1966. Concentrating mainly on Troeltsch's two most celebrated works, *The Social Teaching of the Christian Churches* and *Historicism and Its Problems*, Reist analyzes Troeltsch's impressive attempt at laying the basis of a theology of culture and of Christian involvement in a pluralist social environment. He concludes that Troeltsch's failure to resolve his doubts about the uniqueness of Christianity was nevertheless a fertile failure in that it helped set the agenda for a continuing debate.

Rubanowice, Robert J. *Crisis in Consciousness: The Thought of Ernst Troeltsch.* Tallahassee: University Presses of Florida, 1982. This recent account of Troeltsch's development as teacher, as thinker, and as politician attempts to evaluate his career as a whole. The author places Troeltsch firmly and convincingly within the context of twentieth century intellectual history, especially in regard to his philosophy of history, his historical method, and his political thought.

*Donald Sullivan*

# LEON TROTSKY
## Lev Davidovich Bronstein

*Born:* November 7, 1879; Yanovka, Ukraine, Russian Empire
*Died:* August 21, 1940; Mexico City, Mexico
*Areas of Achievement:* The military, journalism, government, and politics
*Contribution:* Trotsky was a preeminent leader of the 1917 Russian Revolution. Along with Vladimir Ilich Lenin, he directed and guided the revolution and became one of its leading political, military, and intellectual figures. Ousted from political power by Joseph Stalin in 1927 and exiled from the Soviet Union two years later, Trotsky continued to publish on a wide variety of political issues until his murder by a Soviet secret police agent in 1940.

### *Early Life*

The small farming village of Yanovka, in the southern Ukraine, was the birthplace of the Russian Revolutionary leader Leon Trostky. Trotsky was born Lev Davidovich Bronstein, in November, 1879, a period of considerable change in Imperial Russia. His parents were well-to-do farmers and, although barely literate, were committed to securing an education for their son. The Bronstein family was Jewish, although not particularly religious. While maintaining Jewish cultural traditions, they also assimilated much of the Russian and Ukrainian culture that surrounded them. By naming their son "Lev," the Russian word for lion and the Hebrew word for heart, they combined both Jewish and Russian traditions.

Lev Bronstein began his formal education in the port city of Odessa. One of the most Westernized of Russian cities, Odessa was a mecca for students and foreigners. Bronstein attended a German school, and it was at this school and in this cosmopolitan city that he developed an understanding of and appreciation for the West. He completed his schooling in the provincial city of Nikolayev. As Odessa had made him a man of the West, Nikolayev made him a man of politics. In Nikolayev, Bronstein met a group of young radicals and initially opposed their Marxist ideas. He maintained a passionate rivalry with Alexandra Lvovna Sokolovskaya, one of the most articulate Marxists in the group and the woman who became his first wife. In the spring of 1879, the radicals of Nikolayev, under Bronstein's leadership, organized the illegal and underground South Russian Workers' Union. The organization was short-lived, and in less than a year the members were arrested and exiled to Siberia. Before leaving for the Siberian wasteland, Bronstein and Sokolovskaya were married in a Moscow prison.

During his imprisonment and exile, Bronstein became increasingly convinced of the philosophical concepts of Marxism. During this time, he first encountered the works of Lenin. Exiled in the far reaches of Siberia, Bronstein read Lenin's plan for revolution, *Chto delat?* (1902; *What Is to Be Done?*, 1929). It was as if Bronstein had heard a calling. In 1902, leaving his wife and four-month-old daughter behind, Bronstein escaped from Siberia and journeyed to London to meet Lenin. In order to cross the Russian border undetected, Bronstein secured a false passport in which he penned the alias Trotsky, the name of his former jailer in Odessa, and the name that would be his for the remainder of his life.

### *Life's Work*

Trotsky's pen was his most valuable asset. In London, he joined the editorial board of *Iskra*, the newspaper and the organizational nucleus of the Russian Social Democratic Labor Party (RSDLP). Trotsky's fiery prose won for him praise among his fellow émigrés. He did not restrict his writing to revolutionary tracts. Trotsky was deeply interested in culture and literature. Later in life he wrote penetrating literary criticisms and critiques on the development of culture and its relationship to the proletariat. Trotsky was nicknamed "Pero" (the pen) by his contemporaries.

The year 1903 holds particular importance in Trotsky's life. He traveled to Paris on a lecture tour and met Natalia Sedova, who became his second wife and who remained with him in triumph and defeat until his death. It was also the year of the Second Congress of the RSDLP. During the congress, bitter disagreements between factions in the RSDLP caused a schism, creating two parties, the Bolsheviks, headed by Lenin, and the Mensheviks, headed by L. Martov. Trotsky sided with Martov and against Lenin on the issue of party structure. An ideological opponent of Lenin and the Bolsheviks for more than a decade, Trotsky also had his differences with the Mensheviks, and, although he supported some of their programs, he remained independent, not joining either political party.

The 1905 revolution brought Trotsky back to Russia. Writing for both the Bolshevik and Menshevik presses, Trotsky became a popular spokesman for the revolution. In October, he was elected chairman of the Soviet of Workers' Delegates. By December, however, the revolution had run its course and the czarist regime regained authority and arrested leading members of the Soviets. Trotsky was again deported to Siberia, this time for life. Once again he escaped. Back in Europe, Trotsky turned to writing, composing his first major work.

Trotsky, now notorious, traveled from country to country as a political journalist. It was during this time that he developed his most important contribution to Marxist ideology, the theory of "permanent revolution." The theory rests on several basic principles: the application of Marxist ideas of revolution to backward or less developed nations, the constant or permanent relationship between democracy and socialism during and after the political phase of revolution, and the linkage between the fate of the revolution in

Russia and a continued international revolution. In February, 1917, Trotsky was in New York writing for a Russian radical newspaper when he received news that the czarist government had collapsed.

Trotsky arrived in Petrograd on May 4, 1917; the revolution was already ten weeks old. Lenin had returned from exile one month earlier. Although in the past Lenin and Trotsky had had strong ideological differences, the paths of the two great political thinkers, so long divergent, now met. Upon Trotsky's return, Lenin asked him to join the Bolsheviks. Trotsky shared many views with the Bolsheviks; he opposed the new provisional government, wanted an immediate end to the war, supported redistribution of land to the peasantry, and believed that all power should rest in the hands of the Soviets. Trotsky did not immediately accept Lenin's offer; his was a gradual evolution to the Bolshevik Party. It was not until September that he openly referred to himself as a Bolshevik. From that time forward, Trotsky's name was synonymous with Bolshevism. He became the number two man in the Party. While many in the Bolshevik inner circle resented Trotsky's meteoric rise within the Party, they also had to acknowledge his firmness, clarity, intellect, and fiery oratory.

Trotsky assumed the leadership of the Military Revolutionary Committee of the Bolshevik Party in September, the same month he was elected President of the Petrograd Soviet. From the Smolny Institute, headquarters of the Bolshevik Party, Trotsky planned the overthrow of the provisional government. On October 25, 1917, radical soldiers led by the Military Revolutionary Committee stormed the Winter Palace, where the provisional government was meeting, and staged a successful *coup d'état*. That same evening the All-Russian Congress of Soviets, consisting of the divergent radical groups in Russia, convened. At the congress, Socialist groups opposed to the Bolsheviks denounced the seizure of power and withdrew from the congress, prompting Trotsky's famous comment: "To those who have left . . . [y]ou are miserable bankrupts, your role is played out; go where you ought to go: into the dustbin of history!"

The first aim of the revolution was to end Russia's involvement in World War I. Trotsky was named commissar of foreign affairs and went to Brest-Litovsk to sign a peace treaty with Germany. No sooner was World War I over than the Russian Civil War began. The Bolsheviks faced their most serious challenge as anticommunist forces organized the White Army. Trotsky, who had no prior military experience except for leading the October coup, was placed in charge of the Red Army. From 1918 to 1921, Russia endured a long and bloody civil war. During this time of great chaos, Trotsky led the Red Army to a decisive victory over the Whites. He was hailed as the savior of the revolution. Never in his career was his reputation higher.

Shortly after the death of Lenin in 1924, Trotsky's political fortunes began to wane. It became clear that Trotsky's preeminence in the Party was the result of Lenin's support. Now with Lenin's death, the veteran functionaries of the Party such as Stalin, Lev Kamenev, and Grigori Zinovyev organized a "troika," a three-man political clique, to prevent Trotsky from taking power. Although Trotsky had a strong following in the rank and file of the Party, the leadership resented his rise to power, his arrogance, his intellect.

In the years following Lenin's death, Trotsky continued to promote his own views for the continued development of the Soviet state. He advocated a move away from the New Economic Policy (NEP) adopted in 1921 and a more open, less bureaucratic party. The Left Opposition, organized by Trotsky and forty-six prominent Bolsheviks, opposed Stalin's troika and called for a more balanced economy and great democratization within the Party. Trotsky's political program came under scathing and brutal assault by Stalin and his followers.

Trotsky's personality was as much under attack as his political programs. His Western cosmopolitanism and Jewish background further alienated him from the Party leadership. Trotsky never fully understood that his late arrival into the Party and his vituperative disagreements with Lenin in the years prior to the Revolution would work against him. Although a powerful intellect, Trotsky was neither an adroit bureaucrat nor a skillful political opponent. By 1927, Stalin marshaled sufficient forces to oust Trotsky from the Party. He was exiled to Alma-Ata in Soviet Turkestan in 1928 and in 1929 was banished from the Soviet Union.

Even in exile Trotsky and his pen remained a threat to Stalin. On August 20, 1940, Roman Mercador, a Soviet secret police agent, under the direction of Stalin, assassinated Trotsky by a blow to the head with an ice pick.

*Summary*

In exile Leon Trotsky continued to speak and write defiantly. His pen was once again his only weapon. He warned against the totalitarian model being applied in the Soviet Union by Stalin and railed against the evil of Fascism and its destructive forces. His analysis of the development of Stalinism and Fascism are classics of modern political theory. His most enduring works of this period are his autobiography *Moya zhizn: Opyt avtobiografi* (1930; *My Life: An Attempt at an Autobiography*, 1930), the monumental *Istoriya russkoy revolyutsii* (2 volumes, 1931-1933; *The History of the Russian Revolution*, 3 volumes, 1932-1933), and his prophetic exposé on the dangers of the Stalinist dictatorship, *The Revolution Betrayed: What Is the Soviet Union and Where Is It Going?* (1937).

Trotsky was a man of words and action and lacked political acumen. He found the business of politics, of manipulating men and creating self-promoting situations, crude and distasteful. His arrogance and his intolerance for the realities of political life made him vulnerable to the shrewder first secretary of the party, Stalin. Trotsky remains *persona non grata* in the Soviet Union. Much of his written work is banned. His role during the Revolution and Civil War are not officially recognized; not even his photograph is to be found in encyclopedias or textbooks. Outside the Soviet Union, Trotsky's many contributions are more widely recognized.

*Bibliography*


Carr, E. H. *A History of Soviet Russia*. Vols. 1-3, *The Bolshevik Revolution*. New York: Macmillan, 1951. A comprehensive general account of Trotsky's role in the Russian Revolution.

Deutscher, Isaac. *The Prophet Armed*. New York: Oxford University Press, 1954.

___________. *The Prophet Unarmed*. New York: Oxford University Press, 1959.

___________. *The Prophet Outcast*. New York: Oxford University Press, 1963. Deutscher's trilogy is a historical classic. Based on extensive research at the Trotsky archives at Harvard University, this work is the most comprehensive biography on the life and works of Trotsky.

Howe, Irving. *Leon Trotsky*. New York: Viking Press, 1978. A short and eloquently written biography.

Krasso, Nicolas, ed. *Trotsky: The Great Debate Renewed*. New York: New Critics Press, 1972. A book that reflects the continued controversy over Trotsky's ideas and his contribution to Marxist theory.

Trotsky, Leon. *History of the Russian Revolution*. Translated by Max Eastman. Ann Arbor: University of Michigan Press, 1957. Written in 1932, this monumental three-volume work is considered Trotsky's greatest work. The book is an epical and passionate narrative and analyzes the events of the Russian Revolution.

___________. *My Life*. New York: Grosset and Dunlap, 1960. Trotsky's autobiography written in 1930 while he was in exile in Turkey.

___________. *The New Course*. Translation by Max Shachtman. London: New Park Publications, 1956. Written in 1923, this series of articles is Trotsky's response to attacks made against his political views.

Wolfe, Bertram D. *Three Who Made a Revolution*. 4th ed. New York: Dell, 1964. A study of Lenin, Trotsky, and Stalin. Contains particularly good chapters on Trotsky's early life and his role in the revolution.


*Shlomo Lambroza*

# FRANÇOIS TRUFFAUT

*Born:* February 6, 1932; Paris, France
*Died:* October 21, 1984; Neuilly-sur-Seine, France
*Area of Achievement:* Film
*Contribution:* A film critic whose auteur theory helped revolutionize film analysis, Truffaut was a leader of the New Wave directors who changed filmmaking itself.

## *Early Life*

François Truffaut was born February 6, 1932, in Paris, the only child of Roland Truffaut, a draftsman, and Janine de Montferrand, a typist. Young Truffaut was neglected by his parents, who were either working or engaged in his father's enthusiasm for camping. Truffaut spent his first eight years with his maternal grandmother, and, when she died, his parents reluctantly took him back. He frequently skipped school with his friend Robert Lachenay to go to see films, and, in 1943, he ran away from home but was eventually retrieved by his father.

Truffaut later ran away again and lived with Lachenay for a time. In 1947, they bought a print of Fritz Lang's *Metropolis* (1927) and launched a club for film enthusiasts. When this venture failed because of competition from another nearby club, Truffaut met its head, André Bazin, who became the most important influence on his life. They remained inseparable until Bazin's death at forty on November 10, 1958, the first day of shooting on Truffaut's *Les Quatre Cents Coups* (1959; *The 400 Blows*). Bazin's club folded shortly after Bazin and Truffaut met because of Bazin's poor health, and Truffaut became a petty thief. His father sent him to a reform school at Villejuif, but in March, 1948, he was released into the protective custody of Bazin, who had legal responsibility for him thereafter. After being rejected by a young woman, Truffaut joined the French army in December, 1950, but soon deserted. Bazin helped him obtain a dishonorable discharge in 1952.

Truffaut lived in the attic of the home of Bazin and his wife for the next year. Bazin helped Truffaut become film critic of the cultural magazine *Arts*, and Truffaut also began writing for *Cahiers du cinéma*, founded by Bazin and Jacques Doniol-Valcroze while Truffaut had been in the army and soon to be the world's most influential film journal. In his articles, Truffaut praised low-budget American films for their honesty and attacked recent French films as pedantic and artificial. These essays established his reputation as a confrontational critic and clearly stated his critical principles, influenced not only by Bazin but also by Henri Langlois, cofounder and director of the Cinémathèque Française. At the Cinémathèque, Truffaut and such friends as Jean-Luc Godard, Eric Rohmer, and Jacques Rivette, all future directors, saw silent films, the works of the German Expressionists and the

Italian Neorealists, and the American films that had been banned during the Nazi Occupation. They were particularly impressed by the American *films noirs* of the 1940's.

Truffaut's passion for the cinema showed in his approach to reviewing, treating each film as if he were personally involved in determining its fate. In Truffaut's most famous essay, "Une Certaine Tendance du cinéma français" (a certain tendency in French cinema), in January, 1954, he ridiculed the work of such directors as René Clement and Jean Delannoy as being too literary and for failing to recognize the visual aspects of film. According to Doniol-Valcroze, "What many uttered under their breaths he dared to say out loud." In contrast, Truffaut championed the efforts of such American B-film directors as Samuel Fuller and Edgar G. Ulmer for exploiting the relative freedom that low budgets provide to create films bearing the imprints of the director's personality and style.

Truffaut's affection for films was such that criticism could not satisfy him. Truffaut worked briefly for Max Ophüls during the making of *Lola Montès* (1955) and spent two years collaborating on three unproduced screenplays with Roberto Rossellini, the latter experience particularly helping him make the transition to filmmaker. He was to continue writing about films even after becoming a director. His best-known publication is *Le Cinéma selon Hitchcock* (1966; *Hitchcock*, 1967), based on fifty hours of interviews in 1962 with his favorite Hollywood director.

On October 29, 1957, Truffaut married Madeleine Morgenstern, daughter of Ignace Morgenstern, one of the most powerful film distributors in France. Their daughter Laura was born in 1959, and another daughter, Ewa, was born in 1961. They were later divorced.

### *Life's Work*

After directing two short films and codirecting a third with Godard, Truffaut made his first feature, *The 400 Blows*, for slightly less than eighty thousand dollars. Because he had criticized people like his father-in-law so much, he was given a third of his budget by Ignace Morgenstern, who challenged him to prove he could make a theatrical film. This highly autobiographical account of the life of a young delinquent won the Grand Prix at the 1959 Cannes Film Festival. *The 400 Blows* stars thirteen-year-old Jean-Pierre Léaud, chosen from sixty boys who answered an advertisement in *France-Soir.* The son of a screenwriter and an actress, Léaud had a difficult childhood and developed a relationship with Truffaut similar to that between the director and Bazin. He was to appear in six additional Truffaut films, playing the Antoine Doinel character from *The 400 Blows* in four.

Truffaut did not savor this success and that of his friend Godard's *À bout de souffle* (1960; *Breathless*), which he cowrote, as much as he might have, because of the loss of his mentor. He was depressed by Bazin's death throughout the making of *Tirez sur le pianiste* (1960; *Shoot the Piano Player*), based on an American pulp novel by David Goodis. Packed with allusions to other films, especially American *films noirs*, and more visually experimental than *The 400 Blows*, *Shoot the Piano Player* was a commercial failure, disturbing the director, who believed himself in tune with public taste. Truffaut recovered with *Jules et Jim* (1962; *Jules and Jim*), which has since been considered his masterpiece. Based on an Henri-Pierre Roche novel, the film is a very unliterary adaptation, comprising almost a catalog of the visual language of the cinema. This depiction of the tragic relationship between two men and a woman was condemned by the Catholic church for its liberated attitude toward sex and adultery. It was an enormous popular success in France and confirmed Truffaut's international status as a major director.

Firmly established, Truffaut began imitating the American directors of whom he was so fond by becoming what critic Wheeler Dixon calls "a compulsive movie-maker." When the shooting of *Fahrenheit 451* (1966) was delayed, Truffaut hurriedly made *La Peau douce* (1964; *The Soft Skin*), a badly received tale of adultery and murder. *Fahrenheit 451*, from the Ray Bradbury novel, was another critical and commercial failure. Truffaut's only English-language film (made in England), it may have suffered from the director's discomfort with working in another language. (Truffaut turned down several Hollywood projects during this period because of the language barrier.) *La Mariée était en noir* (1968; *The Bride Wore Black*), another uneven film, is his most obvious homage to Hitchcock.

Truffaut recovered somewhat with a return to his autobiographical account of the young adult life of Antoine Doinel in *Baisers volés* (1968; *Stolen Kisses*). He and Léaud had previously continued the character's story in "Antoine et Colette" as part of the *L'Amour à vingt ans* (1962; *Love at Twenty*) anthology. He made the film during afternoons while spending his mornings protesting the firing by the Ministery of Culture of Langlois from the Cinémathèque. The Langlois dismissal helped set off massive student demonstrations against the Charles de Gaulle government in May, 1968, and Truffaut and Godard forced the Cannes Film Festival to close in sympathy with the demonstrators. Truffaut won Langlois's reinstatement by having other directors threaten to withdraw their films from the Cinémathèque.

After another failure, the glossy romance *La Sirène du Mississippi* (1969; *Mississippi Mermaid*), Truffaut realized he was not destined to be a director of commercial entertainments and decided to make only smaller, more personal films. The first of these, *L'Enfant sauvage* (1970; *The Wild Child*), represents a return to the stylistic simplicity and thematic sincerity of *The 400 Blows*. This account of the education of a boy discovered living wild in a forest tells virtually the same story of alienation, rebellion, and lost innocence as Truffaut's first film and seems almost a dramatization of the Bazin/

Truffaut and Truffaut/Léaud relationships. Like his beloved Jean Renoir, Truffaut turned actor, playing the leading role of the doctor in charge of the boy. Short, thin, dark, intense, Truffaut was a good if limited actor. *The Wild Child* was better received by the critics than any of the director's efforts since *Jules and Jim*, with a new maturity and confidence found in his work.

After *Domicile conjugal* (1970; *Bed and Board*), focusing on Antoine Doinel's marriage and infidelity, Truffaut adapted another Henri-Pierre Roche novel. *Les Deux Anglaises et le continent* (1971; *Two English Girls*) is a somber treatment of doomed love. After *Une Belle Fille comme moi* (1972; *Such a Gorgeous Kid Like Me*), a low-key black comedy and perhaps his weakest film, Truffaut followed with one of his masterpieces, *La Nuit américaine* (1973; *Day for Night*). This story, loosely based on his experience with *Mississippi Mermaid* of the travails of making a hack film in a Nice studio with insecure, temperamental actors, is considered the best and most accurate film about filmmaking. Truffaut, who plays the director, uses the film to express his belief that films and life are inseparable, that he is alive only when making films. In spirit, if not in details, it is as autobiographical as *The 400 Blows*. *Day for Night* won the Academy Award as best foreign-language film of 1973.

Alternating between light and dark attitudes toward humanity, Truffaut next made *L'Histoire d'Adèle H.* (1975; *The Story of Adèle H.*), an account of the obsessive love of Victor Hugo's daughter for a soldier. After making *L'Argent de poche* (1976; *Small Change*), a much brighter picture of childhood than *The 400 Blows*, and playing a scientist (speaking French only) in Steven Spielberg's *Close Encounters of the Third Kind* (1977), he made *L'Homme qui aimait les femmes* (1977; *The Man Who Loved Women*), a romantic comedy; *La Chambre verte* (1978; *The Green Room*), an adaptation of Henry James's "The Altar of the Dead," with Truffaut as a man obsessed with death; *L'Amour en fuite* (1979; *Love on the Run*), the last and slightest of the Doinel series; *Le Dernier Métro* (1980; *The Last Métro*), a look at a Paris theatrical group during the Nazi Occupation; *Le Femme d'à côté* (1981; *The Woman Next Door*), another tale of adultery; and *Vivement dimanche* (1983; *Confidentially Yours*), a light tribute to *films noirs*. Truffaut spent his last years with Fanny Ardant, star of his final two films, and their daughter, Joséphine, was born in 1983. As with Bazin's fatal illness, he kept the fact that he was suffering from brain cancer from all but his closest friends. Truffaut died on October 21, 1984, at Neuilly-sur-Seine.

### *Summary*

By helping to create the auteur theory, François Truffaut pioneered recognition of the contribution of the film director to both obviously artistic films and low-budget genre films, bringing a new seriousness to film criticism. As auteur criticism became the most legitimate way of looking at films and works by Truffaut, Godard, Rohmer, and others in the New Wave showed the benefits of allowing directors the freedom to make personal statements, a new respect for the film director was created. The enthusiasm and humanity in such films as *The 400 Blows* and *Jules and Jim* have had a profound influence on directors throughout the world.

Except for his actions of 1968, Truffaut was a relatively nonpolitical person, saying he never voted because he did not think of himself as a citizen. His films have been attacked, especially in France, for lacking any political context. He has also been justifiably criticized for being too indiscriminate in his choice of material, for making more mediocre films that great ones. Ironically, despite the freedom he espoused for directors, Truffaut may have preferred working in the old Hollywood studio system in which he could have risen to the challenge of imposing his personality on formula films. He was being modest only to a degree when he called himself "the least modern and the least intellectual of all the New Wave directors."

Truffaut is clearly an auteur himself. The predominant theme in his films is his sympathy for outsiders. According to Truffaut, his "characters are on the edge of society" and he wants them "to testify to human fragility." His films illustrate how people, especially those in love, fail to make the necessary connections that could bring them happiness. Of all French directors, Truffaut most admired Jean Vigo, Jean Renoir, Jean Cocteau, and Robert Bresson. The compassion for human frailties in his films has made him their equal.

*Bibliography*

Allen, Don. *Finally Truffaut*. New York: Beaufort Books, 1985. An analysis of Truffaut's films combined with biographical details. Based on fifteen years of interviews with the director.

Crisp, C. G. *François Truffaut*. New York: Praeger, 1972. A commentary on Truffaut's films emphasizing the autobiographical element, providing considerable information about the director's life. Sees Truffaut's characters as torn between dream and reality, art and life, savagery and civilization. Includes critical essays by Truffaut.

De Gramont, Sanche. "Life Style of Homo Cinematicus." *The New York Times Magazine*, June 15, 1969: 12-13, 34-47. An excellent profile revealing details of Truffaut's life, method of making films, and personality.

Dixon, Wheeler. "François Truffaut: A Life in Film." *Films in Review* 36 (1985): 331-336, 413-417. An excellent biographical sketch. One of the best sources of details about Truffaut's life.

Insdorf, Annette. *François Truffaut*. New York: Simon & Schuster, 1989. A good overview of Truffaut's life and career. Discusses the influence of Renoir and Hitchcock.

Monaco, James. *The New Wave: Truffaut, Godard, Chabrol, Rohmer,*

*Rivette*. New York: Oxford University Press, 1976. Analysis of Truffaut's films in context of the New Wave movement. Includes biographical details of his early life.

Roud, Richard. *A Passion for Films: Henri Langlois and the Cinémathèque Française*. New York: Viking, 1983. A biography of one of the most significant influences on Truffaut's life and career. Gives details of Truffaut's successful effort to save Langlois's job.

Truffaut, François. *The Films in My Life*. Translated by Leonard Mayhew. New York: Simon & Schuster, 1978. A collection of Truffaut's reviews and essays written between 1954 and 1974. This is the best source of examples of his passion for American films. The introduction summarizes his career as a critic.

___________. *Truffaut by Truffaut*. Compiled by Dominique Rabourdin. Translated by Robert E. Wolf. New York: Harry N. Abrams, 1987. An illustrated account of Truffaut's career. Includes interviews with the director and essays, reviews, and letters by him.

*Michael Adams*

# MOISE TSHOMBE

*Born:* November 10, 1919; Musamba, Katanga, Belgian Congo
*Died:* June 29, 1969; under house arrest in a secret location near Algiers, Algeria
*Areas of Achievement:* Government and politics
*Contribution:* Tshombe believed that a confederation of provinces held together by a weak central government comprised the key to national unity in the postcolonial Congo. In spite of formidable opposition, Tshombe tried to carry out his unification program by emphasizing ethnicity over pan-Africanism and by using European money, men, and material.

*Early Life*

Moise Kapenda Tshombe was the eldest of eleven children of Joseph Kapenda Tshombe, a wealthy businessman. Tshombe was reared in a devout Christian atmosphere and educated in American Methodist mission schools in Katanga (now Shaba). He also earned a correspondence accounting degree. He married Ruth Matschik, the daughter of Paramount Chief Mbaku Ditende of the Lunda, and they had ten children. By the early 1950's, Tshombe's life had been shaped by business, religion, and royalty; these influences encouraged his European life-style. As the eldest son, Tshombe inherited his father's business at Elisabethville (now Lubumbashi) in 1951. Shortly thereafter, he was elected president of the African Chamber of Commerce. Tshombe's business success was hampered by his own mistakes and colonial restrictions. Realizing both shortcomings, he turned over what remained of the family business to his brothers and launched his political career.

*Life's Work*

In 1951, Tshombe replaced his father as a member of the Katanga provincial council and began to expand his political base. Drawing on experience acquired from a variety of political offices, Tshombe helped form CONAKAT, the Lunda-dominated Confederation of Tribal Associations of Katanga, in October, 1958. CONAKAT was created to promote Lunda politicians, repatriate non-Lunda immigrants, create an autonomous Katanga within a loose confederation, and collaborate with European mining interests.

At decolonization talks in Brussels in January, 1960, Tshombe led the CONAKAT delegation and argued for autonomous provinces within a loose confederal state. He was opposed by African nationalists, who accused him of being in the pay of Belgian mining interests. Of Tshombe's two major opponents, Joseph Kasavubu led ABAKO, the Bakongo-dominated Alliance of the Bakongo, and also supported federalism. Tshombe's other opponent,

Patrice Lumumba, led MNC, the multiethnic, Soviet-supported National Congolese Movement. Lumumba advocated a strong central government and pan-Africanism. The conference produced a compromise in which the state's unitary character was expressed through a president, prime minister, and bicameral legislature while the provinces joined in a federation of separate governments and legislatures. Independence was set for June 30, 1960.

Preindependence elections and Belgian support combined to make Tshombe president of Katanga. At the national level a coalition government was formed between Prime Minister Lumumba and President Kasavubu but ran into trouble immediately. By mid-July, army units, disillusioned with the slow pace of Africanization, mutinied. As violence spread throughout the Congo, the European-dominated civil service fled. Organized government collapsed. Lumumba appealed to the United Nations for help.

Tshombe also called on foreign intervention to end Katangan unrest. After Belgian paratroopers restored order, Tshombe proclaimed Katanga's secession on July 11, 1960. The weakness of Lumumba's central government, the encouragement from Belgian commercial and mining interests who preferred Western-oriented Tshombe over Soviet-supported Lumumba, and the ethnic desire to retain Katangan wealth within Katanga contributed to Tshombe's action. Katanga's major employer, Union Minière du Haut-Katanga, supported Tshombe's secession with armaments, taxes diverted from the central government, and the cover of employment for European mercenaries to prop up the secession. Lumumba broke diplomatic relations with Belgium because of that country's support for the secession. The Congo fragmented further when President Kasavubu and Prime Minister Lumumba quarreled over Soviet aid and dismissed each other. Mobutu Sese Sekou, head of the army, settled the dispute by seizing power on September 14, 1960.

By November, U.N. troops had entered a chaotic Congo, sided with Kasavubu's government, and detained Lumumba in Léopoldville. Lumumba fled U.N. custody for his supporters in Stanleyville, but Kasavubu's soldiers captured him en route, interned him, and then transferred him to Katanga, where he was immediately executed under mysterious circumstances. His supporters continued his centralist, pan-Africanist government while accusing Tshombe of complicity in the execution.

From January 25 to February 16, 1961, national reconciliation talks took place at Léopoldville. Discussion continued from March 8 through March 12 in Tananarive (now Antananarivo), Madagascar, where Tshombe's influence was paramount. Delegates recommended a loose, autonomous confederation, a shared foreign policy, and a national president. Yet what Tananarive had been to Tshombe, Coquilhatville (now Équateur) would become to Kasavubu. During discussions from April 23 to May 30, the Tananarive accords were replaced with a federal structure composed of a strong central government, U.N. protection, and the U.N.-forced reintegration of Katanga.

Tshombe walked out in protest, was arrested, and was threatened with trial. The agreement that Tshombe signed promising to reunite Katanga with the Congo was rejected by the Katangan government on the grounds that Tshombe had signed under duress.

Tshombe did not attend the central government convocation in Léopoldville (now Kinshasa) in July. Mobutu, Kasavubu, and Lumumba's successors accepted Cyrille Adoula as a compromise prime minister, restored constitutional government, and reestablished diplomatic relations with Belgium. With a central government now back in place, the U.N. could address the issue of mercenaries in Katanga. In late August, U.N. troops occupied key points in Katanga. After fighting broke out, Tshombe declared total war on U.N. forces. United Nations Secretary-General Dag Hammarskjöld was killed in an airplane crash en route to arrange a ceasefire.

Within weeks, the United Nations and Belgium took stronger measures against Tshombe. On November 24, 1961, the United Nations passed a resolution permitting U.N. forces to expel Katanga's mercenaries. Belgium ordered its nationals serving Katanga to leave, revoked the passports of Belgian mercenaries, condemned Katangan secession, and encouraged Tshombe to open negotiations with Adoula. Tshombe met Adoula on December 19, 1961, and agreed to recognize the indissoluble unity of the Congo, conceded the central government's authority over Katanga, and promised to help draft a new constitution. Yet Tshombe continued to delay. U.N. forces took control of most of Katanga on January 14, 1962. Tshombe marked the end of Katanga's secession and approval to the United Nations' reconciliation plan by going into exile.

Central government problems did not end with the reunification of Katanga. Kasavubu again fell out with a prime minister—this time over the draft of a new constitution. On September 29, 1963, Kasavubu prorogued parliament and declared a state of emergency. It was well timed—revolutionaries had captured about two-thirds of the Congo. Nevertheless, a special constituent assembly was convened in Luluabourg (now Kananga) on January 10, 1964, and established a U.N.-advised, unitary-federal constitution creating the Democratic Republic of the Congo.

Central government leaders invited Tshombe to return from exile and create a provisional government to implement the new constitution and end revolutionary activity. In July, 1964, Tshombe replaced Adoula as prime minister, created a coalition government in which he retained five of twenty portfolios, negotiated with rebel leaders, and released political prisoners.

Much of the country remained suspicious. In early August, Stanleyville (now Kisangani) fell to Lumumba's successors. Tshombe, now not so gregarious and exuberant, blamed corrupt centralized government and Chinese and Soviet aid for the success of the revolutionaries. Risking the opprobrium of African nationalists and the Organization of African Unity, Tshombe hired white mercenaries to restore order. By the end of 1964, Tshombe's combined mercenary-national forces had the revolutionaries in retreat. In response, Congolese revolutionaries held some eighteen hundred European hostages for bargaining purposes. Tshombe permitted Belgian paratroopers to fly in on U.S. airplanes to Stanleyville during November 24-26, 1964, to rescue them. The city was recaptured and most hostages freed, but about two hundred Europeans and many more Africans were killed before all revolutionary areas were liberated.

By May, 1965, Tshombe had gained the support of some African nations, reestablished international credit, met Charles de Gaulle and Pope Paul IV, held national elections, and, through his forty-nine-party CONACO coalition, the National Congolese Convention, won a majority in the forthcoming parliament. Tshombe seemed poised for an important role in shaping the Congo's future.

When the new parliament opened on October 13, 1965, Kasavubu, out of fear that Tshombe wanted the presidency, dismissed Tshombe and nominated another Katangan, Evariste Kimba, prime minister. When parliament rejected Kimba on November 14, 1965, Kasavubu nominated him again. Kasavubu's third constitutional deadlock was broken for the second time by Mobutu. On November 24, 1965, the general overthrew the government and declared himself temporary president. Shortly thereafter, Mobutu assumed the presidency for five years and appointed some of Tshombe's opponents to office. Tshombe returned to exile.

Mobutu further consolidated his power by seizing the property of Tshombe's longtime supporter, Union Minière, disbanding Tshombe's Katangan Regiment, and putting the former prime minister on trial in absentia. Tshombe was convicted of treason and sentenced to death by a three-man military court on March 13, 1967.

After almost two years of exile and intrigue, Tshombe's fortunes took another tumble. His airplane was hijacked over the Mediterranean and forced to Algiers on June 29, 1967. Still, the Algerian government refused to extradite Tshombe. Instead, Tshombe was confined to military barracks and various villas. He died of natural causes in his sleep ironically on double anniversaries: the independence date of the Congo and the date of his hijacking. Tshombe was buried at the Protestant church of Champ-de-Mars, Brussels, on July 4, 1969.

### *Summary*

Politics tossed Moise Tshombe and controversy together. At one time or another he was praised and condemned by most major contributors to the Congo crisis. In fact, Tshombe symbolized both the Congo's hope and its hopelessness. Much of his complicated life remains mysterious. Tshombe's defenders, generally a combination of Lunda, neocolonial, imperial, collaborative, and Christian forces, argued that the United Nations and various self-serving nations had slandered him. To his supporters, Tshombe's diplomatic skills, Western education, wardrobe, entourage, and manners opened doors slammed shut to some African nationalists. Cultured and articulate, Tshombe was to many Europeans an intelligent, moderate African nationalist. His downfall was blamed more on the intrigue of the U.S. Central Intelligence Agency (CIA) than his own mistakes.

From the perspective of most African nationalists, however, Tshombe had betrayed Africa. Tshombe was accused of being out of touch with *négritude* and rising African nationalism by relying on white mercenaries and living like a European. Denounced by detractors as an embezzler and bribe-taking lackey of Belgian mining interests, Tshombe was seen as an opportunist who sought personal gain and Lunda supremacy over the Congolese people, an accomplice to the murder of Lumumba and perhaps Hammarskjöld, and a Cold War propagandist who slandered his political opponents with communist labels. Whether seen as a popular, pragmatic confederalist and diplomat or as a selfish sunderer of the Congo and collaborator with imperialists, Tshombe stirred strong feelings in everyone who knew him.

*Bibliography*

Bouscaren, Anthony. *Tshombe*. New York: Twin Circle, 1967. Well-written, well-researched, and sympathetic from a Western perspective; contains a pro-Tshombe statement by Senator Thomas Dobb.

Bustin, Edouard. *Lunda Under Belgian Rule: The Politics of Ethnicity.* Cambridge, Mass.: Harvard University Press, 1975. An important study that places Tshombe and his ethnic group within Congolese and Katangan contexts. Last chapter considers Tshombe's activities in Katanga.

Colvin, Ian. *The Rise and Fall of Moise Tshombe*. London: Leslie Frewin, 1968. Probably the most pro-Western, sympathetic account of Tshombe. Colvin interviewed him and blamed the CIA for his downfall. The book is considered reactionary by African nationalists.

Gordon, King. *The United Nations in the Congo*. New York: Carnegie Endowment for International Peace, 1962. Written by an employee of the United Nations who was in the Congo. Assessment of the relationship among Tshombe, the Congo, and the United Nations is splendid. Best when read in conjunction with Lefever.

Kaplan, Irving, ed. *Zaïre: A Country Study.* 3d ed. Washington, D.C.: The American University, Foreign Area Studies, 1979. Contains the U.S. government's view of events in the Congo. CIA involvement in Tshombe's downfall is not considered. Important bibliographies are included.

Lefever, Ernest W. *Crisis in the Congo: A United Nations Force in Action*. Washington: The Brookings Institution, 1965. A fine summary of U.N. activity in the Congo. Tshombe is considered throughout. Contains useful appendices, including U.N. resolutions on the Congo. Best when read in conjunction with Gordon.

Nkrumah, Kwame. *Challenge of the Congo*. New York: International, 1967. Valuable from an African nationalist perspective of Tshombe. Particularly useful is Nkrumah's letter to African leaders that symbolically devastates Tshombe.

Tshombe, Moise. *My Fifteen Months in Government*. Translated by Lewis Barnays. Plano, Tex.: University of Plano, 1967. Although Tshombe reflects on Africa, his premiership, and his resignation, he is very selective in recollecting his most controversial activities. Spotty and hastily written.

*Kenneth Wilburn*

# KONSTANTIN TSIOLKOVSKY

*Born:* September 17, 1857; Izhevskoye, Russia
*Died:* September 19, 1935; Kaluga, U.S.S.R.
*Area of Achievement:* Aeronautics
*Contribution:* Tsiolkovsky was the first scientist to discover the mathematical theories of rocketry and astronautics on which modern space travel is based. Along with contemporary scientists Hermann Oberth of Germany and Robert Goddard of the United States, he pioneered the concepts of reaction propulsion as a means to lift a rocket into space, liquid-fueled rocket engines, and manned space travel.

## *Early Life*

Konstantin Eduardovich Tsiolkovsky, a Russian schoolteacher who would become one of the founding fathers of modern astronautics, was born in the rural town of Izhevskoye, Russia, on September 17, 1857. Tsiolkovsky's father, Eduard Ignatyevich Tsiolkovsky, a forester, was a dominant figure in Konstantin's early life. The elder Tsiolkovsky's passion for invention led him to design and build model homes and machines that significantly influenced his son's interest in the inventive process. At the age of nine, Konstantin became ill with scarlet fever, which forced him into bed and into a process of disciplined self-study and experimentation that would be his primary means of education throughout his life. Using the books in his father's library, Tsiolkovsky taught himself the fundamentals of literature, history, and the subjects that he found most interesting, mathematics and physics.

Konstantin's passion for reading and study led him as a teenager to follow in his father's footsteps and become an inventor. By the age of sixteen, he had designed and built a miniature model of a wind-driven horseless carriage, windmills, pumps, and a unique device for measuring heights and distances, among other things. Tsiolkovsky would use his skills as an inventor and a craftsman to build equipment and conduct experiments to prove the theorems he would study in books. It was this practice that led him to the development of the theories of reaction propulsion and astronautics that would later make him world-famous.

Also at sixteen, Tsiolkovsky's father (his mother died when he was thirteen) sent him to Moscow to further his education. It was the elder Tsiolkovsky's hope that Konstantin would be able to gain admission to the Moscow Technical School to allow him to become a teacher. Unfortunately, Tsiolkovsky was unable to gain admittance to the school and was forced to continue his self-study efforts, using the books in the Moscow Technical School's library. Living on nothing but bread and water for months on end, Tsiolkovsky spent most of the meager allowance his father sent him on equipment and supplies for his experiments. Many of his experiments centered on designing new methods of construction of dirigibles, the airships of his day. One of his primary fascinations at this time, however, was the thought that humans could use the principles of physics to free themselves of gravity and move into the space beyond the atmosphere. His first unsuccessful experiment in this area left him shaken but emotionally challenged by the prospect of flight into space.

At the age of nineteen, Tsiolkovsky returned to his hometown to work as a tutor for young children in physics and mathematics. Two years later, he received a teaching certificate in arithmetic and geometry and was given a job as a teacher in Borovsk, in the Kaluga Province. He would live in Kaluga for the remainder of his life. In Kaluga, Tsiolkovsky continued to theorize and experiment in many areas of science. By the time he was twenty-four, the young schoolteacher had submitted a rudimentary technical paper to the St. Petersburg Society of Physics and Chemistry on the movement of gases. His second paper, which followed shortly after his first, gained for him full membership in the society—his first official recognition as a scientist and theorist. This development set the stage for his later successes in rocketry and astronautics.

### *Life's Work*

In 1883, Tsiolkovsky came upon the historic idea that one could use gases escaping from an opening in a pressurized chamber as a method of propelling an object through the air and, ultimately, through the airless, gravity-free void of interplanetary space. This theory, called reaction propulsion, uses Isaac Newton's laws of motion by throwing off particles of matter to propel an object through space. Tsiolkovsky explained his theory by noting that opening a hole in a cask or barrel filled with pressurized gas would push the cask through space. The number of holes in the cask would regulate the flow of escaping gas and control the direction and speed of the cask's movement through the air. Tsiolkovsky's principle is also demonstrated by the way air released through the end of an inflated balloon causes the balloon to fly around a room.

By August, 1898, after years of experimentation into his theory, Tsiolkovsky had worked out the first mathematical formulas for the amount of thrust that would be necessary to lift objects into space and the speed at which the object would have to travel in order to develop the centrifugal force needed to balance the pull of Earth's gravity and remain in orbit. The following year he received a grant from the Academy of Sciences that he used to develop and refine his theories through rudimentary experiments and exhaustive computations.

While Tsiolkovsky was in the process of developing his theories on space travel, he began writing popular stories of science fantasy and fact that captured the imagination of the reading public in Russia. His fiction and narrative fantasies helped him communicate his dream of manned space exploration and the prospect of establishing colonies on other planets. These stories also helped the theorist to refine his scientific thought process and seek realistic applications for his theories. In 1903, Tsiolkovsky's first article on rocket-powered spaceflight, entitled "Issledovanie mirovykh prostranstv reaktivnymi priborami" (exploration of space with reactive devices), was published in *Naootchnoye Obozreniye* (scientific journal). This short article is considered the seminal work in the fields of rocketry and orbital mechanics. It would also, as the years passed, gain for Tsiolkovsky much recognition as a scientist within the Western world and what would later be the Soviet Union.

In the article "Issledovanie mirovykh prostranstv reaktivnymi priborami," Tsiolkovsky diagrammed his ideas for the construction of a rocket engine and the rocket it would power. Using liquid oxygen and hydrogen as fuels—the same materials that would later be employed by Robert Goddard, Wernher von Braun, Sergei Korolev, and other practical developers of manned and unmanned launch vehicles—Tsiolkovsky speculated that the mixing of the two substances in a narrow combustion chamber within the rocket would produce enough power through a nozzle at the rocket's end to power it through space.

In his most famous article, and in later published works, Tsiolkovsky would be the first scientist to explore the concept of stacking several rockets on top of one another to produce the momentum necessary to move into Earth orbit and beyond the planet's gravity. Tsiolkovsky developed this idea, the first multistage rocket, because his calculations showed him that a single-stage rocket would have to be of immense dimensions in order to place an object of any size into space. Tsiolkovsky's theory was that, after the first rocket had used its fuel, a second stage would be able to use the momentum developed by the first to increase the vehicle's speed to orbital, or escape, velocity. The second and later stages of the rocket would be succeedingly smaller, since less thrust would be required to push the vehicle as it got lighter after discarding each empty stage. Tsiolkovsky's first manned multistage design, called a passenger rocket train, included twenty rockets and was more than three hundred feet tall.

Two years after the Russian Revolution that brought Vladimir Ilich Lenin to power in what was now called the Union of Soviet Socialist Republics, Tsiolkovsky was elected to membership in that nation's premier scientific body, the Socialist Academy. This organization, the forerunner of the modern U.S.S.R. Academy of Sciences, was responsible for leading the development of scientific theory in the Soviet Union. Shortly after his election to the academy, Tsiolkovsky was given a pension to support his studies in Kaluga.

After his rise to fame, Tsiolkovsky became an icon for his contemporaries and for students of the budding science of rocket research. Oberth, the man who would later build upon Tsiolkovsky's theories and propose the first space-station design, began a substantial correspondence with the former schoolteacher. Korolev, the man who would later found the Soviet Union's missile and space programs, would also build a relationship with Tsiolkovsky, whom Korolev considered his scientific mentor. During much of the period of his earliest space travel computations, Tsiolkovsky continued to teach at the children's school in Kaluga. He had, it was said, a special rapport with the children he taught, and it is speculated that the young people's own imaginations helped their teacher continue to expand his own.

Although he never actually built a rocket or launch vehicle of any kind to substantiate his theories, Tsiolkovsky continued to promote the potential values of space travel and to work for a greater public understanding of the laws of physics and nature behind them. He was a strong role model for many of the young men who founded, in the 1930's, the first rocketry club in the Soviet Union, which built Russia's first successful liquid-fueled rocket. Among the members of the group were Friedrich Tsander, the famous Soviet aircraft designer, and Korolev, the future chief designer of the Soviet space program.

At the age of seventy-eight, in September, 1935, only two days after his birthday, Tsiolkovsky, still considering himself a humble but visionary schoolteacher, died in his home in Kaluga. At the time of his death, he had authored more than sixty works of fiction, fantasy, and fact. Numerous tributes to him have been established in the years following his death, most particularly since the establishment of the Soviet space program in the late 1950's.

### *Summary*

The mathematical theories and formulas developed by Konstantin Tsiolkovsky, coming as they did during the earliest days of aeronautic research, were part of a period of time in which one of the most rapid expansions of mankind's attainable horizons was occurring. In a space of less than twenty years, mankind went from being virtually earthbound to having the capacity to move through the skies and, in quantifiable theory, beyond the atmosphere into interplanetary space. Tsiolkovsky's studies essentially offered the blueprint for future reaction propulsion-powered travel by way of the rocket engine, the multistage rocket for launch vehicles and spacecraft, and the jet engine that would be used on modern aircraft. All major rocketry pioneers after Tsiolkovsky—Goddard, Oberth, von Braun, and Korolev—acknowledged him as the father of their fledgling science.

Tsiolkovsky was also part of a long series of events that allowed for the expansion and reshaping of the understanding of science and the world. Tsiolkovsky's popular writings showed the layperson the practical benefits of scientific endeavor, in much the same way that Jules Verne, Hermann

Oberth, Isaac Asimov, and other scientists in the second half of the nineteenth century to modern times have done. He helped bring science, the study of the real world, and all the possibilities it holds into the frame of reference of laypersons.

*Bibliography*

Braun, Wernher von, and Frederick I. Ordway III. *The History of Rocketry and Space Travel*. New York: Thomas Y. Crowell, 1966. This compendium of information about the early days of the American space efforts and the history of rocketry gives an excellent, easy-to-read narrative by one of the pioneers in space travel.

Clark, Phillip. *The Soviet Manned Space Program: An Illustrated History of the Men, the Missions, and the Spacecraft*. New York: Orion Books, 1988. Clark is one of the acknowledged Western experts on the Soviet space program, and this is one of the most comprehensive books on the subject.

Daniloff, Nicholas. *The Kremlin and the Cosmos*. New York: Alfred A. Knopf, 1972. This book, by a noted American journalist, gives an insightful look at the early days of the Soviet space program and how space research developed in the closed society of the Soviet Union.

Kosmodemianskii, Arkadii Aleksandrovich. *Konstantin Tsiolkovsky: His Life and Work*. Moscow: Foreign Languages Publishing House, 1956. This book, one of the very few English-language biographies available in the West, is a propagandist view of Tsiolkovsky's life. It is interesting nevertheless and offers good information about his work.

McAleer, Neil. *The Omni Space Almanac: A Complete Guide to the Space Age*. New York: World Almanac, 1987. This book is an excellent beginner's resource on the history of space travel, from before Tsiolkovsky to modern times and beyond.

Oberg, James E. *Red Star in Orbit: The Inside Story of Soviet Failures and Triumphs in Space*. New York: Random House, 1981. Oberg is one of the Western world's leading experts on the Soviet space program. In this, his most famous book, he carefully details, in entertaining and informative language, the development of the cosmonauts' march to space. Through his discussions of Tsiolkovsky, Korolev, and other leading space figures in the Soviet Union, the reader is given a panoramic yet very human view of one of the world's two great space efforts.

Tsiolkovsky, Konstantin. *Beyond the Planet Earth*. New York: Pergamon Press, 1960. This English-language translation of one of Tsiolkovsky's popular accounts of space travel is a fascinating look at the work of the founder of modern rocketry principles.

*Eric Christensen*

# MARINA TSVETAYEVA

*Born:* October 9, 1892; Moscow, Russia
*Died:* August 31, 1941; Yelabuga, U.S.S.R.
*Area of Achievement:* Literature
*Contribution:* Tsvetayeva, whose life and work bridged the Bolshevik Revolution, was one of the greatest Russian poets of the twentieth century. Her poetry and her correspondence illuminate the time in which she lived, and her mastery of the technique of writing poetry led to innovative poetic forms and rhythms.

## *Early Life*

Marina Ivanovna Tsvetayeva was born in Moscow on October 9, 1892, the eldest daughter of Maria Alexandrovna, who was the second wife of Professor Ivan Vladimirovich Tsvetayev. Tsvetayeva had a stepsister, Valeria, who was ten years older, and a stepbrother, Andrei, only two years older. Two years after Tsvetayeva's birth, her sister Anastasia was born.

Tsvetayeva's mother was an outstanding pianist who not only had been forbidden to play professionally but also had been forced to marry a man she did not love. Tsvetayeva's father, a professor of Roman literature and of fine arts at the University of Moscow and director of the Rumyantsev Museum, was more interested in his work than in his children. He was also still in love with his dead first wife. Maria Alexandrovna was determined that her eldest daughter would become a concert pianist. Tsvetayeva was required to practice several hours daily and was punished for reading. Her mother feared that literature might distract her from the piano. Tsvetayeva's isolation in this family of emotionally detached people undoubtedly provided her with the inner strength that sustained her throughout her life.

At the age of nine, Tsvetayeva began school but was almost immediately removed to accompany her mother, suffering from tuberculosis, and sister to Italy for treatment. The two Tsvetayeva sisters were sent to boarding school in Lausanne, Switzerland, until they all returned to Moscow, where Maria Alexandrovna died in June, 1906.

Ivan Tsvetayeva then sent his young daughters to a boarding school, did not require Marina to pursue the piano, and in 1908 permitted her to study French literature at a Sorbonne summer school. During these years after her mother's death, Tsvetayeva began to write poetry reflecting her adoration of heroes such as the Russian poet Alexander Pushkin, Napoleon I and his son, the actress Sarah Bernhardt, and the playwright Edmund Rostand. Based on Russian folktales or everyday trivia, written in simple and clear language using traditional Russian meters, these early poems reveal Tsvetayeva's inherent talent and originality and her skillful use of language.

When Tsvetayeva published her first collection of poetry, *Vecherny albom*

(1910; evening album), she was praised by Nikolai Gumilyov, husband of Anna Akhmatova and the leader of the Acmeist movement in Russian poetry, for her spontaneity and originality and by the eminent critic Max Voloshin. This praise and adulation opened up to Tsvetayeva and her sister Anastasia the society of poets in Moscow and at Voloshin's *dacha* at Koktebel in the Crimea. This was a passionate world not only of the mind but also of the heart and spirit, a world with powerful attraction for Tsvetayeva.

*Life's Work*

Tsvetayeva's life's work was her poetry, but that was not her only life's work. Her energies were devoted to other people as well—lovers, children, husband, and friends. This intercourse was both the source of poetry for her and the source of life. At Koktebel in 1911, Tsvetayeva met Sergei Yaklovlevich Efron. Called Seryozha by his friends and family, he represented to Tsvetayeva a knight in shining armor. In January, 1912, Tsvetayeva and Efron married, and in September their first daughter, Ariadna, was born. Tsvetayeva also published her second book of verse, *Volshebny fonar* (1912; the magic lantern), but at this time writing was not her first priority. For the moment her family was.

During these years, Tsvetayeva's husband, Seryozha, was a student at the University of Moscow. When World War I broke out, he was eager to serve, partly for patriotic reasons and partly because Tsvetayeva's attention was focused elsewhere. As she continued to write in Moscow and the Crimea, Tsvetayeva met and cultivated infatuations with the Surrealist poet Tikhon Churilin and the Symbolist poet Osip Mandelstam as well as pursuing an openly lesbian relationship with Sophia Parnok, who became a poet only later. Even so, her attachment to her husband remained strong.

The 1917 February Revolution, which found Tsvetayeva in the Crimea, initiated a time of great confusion and hardship. Although Tsvetayeva was unconcerned with politics, Efron by chance fought in the White Army against the Bolshevik forces. From 1917 to 1922, Tsvetayeva lived in Moscow with her daughters, struggling to stay alive in the face of economic hardship and widespread famine, while her husband fought in the south on the losing side.

During these years on her own, Tsvetayeva's physical strength was tested by hunger that eventually led to the starvation death of her second daughter, born in April, 1917, and her emotional stamina was tested by the uncertainty about politics and Efron. Neverthelesss, she continued to write and to love passionately. Sophia Holliday, Pavlik Antokolsky, and other actors aroused her attention as she wrote verse plays. In 1920, she read her poem "Tsar-devitsa" (1922; czar maiden) at the Palace of the Arts, home of the Moscow Writers' Union, and the following year she read poems from *Lebediny stan* (swan's encampment), which were composed between 1917 and 1921 but not published until 1957. The *Lebediny stan* poems praised the White Army, and, in Bolshevik Moscow, reading them was a considerable risk. Since 1916 Tsvetayeva had also been writing a series of poems dedicated to the great Russian Symbolist poet Aleksandr Blok. These poems, *Stikhi k Bloku* (1922; verses to Blok), were published in Berlin in 1922, a year after Blok's death.

The Bolshevik victory was consolidated in 1921, and liquidations of counterrevolutionaries began. Tsvetayeva was ecstatic to learn that Efron had survived the civil war and had escaped to Prague, where a sympathetic Czech government provided subsidies to a number of Russian émigrés. Tsvetayeva applied for a passport to leave Moscow in the spring of 1922 just as her poetry was beginning to be published; *Vertsty I* (1922; mileposts I) appeared and was greeted enthusiastically by Moscow writers, including Boris Pasternak.

On May 15, 1922, Marina and her daughter Ariadna, or Alya, as she was called, arrived in Berlin, where they found a sizable Russian émigré population, three daily newspapers, five weeklies, and seventeen Russian publishing houses. Tsvetayeva worked feverishly and productively in spite of the harsh living conditions while she waited for Efron to arrive from Prague. During these months in Berlin, Tsvetayeva began a passionate correspondence with Pasternak that continued to fuel her creativity during the next years.

In August, Tsvetayeva, Efron, and Ariadna settled in Prague, where Efron received a government stipend to attend the university and Tsvetayeva received an allowance for her own writing. She entered the literary life of Prague and continued to write, while taking care of her husband and daughter even as she began to separate from them both emotionally and psychologically.

At thirty Tsvetayeva was entering her most vibrant and productive period both as a writer and as a lover. During the years in Prague, Tsvetayeva produced all the remaining poetry—lyrics, long poems, and verse drama—ever to be published during her lifetime. It is significant that during these years she continued the stimulating correspondence with Pasternak, initiated another equally sensual, although in the end platonic, correspondence with Aleksandr Bakhrahk, a critic in Berlin, and lived through a grand passion, certainly not platonic, with Konstantin Rodzevitch in Prague. Rodzevitch loved Tsvetayeva as she had always dreamed of being loved, but he could not live with the intensity of her passion or without the economic security that Tsvetayeva could not give him. In the end, Tsvetayeva transfigured the misery of this love affair into two poem cycles that are the most sophisticated of her lyric poetry: *Poema gory* (1925; poem of the mountain) and *Poema konca* (1926; poem of the end).

These poems and the epic poem "Molodec" (1924; the swain) show that

Tsvetayeva had refined the intuitive and creative uses of language that had been apparent in the earlier *Versty I* poems: the mixture of meters in one poem and even in one line; the unusual rhythms and elliptic imagery; the verblessness, syntactic ellipsis, and one-word sentences; the use of archaisms and eighteenth century Russian words and images reminiscent of the Russian Symbolist and Acmeist poets as well as the use of colloquial, uneducated, and peasant speech forms characteristic of a peasant genre of poetry. Tsvetayeva's mature style, concise with an almost mystical bond between the shape and sound of a word and the object it designates, places her in the company of the European Futurist poets of the early 1920's while the musical richness and complexity of her verse ensures her uniqueness.

In February, 1925, Tsvetayeva and Efron's son was born and named Georgi after the patron saint of Moscow. Desperate to make a living, Efron moved his family to Paris. Although Tsvetayeva's poetry was well received, and Efron and Ariadna were able to get jobs on newspapers soon after their arrival, the émigré community began to distrust the Efrons. Efron became involved with a reformist Bolshevik group sympathetic to Bolshevism. In 1928, Tsvetayeva welcomed the Bolshevik Russian poet Vladimir Mayakovsky to Paris. A long poem about the civil war written in 1929 managed to offend both monarchist émigrés and revolutionary sympathizers. In 1932, Efron and Ariadna joined the Union for Repatriation of Russians Abroad; members were widely suspected of being Soviet agents. The Efrons were further tainted by Tsvetayeva's meetings with Sergei Prokofiev, a visiting Soviet composer, and Boris Pasternak, who came to Paris as a delegate to a Communist-sponsored Congress of Writers in Defense of Culture. Although art not politics was the subject of the conversations, the émigré community punished Tsvetayeva's political naïveté by refusing to publish her poetry and her prose. Living in Paris became more difficult as the Efron resources diminished. In 1937, Ariadna was finally granted a visa to return to Moscow; gladly she left Paris. Soon after that, Efron was accused of involvement in the assassination of a Soviet agent who had renounced Bolshevism. He, too, left for the Soviet Union.

On June 15, 1939, Tsvetayeva, with her son Georgi, followed her husband to Moscow—Tsvetayeva resigned but full of foreboding and Georgi eager to see his homeland for the first time. Shortly after their arrival, both Ariadna and Efron were arrested and sent to prison; Tsvetayeva's sister Anastasia had already been sent to a camp. Although Tsvetayeva was not arrested, she had difficulty getting anything but menial work even with the assistance of Pasternak. She and her son could find no suitable lodging. With the German invasion on June 22, 1941, Tsvetayeva became increasingly concerned about Georgi's safety and decided to emigrate to the Tatar region.

The burden had become too heavy. Rejected by the Writers' Union, without work or a place to live, with her husband and daughter far away in prison—by this time, Efron had been shot, although Tsvetayeva did not know it—she decided that her rebellious son would be better off without her. On Saturday, August 31, 1941, at the age of forty-eight in the village of Yelabuga in the Tartar Autonomous Republic, Tsvetayeva, lonely and exhausted, hanged herself.

*Summary*

Throughout her life, Marina Tsvetayeva was passionately devoted to poetry and to people. During years of unbelievable hardship, she continued to write and to develop her poetic style without regard to politics or to fame. She wrote because she could do nothing else. Her poetry was personal, confessional, and both intuitive and intellectual in the way she used words. The passion she needed to inspire her creative soul she acquired from human relationships through conversation and correspondence.

After the death of Joseph Stalin in 1953, Tsvetayeva's sister and daughter were freed from the concentration camps. Tsvetayeva's friends arranged to have her writings, all banned in the Soviet Union, published in New York. From that time on, her work has appeared in Russian-language journals published abroad. Her poetry began to appear in anthologies within the Soviet Union in 1956 and to circulate secretly among the Russian population in manuscript. During the 1960's and 1970's, Tsvetayeva emerged as one of the poets most beloved by Soviet youth.

*Bibliography*

Feinstein, Elaine. *A Captive Lion: The Life of Marina Tsvetayeva*. London: Hutchinson, 1987. A popular biography with annotation and a selected bibliography, this work draws on material from scholars and presents Tsvetayeva as a humanist and feminist interested in art, not politics.

Hingley, Ronald. *Nightingale Fever: Russian Poets in Revolution*. New York: Alfred A. Knopf, 1981. An excellent collective biography of four contemporary Russian poets (Akhmatova, Pasternak, Mandelstam, and Tsvetayeva) in the context of their time. Includes a bibliography and notes.

Karlinsky, Simon. *Marina Cvetaeva: Her Life and Art*. Berkeley: University of California Press, 1966. The early version of the definitive biography divided into a biographical section and one of Tsvetayeva's poetry.

__________. *Marina Tsvetaeva: The Woman, Her World, and Her Poetry*. Cambridge, England: Cambridge University Press, 1985. A revised, updated, and definitive biography based on the poetry and prose of Tsvetayeva as well as the memoirs of her relatives. Material about her life and her writing are integrated in the text. Includes an excellent bibliography and notes.

McDuff, David. "Marina Tsvetayeva." *Parnassus: Poetry in Review* 12-13

(1985): 117-143. Good analysis of the poetry as it relates to biographical information about Tsvetayeva.

Pasternak, Boris, et al. *Letters, Summer 1926*. Edited by Yevgeny Pasternak, Yelena Pasternak, and Konstantin M. Azadovsky. Translated by Margaret Wettlin and Walter Arndt. San Diego: Harcourt Brace Jovanovich, 1985. The correspondence between Tsvetayeva, Pasternak, and Rainer Maria Rilke during the last year of Rilke's life. Discussion of poetry illuminated by the passion of relationship.

Proffer, Ellendea, ed. *Tsvetaeva: A Pictorial Biography.* Translated by J. Marin King. Introduction by Carl R. Proffer. Ann Arbor, Mich.: Ardis, 1980. An excellent collection of annotated photographs of Tsvetayeva throughout her life.

*Loretta Turner Johnson*

# WILLIAM V. S. TUBMAN

*Born:* November 29, 1895; Harper, Liberia
*Died:* July 23, 1971; London, England
*Areas of Achievement:* Government and politics
*Contribution:* Tubman, who was President of Liberia for twenty-seven years, held that office longer than anyone else in the history of Africa's first republic. During his tenure, he instituted several political, economic, and social reforms, which had important consequences for Liberian society.

## *Early Life*

William Vacanarat Shadrach Tubman was born in Harper, Maryland county, Liberia, on November 29, 1895. His ancestors were freed slaves, who emigrated from Georgia and settled in Liberia in the mid-nineteenth century. His father, a Methodist minister, also served as speaker of the House of Representatives and was later elected a senator. Tubman's parents were very religious and were strict disciplinarians; their six children were required to attend daily family prayers and weekly church services. Tubman attended Cape Palmas Seminary and Cuttington College and Divinity School. As a young man, he served with the Liberian militia and rose to the rank of colonel. He took part in several military encounters between forces of the Americo-Liberian government and the indigenous peoples. He founded a military unit known as the "Tubman Volunteers," which later became part of the Liberian National Guard. After his ordination as a Methodist minister in 1914, Tubman began teaching at the seminary he had attended, while studying law at the same time. He also served temporarily as collector of internal revenue for Maryland county. He was admitted to the bar in 1917 and two years later was appointed county attorney. He soon established a reputation for legal competence and eloquence in the courtroom. "The poor man's lawyer," as he became known, Tubman gave free legal advice and represented many poor clients who could not afford his fees. As a result, his popularity increased, and he developed friendships with ordinary men and women, which later served him well in his political career. Tubman joined the True Whig Party, which had been in power since 1878, in order to further his political aspirations. In 1923, he was elected to the senate, and at twenty-eight became the youngest senator in Liberian history. He was reelected for another six-year term in 1929.

## *Life's Work*

Tubman's political career received a temporary setback after the League of Nations inquiry into the Fernando Po scandal. In 1930, a Commission of the League concluded that Liberia (a member of the League of Nations) was guilty of selling its citizens to cocoa planters on the Spanish island of Fernando Po. This finding prompted the resignations of the President of Liberia, Charles D. B. King, and the vice president, Allen N. Yancy. Tubman, who had served as legal adviser to the vice president, resigned from the senate in 1931. Ironically, this incident afforded him the opportunity of gaining greater knowledge of the Liberian political system, when he defended the officials who were involved. Although Tubman returned to the senate in 1934, he again resigned three years later, when he was appointed an associate justice of the supreme court. Nevertheless, his responsibilities on the nation's highest court did not preclude him from remaining active in the ruling True Whig Party.

In 1943, Tubman was elected the eighteenth President of Liberia, for the first of seven successive terms. When Tubman, as president-elect, and President Edwin Barclay visited the United States as guests of President Franklin D. Roosevelt later that year, they became the first black guests to spend the night in the White House and the first to be entertained there since Booker T. Washington had visited President Theodore Roosevelt in 1901.

Tubman's inauguration in January, 1944, heralded major political, economic, and social changes in Liberia. Since the early nineteenth century, Liberian society had consisted of two distinct and separate societies: the Americo-Liberians, who were descended from freed American slaves who first arrived there in 1822, and the indigenous ethnic peoples. Although constituting only a small percentage of the total population, the Americo-Liberians soon became the ruling class and the established political and social elite. Tubman introduced two cardinal policies that were the pillars of his administration: the "Open Door Policy" and the "National Unification Policy." The Open Door Policy encouraged foreign investment and trade, and exploitation of the country's natural resources. This policy sought to reverse the policies of previous administrations, which isolated the indigenous peoples from economic development and modernization.

The National Unification Policy instituted by Tubman was aimed at improving the political and social relations between the Americo-Liberian minority and the indigenous majority. In his first inaugural address, he condemned the exploitation of the indigenous peoples and pledged himself to improving their political and educational opportunities. The constitution was amended to extend the suffrage to women and the ethnic majority, and legal barriers which prevented the latter from owning property on a freehold basis were eliminated. Non-Americo-Liberians were also represented in the legislature and were appointed to the cabinet. Tubman also traveled widely in the interior, forging personal contacts with the chiefs and ordinary people and listening to their grievances. Of symbolic importance was the deliberate policy to end public distinctions between Americo-Liberians and native, or tribal, peoples.

Liberia experienced rapid economic growth in the 1950's and early 1960's as a result of foreign investment and economic and technical assistance. Major concessions were given to foreign companies, such as the Firestone Corporation, for the exploitation of the country's natural resources. Many Liberians were employed in mines, plantations, and rapidly growing towns. The prices of Liberia's primary commodity exports—iron ore and rubber—also increased significantly. Between 1950 and 1970, the gross domestic product rose from $48 million to more than $400 million, and the national budget increased from $14 million to more than $60 million. With this relative prosperity, schools, bridges, markets, and hospitals were built. Monrovia, the capital, which had been a sleepy coastal town of 12,000 people in 1939, was transformed into a bustling city of 134,000 in 1970.

Yet, under Tubman's Open Door Policy, foreign entrepreneurs, rather than Liberians, controlled the economy. The terms of concession agreements were highly favorable to foreign investors, and there was no scrupulous enforcement of tax obligations and correct accounting practices by foreign companies. Most Liberians were employed as unskilled or semiskilled workers, and few provisions were made for the training and hiring of qualified Liberians for managerial positions. Nevertheless, the leading politicians and government officials benefited from increased foreign involvement in the economy, and many owned large rubber estates and shares in foreign companies. Starting in the late 1960's, Liberia faced severe economic problems and entered a period of stagnation as the international prices for iron ore and rubber slumped. Although Tubman instituted austerity measures, government officials continued their lavish life-styles, which put a further drain on the national treasury.

In the early years of his presidency, Tubman adroitly began to consolidate his political power. He undermined the bases of power of Americo-Liberian rivals, by coopting many of them into his administration. In addition, he broadened his base of support among the indigenous peoples. As his position became more secure, Tubman tolerated no challenges to his authority and used the police, army, and security forces to quell domestic opposition to his rule. Elections became a mere formality within the context of the single-party system of government.

As Liberia was one of only a few independent African countries at the end of World War II, Tubman became a leading spokesman for African independence. He used the major international forums to draw attention to the decolonization struggle and racial discrimination in southern Africa. In 1960, Liberia became the first African state to have a seat on the United Nations Security Council, and nine years later the Liberian delegate to the United Nations, Angie Brooks-Randolph, became the first African president of the General Assembly. On the continental level, Tubman hosted several important inter-African conferences, notably the Monrovia Conference of 1961.

The conference brought together what at the time was the largest number of African states and favored functional cooperation over continental political unification, which was advocated by the more radical Casablanca Group of States. The Monrovia Conference played an important role in the creation of the Organization of African Unity in May, 1963. Having acquired the stature of an elder statesman, Tubman was often called upon to mediate disputes between African states.

*Summary*

Throughout his long presidency, William V. S. Tubman proved to be the consummate politician: shrewd, astute, and tenacious. He was, in Niccolò Machiavelli's dictum, "a fox in order to recognize traps, and a lion to frighten off wolves." Although the True Whig Party, the only legitimate political party during his tenure, was still dominated by Americo-Liberians and the key positions in the government, judiciary, and bureaucracy remained in their hands, Tubman broadened the base of Liberian politics and gave greater political and educational opportunities to the indigenous people. The political system during his presidency was not monolithic, and he developed and expanded the central and local institutions of government.

Although a member of the Americo-Liberian aristocracy, Tubman established strong personal ties with Liberians of different classes and ethnic backgrounds. Affable and accessible and with a dynamic personality, Tubman enjoyed wide support. He was largely responsible for bringing Liberia into the modern age. Tubman was able to maintain political stability in a period of tremendous political, economic, and social change, not only in Liberia but also throughout the African continent. He died in London on July 23, 1971.

*Bibliography*

Liebenow, J. Gus. *Liberia: The Evolution of Privilege*. Ithaca, N.Y.: Cornell University Press, 1969. A readable, analytical, and dispassionate account of the political structure of Liberian society. It contains many insights into the emergence and nature of the Americo-Liberian elite.

____________. *Liberia: The Quest for Democracy.* Bloomington: Indiana University Press, 1987. This is a discussion of Liberia's efforts at democracy and development. It has a stimulating interpretation of Tubman's contribution to the "cult of the presidency."

Lowenkopf, Martin. *Politics in Liberia: The Conservative Road to Development*. Stanford, Calif.: Hoover Institution Press, 1976. A competent treatment of Liberian development that blends politics, history, economics, and sociology. Includes a detailed discussion of the Tubman era. A major limitation is its use of the outdated "modernization school" approach to development.

Smith, Robert A. *William V. S. Tubman*. Amsterdam: Van Ditmar, 1967. A useful biography of Tubman. It conveys a good sense of the nature of the Tubman presidency.

Wreh, Tuan. *The Love of Liberty: The Rule of President William V. S. Tubman in Liberia*. London: C. Hurst, 1976. A short and lively biography that is critical of Tubman. Despite lapses in style, it focuses attention on some of the drawbacks of the Tubman era.

*Abiodun Williams*

# ANDREI NIKOLAYEVICH TUPOLEV

*Born:* November 10, 1888; Pustomazovo, Russia
*Died:* December 23, 1972; Moscow, U.S.S.R.
*Area of Achievement:* Aeronautics
*Contribution:* Tupolev was among the world's leading designers of military and civilian aircraft. He worked in the Soviet aircraft industry for half a century and designed more than 120 planes, many of which have held world records for being the heaviest, fastest, or largest built. He was first in the U.S.S.R. to build all-metal aircraft, was a member of the Academy of Sciences of the U.S.S.R., and was a recipient of many state prizes.

## *Early Life*

Andrei Nikolayevich Tupolev was born in Pustomazovo, Russia (modern Kalinin Oblast), on November 10, 1888. He was the son of the village notary public. In 1908, he entered the Moscow Higher Technical College (MVTU), from which he was graduated in 1918. There, he studied under Nikolay Yegorovich Zhukovsky, a lecturer in mechanical engineering. Zhukovsky, also known as "the father of Russian aviation," organized an aeronautical study group of interested students at MVTU, Tupolev being among them. While a student, Tupolev, working with Zhukovsky, was instrumental in developing the first wind tunnels. During the Russian Civil War, Leon Trotsky charged Tupolev and Zhukovsky with the task of creating a multiengine bomber to replace the very effective *Il'ya Muromets*. They designed a twin-engine triplane that failed, but the idea nevertheless did much to increase Soviet interest in building heavy bombers.

During his student years, Tupolev also worked on the Central Aero and Hydrodynamics Institute (TsAGI), established by Zhukovsky. From 1923 to 1938, he served as the chief engineer, and he continued an association with the institute during most of his career. In the early 1930's, this was the only organization in the Soviet Union dealing with aeronautics. Tupolev's first aircraft design, the ANT-1 (the letters were his initials), was a small, thirty-five-horsepower craft. It was built in 1922, the year that Zhukovsky died.

## *Life's Work*

Following his early research on wind tunnels and training gliders, Tupolev became involved in aerodynamics and the use of metal in aircraft construction. He was the first Soviet engineer to build an all-metal craft. In 1922, he organized a group at TsAGI for the purpose of working on all-metal planes and aerosleighs. In 1925, this group was named Aviation, Hydroaviation, and Special Design. The ANT-1 (1922) was made mostly of aluminum, and the ANT-2 (1924) was made entirely of metal. Both of these were single-engine monoplanes. These early aircraft were often used for propaganda purposes. The ANT-3, completed in 1926, received widespread acclaim when in late summer of that year Mikhail Gromov, in an ANT-3 named *Proletari*, made a forty-five-hundred-mile flight around various European capitals in approximately thirty-five hours of flying time. The next year, Semyon Shestakov flew *Nash otvet* (our reply) over Siberia to Tokyo.

Tupolev's ANT-4 first flew in 1925 and, despite protests from the Germans regarding infringed patents, was quickly put into series production. In 1929, an ANT-4 known as *Land of the Soviets* flew from Moscow to San Francisco to New York covering 13,600 miles in 153 flying hours. The wheels were replaced with floats before the flight across the Pacific. This twin-engine plane was developed by the military into a heavy bomber—the TB-1. It was also designed as a naval torpedo plane, the MTB-1. These were being built in the U.S.S.R. in the early 1930's, as were fighter planes, also designed by Tupolev. Having been instructed to design fighters in 1928, Tupolev produced the ANT-5 or I-4. The I-4 was in service to the Soviet air force until 1933. The ANT-6 or TB-3 was being produced by 1932, and by 1938 it had replaced the ANT-4 or TB-1 as the main Soviet bombing craft.

Tupolev was also a leader in developing planes for civilian transport, and several of his ANT designs were used for this purpose. The ANT-9 had three engines and carried nine passengers, and the ANT-14 had five engines and could seat thirty-six. The passenger plane of the early 1930's was the ANT-20 named *Maxim Gorky.* It could carry fifty passengers, making it the largest civilian plane in the world, and could be converted into a bomber or a military transport quite easily. It was developed primarily for propaganda purposes and received much news coverage. It had eight engines and weighed forty tons. It included a radio station, a printing press, a photographic laboratory, loudspeakers, a telephone switchboard, illuminated signs, and recording and projection equipment. It was taken, in 1935, for a demonstration flight and was escorted by a fighter plane that was painted red so people on the ground could easily compare the size of the two planes. The pilot of the fighter plane was a famous stunt pilot who was going through various dives and loops and in the process miscalculated and hit the *Maxim Gorky.* The plane crashed, killing the forty-nine passengers, all award-winning workers who were on the flight in recognition of their achievement.

Tupolev visited England in 1934 with other Soviet air force officers. In 1935, he completed designs for the ANT-22, a flying boat that set a record by reaching 6,370 feet carrying 22,000 pounds. His ANT-25, also designed in 1935, flew from Moscow to California by crossing the North Pole, traveling 6,262 miles in sixty-two hours and two minutes. The plane brought glory to the U.S.S.R. but never became the long-range bomber as had been intended.

Between 1933 and 1938, there were two aircraft design establishments serving the Soviet air force: Tupolev's Experimental Aero-Design Division and Sergey Ilyushin's Central Design Bureau. There was much rivalry and jealousy between these two establishments. Nikolai Polikarpov, who headed the Central Design Bureau, was, like Tupolev, an uncompromising person. Polikarpov modeled his management style after that of Joseph Stalin, who worked with a small group of loyal followers, while Tupolev insisted that only a large organization could effectively use the talent and have the experience necessary to succeed in the world of complex design. Polikarpov wanted to create aircraft that were superior to those in the West. That was the only way he would feel successful. Tupolev believed that such competition was pointless and that success was measured by designing a craft that served a function required by the Soviet air force.

Tupolev visited the United States and Germany in 1936. In the United States, he studied industrial design at both the Douglas plant in Santa Monica, California, and the Ford plant in Detroit, Michigan. Later that year, he was arrested during the Stalinist purges and was sentenced to five years in prison. He was charged with having sold plans for fighter planes to Germany. Supposedly the Germans used these plans for the construction of the Messerschmidt-109. Tupolev was also said to have opposed the purge trials, during which millions were held without evidence, implying that he was willing to testify against Stalin. Tupolev was followed to prison by most of his senior staff; it is estimated that 450 aircraft designers from his bureau were arrested between 1934 and 1941, fifty being executed and one hundred dying in labor camps. Tupolev himself was originally sentenced to death, but Stalin recognized his value to the Soviet Union and established a design bureau in prison so he could continue to work for the good of his country. He later obtained his freedom for having produced a successful attack bomber, the TU-2, which was used extensively during World War II. For this he received a Stalin Prize in 1943. Later when Stalin wanted him to design an attack bomber that could reach the United States and return to the Soviet Union without refueling, Tupolev refused. While his stay in prison silenced his earlier criticism of the Soviet government and philosophy, he still dared to defy Stalin when he knew that he was being requested to perform an impossible task given the existing limits of technology. The arrest bothered Tupolev, and, after Nikita Khrushchev became head of the party, Tupolev asked him if it would be possible to remove his arrest record as it was a black mark on the careers of his children as well as his own. Khrushchev, who considered Tupolev to be his country's greatest airplane designer, agreed. In 1953, after Stalin's death, Tupolev was given full membership in the Academy of Sciences.

After being released from prison in 1941, Tupolev served as a lieutenant general of the Engineering Technical Forces. In 1944, when three B-29's were impounded after being forced to land near Vladivostok following raids over Japan, Tupolev was assigned the task of producing a similar plane. In response, he designed the TU-4, which was put into production in less than a year. The Soviets built around fifteen hundred of these planes before they stopped production in 1954. The TU-4's could reach the United States and return to the Soviet Union if they were refueled in the air. Yet despite the superiority of the B-29 during World War II, by the time the TU-4 was in use it was outdated as the United States was already producing superior models.

Tupolev was a very practical person. Sometimes his airplanes did not turn out to be good for their intended use. The TU-95 was a turboprop bomber that could fly around 850 kilometers per hour and could not go higher than eighteen thousand meters. It had an excellent range, but its speed and altitude limitations would make it very easy to shoot down. Tupolev suggested that he be allowed to modify it for civilian uses. The TU-95 thus became the TU-114, the first nonstop passenger plane between Moscow and Washington.

Toward the end of World War II, Tupolev became concerned with developing jet-propulsion engines. He used British and German engines on his TU-2's to create a prop-jet. This was called a TU-2A and first appeared in 1947. Within two years, Tupolev was made a Hero of Socialism and received the Order of Lenin and two more Stalin Prizes. In 1948, his tactical jet bomber, TU-10, appeared, and in three years this plane was being used at bases in Eastern Europe. By the early 1950's Tupolev had developed a long-range strategic bomber, the TU-75, used in the Far East. In 1952, this brought Tupolev and his associates another Stalin Prize. His TxAGI-428 was similar to the B-52 and could deliver a hydrogen bomb. In 1956, his TU-104 transport was flown to England. It had a capacity of fifty persons and was considered well in advance of anything likely to be developed soon in the West. Tupolev visited England in 1956 with Khrushchev and announced that he was in the process of completing designs for a jet airliner. In September, 1957, his TU-114, capable of carrying 220 persons, was in operation. The culmination of his career came in 1968, when the supersonic TU-144 made its first flight. By 1971, it was in production. Foreign engineers had started work on the Concorde two and a half years before Tupolev began the project. On May 25, 1971, a TU-144 landed in Paris on its first flight West with its designer on board. A little more than a year later, at age eighty-four, Tupolev died.

*Summary*

Born before the advent of flight, Andrei Nikolayevich Tupolev lived to witness and be a primary contributor to spectacular advances in aviation history. Having devoted more than fifty years of his life to keeping his country on the leading edge of aeronautical technology, he made a greater impact on the development of Russian aviation than anyone else. Tupolev had special problems as a Soviet designer. Not only did his planes have to be able to operate in and withstand the fierce winters of Siberia, but also, as late as 1960, there were still runways in major cities that were unpaved. Yet from monoplanes to fighters to supersonic jet transport, Tupolev's design bureau led the way. Because of his efforts, within a decade after the end of World War II, the Soviets had considerably diminished the United States' lead in air power.

Tupolev loved to travel to air shows in the West to obtain ideas to help him in his work. His last visit was to Paris in 1967. He also served as host to foreign visitors in his own country, graciously showing them his facilities near Moscow. Neil Armstrong was among the last of such guests, visiting with Tupolev in 1970. In a time when the Soviet Union remained quite isolated from capitalist societies, Tupolev did much to improve communications. Khrushchev, always an admirer of Tupolev for his enormous technical achievements, his passionate commitment to his work, and his personal warmth and humor, believed that while "there were other talented designers, Andrei Nikolayevich was head and shoulders above" the rest.

*Bibliography*

Bailes, K. E. "Technology and Legitimacy: Soviet Aviation and Stalinism in the 1930's." *Technology and Culture* 17 (January, 1976): 55-81. Discusses Stalin's use of the aircraft industry for propaganda purposes and his establishment of a special design bureau in prison camp. Tupolev's work figures prominently in the article.

Boyd, Alexander. *The Soviet Air Force Since 1918*. London: Macdonald and Jane's, 1977. Includes considerable information about Tupolev but puts him in the context of the development of the Soviet air force, indicating the significance of his contribution in relation to the many other engineers and designers who were working during the same period.

Higham, Robin, and Jacob W. Kipp, eds. *Soviet Aviation and Air Power: A Historical Review.* Boulder, Colo.: Westview Press, 1978. This is perhaps the best volume existing on the subject of Soviet air power, and it contains articles covering all aspects of Soviet aviation from the creation of the Central Aerohydrodynamic Institute to missile and cosmic research. Puts Tupolev's work in perspective.

Khrushchev, Nikita. *Khrushchev Remembers*. 2 vols. Translated and edited by Strobe Talbott. Boston: Little, Brown, 1970, 1974. In volume 2, chapter 3, Khrushchev gives a personal account of his association with Andrei Tupolev and discusses the accomplishments of the man he considers to be the Soviet Union's greatest aircraft designer. This is a very useful discussion.

Taylor, John W. R., ed. *Combat Aircraft of the World: From 1909 to the Present.* New York: G. P. Putnam's Sons, 1977. This allows comparisons of Tupolev's military craft designs with those of other Soviet and world designers, beginning with the ANT-3, the first mass-produced Soviet craft.

__________. *Jane's All the World's Aircraft, 1970-1971.* New York: McGraw-Hill, 1970. This volume includes complete descriptions and pictures of all aircraft designed by Tupolev from the TU-16 (*Badger*) in 1954 to the TU-154 (*Careless*), which went into production in the late 1960's.

*Nancy L. Erickson*

# DESMOND TUTU

*Born:* October 7, 1931; Klerksdorp, South Africa

*Areas of Achievement:* Religion, civil rights, and social reform

*Contribution:* Tutu became the first black Anglican Bishop of Johannesburg and head of the South African Anglican church. He is a leader of the anti-apartheid movement, and his 1984 Nobel Peace Prize was a recognition of his contributions to nonviolent resistance to apartheid.

*Early Life*

Desmond Mpilo Tutu was born in the gold-mining town of Klerskdorp, Witwatersrand, Transvaal, South Africa, on October 7, 1931. His father, Zachariah Tutu, was a schoolteacher, and his mother, Aletta, was a domestic servant. Although Tutu was baptized a Methodist, his parents later joined the Anglican church.

From an early age, he was profoundly influenced by the idealism of his parents. When he was twelve, the family moved to Johannesburg. His mother was employed as a cook at a missionary school for the blind, where Tutu's desire to serve the underprivileged was kindled. It was also at that school that he met the Anglican priest Father Trevor Huddleston, who had a profound influence on his life. Father Huddleston was a parish priest in Sophiatown, a black slum, and as Bishop Huddleston, became a leading antiapartheid activist in the United Kingdom.

When Tutu was graduated from Western High School in Johannesburg, he was unable to fulfill his ambition of becoming a doctor as his parents could not afford the tuition fees. As an adolescent, he earned money by selling peanuts at suburban railway stations and caddying at Johannesburg's exclusive Killarney golf course.

Having decided to pursue teaching as a career instead, he took a diploma at the Bantu Normal College in Pretoria and a B.A. degree at the University of Johannesburg. From 1954 to 1957, he taught high school in Johannesburg and Krugersdorp. A happy personal event occurred during this period, when he married Leah Nomalizo Shenxane in 1955. His career as a teacher was short-lived, for Tutu resigned in 1957 to protest the "Bantu Education Act," which introduced a discriminatory and inferior educational system for blacks.

Tutu subsequently joined the Community of the Resurrection, the religious order to which Huddleston belonged. Although Tutu has said that he was not motivated to join the ministry by high ideals, his religious conviction grew while studying theology at Saint Peter's Theological College in Johannesburg. He became a deacon in 1960 and was ordained as an Anglican priest in 1961.

*Life's Work*

After serving as curate of two churches in Benoni and Alberton, Tutu left for England in 1962. During the four years he spent in London, he earned the bachelor of divinity and master of theology degrees from King's College. He was also assigned to St. Alban's parish in London and St. Mary's parish in Bletchingley, Surrey. When he returned to South Africa in 1967, he lectured at the Federal Theological Seminary in the Ciskei and from 1969 to 1971 at the University of Botswana, Lesotho, and Swaziland, which later became known as the National University of Lesotho at Roma. Tutu returned to England in 1972 as associate director of the Theological Education Fund based in Bromley, Kent. During the next three years, he was responsible for administering scholarships for the World Council of Churches and traveled widely in sub-Saharan Africa and Asia.

Tutu was rising rapidly in the ranks of the church, and, when he returned to South Africa in 1975, he was appointed the first black Anglican dean of Johannesburg. The following year he was consecrated Bishop of Lesotho. Tutu was becoming more active in the struggle against apartheid, South Africa's oppressive system of institutionalized racism that denies the black majority any political rights. A few weeks before the Soweto riots on June 16, 1976, during which six hundred young blacks were murdered by the security forces, Tutu wrote an open letter to B. J. Vorster, then prime minister, warning him of the dangerous and volatile situation. Vorster dismissed the letter as a "propaganda ploy," and, since the uprising at Soweto, South Africa has faced continuing unrest and instability.

In 1978, Tutu became the first black general secretary of the South African Council of Churches (SACC). The largest ecumenical organization in the country, SACC represents thirteen million Christians (black and white) and is the national representative of the World Council of Churches. Under his leadership, SACC became an important force in the opposition to apartheid and filled the vacuum created by the banning of antiapartheid political parties. Tutu campaigned vigorously against the Pass Laws, the discriminatory and unequal educational system, and the forced relocation of blacks to Bantustans, or so-called homelands. Tutu began the call he has repeated over the years for the imposition of economic sanctions and an end to foreign investment in South Africa. Although the South African government confiscated his passport in 1979, Tutu continued his courageous opposition to its iniquitous system. Like Mahatma Gandhi and Martin Luther King, Jr., Tutu advocated civil disobedience and led many peaceful antigovernment demonstrations. With faith, resoluteness, and dynamism, he became a symbol of peaceful resistance to racial oppression and a leading apostle of interracial conciliation. He gained worldwide prominence, and his stature and reputation were enhanced internationally.

After the South African government restored his passport in 1981, Tutu traveled to the United States and Europe. In speeches and statements during his tour, Tutu reiterated the message that it was necessary for Western nations to apply diplomatic, political, and economic pressure on the South African government if there was to be peaceful change in South Africa. Upon his return to South Africa, his passport was again confiscated by the government. In 1982, Tutu was awarded an honorary doctorate of sacred theology by Columbia University but was denied permission to travel to New York to receive the degree. Michael Sovern, the president of Columbia, then traveled to Johannesburg to confer the degree on him. With his passport revoked, when permitted to leave South Africa, Tutu had to carry "travel documents" that stated that he was of "undetermined nationality."

In 1984, the South African government adopted a new constitution under which Parliament consisted of three segregated chambers, one each for whites, coloreds, and Asians. Blacks, who constitute 73 percent of the population, were still excluded from any political participation in their country. Tutu was an articulate spokesperson for the widespread opposition to the constitution. He denounced it as a "monumental hoax," a scheme to entrench further white minority rule and to give the impression to the world community that apartheid was being dismantled. Also in 1984, Tutu's efforts as a nonviolent crusader for civil and political rights received international recognition when he was awarded the Nobel Peace Prize. He received the news at General Theological Seminary in New York, where he was serving as a visiting professor. Tutu emphasized that the award was not for him alone but was a moving tribute to all those who had played a part in the struggle for racial equality and justice. He announced that he would put the $193,000 prize money into a trust fund for scholarships for black South Africans. Shortly after receiving the Nobel Prize, a synod of twenty-three bishops appointed Tutu the first black Anglican Bishop of Johannesburg.

South Africa had been in a state of turmoil since the introduction of the new constitution. As disenfranchised blacks vented their rage in protests across the country, the government imposed a state of emergency and a ban on mass funerals for the victims of apartheid in the summer of 1985. Tutu defied the government's ban on "political" funerals and continued his efforts to prevent civil war and massive racial bloodshed. He received increasing support from the international community as many companies and financial institutions disinvested in the South African economy. Members of the House of Representatives in the United States Congress adopted legislation banning the importation of Kruggerands into the United States, prohibiting new U.S. bank loans to South Africa and the export of computers and nuclear technology.

In 1986, Tutu set another milestone with his election as Archbishop of Cape Town and head of the Anglican church in South Africa. His installation ceremony at St. George's Cathedral was attended by more than fourteen hundred guests from around the world, including Coretta Scott King, widow of Martin Luther King, Jr., and John T. Walker, the Episcopal Bishop of Washington, D.C.

*Summary*

For most of his life, Desmond Tutu has been in the vanguard of the struggle for racial justice and equality in South Africa. Viewed as a troublemaker and a subversive by the South African government, he has been courageous and outspoken in his denunciation of apartheid. In sermons, speeches, and other public statements, he has drawn attention to the inequalities in South African society and the urgent need of redressing them in order to prevent a catastrophe. He has become a familiar figure leading demonstrations, sometimes risking his own life in confrontations between protesters and security forces. As the Nobel citation stated, Tutu "has shown that to campaign for the cause of peace is not a question of silent acceptance, but rather of arousing consciences and a sense of indignation, strengthening the will and inspiring the human spirit so that it recognises both its own value and its power of victory."

Tutu has been a "pathbreaker" in a racially segregated society. He has helped to open doors previously closed to blacks, and as head of the Anglican church (to which 75 percent of the South African people belong) he has used his position to be a peacemaker as well. Although Tutu is first and foremost a religious leader, the scope of his activities and influence go far beyond the religious domain into the political and social spheres. When interpreting the Gospel, he stresses its revolutionary aspects; he believes that Christians have a special obligation to become involved in the liberation struggle. Tutu demonstrates that the struggle for political, social, and economic justice in South Africa has made politics and religion a "seamless garment."

*Bibliography*

Bunting, Brian. *The Rise of the South African Reich*. Reprint. Cambridge, Mass.: International Defence and Aid Fund, 1986. This book, which was first published in 1964, traces the origins and the rise to power of the Nationalist Party, showing the marked similarities between its ideology and that of Nazism. It gives a good illustration of the pillars of apartheid and the manner in which they were erected. It is well documented and highly readable.

Du Boulay, Shirley. *Tutu: Voice of the Voiceless*. Grand Rapids, Mich.: William B. Eerdmans, 1988. This book is an excellent biography of Tutu. It contains many intriguing anecdotes.

Hope, Marjorie, and James Young. *The South African Churches in a Revolutionary Situation*. Maryknoll, N.Y.: Orbis Books, 1981. An insightful book that examines the role of churches within the context of South Africa's apartheid system. It includes a short but lucid portrait of Tutu.

Lodge, Tom. *Black Politics in South Africa Since 1945*. New York: Longman, 1983. A detailed history of black resistance to apartheid. Although it includes a chapter on early methods of resistance, its strength lies in its analysis of protest movements after World War II.

Murray, Martin J. *South Africa: Time of Agony, Time of Destiny.* London: Verso, 1987. An informed study of the roots and diversity of black opposition to apartheid. It is particularly useful on the new forces that have shaped the resistance groups since the Soweto uprising of 1976.

*Abiodun Williams*

# WALTER ULBRICHT

*Born:* June 30, 1893; Leipzig, Germany
*Died:* August 1, 1973; East Berlin, East Germany
*Areas of Achievement:* Government and politics
*Contribution:* As Moscow's loyal ally, Ulbricht helped to found East Germany and make it into the most stable and prosperous Socialist state in Eastern Europe. His oppressive rule in the 1950's and 1960's, including the building of the Berlin Wall in 1961, prolonged the Cold War and cemented the political division of Germany.

## *Early Life*

Walter Ulbricht was born in Leipzig, Germany, on June 30, 1893. Son of an impoverished Social Democratic tailor, he learned about radical socialism at home and in the city's seamy Naundörfchen workers' district. The family's poverty forced "Red Walter"—as he was known to classmates—to leave school at the age of fourteen and apprentice himself to a cabinetmaker. Ulbricht's political education continued, however, first in Leipzig's Socialist youth movement, and, after his journeyman travels across Europe in 1911 and 1912, in the Social Democratic Party (SPD). It was in this prewar, proletarian environment that his dogmatic Marxist outlook took shape.

World War I pushed this shy but talented young Socialist in radical new directions. In August, 1914, he joined revolutionary Social Democrat Karl Liebknecht in condemning his party's support for the kaiser's war. Drafted in 1915, he served unwillingly on the Macedonian front and, in 1918, on the Western Front, where he twice tried unsuccessfully to desert. Following the November, 1918, revolution, Ulbricht returned to Leipzig, where he helped to found the local Communist Party (KPD).

The 1920's provided Ulbricht with the opportunity to work his way up through the ranks of the Communist Party. By 1921 he had been named to a salaried Party post in Thuringia; in 1923 he was elected to the KPD's central committee and transferred to Berlin as a paid Party functionary. By the end of the decade he had also taken charge of the Party's pivotal Berlin organization. In addition, Ulbricht was elected to the Thuringian State Assembly in 1926, and then in 1928 to the Reichstag, a seat he held until 1933.

Ulbricht's steady advance was the result in large part of his organizational talent, tireless capacity for work, and personal dedication. Another reason was his ability to avoid taking sides in factional disputes within the Party. By proclaiming his loyalty to Moscow and the Communist International (Comintern), he elevated himself above Party wrangling. Trips to Moscow in 1922 and 1924 sealed Ulbricht's allegiance. Thereafter he dutifully followed the Comintern line, including orders in the early 1930's to attack Social Democrats and the Weimar Republic rather than National Socialism.

*Life's Work*

When Adolf Hitler came to power in January, 1933, Ulbricht was forced to emigrate, first to Paris, where he joined the KPD's exile organization, and eventually to Moscow, where he served as the KPD's permanent representative to the Comintern from 1938 to 1943. He loyally defended Joseph Stalin's every move, from the bloody purges to the Nazi-Soviet Nonaggression Pact of 1939, and thus survived the violence that eliminated so many other German exiles. During World War II, he distributed Soviet propaganda among German prisoners of war and prepared small groups of German Communists to implement Stalin's plans for a postwar bourgeois democratic republic in Germany.

The most crucial phase of Ulbricht's career began on April 30, 1945, when he and a small hand-picked group of German Communists returned to Berlin in a Red Army plane. Subordinated to Soviet military directives and overshadowed by better known KPD survivors such as Wilhelm Pieck and Otto Grotowohl, Ulbricht nevertheless exercised considerable influence over postwar reconstruction in the Soviet occupation zone. He engineered the reorganization of local administration, helped to create the Communist-dominated Socialist Unity Party (SED) in 1946, and took charge of de-Nazification and economic reorganization. When Moscow's plans for Germany changed and integration into the Soviet bloc became the top priority in 1947, Ulbricht ruthlessly pushed through the required Sovietization.

Ulbricht also used every opportunity to consolidate his own authority within the SED. During the occupation period (1945-1949), he outmaneuvered or neutralized political rivals who questioned his Moscow-backed authority. With the establishment of East Germany in 1949, Ulbricht stepped directly into the political spotlight, assuming the key post of SED general secretary a few months later. A decade later he added the positions of head of state and chairman of the National Defense Council. Thereafter he controlled every major decision affecting central economic planning, forced socialization, military expansion, and Soviet East German relations.

Yet governing a socialist state in Eastern Europe during the height of the Cold War was no easy task, especially when that country was German. For Ulbricht it meant a difficult balancing act that required him to implement Moscow's orders, appease Eastern Europe's suspicions, and maintain strict controls over an untrusting East German citizenry. As long as Stalin lived, he could depend on Soviet backing and leadership. When the Soviet dictator died in 1953, however, Ulbricht encountered a series of challenges that tested his authority and demonstrated the precarious nature of Socialist rule in Eastern Europe.

The most serious challenge came after Stalin's death in 1953. As a post-Stalinist political "thaw" swept Eastern Europe, disaffected construction workers in East Berlin staged a public protest against increased work norms, which, on June 17, 1953, mushroomed into a nationwide uprising against the East German state. Soviet troops had to be called in to suppress this workers' revolt against the workers' state. Coming at a time when rivals in the SED and their allies in Moscow were poised to replace the general secretary with a more reform-minded leader, the workers' revolt discredited the opposition and saved Ulbricht's political career. His harsh, Stalinist methods now seemed the only way to keep East Germany in the Soviet camp.

Another challenge to Ulbricht's authority came with de-Stalinization in 1956. Shocking revelations about Stalin's past raised new questions about the SED leader and forced relaxation of a number of arbitrary Stalinist controls. Before serious opposition to Ulbricht could form, however, revolts in Poland and Hungary once again undercut the reform movement, leaving the SED dictator free to restore his hard-line rule.

Economic problems also haunted Ulbricht in the late 1950's. He might boldly promise that rapid socialization would enable East Germany to overtake West Germany economically by the 1960's, but East Germans remained skeptical. In fact, lagging economic growth and ruthless agricultural collectivization in 1960 were driving thousands to flee the country through the open door of West Berlin. To halt this mass exodus of human resources, a flight that reached two thousand a day by mid-1961, Ulbricht demanded and received Soviet approval to begin building the Berlin Wall on August 13, 1961. The Berlin Wall provoked yet another Berlin Crisis, and it was heralded in the West as a monument to socialist failure, but it also began an economic turnaround in East Germany that rapidly transformed this nation of seventeen million into Eastern Europe's most prosperous state.

To Westerners, Ulbricht's strict rule changed little during the 1960's. His endless diatribes against West German imperialism, stern warnings to East European leaders about the dangers of reform, leading role in suppressing Czechoslovakia's 1968 reform movement, and ruthless elimination of dissent at home inspired little but enmity and disdain. Yet despite his well-deserved reputation as a servant of Moscow and Sovietization, Ulbricht spent the years after 1963 distancing East Germany from the Soviet model and emphasizing East Germany's independent achievements. Outsiders overlooked Ulbricht's flexibility in questions of economic reform, his progressive approach to education and social services, and the mounting respect he enjoyed in both Eastern Europe and the Soviet Union.

In the end, however, Ulbricht fell victim to his quest for independent leadership in the Soviet bloc. As Soviet Party leader Leonid Ilich Brezhnev sought to ease tensions with the West in the early 1970's, Ulbricht's rigid opposition to détente, especially with regard to Berlin, became intolerable to Moscow. His recalcitrance combined with mounting SED reservations about Ulbricht's grasp of contemporary problems (he was, after all, seventy-eight and ailing) led to his dismissal on May 3, 1971. He retained several ceremonial posts, including that of head of state, until his death on August 1, 1973, but his influence in these last years remained negligible. After a quarter century in power, not one foreign official mourner participated in his state funeral.

*Summary*

Walter Ulbricht belonged to the first generation of European Communist leaders. More "apparatchik" than political revolutionary, he rose to prominence because of his close ties to the Soviet Union. Yet his success also resulted from exceptional personal diligence and political acumen. To be sure, he lacked the personal warmth, public charisma, and intellectual temper to give Communism a human face. He was too uninspiring, peremptory, and pitiless for that. Yet Ulbricht did possess the personal commitment, organizational talent, and administrative efficiency to make Socialism work better in East Germany than in any other Soviet bloc country.

Despite his Moscow orientation, however, he always remained more German than Socialist. Contemporaries remember him for his wiry goatee beard trimmed close in the imperial style, his fluting, sing-song voice, and his strong Saxon accent. His penchant for Prussian formality and order, and his clear feelings of national pride were also very German. He lived simply, devoting little time to family or personal interests—except sports. Almost every minute of every day was spent attending to the affairs of state, and as time passed it seemed as if no detail escaped his personal attention. His authoritative pronouncements in later years covered everything from architecture to fishing, from history to art, and they raised eyebrows even among loyal East Germans. Yet despite advancing age and mounting infirmities, he never weakened in his determination to keep the SED in power and East Germany in the vanguard of world socialism.

*Bibliography*

Childs, David. *The GDR: Moscow's German Ally.* London: Allen & Unwin, 1983. This is the most comprehensive examination of East Germany available in English. Childs locates Ulbricht effectively in the context of his times and crises.

Lippmann, Heinz. *Honecker and the New Politics of Europe*. Translated by Helen Sebba. New York: Macmillan, 1972. A political biography of Ulbricht's chief protégé and successor by a former SED functionary who witnessed firsthand Ulbricht's dominant role in East Germany.

Ludz, Peter C. "Continuity and Change Since Ulbricht." *Problems of Communism* 21 (March/April, 1972): 56-67. This article provides an excellent analysis of Ulbricht's lasting political legacy at home and abroad. The author, a professor of political science at the University of Bielefeld in West Germany, has studied the East German political elite for a number of years.

Sandford, Gregory W. *From Hitler to Ulbricht: The Communist Reconstruction of East Germany, 1945-46*. Princeton, N.J.: Princeton University Press, 1983. An excellent study of the origins of Communist rule in East Germany that explains the transition from Soviet military occupation to SED rule. Ulbricht's role is discussed only in broad outlines.

Sodaro, Michael J. "Ulbricht's Grand Design: Economics, Ideology, and the GDR's Response to Détente—1967-1971." *World Affairs* 142 (1980): 147-168. This article describes Ulbricht's unsuccessful attempt to develop an economic and political policy that would prevent détente with the West and preserve East German influence in the Soviet bloc.

Stern, Carola. *Ulbricht: A Political Biography.* New York: Praeger, 1965. The only full-scale biography available in English. The book attempts to assess Ulbricht evenhandedly but is limited by numerous gaps and its 1964 publication date.

Wilhelm, Berhard, "Walter Ulbricht: Moscow's Man in East Germany." In *Leaders of the Communist World*, edited by Rodger Swearingen. New York: Free Press, 1971. A short biographical article emphasizing Ulbricht's fanatical loyalty to Soviet Communism and dictatorial control in East Germany. It is based on East and West German sources and provides important information about Ulbricht's pre-1945 career and major challenges to his authority between 1949 and 1968.

*Rennie W. Brantz*

# MIGUEL DE UNAMUNO Y JUGO

*Born:* September 29, 1864; Bilbao, Spain
*Died:* December 31, 1936; Salamanca, Spain
*Area of Achievement:* Literature
*Contribution:* One of the outstanding Spanish men of letters of the twentieth century, Unamuno wrote everything from poetry and novels to philosophy, drama, and cultural criticism; he served the cause of Spanish republicanism, was a key figure in the expression of the existentialist tension between reason and faith, and influenced two generations of Spanish students at the University of Salamanca.

## *Early Life*

Miguel de Unamuno y Jugo was born September 29, 1864, in Bilbao, Spain, the first son and third of the six children of Félix de Unamuno and Salomé de Jugo. His father had gone to Mexico as a young man, accumulated some money, and then returned to marry his much younger niece, Salomé. He had also acquired several hundred books on philosophy, history, and the physical and social sciences, which helped form his son's mind. From an early age, death preoccupied Miguel. His father, two of Miguel's sisters, and a school friend died by 1873, producing a mysterious fear in the young boy. Unamuno's struggle to accept his own mortality became one of the major themes of his religious, philosophical, and literary work.

Miguel completed a traditional, Catholic secondary education at sixteen and then was enrolled in the Central University of Madrid, torn between his love for his childhood sweetheart, Concepción ("Concha") Lizárraga, and a mystical belief that God wanted him to become a priest. Fascinated with language since listening to his father talk with a Frenchman in French, Unamuno wrote his doctoral dissertation on the origins and prehistory of the Basque race. In Madrid he applied reason to his religious faith and lost it. He struggled for the remainder of his life to overcome his doubt. After receiving his doctorate in 1884, he returned to Bilbao, competed for a university teaching position, taught private classes, and wrote for local periodicals. Impatient to wait until securing a permanent teaching position, he married Concha on January 31, 1891, and, under the influence of his wife and his mother, began religious observance again. In 1891, he also won a competition for the chair in Greek language and literature at the University of Salamanca.

## *Life's Work*

In the provincial university town of twenty-three thousand, with the faded glory of its medieval university and magnificent, café-lined central plaza, Unamuno found the tranquillity to read voraciously and widely, ponder the human condition, write insatiably, and rear his family. Yet he soon lost interest in teaching Greek: given the desperate problems facing Spain, he decided that the nation really did not need more Hellenists. Although he conscientiously met his pedagogical responsibilities, Unamuno devoted the rest of his time to writing novels, poetry, and essays intended to illuminate the solution to Spain's problems and his own concerns about man's condition. He also associated himself with Spanish socialism, believing it offered man his best hope of liberty through a religion of humanity, but refused to join the party. In fact, his interest in socialism was primarily religious and ethical; Unamuno's heart was anarchist.

Transcendental questions troubled Unamuno. In 1896, Raimundo Jenaro, the third of his nine children, was born, but shortly after birth the infant contracted meningitis, which produced fatal encephalitis, although the child lingered until 1902. His child's condition agonized Unamuno. Why was God punishing an innocent child? Was it because of Unamuno's own sins, perhaps for having abandoned his Catholic faith? He was desperate for consolation, spent days in meditation and prayer, yet remained anguished. God did not answer, and Unamuno was obsessed with suicide and beset with angina, insomnia, and depression. Not only was reason unable to bring him to a knowledge of God, but it told him that God did not exist, that death brought the finality of nothingness. Yet Unamuno's despair at the inevitability of death forced him to hope and led him to the paradoxical solution of creating God for himself through his own faith. When he began reading the works of Søren Kierkegaard in 1900, he discovered a kindred being, although Unamuno had already developed the fundamentals of his own thought.

Meanwhile, Unamuno poured forth articles for Spanish and Latin American periodicals plus novels, plays, and criticism to supplement his meager academic salary. In 1895, he published a series of essays, later reedited as *En torno al casticismo*, which urged a return to the bedrock of tradition, to the study of the Spanish people, as the first step in confronting the nation's decadence. *Paz en la guerra* (1897; *Peace in War*, 1983), sometimes called the first existentialist novel, reflected his experiences during the Carlist siege of Bilbao (1874-1876). Two plays, *La esfinge* (1898) and *La venda* (1899), and an analysis of Spanish higher education, *De la enseñanza superior en España* (1899), soon followed, as did *Nicodemo el fariseo* (1899), which used Saint John's account of Nicodemus' meeting with Christ as a dramatic vehicle for stating the basic theme of all his remaining work: man's desire for God and his existential will to believe.

In 1900, Unamuno became rector of the university, despite opposition from conservatives who disliked the outsider from Bilbao for his socialist rhetoric and his unorthodox religious views. On taking office, he appointed himself to a new chair of the history of the Spanish language, declared that Spain was ready to be discovered, and urged that the students study popular culture. Dressed idiosyncratically in his "uniform," he appeared a cross between a Protestant minister and an owl; he wore a dark suit, with vest and white shirt buttoned to the top, but no tie, and metal-rimmed eyeglasses, and had an aquiline nose and a closely cropped and pointed graying beard.

Unamuno energetically joined in the campaign of the "Generation of 1898" to renew Spain following the loss of its last overseas colonies in 1898. Yet while others called for Spain to emulate the science, technology, and democracy of northern Europe and the United States, Unamuno rejected mass society and focused upon the potential of the individual. His essays entitled *La Vida de Don Quijote y Sancho* (1905; *The Life of Don Quixote and Sancho*, 1927) he considered genuine Spanish philosophy. Subjectively choosing parts of Cervantes' novel and ignoring relevant scholarship, Unamuno resurrected Quixote in his own image, a man who recreated the world around him through his own will to believe. Although some Spanish republicans looked to Unamuno to lead, or at least to participate in a revolution against the decadent monarchy, he opposed all revolution except in the individual heart. He found José Ortega y Gasset and other Spanish intellectuals too enamored of modern science and declared that Spain should let the northern Europeans invent and then apply their inventions.

Unamuno's religious thought received its fullest expression in *Del sentimiento trágico de la vida en los hombres y en los pueblos* (1913; *The Tragic Sense of Life in Men and Peoples*, 1921). Then, in 1914, the government unexpectedly and without explanation removed him as rector. Liberals and socialists supported him in the ensuing controversy. During World War I, he supported the Allied powers. His novel *Abel Sánchez: Una historia de pasión* (1917; *Abel Sánchez*, 1947) portrayed Cain as Abel's victim and questioned why God accepted the latter's smug offerings while rejecting those of his brother. In his powerful *El Cristo de Velásquez* (1920; *The Christ of Velázquez*, 1951), art and spiritual longing seek in Christ the possibility of redemption from death, while Unamuno eschews all dogma and cult.

For publishing in Valencia an article critical of the monarchy, a court there condemned Unamuno in 1920 to sixteen years' imprisonment. At the same time he was presented in both Bilbao and Madrid as a candidate for the national parliament but refused to campaign and was not elected. With his sentence under appeal, the faculty at Salamanca elected him vice-rector in 1922. Then, to the dismay of his supporters, he agreed to meet with the king, leading to criticism that he was self-serving and only wanted the rectorship. While awaiting appeal of his sentence, he took care to avoid offending the monarchy but became convinced that Spain was headed for dictatorship. Time bore out his forebodings, and General Miguel Primo de Rivera seized power with the connivance of Alfonso XIII. In early 1924, Primo de Rivera exiled Unamuno to the Canary Islands, stripping him of his salary and positions at Salamanca despite national and international protests. At Fuerteventura, he planned with some French friends to escape, but Primo de

Rivera granted him amnesty, although subjecting him to certain restrictions upon his return. Unamuno refused to return and went into voluntary exile in France to wait for the fall of the dictatorship.

Unamuno passed the years of exile, first in Paris and then in Hendaye along the Basque border. They were years of despair and loneliness, since he refused to let members of his family take turns living with him, wanting his exile to be a moral protest. While in Paris, he published *L'Agonie du christianisme* (1925; *The Agony of Christianity*, 1928), a difficult but intense and poetical restatement of his anguish caused by loving an unreachable God, from which torment the only respite was death. With Primo de Rivera's fall, Unamuno reentered Spain on February 9, 1930, and returned to Salamanca. Faculty, students, and workers demanded his reinstatement as rector. His greatest novel, *San Manuel Bueno, mártir* (1933; *Saint Manuel Bueno, Martyr*, 1956), soon appeared. It tells the story of a priest who loses his faith but assumes the ethical obligation of protecting his parishioners from disbelief by setting an example of saintliness, teaching them to pray, and consoling himself by consoling them.

With the abdication of Alfonso XIII, Spain became a republic on April 14, 1931, and the municipal government of Salamanca named Unamuno an honorary magistrate for his role in the triumph of republicanism. The university cloister also appointed him rector, and some rumored that Unamuno wanted to be President of Spain. On April 27, the republic designated him president of the Council of Public Instruction, and Salamanca elected him as one of its representatives to the constituent assembly. In its deliberations Unamuno rarely participated except to stress unity, hoping to ward off regionalism. Increasingly disturbed by the factionalism and the anti- or irreligious stance of the leftists, he became openly critical of the republic, refused to be a candidate in the 1933 elections, and resigned from the Council of Public Instruction. Adding to his despondency were the deaths of his wife and eldest daughter in 1934. He retired from his university chair that September at age seventy, but the President of Spain decreed Unamuno rector of Salamanca for life and created a special chair in his name for him. The following year the republic named him a citizen of honor, and in 1936 the University of Oxford gave him an honorary doctorate.

After the outbreak of the civil war in July, 1936, the government removed Unamuno as rector because of his criticism of the republic. The Nationalists, however, soon captured Salamanca and rewarded Unamuno's support by reappointing him rector. Yet Unamuno had come to see the war as national insanity. In a ceremony on October 12 attended by faculty, some Nationalist military leaders, and townspeople, he courageously denounced the speech of a general who had exalted anti-intellectualism and death. Confined to his home for his protest, Unamuno died on December 31, 1936.

*Summary*

Paradoxical and prickly, egocentric and sincere, Miguel de Unamuno y Jugo inevitably generated controversy. In his fiction and poetry, he sacrificed art to philosophical concerns, especially his religious despair and struggle for faith. Yet to Rubén Darío, the great Latin American poet, Unamuno was first and foremost a poet himself. His philosophy was not systematic and careful, and his assertions were sometimes outlandish and exaggerated. Scholars and critics even disagree regarding Unamuno's religious views, some arguing that he was an atheist and others that his belief was sincere. Certainly he constituted a thorny problem for Spanish Catholicism, which eventually banned several of his works.

Yet through the paradox, the rant, and the self-preoccupation, Unamuno's energy, determination, despair, and hope are unmistakable. The volume of his work was tremendous, and its breadth and weight placed him in the vanguard of Spanish intellectual life. With Kierkegaard and Friedrich Wilhelm Nietzsche, he laid out the existentialist dilemma, preparing the way for Martin Heidegger, Karl Jaspers, and Jean-Paul Sartre. He loved Spain deeply, despite its flaws, and became a sort of Quixote himself, tilting at transcendental windmills and giants that few had the courage or will to perceive.

*Bibliography*

Ellis, Robert R. *The Tragic Pursuit of Being: Unamuno and Sartre.* Tuscaloosa: University of Alabama Press, 1988. A short comparison of the existentialism of Unamuno and Sartre.

Ferrater Mora, José. *Unamuno: A Philosophy of Tragedy.* Translated by Philip Silver. Berkeley: University of California Press, 1962. An excellent, brief survey of Unamuno's philosophy.

Ilie, Paul. *Unamuno: An Existential View of Self and Society.* Madison: University of Wisconsin Press, 1967. Considers Unamuno's contributions to existentialism in relation to Kierkegaard, Nietzsche, Heidegger, Jaspers, and Sartre.

Marías, Julían. *Miguel de Unamuno.* Translated by Frances M. López-Morillas. Cambridge, Mass.: Harvard University Press, 1942. Old but insightful, this work analyzes Unamuno's contribution to philosophy, with occasional biographical references.

Nozick, Martin. *Miguel de Unamuno.* New York: Twayne, 1971. Together with a short biography, this work is an analysis of Unamuno's thought and an evaluation of his literary art. Contains a good bibliography.

Rudd, Margaret Thomas. *The Lone Heretic: A Biography of Miguel de Unamuno y Jugo.* Austin: University of Texas Press, 1963. The most thorough biography in English but problematic in some of its details and interpretations.

*Kendall W. Brown*

# PAUL VALÉRY

*Born:* October 30, 1871; Sète, France
*Died:* July 20, 1945; Paris, France
*Area of Achievement:* Literature
*Contribution:* Valéry was one of the most important French poets of the early twentieth century; he also made significant contributions to literary criticism.

## *Early Life*

Paul Valéry was born in Sète, France, in the western Mediterranean, on October 30, 1871. The family moved to the larger town of Montpellier in 1884 when Valéry was thirteen; he was already writing poems at this early age, but the family expected him to become a lawyer. The expectations of his family were increased when Valéry's father died in 1888, and so a year later Valéry entered the University of Montpellier to study law. After reading works by Stéphane Mallarmé, however, Valéry knew that his true vocation was as a poet not a lawyer. He began to acquire a circle of friends who shared his interests in literature, including his lifetime friend, André Gide. In 1891, he published two important poems, "La Fileuse" and the much praised "Narcisse parle," in a small review. He was established as a poet, and so he moved to Paris, where he became a friend of his master, Mallarmé.

## *Life's Work*

Valéry's early poems celebrate the wonders of nature; their major stylistic features are an evanescent mood and lush imagery. "Le Fileuse" portrays those powers of nature operating while an old woman who is spinning a thread falls asleep. Nature is the active agent; a spring waters the flowers and a stem bends to the wind. The human spinner dreams and sleeps.

> The rose, your sister, where a saint delights
> Perfumes your vague brow with her innocent breath;
> You languish . . . you are an innocent light
> At the blue window, where you spun the thread.

Nature, although invisible, is the real power and presence in the poem; the woman is a mere receptacle.

"Narcisse parle" is a longer and more important poem that uses the myth of Narcissus. Valéry was obsessed with the figure of Narcissus and wrote about him a number of times. In this early poem, Narcisse wanders in nature seeking "Some face that never wept." He is divided and incomplete, an early exploration by Valéry of consciousness and the failure to achieve unity. Once more, much of the poem is devoted to the force and activity of nature.

For example, Narcisse speaks of the "waters" as a God. He cannot, however, find the peace of the old woman in "Le Fileuse"; he remains "restless" until the union with this shadowy other is consummated. At the end of the poem, he remains solitary and can only bid farewell to what cannot be.

> Alas: wretched flesh, it is time to be at one . . .
> Lean: Tremble in all thou art:
> Possessed, the love it has been thine to promise me
> Is passing; its tremor shatters Narcissus and fails . . .

After this early success, Valéry was forced to decide whether to continue with poetry or to "cultivate his mind." Should he be Orpheus or Narcissus? He had always been interested in the human consciousness and the best way to achieve the "true self," or unity, and poetry was only one aspect of the human mind. It has been suggested that this crisis came about as a result of an unhappy love affair. Whatever the reason, Valéry decided in 1892 to abandon poetry. He moved to Paris, began to study and to record his thoughts in notebooks. These labors led to a study of Leonardo da Vinci, a figure who was not restricted to one mode of creation, and to the books on his character Monsieur Teste.

"Introduction à la méthode de Léonard de Vinci" (1895; "Introduction to the Method of Leonardo da Vinci," 1929) is an attempt by Valéry to reconcile the conflicting claims of the artist and the thinker in the figure of Leonardo. Valéry had been forced to choose thought over art and could not reconcile them in his own person. The essay reveals much about Valéry's inner conflict. He contrasts the fragmented "consciousness" that can only end in "exhaustion" and despair, while the universal genius, such as Leonardo, can turn his hand to any activity and create something. He can accomplish this by restraining his ego. This formulation seems to be very similar to that of John Keats. Keats contrasted the poet of the "egotistical sublime," who could only create out of himself, with the one who had achieved "negative capability" and could, therefore, create any type of character. For Valéry, the best poetry was not a turning loose of emotion but a process of the mind.

The cycle on Monsieur Teste is a continuation of the Leonardo essay. Teste is seen as a thinking machine, a pure intellect. Teste is discovered, for example, doing material "gymnastics," discovering "angles" while others waste their time and minds and fail to perceive the patterns around them. Such an abstract thinking machine might seem repellent to those schooled in the Romantic tradition, but to Valéry it was an antidote to Romantic self-indulgence. He continually celebrated the discipline of the human mind and sought unity of consciousness.

In 1913, Valéry returned to poetry. He wrote a few minor poems, but he worked on one poem from 1913 to 1917 and published it as *La Jeune Parque* (1917; the young fate). The poem is very obscure but has a lulling sound and beautiful imagery; it also tantalizes the reader to decipher its meaning. For any or all these reasons, the poem became an immediate success, and Valéry was recognized as an important modern poet. One possible way to explicate the poem is to divide it into three parts. The first part is the awakening of the youngest Fate to sexual feelings, which are symbolized by the snake. This awakening is described with images of burning, coiling, and rioting; it is discomfiting but cannot apparently be resisted. The second part of the poem turns from the disturbances of the senses to a joyous celebration of nature. This moment of ecstasy, however, cannot be sustained, and the Fate accepts life with all its questions and uncertainties. This acceptance is a prominent theme in the major poems of Valéry and can be discovered in his own rejection of and return to poetry.

After the success of *La Jeune Parque*, Valéry published a collection of poems that he called *Charmes, ou poèmes* in 1922. There is one poem in *Charmes, ou poèmes* that has been recognized as Valéry's masterpiece—"Le Cimetière marin" ("The Graveyard by the Sea," 1946). The situation is one with which many poets have dealt: the poet in the graveyard. At first, Valéry notes the "forms" of nature surrounding him in the incessant activity. The moment of peace vanishes as he contemplates his self as a changing being and the dead as reduced to nothing. He then attempts to provide some compensation by seeing death as a "womb"; however, he quickly rejects that easy answer as mere feigning and falls into despair. He soon triumphs over the despair brought on by the "worm unanswerable" and the paradoxes of Zeno. He turns back to life, to nature, and resolves: "We must try to live!" The ending is very similar to the acceptance found at the end of *La Jeune Parque*.

In 1925, Valéry was elected to the Académie Française. Having thus achieved recognition as one of France's greatest poets, he set about to make himself a man of letters, not simply a poet. He published many essays, introductions, prefaces, and extracts from his *Les Cahiers* (1957-1961; notebooks). Perhaps of greatest interest are his essays on poetry and the nature of the poet. Valéry makes a distinction between the Romanticism of Victor Hugo and the classicism of Charles Baudelaire; the difference is that Baudelaire subjects the material in his poetry to an unrelenting criticism, an intellectual technique of analysis. Valéry, however, did not discount the importance of inspiration for the poet; he believed that, while feeling may be the origin of the poem, the poet must discipline and contain it by analysis, by the mind. In addition, on many occasions Valéry also insisted that poetry must be "pure." He tried to connect poetry to music and create a poetry in which the formal aspects, the internal relationships, are dominant.

In 1937, Valéry was appointed to the chair of poetics at the Collège de

France, and he continued lecturing during the war years and German Occupation; he courageously resisted any attempts to censor his thought. A collection of poems written at various times was published in 1942. In 1945, Valéry, still busily at work, died on July 20. Two significant works were published after his death, *Mon Faust* (1946; *My Faust*, 1960) and "L'Ange."

*My Faust* is a fragment of a play in the form of a dialogue. In the early part of the play, Faust has reversed the traditional position and now dominates Mephistopheles. Mephistopheles attempts to tempt Faust by offering him, among other things, the glory of completing a book he has been contemplating. Faust rejects Mephistopheles by claiming that mankind has got beyond the narrow range of views that the devil represents. Even good and evil are to be questioned, although it is clear that the soul is immortal. In the last section, Faust leads Mephistopheles to the heights of a cliff to contemplate mankind below. Faust is uncertain that man can rise above his limited perspective and rise to the heights that only mind can give. It is a plea for a higher consciousness and a recognition of limitations. Valéry does not provide an answer but a goal to seek.

### *Summary*

Paul Valéry remains an important poet and thinker. He always doubted the value of poetry but must be ranked as one of the most important French poets of the early twentieth century. His masters and models, however, such as Baudelaire and Mallarmé, are of the nineteenth century. He was not an innovator as the Surrealists or Dadaists were; he was, in fact, one of the last poets to follow the classical rules of French verse. His poetry is marked by lush imagery and lulling sound effects. Within the "pure" poetry, Valéry is constantly exploring and seeking the unified self, the true self. The main concern of his life and his work is the human consciousness. He was not a Leonardo or a Monsieur Teste but one who was aware of the possibility of a higher and more complete human being. His major works from "Narcisse Parle" through *La Jeune Parque* to the final meditations of Faust deal with the conflict of a divided self and the search to attain a unified one.

### *Bibliography*

Crow, Christine M. *Paul Valéry: Consciousness and Nature*. Cambridge, England: Cambridge University Press, 1972. A scholarly treatment of Valéry's various views on the human mind. The book is very good on the sources of Valéry's thought. It also deals in depth with Valéry's treatment of nature, which other critics ignore.

Grubbs, Henry A. *Paul Valéry*. New York: Twayne, 1968. A broad view of Valéry's life and works without much detailed discussion of specific works. While it does not significantly explore Valéry's theories of consciousness, this volume provides a useful introduction for students.

Hytier, Jean. *The Poetics of Paul Valéry.* Translated by Richard Howard. Garden City, N.Y.: Anchor Books, 1966. The best book on Valéry's poetics. There is a detailed discussion of the intellectual background of Valéry's work, the uses of inspiration, and Valéry's methods of composition.

Mackay, Agnes Ethel. *The Universal Self: A Study of Paul Valéry.* Toronto: University of Toronto Press, 1961. An excellent study of Valery's major works. The author provides detailed, specific, and enlightening discussions of the major works. The discussion of consciousness is directly connected to the major works.

Thomson, Alastair W. *Valéry.* London: Oliver and Boyd, 1965. A very short though rather in-depth volume that traces Valéry's life and poetry from the early years to the late. Contains a bibliography.

*James Sullivan*

# EDGARD VARÈSE

*Born:* December 22, 1883; Paris, France
*Died:* November 6, 1965; New York, New York
*Area of Achievement:* Music
*Contribution:* Varèse was one of the first composers to appreciate the opportunities presented by electronic music and advanced recording techniques. His influence has been felt by many modern composers and has percolated into the rock music field.

## *Early Life*

Edgar Victor Achille Charles Varèse (he would later add a "d" to his first name) was born in Paris on December 22, 1883; his father was from the Piedmont region and his mother was a Parisienne. As his father's work entailed much travel, Varèse was several weeks old when he was entrusted to the care of his uncle Joseph and his wife, who lived in Villars. When Varèse was seven, his father moved his family to Turin. Varèse felt very isolated there and grew estranged from his father. Varèse attended his first concerts in Turin and was exposed to the music of Richard Wagner, Richard Strauss, Claude Debussy, and Jean Sibelius. Varèse began when he was seventeen to spend his pocket money secretly taking harmony and counterpoint lessons from the director of the conservatory, Giovanni Bolzoni.

When Varèse was eleven, he composed his first "opera," *Martin Paz*, based on a Jules Verne novel, to amuse his friends. His childhood was divided between Paris and relations in Burgundy. Varèse's father attempted to mold his son into following him in business, insisting that he take courses in engineering and mathematics. His father was not pleased with Varèse's choice of profession, preferring him rather to pursue a career in either mathematics or science. When Varèse found his son becoming too interested in the grand piano in the family home, he locked the keyboard shut. The strain between Varèse and his father grew so great that, after Varèse moved to Paris, he never saw his father again. By the age of fourteen, Varèse had already set his sights on being a composer.

In 1903, Varèse left home for Paris and the following year entered the Schola Cantorum. Varèse left the school in 1905 and entered the Conservatoire National de Musique et de Déclamation to study composition under Charles Widor. Varèse supported himself during these hard times by working as a musical copyist and later found employment in a library.

## *Life's Work*

While at the Schola Cantorum, Varèse met avant-garde artists from fields other than music; he numbered Max Jacob, Pablo Picasso, and Juan Gris among his acquaintances. Varèse's sources of inspiration frequently came from outside the musical sphere; he studied topics as diverse as alchemy and Leonardo da Vinci's notebooks. He later observed that music was the "art-science." Given his scientific education, he was particularly drawn to the work of physicists. Unfortunately, none of his works from this period has survived. In 1906, Varèse founded the choral society of the people's university, an educational establishment for working-class people in the faubourg Saint-Antoine. Varèse's personal life was also settling down; on November 5, 1907, he married Suzanne Bing.

Varèse in late 1907 left Paris for Berlin, where he would remain for most of the next six years; he had been impressed by Ferruccio Busoni's *A New Aesthetic of Music* and wanted to study under him. Busoni encouraged Varèse, and Varèse was later to state, "I owe him a debt of gratitude." He also met Debussy and Maurice Ravel around this time. In early 1909, Varèse finished his symphony *Bourgogne* and began work on a symphonic poem, *Gargantua*. He continued to support himself and his wife by copying music. He met Gustav Mahler and Strauss during this period, and Strauss made representations on Varèse's behalf to help him find work. In 1910, Varèse's daughter Claude was born. On December 15, 1910, *Bourgogne* was performed in Berlin, where its reception was stormy. Varèse would later destroy the score, his last link with his prewar past.

Despite the controversy, Varèse continued composing. Three years later, Suzanne Varèse decided to return to Paris to resume her acting career, and they were amicably divorced. The outbreak of World War I caught Varèse in Paris, and he was unable to return to Berlin until after the war in 1922, when he discovered that the warehouse in which his manuscripts had been stored had been completely destroyed by fire.

Varèse entered the military in April, 1915; after six months he asked for a transfer, but a medical examination showed that he was unfit for military service, and he was discharged. Varèse then decided to try his chances in the United States and arrived in New York on December 29, 1915, with ninety dollars in his pocket and knowing two words of English. He had originally planned to stay only a few weeks, but he eventually settled for good. The heady atmosphere of the Big Apple was introduced to him by a close friend from Berlin, Karl Muck, who was then conductor of the Boston Symphony Orchestra. Varèse's larger interests also put him on the edge of Dadaist groups. Once again, Varèse turned to music copying to keep body and soul together. Varèse was clear on what he wanted to achieve with his music, commenting to one reporter, "our musical alphabet must be enriched; we also need new instruments very badly."

Varèse made his New York conducting debut on April 1, 1917, with Hector Berlioz's *Requiem*; his performance was very favorably received. Conducting engagements now began to trickle in. Varèse remarried, taking as his bride Louise McCutcheon, a writer. In 1920, Varèse began to work on

*Amériques*, which was premiered in 1926. It was scored for 142 instruments, including two sirens. Varèse also helped found the International Composers' Guild with Carlos Salzedo at this time to encourage and support progressive composers. In the guild's six-year existence, it organized performances of works by Igor Stravinsky, Anton von Webern, Alban Berg, and many others.

In 1922, Varèse premiered *Offrandes*; the form of the work with soprano vocal and strings still had recognizable links with European tradition, but it was the last work Varèse composed that was so "conventional." The International Composers Guild staged the first performance on March 4, 1923, of Varèse's *Hyperprism*; scored for sixteen percussionists and ten wind instruments, the piece's debut was stormy. One listener, the London music publisher Kenneth Curwen, was sufficiently stirred to offer to publish Varèse's scores. One music critic observed of Varèse that he was the cause of peaceable music lovers coming to blows and using one anothers' faces for drums. Subsequent performances generated similar polarized criticism. When the British Broadcasting Company the following year broadcast a performance of *Hyperprism*, one critic complained of "musical Bolshevism." In reply to his critics, Varèse observed that "there has always been misunderstanding between the composer and his generation. . . . Music is antiquated in the extreme in its medium of expression compared to the other arts." One conductor who was to consistently champion Varèse's work was Leopold Stokowski, who premiered *Amériques* in 1926 in Philadelphia.

Despite maintaining his residency in the United States and eventually acquiring American citizenship, Varèse made a number of brief trips to Europe in the 1920's, and in 1928 began a long stay in Paris. One work was begun during this period, *L'Astronome*, but never completed. A second piece from this period, *L'Éspace*, was also never finished, although Varèse continued to tinker with it into the 1940's. As originally conceived, *L'Éspace* was a massive undertaking; in its most highly developed shape it was to involve simultaneous broadcasts by musicians scattered across the globe.

Varèse moved a step further to his concepts of *musique concrète* with his 1931 piece, *Ionisation*; the work explored more thoroughly than any other nonelectronic composition the structural values of all nonpitch properties of sound. The score was written for a thirteen-piece percussion ensemble. According to Louise Varèse, *Ionisation* was the piece of music that Varèse himself was most proud of and satisfied with. Varèse called the work, "cryptic, synthesized, powerful, and terse."

Varèse left Paris in 1933; before his departure he attempted to raise funds for a center of electronic instrument research from both the Bell Telephone Company and the Guggenheim Foundation, but the effort failed. Varèse's failure threw him into a deep depression which lasted for many years. In 1936, Varèse completed the work *Density 21:5*; he then wrote nothing for a decade. The following year, he gave classes in Santa Fe, New Mexico, at the Arsuna School of Fine Arts. Varèse moved in 1938 to Los Angeles and attempted to interest film producers in the possibilities of his concepts of "organized sound" for film scoring, but the conservatism of Hollywood doomed his efforts to failure. Returning to New York, Varèse organized the Great New York Chorus for performances of Renaissance and Baroque music. In 1948, he taught courses at Columbia on twentieth century music and composition. In 1950, he taught summer courses in Darmstadt, Germany.

In 1953, an anonymous donor provided Varèse with a tape recorder, a tool which finally allowed him to begin to explore more fully the possibilities of mixing live music and electronic prerecorded material. He began to record sounds for use in *Deserts*, a piece that he had begun to score three years previously for wind, percussion, and tape. In 1955, the work was broadcast in live concert form in stereo on French national radio, the first work to be so presented in France. At the Brussels Exhibition in 1958, Varèse had his *Poème électronique* performed. *Poème électronique* was a work for tape alone; relayed over four hundred loudspeakers and subsequently recorded, the work was very influential.

The last few years of Varèse's life brought him increasing recognition and renown. Performances of his works were staged much more frequently, and prominent younger composers such as Pierre Boulez and Robert Craft made recordings of his works. He received a number of academic and artistic honors, among them election to the National Institute of Arts and Letters and the Royal Swedish Academy. The one thing missing from this period of Varèse's life was new compositions. One of Varèse's confidants offered an explanation. In 1949, the composer Chou Wen-chung began to study with Varèse and eventually became his closest musical colleague as well as the executor of Varèse's musical estate. According to Chou, the reason for a lack of completed works by Varèse after 1960 is that he was "fundamentally writing a single work, despite the number of titles he worked with." Chou stated that shortly before Varèse's death he discarded a great number of manuscripts.

### *Summary*

Edgard Varèse's most important contributions to music began in the 1920's; like a number of his contemporaries, such as Stravinsky, he was aware that new modes of making music would be necessary to produce what he called organized sound. Varèse was one of the first composers to become interested in *musique concrète*, and as early as the 1950's he composed two of the earliest pieces in the classical mode employing taped effects. The great tragedy of Varèse's career was that his ideas outran the technology of the day; he would have been quite at home with the modern electronic revolution of synthesizers and digital sampling. Varèse did not leave a large body of work—total playing time for the pieces he wrote between 1920 and

1960 is about two hours; his influence nevertheless is immense. Varèse used rhythm as the primary base of his musical language at a time when other composers relied on melody and harmony.

*Bibliography*

Austin, William W. *Music in the Twentieth Century.* New York: W. W. Norton, 1966. This work fits Varèse and his accomplishments into the larger context of post-1900 musical development. While many surveys tend to concentrate on Varèse's earlier, more "heroic" works, Austin deals with Varèse's accomplishments as a unity.

Julius, Ruth. "Edgard Varèse: An Oral History Project, Some Preliminary Conclusions." *Current Musicology* 25 (1978): 39-49. Julius conducted interviews with fourteen composers living in the New York metropolitan area, all of whom had known Varèse. Among the composers were John Cage, Charles Wuorinen, and Vladimir Ussachevsky. The article is an interpretive documentation of the interviews; the transcripts of the interviews are in the City University of New York Oral History Archives. Julius was interested not only in biographical information about Varèse but also in the composers' thoughts and observations on the music itself.

Ouellette, Fernand. *Edgard Varèse.* Translated by Derek Coltman. New York: Orion Press, 1968. Ouellette's work remains the best biography of Varèse. The author had the benefit of a number of conversations with Varèse, and Varèse's widow read and commented upon his manuscript before it went to press. The work contains an extensive bibliography of works on Varèse.

Van Solkema, Sherman, ed. *The New Worlds of Edgard Varèse.* Brooklyn: Institute for Studies in American Music, Brooklyn College, 1979. This monograph collects papers delivered at a symposium concerning Varèse's work conducted at the City University of New York in April, 1977. The papers are primarily analytical and technical; of particular interest is Chou Wen-chung's treatise on Varèse's *Ionisation.*

Varèse, Louise. *Varèse: A Looking-Glass Diary.* New York: W. W. Norton, 1972. Mrs. Varèse calls this work "a personal remembering." The work was to be the first of several volumes and offers an intimate portrait of the composer up through 1928.

*John C. K. Daly*

# NIKOLAI IVANOVICH VAVILOV

*Born:* November 26, 1887; Moscow, Russia
*Died:* January 26, 1943; Saratov, U.S.S.R.
*Areas of Achievement:* Genetics and botany
*Contribution:* Vavilov is noted for his pioneering work on the origins, distribution, and genetics of crop plants. He postulated a law of homologous series in variation whereby variation (and thus characteristics of possible cultivars) of a plant could be predicted from variation in related species. He also mapped centers of origin and genetic diversity of cultivated plants on a worldwide scale as well as personally organizing and leading numerous botanical expeditions and establishing a network of agricultural experiment stations in the Soviet Union.

## *Early Life*

Nikolai Ivanovich Vavilov was born in Moscow on November 26, 1887, the eldest child of Ivan Vavilov, a prominent Moscow merchant. The Vavilovs were able to provide an excellent education for all three of their surviving children. Vavilov entered the Petrovsko Agricultural Institute (later the Timiraezev Academy) in Moscow in 1906, studying soils and plant chemistry. When he was graduated in 1910 his dissertation received an award from the Bogdanov Museum in Moscow.

After graduation Vavilov worked as an assistant at the Poltava Experiment Station, studying the immunity of plants to parasitic fungi and anatomical variation in grasses, subjects which were to continue to interest him throughout much of his professional career. In 1911, he moved to St. Petersburg, where he worked with the noted botanists R. E. Regel and A. A. Yachevsky, studying immunity and variability in plants. These men arranged for him to study in biological laboratories in continental Europe and in England, where in 1913-1914 he studied with Great Britain's pioneer geneticist William Bateson and Rowland Biffen, a noted cereal breeder.

In the early years of the twentieth century, botany was in the process of transition from a predominantly field-and-taxonomy-oriented discipline to a more experimental and laboratory-oriented science. Vavilov, who received an excellent education in both approaches, combined them successfully throughout his career. He returned to Russia in 1914, where he completed his M.S. dissertation. In 1917, he was appointed professor of genetics, plant breeding, and agronomy at the Agricultural Institute of Voronezh in central Russia and at the University of Saratov on the Volga. In these early years of the Soviet era, his legendary energy and devotion to agricultural science enabled him to carry on an ambitious program of research into the systematics and breeding of crop plants, despite the disruptions of revolution and civil war. In 1920, he organized a congress of plant breeders in Saratov, at which he presented his classic paper on the law of homologous series in variation, which was also presented at the International Agricultural Congress in the United States the following year and received immediate international acclaim. Some measure of Vavilov's zeal and vision can be deduced from the fact that the 1920 Saratov congress took place in a region devastated by famine and civil war, despite an almost complete breakdown of modern transport, while Vavilov was forming the groundwork for crop-breeding programs as ambitious as any being contemplated in the United States and Western Europe. Vavilov married Elena Ivanovna Barulina, a fellow plant scientist, and the couple had two sons.

*Life's Work*

In 1920, Vavilov was appointed to succeed Regel as chairman of the department of economic botany and plant breeding in the Agricultural Institute of Petrograd. He held this appointment until the institute was reorganized in 1924 as the All-Union Institute of Economic Botany and New Cultures, with Vavilov as its head. In 1966, following Vavilov's rehabilitation, it was named the Vavilov Institute of Plant Industry.

Vavilov had a utopian vision of the transformation of Russian agriculture through plant breeding. His sweeping revolutionary views attracted favorable attention from Vladimir Ilich Lenin, which enabled him to establish a rapport with the Bolshevik hierarchy and obtain scarce funds for agricultural research. With energetic leadership and the full support of the government, agricultural research in Russia grew at a rapid pace. The number of research stations doubled from 1914 to 1929, and the number of trained specialists tripled. Vavilov undertook numerous expeditions to many parts of the world, including Central Asia, Afghanistan, the Mediterranean area, Italy, Ethiopia, China, Japan, Mexico, Central America, and South America to collect stocks of cultivated plants and their wild relatives. These collections, grown in field plots and maintained as viable seed in various parts of the Soviet Union, provided a rich gene bank from which to draw useful characteristics for plant-breeding programs. Unfortunately, they were not well maintained following Vavilov's death, and many irreplaceable strains have been lost.

Vavilov drew on his experience as a field botanist and his work in plant breeding to propose two important principles of economic botany: the law of homologous series in variation and the definition of centers of origin of cultivated plants. The law of homologous series states that a variation found in one species is likely to be found in related species. Vavilov based his principle on observation of thousands of cultivars of grasses and legumes, species of wild plants, and even fungi. It is not a law in the sense of a physical principle (such as the laws of gravity), but it accurately summarized observations and provided a framework for systematic plant breeding.

Vavilov's main work on the centers of crop-plant origin and diversity was unpublished during his lifetime but has since been reconstructed from manuscripts by P. M. Zhukovsky, a younger colleague. He mapped eight (later increased to twelve) macrocenters of crop-plant origin, which in general coincide with the present areas of highest diversity of cultivars and the distributions of wild forebears, both important sources for useful genes, especially for resistance to diseases and pests. Vavilov was honored at home and abroad for his contributions to agricultural science. In 1923, he was elected corresponding member, and in 1929 a full member, of the U.S.S.R. Academy of Sciences and was director of its Institute of Genetics. He received the Lenin Prize for his work on plant-immunity breeding in 1926. Although not a Communist, he was a member of the Soviet Central Executive Committee. He participated in International Agricultural Congresses in the United States in 1922 and 1929, and in the International Genetics Conference in Ithaca, New York, in 1932.

As the foremost Russian geneticist of his day and a prominent figure in science and politics, Vavilov became involved with the scientific demagogue Trofim Denisovich Lysenko in a bitter controversy that ultimately destroyed both Vavilov and genetics in the Soviet Union. Ironically, Lysenko was aided in his early career by the growth of agricultural science under Vavilov's direction. Although he had some success in practical agricultural research, which gave him a certain plausibility, Lysenko was intellectually unable to master theoretical genetics. Instead, he became convinced that he had demonstrated inheritance of acquired characteristics (Lamarckian as opposed to Mendelian genetics), a position that was appealing to the new Soviet leadership under Joseph Stalin for a number of reasons. First, it promised a quicker route to producing improved varieties than laborious crossing experiments. Second, especially as applied to human genetics, inheritance of acquired characteristics was more palatable to Marxists than a doctrine teaching that one cannot by one's own actions change an offspring's genetic inheritance, which as a corollary admits at least the theoretical possibility that there are inherently genetically inferior classes or races of people. Finally, forced collectivization had been a disaster for Russian agriculture, and agricultural science provided a convenient scapegoat. At first, Vavilov attempted to compromise with Lysenko but found himself pushed into an increasingly untenable position. In 1935, he was dropped from the Central Executive Committee and in 1936 relieved of his duties as president of the All-Union Academy of Agricultural Sciences. An offer to chair the International Genetics Conference in Edinburgh in 1939 had to be declined, because he was no longer able to travel abroad, and a proposed International Genetics Congress in the U.S.S.R. in 1940 was abruptly and inexplicably dropped in the planning stages.

The stronger his enemies became, the harder he fought. In 1936, his criticism of Lysenkoism was mild; in 1939, he denounced it as ignorant and irrational. Finally, on August 6, 1940, while on a collecting trip in Moldavia, Vavilov was arrested as an enemy of the people. The charges against him consisted of fictitious allegations of sabotage and espionage in agricultural institutes, brought under duress by a subordinate who was himself in prison, plus a somewhat subtler charge of fascism based on association of Mendelian genetics with notions of racial superiority, a doctrine never espoused by Vavilov. He was interrogated in Moscow, then transferred to a prison in Saratov, on the Volga River, where he died of "dystrophy and edematous disease," according to the official death certificate, on January 26, 1943. Conflicting information appears in the literature regarding the date, place, and circumstances of his death, which only became known in the West after World War II. Mark Popovsky suggests that he may have been murdered at some earlier date when the Germans threatened Saratov, but the witnesses he quotes tend to support the official story. The hunger, cold, and brutality endemic in Soviet prisons at the time undoubtedly hastened the death of a vigorous, athletic man, who was only fifty-five years old.

*Summary*

To his contemporaries, Nikolai Ivanovich Vavilov was a charismatic man, who seemed almost superhuman in his energies, persuasive, capable of inspiring loyalty, and capable, some might say, of working a miracle such as pulling Russian agriculture out of the dark ages into the twentieth century. He failed, not through an inappropriate approach or through lack of effort but through being unable to judge accurately the evolving political climate in which he worked. In retrospect, Vavilov's accomplishments as a geneticist are solid and were very influential in the period between the wars, although modern crop science looks to other models and his predictions about the future of genetics contained too much guesswork to be considered prophetic. It is a great misfortune that the collections he so laboriously built up did not survive intact and that the system of agricultural research he helped so much to foster was crippled by two decades of charlatanism.

In the end, then, it may well be in the unsought role of the most prominent martyr for science that Vavilov is longest remembered. His fate serves as a reminder that science and government are inextricably interconnected and that even in the twentieth century the rational can be overcome by the irrational in a scientific discipline when the wrong people are called upon to be judges.

*Bibliography*

Bakhteev, F. T. "To the History of Russian Science: Academician Nicholas Ivan Vavilov on his Seventieth Anniversary (November 26, 1887-August 2, 1942)." *The Quarterly Review of Biology* 35: 115-119. A testimonial biography of a type commonly published in Soviet scientific journals on significant anniversaries in the life of prominent scientists, this paper coincides with efforts to rehabilitate Vavilov in the Soviet Union. It emphasizes the international character of his work and the respect with which Vavilov was regarded abroad and details his position and the honors he received in the Soviet Union.

Mangelsdorf, Paul C. "Nikolai Ivanovich Vavilov." *Genetics* 38, no. 1 (1953): 1-4. A belated obituary and testimonial in the leading American genetics journal. Vavilov's contributions to genetics are clearly summarized. Vavilov is characterized as Russia's most distinguished geneticist, and the writer comments on the irony that the free world was reaping substantial benefits from the work which the Soviet Union disdained.

Medvedev, Zhores A. *Soviet Science*. New York: W. W. Norton, 1978. Medvedev concentrates his attention on the failures of Soviet science and conditions in the Soviet system that discourage scientific innovation. A considerable portion of the book is devoted to the flowering of genetics in the Soviet Union in the 1920's and its subsequent stifling under the influence of Lysenko. In Russia, Medvedev was among those responsible for defending and rehabilitating Vavilov; he subsequently emigrated to the United States.

Popovsky, Mark. *Manipulated Science: The Crisis of Science and Scientists in the Soviet Union Today*. Garden City, N.Y.: Doubleday, 1979. A Russian specialist in scientific journalism who emigrated to the United States, Popovsky presents a historical overview of the practice of science in the Soviet Union. The emphasis is on failures and weaknesses of the system and the dismal record of natural sciences under Stalin. An admirer of Vavilov, he devotes considerable space to the conflict between Vavilov and Lysenko and Vavilov's imprisonment.

___________. *The Vavilov Affair*. Ann Arbor, Mich.: Archon, 1984. The first two chapters of this book summarize Vavilov's contributions to genetics; the remainder is devoted to the conflict with Lysenko and Vavilov's arrest, trial, and imprisonment. Included are summaries of interviews with contemporaries and commentary on the position of scientists under a totalitarian regime.

Zirkle, Conway, ed. *Death of a Science in Russia*. Philadelphia: University of Pennsylvania Press, 1949. The conflict between Mendelian geneticists and Lysenko and his followers, who espoused a form of Lamarckianism, is documented chronologically in a series of excerpts from the Soviet press, interspersed with interpretive chapters by American scientists. The introductory chapter gives a clear explanation of the background of the controversy, the differences between the two views of inheritance, and factors in the Soviet Union that encouraged Lysenko.

*Martha Sherwood-Pike*

# ELEUTHÉRIOS VENIZÉLOS

*Born:* August 23, 1864; Mournies, Crete, Ottoman Empire
*Died:* March 18, 1936; Paris, France
*Areas of Achievement:* Government and politics
*Contribution:* Venizélos is the outstanding national figure of modern Greece. In and out of power he was the country's leading statesman in the first part of the twentieth century.

## *Early Life*

Eleuthérios Venizélos was born in 1864 in the small village of Mournies near Canea in Crete. His father was the merchant Kiriakos Venizélos Krivatos, whose family had emigrated from Morea (the Peloponnesus) in 1770, and was a leader of the Greek national movement on the island attempting liberation from the Ottoman Empire and union to the Kingdom of Greece. The elder Venizélos had spent many years in exile on the island of Siros as a result of his activities. Eleuthérios was the fourth of six children born to the Venizéloses, the first to survive, and according to one account he was named for a local saint whose name derived from Eileithyia, the ancient goddess of childbirth. In 1866, after the great uprising of that year on Crete, the government deported Kiriakos Venizélos to Siros once again. The family, including Eleuthérios, then only two years old, followed. After the boy had finished elementary and part of secondary school in Siros, the family was allowed to return in 1872 to Canea, where Eleuthérios continued his education and then went on to private study in Athens and also classical studies at *lycées* in Athens and Siros. After Eleuthérios completed these studies, the elder Venizélos wanted his son to remain on Crete in the family business. Eleuthérios, however, wanted a career in law, and a friend of the family, the Greek consul at Canea, persuaded his father to allow it.

In 1881, Venizélos entered the University of Athens, where he gained public recognition when, as leader of the Cretan students' union, he put the island's cause for independence before Joseph Chamberlain, a leader of the British Liberal Party, then traveling in the Near East. While Venizélos was at the university, his father died, so in addition to his studies he was obliged to care for the family business. In 1886, he received his degree and went back to Crete to practice law and continue the struggle for independence. He also worked as a journalist and within a year was elected a deputy to the island's assembly and became the leader of the newly formed Liberal Party. Although he had planned to continue his studies in Germany in 1890, he chose instead to remain at home in order to marry Maria Catelouzu.

## *Life's Work*

Venizélos' real goal was the independence of Crete. When a new insurrection broke out in 1897, he was at the forefront. The Great Powers intervened and appointed a mixed international naval commission to oversee the governing of the island. Venizélos greeted the arrival of the Russian, French, English, and Italian admirals on behalf of the assembly. In December, 1898, Prince George, the younger son of the Greek king, George I, came as the High Commissioner of the Powers. Venizélos was appointed to the island's executive committee and soon became the dominant figure. Yet irreconcilable differences arose between him and Prince George.

Venizélos' anti-Turkish activities and insistence on pushing the government of the island to complete independence led to a new insurrection in 1905 against the wishes of the Great Powers and the commissioner. Prince George abdicated the following year. Venizélos emerged as a Greek hero, but Crete still remained in Turkish hands. In October, 1908, in the wake of the "Young Turk" revolution, Venizélos, without consulting Commissioner Alexandros Zaïmis, who had replaced Prince George, led the Cretans in declaring their independence with the hope of joining Greece; he also became prime minister of a provisional government.

Then an uprising by the junior officers of the Military League in Athens led to an invitation to Venizélos to become the Greek prime minister in 1910—the first of five times he held that post. Venizélos, with the support of the Military League and its backers, swept the elections of 1910. He assumed the leadership of the Greek Liberal Party and carried out major modernizing reforms in the constitution and government. Although he was very popular, he also had many bitter enemies, including the Conservative Party, members of the royal household, particularly the king's sons, and some members of the military.

Venizélos as prime minister also modernized the Greek army with British and French assistance and came to agreements with his Christian neighbors, Bulgaria, Serbia, and Montenegro, to prepare the final exodus of Turkey from Europe. The Balkan Wars of 1912-1913, the first against Turkey and the second against Bulgaria, gave Greece much of Macedonia, Thrace, and Epirus as well as Crete and the Aegean Islands.

In 1913, King George was assassinated and succeeded by his son, King Constantine I, who was less accommodating to Venizélos. The outbreak of World War I exacerbated relations between Venizélos and the monarch as the former wished Greece to join the Allies, but Constantine, loyal to his brother-in-law, William II of Germany, steadfastly chose to remain neutral. Venizélos resigned his post in March, 1915, but in the summer won a strong majority in parliament and began his second administration. His pro-Allied stance, however, caused the king to ask for his resignation within a few weeks.

The next year, the Allies, trying to establish a second front in Greece, invaded Athens and forced the government to expel the missions of the

Central Powers. In September, Venizélos declared a Greek republic in Crete and then moved to Salonika, where large numbers of Allied troops were stationed. Great Britain and France enthusiastically recognized him. King Constantine persuaded the Metropolitan of Athens to swear a curse of anathema on Venizélos and then left the country with Prince George. In 1917, however, the royal family under Prince Alexander, Constantine's younger son, made its peace with Venizélos. The monarchy was restored and joined the Allied side.

After the war was over, Venizélos journeyed to Paris as the Greek representative at the peace conference and came away with great gains from Bulgaria and Turkey. Yet he had hoped to obtain Constantinople as well as more of Asia Minor for Greece. Although the Allies had promised this as a consideration, they were reluctant to hand the Turkish capital over to Athens. Venizélos returned from Paris in September, 1920. Despite his triumphs, his long absence and the continuation of wartime conditions in Greece pending the resolution of the Turkish dispute led to his loss of popularity. Furthermore, a month after his return, King Alexander died from illness contracted when bitten by his pet monkey. Then, in the November elections, the Conservative Party won a stunning upset. Constantine returned, and Venizélos went to Paris in self-imposed exile.

By this time the Greek army had moved into the interior of Asia Minor to enlarge its war gains. Mustafa Kemal (later Atatürk), however, organized the Turkish defense that delivered a stunning defeat to the Greek forces. An armed insurrection followed, and Constantine abdicated a second time. His son George became king, and Venizélos once more entered the Greek service, representing the monarchy at the peace talks at Lausanne between the Allies and Turkey.

Another insurrection in 1924 forced George into exile, and Venizélos became prime minister for the fourth time. He did not wish to end the monarchy as his associates did, however, and, using illness as an excuse, he resigned in four weeks and returned to Paris. Yet in 1928 he came back for his fifth term as prime minister and was confirmed when the country gave the Liberal Party a large electoral victory. These were turbulent years for Greece, with army insurrections, periods of military dictatorship, and the struggle between the monarchists and the republicans. Prime Minister Venizélos was able to come to peace terms with his neighbors, including Turkey, but the Great Depression had grievous economic effects for Greece, and the Conservatives swept him from power in 1932. After an unsuccessful run for the presidency in 1934, he went into exile a third time but continued to interfere in the chaotic politics of Greece, including another attempted *coup d'état*. In 1935, Ioannis Metaxas, a royalist general, reestablished the monarchy under his dictatorship. Venizélos died in March, 1936, at seventy-one from pneumonia after a short illness. He was survived by his second wife and two sons, Sophocles, who became prime minister of Greece in 1944, and Kyriakos.

*Summary*

Eleuthérios Venizélos is the towering figure of contemporary Greece. More than the monarchs whom he served and battled, he stands as the symbol of the twentieth century Hellenes. He was a nationalist who fought for the *Megali Idhea* (great idea) of great Greece but was willing to embrace the precepts of peace, equality, and justice. He was trained in the liberal tradition of the classics and law, and his ideas and deeds were a mixture of conservatism, progressivism, and radicalism that earned for him many friends and as many enemies. Under Venizélos, Greece fulfilled much of its dream of gaining Turkish territory, almost doubling in size. Venizélos' charisma and his political and oratorical gifts made him the ideal statesman to lead the Greek cause in the early twentieth century. His family tradition of Greek nationalism and rebellion as well as his nativity in Turkish-held Crete also aided his career. Much of Venizélos' success had a serendipitous aspect—being in the right place at the right time. He was a leader of Crete and then Greece during the final days of the Ottoman Empire. He chose the side of the winning Allies at a time when his monarch, a political rival, chose the losing Germans. He was out of power when Greece suffered its major defeat at the hands of Atatürk. Yet often fortune frowned on him. He lost his popular mandate after one of his greatest triumphs at the 1919 Peace Conference at Paris; he also bore the full brunt of censure for the unsuccessful military *coups d'état* of 1933 and 1935. (He actually was involved only in the latter.)

Venizélos was a stormy figure whose politics and actions called forth either unqualified adulation or bitter enmity. Like the monarchs he opposed, he alternated between holding the supreme rule in his state and living in exile. His political gifts of sagacity and moderation were also in part the cause of his downfall at a time when Greece, like many countries entering into the modern world, swung from one extreme to the other, from republicanism to monarchy, and indeed at a time when extremes of both Right and Left came to dominate much of European politics. As a national leader, Venizélos could only meet with success, but, when the boundaries of the new state had been won, he was unable to compete in the domestic political wars.

*Bibliography*

Alastos, Doros. *Venizélos: Patriot, Statesman, Revolutionary.* London: Percy Lund Humphries, 1942. A hagiographic biography of Venizélos that emphasizes his life to 1924 and has an appendix covering Greece from his death to the country's involvement in World War II. Includes maps.

Chester, Samuel Beach. *Life of Venizélos*. New York: George H. Doran, 1921. A sympathetic look at Venizélos' career to World War I. Contains a map of Greece.

Dakin, Douglas. *The Unification of Greece: 1770-1923*. New York: St. Martin's Press, 1972. A history of Greece including the period of Venizélos' early political career, putting his role in context. Very sympathetic to the Greek point of view. Contains tables, notes, a bibliography, and an index.

Falls, Cyril "The Greek Anatolian Adventure." *History Today* 16 (July, 1966): 452-458. An analysis of the Greco-Turkish war of 1919-1922 with an evaluation of Venizélos as well as the Turkish leaders.

Kerofilas, Costas. *Eleftherios Venizélos: His Life and Work*. Translated by Beatrice Barstow. London: John Murray, 1915. A brief biography of Venizélos written for wartime propaganda.

*Frederick B. Chary*

# PANCHO VILLA
## Doroteo Arango

*Born:* June 5, 1878; San Juan del Río, Mexico
*Died:* July 20, 1923; near Parral, Mexico
*Area of Achievement:* The military
*Contribution:* Villa played a central role in the Mexican Revolution as a rough, crude, and sometimes brilliant general from 1910 to 1920. Villa's exploits on and off the battlefield have broadened into legends that remain an integral part of Mexican history and folklore.

*Early Life*

Francisco "Pancho" Villa was born June 5, 1878, on a large estate, or "hacienda," in San Juan del Río, State of Durango, Mexico. His parents, who worked as laborers on the hacienda, named their son Doroteo Arango. Mexico at that time was ruled by Porfirio Díaz. Under the dictatorship of Díaz, landless peasants enjoyed few rights and remained caught in a cycle of poverty from which there was no escape.

As a young boy, Doroteo taught himself to ride horses, explored the mountainous terrain near his home, and acquired valuable skills that later enabled him to survive as a fugitive. Doroteo was only twelve years old when his father died and left him head of the family. At age seventeen, Doroteo was forced to leave his home after he killed a man who had attacked his sister. Although he was captured by police, Doroteo managed to escape into the mountains of northern Mexico. There he joined a group of bandits led by Ignacio Parra and adopted the name of a notorious, early nineteenth century bandit, Pancho Villa. After Parra was killed, Villa became leader of his own band of bandits and gained a reputation as a benevolent bandit who plundered the rich and shared his stolen goods with the poor. Villa's activities at this time included robbing banks and trains, and murdering those who challenged his outlaw existence.

From about 1896 to 1909, Villa extended his influence beyond Durango to Chihuahua, in the northern part of Mexico along the border with the United States. In 1910, however, Villa abandoned his outlaw career to join Francisco Madero in the revolution against the Díaz regime.

*Life's Work*

The Mexican Revolution of 1910 to 1920 was a dramatic and convulsive period that became a revolt of the landless masses against oppressive rulers, cost millions of lives, and produced vast destruction of property and resources. From this struggle, Villa emerged as a folk hero to the Mexican people and became one of the most colorful personalities of the Revolution. Regional and personal conflicts as well as betrayals confused and symbolized the course of the Revolution.

When Madero rallied others against the despotic and dictatorial government of Díaz in 1910, Villa joined the movement to reform Mexico. Within a short period of time, Villa controlled a loosely organized force of men dedicated to the democratic ideals espoused by Madero. At the end of 1910, Villa led his troops in capturing the small town of San Andrés in Chihuahua. This victory, the first of many, established Villa as one of the most daring and competent military leaders of the Revolution. By May, 1911, Villa confirmed his reputation with a stunning victory over federal troops when he captured Ciudad Juárez. The control of this valuable border city by the rebel army forced the resignation and exile of Díaz and allowed Madero to assume the presidency.

Acquiescing to the demands of the new president, Villa reluctantly agreed to serve under the command of Madero's general Victoriano Huerta. Villa soon challenged the authority of Huerta, however, was arrested, and then sentenced to die. In June, 1912, while he was smoking the traditional last cigarette before he faced the firing squad, Villa won a reprieve when a last-minute pardon from Madero arrived. Transferred to the prison in Mexico City, Villa there sought the assistance of a fellow inmate to improve his reading and writing skills. In December of the same year, Villa and his tutor both escaped. Traveling north, Villa left Mexico and entered the United States at El Paso, Texas, where he organized supporters, plotted against Huerta, whom he believed had abandoned the ideals of the Revolution, and planned his return to Mexico.

In March, 1913, word reached Villa in El Paso that Huerta had murdered Madero and usurped the presidency. Acting on this information, Villa gathered his forces, reentered Mexico, and began to contest Huerta's control. By October, Villa emerged as the undisputed leader of the anti-Huerta forces in the north. Demonstrating remarkable military skills and utilizing daring strategies, Villa and his army, the Division of the North, cleared Huerta's forces from the state of Chihuahua. At the end of 1913, in one of the bloodiest battles of the Revolution, Villa recaptured Ciudad Juárez. While controlling that city, Villa undertook reforms that increased the food supply for the populace, improved the water system, and repaired the power plant to provide electricity for public and private use.

By 1914, Villa, now dubbed the "Centaur of the North," had become the symbol of the Revolution to his countrymen. Motivated by a desire to return Mexico to the Mexican people, and with few ideological purposes, Villa successfully commanded his forces in victories against the Huerta government. Although he brutally ordered foreigners to leave areas under his control, in the early stages of the Revolution Villa courted the friendship and goodwill of the United States. As an uneducated and unsophisticated general, Villa nevertheless understood the importance of propaganda and publicity to secure favorable public opinion in the United States. When President Woodrow Wilson in 1914 ordered the occupation of the port city of Veracruz after an affront to a ship of the United States Navy, Villa alone among Mexican leaders refused to condemn Wilson's actions. The United States at that time viewed Villa as the one revolutionary capable of establishing and maintaining order in Mexico, yet hesitated to recognize any clear leader.

In the middle of 1914, rebels supported by the United States overthrew the Huerta regime. At this point, the political climate in Mexico disintegrated into chaos. Although quarrels among the various factions had surfaced earlier, fundamental differences in direction and goals caused the Revolution by 1915 to degenerate into an anarchy characterized by civil wars in different regions of the country. During this period of intense bloodshed and destruction, a conflict between Venustiano Carranza and Villa dominated the Revolution. Carranza, as leader of a large rebel group that called themselves the Constitutionalists, and Villa, as commander in Chihuahua, both claimed control of Mexico. Failure to resolve this contest undermined the political stability of the country. Central to their dispute was a basic difference in attitude, education, and personality. Villa, a colorful, unorthodox, sometimes crude bandit-turned-general, denounced the supremacy of the courtly, well-bred Carranza. Yet, after General Álvaro Obregón, a supporter of Carranza, defeated the Centaur of the North at the Battle of Celaya in April, 1915, Villa's influence waned. Shortly thereafter, President Wilson recognized the government of Carranza as the legitimate authority in Mexico.

Resenting the official recognition of Carranza and attempting to demonstrate that his opponent did not control all of Mexico, Villa initiated attacks against the United States in towns along the border. These skirmishes culminated in a raid against Columbus, New Mexico, in March, 1916, when four hundred of Villa's men crossed the border before dawn, brutally murdered seventeen American citizens, then burned the center of the town before they escaped.

The reaction of the United States to Villa's wanton act of violence and disregard for international law was swift. Troops under the leadership of General John J. Pershing formed the Punitive Expedition that marched to Mexico in an attempt to capture Villa and disperse his forces.

Even though permission to enter Mexico remained a disputed issue between Carranza and Wilson, Pershing pursued Villa's army for more than ten months. Although never able to capture Villa, the Expedition succeeded in disrupting his organization and reducing his control in northern Mexico. Villa continued sporadic campaigns against the Carranza government until Carranza's murder in 1920. At that time, Villa surrendered his remaining army to the new president and retired to a ranch provided for him by the Mexican government. By then a hero to the Mexican people, Villa spent the next three years peacefully as a rancher in Chihuahua, outside the political sphere. On July 20, 1923, assassins hired by his old enemies murdered Villa and his bodyguards near the town of Parral.

*Summary*

Pancho Villa, who began his career as an outlaw and bandit, became a symbol of the Revolution to Mexican peasants during and after his death. Despite documented evidence of his cruelty and perverse disregard for human life, Villa has dominated Mexican folklore as a champion of the poor and landless masses. Numerous myths and legends, popularized in songs and romanticized tales recount Villa's feats. Villa's support came from the lower classes, who saw in him a charismatic figure capable of winning for them an opportunity to gain a place in Mexican society and to improve their fortunes in life. As a military leader, Villa demonstrated extraordinary skill in routing his enemies on the battlefield. To his troops, Villa seemed to be the epitome of Mexican masculinity, with his fearless exploits and daring attacks against superior forces. Chased by Pershing's troops for more than ten months, Villa and his followers outwitted and eluded the more powerful and domineering United States. This feat not only brought Villa worldwide attention but also advanced Mexican nationalism during a period of violence and confusion. In the final analysis, Villa remained loyal to his cause during a time in Mexican history noted for betrayal and emerged as one of the foremost personalities of the Revolution. Yet Villa persists as an enigma. To some, Villa's brutality and atrocities inspired fear and hatred, while others responded to his leadership and acts of kindness with respect and adulation. Despite conflicting interpretations of his motives and actions, Villa influenced the course of Mexican history and has endured as a hero to his countrymen.

*Bibliography*

Braddy, Haldeen. *Cock of the Walk: The Legend of Pancho Villa*. New York: Kennikat Press, 1955.

____________. *The Paradox of Pancho Villa*. El Paso: Texas: Western Press, 1978. Both studies present a highly romanticized figure of Villa, with an emphasis on legends and myths that have developed since his death.

Clendenen, Clarence C. *The United States and Pancho Villa: A Study in Unconventional Diplomacy*. New York: Kennikat Press, 1961. This work stresses that events in Mexico during the Revolution had a profound impact on the United States. The study is based on excellent research that explores Villa's actions and the diplomatic consequences.

Cumberland, Charles C. *Mexican Revolution: The Constitutionalist Years*. Introduction and additional material by David C. Bailey. Austin: University of Texas Press, 1972. This scholarly account of the Revolution, when Villa was most active, provides informative biographical information on the period's leading figures with insightful interpretations of the factional disputes during a very confusing time in Mexican history.

Lansford, William Douglas. *Pancho Villa*. Los Angeles: Sherbourne Press, 1965. This fictional account, based closely on facts, provides insight into why Villa acted as he did before and during the Revolution.

Machado, Manuel A., Jr. *Centaur of the North: Francisco Villa, the Mexican Revolution, and Northern Mexico*. Austin, Tex.: Eakin Press, 1988. A well-written, well-researched, and favorable biography, with numerous pictures, that emphasizes Villa's pivotal role as a military leader in the Revolution.

Mason, Herbert Mollory, Jr. *The Great Pursuit*. New York: Random House, 1970. This detailed military history of the Punitive Expedition, with recollections by those involved on both sides, concentrates on the activities of the United States Army. The author claims the Expedition was successful because it dispersed Villa's troops and gave the United States experience to draw upon in World War I.

Peterson, Jessie, and Thelma Cox Knowles, eds. *Pancho Villa: Intimate Recollections by People Who Knew Him*. New York: Hastings House, 1977. These essays, composed by those who knew Villa as friend and enemy, capture the intensity of the Revolution and highlight his central role.

White, E. Bruce. "The Muddied Waters of Columbus, New Mexico." *The Americas* 32 (July, 1975): 72-98. This historiographical essay for the serious student explores why Villa raided Columbus, New Mexico. The author argues that the reason for the raid is less important than the result, since the Punitive Expedition helped the United States Army better prepare for World War I.

*Judith R. Johnson*

# HEITOR VILLA-LOBOS

*Born:* March 5, 1887; Rio de Janeiro, Brazil
*Died:* November 17, 1959; Rio de Janeiro, Brazil
*Area of Achievement:* Music
*Contribution:* Villa-Lobos' compositions number more than two thousand in authentic Brazilian style, which he cultivated and popularized throughout the world. He has also been a champion of Brazilian folk melodies, traveling through all areas of Brazil in search of melodies and rhythms that he has published and used as bases for compositions.

*Early Life*

Heitor Villa-Lobos was born on March 5, 1887, in Rio de Janeiro, Brazil. He showed great interest in music as a young child and enjoyed sitting quietly as he listened to simple songs long before he could speak. At the age of six, Villa-Lobos began studying cello with his father as teacher. He held great interest in the sounds and technique of all musical instruments and learned throughout his life to play most, if not all, of the instruments commonly used in the symphony orchestra. Villa-Lobos attended school as a child in Rio de Janeiro, working on his music training after school with his father and anyone else he could find to teach him.

Tragedy struck the Villa-Lobos family when in 1898 Heitor's father died. The family was forced to find small jobs to provide income in a very depressed economy. Young Villa-Lobos, being only eleven years old, was forced to quit his formal schooling and perform in café and theater orchestras that were small and amateur. Rehearsal times made it impossible for Villa-Lobos to attend school, and he continued to study on his own, in what spare time he could find.

During this financially strained period of time, music became more of a means of survival than a course of study to Villa-Lobos, and, except for a few lessons in harmony and counterpoint from Agnello Franca and Francisco Braga, Villa-Lobos became a self-instructed musician and composer, as he spent many hours after his local jobs poring over borrowed scores and music texts. Because of his lack of training in traditional methods, Villa-Lobos ventured into his own realm of music construction. His originality and impatience with accepted harmonic rules manifested themselves very early in his career.

*Life's Work*

In 1905, the interest that Villa-Lobos had found in Brazilian folk music led him on an extended trip through the northern states of Brazil, collecting popular folk songs and rhythmic patterns. Finally, in 1907, the financial position of his family had settled somewhat to where he could again enter school. Villa-Lobos began music composition studies at the National Institute of Music, where he studied intently with Frederico Nascimento. In between his studies, he continued to travel throughout Brazil in search of new songs and techniques.

In 1912, Villa-Lobos undertook his fourth and longest expedition deep into the interior of Brazil, accompanied by another musician named Gaetano Donizetti. During their three-year journey, they gathered a rich collection of folk songs from deep within the country, where the natives provided them with all the music they could gather. This experience in the Indian and Negro music forces influenced Villa-Lobos in many of his later compositions as he was able to call upon these remembered experiences for an almost unending source of musical suggestions. Returning to Rio de Janeiro in 1915, after three years of travel, Villa-Lobos presented a concert of his music on November 13, creating a sensation throughout the audience by the exuberance of his melodies and rhythms and the radical character of his idiom.

An ardent patriot of his homeland, Villa-Lobos resolved from his earliest steps in composition to use Brazilian song materials as the source of his thematic inspiration. Occasionally he used actual quotations from folk songs. Much more often, however, he used the folk songs as thematic germs, or suggestions, from which he wrote melodies in an authentic Brazilian style but of his own invention. In his desire to relate Brazilian folk resources to universal values, he wrote a unique series of compositions entitled *Bachianas brasileiras*, which consists of five suites. Number one is for the very unexpected instrumentation of eight celli; number two is for eight celli and soprano voice. Number three reaches the largest use of forces as it is composed for solo piano and orchestra, and number four begins to decline in numbers again, as it employs solo voice and small chamber orchestra. Number five, the last of the suites, returns to the use of eight celli and voice. Starting small, peaking in the middle, and shrinking to the end, these pieces are a fine example not only of Villa-Lobos' imagination but also of his orchestral techniques. Writing for eight celli is a challenge that Villa-Lobos completed very successfully. This set of five suites features Brazilian melorhythms being treated by almost Bach-like traditional counterpoint, which creates a sensation of exciting dance rhythms with flowing accompaniments.

In 1916, Villa-Lobos met the famous and artistically perfect pianist, Arthur Rubinstein, who became his ardent admirer. Rubinstein subsequently performed many of Villa-Lobos' pieces at concerts throughout Europe and the United States, including the very difficult composition *Rudepoema*, which Villa-Lobos had dedicated to Rubinstein. Through the worldwide success of Rubinstein, the compositions of Villa-Lobos began to have an impact on the international scene and were no longer kept within the borders of Brazil.

The five-year period from 1916 to 1921 saw the creation of Villa-Lobos' first six symphonies. The first three are written for traditionally organized symphony orchestra, while the fourth adds to the orchestra a large chorus. Symphony number five employs the orchestra, chorus, and symphonic band. Villa-Lobos' last symphony of this period, number six, is the only one of his first group of symphonies to be remembered by a subtitle, *The Indian Symphony.*

In 1923, Villa-Lobos was surprised to receive a stipend from the Brazilian government to study abroad. This government-sponsored opportunity was almost unheard of in most parts of the world and especially in Brazil, but with the surprise came an opportunity that Villa-Lobos had long secretly awaited: to study in Europe. His visit to Europe extended to nearly four years; he lived in Paris but enjoyed many excursions to London, Vienna, Lisbon, and Berlin. His main source of inspiration came through the French Impressionist musician Darius Milhaud, who introduced him to many other European composers.

A purely Brazilian form that Villa-Lobos successfully cultivated is the *choros*, a popular dance marked by incisive rhythm and songful balladlike melody. Villa-Lobos expanded the *choros* to embrace a wide variety of forms, from a solo instrumental to a large orchestral work with chorus. Villa-Lobos wrote his fourteen *choros* pieces between 1920 and 1929. According to Villa-Lobos, *choros* means "serenade," and is a synthesis of the various elements in Brazilian music, Indian, African, and popular folk melody, in which the harmonic treatment represents a stylization of the original material. These striking compositions are rhapsodic and free in structure.

Villa-Lobos returned home to Rio de Janeiro in 1926, determined to continue his career in composition with his new-found love of Impressionism. Composition had to take a backseat for some time, however, as he was engaged as director of musical education for the São Paulo public school system in 1930. After two successful years in this position, he assumed the important post of superintendent of musical and artistic education in Rio de Janeiro. In these positions he introduced bold innovations of using the cultivation of Brazilian songs and dances as the basis of music study in the public schools.

In 1929, after many careful years of study and categorization of pieces, Villa-Lobos published a book of Brazilian folk music under the title *Alma do Brasil*. He also compiled a selection of folk songs arranged for chorus, entitled *Guia Pratico*, which has been widely used in the public school system of Brazil and teaches music basics to students, while introducing them to their homeland culture.

An experimenter by nature, Villa-Lobos devised a graphic method of composition, using as material geometrical contours of drawings, shapes, structures, and the like. In 1940, Villa-Lobos used this method as he composed

*The New York Skyline* for the World's Fair, in which he used as his source of inspiration a photograph of the city, from which he devised his melodic material.

In 1944, Villa-Lobos made his first tour of the United States, conducting many of his own works. During this period of personal unrest as well as world unrest, Villa-Lobos established the Brazilian Academy of Music in Rio de Janeiro in 1947. With this establishment came the desire to make Rio his permanent home, from which he continued to venture out on conducting tours but to which he always returned.

Between 1945 and 1956, Villa-Lobos wrote six more symphonies. His seventh, subtitled the *American* symphony was premiered in 1945. Villa-Lobos received praise throughout the United States when his eleventh symphony was premiered in Boston on March 2, 1956, with Villa-Lobos conducting. His last symphony, number twelve, followed close behind with the premier performance at the American Music Festival in Washington, D.C., April 20, 1958.

An exceptionally prolific composer, Villa-Lobos also wrote many operas, ballets, chamber pieces, choruses, piano works, solo songs, and instrumental solo pieces. His list of works numbers more than two thousand, and many of his most popular compositions are for massive and diverse musical forces. Villa-Lobos holds the record for the largest performance at any one time as he conducted more than forty thousand voices in a stadium outside Rio de Janeiro. For one composer to run the gamut of solo music to vast combinations of performers is remarkable enough but to be successful and competent in this endeavor is left to only a few composers, such as Wolfgang Amadeus Mozart, Ludwig van Beethoven, Gustav Mahler, and Villa-Lobos.

In addition to his work as a composer and conductor, Villa-Lobos was a champion of music education. He organized the Orfeao de Professores, a training school for teachers through which his system of music education has been carried throughout the nation of Brazil. He made enormous and exhaustive collections of folk and popular Brazilian music and arranged, classified, and traced to their original sources these melodies. Because of his care and interest in national musical pride, Villa-Lobos represented Brazil at the 1936 International Congress for Music Education in Prague, where he was honored for his nationalistic efforts. His music has long been known in Europe, and two festivals of his works were given in Paris in 1927 in conjunction with the Concerts Lamoureaux, and another concert was given in 1929. In 1938, Villa-Lobos was represented at the sixth International Festival of Contemporary Music in Venice.

### Summary

Heitor Villa-Lobos is one of the most original and imaginative composers of the twentieth century. His lack of formal academic training has never been considered a detriment to his work but rather the element that compelled him to create a technique all his own, curiously eclectic yet admirably suited to his musical ideas. In the ever-changing patterns and styles of the mixed-up twentieth century, it takes a determined artist to know what he wants to achieve and to know what to take from the popular society and what to discard in order to fulfill his purposes. Villa-Lobos was such an artist.

*Bibliography*

Austin, William W. *Music in the Twentieth Century: From Debussy Through Stravinsky.* New York: W. W. Norton, 1966. This source discusses the vast amount of music composed by Villa-Lobos and describes in detail some of his most famous works.

Chase, Gilbert. *The Music of Spain.* 2d ed. New York: Dover, 1959. This book provides a lengthy bibliography that provides further study into the life of Villa-Lobos and Spanish music in general.

Ewen, David. *David Ewen Introduces Modern Music.* Philadelphia: Chilton, 1962. Ewen provides an interesting life sketch and a chronological list and description of Villa-Lobos' works. Good reading for young people.

Mariz, Vasco. *Heitor Villa-Lobos.* 2d rev. ed. Washington, D.C.: Brazilian American Cultural Institute, 1970. This book discusses the life and works of the great composer, providing insights, explanations, and details from a Brazilian point of view.

Myers, Rollo H., ed. *Twentieth Century Music.* New York: Orion Press, 1968. A discussion of the various instruments and sounds needed to produce Villa-Lobos' music. It also discusses score techniques and musical comparisons to the works of other composers.

Salzman, Eric. *Twentieth-Century Music: An Introduction.* Englewood Cliffs, N.J.: Prentice-Hall, 1967. This text compares Villa-Lobos' Brazilian nationalisim with his studies in French Impressionism, providing a brief summary of the subject.

Slonimsky, Nicolas. *Music of Latin America.* Reprint. New York: Da Capo Press, 1972. This book provides interesting reading about the sources of inspiration for much of Villa-Lobos' music as well as details into the composer's life that endear him to the reader.

*Robert Briggs*

# VO NGUYEN GIAP

*Born:* September 1, 1912; An Xa, Vietnam, French Indochina

*Areas of Achievement:* The military, government, and politics
*Contribution:* As chief Vietnamese Communist military strategist and expert guerrilla warfare tactician, Giap was architect of the Viet Minh victory over the French in 1954 (which ended French colonialism in Southeast Asia). Afterward he officially served as North Vietnam's defense minister and directed the military campaigns of the 1960's and 1970's that led to final victory over U.S. and South Vietnamese forces in 1975.

## *Early Life*

Vo Nguyen Giap, whose first name means "force" and last name means "armor," was born at An Xa in Quang Binh Province, a poor region of central Vietnam. He was reared in a lower-middle-class family of high educational attainment. His father, an ardent anticolonialist scholar who supported the family by cultivating rice, was determined to have his son educated and scraped together enough money to send him to a private school, Quoc Hoc Secondary School, in Hue. It was run by Ngo Dinh Kha, the father of Ngo Dinh Diem (future president of South Vietnam and enemy of Giap).

Quoc Hoc Secondary School was also attended by Ho Chi Minh, and there the young Giap began to read Ho's pamphlets, smuggled into Vietnam from abroad. Giap also acquired anticolonial and nationalistic political ideas from Phan Bio Chau, a veteran revolutionary who was then under house arrest at Hue but who was allowed to chat informally with interested parties. While still a student at Hue in 1926, Giap joined the Vietnamese Revolutionary Youth Association, known as the Thanh Nien, which Ho had helped to establish. At age fourteen, he was already becoming a bona fide revolutionary and disciple of Ho.

In 1930, at age eighteen, Giap was arrested by French security police as a supporter of revolutionary agitation. He had been helping to lay the groundwork for the Indochinese Communist Party, which was organized by Ho that year with the help of members of the Thanh Nien in Hanoi, Saigon, and Hue (where young Giap was involved). Giap was sentenced to three years in prison but was paroled after a few months. After his release from jail, he resumed his involvement in nationalistic anticolonial politics as well as the Communist Party, of which he became a recognized founding member.

Giap left Hue for Hanoi in order to study law at the French-run University of Hanoi. In 1937, he obtained a doctorate and went to work at Thang Long College, teaching history and writing articles in French and Vietnamese for nationalist newspapers. Giap converted many fellow teachers and students to his political views. In 1938, Giap married Minh Thai, daughter of the dean of the faculty of letters at the college; together they worked to further the Indochinese Communist Party. Their life together was not a long one. In 1939, just before the Japanese occupation of Indochina, the Party was outlawed. Giap went to China to get military help, but his wife was arrested by the French and died in prison in 1941, along with their infant daughter. Giap's sister-in-law, arrested for terrorism, was guillotined in Saigon at the same time. Those events left Giap with profound anti-French feelings as he entered a new and intense phase of his life.

*Life's Work*

As a teacher in Hanoi in 1937 and 1938, Giap developed a great admiration for Napoleon I, with whom, as a military leader, he later was said to identify. Decades afterward, former students recalled his lectures on Napoleon's campaigns, how he recounted the battles in brilliant detail as though he were the great commander himself or preparing to become one like him. After 1939, Giap would spend much of his life practicing the same profession as the man whom history had taught him to admire so much. It is ironic that the profession was practiced against Napoleon's homeland.

Once in China, Giap joined his political mentor, Ho, and became his military aide. When France was defeated by Germany in 1940, Ho, Giap, and Pham Van Dong worked out plans to advance Vietnamese nationalist goals. Crossing the border from China into Vietnam in January, 1941, the trio prepared to organize the League for the Independence of Vietnam, a coalition of various exile forces dedicated to liberating their country from foreign occupation or rule. Better known as the Viet Minh, the League was created in May of 1941. At Ho's direction, Giap also organized a Viet Minh army of liberation and trained it with China's help. By December, 1944, Giap's army began to wage guerrilla warfare against the Japanese, who had completely overrun Indochina.

Described as a cynic in action, Giap first collaborated with the French when they were driven into the mountains by the Japanese. His commandos moved against Hanoi, the occupied Vietnamese capital, in the spring of 1945, but, after the bombing of Hiroshima (early August, 1945), Giap made overtures to the Japanese, from whom he hoped to get arms. Giap's brief collaboration with the Japanese paid off in late August, 1945, when they let his forces into Hanoi ahead of the Allies. The Allies were then put in the position of having to deal with Giap and Ho.

With the abdication of Emperor Bao Dai, Ho proclaimed Vietnamese independence in September, 1945. He became president of the new nation, and Vo Nguyen Giap was selected as minister of defense and state. Unfortunately, Giap, who was already viewed as being Moscow-oriented, could not refrain from passionately expressing hatred for France at a time when Ho was trying to foster a favorable public image of his government, especially on the international scene. Giap, therefore, was dropped briefly from the cabinet. Ultimately, however, the French were unwilling to give up their claims to Vietnam by recognizing its independence. When frustrating negotiations finally broke down altogether, Ho declared a national war of resistance. Giap, still commander in chief of the army, returned to the cabinet as minister of defense.

Actually, it was Giap who issued the first call to arms on December 19, 1945 (the official starting date for the French Indochina War), as Ho was sick in bed at the time. Outnumbered and poorly supplied at times, Giap took his ragtag army into the northern Tonkinese Mountains, built it into a sixty-thousand-man guerrilla force, and prepared a plan of calculated harassment of the French. In Giap's strategy, guerrilla resistance was to be the initial phase, preparatory to more conventional warfare which could culminate in a full-scale counteroffensive and final defeat of the enemy. Giap's training manual, a refinement of Mao Tse-tung's ideas, stressed the importance of surprise in guerrilla warfare. The feint, the ambush, and the diversion were important tactical elements. Though an army might be outnumbered ten to one strategically, careful use of guerrilla tactics could cause the opponent to disperse his force so widely that he then would become outnumbered ten to one at the point chosen for attack. Giap also taught the necessity of maintaining the allegiance and support of the peasantry.

General Giap began his drive against the French gradually by harassing the most isolated French garrisons, bottling up their defenders so as to leave the countryside open to the Viet Minh. As his strength increased, Giap accelerated the pace of his attacks and directed them against larger French garrisons. Sometimes the French would withdraw from positions, abandoning precious artillery, mortars, thousands of rifles, and thousands of tons of ammunition.

In 1951, Giap lost momentum by overstepping his own plans and attacking key sectors rashly and prematurely, aiming to dramatize his supremacy over the French. Yet after pulling back and learning from his errors, Giap's forces regained the initiative and enjoyed success. By late 1953, the French were tiring of a war which had already cost them 170,000 casualties and $10 billion. Their commanders decided that Dien Bien Phu would become the mooring point from which they could stop Giap and inflict a stunning defeat on the Vietnamese that would end the war.

The French fortress of Dien Bien Phu was located in a valley 180 miles west of Hanoi. By early 1954, the French had parachuted more than twelve thousand men into the area. Not knowing that Giap had acquired one hundred American-made 105-mm howitzers, that he had spent three months deploying fifty thousand men at the site, and that the Viet Minh had dragged the artillery up to the heights above the valley, the French hoped to lure the Vietnamese general into battle there. (They need not have worried about

Giap failing to engage them.) Equally important was the fact that of the thirteen-thousand-man French fighting force, only half were qualified for combat, a fact discounted by French leadership because of their arrogance and vanity. Giap's army trapped the French within the bastion, and, after fifty-five days of bombardment, the few survivors surrendered to Giap, having lost four thousand dead and almost eight thousand missing. Giap thus became the first military leader to defeat a major Western army on the Asian continent and was known as the Tiger of Dien Bien Phu.

At Geneva, Switzerland, in July, 1954, the Vietnamese and French signed an official cease-fire agreement. Representatives of world powers also concluded that Vietnam was to be divided at the seventeenth parallel, into northern and southern sections. The Communist government of Ho Chi Minh would rule in North Vietnam (officially called the Democratic Republic of Vietnam), while the French would have some voice in a South Vietnamese government until the Vietnamese people themselves, voting in a 1956 national election, would decide the fate of their entire country. Those elections were never held, and gradually the United States replaced the weary French as the Western power in South Vietnam.

Despairing of ever reunifying Vietnam through legal means, nationalists in South Vietnam went underground and formed the Viet Cong guerrilla force, which began conducting an armed revolt against the U.S.-sponsored regime of Ngo Dinh Diem. Upon the division of Vietnam in July, 1954, General Giap had become deputy prime minister, minister of defense, and commander of all the armed forces of North Vietnam. He began sending aid to the Viet Cong, and the United States reciprocated with aid to the south. This mutual intervention escalated into full-fledged war in 1965. Giap sent whole divisions of North Vietnamese regulars into the south to fight alongside the Viet Cong and assigned his associate, General Nguyen Chi Thanh, to direct operations in the south. Giap and Thanh often disagreed over the conduct of the war, and when the latter was killed in action in 1967 Giap took direct control of Communist military operations in the south.

Giap's masterstroke of 1968 was his execution of the Tet Offensive, in which he led the Americans to believe that he was planning a Dien Bien Phu-type attack on the Marine outpost at Khe Sanh. Then, during the Tet (lunar new year) holiday, while Americans were concentrating on Khe Sanh, Giap launched a sweeping offensive against cities as well as military and government compounds throughout South Vietnam with a Communist force of more than thirty-six thousand troops. Though his losses numbered some fifteen thousand, Giap's bold move was regarded as a moral and psychological victory, demonstrating that the Viet Cong, with the help of the peasantry (which Giap had advocated for many years), could strike at will all over South Vietnam against the world's mightiest military power. The Tet Offensive also reminded the world of Giap's brilliance and strength of will. From

1976 (when the two Vietnams were finally reunited) to 1980, Giap served as Vietnam's national defense minister and was confirmed as the united country's deputy prime minister. He was a full member of the Politburo of the Vietnamese Communist Party until 1982.

*Summary*

Throughout the long years of his military service, Vo Nguyen Giap came to be seen as indispensable to the cause of an independent, unified Vietnam, even in the face of resentment from some Vietnamese. His successes boosted him to a position of popular hero second only to Ho but at the same time displayed the great brutality of which he was capable. In 1969, he admitted that North Vietnam had then already lost half a million troops against the United States and South Vietnamese regime, but he would have his forces continue to fight for another fifty years if necessary. Twenty-five years earlier, as he led his liberation army into the Dinh Ca Valley and liquidated government officials as well as wealthy farmers, he gave cruel force to his oft-repeated slogan: Every minute 100,000 men die all over the world—life and death of human beings means nothing.

Giap is to be regarded as Vietnam's most important modern military leader, theoretically and practically. He is universally recognized as an authority on and practitioner of modern guerrilla warfare. Giap's brilliance as a military strategist and tactician not only led to the end of the French colonialist regime in Vietnam but also was responsible for driving the Americans from the country and bringing about the fall of South Vietnam in 1975. Giap's genius lay in his ability to articulate and carry out the relationship of Communist ideology to military strategy. He was able to animate a conservative society and turn a group of medieval peasants into an army capable of defeating world powers.

Without question Giap was unbending on matters of duty. A veteran French officer of the first Indochinese War once summed up the tiny general (he was only five feet in height) succinctly when he said he was an implacable enemy and would follow to the end his dream and his destiny. Giap was more like Napoleon than the French themselves realized.

*Bibliography*

Fall, Bernard B. *The Two Viet-Nams: A Political and Military Analysis*. New York: Frederick A. Praeger, 1963. Though written at a time when the U.S. military was beginning to escalate its involvement in South Vietnam, this scholarly work provides an excellent discussion of the conflicts and wars in Vietnam that arose out of colonialism and outside (especially Western) involvement in that country. Against this backdrop, Fall presents fascinating glimpses of Giap, his thinking, and his role in revolutionary activities.

Gerassi, John. *North Vietnam: A Documentary.* Indianapolis: Bobbs-Merrill, 1968. Written by a reporter and member of the first investigating team for the International War Crimes Tribunal, this book is a collection of documents (along with the author's observations) prepared by the North Vietnamese concerning U.S. aggression in North Vietnam. Its value for a study of Giap is its presentation of some twenty pages of material eloquently written by Giap detailing the United States violations of the 1954 Geneva Agreements. The book is polemical in nature in that it is antiwar.

Huyen, N. Khac. *Vision Accomplished? The Enigma of Ho Chi Minh.* New York: Macmillan, 1971. A native of Indochina, Huyen lived under Ho's regime for seven years. Though specifically not about Giap, the work nevertheless presents, in thorough fashion, the important association and points of contact between Giap and Ho—the twin pillars of Vietnamese nationalism. It is virtually impossible to understand Giap thoroughly without understanding something of his connection with Ho.

Karnow, Stanley. *Vietnam: A History.* New York: Viking, 1983. Perhaps the finest single volume on the history of war in Vietnam, Karnow does an excellent job of tracing Giap's role in fighting the first and second Indochinese wars against the background of the whole history of the country.

O'Neill, Robert J. *General Giap: Politician and Strategist.* New York: Praeger, 1969. Though deficient in some respects, this modestly sized work (219 pages) represents the first book-length English-language biography on Giap. The author traces his intellectual, political, and military development against the background of the growth of nationalism and Communism in Indochina. The author served in the military in Vietnam from 1966 to 1967. The weakness of the book is its failure to discuss in greater detail Giap's contributions to guerrilla warfare by creating an army out of peasants.

Roy, Jules. *The Battle of Dienbienphu.* Translated by Robert Baldick. New York: Harper & Row, 1965. This outstanding work discusses what some consider to be Giap's greatest success—victory over the French. The most significant aspects of the book are not the details of the battle itself but the motives and reasoning of the leaders of the two combatants. Giap's ability comes through clearly in this well-written account.

Vo Nguyen Giap. *Banner of People's War: The Party's Military Line.* New York: Praeger, 1970. This short book written by the general himself constitutes a statement on Communist political and military strategy in the Vietnamese war against U.S. intervention. An important theme in Giap's text is that the Vietnamese Communist Party's military ideology is part of the two-thousand-year history of Vietnamese resistance to foreign aggression. He sees the struggle as a just war of national liberation against a bully.

*Andrew C. Skinner*

# ÉDOUARD VUILLARD

*Born:* November 11, 1868; Cuiseaux, France
*Died:* June 21, 1940; La Baule, France
*Area of Achievement:* Art
*Contribution:* Vuillard's wide experience in graphic art for the theater taught him to paint large-scale decorations, and, through his experiments with the formal elements of painting, he helped the Nabis school of painting to fulfill its primary ambition: to gain acceptance for decorative paintings.

## *Early Life*

Jean-Édouard Vuillard, the youngest of three children, was born at Cuiseaux, Saône-et Loire, in France, on November 11, 1868. After Édouard's father retired as a colonial officer, he married Marie Michaud, the daughter of a textile manufacturer. He died in 1883, and his wife, Marie, went into business as a corset maker in order to support the family. The household, though frugal, was not poverty-stricken. Marie, Vuillard's mother, worked hard and performed her daily duties with courage and a cheerful air. She remained close to her bachelor son until her death in 1928—when he was sixty years old—and she exerted a strong influence on him throughout her life.

Vuillard's habit of collecting colored boxes and pictures demonstrated an interest in art at an early age. He began his schooling under the stringently ascetic Marist Brothers, continued at the École Rocroy, then attended the Lycée Condorcet, where he met the two young painters who were to be the most important influences upon him: Ker-Xavier Roussel and Maurice Denis. (Denis is given credit for "recruiting" Vuillard into the Nabis.) Vuillard failed twice in his attempt to gain acceptance at the École des Beaux-Arts, but he was accepted on his third try. After two years of study in the crude barracks atmosphere there, the three young painters gradually began to spend more time at the Académie Julian, where they studied under Adolphe-William Bouguereau and Tony Robert Fleury. At this new school they met Pierre Bonnard and Paul Sérusier, the student monitor (*massier*) and leader of the Nabis, a secret brotherhood of discontented students. The Hebrew word, *nabis* means prophet, and these young men considered themselves to be prophets of Paul Gauguin's radical new synthetist discoveries.

## *Life's Work*

The year 1889 marked an important turning point in Vuillard's life. His first drawing was accepted for exhibition at the Salon, and this was the year that Gauguin, Émile Bernard, and their friends staged a significant exhibition at the Café Volponi. In 1889, he was still more interested in naturalism and the Barbizon school painters at the Palais des Beaux-Arts than in Gauguin's ideas, but a year later Denis had succeeded in recruiting him as a member of the Nabis.

Sérusier was the early spokesman for the Nabis: In reaction to photography's encroachment upon the domain once occupied by artists and in direct contrast to the attitude of the Impressionists, he maintained that painters—to avoid becoming machinelike copyists—should work only from memory. This practice was intended to simplify the forms and exaggerate the colors that nature inspired. This idea stems directly from the earlier concept that Bernard had persuaded Gauguin to accept. Bernard believed that the imagination retained only that which is essential and thus simplified the image because only the significant and the symbolic are retained by memory. This practice, he believed, generated a simplified, rather flat, silhouette and preserved the purity of color.

Denis had published an article, which came to exert an important influence on Vuillard's direction, in 1890 in which he argued for the primacy of formal elements over content in order to convey emotion in the New-Traditionism: "[A] painting, before it is a war horse, a nude woman or some anecdote, is first and foremost a flat surface covered with colours arranged in a certain order." Consequently, late in 1889 Vuillard wrote in his notebooks that he had begun to work from memory, painting what he called "little daubs" (*petites salissures*). He painted these little daubs quickly using a flat, simplified technique—sometimes with textured dots—on small panels or pieces of cardboard. In 1890 he began to use raw saturate color in some of his paintings and in the programs he designed for the Théâtre Libre, but he never entirely deserted his earlier use of low-key tones of color, carefully adjusted in value to avoid strong contrast in dark and light.

Vuillard, like the other Nabis, attempted to exploit the symbolic in order to express emotion and experience. He wrote that a woman's head created a certain emotion in him, and he wanted to paint only that emotion; he believed that details such as a nose or an ear were of no importance. Both the strong, raw color and the simplified silhouette—much like the Japanese woodblock prints which were so common in Paris during this period—were critical elements in this attempt to express emotion.

During the early 1890's, Vuillard began to enjoy some success; the critics were writing about him, and several collectors began to buy his work. He had his first two shows in 1892: the first at the offices of *La Revue blanche*, the second at le Barc de Boutteville's gallery. After 1894, his work was widely exhibited in galleries and exhibitions.

The graphic arts were enjoying a strong revival during the 1890's, and Vuillard worked in several media: prints, stained glass, colored lithographs, stage sets, and advertising playbills for the theater. The playbills and stage sets—including sets for Henrik Ibsen's plays—that he painted for the experimental Théâtre de l'Oeuvre are recognized as an important step in the development of his style.

During the last decade of the nineteenth century, Vuillard kept his pictorial space ambiguous and rather shallow—nearly flat—in the mode of the day: His designs and flat pictorial space often suggest tapestries. Like Gauguin, Pierre-Cécile Puvis de Chavannes, and most of the decorative painters of his time who sought to avoid the reflective surface and the illusion of depth associated with oil paint, Vuillard preferred a dry matte paint surface. Consequently, he used distemper as a medium in the four panels and continued thereafter to use this medium almost exclusively in both his decorative panels and his easel painting. This medium, coupled with his tendency to build up his surfaces quickly without allowing time for the first coats to dry, has led to severe cracking in some of his paintings.

Vuillard was not interested in painting posed figures or picturesque views, so he acquired a box camera in 1897 that he constantly used, as some painters use drawings, to record the candid, lifelike visual information that he painted: informal groupings and conversations, in public or at home. By 1898 his paintings were becoming more complex, rather than simplified and reductive. He began, perhaps with the help of the camera, to record the cluttered details and patterns of interior settings.

After the turn of the century, Vuillard abandoned the shallow, ambiguous pictorial space and flat figures of his earlier paintings and began to paint street scenes and landscapes in which he depicted a considerable amount of depth. These paintings featured a more volumetric treatment of the figure and a more realistic, wide-angle depiction of space, much like the fish-eye lens on an early camera. Influenced by Paul Valéry, he began to observe and paint details with more complexity.

The Nabis disbanded toward the end of the 1890's as the stronger talents achieved independent fame and no longer identified with the group. In 1899, at an exhibition of the Nabis and the Neoimpressionists at the Durand-Ruel Gallery, critics singled out Vuillard and Bonnard as the best artists in the exhibition. During the first years of the twentieth century, both Bonnard and Vuillard regularly exhibited and sold paintings at the Bernheim-Jeune Gallery and consequently enjoyed a great degree of financial security. Vuillard was given many commissions for both decorations and portraits between 1910 and 1914. In 1905, the year of the Fauves and their color revolution, the critic François Monot wrote that Vuillard was one of the first colorists of the time. Yet he was often criticized for carelessness in technique because of areas left blank or treated too quickly. He left blank areas of warm brown cardboard to harmonize with his color, and this was sometimes criticized as an affection, a passing fad.

During the last twenty years of his life, Vuillard's work focused on portraiture. The composition in these portraits is often organized in traditional "compositional climax." The bottom and particularly the top sections of the painting are simplified and composed of large inactive areas, while a transition is made toward the middle area of smaller more complex shapes and details, creating an area of visual activity. Toward the end of his life, his paintings moved toward realism, complexity, and detail, finally to create a writhing surface of detailed and complex minutiae. Yet, when Vuillard was consulted about the selection of more than three hundred of his works to be shown at the major retrospective exhibition at the Pavillon de Marsan in 1938, almost half of the works included in this exhibition had been executed during that early reductionist period before 1900. At the age of seventy-one years, Vuillard died at La Baule, France, on June 21, 1940.

*Summary*

Édouard Vuillard—the most famous member of the Nabis school of painting as well as an excellent realist painter—was best known for his "decorative" paintings of French gardens and interiors and his portraits of public men. Vuillard disliked theory and, influenced by Gauguin, relied on personal symbol, sensation, and instinct to express his emotional reaction to experience. During the course of his early career, Vuillard simplified his reductionist form and silhouette with ruthless discipline and relentless restraint to eliminate all unnecessary detail, but after the turn of the century he reversed priorities and direction to create a complex image of activity and detail.

During the first part of the twentieth century, the crucial split between the painters of classicism and the painters of genre in France was exemplified by Vuillard, the genre painter, and Denis, the classicist. Though Andy Warhol has been given credit for having reversed priorities in the relationship between fine art and graphic art, his accomplishment was preceded by the successes of Gauguin and Vuillard's group, the Nabis. Their efforts were directed primarily toward creating a decorative graphic art of such quality that it would have to be accepted in the same spirit, with the same respect, as the works of so-called fine artists. The success of this effort is demonstrated by the attention still accorded their work and their continuing influence upon painters during the twentieth century.

*Bibliography*

Boyer, Patricia Eckert, ed. *The Nabis and the Parisian Avant-Garde*. With essays by Patricia Eckert Boyer and Elizabeth Prelinger. New Brunswick, N.J.: Rutgers University Press and Jane Voorhees Zimmerli Art Museum, 1988. This 195-page book is an excellent catalog of the Voorhees Zimmerli Art Museum's exhibition of paintings from the Nabis group of painters. Several sections are devoted to Vuillard's place within the school, and it features a good chronology of the Nabis with 232 illustrations, forty in color.

Marx, Claude Roger. *Vuillard: His Life and Work*. New York: Éditions de la

Maison Française, 1946. Marx was Vuillard's original biographer, an early champion of the applied arts, and he has written extensively on Vuillard, beginning in the 1890's. The book (212 pages, 204 illustrations, eight in color) is well written and accurate.

Mauner, George L. *The Nabis: Their History and Their Art, 1888-1896*. New York: Garland, 1978. Though apparently a product of a subsidy press, this dissertation was written under the supervision of Meyer Shapiro. It is a solid scholarly work and the best-documented history of the Nabis school. Vuillard's contribution is well documented, and the book features 326 pages of text and 159 black-and-white illustrations—forty-seven by Vuillard.

Thompson, Belinda. *Vuillard*. New York: Abbeville Press, 1988. Brief and easy to read but accurate and incisive, this is an excellent book for the general reader. Contains 139 illustrations (about half in color). Documents his early life and training, his relationship with the Nabis, his success, and his role in the theater. A good select bibliography is to be found at the end of the book.

Vuillard, Édouard. *Edouard Vuillard*. Text by Stuart Preston. New York: Abrams, 1972. This is an excellent picture book with forty-six pages of text interspersed with seventy-three black-and-white illustrations, followed by forty full-page color plates, each accompanied by a page of text about the painting. In the back is a select bibliography of books and articles; most are written in French.

*William V. Dunning*

# JOACHIM WACH

*Born:* January 25, 1898; Chemnitz, Germany
*Died:* August 27, 1955; Orselina, Switzerland
*Area of Achievement:* Religion
*Contribution:* Wach distilled the descriptive requirements for a scientific definition of religious experience from his general theory of knowledge and understanding. He created the modern academic field of the history of religions out of and in contrast to preceding notions of comparative religion.

## *Early Life*

Joachim Wach was born in 1898 at Chemnitz in Saxony, the eldest child of three, to Felix Wach, who was food comptroller of Germany during World War I, and his wife, Katharina von Mendelssohn-Bartholdy. Joachim's paternal grandparents were Adolf Wach, prominent juridical counsellor to the King of Saxony, and subsequently professor of law, first at the University of Rostock, later at the University of Leipzig, until his death in 1926; and Lily, the youngest daughter of the composer Felix Mendelssohn. Joachim's mother was the granddaughter of Paul, brother to the composer Felix. While the two lines were thus related, they distinguished by the hyphen in the name their common descent from the brothers' grandfather, the eminent Jewish philosopher Moses Mendelssohn.

The immediate family had means and influence in imperial Germany. Joachim, while of remote Jewish ancestry and prosperity, was reared Lutheran, though with a governess who was devoutly Roman Catholic. Through her he had a childhood audience with the Bishop of Wurzburg, who gave him religious pictures that entered into his play at mass with his brother and sister.

The Latin of that tradition came as easily into his formative years as did the variety of cultural influences of his exposures to international acquaintances connected with both the academic world and the royal courts of Saxony and, through an aunt, Sweden. The family estate overlooked the Elbe River near Dresden, but, with the family fortune, it was confiscated by Adolf Hitler.

Aside from familial contacts and activities, involving music, drama, literature, and poetry—read and performed—Joachim's early education included classical and modern languages. In 1916, he completed examinations at the Vitzhumsche Gymnasium in Dresden, was commissioned a German army officer, and was sent to the Russian front, accompanied by his boxes of books. He learned Russian and Arabic while on duty, completed a summary of the history of Greek philosophy for his sister, and was forced to encounter, both as a philosophical and as an existential issue, the matter of death.

These ingredients came together in his personal religious life and in his intellectual development.

*Life's Work*

At the end of World War I, Wach began his serious studies in the history and philosophy of religion at Leipzig. He spent the year 1919 at the University of Munich, under the tutorage of a slightly older, comparably minded instructor, Friedrich Heiler, with whom Wach, at the other's insistence, read Sanskrit, and by whom he was introduced to Rudolf Otto's *Das Heilige* (1920; *The Idea of the Holy*, 1923). After the year 1919, Heiler went to Uppsala, Sweden, to study with Archbishop Nathan Soderblom, who had previously held the chair of religions at Leipzig. Heiler returned in 1920 to the position at Marburg, which he held for the rest of his life, and remained a close friend and continuing influence on Wach.

Wach went on to Berlin, where he came into contact with the major historians of Christian thought and institutions, Adolf von Harnack and Ernst Troeltsch, before returning in 1922 to Leipzig to receive his doctor of philosophy degree for a dissertation begun with Heiler. The method, scope, and structure of Wach's mind were already in evidence in this preliminary work.

Wach's concern for phenomenology grew out of his contact with Edmund Husserl at Freiburg, and similar attentiveness to the history of literature was a by-product of his attending the lectures of Friedrich Gundolf at Heidelberg. By early 1924, Wach had completed a more systematic study on *Religionswissenschaft: Prolegomena zu ihrer wissenschaftstheoretischen Grundlegung* (1924; the science of religion: prolegomena to its epistemological foundations) and was appointed privatdocent in the faculty of philosophy at Leipzig, where his grandfather was still active. Successively thereafter, Wach published (1925) a summary of the fundamental notions of Mahayana Buddhism and a survey of the influence of Friedrich Adolf Trendelenburg upon Wilhelm Dilthey, whose philosophy of history was crucial to Wach's own thought.

Wach was ready to lay out his major study of human "understanding," *Das Verstehen: Grundzuge einer Geschichte der hermeneutischen Theorie im 19. Jahrhundert* (1926-1933), in a series of three volumes illustrative of sequential developments in general interpretive theory. The first volume appeared in 1926 and explained the general German intellectual situation in "hermeneutics," or theory of interpretation, at the outset of the nineteenth century, with focal attention upon the liberal Berlin court preacher and theologian, Friedrich Schleiermacher. The second volume followed in 1929 with a survey, after a lengthy and erudite introduction, of the divergent notions of interpretation applied to biblical materials from Schleiermacher, through twenty-two mid-century German academics, to the conservative proponent of the Erlangen "school," Johann Hofmann. In that same year, Wach gave his inaugural lecture as professor in Leipzig on the philosophical history of the nineteenth century and the theology of history, and, in 1930, he was awarded the degree of doctor of theology from Heidelberg. Volume three, dealing with "understanding in historical research" from before Leopold von Ranke at the outset of the nineteenth century to the positivistic Germans who dominated its mid-years, did not appear until 1933.

The interim had seen Wach's publication of *Einführung in die religionssoziologie* (1931; introduction to religious sociology) and *Typen religiöser Anthropologie* (1932; types of religious anthropology). The former was systematic, the latter comparative of Eastern and Western intellectual traditions. In 1934, Wach brought to fruition his consideration of *Das Problem des Todes in der Philosophie unserer Zeit* (1934; the problem of death in the philosophy of our times). All of this output, and much of its mode of treatment, suffered a severe and jarring impact from the Nazi movement, which forced the government of Saxony to dismiss Wach from his academic post on April 10, 1935.

Fortuitously, Wach had received but days before, from an old friend, Robert Pierce Casey of Brown University, Providence, Rhode Island, the invitation to be visiting professor. In spite of concern for his family and friends, whom he would have to leave behind to the terrible events of war and holocaust, Wach accepted. His family moved into a small villa at Orselina above Locarno in Switzerland, to which he could be a periodic visitor. His father died late in the war, his spirit broken by the tragedy of such vast destruction to all that had been their previous life; his brother survived to become a Lutheran pastor in the new East Germany.

Wach never turned back. He settled readily into the life of the United States and was naturalized as a citizen in 1946. He became an active communicant in the Protestant Episcopal church. His visiting professorial status was regularized in 1937 at Brown, and he was called to head a newly created department of the history of religions at the University of Chicago in 1946. At Chicago, Wach had doctoral candidates, and the desired involvement in the total life of a theological faculty. In both institutions, he displayed concern not merely for the relation of religion to the modern secular university but especially for the students under the impact of secular modernity. He gave generously of time and energy to collective student affairs and to individual counseling needs.

Wach was a devout churchman, though never ordained. He was ill-equipped to handle modern gadgets, even something as simple as the plugging in of a radio, for which he depended upon those students of whom he was most fond and whose company he enjoyed. He got acquainted easily and remained available—a most comforting figure among awesome faculty to the new student. He knew one by name from the first introduction. Yet his systematic mode when lecturing would not tolerate a late arrival.

Wach had the disciplined mind of one trained in the late nineteenth century's academic ideals of "abandoning the haphazard" in scholarship, with none of the arrogance of an elitist. He demanded a precision of time, of vocabulary, and of style—illustrating a touch of formality within a gentle warmth of humanity. He knew the key figures of the world's religions and tried to make them accessible to his students, not only in books but also in person—Hindu, Buddhist, Muslim, and the various kinds of Christian—at a level of both intellectual rigor and spiritual depth.

He was working on a major synthesis, *The Comparative Study of Religions* (1958), when he was stricken, while visiting his mother and sister, by a severe heart attack from which he succumbed within a few weeks. This study and other manuscripts survived and have received posthumous publication.

Ironically, only weeks before Wach's death, in an effort to recompense "that great injustice which the Nazi government had done to this outstanding representative of German science," as his lifelong friend Heiler expressed it, the state of Hesse offered Wach the chair of systematic theology at Marburg once held by Rudolf Otto. In commitment to all that had become the new repository for his life's work, he declined to accept.

### *Summary*

Joachim Wach tried to find those few unifying definitions by which the great variety of phenomena of religious experience could be understood. He perceived that it was not humanly possible to express with finality those dimensions that were traditionally described as godlike or divine or revelatory. He did think it conceivable to arrive at some generalizations indicative of the human responsive posture toward the essential and substantive activities. Encounters at Chicago with theologians and philosophers of emergent naturalism may have been at odds with Wach's inherent Kantianism, but, when mediated by the Anglican archbishop, William Temple, "process" thought provided the kind of medium through which his own bent toward historically conditioned sociology could be given its dynamic form.

Wach identified the descriptive requirements for a scientific definition of religious experience in a few fundamental propositions. Religious experience is the total response of the total human personality to that which is apprehended as ultimate reality. This experience is the most intense of which the human is capable, and this experience impels the human to act. In the analysis of the religious experience, all expression falls within three categories: theoretical, practical, and sociological. Wach affirmed that religion cannot be the perspective of one. Even the psychological dimension of the experience must have a communal component, if it is to qualify as religious.

In contrast to Mircea Eliade, who succeeded Wach at Chicago and who sought to create a "history of religions" from the diverse phenomena without reference to variations in time and space, Wach saw the unity and universality of all religious experience within a system of metaphysical principles whose fundamental ingredient was "understanding." That understanding required expression, with due reference to the whole history of human "modes of thought" and conscientious concern for a theory of human inquiry. Only then might one propound the nature of "revelation" as the empirical element in knowledge, which does not exclude but lies beyond human thought. Wach concluded that "the real history of man is the history of religion."

*Bibliography*

Alles, Gregory D. "Wach, Eliade, and the Critique from Totality." *Numen* 35 (1988): 108-138. An evaluative essay reflecting upon the comparisons and contrasts between Wach and his successor.

Eliade, Mircea, and Joseph M. Kitagawa, eds. *The History of Religions: Essays in Methodology.* Chicago: University of Chicago Press, 1959. Within a volume collected in honor of Wach, Kitagawa's initial essay, "The History of Religions in America" (pages 1-30), places Wach within the context whereby a field of academic study was defined by his transitional role.

Kitagawa, Joseph Mitsuo. "The Life and Thought of Joachim Wach." In *The Comparative Study of Religions*. New York: Columbia University Press, 1958. To accompany the posthumous publication of the manuscript, upon which Wach was working at the time of his death, his former student and colleague wrote a major biographical statement. The volume is an outgrowth of a series of lectures given in India in 1952 and in American universities in 1954-1955.

__________. "The Nature and Program of the History of Religions Field." *The Divinity School News* 23, no. 4 (November 1, 1957): 13-25. The reconstruction of a department after the death of Wach and before the assumption of dominance by Eliade provided occasion to discuss Wach's understanding of "the history of religions" and the two kinds of "sociology of religion."

Wach, Joachim. "The Meaning and Task of the History of Religions (*Religionswissenschaft*)." In *The History of Religions: Essays on the Problem of Understanding*, edited by Joseph M. Kitagawa, Mircea Eliade, and Charles H. Long. Chicago: University of Chicago Press, 1967. In the first volume of a series of "Essays in Divinity," reflecting "the Chicago school," a translation of an article from Wach's German of 1935 was given priority of place to demonstrate the complete difference in method and interest of history of religions from comparative religion, whose transition Wach's appearance at Chicago had accomplished.

__________. *Understanding and Believing: Essays*. Edited with an introduction by Joseph M. Kitagawa. New York: Harper & Row, 1968. A series of minor writings on a variety of topics, some unpublished, some newly translated, were offered as memorial when Wach's manuscripts were gathered. A bibliography of Wach's works from 1922 to 1955 is included.

Wood, Charles Monroe. *Theory and Religious Understanding: A Critique of the Hermeneutics of Joachim Wach*. Missoula, Mont.: American Academy of Religion, 1975. Originally a doctoral dissertation at Yale (1972), this study examines Wach's method of interpretation as a derivative of his philosophical perspective on human knowledge and understanding.

*Clyde Curry Smith*

# LECH WAŁĘSA

*Born:* September 29, 1943; Popowo, Poland

*Areas of Achievement:* Trade unionism, government, and politics

*Contribution:* Wałęsa's receipt of the Nobel Peace Prize in 1983 underlined his contributions to peaceful political evolution in the Eastern Bloc. Wałęsa's role since 1980 as leader of Solidarnost (Solidarity) in pressuring the Polish leadership for recognition of proletariat demands that were not addressed by the country's government-controlled trade unions was capped by the Polish authorities in 1989 with the holding of free elections and the subsequent victory of the Solidarity-led ticket.

## *Early Life*

Lech Michal Wałęsa was born in Popowo, Poland, north of Warsaw on September 29, 1943, the son of a carpenter, Boleslaw Wałęsa, and his wife, Fela Kaminska. His father died of deprivations suffered during World War II in a Nazi concentration camp when Lech was eighteen months old; his mother later married her deceased husband's brother, Stanisław. Lech was reared with seven siblings in the straitened circumstances of postwar Poland.

Wałęsa was trained in a state agricultural school at Lipno as an electrician and, after completing his studies, served two years in the army. Wałęsa moved to Gdańsk in 1966, where he began working in the Lenin Shipyards as an electrician. Wałęsa was working in the shipyards in 1970 when rioting erupted over the high cost of food; more than one hundred people were killed in the subsequent unrest. The demonstrations brought down Władysław Gomułka's government, but little was ultimately achieved. The same year, Wałęsa married, and he and his wife eventually had eight children.

## *Life's Work*

Wałęsa was dismissed in April, 1976, for participating in protests over the decline in living standard concessions made in 1970 by the authorities to the workers after riots over declining living standards. Wałęsa was unemployed for the next four years, during which time he supported his family by taking odd jobs. During this period he participated in meetings of the Workers Self-Defense Committee and edited an underground paper, *The Coastal Worker*, critical of the government. In 1978, Wałęsa also became a founding member of the Free Trade Union of the Baltic Coast, which would later provide many leaders and ideas for Solidarity. As Wałęsa's political awareness grew, so did his scrapes with the authorities; by his own estimate, he was detained more than one hundred times by the authorities during 1976-1980. Polish consciousness was heightened in October, 1978, with the election of Cardinal of Kraków Karol Wojtyła as Pope John Paul II. John Paul returned to Poland in

June, 1979, for a nine-day visit to scenes of extraordinary national rejoicing.

Wałęsa's star again rose in August, 1980, when workers across Poland engaged in wildcat strikes protesting price increases. On July 1, the government had raised the prices of several types and cuts of meat 60 to 90 percent. In the Gdańsk Lenin Shipyards, events that summer were brought to a head by the dismissal for labor agitation of Anna Walentynowicz, an elderly woman who was six months short of receiving her retirement benefits. On August 14, the day that the strike began, Wałęsa climbed the fence and joined strikers in the Lenin Shipyards. The strike quickly spread throughout Poland, from the steelworkers at Nowa Huta to the Silesian coal mines. Intellectuals, peasants, and working men throughout Poland joined the labor unrest. More than 300,000 workers were shortly out on strike. The Gdańsk Lenin Shipyards' Inter-Factory Strike Committee, chaired by Wałęsa, presented a list of twenty-one demands to the government.

On August 31, 1980, the Polish government signed an accord with Wałęsa that granted unprecedented rights to labor organizations in a Communist country. Shortly thereafter, the first secretary, Edward Gierek, was dismissed. The right for workers to form independent trade unions was recognized, wage and benefit increases were granted, Catholic mass was broadcast on Sundays, censorship was eased, and political dissidents were freed. The 1980 strike that led to the formation of Solidarity drove Gierek's government from power. While Solidarity sought change from the authorities, it was careful not to offer challenges that would force the government's hand. Wałęsa and Solidarity called their innovations a "self-limiting revolution." As chairman of the National Commission of Solidarity, Wałęsa had enormous visibility.

Solidarity immediately attracted many followers; shortly before the imposition of martial law, Wałęsa numbered its followers at ten million. Wałęsa once described his role as that of a "democratic dictator"; goals are developed in a democratic context, and Wałęsa then sets himself to realize them. Despite his prominence and popularity, Wałęsa as the head of a broad democratic movement spent much of his time attempting to calm militants within his organization and striking to head off confrontation with the authorities. Such a broad-based movement had many shades of opinion within it, and Wałęsa as a realist attempted to rein in its more extreme members.

The Soviet Union began to take an increasingly harsh line toward its unreliable Western neighbor and ally. Most menacing was the massing of fifty-five Soviet divisions near Poland's eastern frontier. The nervous Polish government began to see Soviet intervention as an increasingly likely possibility.

Events continued to show the increasing influence of Solidarity; on March 27, 1981, the biggest organized protest in the Eastern Bloc occurred when thirteen million workers staged a four-hour strike to protest the beatings in Bydgoszcz of several Solidarity activists. Solidarity's influence extended into the countryside with the formation of Rural Solidarity, making possible a coalition of workers and peasants. The government responded to the increasing unrest by appointing General Wojciech Jaruzelski Party leader in addition to premier on October 18, 1981.

After the imposition of martial law on December 13, 1981, the Polish authorities began a campaign of vilification against Wałęsa, describing him as the "former head of a former union." Nearly six thousand individuals were taken into immediate custody, among them Wałęsa and the rest of the Solidarity leadership. The number interned rose eventually to more than ten thousand. More than ninety thousand were tried by civil courts in the first six months of martial law. All labor unions, including Solidarity, were dissolved by a law introduced on October 6, 1982. A protest strike at the Lenin Shipyards in Gdańsk was ended when the authorities militarized the shipyard. When Solidarity attempted to organize a nationwide protest strike in November, it failed miserably.

On the day Wałęsa was released from prison he stated, "In my future conduct I will be courageous, but also prudent, and there is nothing negotiable in this regard. I will talk and act, not on my knees, but with prudence." Wałęsa was restored to the Lenin Shipyard's payroll in January, 1983, although he did not formally return to work until April. Wałęsa continued to work to restore Solidarity's role in national affairs; shortly after his return to work he prophetically declared that Solidarity "was a moral force without whose participation Poland could not get out of the crisis." He constantly reiterated that it was not Solidarity's intention to overthrow the government but to better workers' lives. Solidarity banners were unfurled at rallies, and, despite the authorities' best efforts, Solidarity's underground continued to keep the organization and its values alive.

Martial law was suspended on December, 1982, and lifted on July 22, 1983. Despite the government's attempts to bury him in oblivion, Wałęsa and his vision continued to thrive. His contributions to human values were recognized in 1983 when he was awarded the Nobel Peace Prize. The news was given to him by Western correspondents; Wałęsa observed, "The world recognizes Solidarity's ideals and struggles."

As the Polish government continued to grapple with its problems, it considered approaching Wałęsa for assistance. In 1987, Jaruzelski created a consultative council to include people of disparate political views and extended an invitation to Wałęsa, who declined to join. Wałęsa's refusal was based on his observation that the new council would only have the ability to debate issues and policy but lack the ability to legislate change.

Wałęsa again reemerged as a force in Polish politics in the autumn of 1988, when the government initiated talks with him. Faced by an outbreak of wildcat strikes, the government proposed to Wałęsa that it would open talks about relegalizing Solidarity if Wałęsa would persuade the workers to return to work. After hard bargaining, Wałęsa ended the strikes. Wałęsa's durability has proven remarkable; the loyalty that Solidarity retained during its period of repression combined with other factors to force the Polish government to hold elections in the summer of 1989, in which Solidarity candidates did remarkably well. Wałęsa proved himself a masterful and patient politician.

Despite official hostility, Solidarity continued to prove a potential alternative to the country's increasingly desperate financial problems. Wałęsa waited and on April 5, 1989, signed an agreement lifting the governmental ban on Solidarity, allowing the organization to participate in the upcoming elections for the Sejm. The government had proven itself unable to cope with its accumulated financial problems; inflation had reached 200 percent and the foreign debt stood at $39 billion. The result was a very unpleasant surprise for the Polish Communist Party; of 261 contested seats, Solidarity won 260.

A further element strengthening the forces of change was the visit of U.S. President George Bush to Poland in July, 1989. Both the Polish government and Wałęsa appealed to Bush to extend aid in the form of credits and loans to Poland to an eventual level of $10 billion in order to strenghten the forces pushing toward a mixed economy. Bush unfortunately offered about one hundredth of the amount requested, putting a severe strain on Polish reformers who wish to avoid seeking Eastern Bloc support. Wałęsa negotiated with the Polish president Jaruzelski throughout August and September, 1989, to prepare the way for forming a government led by a Solidarity activist. Solidarity proved its influence by largely halting strikes during this period.

*Summary*

Lech Wałęsa's contribution to the liberalization of Polish political life cannot be overstated. A proletarian from a working-class background, Wałęsa had the courage and skill to force a government holding power to admit by its actions that it simply represented a dictatorship. Wałęsa consistently showed the greatest courage from the beginning of his organizing activities, suffering punishment for his efforts. A deeply religious man, he consistently displayed moderation in the face of provocation by the authorities. In the early days of Solidarity, his abilities to compromise avoided splitting the movement between the moderate and more extreme elements.

The election on August 24, 1989, and subsequent appointment of longtime Solidarity supporter Tadeuz Malowiecki, a lay Catholic lawyer and journalist, as prime minister represents the first time since 1945 that a government in Eastern Europe has been led by a non-Communist. While the Communist Party retains four influential ministerial portfolios to Solidarity's eight positions, Solidarity has been able to achieve the first coalition government in the Eastern Bloc led by non-Communists since 1945. The example that Solidarity provided to the rest of the Eastern Bloc had profound reverberations in 1989 in East Germany, Czechoslovakia, Hungary, Romania, and Bulgaria.

Wałęsa's and Solidarity's examples of nonviolent resistance will continue to influence Eastern European politics for many years to come. Despite Poland's crippling economic legacy from its Communist rulers, Solidarity's government has the immense advantage that it truly represents a "government of the people," the first that Poland has had since World War II. It is a mark of the high esteem in which Wałęsa is held worldwide that when he visited Washington in late 1989, he was invited to address a joint session of Congress, being only the second foreigner ever to be accorded this honor. Wałęsa intends to pursue a peaceful middle path; he stated, "we want to take what is good from capitalism—what is good for the people, what the people will take from it, but we also want to take what is good from socialism." It is to the world's advantage that he succeed.

*Bibliography*

Ascherson, Neal. *The Polish August: The Self-Limiting Revolution*. New York: Viking, 1982. Ascherson, a British correspondent, was in Poland during the heady days of Solidarity; the work covers the history of the country from 1939 to the imposition of martial law.

*The Book of Lech Wałesa*. Introduction by Neal Ascherson. New York: Simon & Schuster, 1982. A collection of various comments and statements of the leader of Solidarity with a good introduction providing some basic background.

Garton Ash, Timothy. *The Polish Revolution: Solidarity, 1980-1982*. New York: Charles Scribner's Sons, 1984. Ash is a British historian specializing in Eastern Europe. His account is vivid and authoritative, covering the period from the beginnings of Solidarity to the imposition of martial law.

Labedz, Leopold, ed. *Poland Under Jaruzelski*. New York: Charles Scribner's Sons, 1984. A collection of sixty-five articles by specialists on Eastern Europe analyzing Solidarity's influence and the immediate aftermath of martial law.

Wałęsa, Lech. *A Way of Hope: An Autobiography.* New York: Henry Holt, 1987. This work remains the best source for Wałęsa's early years and his experiences as leader of Solidarity. Despite its being published in 1987, Wałęsa's reminiscences end in 1984; as a result, the work does not contain his thoughts on the most recent dramatic changes in Poland.

*John C. K. Daly*

# LÉON WALRAS

*Born:* December 16, 1834; Évreux, France
*Died:* January 5, 1910; Clarens, near Montreux, Switzerland
*Area of Achievement:* Economics
*Contribution:* Walras, along with Herman Heinrich Gossen, William Stanley Jevons, and Carl von Menger, discovered the concept of marginal utility. His long-term influence rests on his system of general equilibrium, which was a far more comprehensive analysis of value and price, demand and supply than any postulated up to his time. Many economists, however, believe that his pioneering use of mathematics in economic theory is his most lasting contribution to the science.

## *Early Life*

Marie-Esprit-Léon Walras was born in Évreux, a provincial town in Normandy, France, on December 16, 1834. His father, Antoine-Auguste Walras, though he never held an economic post, also wrote on economics and greatly influenced Léon throughout his life and career. The younger Walras later used many of his father's ideas and terms in his own works.

Léon received a standard education for a boy of his class and time, and was graduated from secondary school in 1852. He then attempted to enter an engineering school in Paris but failed the mathematics paper in the entrance examinations two years in a row. This is ironic in view of the fact that many think of him as the economist above all others who brought mathematical methodology into the theory of economics. While studying for these exams, he read the works of Augustin Cournot, who in 1838 had published a book on wealth using mathematical economics. Cournot, along with Walras' father, was the main influence on Walras' economic writings. Walras entered a less prestigious engineering school in 1854 but withdrew after a year and spent the following four years pursuing his interests in philosophy and literature. He published a novel in 1858 which is generally regarded as being very poor. That same year, he was finally persuaded by his father to devote himself to economics.

It took him twelve years to obtain an academic post in the discipline. His unwillingness to conform and his unpopular economic ideas, which included the nationalization of land, are usually cited as the reason for the many rejections. Meanwhile, he worked as a journalist for two publications and was dismissed from both for his independent viewpoints. Failing to establish his own journal, he worked with a railway company and afterward co-founded a bank, which went bankrupt in 1868.

Walras was very poor during this period and struggled constantly to support his wife and family. Indeed, only on his second marriage to a rich widow in 1884, his first wife having died, was he able to obtain financial security. Finally in 1870, he applied for the chair of political economy in the faculty of law at the Academy of Lausanne in Switzerland and was appointed to the post by a narrow majority. His financial situation was such that the academy had to advance him some money from his salary to meet his travel expenses.

*Life's Work*

Walras held his position at Lausanne for twenty-two years, until 1892, when he retired for health reasons. His major work *Éléments d'économie politique pure* (1874; *Elements of Pure Economics*, 1954) was first published four years after his appointment and went through many revisions and additions. He intended it as the theoretical portion of a three-part study, the others being the application of economic theory and the social implications and ethics of this application. In philosophical terms, he referred to this division of the study of economics as the True, the Useful, and the Just. Yet it is as a theorist that he is remembered. His lasting contribution to economic theory was his analysis and outline of the concept of general equilibrium, that is, a situation in which the market and the economy show no tendency to move away from the current position. In this situation, each individual consumer receives the maximum possible satisfaction from exchange; the supply of each commodity equals the demand and the price of each product equals its cost of production.

Walras was the first economist to show the complete interdependence of all elements in an economic system. For example, a change in the demand for one commodity will affect the demand for all other commodities in the market, and it will also change the prices of the factors of production (land and labor, for example) used in producing the commodities. In his analysis, Walras used the term *rareté* (scarcity), which is now referred to as marginal utility. It signifies the utility or satisfaction obtained by the consumer from the last unit purchased of a commodity. This is in contrast to total utility, which is the satisfaction obtained from the total number of units of the commodity consumed. Walras assumed perfect competition for his analysis, that is, a market where a large number of small firms compete to sell their products to consumers who are perfectly rational in their buying and where full market information is freely available to all.

He thought of his marginal utility theory as the subjective theory of value to distinguish it from classical economics, which assumed all value comes from the supply side, that is, the sum total of the factors of production that are used in producing a commodity. Yet he also used marginal utility analysis on the supply side: The firms who produce the goods buy the factors of production, so they also gain a marginal utility from each unit of the factor they buy. Logically each firm on the supply side will also seek to maximize utility or satisfaction by equalizing the marginal utility gained from the purchasing of units of the different factors of production. For example, they will substitute land for labor if greater utility is obtained by doing this. Walras' great contribution was to demonstrate mathematically the tendency for market and prices to go toward equilibrium, where each firm and consumer gains maximum satisfaction. He did this with a series of simultaneous equations in which the price and quantity of the product and the factors of production are the unknown variables. *Tatonnements*, or gropings, was the catchword he used to express the idea of each price, each quantity produced and consumed in all markets tending to move toward the equilibrium value—the value wherein all of his equations are equalized and all satisfactions are maximized.

Walras corresponded with almost every economist of note before his death, mainly to convince them of the validity of his theories. On the whole, however, he met with little success in his advocacy. English economists, with the exception of Jevons, dismissed him out of hand, as indeed he did them. He was the recipient of even greater indifference in his native France, though he continued to try to obtain an economic post there with a view to a higher salary. The German universities and the Austrian school ridiculed his mathematics, and only in Italy, and to some extent in the United States, was he read and studied.

He was convinced of the need to develop economics as a pure science whose theory could be compared with the physical sciences. This was the reason he separated applied economics from the theory. He never wrote the systematic works he had planned on the social and applied aspects of economics. Instead, he published *Études d'économie sociale* (1896; studies in social economy) and *Études d'économie politique appliquée* (1898; studies in applied political economy), collections of his papers. His most controversial idea in applied economics was that of the nationalization of all land. In this theory, the state would rent land to people and businesses and the revenue obtained would eliminate the need for taxation. The proposition has led to Walras being labeled a communist, but this is inaccurate, since he strongly defended the idea of private property and emphasized the need for competition in the marketplace.

Walras resigned from his post at Lausanne in 1892 on the ground of exhaustion. He was succeeded by Vilfredo Pareto, one of his followers, who continued with the mathematical expression of economic theory. Eventually, however, Walras believed that Pareto had betrayed him and they quarreled publicly on many occasions. Walras was a difficult man to get along with, often suffering from paranoia and hypochondria. He was aggrieved when recognition of his achievements was not forthcoming. He put his name forward for the Nobel Peace Prize in 1906, but the award went instead to Theodore Roosevelt. Walras continued to work until his death in 1910 near Montreux, Switzerland.

### *Summary*

Léon Walras was one of the most controversial of all economists. Partly this was a result of his fiery, impatient, forceful personality and a strong propensity to engage in personal arguments. Yet his ideas were often unjustly represented and ignored. In some ways he was a man ahead of his time, with his insistence on the validity of using mathematics, an advocacy which has certainly been vindicated with the passage of time. Indeed Walras' stock has risen enormously since his death. Until the 1930's, he was hardly acknowledged in many textbooks, and his major work, *Elements of Pure Economics*, was not translated into English until 1954. Yet by the late 1940's, Milton Friedman could say: "We curtsy to [Alfred] Marshall, but we walk with Walras." Another great twentieth century economist, Joseph Schumpeter, wrote in 1952: "As far as pure theory is concerned, Walras is in my opinion the greatest of all economists."

He is most often compared to his contemporary Alfred Marshall, the great English economist. Marshall received the lion's share of the credit for equilibrium analysis both when he wrote, in the late nineteenth century, and afterward. This fact resulted mainly from the obscurity of much of Walras' writing with its strong mathematical content. Walras wrote for his fellow economists. By contrast, Marshall wrote for businessmen and the intelligent layperson, and, though he was the superior mathematician of the two, he consigned his mathematics to appendices. It has also been argued that Marshall is closer to life and that Walras is unduly abstract and too simplistic in his assumptions. Yet the economists of the 1920's and 1930's successfully related empirical data to Walras' model and gave it operational validity. What is certain is that, along with Jevons and Menger, Walras broadened the scope and methodology of economics and that only later was proper acknowledgment given to his achievements.

### *Bibliography*

Blaug, Mark. *Economic Theory in Retrospect.* Homewood, Ill.: Richard D. Irwin, 1962. A difficult book for the layperson, with its detailed exposition of Walras' mathematics; nevertheless, it probably presents his mathematics in the simplest form possible, while doing justice to its complexity.

Cirillo, Renato. "Léon Walras and Social Justice." *American Journal of Economics and Sociology* 43 (January, 1984): 53-60. A very well-written and clear discussion of Walras' ideas on the best way to achieve justice for all through economic policies.

Deane, Phyllis. *The Evolution of Economic Ideas*. Cambridge: Cambridge University Press, 1978. A brief, scholarly, but very readable overview of the history of economic ideas from Adam Smith to the modern times. It discusses Walras very much in his context among other theorists of this period rather than individually.

Ekelund, Robert B., Jr., and Robert F. Hebert. *A History of Economic Theory and Method*. New York: McGraw-Hill, 1975. Places Marshall and Walras in the same chapter and offers a very technical and exhaustive comparison and contrast of the two, though in their overview they also write in a nontechnical manner.

Gill, Richard T. *Evolution of Modern Economics*. Englewood Cliffs, N.J.: Prentice-Hall, 1967. Excellent short introduction to Walras and other major economists that is written in a simple, nontechnical style and could be understood by someone with no background in economics.

Jaffé, William. "The Antecedents and Early Life of Léon Walras." *History of Political Economy* 16, no. 1 (1984): 1-57. An interesting, anecdotal account of Walras' early life and that of his father.

__________. *William Jaffé's Essays on Walras*. Edited by Donald A. Walker. Cambridge: Cambridge University Press, 1983. A collection of essays varying from pure biography to Walras' correspondence to involved discussions of aspects of his theories. Written by the foremost authority on Walras.

Spiegel, Henry William. *The Growth of Economic Thought.* Englewood Cliffs, N.J.: Prentice-Hall, 1971. A very well-written book that lies halfway between Gill's and Blaug's books in its treatment of Walras and its accessibility to the noneconomist.

*Philip Magnier*

# WANG CHING-WEI

*Born:* May 4, 1883; Sanshui, near Canton, China
*Died:* November 10, 1944; Nagoya, Japan
*Areas of Achievement:* Government and politics
*Contribution:* Wang, an early disciple of Sun Yat-sen and a founding member of the T'ung-meng hui, was contender for leadership of the Kuomintang after Sun's death in 1925. He was initially identified with the left wing of the party, then became an anticommunist and favored appeasement of Japan as leader of the government between 1932 and 1936; in 1937, he defected to form a puppet government in Japanese-occupied China in 1940.

## *Early Life*

The Wang family came from Shao-hsing in Chekiang Province. Wang Ching-wei was born in Sanshui near Canton, on May 4, 1883, the tenth and last child and fourth son of Wang Shu, and his second wife. His given name was Wang Chao-ming. The elder Wang, then sixty years old, was a government legal secretary and, because of his large family, was compelled to work until failing eyesight necessitated his retirement at age seventy. Although the family was not well-off, Wang had a happy childhood until he was twelve, when his mother died, followed by the death of his father the next year and of several siblings in the following years. Supported by his eldest brother, he continued his schooling and worked part-time as a tutor from age seventeen, in order to contribute to the family's income. His early education was typical for the time; it emphasized training in the classics, history, philosophy, and literature. He was later noted for his persuasive writing style and fine calligraphy. He also wrote poetry and published a volume of his poems.

In 1902, he placed third in the first level, or county, examination. Later that year he came in first in the provincial exam held at Canton, a great achievement considering his youth and the stiff competition. Despite this early scholarly success, Wang decided not to proceed to compete in the metropolitan exam but, influenced by new Western ideas, to pursue a modern education in Japan, for which he won a government scholarship in 1904. He quickly learned Japanese and attended the Tokyo Law College, where he obtained a degree in 1906. While in Japan he became attracted to anarchism, but, more important, he met Sun Yat-sen and other Chinese revolutionaries, joined Sun's T'ung-meng hui (United League) when it was formed in 1905, and contributed eloquent pro-republican articles to its publication, the *Min Pao*, waging pen battles with exiled supporters of a constitutional monarchy in Japan. His notoriety led his eldest brother to expel him from the family, lest its members in China should be blamed for his activities. When the Ch'ing government successfully persuaded Japanese authorities to expel Sun from Japan in 1907, Wang accompanied him on a recruiting and fund-raising trip to Southeast Asia. During this trip, he met Ch'en Pi-chun, the daughter of a wealthy overseas Chinese family in Malaya and an enthusiastic follower of Sun. He married her in 1912. She continued to be active in Kuomintang politics throughout her life. Against the advice of Sun and his other colleagues, Wang returned to China, was involved in a bungled attempt to assassinate the prince regent in 1910, was arrested, tried, and sentenced to death. The sentence was commuted to life imprisonment, but he was released in 1911 at the outbreak of the revolution. He and his wife lived in France from 1912 to 1917, during which time he wrote Chinese poetry but did not learn much French.

*Life's Work*

Wang returned to China in 1917, again became active in Sun's movement, and served in various high positions in Sun's government in Canton. Although he had initially advised Sun against entering into an alliance with the Communists, once Sun embarked upon it, Wang, like other members of the Kuomintang, acquiesced in the decision. At the first Kuomintang Congress held in Canton in 1924, Wang was elected a member of the Central Executive Committee and was appointed as the party's minister of propaganda and to other key posts. He was among Sun's entourage when the latter made his final trip to Peking in 1924. Sun's aim was to negotiate with the warlords who ruled north China with the goal of establishing a unified government, but he fell terminally ill with cancer and died in 1925. Wang was the author of Sun's last will and testament.

After Sun's death, Wang became the leader of the left wing of the Kuomintang, which favored continuation of the alliance with the Soviet Union and cooperation with the Chinese Communist Party that Sun had forged in 1922, and contended for leadership of the party with right-wing leader Hu Han-min and centrist Chiang Kai-shek. Neither Wang nor Hu held military power, while Chiang, who was junior to both in the Kuomintang, became its rising star as commandant of the party's military academy and commander in chief of the new party army that he had been appointed by Sun to organize. In 1926, Chiang led the Kuomintang army in the successful Northern Expedition to unify China; Wang headed the Kuomintang civilian government, which had moved to Wu-han along the lower Yangtze River Valley at the beginning of 1927. In the spring of 1927, when Chiang and his right-wing allies, who had established themselves in Nanking, purged the Communists from lands that they controlled, Wang and his left-wing supporters in Wuhan refused to do so, and continued their cooperation with the Chinese Communists and Soviet advisers headed by Mikhail Borodin. They waited until July, 1927, when evidence proved beyond a doubt that the Soviet Union intended to use the Kuomintang to propel the Chinese Communist Party to power. The Wang-led Wu-han government dissolved itself after it, too, expelled the Soviet advisers and purged the Chinese Communists. From then until his death, Wang would be a staunch anticommunist; he regarded Communism and the Soviet Union as China's greatest threat. He left China in disgrace late in 1927 for France but soon returned to head a group called the Reorganizationists, and joined in various movements against the central government in Nanking headed by Chiang between 1928 and 1931, all of which, however, failed.

Japan's invasion of Manchuria in 1931 forced the factions of the Kuomintang to mend their differences and resulted in Wang's heading the civilian government as president of the executive yuan (premier) and foreign minister between 1932 and 1935, while Chiang led and modernized those units of the military under the central government's control and organized campaigns against the Communist insurgents. The cooperation between Chiang and Wang was an uneasy one. While Chiang and his allies controlled the major portions of the military and the party machinery, Wang, who had only a small corps of personal supporters, was clearly relegated to a junior position. Wang and Chiang were however agreed that weak and disunified China was in no condition to resist Japan and that, while they implemented programs to modernize China, they must negotiate with the Japanese and make concessions if necessary. Both men, but especially Wang, became targets of hostile public opinion, expressed in the press and in student demonstrations, for their nonresistance and concessions to Japanese aggression. In November, 1935, Wang was wounded in an attempted assassination by an army officer bitter about Wang's appeasement of Japan. He left for convalescence in Europe in early 1936, returned to China a year later, and found Chiang riding a crest of popularity as national leader in an incipient united front against Japan. When the Japanese invasion of north China in July, 1937, resulted in all out war, Chiang came to symbolize resistance and gained even greater power as commander in chief and as party leader in 1938; Wang was named deputy party leader, again superseded by Chiang, whom Wang regarded as a junior in party seniority.

Dissatisfied with his subordination to Chiang and pessimistic over the sufferings in a war against Japan that he saw as hopeless for China, Wang secretly left Chungking, China's wartime capital, in December, 1938. He surfaced in Hanoi in French Indochina and began actively to campaign for peace with Japan. He offered to lead that movement and placed himself and his supporters as alternatives to the Chinese government in Chungking led by Chiang. While he was in Hanoi, there was an attempt to assassinate him, probably instigated by some members of the Chungking government. Although he escaped unscathed, this event marked a point of no return for Wang's "peace movement." After two visits to Tokyo, Wang signed a secret treaty with Japan that permitted him to set up and head a "reform government" in Nanking in March, 1940. Aside from several long time associates, no one of note deserted the Chungking government to join Wang's puppet regime. Anti-Chiang politicians and dissident warlords alike denounced Wang for treason. He had clearly miscalculated disastrously; Chiang's prestige had soared as leader in a war of national salvation, and, among nationalistic Chinese, anti-Chiang did not mean pro-Japan. The Wang regime aped the legitimate Chinese government in its party structure and government organization, professed allegiance to Sun's ideology, and even used the same national flag, to which it added a yellow tab that read "peace, anti-Communism and reconstruction."

Japan had hoped that its installation of the Wang regime would bring about the collapse of the government at Chungking and continued Chinese resistance. When these things did not happen, Japanese support for Wang waned. Thus it did not formally recognize his Nanking regime until November, 1940, and conceded to it only nominal control of Japanese-occupied areas in central and south China, while earlier established puppet regimes in inner Mongolia and north China continued to exist separately. For its part, the Wang regime recognized Manchukuo, the first Japanese-created puppet state in China. It received diplomatic recognition from only the Axis powers and their client states.

The two most powerful offices in Nanking throughout the life of the Wang regime were Japan's Supreme Military and Economic Advisory Commissions, which supervised important activities in areas nominally under Chinese control. Several trips by Wang to Japan netted a treaty in 1943 in which Japan relinquished its extraterritorial rights in China and recognized the Wang regime as an ally in Japan's scheme of Greater East Asia. These were empty gestures, because Japanese troops remained in occupation of conquered China, where Japan continued to enjoy enormous economic and political privileges. Strains over the Pacific War led Japan to permit a greater role for Wang's puppet troops in the China theater after 1943, even as the same strains resulted in greater material demands on Chinese in occupied areas.

The turning tide of war enveloped the Wang regime in pessimism, evidenced by Wang's frequent raging temper outbursts and heavy drinking and a live-for-today attitude among his associates. Failing health and persistent trouble from the assassin's bullet wound led Wang to enter the Nagoya University Hospital in Japan in March, 1944. Even though he was given the best medical treatment available, Japanese authorities guarded his sick bed and prevented him from speaking to journalists. He died on November 10, 1944, from pneumonia. His body was flown back to Nanking, and he was given a huge public funeral and buried near to Sun's mausoleum outside Nanking. His demoralized regime ended with Japan's defeat and the end of World War II. After the war, Wang's tomb was destroyed by order of the Nationalist government. His associates and widow (who had been active politically and held high positions under the puppet regime) were tried by the Nationalist government for treason. Some were executed upon conviction, and Mrs. Wang was sentenced to life imprisonment, which she served out under the Communist government.

*Summary*

Wang Ching-wei was a key figure in modern Chinese history. His eloquent writings in favor of the overthrow of the Ch'ing Dynasty and in support of Sun's ideology contributed to the cause of revolution, as did his willingness to sacrifice himself in the failed attempt to assassinate the prince regent. He was widely admired for his good looks, his elegant bearing, his charismatic speaking style, and his persuasive writing. The darker side of his personality includes his vaulting ambition, which drove him to sacrifice principle for personal political gain, and his mercurial temperament. His quest to be successor of Sun led him to oppose Hu Han-min, another leading disciple of Sun, and to espouse the alliance with the Soviet Union and the Chinese Communist Party. After the exposing of Joseph Stalin's goal in China and the discrediting of the left wing Kuomintang that he led, Wang joined in a series of makeshift alliances with warlords that waged civil wars against the new national government in Nanking led by Chiang. Even after his rapprochement with Chiang and installation as head of the civilian government in Nanking after 1932, he continued to chafe under Chiang's greater overall authority. He frequently used histrionics and real or pretended illnesses to threaten resignation and to gain political leverage. Popular opinion turned increasingly against him for his policy of nonresistance against Japanese aggression and for China's territorial losses to Japan under his stewardship; after he turned quisling and organized a puppet regime in Japanese occupied China in 1940, he became execrated as a traitor. Even those sympathetic to him condemned his collaboration with Japan as a hopeless and pointless endeavor. A revolutionary who had devoted much of his life in the cause of Chinese nationalism, he had disastrously misjudged its character when he deserted to the Japanese camp. In his last testament, he claimed that he acted to save the Chinese from the horrors of a prolonged war he saw as doomed and from the dangers of Communism that he saw as worse for China than Japanese imperialism.

*Bibliography*

Boyle, John Hunter. *China and Japan at War, 1937-1945: The Politics of Collaboration*. Stanford, Calif.: Stanford University Press, 1972. An analysis of why Wang and others collaborated with Japanese conquerors.

Bunker, Gerald E. *The Peace Conspiracy: Wang Ching-wei and the China War, 1937-1941*. Cambridge, Mass.: Harvard University Press, 1972. A sympathetic account of Wang's motives for collaborating with Japan. Examines the frustrations and achievements of his regime.

Shirley, James R. *Political Conflict in the Kuomintang: The Career of Wang Ching-wei to 1932*. Ann Arbor, Mich.: University Microfilms, 1965. Deals with Wang's rise and early career. Good explanation of the Kuomintang.

T'ang, Leang-li. *Wang Ching-wei: A Political Biography.* Peiping: China United Press, 1931. A laudatory account written by a Wang supporter, this book goes fairly in depth in biographical information.

Wang, Chao-ming. *China's Problems and Their Solution*. Shanghai: China United Press, 1934. Wang wrote these while he headed China's government to justify his policy. The listing of his name here is a variant spelling.

*Jiu-Hwa Lo Upshur*

# FELIX WANKEL

*Born:* August 13, 1902; Lahr, Germany
*Died:* October 9, 1988; Lindau, West Germany
*Areas of Achievement:* Invention and technology
*Contribution:* As early as 1924, Wankel began to sketch models for rotary piston engines; in 1929, he obtained his first patent for an engine that has a reciprocating piston housed in a horizontal cylinder, the earliest Wankel engine, that has since been perfected to the point that it can power automobiles and other motorized vehicles.

## *Early Life*

Felix Wankel was born in Lahr in that southwestern reach of Germany near the Alsace province of France, practically on the Swiss border. His father, Rudolf, a forest commissioner killed in the first month of World War I, left his wife, Gerty Heidlauff Wankel, and his twelve-year-old son, Felix Heinrich, to fend for themselves. They were financially comfortable. Their security, however, was sufficiently eroded by the raging postwar inflation that nineteen-year-old Wankel lacked the means to continue his education beyond the secondary level.

Wankel, leaving Lahr and its stolid people behind him, moved to Heidelberg and was employed there by a publisher of scientific books. Within three years, he had opened a mechanical shop and begun his early work with motors. He quickly learned the need for precision and meticulous craftsmanship in mechanical work. He began to dwell on the problem of finding more efficient engines than those then in common use: gas turbines, Diesel engines, free-piston engines, steam engines, electrically powered engines, fuel cells, Stirling engines, and combinations of these.

By 1924, he had conceived the basic idea for the Wankel engine. Working from his sketches of it, he eventually forged models that represented a dramatic departure from all engines of the past. The concept of such an engine was not new; mechanics and engineers had puzzled over the idea for more than a century, but Wankel was the first to conceive of a model that would work and that, providing the requisite power to propel vehicles, could function economically without undue wear.

The concept behind Wankel's engine was that energy could be conserved if an engine were developed that rotated rather than pumped vertically. Because the wheels of vehicles are round, the energy from piston-driven engines, once it is produced, must be converted to a rotary motion. Wankel found this conversion, with its accompanying loss of energy, inefficient.

The practical problem he had to solve was that of developing a working model of an engine that, housed in a horizontal chamber, would seal the gap created by the motion of the rotor. In piston engines, the only gap that has to be sealed is that between the piston rod and the walls of the cylinder into which it plunges. Wankel realized that if a rotor is packed into its chamber too tightly, it loses energy through friction. It the rotor is packed too loosely, the seal is not tight, so the cylinder leaks energy. Wankel packed the rotor in various materials, none of which worked.

*Life's Work*

Unable to support himself from his workshop in Heidelberg, Wankel continued to work for a publisher of scientific books until 1926. By 1927, he had a detailed working sketch of his engine, but he had not solved the sealing problem. Despite this, he had progressed sufficiently by 1929 to obtain his first patent for a rotary engine.

The sealing problem, however, continued to plague Wankel for the next two decades. The substantial reputation he gained for his work grew during World War II, when he served Germany by working on torpedoes, although this work diverted him from his main purpose. As Adolf Hitler was rising to power, Wankel joined the Hitler Youth Movement, as did the woman he married. He remained a supporter of the dictator during the early years of Nazism but fell from grace, was arrested, and was imprisoned soon after he broke from the Nazi Party in 1932.

Wilhelm Keppler, a staunch supporter of Hitler, had become an enthusiastic advocate of Wankel and his invention. Through his intervention and that of the chief engineer of Daimler-Benz, Otto Nibel, Wankel was released from prison in 1933 and returned to his experimental work, now with Daimler-Benz, quitting a year later when he had a dispute with the general manager. He then went to work for Bayerischen Motoren Werke (BMW) in Munich, assigned to develop a piston engine with rotary valves.

The basic sealing problem Wankel encountered was that the seal edge in his previous designs was too wide. Every means he conceived of for sealing the cylinder resulted in lost energy and rapid wear, rendering the engine impractical.

Wankel's personality was such that people could not work easily with him, resulting in his usually having to attack problems independently that several minds working harmoniously might have resolved more quickly than Wankel alone could. Keppler, realizing his protégé's potential, used his influence to help Wankel receive a government subvention in 1936 that enabled him to establish a workshop that grew into an institute in the island town of Lindau, Bavaria, at the Lake of Constance, where he would settle permanently. There this man of average height, his hair growing thin and his eyes obscured behind thick glasses, proceeded with his solitary work.

Finally, after experimenting with various materials, Wankel devised thin strips of metal that represented a major step toward resolving the persistent sealing problem. His wartime work with the Goetz corporation, which made piston rings, added another possibility to Wankel's means of sealing his motor. Goetz developed an ultrastrong metal alloy, IKA, that would figure prominently in the development of sealing devices for rotary engines.

Wankel overcame another crucial obstacle when he discovered that he could use the gas pressure built up in the engine as the gas tries to escape to work for rather than against sealing it. He used this gas buildup to put pressure on the seals, thereby fixing them tightly enough to prevent significant leakage and obviating the need for springs beneath the plates of his engine.

At the war's end in 1945, the French occupied Lindau. Wankel was arrested, his institute disbanded, and most of the thousands of sketches for his engine destroyed. This seeming disaster turned into a blessing for Wankel, who was now forced to rethink his work from the beginning, unhindered by the lingering ghosts of his past work. By 1951, when he reestablished his institute, he began the tedious, gargantuan task of classifying the thousands of possible configurations for his engine, not publishing his results until 1963. By January, 1954, however, he had drawn the design for rotary engines that finally powered automobiles in the 1970's. It consisted of a double circle housing for a rotor with three convex sides, a fat, triangular figure rotating within a figure eight.

During the 1950's, automotive manufacturers in Japan, the United States, Germany, and France grew interested in Wankel's experiments, and with their help the first Wankel rotary engines stood endurance tests in 1959. Because such engines could deliver acceptable power economically with minimal air pollution, the idea was appealing to automobile manufacturers and environmentalists alike. The Wankel, half the weight of conventional six-cylinder engines but capable of delivering more power, had potential popular appeal.

General Motors committed fifty million dollars to buying the Wankel license but had difficulty bringing rotary-engine cars into production. Meanwhile, however, Toyo Kogyo of Japan produced an economically viable rotary engine car, the Mazda R-100 and later the Mazda RX-2, for the American market. The first of these cars reached the United States in May, 1970. Despite early customer skepticism and some negative reports, they enjoyed considerable popularity in the geographically limited market in which Toyo Kogyo first marketed them. Soon, Mazda's rotary engine models ranked fourth in sales in the markets where they were sold.

The only problem to emerge was that Wankel engines did not endure. Often the entire engine had to be replaced before thirty thousand miles. Enthusiasm for the Wankel engine waned as the end of the 1970's approached. Although several major automotive manufacturers bought the license to manufacture the engine, the piston engine still dominates the automobile industry.

*Summary*

Despite its present lack of popular acceptance, the Wankel engine holds many appealing possibilities, particularly in its ability to produce sufficient power to propel automobiles smoothly and quietly at high speeds with much less air pollution than conventional engines create and with relatively modest consumption of fuel.

Felix Wankel became rich because he ensured that his early patents were airtight. Subsequent patents—more than thirty of them between 1955 and 1958 alone—were carefully drawn to protect Wankel's financial interests fully. His arrangement with the Necharsulm Strickmachinene Union (NSU), for example, gave him 40 percent of the profits from NSU's rotary engines, even though Wankel had been on their payroll when he developed them. Despite his wealth, Wankel always lived frugally and was not renowned for his beneficence, although he founded a refuge for dogs and cats and contributed money to cancer research.

*Bibliography*

Ansdale, Richard F. *The Wankel RC Engine*. New York: A. S. Barnes, 1968. This book by Wankel's translator is definitely for specialists although valuable general information can be gleaned from it. Ansdale's writing style is often unclear, resulting in an unnecessary complexity in a book whose subject is itself complex and highly technical in many of its essential aspects.

Burstall, Aubrey F. *A History of Mechanical Engineering*. New York: Pitman, 1963. This book provides as solid a brief overview of Wankel and his work as any in print. Although written with an audience of engineers in mind, the book is not so technical as to bewilder more general readers. It makes a reasonable, well-focused starting point for those unfamiliar with Wankel and his inventions.

Faith, Nicholas. *Wankel: The Curious Story Behind the Revolutionary Rotary Engine*. New York: Stein & Day, 1975. Faith's is the most accessible source for readers who do not require a highly technical approach. His exposition is lucid and appealing. Faith avoids scientific jargon, often defining key terms in context. His research is thorough and accurate. He is totally in control of all the basic writing by and about Wankel to the mid-1970's. The index is extensive and useful.

Inman-Hunter, Marcus C. *Rotary Valve Engines*. New York: Hutchinson's Scientific and Technical Publications, 1951. This book pays considerable homage to Wankel although it was published before his ideas had progressed to the point of making rotary engines reasonable alternatives to conventional piston engines. The book is interesting primarily for its historical review of Wankel's work at a time when the practicality of his inventions was questionable.

Norbye, Jan P. *The Wankel Engine: Design, Development, Applications*. Radnor, Pa.: Chilton, 1971. Norbye, automotive editor of *Popular Science Monthly*, has produced a highly detailed book on the Wankel engine, profuse with clear, helpful illustrations. The book is more technical than Faith's, but it is generally comprehensible to nonspecialists. Norbye has an encyclopedic knowledge of the engines in general use and understands them technically. Although his emphasis is on engines rather than on the man, Norbye provides substantial biographical information.

Wankel, Felix. *Rotary Piston Machines*. Translated by Richard F. Ansdale. London: Iliffe Books, 1965. Wankel's own book provides an excellent resource for the specialist but is not valuable for beginners because it tends to be overly technical. Much of the material in this book is replicated in Ansdale's book cited above, but neither book is recommended for the novice.

*R. Baird Shuman*

# MAX WEBER

*Born:* April 21, 1864; Erfurt, Prussia
*Died:* June 14, 1920; Munich, Germany
*Area of Achievement:* Sociology
*Contribution:* A German social scientist and theorist widely acclaimed as the "father of sociology," Weber is best known for his thesis of the Protestant ethic, which links the psychological effects of Calvinism with the development of modern capitalism.

## *Early Life*

Max Weber was the first child of Max and Helen Fallenstein Weber. His father was a prominent lawyer and aspiring politician whose family had attained considerable wealth in the German linen industry. An ardent monarchist and Bismarckian within the German Reichstag, the elder Weber was to his son the epitome of a patriarchal, amoral creature-of-pleasure who knew real politics and the art of compromise. His mother, on the other hand, was a highly educated, moralistic woman, intensely preoccupied with religious and social concerns, particularly with charity work for the poor. The hedonistic father and humanitarian mother shared little in common, and Weber grew to maturity in a household charged with open tension and hostility.

Weber received an excellent early education in select German private schools. In addition, because of the political prominence of his father, a considerable circle of famous personalities—such as Wilhem Dilthey, Heinrich von Treitschke, Levin Goldschmidt, and Theodor Mommsen—frequented the Weber household. Meeting and engaging in political discussion with such men of prestige not only stimulated young Weber's intellectual curiosity but also provided him with contacts who would help promote his career in later life.

Weber began his university studies in 1882 at Heidelberg—his mother's home during her youth—taking courses in law, history, and theology. At his father's suggestion (and against his mother's wishes), he also joined the student fraternity, an activity which consumed much of his time in drinking bouts and duels. In 1883, Weber moved to Strasbourg to fulfill his one-year military obligation in the National Service. There, Weber visited and developed a close attachment to his aunt and uncle: Ida Baumgarten, an intensely devout woman much like his mother, and Hermann Baumgarten, a professor of history who, unlike his father, was highly critical of the Bismarckian empire.

Hoping to extricate young Weber from the influence of the Baumgartens, the elder Weber encouraged his son to resume his studies back home at the University of Berlin. Weber returned to Berlin, and, except for one semester in school at Göttingen and several months away on military exercises, Weber spent the next eight years at home. In 1889, Weber was graduated magna cum laude and then began preparing for his *Habilitation* (a higher doctorate required to teach in German universities), which he received in 1891. While pursuing his advanced studies, Weber worked intermittently as a lawyer's assistant and a university assistant—two unremunerative apprenticeships. Hence at age twenty-nine, Weber was still residing in his parents' home, financially dependent on their income and continually subject to their conflicting claims on his loyalty.

In 1893, Weber married his second cousin, Marianne Schnitger, an intelligent woman who later achieved some prominence in the German feminist movement. The marriage lasted until Weber's death but never was consummated. Although their marriage was without affection, Weber and Marianne were intellectually compatible. Following Weber's death, Marianne published a seven-hundred-page biography of her late husband that contained not a negative word regarding their union.

### *Life's Work*

A workaholic with strong academic credentials and political contacts, Weber rose rapidly in the teaching profession. After a brief appointment in Berlin, Weber in 1894 became a full professor in economics at the University of Freiburg. Two years later, he was called to the University of Heidelberg to succeed the preeminent professor of political economy, Karl Knies. As a professor, Weber advocated what he called "freedom from value-judgment" in lecturing. This doctrine demanded that teachers present to their students the established empirical facts without expressing their evaluations as to whether the facts were satisfactory or unsatisfactory. Weber also was an avid researcher and writer. During these years, however, his research interests focused on rather mundane economic issues of immediate application.

Weber's academic career, however, was cut short in 1898 when he suffered a severe mental and physical breakdown that virtually incapacitated him for four years and prevented him from returning to the classroom until 1918. The symptoms of the illness included insomnia, inner tension, exhaustion, bouts of anxiety, and continual restlessness. Biographers have speculated that familial problems triggered this neurosis. In 1897, Weber had a violent dispute with his father over the authoritarian way his father treated his mother. Following the argument, his father stormed away from Weber's Heidelberg home, promising never to return. Shortly thereafter, the elder Weber died of a gastric hemorrhage. His mother quickly recovered from her grief, but Weber harbored intense feelings of guilt. Throughout his life, Weber had been intellectually torn between the moralistic idealism of his mother and the practical realism of his father. Outwardly, he resembled his father; inwardly, he aspired for the moral certitudes of his mother. Perhaps the tragic circumstances of his father's death locked the two sides of his personality in a paralyzing symbiosis.

Whatever the cause, Weber's neurotic breakdown had a dramatic impact upon his future thought and career. The prolonged agony of his personal crisis led him to develop insights into the relationship between religious ethics and social and economic processes that would distinguish his subsequent scholarship. His illness also freed him from the burden of the classroom. After a lengthy leave of absence, in 1903 Weber resigned from his university position and accepted the editorship of *Archiv für Sozialwissenschaft und Sozialpolitik* (social science and social political archives). This position provided Weber with a place to publish his own materials without passing an outside review. It also provided him with the leisure to write at his own pace. Except for a brief tenure as a German military hospital administrator during World War I, from the time of his partial recovery in 1903 until his return to academe in 1918, Weber was not obligated to any duties other than the editorial work he took on himself. All of Weber's most important works were written during these years between the worst part of his illness and his death. As tragic as his personal crisis was, without it he would not have achieved the greatness for which he is remembered.

Weber published his most famous piece, *Die protestantische Ethik und der Geist des Kapitalismus* (*The Protestant Ethic and the Spirit of Capitalism*, 1930), in the journal he edited during the years 1904 and 1905. In this work, Weber noted the correlation in German communities between the expansion of capitalism on the one hand and Protestant ideology on the other. He attributed this relationship to accidental psychological consequences of the Puritan doctrine of predestination. This doctrine, Weber postulated, produced an extreme condition of anxiety among Calvinist believers, which served to motivate them to discipline their lives in every respect. Calvinists worked hard, avoided idleness and waste, and, as a consequence, accumulated considerable wealth. Ironically, however, as capitalism grew and Calvinists became rich, puritanism began to fade. The Protestant ethic, in the end, transformed the world but in so doing eventually undermined itself.

After completing his study of Protestant ethics, Weber focused attention upon other world religions: Judaism, Confucianism, Taoism, Hinduism, and Buddhism. In all of his works on the sociology of religion, Weber emphasized the "universal historical relationship of religion and society." His studies attempted to show how different religious worldviews have affected the development of their cultures. In contrast to Karl Marx, who viewed religion as simply a reflection of the material basis of society, Weber argued that religious beliefs have significant impact upon economic actions and, in the case of Protestantism, were themselves the basis for the emergence of modern capitalism.

In 1909, Weber agreed to edit a new edition of an academic encyclopedia intended to cover every area of economics. In addition to arranging other contributors for the project, Weber planned to write for the volume a section on the relationship between economy and society. Although he never finished this work, Weber's involvement in the project provided him with the occasion to work out a comprehensive sociology. At the time of his death, he had written nearly fifteen hundred pages of text, but the work still was incomplete. The disordered and fragmentary manuscript was edited and published posthumously under the title *Wirtschaft und Gesellschaft* (1922; *Economy and Society*, 1968). This book contains many of Weber's thoughts on politics, law, bureaucracy, and social stratification.

Perhaps Weber's greatest impact on his contemporaries came near the end of World War I when he crusaded against Germany's annexationist war goals and policy of submarine warfare. His journalistic attacks at this time frequently placed him in conflict with the military censors. After Germany's defeat, Weber assisted in the drafting of the new constitution and in the founding of the German Democratic Party.

Weber briefly returned to the classroom, accepting in 1918 a professorship at the University of Vienna and the following year at the University of Munich. In early summer of 1920, Weber became ill with influenza, which soon turned into pneumonia. Weber died at his home in Munich on June 14, 1920.

### *Summary*

In a strictly scientific sense, Max Weber did not develop a new sociological theory. His works instead consisted of a cloud of axioms, hypotheses, suggestions, and a few theorems—the details of which generally have been discredited by specialists in their respective fields. Weber also did not discover any new problematic area which had not been discovered by others before him. Sociologists previous to and independent of him, for example, had delved into matters relating to the origins and effects of modern capitalism. Moreover, largely because little of his work was published in book form while he was alive, Weber did not stand in the center of sociological discourse during his own life. Much to his dismay, few of his peers welcomed his "freedom from value-judgment" doctrine, which was Weber's major methodological contribution to social science disciplines.

Yet, today Max Weber is almost the canonized saint of sociology who is widely acclaimed as the most influential and, perhaps, the most profound of twentieth century social scientists. His greatness does not lie in cerebral consistency, for much of his work is ambiguous and inconclusive, if not contradictory. Instead, Weber's fame is a result of his multisided, far-reaching intellect. Weber was a genius whose work crossed all the boundaries of sociology, law, economics, history, and religion. His multidimensional works influenced thinkers as diverse as C. Wright Mills, H. Richard Niebuhr, György Lukács, and Carl Schmitt. Weber's works remain "classic" because they call scholars away from the narrow perspectives of their individual disciplines to ask the grand questions about the meaning of human culture for which there are no easy answers.

*Bibliography*

Bendix, Reinhard. *Max Weber: An Intellectual Portrait*. Garden City, N.Y.: Doubleday, 1960. An older, but still one of the better single-volume portraits in English on the work of Weber.

Collins, Randall. *Max Weber: A Skeleton Key.* Beverly Hills, Calif.: Sage, 1986. An excellent brief introduction to Weber's life and thought. Beautifully written. Highly recommended for readers interested in a concise synopsis of Weberian thought.

Giddens, Anthony. "Marx, Weber and the Development of Capitalism." *Sociology* 4 (September, 1970): 289-310. An interesting summation of the works on the origins of capitalism of these two great thinkers.

Kasler, Dirk. *Max Weber: An Introduction to His Life and Work*. Translated by Philippa Hurd. Chicago: University of Chicago Press, 1988. This English translation of Kasler's *Einfuhrung in das Studium Max Webers* is a scholarly interpretation of the work of Weber. Balanced and insightful, but definitely intended for the advanced reader. Includes an extensive bibliography of Weber's works listed in chronological order.

MacRae, Donald G. *Max Weber.* New York: Viking Press, 1974. A 111-page volume in the Modern Masters series edited by Frank Kermode. A very readable and informative work which briefly analyzes the components of Weber's genius and suggests some reasons for Weber's overrated reputation.

Weber, Marianne. *Max Weber: A Biography.* Translated by Harry Zohn. New York: Wiley, 1975. A biography written by the wife of Weber. Although not to be taken at face value, this work is an interesting and sometimes entertaining volume that sheds considerable light on the humanness of this academic giant.

Weber, Max. *The Protestant Ethic and the Spirit of Capitalism*. Translated by Talcott Parsons, with an introduction by Anthony Giddens. New York: Charles Scribner's Sons, 1976. A translation of Weber's most famous work. Required reading for all students interested in the thought of Weber.

*Terry D. Bilhartz*

# ANTON VON WEBERN

*Born:* December 3, 1883; Vienna, Austro-Hungarian Empire
*Died:* September 15, 1945; Mittersill, Austria
*Area of Achievement:* Music
*Contribution:* Webern brought to the second Viennese school a unique and highly individual compositional approach. Like his mentor Arnold Schoenberg, Webern broke with existing musical traditions and developed a new compositional language and perspective. His adaptation of Schoenberg's twelve-tone method, based upon his own contrapuntal proclivity and concise musical rhetoric, proved to be the major influence on the subsequent generation of composers.

## *Early Life*

Anton Friedrich Wilhelm von Webern was born in Vienna on December 3, 1883. His father Karl, a mining engineer and government official, had an aristocratic lineage; vacations at the Preglhof, the family estate, fostered Anton's lifelong love of nature and mountain climbing, and provided a summer retreat for composition. Karl was well-read but not particularly artistic, and planned for his son to pursue an agricultural career. Webern's mother, Amalie (née Gehr), was an amateur pianist and singer. She taught her son piano from the age of five; with Webern's two sisters, the family often held impromptu concerts. Webern was particularly close to his mother and was deeply affected by her death in 1906; he later declared the majority of his works to be in her memory.

Because of Karl's career, the family moved from Vienna to Graz and finally settled in Klagenfurt in 1894. Webern received his first true music instruction there, studying cello, piano, and elementary harmony with Edwin Komauer, who also introduced Webern to contemporary works through piano reductions. Although Webern's musical inclinations were by now clear (his graduation from *Gymnasium* was celebrated with a pilgrimage to Bayreuth in 1902), his compositional proclivity was not as yet apparent. He entered the University of Vienna in 1902 to study musicology with Guido Adler; Webern's study of the Flemish composer Heinrich Isaac for his Ph.D. would later motivate the importance of counterpoint in his own compositional style. He continued to study cello and piano, and also studied harmony with Hermann Graedener and counterpoint with Karl Navrátil. Webern's work in composition to this point consisted of, for the most part, student efforts, but his increasing interest and productivity led him to seek out a true composition teacher. After a failed attempt to study with Hans Pfitzner, Webern began lessons in 1904 with Arnold Schoenberg, who, at nine years Webern's senior, was just beginning to attract attention, if not notoriety, in Viennese music circles. Schoenberg's instruction and the ensuing friendship that evolved proved to be the most crucial event in Webern's development; Schoenberg remained a profound artistic influence and close friend throughout Webern's life.

*Life's Work*

The four years of Schoenberg's tutelage brought Webern's work to maturity, evident in the mastery of harmonic and formal considerations in the *Passacaglia* Op. 1 (1908). Yet the competence of the *Passacaglia* hardly foreshadows the unique traits that would evolve to characterize Webern's style: brevity, textural clarity, dynamic restraint, motivic conciseness, contrapuntal dexterity, harmonic stasis, and a delicate objectivity. While these traits evolved continually, Webern's oeuvre does not display the drastic changes of style that mark Schoenberg's evolution. Rather, Webern's development loosely paralleled that of his mentor, tempering each stylistic advance with his own compositional sensibilities.

This process is clearly evident in the evolution of the remarkable series of aphoristic instrumental miniatures, Opp. 5-11. The energetic terseness in the taut motivic construction of the Five Movements for String Quartet Op. 5 (1909) devolves into the fleeting ephemerality of the Six Bagatelles for String Quartet Op. 9 (1911-1913). Also, the surprisingly delicate, chamberlike scoring that belies the massive forces of the Six Pieces for Large Orchestra Op. 6 (1909) is distilled into the exotic instrumentation of the Five Pieces for Orchestra Op. 10 (1911-1913), which further explores the technique of *Klangfarbenmelodie* (tone-color melody, in which the progression of instrumental timbres becomes a prime developmental consideration), first developed in Schoenberg's Five Orchestral Pieces Op. 16 (1909). That coloristic effect has now become an integral aspect of development rhetoric and is apparent in the Four Pieces for Violin and Piano Op. 7 (1910) but is particularly so in the Three Little Pieces for Cello and Piano Op. 11 (1914), whose extreme brevity (the total of thirty-two measures lasts no more than two minutes) demonstrates the ultimate compression of musical development. While Webern's work would never again approach such extreme brevity, he found little need for extensive rhetoric in any of his work; at 269 measures (about ten minutes), the *Passacaglia* remained his most expansive single movement.

By 1910, his artistic development had convinced Webern of his compositional métier. Yet composition would never prove to be his livelihood nor the source of much local recognition. Rather, after receiving his Ph.D. in 1906, Webern embarked on a career as a conductor, a vocation that he appears to have taught himself. After a series of unsuccessful appointments in theater in Ischl, Teplitz, Danzig, Stettin, and Prague, he eventually settled in Mödling in 1918 in order to be near Schoenberg, conducting the Vienna Workers' Symphony Concerts and Chorus (1922-1934). Conducting did not prove lucrative, however, and recognition of his compositions was late in coming (it was not until 1921 that his music was published by Universal Edition); he found it necessary to supplement his income by consulting for the Austrian radio station and by making arrangements for Schoenberg and the Verein für Musikalische Privataufführungen (Society for Private Musical Performances, 1918-1922). Webern also taught piano at the Jewish Cultural Institute for the Blind (1925-1931); besides his periodic private students, this would be Webern's sole teaching position. Financial difficulties plagued Webern throughout his life; he periodically received loans and gifts from his publisher, friends, family, and patrons, often through Schoenberg's intercession. Financial constraints did not, however, markedly alter Webern's reserved and prudent life-style; he was throughout his life a dedicated family man, devoted to his wife Wilhelmine (née Mörtl), a cousin whom he married in 1911, and their four children.

Given the evident stylistic limitations of the aphoristic miniatures of 1909-1914, Webern turned in 1914 to writing songs, the use of text thus providing for and even dictating formal expansion. In fact, Opp. 12-18, spanning 1914-1925, are exclusively songs and accompaniments ranging from piano to small mixed ensembles to chamber orchestra. Yet genre and length are not the only aspects different from the preceding works. Stylistically, the songs tend toward a heightened emotional tension, reflecting attitudes prevalent in the expressionist movement as manifested in music by the second Viennese school (that is, Schoenberg, Webern, and Alban Berg, Webern's fellow pupil and close friend). Wide, dramatic leaps, exaggerated by sudden dynamic contrasts, mark the vocal lines, as they develop within an unsettling atonal harmonic context. Even with Webern's adoption of Schoenberg's twelve-tone method, consistently applied from the *Three Traditional Rhymes* Op. 17 (1924-1925) onward, no sudden stylistic change is apparent. Rather, Webern's individual style characteristics evolved throughout the series of songs. Leaps of major sevenths, minor ninths, and tritones become prominent, obscuring a sense of voice-leading. Melodic lines tend toward fragmentation, emphasizing motifs of only two to four notes. Natural and sacred imagery abounds in the texts (the authors range from Li T'ai-po to August Strindberg and Georg Trakl), reflecting Webern's deep spirituality that often expressed itself in his lifelong reverence of nature. Most characteristic, however, is the increasing importance of strict contrapuntal techniques, particularly evident from the *Five Canons on Latin Texts* Op. 16 (1923-1924) through the rest of his oeuvre. A lasting impression from his study of the Flemish composers, Webern's contrapuntal dexterity allowed for the coalescence of all of these varied traits into the unique style characteristic of his late works.

The ordering principles inherent in the twelve-tone method brought renewed structural coherence to Webern's work, which allowed for a return to purely instrumental works of greater expanse, beginning with the String Trio Op. 20 (1926-1927) and the Symphony Op. 21 (1927-1928). Beyond changes in length and genre, Webern's application of the technique explored its powerful structural possibilities, both within the tone-row itself and by using the row as the generator of the form of larger structures. Webern's general concern with contrapuntal clarity typically leads to the stratification of various row forms among the individual lines. Similarly, his predilection toward symmetrical and palindromic forms shaped not only the larger formal structures but also the internal structure of the rows as he devised them; internal motivic cells generate the row itself. Thus, the four-, three-, and even two-note motifs found within the rows carry on the motivic fragmentation characteristic of the earlier experiments in *Klangfarbenmelodie*, a process giving rise to musical pointillism. These formalistic concerns supersede earlier concerns of coloristic and melodic effect, giving late works such as the Piano Variations Op. 27 (1935-1936), the String Quartet Op. 28 (1937-1938), and the Variations for Orchestra Op. 30 (1940) a detached, objective quality. Yet Webern's eminently humanistic stance provides the motivation for his two Cantatas Op. 29 (1938-1939) and Op. 31 (1941-1943), the texts of which, written by his close friend Hildegard Jone, reflect his profound respect for nature through a simple spirituality.

The quantity of Webern's creative output steadily declined after the burst of compositional activity of 1909-1914, a decline balanced, however, by the continual development of his individual artistic voice. External economic, social, and political factors had their effect here; events such as the sale of the Preglhof retreat by Webern's father in 1912, Webern's volunteer efforts in World War I (along with his efforts to secure Schoenberg's release from duty), and his continual dependence on conducting for financial support all hampered his compositional activities. While his renown as a conductor was both local and international in scope (he made numerous conducting tours throughout Europe), his compositions sparked more interest abroad than at home. This situation worsened with the rise of the Nazi regime, which not only outlawed Webern's work as "degenerate art" but also disbanded the Vienna Workers' Concerts, Webern's major source of income. World War II brought numerous tragedies, including the death of Webern's son Peter in 1945, the emigration or death of numerous friends and colleagues (Schoenberg had fled to the United States in 1933), and the flight of his family to Mittersill to escape the bombings of Vienna. On September 15, 1945, Webern was accidentally shot and killed by a soldier from the occupying American forces during an attempt to arrest his son-in-law for black-marketeering.

### *Summary*

Much of the initial recognition of Anton von Webern's work was inextricably linked, often in a derogatory fashion, to his close relationship with

Schoenberg as student, colleague, and friend. Webern's veneration of Schoenberg, at times carried to extremes of obsessive idolization, did little to diffuse misunderstanding about the development of their individual musical styles. Basic to the dynamics of their relationship were the marked differences of their personalities. With fierce independence garnered from enduring years of harsh criticism, Schoenberg demanded utter loyalty from his coterie; Webern, more reserved and reticent, thus often appeared subsumed. Schoenberg left a legacy of students, textbooks, and critical writings; Webern, who taught only occasionally and left few writings, often deferred what little recognition he did attain to his mentor. Yet the two continually exchanged reciprocal support throughout their lives on artistic, personal, and financial planes.

Such reciprocity extended to the musical plane as well, often leading to the conflation of their individual and communal (including Berg) stylistic development. Schoenberg is often characterized not only as the mentor but also as the sole innovator, which relegates Webern's development to a mere reinterpretation of Schoenberg's advances. Their creative interaction, however, was more symbiotic than this perspective implies. For example, while the exploration of *Klangfarbenmelodie* in Schoenberg's Five Orchestral Pieces Op. 16 (1909) predates Webern's Six Pieces for Large Orchestra Op. 6 (1909) by some months, the process of miniaturization seen in Webern's Opp. 5-11, begun in 1909, is only taken up by Schoenberg in his Three Orchestral Pieces (1910) and the Six Little Piano Pieces Op. 19 (1911). In similar fashion, Webern's application of Schoenberg's twelve-tone method is important not only as a demonstration of its stylistic flexibility but also for its deeper exploration of aspects of the method as reflected by Webern's own musical proclivities. Whereas Schoenberg viewed the tone row as able to provide compositional unity through motivic manipulation of the row, Webern turned to motivic connections within the row itself not only to generate the row but also to provide compositional unity, a significant shift in compositional perspective. To Webern, this reflected the balances he observed in nature, where each component works in perfect balance not only as part of a larger system but also as an individual, self-contained aspect.

The continual distillation and atomization apparent in the evolution of the various aspects of Webern's style grew to be of great influence to the succeeding generation of composers, particularly in Europe. Through courses taught by Webern's student René Liebowitz at the Kranichstein Summer School at Darmstadt, many younger composers of the 1950's took Webern to be their stylistic progenitor, most notably Karlheinz Stockhausen, Pierre Boulez, and Luciano Berio. These composers, whose compositional view in turn grew to great prominence, further distilled the serial, pointillistic, and objective aspects of Webern's style, to extremes perhaps far beyond Webern's broadest intentions, to a point at which musical rhetoric became solely an explication of compositional process. Thus, while in part construed in a manner seemingly at odds with his typically humanistic and deferential approach, Webern's influence on the development of music in the twentieth century has been pervasive.

*Bibliography*

Griffiths, Paul. "Anton Webern." In *Second Viennese School: Schoenberg, Webern, Berg*. Vol. 16 in *The New Grove Dictionary of Music and Musicians*, edited by Stanley Sadie. New York: W. W. Norton, 1983. *Second Viennese School* is part of The New Grove Composer Biography series. This article provides a concise survey of Webern's life and work as well as a brief discussion of his style and ideas. A thorough list of works and bibliography is appended.

Kolneder, Walter. *Anton Webern: An Introduction to His Works*. Translated by Humphrey Searle. Berkeley: University of California Press, 1968. Following a short biographical sketch, Kolneder examines Webern's works in chronological order, with emphasis on the evolution of stylistic traits. Chapters on Webern's personality and influence round out the study. Includes a list of works and an extensive, if somewhat outdated, bibliography.

Moldenhauer, Hans, and Rosaleen Moldenhauer. *Anton von Webern: A Chronicle of His Life and Work*. New York: Alfred A. Knopf, 1979. The most extensive and thorough biography available. Through interviews with Webern's family and associates, coupled with exhaustive gathering of surviving letters, documents, and manuscripts, the Moldenhauers augment existing information with important and insightful new research. Chapters alternate between Webern's life and works; the compendious detail is balanced by Moldenhauer's lively prose style. Includes Webern's own extensive analysis of his String Quartet Op. 28. The appended work lists are perhaps the most comprehensive available, and the select bibliography is also thorough.

Rognoni, Luigi. *The Second Vienna School*. Translated by Robert W. Mann. London: John Calder, 1977. A study of the stylistic derivation of expressionism, as applied by Schoenberg, Berg, and Webern, and its relationship to other contemporaneous artistic trends. Webern's works are described in chronological order, with emphasis on stylistic evolution rather than biographical context.

Webern, Anton. *The Path to the New Music*. Edited by Willi Reich. Translated by Leo Black. Bryn Mawr, Pa.: Theodore Presser, 1963. Given the dearth of Webern's extant critical prose, this transcription from shorthand of sixteen lectures given by Webern in 1932-1933 provides important insight into his aesthetic motivation. Traces the historic justification of the innovations in musical language developed by the second Viennese school. Includes as a postscript a number of personal letters from Webern to Reich.

Wildgans, Friedrich. *Anton Webern*. Translated by Edith Temple Roberts and Humphrey Searle. London: Calder and Boyars, 1966. Wildgans discusses the evolution of Webern's style in a biographical context, followed by a short critical description of the works in chronological order. Five tributes to and by Webern are appended. The short bibliography and discography have been surpassed.

*Paul A. Siskind*

# ALFRED WEGENER

*Born:* November 1, 1880; Berlin, Germany
*Died:* Winter of 1930; Greenland
*Areas of Achievement:* Geology and physics
*Contribution:* Wegener was a German meteorologist and Arctic explorer who receives credit for the first clear statement of the hypothesis of continental drift. Although his ideas were scornfully dismissed by most geologists in his own time, they were enthusiastically revived by oceanographers in the mid-1960's as the precursor to the well-known plate tectonics theory.

## *Early Life*

Alfred Lothar Wegener was born in Berlin, Germany, on November 1, 1880, the son of a preacher in the Evangelical church. He was educated at the Köllnisches Gymnasium in Berlin and subsequently attended the Universities of Heidelberg, Innsbruck, and Berlin. He received his Ph.D. degree in astronomy from the University of Berlin in 1905, and his doctoral thesis was on the conversion of a set of thirteenth century tables of planetary motion from a number system based on multiples of sixty to the decimal system.

As a youth Wegener became fascinated with the vast, ice-covered island of Greenland. At that time nothing was known of Greenland's interior as exploration had been limited to the coastal areas only. In order to prepare himself for the longed-for trip to Greenland, Wegener spent much of his spare time in a rigorous program of endurance training, which consisted of gymnastics and all-day bouts of walking, ice skating, mountain climbing, and skiing.

Following his graduation from the University of Berlin in 1905, Wegener found that he had lost interest in the field of astronomy, and he turned his attention to the newly established science of meteorology instead, taking a position as an assistant at the Royal Prussian Aeronautical Observatory at Lindenberg. There he experimented with kites and balloons, and in 1906 he and his brother Kurt broke the world's record for long distance in a free balloon, drifting for fifty-two hours from April 5 to 7 across Germany, Denmark, and adjacent water bodies.

Also in 1906, the long-awaited opportunity to visit Greenland finally presented itself, and Wegener resigned his position at the observatory in order to join the 1906-1908 Danmark Expedition to Greenland. He served as official meteorologist to the expedition, which successfully explored the northeastern part of the island and made important weather measurements. Wegener returned safely to Germany at the expedition's end, but its leader, Ludvig Mylius-Erichsen, did not. He and two companions died while on a side trip northward toward the pole, a tragic premonition of Wegener's own death on the Greenland ice cap in 1930.

Upon his return to Germany in 1908, Wegener went to the University of Marburg as a lecturer. There he taught courses in meteorology, practical astronomy, and cosmic physics, meanwhile continuing his meteorological investigations. He also published a book on the thermodynamics of the atmosphere in 1911, but his academic career was abruptly halted in 1914 when World War I broke out, and he was called up as part of the general mobilization.

*Life's Work*

Wegener is chiefly noted for the hypothesis of continental drift. In it he contended that the earth's continents had once been joined together but then had broken apart and begun drifting about the surface of the globe much as icebergs drift about the sea. The subject of drift had claimed his attention as early as 1903 when he pointed out the remarkable "fit" between the continents on the opposite sides of the Atlantic to a fellow student at the University of Berlin. Then in 1910, when he was examining world maps in a handsome new atlas, the idea of drifting continents came over him in its full force, but he relates that he instantly rejected the idea as being "too improbable." In 1911, however, he stumbled "quite by accident" on a study summarizing the similarities between the fossil animals found in Africa and in Brazil. The study attributed these similarities to a former land connection—now submerged—between the two continents; Wegener, however, believed otherwise. He was convinced that Africa and Brazil had once been joined together and subsequently had drifted apart.

Wegener presented his new ideas to the scientific community during January of 1912, first addressing the Geological Association in Frankfurt and then the Society for the Advancement of Natural Science in Marburg. A paper on the subject quickly followed, but next came two interruptions. The first was a return to Greenland in the spring of 1912, accompanied by J. P. Koch, a Dane whom he had met on the 1906-1908 expedition. After lengthy preparations, they made the first successful east-west crossing of the ice cap at its widest point, using sledges hauled by ponies for the 1,100-kilometer trip. The second interruption came in 1914 with the outbreak of World War I when Wegener was called into the army.

Wegener served with distinction and was wounded twice. In his spare time, however, he still managed to continue working on his Greenland data, to make meteorological observations, and to refine his thinking on the subject of continental drift. While on sick leave in 1915, he even managed to set down his ideas in a slender volume, which came out under the title *Die Entstehung der Kontinente und Ozeane* (1915; *Origin of Continents and Oceans*, 1922). This book spelled out the basic tenets of continental drift, along with supporting evidence. In essence, Wegener proposed that the continents had not always occupied their present positions but were originally gathered together as a large supercontinent, which he called Pangaea (literally, all-earth). Pangaea had occupied half the globe, with the other half being covered by water—the ancestral Pacific Ocean.

Beginning in the Mesozoic era, however—some 200 million years before the present—Wegener believed that the continents had begun detaching themselves from Pangaea and started drifting toward their new locations, much as icebergs plow through water. He proposed that the Atlantic Ocean had been formed when Pangaea split in two, with North America, South America, Antarctica, and Australia originating from the strip of continental crust on the west. As this strip plowed westward across the Pacific, Wegener believed that great wrinkles had appeared along its leading edge which now form the mountain chains that extend from the Andes to Alaska. He also proposed that the towering Himalaya Mountains had been created in a similar fashion when northward-drifting India crashed into the continent of Asia.

Wegener spent the years following 1915 marshaling the evidence to support his hypothesis. First there was the behavior of earthquake waves; they seemed to indicate that the continents were composed of lightweight rocks floating on the heavier rocks of the ocean floor. Then came the jigsaw-puzzle "fit" between continents on the opposite sides of the Atlantic; by including with the continents the submerged lands adjacent to their shoreline—the so-called continental shelves—he obtained an even better "fit" than was possible by merely juxtaposing coastlines.

A third line of evidence was the presence of similar geologic features on continents that are now widely separated. The rocks of Brazil strongly resemble those of Africa, for example, and mountain trends even seem to match when the continents are restored to their predrift positions. Wegener also cited similarities in fossil plants and animals found in continents that are now far distant from one another.

An ingenious line of evidence was based on glacial activity in pre-Mesozoic times. Distinctive deposits of ancient glacial debris are found in such diverse localities as southern South America, Antarctica, Australia, South Africa, and parts of India. Worldwide glaciation cannot explain these deposits, because tropical climates existed side by side with glaciated areas. Pangaea provided a likely explanation, however, because when the continents are restored to their predrift positions, all these glaciated areas become contiguous, suggesting a single large ice cap located at the South Pole. A final line of evidence was the apparent changes in the longitude of various localities on the globe. Such changes would have supported his hypothesis by demonstrating that the continents were still moving. Unfortunately, the methods used for measuring longitude in those days were not sufficiently precise to provide the confirmation he needed.

After the war's end, Wegener accepted a teaching post at the University of Hamburg and while there conducted experiments related to another one of his theories, namely that the moon's craters had originated as a result of meteoric bombardment, rather than through volcanic action. Continental drift remained his primary obsession, however, and he brought out revised and expanded editions of *Origin of Continents and Oceans* in 1920 and 1922. His hypothesis had attracted attention outside Germany by now, and French, English, Spanish, and Russian translations of the 1922 edition appeared in 1924. In the same year, Wegener was also appointed to the chair of meteorology and geophysics at the University of Graz in Austria, an important upward step in the academic world.

The growing attention to his ideas resulted in a swelling controversy, however, which reached its climax in 1926 when the American Association of Petroleum Geologists organized a symposium concerning continental drift as part of its annual meeting in New York City. Wegener attended, as did noted geologists from Europe and the United States. The hypothesis suffered a major setback as far as acceptance by the scientific world was concerned, however, because of the effective way in which his opponents presented their arguments. Undaunted, Wegener put out a fourth edition of his book in 1929, incorporating in it his rebuttals to the arguments advanced at the symposium. He also agreed to make another trip to Greenland, as leader of the German Inland Ice Expedition of 1930. The jet stream, that fast-moving current in the upper atmosphere which circles the earth in northern latitudes, had just been discovered, and the expedition's goal was to establish three year-round stations on the ice cap in order to study jet stream flow. The expedition was also to make pioneering measurements of the thickness of the ice cap using echo-sounding techniques.

Two of the three stations were to be on opposite coasts, and the third—named "Eismitte" (mid-ice)—was to be in the center of the ice cap at an elevation of 3,000 meters. Two members of the expedition had already set up a temporary camp there by the fall of 1930. Their quarters consisted of a pit dug into the ice and roofed over. Wegener and a fourth member followed with the necessary supplies but did not arrive until October 29 because of bad weather. Because most of the supplies had been lost en route, Wegener and his Eskimo companion decided to return to the coastal base before the polar night set in. They never made it. Wegener's body was later found halfway back, neatly sewn into his sleeping bag and buried in the snow with upright skis as a marker. His Eskimo companion apparently had gone on, but no trace of him or his sledge was ever found.

### *Summary*

Alfred Wegener's scientific reputation rests primarily on his advocacy of continental drift. Although he was not the first to speculate about drifting continents—Sir Francis Bacon had called attention to the similar shapes of Africa and South America in 1620—he was the first to present a unified hypothesis, together with evidence drawn from many scientific disciplines. This was a remarkable achievement in itself in that era of the Germanic tradition of specialization. Wegener was also the first scientist supporting continental drift who was taken seriously. His book went through four editions and was translated into as many languages. A symposium was even arranged by the prestigous American Association of Petroleum Geologists, and world-famous scientists met to discuss his ideas. Unfortunately, their verdict was negative, and this led to continental drift's being consigned to the academic scrap heap for the next thirty-five years.

Numerous factors led to the hypothesis' rejection. There were some flaws in his reasoning, to be sure, and some of the evidence proposed later proved to be inaccurate. More telling, however, was Wegener's inability to provide a convincing mechanism for moving continents around the globe. In fact, he was unable to demonstrate that the continents were moving at all. Being an "outsider" did not help either—his doctorate was in astronomy, his research had been in meteorology, and his professional reputation rested on his exploits as a balloonist and as an Arctic explorer. His credentials in geology were nonexistent. No wonder the reception that he received from the professional geologists at the New York City symposium ranged from politely skeptical to openly sarcastic.

After Wegener's death in 1930, the hypothesis of continental drift was no longer given serious consideration by the scientific world. It had been too radical a departure from the accepted thinking of the day. As one of the participants in the 1926 symposium put it, "If we are to believe in Wegener's hypothesis, we must forget everything which has been learned in the last seventy years and start all over again." That, of course, was exactly what was going to have to happen. A revolution in geological thinking was coming, but regrettably Wegener did not live to see it. It was not until the mid-1960's, when oceanographers proposed the radically new plate tectonics theory, that scientists around the world realized how forward-looking Wegener had been.

*Bibliography*

Calder, Nigel. *The Restless Earth: A Report on the New Geology.* New York: Viking Press, 1972. A concise overview of plate tectonics, suitable for high school level readers and the interested lay person. Well illustrated with diagrams, black-and-white photographs, and superb color plates. Wegener's contributions to the development of the plate tectonics theory are presented in summary form and are evaluated in terms of the overall framework of plate tectonics.

Dott, Robert H., and Roger Lyman Batten. *Evolution of the Earth.* 4th ed. New York: McGraw-Hill, 1988. A well-written and well-illustrated text. It presents an up-to-date account of earth history from the viewpoint of plate tectonics and describes the evidence that has been advanced to support this theory. Wegener's contributions are described and are compared with the contributions of others. Suitable for college-level readers.

LeGrand, H. E. *Drifting Continents and Shifting Theories*. Cambridge, England: Cambridge University Press, 1988. An up-to-date analysis of the thinking that led to the plate tectonics theory. Written for the college-level reader or lay person with some technical background. Wegener's work is described against the backdrop of the other theories of crustal evolution, and there is a very extensive bibliography of sources dealing with continental drift and plate tectonics.

Marvin, Ursula B. *Continental Drift: The Evolution of a Concept*. Washington, D.C.: Smithsonian Institution Press, 1973. A comprehensive study of the scientific debate on continental drift, with an exhaustive review of the evidence proposed by Wegener in support of his hypothesis and of the arguments advanced by his critics against it. The extensive bibliography contains a list of Wegener's publications dealing with continental drift.

Sullivan, Walter. *Continents in Motion: The New Earth Debate*. New York: McGraw-Hill, 1974. The author uses the historical approach to present the subject of plate tectonics in a manner that is both understandable and exciting for the average reader. A full chapter is devoted to Wegener, and the references accompanying this chapter list the important sources of bibliographical material pertaining to him.

Wyllie, Peter J. *The Way the Earth Works: The Introduction to the New Global Geology and Its Revolutionary Development*. New York: John Wiley & Sons, 1976. An overview of the plate tectonic theory that is suitable for high school level readers and the interested layperson. Wegener's role is clearly described and much useful biographical information is included. The information relating to his Greenland expeditions is particularly useful, and there are also lists of suggested readings covering the various aspects of plate tectonics.

*Donald W. Lovejoy*

# SIMONE WEIL

*Born:* February 3, 1909; Paris, France
*Died:* August 24, 1943; Ashford, Kent, England
*Areas of Achievement:* Philosophy and religion
*Contribution:* Perhaps even more than her writing, the life of Weil, twentieth century French mystic and philosophical thinker, has for several generations both fascinated and perplexed many. Weil's passion and originality, her intense sense of commitment toward eternity and her fellowman, and her willingness to sacrifice her life for her truths remain her principal legacy.

## *Early Life*

Simone Weil was the second child and only daughter of a prosperous and highly cultured professional family. Her father, Bernard Weil, an eminent physician, was born in Strasbourg; Salomea Reinherz Weil, her mother, was from Rostov-na-Donu. The family was extremely close, and the influence of Weil's mother was particularly strong. Although Weil's parents were both of Jewish descent, they were agnostics and maintained no Jewish identity. Simone's attitude toward her own Jewishness was to remain problematical throughout her lifetime. A sickly child almost from birth, Weil experienced normal health for only a few years of her life. Although much of Weil's time was spent reading and studying, from a young age she also demonstrated an exceptionally acute moral sensibility and an unusual concern for the poor and oppressed.

An enlightened Parisian family, the Weils spared no expense in obtaining the best education for their children. They soon perceived, however, that André, Weil's brother, was the more intellectually gifted of the two children. Considered something of a genius, he passed the *baccalauréat* at the age of fourteen and later was to become one of the outstanding mathematicians of his time. Intimidated by her brother's achievements and discouraged by several unsympathetic teachers, Weil suffered through a period of deep depression in her early teens.

When Weil entered the Lycée Henri IV in 1925, she became acquainted with a man who was to exert the strongest and most lasting influence on her philosophy: Émile-Auguste Chartier, better known by his pseudonym, Alain. During her time at Henry IV (1925-1928), Weil continued her social activism. In particular, she became passionately committed to the revolutionary syndicalist, or trade unionist, movement. At this time she also began teaching in a type of free university organized for railroad workers. She was to devote much time and effort to this kind of project throughout her life because of her deep conviction that the proletariat—not merely the privileged few—could appreciate education and culture.

### *Life's Work*

In 1927 the École Normal Supérieure had only begun admitting women, but, when the results of the entrance examination in 1928 were announced, two women were at the top of the list. Weil was first, and Simone de Beauvoir was second, followed by thirty male students.

During her years at the École Normale Supérieure, Weil gained a reputation as an intransigent revolutionary and was nicknamed the "Red Virgin." Upon completion of the agrégation in philosophy in 1931 with a thesis on science and perception in the works of René Descartes, she was assigned to the position of professor of philosophy at the girls' *lycée* of Le Puy, a small town in the Massif Central. This was the first of her five teaching assignments in five different towns during the years of 1931 through 1937. Her organizing activities among the unemployed working classes of the area earned for her continual harassment—even arrest on several occasions—by the municipal authorities.

Believing that any political theory or plan of social action required a firsthand acquaintance with the moral and physical problems that confronted the proletariat, Weil, in 1934, took a one-year unpaid leave of absence from teaching in order to learn by direct contact what kinds of problems most seriously undermined the quality of working-class life. She took on a series of factory jobs to better her understanding. Weil's year of factory work is often regarded as a major turning point of her life. Her most ambitious goal during this year was to discover the means by which to reorganize industrial planning so as to create working conditions in which the proletariat could become truly free. Her probing essays on the subject, *La Condition ouvrière* (1951; factory journal), argued not for the conventional leftist change in ownership and political power but for a more profound transformation of modern work itself.

Pragmatically speaking, the answers that she found to freeing the proletariat were relatively vague. Yet the most lasting effect of the factory experience was one that she had not anticipated: a profound and irrevocable change in her character. She learned that, while the physical suffering of workers was deplorable, it was far less devastating than their slavelike humiliation and degradation. Another change was that a new pessimism about revolutionary activity began to surface in her thinking during this time.

Yet her dissociation from the revolutionary syndicalist movement as a result of this new pessimism was a process that had actually begun some time earlier. As early as 1933, Weil had written an article for the organ of La Révolution Prolétarienne (a humanitarian, anarchist, syndicalist movement with which she had become acquainted while at the École Normale Supérieure) in which she had criticized not only the Stalinist state in the Soviet Union but also the revolutionary syndicalist movement itself for excessive bureaucracy at the expense of the worker.

In August of 1936, Weil traveled to Barcelona to join the anarchist movement in the Spanish Civil War and volunteered for noncombatant service in the Confederación Nacional del Trabajo (CNT). Although she was in Spain only a few weeks, she witnessed enough of the conflict to learn that neither side could be trusted; in her opinion, the war was only a pretext for a battle between the interests of the Soviet Union and those of Germany and Italy.

Weil's involvement in the Spanish Civil War ended abruptly as the result of an injury (she accidentally spilled some boiling oil on her leg). Since Weil's general physical condition was already poor and the complications from her burns weakened her so severely, she was forced to take a medical leave of absence from teaching during the academic year 1936-1937. Although she returned to the classroom in October, 1937, at the Lycée of Saint-Quentin near Paris, by January of 1938 her health was so poor that she had to apply once again for sick leave. She was never to return to teaching.

From the time she ended her factory work in August, 1935, until the autumn of 1938, Weil was in spiritual crisis. One of the first revelations of her sympathy with Catholicism occurred during a visit to Portugal in September, 1935. It was in Santa Maria degli Angeli, in Italy, however, that a force far stronger than she, as she describes it, compelled her to go down on her knees for the first time in her life. Weil spent Holy Week of 1938 at the Benedictine monastery of Solesmes meditating, and it was there, she recounts, that Christ himself came down and took possession of her. She had always admired Christ; from her *lycée* days she had read and used the Bible in her writing, teaching, and personal meditations on history, social justice, and philosophy. Yet her aversion for the Roman and Hebrew civilizations was a major obstacle that for years repelled her from the faith. As a result of her mystical experience, occurring in the autumn of 1938, Weil's life was suffused with a belief that she had encountered Christ and that she belonged to him. Thenceforth the person of Christ was to guide her philosophy.

During the years of Weil's spiritual crisis, she became more and more detached from the revolutionary syndicalist movement. While her faith in political parties had collapsed after her brief participation in the Spanish Civil War, she continued to demonstrate her concern for the working class in her articles on industrial reform. She also attended meetings of the Nouveaux Cahiers, a discussion group organized and attended by industrial executives for the purpose of planning a rational and equitable program of social reform in factory life.

The new emphasis in Weil's political thought at this time was on two rather unpopular causes: anticolonialism and pacifism. Although her views on a policy of gradual decolonization were similar to the policy eventually adopted by the French government in the 1950's, at that time the French public was not yet ready to give up its territorial claims. In retrospect, the pacifist stance in which Weil persisted right up to the German invasion of

Czechoslovakia in March, 1939, was much less justified. She repeatedly underestimated Adolf Hitler's drive for conquest, and she insisted that almost anything was preferable to armed conflict. Yet when news reached France of German soldiers entering Prague, Weil was no longer able to support a pacifist position.

After a few months' stay in Vichy, in October of 1940 Weil moved to Marseilles, where she attended meetings of the Young Christian Workers' Movement and wrote for the French Resistance newspaper, *Témoignage chrétien*. One of the most important associations of Weil's Marseilles years, however, was her involvement with the group that published *Cahiers du sud*, including Jean Ballard, editor in chief, the poet Jean Torrel, and André Gide's son-in-law, Jean Lambert. It was in this journal that Weil published her essays on the *Iliad*, literature and morality, and Provençal Catharism (a form of Christian gnosticism widespread in the region known as Occitania in the eleventh and twelfth centuries).

Ever since her conversion experience, Weil had been exploring very carefully the doctrines and beliefs of the Catholic church. Yet, while she was drawn to Catholicism, she also criticized the Church as a bureaucratic establishment, especially in its inquisitional intolerance, ambiguous morality, anti-intellectualism, and otherworldly impurity. Because of these and other doubts, she never officially joined the Church and was never baptized.

Although she preferred to remain in France and share the hardship of her countrymen, in May, 1942, Weil reluctantly agreed to accompany her parents to New York, where she hoped to leave them in safety. After months of waiting in New York, Weil finally arranged passage to England, where she began working for the Free French movement. Assigned to the Ministry of the Interior, she was to submit written reports analyzing political documents received from unoccupied France. Since these documents concerned the postwar reconstruction of the new republic, they provided the occasion for some of Weil's most detailed political theorizing. While their tentative nature often led to impracticalities and excesses, the essays in *Écrits de Londres et dernières lettres* (1957) offer a useful look at the practical implications of her unusual speculative philosophy.

Ever since leaving France, Weil had drastically restricted her diet in order to share the privations of her countrymen in the Occupied zone. Her revulsion to the fallen material world had always included sexuality, comfort, and other desires—not the least of which was food. Eventually, however, her friends found it necessary to resort to subterfuge to keep her even minimally nourished. Negligent sleep habits also contributed to a general decline in her health involving an aggravation of her chronic migraines, progressive weakening of her physical stamina, and the onset of a tubercular condition.

As she felt her life ebbing away from her, Weil accelerated the pace of her writing. She reportedly spent her last months in a constant state of creativity, continually scribbling down notes on random topics as they occurred to her. The *Cahiers* (1951; *Notebooks*, 1952-1955) contain numerous examples of elliptical thoughts, outlines, and sketches of projects that she was unable to pursue. As such, these tentative explorations might be viewed as footnotes to the definitive formulation of her philosophy.

In April, 1943, Weil's body was no longer able to endure the demands she made upon it, and she was admitted to the hospital with tuberculosis and severe exhaustion. While the doctors believed that her chances of recovery were good, she persistently refused treatment and took food only infrequently. Clearly designed to transgress the boundaries of deprivation that could be reasonably attributed to solidarity with her countrymen, Weil's actions expressed her need for total personal affliction in the suffering world to which she was so sensitive.

On August 17, Weil was transferred to Grosvenor Sanatorium in Ashford, Kent, and on the afternoon of August 24, 1943, she lapsed into a coma and died later that evening. The newspapers in the area announced that the coroner's inquest had ruled her death a case of suicide by starvation, although medical reports were confusing and conflicting. At the age of thirty-four, Weil had reached the end of one of the most unusual and controversial pilgrimages in recent history.

*Summary*

In her short life, Simone Weil was a striking teacher of philosophy, a dedicated left-militant, a provocative essayist on social and religious issues, and an exceptional, though controversial, personality. In her final years and posthumously for a much larger audience (when her essays, notes, fragments, poems, and letters were first published in book form), she gained an even more paradoxical notoriety as a "Catholic saint outside the church."

While her later social thought, exemplified in the political sociology of *L'Enracinement* (1949; *The Need for Roots*, 1952), still emphasized the centrality of the worker and his alienation and oppression, it demonstrates less of her earlier insight. The antipolitics and the libertarianism, egalitarianism, and pacifism had partly submerged themselves into a heightened spiritual quest that undercut merely human social questions. Weil's remarkable intensity and impassioned earnestness, combined with sophisticated philosophical and historical perceptions and abilities, made her a poignant witness to the possible social-religious transcendence of human suffering.

*Bibliography*

Coles, Robert. *Simone Weil: A Modern Pilgrimage*. Reading, Mass.: Addison-Wesley, 1987. In this intelligent and interpretive portrait written by a Harvard psychiatrist and humanities professor, the author describes Weil's major quests and obsessions in an effort to comprehend her inspiring and contradictory nature. Also contains notes and bibliography.

Dunaway, John M. *Simone Weil*. Boston: Twayne, 1984. This brief sketch is intended as an introduction to the subject, primarily for the use of the nonspecialist. A bibliography, extensive notes, and references are also provided.

Fiori, Gabriella. *Simone Weil: An Intellectual Biography.* Translated by Joseph K. Berrigan. Athens: University of Georgia Press, 1989. This lengthy and well-written synthesis of Weil's life and thought is based upon evidence solely provided by individuals closely familiar with Weil and her works. Extensive notes and a bibliography of primary and secondary works are included.

McFarland, Dorothy Tuck. *Simone Weil*. New York: Frederick Ungar, 1983. This brief but very readable study underscores the continuity of Weil's work beneath the seeming reversal of political positions. Also contains footnotes and primary and secondary bibliography.

Pétrement, Simone. *Simone Weil: A Life*. Translated by Raymond Rosenthal. New York: Pantheon Books, 1976. Written by one of Weil's closest friends, this lengthy standard biography of Weil is particularly useful for the documents it contains and for the author's efforts at ordering and dating these documents. Numerous notes and illustrations are also included.

*Genevieve Slomski*

# KURT WEILL

*Born:* March 2, 1900; Dessau, Germany
*Died:* April 3, 1950; New York, New York
*Area of Achievement:* Music
*Contribution:* Weill was one of the outstanding composers of the generation that came to maturity after World War I. He broke away from the Romantic, emotional style of Wagnerian opera to create a revolutionary new form: the opera of sharp social satire. After his emigration to the United States, Weill turned away from his earlier "serious" works to become one of the top composers of Broadway musicals in the 1940's.

## *Early Life*

Kurt Julian Weill was born in Dessau, Germany, on March 2, 1900. His father, Albert, was the cantor at the synagogue in Dessau, and a composer in his own right. His mother, Emma (née Ackermann), loved literature and maintained an extensive library for the family. Weill was reared as an orthodox Jew, along with his two elder brothers, Nathan and Hans Jacob, and his younger sister, Ruth. The Weill children were all taught music, and often attended performances of Wagnerian operas at the Ducal Court Theater, or Hofoper, in Dessau.

Weill had begun to compose by the time he was twelve years old. When he was fifteen, his father arranged for him to study with Albert Bing, a respected composer who served as the associate musical director of the Hofoper. In April, 1918, Weill went to Berlin to attend the Hochschule für Musik. There he studied composition under Wagner disciple Engelbert Humperdinck (composer of the opera *Hänsel und Gretel*, 1893), harmony and counterpoint with Friedrich E. Koch, and conducting with Rudolf Krasselt. He wrote a symphonic poem based on Rainer Maria Rilke's *Die Weise von Liebe und Tod des Cornets Christoph Rilke* (1906; *The Tale of the Love and Death of Cornet Christopher Rilke*, 1932). This piece was considered good enough to be performed by the Hochschule orchestra, and it won for him a scholarship given by the Felix Mendelssohn Foundation. Despite his success, however, Weill felt stifled by the old-fashioned musical ideas taught at the Hochschule, so he left it after one year to return to Dessau. There, he worked for three months as a repetiteur, or singing coach, at the Hofoper under his former teacher, Albert Bing. In December, 1919, he took a temporary staff conducting job with the tiny Lüdenscheid Civic Opera in Westphalia. There, he received a solid training in making music for the theater.

In September, 1920, Weill auditioned and was accepted into the master class in composition at the Berlin Academy of Art, which was taught by Ferruccio Busoni, an avant-garde composer who Weill greatly admired. Weill became one of Busoni's favorite students, and he studied under him for three years, until December, 1923. During that time, Weill wrote several works, including a children's ballet, *Die Zaubernacht*, which was performed in Berlin in 1922 and again two years later in New York under the title *Magic Night*; a *Divertimento* for orchestra and male chorus; his *Sinfonia Sacra* Op. 6; *Frauentanz* (women's dance), a cycle of seven songs for soprano and small instrumental ensemble, which was performed at the Salzburg Festival in 1924 and which won for him a contract with Universal Edition, a leading publisher of new music; and his String Quartet Op. 8. This piece was first performed for the Novembergrüppe, an association of radical artists of which Weill was a member.

*Life's Work*

In 1922, Weill met Georg Kaiser, perhaps Germany's most significant expressionist playwright. In January, 1924, Kaiser offered to collaborate with Weill on a ballet based on Kaiser's play *Der Protagonist* (1922; the protagonist). They worked for two months on the idea before they decided that the piece would work much better as an opera than a ballet. While Kaiser revised his libretto, Weill took the opportunity to compose his best instrumental work to date, a Concerto for Violin and Wind Orchestra, which was first performed in Paris in June, 1925.

Weill visited Kaiser at his country home during the rest of 1924 and early 1925 to complete the music for *Der Protagonist*. While he was there, in the summer of 1924, he became acquainted with an actress named Lotte Lenya (née Karoline Blaumauer). By the end of that year, they had taken an apartment together. They were married on January 28, 1926. Lenya was not Jewish, and Weill's parents disapproved of the match. By that time, however, Weill felt disaffected by the religion of his childhood and rebellious against middle-class conventions in life as well as music, and so his Bohemian, Gentile bride suited him very well. Their marriage was sometimes troubled, and once they divorced and remarried, but then they remained together until he died. Afterward, Lenya protected and promoted Weill's legacy until his music became well known around the world.

Weill and Kaiser completed the opera *Der Protagonist* in April, 1925. It was a fabulous success at its premier at the Dresden State Opera on March 27, 1926, and it marked the turning point in Weill's career. He was now considered one of the leading composers of theatrical music in Germany. Weill started writing another opera with Kaiser, a comic one-act piece called *Der Zar lässt sich photographieren* (1927; the czar has his picture taken) in March, 1927, the same month in which he began one of the most famous collaborations in twentieth century theater: his association with Marxist playwright Bertolt Brecht.

Weill and Brecht began with a plan for a full-length opera called *Aufstieg und Fall der Stadt Mahagonny* (1930; *The Rise and Fall of the City of*

*Mahagonny*, 1957) based on part of Brecht's poetry collection, *Hauspostille* (1927, 1951; *A Manual of Piety*, 1966). In the meantime, however, Weill received a commission for a short, one-act opera to be performed at the Baden-Baden Festival of German Chamber Music that summer. He decided to use the commission to write five songs as a preliminary study for the opera. The result, *Mahagonny Songspiel*, premiered at the Baden-Baden Festival on July 18, 1927, with one of the female roles being sung by Lenya. Brecht then arranged to write the play that would open the new theater managed by impresario Ernst Robert Aufricht. *Die Dreigroschenoper* (*The Threepenny Opera*, 1949) was based on John Gay's *The Beggar's Opera* (1728) and featured songs by Weill. After a turbulent rehearsal period, it opened on August 31, 1928, at the Theater am Schiffbauerdamm in Berlin, to immense and immediate success.

*The Threepenny Opera* brought Weill popularity and financial security. He completed several other commissions before finishing the score for *Rise and Fall of the City of Mahagonny* in April, 1929. During that summer, he and Brecht collaborated on another musical play called *Happy End*, which premiered on September 2, 1929, at the Theater am Schiffbauerdamm. Before it opened, however, Brecht decided that the play was too frivolous, that it violated his belief that theater should teach, not entertain. He renounced his authorship of the play, and it closed after a few performances.

In the six months between the disastrous opening of *Happy End* and the premier of *The Rise and Fall of the City of Mahagonny* at the Leipzig Opera House on March 9, 1930, the stock market experienced its infamous crash that destroyed the economies of countries all around the world. The unemployment crisis in Germany had given the Nazis a new strength, and they put Weill, who was Jewish, on their list of artists that they reviled. On the opening night of *The Rise and Fall of the City of Mahagonny*, the Nazis interrupted the performance by starting fist fights in the aisles of the theater. Performances of *The Rise and Fall of the City of Mahagonny* in other cities were cancelled by Nazi-led town councils. By 1933, the Nazis had succeeded in their campaign to drive the works of Weill off the stages of Germany.

In the meantime, Brecht and Weill were growing apart. Brecht became increasingly autocratic and devoted to Marxism, whereas Weill grew more tolerant, exploring the tensions in his work between the atonality of the modern fashion and the traditional, romantic melodies he remembered from his youth. Their famous, productive partnership came to an end after only three years.

Weill wrote one more opera with Kaiser, *Der Silbersee* (silver lake), which opened simultaneously to good reviews in Leipzig, Erfurt, and Magdeburg on February 18, 1933. On February 27, Adolf Hitler began his crackdown on his political opponents. On March 21, Weill learned that he was about to be arrested by the Gestapo, so he packed a few belongings in a car and escaped to France. Weill's music was popular in Paris, and yet his exile there was unhappy. He felt betrayed by his homeland. Also, he had lost all of his money when he left Germany, and his relationship with his wife had become very strained. He reluctantly agreed to write a final piece with Brecht, a ballet called *Die sieben Todsünden der Kleinbürger* (*The Seven Deadly Sins of the Petit Bourgeois*, 1961), which premiered at the Théâtre des Champs Élysées on June 7, 1933. He composed several more pieces before being commissioned, late in the summer of 1934, to write the score for Franz Werfel's Biblical drama *Der Weg der Verheissung* (1935; *The Eternal Road*, 1936), which tells the story of the wanderings of the Jewish people toward their goal of the Promised Land. Weill's persecution at the hands of the Nazis caused him to reidentify with his Jewish ancestry, and he used the religious music of his youth as the basis for his score. The play was scheduled to open in New York in early 1936, and Weill was to conduct the performance. So, in September, 1935, he and Lenya, with whom he had recently reconciled, sailed for the United States.

For financial reasons, the production of *The Eternal Road* was delayed, so Weill took a commission from the Group Theatre to write the score for *Johnny Johnson*, an antiwar satire written by Paul Green, which opened in New York on November 19, 1936, and closed only sixty-eight performances later, the victim of bad reviews. *The Eternal Road* finally opened on January 7, 1937. Unfortunately, budget overruns doomed this lavish production to financial disaster, even though it played to packed houses.

Weill then collaborated with Maxwell Anderson on a political satire based on Washington Irving's book *A History of New York* (1809). Weill's first Broadway success, *Knickerbocker Holiday*, the score of which includes the famous "September Song," opened at the Ethel Barrymore Theater in New York on October 19, 1938. Weill teamed with Moss Hart and Ira Gershwin for his next Broadway hit. *Lady in the Dark*, starring Gertrude Lawrence and Danny Kaye, opened at the Alvin Theater in New York on January 23, 1941, and ran for two years. His next musical, called *One Touch of Venus*, was written with S. J. Perelman and Ogden Nash. It opened at the Imperial Theater in New York on October 7, 1943, starred Mary Martin, and was Weill's greatest Broadway success.

Weill wrote one more play with Gershwin, along with Gershwin's friend Edwin Justus Mayer, an operetta based on Mayer's play *The Firebrand* (1924). *The Firebrand of Florence*, starring Lenya in only her second American stage appearance, was a complete disaster when it opened on March 22, 1945. After this, Weill deliberately changed his musical style from a slick, Broadway idiom to a simpler, American folk sound. He collaborated with Elmer Rice to write the opera *Street Scene*, based on Rice's 1929 play of the same name. It opened in New York at the Adelphi Theater on January 9,

1947, to critical acclaim but only moderate box-office success. Weill wrote a folk opera, *Down in the Valley,* for the students at the University of Indiana at Bloomington, where it premiered on July 15, 1948. His next musical, *Love Life*, written with Alan Jay Lerner, opened on October 7, 1948, at the Forty-sixth Street Theater in New York, and received only mediocre critical reviews.

Weill's last work was written with his good friend Maxwell Anderson. It was a "musical tragedy" based on the novel *Cry, the Beloved Country* (1948) by Alan Paton. *Lost in the Stars* premiered at the Music Box Theater in New York on October 30, 1949. The production did very well, at first. Weill and Anderson began work on a musical based on Mark Twain's 1884 novel *The Adventures of Huckleberry Finn*. Then, in January, 1950, the box office for *Lost in the Stars* began to deteriorate. Weill became increasingly irritable, and he suffered a terrible attack of the psoriasis that had plagued him all of his life. On the night of March 16, he awoke with chest pains. He was admitted to Flower-Fifth Avenue Hospital in New York, where his condition gradually grew worse. He died there, at 7:00 P.M. on Monday, April 3, 1950, with Lenya and his friends Maxwell and Mab Anderson at his bedside.

*Summary*

From 1924, with the premier of *Der Protagonist*, to 1935, when he emigrated to the United States, Kurt Weill was considered one of the leading composers in Europe. He worked to simplify music to make it more accessible to a popular audience and pioneered the technique of "alienation" in opera music, that is, writing music that goes against the stage action, thereby causing the listener to think about the message of the opera, rather than merely becoming emotionally involved with it. He believed that art should take a political stand against social injustice. In his music, there is always a tension between an atonal, intellectual sound and the melodious, emotional style of music that he heard as a child.

Weill fervently embraced his new home in the United States and totally rejected his German works, as he believed Germany had done to him. Indeed, after his arrival in New York, he never spoke German again. As he strove to write in an exclusively American idiom, his rebellion against sentiment in art mellowed, and his music became more rich and free. Although his American pieces lacked the intellectual sophistication of his European works, they nevertheless retained a sense of social consciousness that was very courageous, especially in the context of an American society that was growing increasingly nationalistic and conservative.

It is ironic that "Mack the Knife" from *The Threepenny Opera*, a play that denounces capitalism, has been used in an advertising campaign to sell McDonald's hamburgers. This fact testifies to Weill's extraordinary success as one of the few twentieth century composers whose music can be considered both "serious" and "popular."

*Bibliography*


Drew, David. *Kurt Weill: A Handbook*. Berkeley: University of California Press, 1987. Drew is the foremost authority on Weill. He presents detailed chronologies of Weill's compositions, as well as a description of his method of composition.

Jarman, Douglas. *Kurt Weill: An Illustrated Biography.* Bloomington: Indiana University Press, 1982. This concise but complete biography serves as an ideal introduction to the composer's life and works.

Kowalke, Kim H., ed. *A New Orpheus: Essays on Kurt Weill*. New Haven, Conn.: Yale University Press, 1986. This is a collection of seventeen essays from the 1983 international conference on Weill held at Yale University. They are arranged according to the chronology of his career and are suitable for general readers.

Sanders, Ronald. *The Days Grow Short: The Life and Music of Kurt Weill*. New York: Holt, Rinehart and Winston, 1980. This detailed biography gives psychological insight to Weill's music. Sanders also outlines the backgrounds of the people and events who were important in Weill's life.

Spoto, Donald. *Lenya: A Life*. Boston: Little, Brown, 1989. Lenya's fame rests mostly on her interpretation of her husband's works. Along with that, however, she led a long and fascinating life. This book reveals some of the details of Weill's and Lenya's troubled marriage.


*Pamela Canal*

# CHAIM WEIZMANN

*Born:* November 27, 1874; Motol, Poland, Russian Empire
*Died:* November 9, 1952; Rehovot, Israel
*Areas of Achievement:* Government, politics, statecraft, and chemistry
*Contribution:* Although a world-class chemist and scientific researcher, Weizmann's greatest contributions and achievements must be regarded as his leadership of the World Zionist Organization for twelve years and his central role in helping to forge the new State of Israel. He was the first president of that new nation from 1949 through 1952.

## *Early Life*

Chaim Azriel Weizmann was born in the small Russian (later Polish) village of Motol, near Pinsk, to a Jewish family that lived amid impoverished circumstances. Motol was situated in the Pale of Settlement, a region along Russia's western frontier and the only place in the country where Jews could reside legally. Even there, however, they existed under the constant threat of persecution and periodic massacres known as pogroms. Life was hard for everyone living within the Pale. Yet Chaim's large family, though of meager means, fared better than many other Russian Jews. Chaim was the third of fifteen children born to his parents, Ozer and Rachel Weizmann. Ozer supported the family as a timber merchant, a somewhat seasonal business that gradually improved over time.

The Weizmann children grew up in an enlightened atmosphere that encouraged learning but that also promoted reverence for tradition. Their home was filled with books written in the Yiddish, Hebrew, and Russian languages. Zionist periodicals also found their way into the house and influenced young Chaim. Ozer Weizmann was determined that his children should learn as much as they could about the world outside the Pale of Settlement. In an unprecedented step for a family living in a village like Motol, the elder Weizmann sent two sons, Chaim and an elder brother, twenty-five miles from home to study at the secondary school in Pinsk. There Weizmann's aptitude for science was fostered, and he decided on a career in chemistry.

At that time Pinsk was a center of Zionist beliefs and the home for an early Zionist group. Young Weizmann increasingly became involved with the movement and absorbed its beliefs. Upon his graduation from the Pinsk Gymnasium in 1891, he thought of himself as a committed Zionist.

After graduation, Weizmann left Russia for Germany and then Switzerland to continue his education, since his own country enforced university quotas restricting the admissions of Jewish students. After an unhappy and financially stressful year (1892) at the Darmstadt Polytechnic Institute, Weizmann returned home for a brief period only to set out again for the

German capital, Berlin, where he was to attend the prestigious Charlottenberg Polytechnic Institute in 1893. In Berlin, Weizmann's Zionism matured as he joined with a group of intellectuals from the Russo-Jewish Academic Society, an organization he later regarded as the cradle of the modern Zionist movement. In 1896, he came under the influence of Asher Ginzberg, better known as Ahad Ha'am, a Hebrew essayist and an early Zionist theoretician. Weizmann adopted the approach of Ha'am, who advocated a slow and careful Jewish settlement process, making Palestine first a spiritual and cultural center for world Judaism, and who also stressed the importance of reaching an agreement with the Arabs of Palestine.

Because a favorite professor joined the staff of the University of Fribourg in Switzerland, Weizmann went there to study in 1897. After three more years of hard work, he obtained a Ph.D. magna cum laude (1900) and shortly thereafter was appointed *Privatdozent* (lecturer) in organic chemistry at the University of Geneva. The adult pattern of Weizmann's life was now established. He would blend a love of science with a passion for Zionism and end up directing the course of an entire race of people.

*Life's Work*

For a half century, beginning in 1900, Weizmann devoted his life to considering the needs and aspirations of his people, deciding how the Jewish world should support Zionism and directing the desire for Jewish national rebirth. By the time of his graduation, he was becoming a well-known member of the World Zionist Organization. It had been created in 1897 by the First Zionist Congress, which Theodor Herzl had convened to bring about the establishment of a Jewish home in Palestine. Weizmann first served as a delegate to the Second Zionist Congress held in 1898 in Basel, Switzerland, while he was finishing his doctorate. At that time he was elected to the Congress Steering Committee (responsible for finances) and immediately began to make formal progress in the leadership of the movement. In 1900, Herzl convened the Fourth Zionist Congress in London, and Weizmann made his first visit to England.

By 1901, Weizmann, at age twenty-seven, found himself at odds with Herzl's ideas and efforts, which he considered too visionary, so he formed the first opposition group in the Zionist movement. This group greatly influenced Zionist affairs for a time and provided the vehicle through which Weizmann rose to prominence. Between 1904 and 1914, Weizmann devoted more time to his scientific career and personal life, though he remained an active Zionist. The death of Herzl in 1904 left the Zionist movement in a state of shock, and Weizmann, Herzl's as-yet-unrecognized heir, wanted time to think and to make a fresh start somewhere. So he set out for Great Britain, taking an academic position at the University of Manchester, where he also became the leader of the Manchester group of Zionists, which he headed for fifteen years. In 1905, in Manchester, he met Arthur Balfour (then Great Britain's prime minister) and convinced him that Palestine was the proper national homeland for Jews. Their meeting established a working relationship that eventually resulted in the Balfour Declaration of 1917.

In 1906, Weizmann married Vera Chatzman whom he had first met in Geneva six years before, when she was a medical student and he a doctoral candidate in chemistry. Two sons were born to them, and, though the marriage would be marked by many work-related separations, they shared a love that bridged these gaps.

In 1907, Weizmann took an important step toward assuming Herzl's mantle of leadership. At the Eighth Zionist Congress, he delivered a major speech on what he termed synthetic Zionism. He attempted to reconcile the two major schools of Zionist thought. Political Zionism, which Herzl advocated, promoted diplomacy and aimed at securing political guarantees for the establishment of a Jewish home in Palestine. While this was important, as Weizmann said, the achievements of practical Zionism—the actual establishment of settlers in the Yishuv (the Jewish Community in Palestine)—would create the strongest possible political base for a homeland. Therefore, Zionist leaders ought to strive for a synthesis between the two concerns.

Shortly after the speech, Weizmann made his first visit to Palestine. While there, he helped to found the Palestine Land Development Company and stepped up his campaign for the Jewish settlement of Palestine when he returned to his home in England, which he had grown to appreciate. In 1910, Weizmann became a naturalized British subject and received two more doctoral degrees while at Manchester (a D.Sc. degree in 1909 and an LL.D. degree in 1919).

With the coming of World War I, international attention was diverted from the Zionist cause, and consensus broke down within the movement. Realizing the difficulty of conducting international Zionist politics under such circumstances, Weizmann focused his attention on helping England with the war effort through scientific research. He created a process for synthesizing acetone, which alleviated a shortage in the manufacture of explosives. He then directed the large-scale manufacture of the invaluable chemical. In 1916, Weizmann was appointed by Prime Minister David Lloyd George superintendent of the Admiralty Laboratories, a position that he retained until 1919.

Not satisfied with the direction taken by the secret Sykes-Picot Agreement of May, 1916 (a pact between the French and British that divided up the Middle East), Weizmann, when he learned of it, used his diplomatic talents to get the British to reconsider the pact as well as the plight of the Jewish people and their desire for a homeland. The result was the Balfour Declaration of November, 1917, a statement that seemed to throw full British support behind the Zionist cause.

By the end of 1917, Weizmann had become, in the eyes of many Jews (and deservedly so), a great emancipator and promoter of Jewish freedom. In 1920, he was elected unopposed as president of the World Zionist Organization. For twelve years Weizmann served as the president of that body (from 1920 to 1931 and again in 1935), trying to appease Zionist opponents and working on compromises between Zionists, Jewish settlers in Palestine, Arabs, and the British. From 1921 onward, he traveled the world at a dizzying pace, preaching Zionist ideology and raising funds at mass rallies. On April 2, 1921, Weizmann arrived in New York City on the first of many trips to the United States to drum up enthusiasm and financial support for his organization. Weizmann managed to turn the United States into Zionism's great provider during the 1920's.

Great Britain, in the 1920's, retreated from its commitment to support a Jewish national home in the face of Arab nationalism and civil strife. A summer-long Arab uprising in 1929 took the lives of more than one hundred Jews. Weizmann's years of negotiations only brought British policy changes unfavorable to Zionist aims. The British restricted Jewish immigration and limited Jews's land purchases. Ardent and extremist Zionists grew impatient and challenged Weizmann's leadership of the Zionist movement by submitting him to a vote of nonconfidence at the 1931 Zionist Congress. He was not reelected as president of the World Zionist Organization and Jewish Agency for Palestine, the expanded Zionist body he had helped form in 1929.

Weizmann returned to his science for a time, founding the Daniel Sieff Research Institute (1934) at Rehovot, Palestine—his second home. Yet, with the rise of Adolf Hitler's Germany and continued British limitation of immigrants to Palestine, Weizmann was returned to the presidency of the World Zionist Organization for one more year. He was surprised over, but happily supported, the recommendation of a 1937 British commission to partition Palestine into Jewish and Arab sectors. Ultimately the plan failed because the Arabs rejected it.

During World War II, Weizmann directed the Sieff Research Institute, which provided essential pharmaceuticals to the Allies; he also helped develop a method for producing synthetic rubber. Because of his denunciation (1945) of underground Jewish guerrilla groups such as the Irgun (led by Menachem Begin), which attacked British military posts and Arabs in Palestine in order to gain independence for a Jewish Palestine, Weizmann incurred the wrath of Zionist leaders. He again lost the presidency of his Zionist organization in 1946.

That the Jewish people as a whole, and many Zionist leaders in particular, continued to revere Weizmann is attested by the fact that he not only appeared before the United Nations as Zionism's most knowledgeable and articulate champion (1947) but also was sent to the United States in 1948 to reconfirm to President Harry S. Truman the rightness of an independent

State of Israel and the importance of including the region known as the Negev within the boundaries of the Jewish state. His intervention led to U.S. recognition of the new State of Israel in May, 1948. In February, 1949, Weizmann was officially elected President of the State of Israel.

After 1949, his work as a theoretician having been accomplished, Weizmann was relegated in effect to a position of bystander in the government. Prime Minister David Ben-Gurion held all the real authority and expected Weizmann to be only a figurehead. The latter participated in no cabinet meetings and had little say in the practical affairs of state as his health and morale deteriorated.

Worn out by demanding itineraries, arduous political strife, and personal frustrations, Weizmann died in November of 1952, only days short of his seventy-eighth birthday. The fallen Zionist leader was mourned throughout the world and was buried on his estate at Rehovot, in the nation he was instrumental in bringing into being.

*Summary*

Chaim Weizmann was a man of many attainments, and his impact on the world was great. The Weizmann legacy is really twofold: a new nation and scientific achievement. His scientific genius influenced the outcomes of two world wars. The Weizmann Institute of Science, built on the foundation of the Sieff Institute, became an important research facility for Israeli and world scientists. Weizmann wrote numerous important scientific papers (more than one hundred), many political essays, and left his memoirs in a book entitled *Trial and Error: The Autobiography of Chaim Weizmann* (1949). He was responsible for registering 110 patents, either singly or in collaboration.

Above all, however, Weizmann dedicated his life to the service of the Jewish people and to the quest of an ideal formulated in his youth. For more than half a century, he worked tirelessly, traveling around the world as leader of Zionism, to see that the Zionist ideal became a practical reality. Weizmann changed the course of history for an entire race of people. More than any other individual, Weizmann—with his powers of persuasion and negotiation, international contacts, passion, intelligence, and vision—enabled the Jewish people to realize a nearly two-thousand-year-old dream. It has been said that the State of Israel was constructed, in part, in the image of Weizmann—even though others tried to keep his influence on government from becoming too great after 1949. Accordingly, his name and ideas are recognized as being an important part of any discussion on Israel's future. Weizmann believed that the issue of Arab-Jewish relations was one of utmost importance. He reminded his followers that Zionism could exist only as it kept justice and the nonviolent resolution of disputes at the forefront of its concerns.

*Bibliography*

Amdur, Richard. *Chaim Weizmann*. New York: Chelsea House, 1988. Written especially for young adults, but by no means juvenile in its presentation, this succinct (one-hundred-page) biography is clearly written and chronicles the major events in the life of Weizmann. Contains many outstanding photographs.

Feis, Herbert. *The Birth of Israel*. New York: W. W. Norton, 1969. Of the voluminous literature on Zionism, this short, easy-to-read book puts Weizmann's life in the context of the birth of the nation over which he presided.

Reinharz, Jehuda. *Chaim Weizmann: The Making of a Zionist Leader*. New York: Oxford University Press, 1985. This very scholarly volume of some length details and analyzes the first half of the life of Weizmann from his ancestry and birth to the outbreak of World War I. Its real strength lies in its extensive notes and its comprehensive bibliography and index.

Rose, Norman. *Chaim Weizmann, a Biography*. New York: Viking Penguin, 1986. This standard comprehensive one-volume presentation of Weizmann's life is balanced (presenting both successes and failures), well written, and well documented. The emphasis is on diplomatic and political history and makes extensive use of Weizmann's letters. Contains two sections of instructive and interesting photographs.

Weisgal, Meyer W., and Joel Carmichael, eds. *Chaim Weizmann: A Biography by Several Hands*. New York: Atheneum, 1963. Written by a group of Weizmann's disciples and admirers in Israel, England, and the United States, the work begins with a survey of the biographical facts of his life. Each following chapter describes and appraises a particular aspect of Weizmann's activity. His contribution to chemistry is well evaluated. The book is illustrated with thirty photographs of Weizmann from childhood to old age.

Weizmann, Chaim. *The Essential Chaim Weizmann*. Edited and compiled by Barnet Litvinoff. New York: Holmes & Meier, 1982. This comprehensive source book presents selections of Weizmann's most significant and penetrating ideas as expressed in his letters, speeches, and writings. Particularly helpful is a succinctly annotated chronology, year by year, of Weizmann's life, which appears at the front of the book.

*Andrew C. Skinner*

# MAX WERTHEIMER

*Born:* April 16, 1880; Prague, Austro-Hungarian Empire
*Died:* October 12, 1943; New York, New York
*Area of Achievement:* Psychology
*Contribution:* Wertheimer pioneered the development of Gestalt psychology, which he and his coworkers Kurt Koffka and Wolfgang Köhler introduced to the European and American psychological communities.

## *Early Life*

Max Wertheimer was born in Prague, which was then in the Austro-Hungarian Empire, on April 16, 1880, into an accomplished middle-class family. His mother was a respected musician, and his father was a school principal. Wertheimer contemplated a musical career and showed interest in writing poetry. Later, while ostensibly studying law at Prague University, he became intrigued by philosophy and psychology.

When Wertheimer was beginning his inquiries into man's ancient questions about the meaning of his life and its relation to the world around him—traditional philosophical issues—the methods of examining such profundities were changing dramatically. Many questions which previously had been the preserve of philosophy were coming under the purview of an increasingly empirical, evolving science subsequently known as psychology. This development led psychologists—Wertheimer among them—into many new areas, with physiological studies acquiring a significance equal to the older philosophies' vital, often rigorously logical yet nonempirical musings and reflections.

Leaving Prague University in 1901, Wertheimer proceeded to the University of Berlin to study philosophy and psychology, then to the University of Württemberg, where in 1904 he received his doctorate. Until 1909, he pursued postdoctoral studies in Prague, Vienna, and again in Berlin. Financial independence permitted such academic mobility. During World War I, he aided Germany's efforts in the development of acoustical devices for its submarines and the improvement of harbor fortifications. These services were short-lived, and he was never a combatant. Thus, from 1916 until 1929 he taught and conducted research at the University of Berlin, accepting a professorship at the University of Frankfurt in 1929 and maintaining it until he abandoned Adolf Hitler's Germany in 1933 for New York City's New School for Social Research. Meanwhile, in 1910, prior to his Frankfurt appointment, Wertheimer launched the psychological investigations that preoccupied the remainder of his life.

## *Life's Work*

Vacationing by train in 1910, Wertheimer made specific observations that gave initial shape to the school of psychology that shortly distinguished him as the founder of Gestalt (or Gestalten). Wertheimer did coin the term *Gestalt,* which had previously appeared in German philosophical-psychological literature, although with a meaning differing from his own. Wertheimer's Gestalt perceptions dealt with, or exposed, the overall configurations of shapes and forms existing prior to the mind's assimilating and making sense of myriad external sensory data imposed upon it. For Wertheimer, human perceptions occurred within an internal field; his evidence suggested that the totality of human perceptual observations constituted more than the sum of their tens of thousands of discrete, externally projected elements. Thus, Wertheimer aborted his 1910 vacation because of impressions drawn while watching scenery pass the train's windows that led him to assumptions about how people actually see "apparent" motion. Immediately afterward, he employed rudimentary tachistoscopes or stroboscopes to measure human perceptions of brief exposures to moving visual stimuli. Light was projected for viewers through two slits, one vertical, the other at an angle of twenty to thirty degrees. When light flashed briefly through the slits, they saw both lights continuously. With slower projections, they saw the lights moving from one place to another.

The results of this commonsensical experiment conflicted with assumptions and approaches of the dominant psychological schools of 1912. The prevalent presumption was that conscious observations could be analyzed into vast numbers of identifiable sensory elements. That is, viewers actually saw each of the bark, branches, and leaves of a tree and these parts imposed upon one's senses then converged in whole form or appeared to be in motion. Since that was deemed accurate, Wertheimer had to explain why, when one motionless object was added to another experimentally, the viewer perceived them to be in motion. Labeling his experimental discoveries the "phi phenomenon," he asserted that "apparent movement" simply existed a priori within the mind and was irreducible to a count of external stimuli affecting perception. "Apparent motion," for him, therefore required no explanation. Thus, although a square was composed of four lines joined in proper relation, the observer did not see four distinct lines; he saw squareness: the whole form instantly. Similarly, irrespective of the keys of instruments selected, when a melody was played, listeners heard neither the individual notes nor instruments. Whether the tune was "Yankee Doodle" or Ludwig van Beethoven's fifth symphony, listeners recognized a total composition. Such investigations were published by Wertheimer as "Experimentelle Studien über das Schen von Bewegung" (1912; "On the *Phi* Phenomenon as an Example of Nativism in Perception," 1965).

Wertheimer's advocacy of Gestalt initially contradicted the perspectives and assumptions of German structural and associationist psychologists, posing a challenge to such of their distinguished leaders as Wilhelm Wundt, who in Leipzig, Germany, then directed the world's first and most renowned psychological laboratory. Wundt was the quintessential elementalist. For him, psychology's task was to identify and calculate the tens of thousands of constituents of mental feelings, images, and sensations, hence the means by which they entered into combination as ideas, concepts, or images. Somewhat like contemporary chemists, Dmitry Mendeleyev, for example, or physicists such as Niels Bohr or Max Planck, Wundt sought to demonstrate that larger matter, forms, or shapes were composed of increasingly smaller, more distinct, and ultimately identifiable parts.

Wertheimer's Gestalt evidence convinced him on the contrary that such discrete elements were not the raw data of man's perceptions, feelings, images, or ideas. The fundamentals of human psychological activities were already structured within the mind and quite ready to assimilate assaults of external sensory stimuli. Men were therefore justified in simply saying "I see a horse" or "I see a house."

His continued investigations of perceptual constancies buttressed his confidence in Gestalt methodology. If, specifically, one stands directly before a window, it projects a rectangle onto the eye's retina. If one then stands to one side, in actuality the window becomes a trapezoid and that change is projected onto the retina. Yet, as Wertheimer's experiments—many along similar lines—demonstrated, one continued to perceive the window as a rectangle. Perception thus remained constant, despite alterations in the image projected onto the retina. He proffered further evidence that this same phenomenon occurs with regard to brightness and to the constancy of objects' sizes. Perceptual experience therefore possessed qualities of wholeness indiscernible in any part of that experience.

In 1922, Wertheimer professionally advanced his famous principles of perceptual organization in his *Untersuchungen zur Lehre von der Gestalt: I. Prinzipielle Bemerkungen* (1923; examination of objects as immediately given to consciousness). A person's perception of objects occurs in the identical simultaneous and unified manner as when he perceives apparent motion. The human mind possesses its own inner, dynamic principles for organizing perceptions.

Like many other psychologists, Wertheimer was interested in learning processes. His evidence, however, took him in different directions from those pursued by Wundt and associationists. Since Gestalt emphasized the salient importance of perceptual processes, Wertheimer consequently opposed the trial-and-error method of learning identified with E. L. Thorndike, as well as John Watson's stimulus-response approach. Ideally, Wertheimer would have teachers begin presentations with an overall view of their subject, proceeding then to their distinct parts.

Gradually, Gestalt psychology earned respect in Germany and much of Europe among psychologists as well as among other scientists who were dissatisfied with the purported sterility and mechanical qualities of Wundtian psychology. While this was occurring, Hitler's rise to power in Germany in 1933 persuaded Wertheimer and Köhler to immigrate to the United States. Wertheimer found a berth as professor of philosophy and psychology on the graduate faculty of the New School for Social Research in New York City. From then until his death on October 12, 1943, he continued experiments and sought to promulgate Gestalt psychology among American psychologists, although he was relatively unknown and, compared to Wundt's fifty-five thousand pages of publication, had published little. His expectations of greater influence were, however, ill-timed. By the 1920's and 1930's, American psychology was dominated by behavioral psychologists such as Watson and Raymond Cattell, and educational psychologists such as Thorndike. At the same time, the profession was assimilating the psychological theories of Sigmund Freud. Only after Wertheimer's death did the profound impact of his work become fully evident.

*Summary*

Notwithstanding nineteenth century precedents for important Gestalt-like initiatives, there is little dispute that Max Wertheimer founded a new and permanent line of psychological and related physiological scientific inquiry. Because professional psychology recorded many significant attainments before and during Wertheimer's career, but in part because he broadly questioned the neglect or disdain of some of these previous endeavors, his conclusions challenged many fundamentals of the predominant psychological theories of his day and of some that preceded him. Traditional experimental psychology, like the natural sciences, had been premised on a reductionism, breaking down investigation of perception, memory, feeling, learning, and thought into distinct elements—indeed, when Wertheimer commenced experimenting, other psychologists had already counted forty-four thousand mental elements that combined to compose human perception and therefore on that basis were accounting for the way humans' minds functioned to make sense of themselves and their world.

Without ignoring physiological constituents of perception and comprehension, Wertheimer's evidence questioned, as the reigning theories did not, whether man was a mere apparatus, "a combination of cameras, telephone receivers, receptors for warmth, cold, pressure," which under external excitation produced a convergence descriptive of man's mental perceptions and reactions. He believed that such subsumptions ignored the basic and immanent human impulses of human actions: "a trend toward sensible, appropriate action, feeling, thought." Worse, from his viewpoint, traditionalists failed evidentially to explain elementary facts of human experiences: what people see when they open their eyes and look about them.

Starting with investigations of the retina, proceeding to explanations of the *phi* phenomenon, then to developing his principles of (mental) organization, advancing further to adducing physiological evidence for his principle of isomorphism, and finally to explications bearing upon productive and creative thought processes, Wertheimer produced substantial descriptions of a more human, thinking human species. These results he attributed to immanent psychological qualities allowing man to perceive himself, his environment, and his problems as wholes. Accordingly, Wertheimer has left a permanent imprint on the daily activities of psychologists.

*Bibliography*

Asch, Solomon E. "Max Wertheimer's Contributions to Modern Psychology." *Social Research* 13 (1946): 81-102. A clearly written, readily comprehensible, authoritative, and professionally sound analysis. Contains a few information footnotes.

Fancher, Raymond E. *Pioneers of Psychology.* New York: W. W. Norton, 1979. Provides a fine contextual setting for a greater understanding of Wertheimer and his followers operating amid other psychological developments. Clearly written both for laymen and professionals alike. Contains several photographs, suggested readings at the end of major sections of this study, end-of-book notes for each chapter, and a very extensive, double-columned index.

Herrnstein, Richard, and Edward C. Boring, eds. *A Source Book in the History of Psychology.* Cambridge, Mass.: Harvard University Press, 1965. A large, authoritative volume written with professional precision and intended for readers with some prior knowledge of psychology. Includes excerpts, abridgments, and translations of important psychological writings that are not easily found elsewhere. An invaluable and exhaustive work in its field. Excerpts are preceded helpfully by brief editorial abstracts. Thorough in its chronological, topical, and personality coverages. Includes an end-of-volume list of excerptions, plus extensive indexes of names and subjects.

Köhler, Wolfgang. "Max Wertheimer, 1880-1943." *The Psychological Review* 51 (May, 1944): 143-146. A tribute to Wertheimer's professional contributions by his distinguished coworker Köhler. The substance of the piece is professional and is devoid of personal information about Wertheimer. Includes an excellent photograph of the elderly Wertheimer. Useful, if not essential.

Neel, Ann. *Theories of Psychology.* New York: Schenkman, 1969. Part 4 deals with Gestalt psychology authoritatively and in its appropriate developmental setting. Excellent for understanding psychology's evolving theories. There are general but often extensive suggested readings at the end of major sections that relate to subject areas covered. Very useful reading for specialists and nonspecialists alike. Contains a very extensive index.

Schultz, Duane P. *A History of Modern Psychology.* New York: Academic Press, 1969. Though the first two chapters provide useful historical background, the book's concentration is on late nineteenth and twentieth century psychologists and their work. A well-written, accurate, and useful survey. Chapter 12 features a fine discussion of Wertheimer and the Gestalt school and the nature and consequences of their work. Suggested readings close every chapter, and there is a useful bibliography and index.

*Clifton K. Yearley*

# ELIE WIESEL

*Born:* September 30, 1928; Sighet, Romania

*Areas of Achievement:* Literature, philosophy, theology, and civil rights
*Contribution:* Wiesel is not only a prizewinning novelist, dramatist, and religious philosopher, but by writing and speaking out on behalf of the world's victims, he has become the conscience of modern times. For his work in this area he was awarded the Nobel Peace Prize.

## *Early Life*

Elie Wiesel was born on September 30, 1928, in Sighet, a small town in the Carpathian Mountains, in an area that belonged to Hungary during World War II but that was Romanian territory before and after the war. Wiesel's father, though a practicing member of the Jewish religious community, questioned traditional Judaism; a tolerant humanist, he emphasized the modern world at large and the need to be a part of it. Wiesel's mother had a lasting and, probably, deeper influence. A devout woman steeped in Hasidism, she hoped that her only son would become a rabbi. To that end, Wiesel studied the Torah and the Talmud in a local yeshiva known for its ascetic mysticism and Cabbalist teachers. This sheltered, bookish existence was irrevocably shattered in the spring of 1944, when the Nazis invaded Hungary and rounded up all its Jews, including Wiesel, his parents, and three sisters.

The fifteen-year-old Wiesel, along with his father, was sent first to Auschwitz and then to Buchenwald, from which he was liberated by American troops on April 11, 1945. (His two elder sisters survived as well.) The horrors he witnessed there, the despair he felt, the anger he directed at God were all to be incorporated in his literary and philosophical writings. Shortly after the war, the young adolescent went to a refugee home in France, where in two years he learned French by carefully reading the classics, especially Jean Racine, whose style he was later to adopt; indeed, French remains Wiesel's preferred written language. In addition, he was developing a lifelong passion for philosophy (starting with Immanuel Kant and Karl Marx) and for philosophical fiction.

From 1948 to 1951, Wiesel studied philosophy, psychology, and literature at the Sorbonne, but, forced to work, he never finished his thesis on comparative asceticism. Instead, he began a career as a journalist, which allowed him to travel extensively; after emigrating to the United States in 1956, he became the United Nations correspondent of an Israeli newspaper, *Yediot Aharonot*.

At the urging of the French Catholic novelist François Mauriac, Wiesel agreed to bear witness to the six million Jews murdered in Europe's concentration camps. From a massive work which he wrote in Yiddish, *Un di*

*Velt hot geshvign* (1956), Wiesel distilled a very brief but exceedingly powerful memoir of the Holocaust, published in French as *La Nuit* (1958; *Night*, 1960). Both a wrenching account of the presence of evil and a terrifying indictment of God's injustice, this book received international acclaim. Wiesel had found his voice and his themes.

*Life's Work*

Following the success of *Night*, Wiesel wrote in rapid succession two short novels presenting the guilty anguish of those who survived the mass slaughter: *L'Aube* (1960; *Dawn*, 1961) and *Le Jour* (1961; *The Accident*, 1962). That every act is ambiguous and implies a loss of innocence and that "God commit[s] the most unforgivable crime: to kill without a reason" are central to the protagonists' conduct and outlook. Little by little, however, Wiesel's characters come to realize that friendship can help them live in the post-Holocaust world. This is especially true in *La Ville de la chance* (1962; *The Town Beyond the Wall*, 1964), where, despite society's indifference to persecution and cruelty, loving and being a friend allow man to attain a kind of equilibrium. Questions about God, evil, and suffering, while they cannot be satisfactorily answered, must nevertheless be asked, since from the beginning such a dialogue has been established between God and His creation. By rejoining his religious community, Wiesel seems to suggest further, in *Les Portes de la forêt* (1964; *The Gates of the Forest*, 1966), that the survivor may finally create joy from despair.

At the same time that he was publishing his novels, Wiesel began writing eyewitness accounts and autobiographical pieces and stories of his life during the Hitler years. After a 1965 trip to the Soviet Union, he described in a series of articles originally published in Hebrew in *Yediot Aharonot* (collected and translated as *The Jews of Silence*, 1966) the plight of Soviet Jewry, as they try to maintain their ethnic and religious identity in the face of often implacable anti-Semitism. His yeshiva and Sorbonne studies, along with more mature and in-depth readings of biblical texts and exegeses, were to form the basis of other nonfiction works, including several studies of Hasidism and Hasidic masters.

The prizewinning novel *Le Mendiant de Jérusalem* (1968; *A Beggar in Jerusalem*, 1970) marked a turning point for Wiesel. The novel shows how, through Israel's victory in the Six Day War, a tormented people came of age; while celebrating this moment, the novel is both a memorial to the dead and an appeal on behalf of the world's "beggars." Although still haunted by the Holocaust, Wiesel could thereafter write about other human issues and problems faced by the next generation. For example, is madness, he asked in the first of several plays, an acceptable option for dealing with persecution (*Zalmen: Ou, La Folie de Dieu*, 1968; *Zalmen: Or, The Madness of God*, 1975)? Is silence a method for overcoming horror (*Le Serment de Kolvillàg*,

1973; *The Oath*, 1973)?

In 1969, Wiesel married Marion Erster Rose, who was to become his principal translator and with whom he would have one son. In the fall of 1972, he began his tenure at the City College of New York as Distinguished Professor of Judaic Studies. This endowed chair gave him the opportunity to teach young students (he considers himself to be an educator first) the celebrations and paradoxes of Jewish theology and the meaning of modern Jewishness and to continue writing in diverse genres. He left this position in 1976 to become the Andrew Mellon Professor of Humanities at Boston University. Meanwhile, Wiesel continued to publish plays, novels, and nonfiction at a prolific pace; in these he again wove post-Holocaust despair and divine cruelty, but above all he denounced the world's forgetfulness of and indifference to man's inhumanity to man.

During this period Wiesel was also involved in various social and political activities, from fighting against racism, war, fanaticism, apartheid, and violence to commemorating the Holocaust. (He was a member of the U.S. Holocaust Memorial Council until 1986, when he resigned in protest over President Ronald Reagan's controversial visit to the military cemetery in Bitburg, West Germany.) For his humanitarian work and his concern for the oppressed everywhere, as well as for his literary achievements, he has received numerous honorary degrees, prizes, and awards, including the Congressional Gold Medal, the rank of *Commandeur* in the French Legion of Honor, and, in 1986, the Nobel Peace Prize.

### *Summary*

The Holocaust and its remembrance, the nature of God and the terrible silence of God: These themes recur throughout Elie Wiesel's novels, plays, personal recollections, and nonfiction. In trying to understand the mystery of theodicy, this modern humanist has encompassed much of Jewish lore, tradition, and memory. In addition, by asking—but without answering—the hard questions that have always plagued man and by relating the Jews' unique experience to the universal legacy of humanity, he has succeeded in creating the quintessential Everyman: "What I try to do is to speak for man, but as a Jew. I make no distinction and I certainly make no restriction."

Against revisionist historians who deny the very existence of the Nazi extermination camps, Wiesel has written with contempt. He has passionately defended the conduct of the murdered and the survivors to his fellow Jews—those who are ashamed of the submissiveness of the victims and those who are skeptical of the survivors' integrity. He has no less passionately criticized novelists and playwrights, television and film directors for trivializing the tragedy of six million martyrs, whose greatest memorialist and bard he has become.

*Bibliography*

Abramowitz, Molly, comp. *Elie Wiesel: A Bibliography.* Metuchen, N.J.: Scarecrow Press, 1974. Dated but still valuable annotated bibliography of works by and about Wiesel.

Berenbaum, Michael. *The Vision of the Void: Theological Reflections on the Works of Elie Wiesel.* Middletown, Conn.: Wesleyan University Press, 1979. Although discussing works published before 1979, this is an excellent study of the Jewish tradition as evident in Wiesel's religious writings and sociocultural position. The bibliography on theological philosophy is quite useful.

Cargas, Harry James. *Harry James Cargas in Conversation with Elie Wiesel.* New York: Paulist Press, 1976. In a series of fascinating and varied interviews, Wiesel speaks not only about the Holocaust but also about his audience, his craft, and his mission as a writer and witness.

__________, ed. *Responses to Elie Wiesel.* New York: Persea Books, 1978. A stimulating collection of articles, interviews, and book chapters (a few are new, most are reprinted), which presents specific aspects of Wiesel's thought. Maurice Friedman's essay on "the Job of Auschwitz" is particularly perceptive; letters, written by Christian philosophers and theologians, show Wiesel's influence in the non-Jewish world as well.

Estess, Ted L. *Elie Wiesel.* New York: Ungar, 1980. In spite of its brevity, this general introduction is well argued and often insightful.

Rosenfeld, Alvin H., and Irving Greenberg, eds. *Confronting the Holocaust: The Impact of Elie Wiesel.* Bloomington: Indiana University Press, 1978. A balanced collection of provocative essays, written by scholars from different disciplines. Also interesting is Wiesel's own short statement, "Why I Write." A highly selective and partly annotated bibliography of his writings is included.

Roth, John K. *A Consuming Fire: Encounters with Elie Wiesel and the Holocaust.* Atlanta: John Knox Press, 1979. This examination by a philosopher of ethics and religion, to which Wiesel contributed an informative prologue, is both thorough and intelligent.

*Pierre L. Horn*

# SIMON WIESENTHAL

*Born:* December 31, 1908; Buczacz, Poland (later Buchach, Ukraine)

*Areas of Achievement:* Law and jurisprudence

*Contribution:* Wiesenthal, a survivor of a dozen Nazi concentration and death camps, became the world's leading independent Nazi hunter. Between 1945 and 1989, Wiesenthal investigated and brought charges against eleven hundred Nazi war criminals. Through his highly publicized cases and publications, he added significantly to the documentary record of the Holocaust—the Nazi destruction of the European Jews—and contributed more than any other individual to bringing the Nazi perpetrators to justice and keeping the historical memory of the Holocaust alive.

## *Early Life*

Simon Wiesenthal is the eldest of two sons of Rosa (Rapp) and Hans Wiesenthal, a prosperous wholesaler and reserve officer in the Austrian army, killed in action during World War I. Wiesenthal grew up in the deeply anti-Semitic Lvov Oblast, then a province of the Austrian Empire. During a pogrom in 1920, the twelve-year-old boy was slashed on the thigh by a mounted, saber-wielding Ukranian officer, leaving a lifelong scar.

Wiesenthal's mother remarried in 1925, restoring some security to the boys' lives. In 1928, Wiesenthal was graduated from the *Gymnasium*. Again, he experienced prejudice when his application to the Polytechnic Institute in Lvov was rejected because of Jewish quota restrictions. In 1932, he received a degree in architectural engineering from the Technical University of Prague. Returning to Lvov, he opened an architectural office and married his wife of more than fifty years, Cyla Muller, a distant relative of Sigmund Freud.

From 1939 to 1941, Wiesenthal practiced architecture in Lemberg, Poland. When the city was seized by the Soviets at the outbreak of World War II, the secret police arrested and killed his stepfather and brother, and the Wiesenthals barely avoided exile to Siberia. When the Germans invaded Russia in 1941, Wiesenthal was arrested and again narrowly escaped execution. He and Cyla were sent to the Janowska concentration camp, outside Lvov, where they worked in the repair shop for German eastern railroads. Wiesenthal was treated decently there by the secretly anti-Nazi German director and deputy director.

By 1942, the Holocaust had begun. Through a combination of luck, skill, friendship, and bribery, Wiesenthal was able to get Cyla out of the camp and, in 1943, to escape himself. Recaptured in June, 1944, Wiesenthal was a prisoner in more than a dozen Nazi concentration camps, escaping death on many occasions by the merest chance. At the end of the war, he arrived by forced march at the Mauthausen camp in Upper Austria, one of 34 prisoners of an original group of 149,000. When U.S. Army units liberated the camp in May, 1945, the six-foot-tall, thirty-seven-year-old Wiesenthal weighed less than one hundred pounds. His terrifying wartime experiences stamped his fearless character and formed the basis for his life's work.

*Life's Work*

After a brief recovery, Wiesenthal assisted the newly arrived U.S. Army War Crimes Section in gathering and preparing evidence to prosecute Nazi war criminals. Wiesenthal worked in anger and despair during the first months of his work. He was amazed to learn that Cyla had survived, and the two were finally reunited late in 1945. They were the only survivors of ninety-one of their family members who perished in the Holocaust. Reunion and the birth of his daughter, Pauline, in 1947 softened his bitterness. He was soon employed by the Office of Strategic Services and the Counter-Intelligence Corps, and the evidence he assembled proved of great value in the preparation for war crimes trials held in the U.S. zone. At first he intended to devote a few years to bringing Nazi mass murderers to justice, and in 1947, he established the Jewish Historical Documentation Center on the Fate of Jews and Their Persecutors in Linz, Austria. Between 1947 and 1954, he built a vast network of informants and collected documentation to help bring Nazi war criminals to justice.

After the trial of the major war criminals at Nürnberg, Germany, however, the major Western powers, under the influence of Cold War ideology, gradually lost interest in prosecution of Nazi criminals and opened their doors to thousands of Nazis as "anti-Communists." By 1954, Wiesenthal, frustrated by lack of support from government authorities, had closed his documentation center and shipped his voluminous files to Yad Vashem Documentation Center in Israel, keeping only one for himself—that on Adolf Eichmann, the Nazi expert who supervised the genocidal destruction of the European Jews. Between 1955 and 1961, Wiesenthal held various social and welfare leadership posts in Austria, which further involved him in assisting Jewish victims of the Nazi regime. In his spare time, he searched for former Nazis, especially Eichmann.

Wiesenthal first gained international recognition for locating Eichmann in Buenos Aires, Argentina, where he was captured by Israeli agents in 1960, brought to Israel for trial, convicted of mass murder, and executed in 1961. Encouraged, Wiesenthal reopened his Jewish Documentation Center, this time in Vienna. Gifted with an extraordinary capacity for finding and evaluating evidence, Wiesenthal assembled, painstakingly scrutinized, analyzed, and cross-referenced every relevant document and survivor account available to him. He compiled a card index of 22,500 names on his Nazi wanted list, assembled dossiers on six thousand cases, and worked on as many as three hundred cases at a time.

In addition to Eichmann, Wiesenthal developed cases against Karl Babor, a Schutzstaffel (SS) captain at the concentration camp in Breslau, Poland, who committed suicide in 1964 after being discovered; sixteen Auschwitz SS officers, tried in Stuttgart, Germany, in 1966, the majority of whom Wiesenthal brought to trial; Joseph Mengele, who selected victims to be gassed at Auschwitz and died in Argentina before capture; Heinrich Müller, Heinrich Himmler's successor as chief of the Gestapo; Walter Kutschmann, former Gestapo leader; and many others.

With his strong interest in Holocaust public education, Wiesenthal has published a number of works on the Nazi perpetrators and their victims, including numerous newspaper and periodical pieces. Among his books are *KZ Mauthausen* (1946; concentration camp Mauthausen); *Grossmufti: Grossagent der Achse* (1947; head mufti, agent of the Axis); *Ich jagte Eichmann* (1961; I hunted Eichmann); and *Verjährung?* (1965; statute of limitations). In the media, books, and many articles, Wiesenthal has presented the philosophy behind his work. He is animated by a deep sense of compassion for the martyrs of the Nazi Holocaust and believes that all victims—Jews, Christians, Gypsies, and all nationalities—are brothers. He believes that forgiveness is a personal matter and that one has the right to forgive what was done to oneself but not what was done to others. He does not condone assassination or other radical measures. Morality, he says, must remain on the side of the accusers, so proper punishment can come only from the courts. Nazi crimes can never be atoned, he believes, nor will all the murderers be caught, but he pursues them relentlessly so that time will not erase their guilt.

Until the 1970's, Wiesenthal rarely left Austria and Germany. Gradually, however, he became involved more directly in the work of Holocaust education, lecturing extensively in West Germany, The Netherlands, and the United States, primarily to university students. During the 1970's, Wiesenthal's activities become known worldwide through such films as *The Odessa File* (1974), for which he was a consultant, and *The Boys from Brazil* (1978), which glamorized the Nazi hunter, but for two decades he resisted all efforts to depict his life in film or biography, fearing distortion. Finally, in 1987, he agreed to give television rights for a documentary based on his memoirs. The production of *Murderers Among Us*, for which he was the primary consultant, was presented in 1988 with Ben Kingsley playing Wiesenthal. He also agreed to the 1990 television dramatization of his 1981 book, *Max und Helen* (*Max and Helen*, 1982), which recounts the intriguing story of a Nazi killer who Wiesenthal decided not to pursue. In April, 1977, he cooperated in the establishment of the Simon Wiesenthal Center for Holocaust Studies and Holocaust Museum at Yeshiva University in Los Angeles, California, with branch offices in New York, Chicago, Washington,

D.C., Toronto, and Jerusalem. Its broad outreach program of Holocaust education and awareness, monitoring and combating neo-Nazi and anti-Semitic hate groups, and Nazi-hunting, reflects Wiesenthal's desire that his work continue.

In his pursuit of Nazis, Wiesenthal has made diverse enemies. Within the Communist Bloc, notably in Poland, a propaganda campaign surfaced in the 1960's against Wiesenthal's exposure of ex-Fascists placed high in the Communist Party apparatus who had instigated an "anti-Zionist" crusade against Israel.

Beginning in the 1970's, Wiesenthal's pursuit of former Nazis embroiled him in bitter disputes in his home country, threatening the future of his Jewish Documentation Center. In 1970, he revealed that some Socialist ministers in Austrian Chancellor Bruno Kreisky's government had Nazi backgrounds. The Socialist Party leadership responded with such vehement attacks that it was feared that the Austrian government was going to close down his Jewish Documentation Center. Only worldwide protests are credited with having saved it. Again, in 1975, antagonisms flared when Wiesenthal accused an Austrian politician of involvement in SS crimes of mass murder. Chancellor Kreisky, who was considering the politician for a governing coalition, attacked Wiesenthal severely. Relations between the two degenerated to personal invective, until Wiesenthal finally brought a libel suit against the chancellor. Only under threat of an official parliamentary investigation of his Jewish Documentation Center, did Wiesenthal finally settle out of court. In 1986, Wiesenthal again became enmeshed in Austrian politics when Kurt Waldheim, the Austrian presidential candidate, was accused by the World Jewish Congress and other organizations of membership in an SS unit implicated in deporting Jews to death camps. The sensational accusations caused a furor in Austria. Wiesenthal took a cautious line in the beginning, but finally in 1987 he called newly elected President Waldheim to resign if an international commission of historians, appointed by the Austrian government to study the case, proved that the military unit of which Waldheim was a member was involved in war crimes.

During the 1980's, Wiesenthal became increasingly an elder statesman of the Holocaust, traveling widely to publicize his Nazi-hunting message, while continuing to develop information on Nazi criminals. United States President Ronald Reagan was a strong supporter and met with him in 1984 to offer assistance. The next year Wiesenthal declined Reagan's invitation to Bitburg, West Germany, where a controversial wreath-laying ceremony to symbolize U.S.-German reconciliation was to mark the fortieth anniversary of the end of World War II. Wiesenthal declined because SS soldiers were buried in the cemetery where the ceremony took place.

In the second half of the 1980's, Wiesenthal expressed his increasing frustration with the Canadian government, which, after twelve years, had failed to prosecute several hundred known Nazis in Canada, many of whom Wiesenthal had identified. For a decade, Wiesenthal had brought increasing pressure on the government, including boycotting visits to Canada, until twenty key Nazis were brought to trial. In 1985, the government expressed its interest in pursuing the many Nazi criminals allegedly living in Canada, and in 1988 the Toronto branch of the Simon Wiesenthal Center presented evidence to the federal justice minister to indict twenty-one accused Nazi war criminals. Yet a Canadian government commission appointed to study the evidence concluded that the estimates of Nazi criminals in Canada had been grossly exaggerated and had made only one arrest by 1988. Toward the end of the 1980's, Wiesenthal and the Simon Wiesenthal Center had generated computer lists of thousands of suspects' names and addresses, which they presented to government authorities in Australia, Canada, England, the United States, and Sweden. These lists included police chiefs, Gestapo officials, and suspected collaborators.

Wiesenthal has received numerous honors and awards, including the Diploma of Honor from the League of the United Nations; a special Gold Medal of the American Congress from President Jimmy Carter in 1980; the Great Medal of Merit from the President of West Germany in 1985; a Nobel Peace Prize nomination in 1985; the French Legion of Honor in 1986; many hononary degrees; and honorary citizenship of many U.S. cities. The state of New York declared June 13, 1984, as Simon Wiesenthal Day. During a trip to the United States in 1988, Chancellor Helmut Kohl of West Germany paid tribute to Wiesenthal at a banquet held by the Simon Wiesenthal Center in New York.

Wiesenthal knew he would never complete his work. The West German government has more than 160,000 names in its war-crimes files, most of them never tried. In the 1980's, it was estimated that fifty thousand Nazi criminals were still at large around the world. Wiesenthal, ailing with a heart condition and in his eighties, continued with a sense of urgency, realizing that he would not outlive all the criminals.

### *Summary*

Throughout a career spanning almost fifty years, Simon Wiesenthal dedicated his life to bringing Nazi war criminals to justice and publicizing the crimes of the Holocaust. With the patience of a great scholar, the structural sense of an architect, and the investigative genius of a keen detective, he developed a brilliant talent for investigative thinking. He brought eleven hundred Nazis to justice, making him the most successful Nazi hunter in the world.

He is motivated by a deep sense of outraged justice; a desire to keep faith with the millions of victims of the Holocaust; a desire that the murderers of 11 million Jews and Gentiles not be allowed "to get away with it"; a desire to deter future anti-Semitism and genocide; and a fear that the world will forget the Holocaust. Master investigator, avenger, prophet of justice, remarkable sleuth, few have become such symbols in the name of justice and loyalty to the victims of the Holocaust. His sense of justice, perseverance, and success evokes admiration and puzzlement, and the mass media has sometimes cultivated the legendary figure of a Jewish James Bond, scourge of Third Reich fugitives.

In 1988, at a reception honoring Wiesenthal, Reagan hailed Wiesenthal as "one of the true heroes" of the twentieth century and saluted the Nazi hunter for his "unswerving commitment to do honor to those who burned in the flames of the Holocaust by bringing their murderers and the accomplices of their murderers to the justice of a civilized world." He then announced his intention to sign into law the international "convention on the prevention and punishment of the crime of genocide," which had languished in the Senate for four decades. Wiesenthal's efforts contributed to the efforts of juridical justice to deal with genocide, the documentation of the Holocaust, Jewish self-identity, and Holocaust remembrance and education, all of which merge in his work.

*Bibliography*

Ashman, Charles, and Robert J. Wagman. *The Nazi Hunters: The Shocking True Story of the Continuing Search for Nazi War Criminals*. New York: Pharos Books, 1988. A competent and admiring treatment of Wiesenthal's life and work within the context of other Nazi hunters. Also presents the work of the Simon Wiesenthal Center and an appendix of selected war criminal cases.

Cooper, Abraham. "Simon Wiesenthal: The Man, the Mission, His Message." In *Genocide: Critical Issues of the Holocaust*, edited by Alex Grobman and Daniel Landes. Los Angeles: Simon Wiesenthal Center and Rossel Books, 1983. This work contains a brief introduction by Wiesenthal's close associate and director of the Simon Wiesenthal Center in Los Angeles.

Noble, Iris. *Nazi Hunter: Simon Wiesenthal*. New York: Julian Messner, 1979. A dramatic, accessible biography of Wiesenthal's life, methods, and main cases, based primarily on his memoirs, for the general reader. Contains a brief bibliography of secondary sources.

Wiesenthal, Simon. *The Murderers Among Us: The Simon Wiesenthal Memoirs*. Edited with a biographical profile by Joseph Wechsberg. New York: McGraw-Hill, 1967. The most detailed memorialization of the author's life and work, told to Wechsberg, including the stories of many of the Nazi crimes that inspired Wiesenthal's searches. Contains illustrations.

Wistrich, Robert S. "Bruno Kreisky and Simon Wiesenthal." *Midstream*, June/July, 1979: 26-35. A detailed, balanced assessment of the bitter conflict between Wiesenthal and the Austrian chancellor during the 1970's. For the general reader.

*Walter F. Renn*

# WILLIAM II

*Born:* January 27, 1859; Berlin, Prussia
*Died:* June 4, 1941; Doorn, The Netherlands
*Areas of Achievement:* Government and politics
*Contribution:* After a quarter of a century of straining the patience and tolerance of his fellow rulers with his ill-advised antics, it was William II's misfortune to lead the German Empire during World War I. Although certainly not solely responsible for that conflict, it is hard to deny that his inability to cope with the demands of the modern state helped to create the climate of instability that eventually led to the rise of Adolf Hitler.

## *Early Life*

Born on January 27, 1859, Prince Friedrich Wilhelm Viktor Albert was the eldest son of Prince Frederick William of Prussia and his wife, Princess Victoria, the eldest child of Queen Victoria and Prince Albert. The delivery was difficult and William's left arm was severely injured. The hand and arm, although healthy, never grew to normal size, thereby producing a lack of bodily balance. This handicap drove the young prince to try harder than his fellows to succeed in areas that required physical stamina, and especially in athletics.

In contrast to his autocratic grandfather, who would in 1871 become the first emperor of Germany, William's parents were liberals who were determined that their son would be educated to govern a democratic state, not an absolute monarchy. Consequently, at the age of sixteen he became the first member of his family to attend a school open to the general public. Having been carefully prepared for entry into the *Gymnasium* at Kassel, William did quite well academically, but he was carefully isolated from his fellow students. Beginning in 1877, he spent four semesters at the University of Bonn, but his real interest lay with the army and not the university.

William began his military training late in 1879 at Potsdam, near Berlin. There William came in close contact with the most conservative elements in German society, the Prussian nobility and the corps of professional officers. At last he could rebel against the ideas and concepts that his parents had tried to instill in him since childhood. His rebellion brought him into conflict with his mother, who was as willful and determined as he was. This tension continued until her death in 1901 and gave rise to a number of unfounded rumors about relations between William and other members of his mother's family.

As was the custom among European royalty, William's marriage was arranged for him, and in February, 1880, he was engaged to Augusta Victoria of Schleswig-Holstein-Sonderburg-Augustenberg, Dona to her family. Reared to concern herself with children and home, she did not provide

William with either the intellectual companionship or direction that he so desperately needed. Yet the marriage, which was solemnized in February, 1881, proved a happy one, and the couple had six sons and one daughter.

During the years that followed his marriage, William was rarely in the public eye, but he was considered important enough to be cultivated by his grandfather's chancellor, Otto von Bismarck. The young prince was flattered by the attention from one whom he greatly admired, and during the last years of the old emperor's life, he seemed to grow closer to the man whom neither his father nor his mother trusted. Then on March 9, 1888, William I died and Fredrick III ascended the throne. His reign was brief; on June 15, 1888, he died of cancer of the throat. At the age of twenty-nine, William II inherited the crown of Germany and began a reign that would last until 1918.

*Life's Work*

Almost completely ignorant of foreign affairs and uncertain of his ability to understand the endless ramifications of his ministers' domestic policies, William II was nevertheless determined to bring under his personal control every aspect of government. Bismarck was equally convinced that to entrust such weighty matters to the care of an immature monarch whose impatience and lack of tact were proverbial might endanger the continued peaceful evolution of the German state. Resolved to manage the young kaiser, and sure of his own indispensable position, Bismarck invoked a long-forgotten cabinet order of 1850 that forbade individual ministers to report to the monarch save in the presence of the chancellor. Having endured Bismarck's arrogance for almost two years, William dismissed him on March 10, 1890.

With the departure of Bismarck, William II assumed complete control of the government, but the only thing consistent about his policies was their inconsistency. Often his instincts were correct, but, aware of his lack of real experience, he repeatedly allowed himself to endorse a course of action that eventually proved injurious to the interests of Germany. Thus, shortly after Bismarck left office, the kaiser was persuaded not to renew the vital Reinsurance Treaty with Russia. This rejection of one of the cornerstones of Bismarck's foreign policy forced Russia into an alliance with France in 1894. This blunder ended the diplomatic isolation of France and left Germany surrounded by potential enemies. The climate of opinion thus created allowed proponents of a two-front war, such as Alfred von Schlieffen, the opportunity to convince William of the inevitable armed conflict with France and Russia.

Determined to counter the Franco-Russian alliance with a diplomatic coup of his own, William used every device at his disposal to form a permanent arrangement with Great Britain. Instead of creating a lasting friendship with the foreign power he most admired, William seemed to lurch from one crisis to another. The African and Asian policies of the two countries were not incompatible, but, when the kaiser finished his diplomatic offensive, relations between the two countries were almost openly hostile. As the possibility of an Anglo-German rapprochement became increasingly remote, William encouraged the passage by the Reichstag of a naval bill that would create a German war fleet. While it was intended to protect Germany's merchant fleet and serve the empire, the British regarded the naval building program as a threat to their continued hegemony on the high seas. All hope of an alliance, formal or informal, was destroyed by the kaiser's continued public support of the Boers in South Africa and his enthusiastic endorsement of the building of a railroad from Berlin to Baghdad.

William's grasp of domestic affairs during the first decade of his reign was equally unsuccessful. In the early days of the empire, Berlin was slowly transformed from a mere royal capital into a city of world stature. Unfortunately, William was completely out of touch with the cultural trends that were sweeping Germany into the mainstream of European life. He turned from the exciting new Berlin of artists and intellectuals, poets and playwrights, politicians and reformers to an older Berlin that still celebrated the martial virtues. Surrounding himself with military personnel, William became increasingly remote from his civilian advisers, a trend that had dire consequences in the early years of the twentieth century.

To their dismay, German diplomats learned of the Entente Cordiale between France and Great Britain in 1904. Undaunted, William proceeded the following year to execute his plan for dislodging the British from their potential alliance with the Third French Republic. Bismarck had encouraged the French to develop a sphere of influence in North Africa, but now William sought to reverse that policy while reawakening British distrust of French colonial ambitions. He recognized the Sultan of Morocco as an independent ruler and paid a visit to Tangier in 1905. To prevent an escalation of this manufactured crisis, the great powers assembled at Algeciras in Spain the following year. The conference was a diplomatic victory for France. It received a free hand in Morocco, the arrangement with Great Britain was strengthened, and in 1907, after months of negotiations begun at Algeciras, Russia was persuaded to settle a number of long-standing differences with Great Britain.

William provoked a second Moroccan crisis in 1911 by sending a German warship to the port of Agadir to protest the French occupation of the city of Fez. The European powers came very close to war, but somehow peace was maintained. Actual fighting in the Balkans the following year had a sobering effect on Europe's leaders, and even the kaiser began to work for the maintenance of peace. The months that followed saw an easing of tensions, and the gala wedding of William's daughter, Viktoria Luise, to Ernst August of Hannover in May, 1912, seemed to mark the beginning of a new era of tranquillity and cooperation. It was to be the last time that the royalty of

Europe would assemble socially, but on that happy occasion war was far from their minds. The development of a rational and peaceful approach to the Continent's problems was welcomed by people of every nationality.

In June, 1914, the kaiser was on holiday when the Archduke Francis Ferdinand was assassinated. Shocked at the loss of an old friend, he promised Germany's moral support to Austria-Hungary, never dreaming that his ally would use that offer to force Serbia into a diplomatic position that could only result in a declaration of war. Ignorant of the exact details of the ultimatum, William nevertheless felt honor-bound to defend Austria-Hungary. Once committed to war, albeit reluctantly, the kaiser threw himself into the fray with his usual energy. His fits of bombastic rhetoric gave the Allies grist for their propaganda mills, but the German people remained loyal until the end. Like all the belligerent powers, Germany censored the news from the front and successfully edited the truth to convince the people of their ultimate victory. The rumor of the armistice and Germany's subsequent admission of defeat seemed to paralyze the nation. Republican elements then seized the opportunity to overthrow the monarchy, which was tainted with failure. On November 10, 1918, William, the last member of the House of Hohenzollern to govern in Germany, crossed the frontier into The Netherlands, an exile.

For more than twenty years, William pursued the life of a country gentleman in the charming castle at Doorn, which he purchased in 1920. Despite repeated Allied demands, the Dutch government refused to extradite him as a war criminal. To ensure his safety, William had only to promise his Dutch hosts that he would abstain from all political activity. This he did, although he never ceased to hope for a restoration. Unfortunately, the suicide of his son Joachim in 1920 and the death of the empress in 1921 made his early years of exile bleak. His marriage to Hermine, the widow of Prince Schonaich-Carolath in November, 1922, marked the beginning of a much happier phase of his life. As the years passed, the former kaiser's public image began to soften, and, with the rise of Hitler, many in Germany and abroad longed for his return. Forgotten were the diplomatic blunders and his open hostility to liberal trends and ideas; instead, his integrity, his patriotism, and his devotion to duty were remembered. When, in November, 1938, William denounced the savagery of Kristallnacht, many of his critics revised their opinions of their former adversary.

When war came in September, 1939, William declined the offer of sanctuary in England, preferring to remain at Doorn. He spent his last months a virtual prisoner of his Nazi guards, but he refused to allow his death on June 4, 1941, to be used to serve the propaganda aims of the Hitler government. He was buried at Doorn and not Berlin. The notice of his death was lost amid the war news, but for those who longed for the return of order and honor he became a symbol of better times.

*Summary*

Although William II was hardly the quintessence of evil portrayed in Allied propaganda during World War I, he does bear a portion of the blame for the outbreak of that most tragic of modern conflicts. Nevertheless, he was also a victim of the system that sucked the great powers into the vortex of war in the second decade of the twentieth century. The last kaiser of Germany was a man of intelligence with the potential for a depth of understanding of the workings of the modern state unparalleled among his fellow rulers, but his erudition was a façade and his learning superficial. William had flair but no substance. By rebelling against the ideals of his parents, he rejected the chance to aid in the transformation of Germany into a modern constitutional monarchy and chose instead to ally himself with those who espoused the outmoded and potentially dangerous military virtues that had helped to unite Germany in 1871. With the death of his father in 1888, William assumed the responsibility of leading his nation into the new century. He was neither professionally trained nor emotionally prepared to bear that burden. Indecisive and hopelessly naïve when it came to international relations, blind to the forces that were transforming Germany, he clung to the past and refused to embrace the future. He was a good man, a courageous man who was chosen to perform a task beyond his capacity. He might have been one of the great men of his time, instead he was one of its greatest failures.

*Bibliography*

Balfour, Michael. *The Kaiser and His Times*. Boston: Houghton Mifflin, 1964. Written in the decade when historians first began to examine World War I and the years that preceded it with real objectivity, this biography remains one of the best treatments of William and his time. The exceptional bibliography, the careful notation, and the charts provided at the end of this work tend to enhance a very scholarly and yet readable book.

Cowles, Virginia. *The Kaiser*. New York: Harper & Row, 1963. Relying on the scholarship of contemporary historians, this popular biography was written with only a passing reference to changing views and attitudes toward the kaiser and his era. Yet it is lively, well written, and very readable, and serves well as an introduction to the subject.

Hull, Isabel V. *The Entourage of Kaiser Wilhelm II*. Cambridge, England: Cambridge University Press, 1982. This fascinating study explores in detail the influence exercised upon the kaiser by his friends, family, and government officials during the thirty years of his reign. Particular attention is given to the often destructive nature of the military elements in William's government and household. The kaiser emerges not as a monster but as a man plagued by indecision and the legacy of Bismarck.

Rohl, John C. G., and Nicolaus Sombart, eds. *Kaiser Wilhelm II, New Inter-*

*pretations: The Corfu Papers*. Cambridge, England: Cambridge University Press, 1982. This collection of eleven essays covers a number of topics ranging from William's relations with his parents and his family in Germany and England to the nature of the empire that he governed for a generation. The questions raised by these scholarly papers delivered at Corfu, the kaiser's favorite vacation retreat, will provide a new generation of historians with subjects for a whole new series of books.

Tuchman, Barbara. *The Guns of August*. New York: Macmillian, 1962. This is without a doubt one of the finest books ever written dealing with the crisis that led to the beginning of World War I. It is the product of thorough scholarship, but it reads like a work of fiction, proving that history is more exciting than any novel.

__________. *The Proud Tower*. New York: Macmillian, 1965. In this fascinating portrait of an age, Tuchman explores the glittering world that existed in the years before the tragedy of World War I. It is, however, a work of limited depth and intended more for the general reader than the serious scholar. Both of these works by Tuchman are useful supplements for the student who wishes to place William in the context of his age.

Viktoria Luise, Duchess of Brunswick and Lüneburg. *The Kaiser's Daughter*. Edited and translated by Robert Vacha. London: W. H. Allen, 1977. This one volume is the English version of the three-part autobiography of the kaiser's only daughter, and it presents an entirely different view of William. In a frank and lively style, Princess Viktoria Luise portrays her father as a devoted husband and father and a patriot with high standards of morality who was anything but the "Beast of Berlin."

*Clifton W. Potter, Jr.*

# LUDWIG WITTGENSTEIN

*Born:* April 26, 1889; Vienna, Austro-Hungarian Empire
*Died:* April 29, 1951; Cambridge, England
*Area of Achievement:* Philosophy
*Contribution:* Wittgenstein is one of the most important and influential philosophers of the twentieth century and perhaps of all time. In his later, mature period, he did not produce a systematic philosophy or even claim to teach new doctrines. Instead, he professed to offer new methods and techniques for work in philosophy.

## *Early Life*

Ludwig Josef Johann Wittgenstein was born into a prominent and highly cultured family in turn-of-the-century Vienna. His father, Karl Wittgenstein, was a leading Austrian industrialist and had in fact made a fortune in the iron and steel industry. Originally educated at home, at the age of fourteen Wittgenstein entered school at Linz in Upper Austria and later attended the Technische Hochschule in Berlin-Charlottenburg. Wittgenstein developed a strong interest in physics, technology, and engineering. In 1908, he went to England, where he experimented with kites at the Kite Flying Upper Atmosphere Station and became a student at the University of Manchester. His early studies took him into airplane engine design, mathematics, and the philosophical and logical foundations of mathematics. He went to Jena, Germany, to visit Gottlob Frege (the "father of modern logic"), where he was advised to study with Bertrand Russell at the University of Cambridge. Russell had published *The Principles of Mathematics* in 1903, and, together with Alfred North Whitehead, had published in 1910 the first volume of their *Principia Mathematica*, a monumental and definitive work in modern logic. In 1912, Wittgenstein was accepted at the University of Cambridge and took up his formal studies there under Russell.

Although Russell and Wittgenstein later drifted apart, there was at this early period a closeness and a mutual seriousness that show themselves in many stories, still told, that date from this time. According to Russell, at the end of Wittgenstein's first term at Cambridge he came to Russell and asked, "Do you think I am a complete idiot?" The idea was that Wittgenstein was thinking about becoming a pilot (if he was an idiot) and a philosopher (if he was not). Russell said to write a paper during the term break. Wittgenstein did, and when Russell saw it he immediately said that Wittgenstein should not become a pilot. On another occasion, Wittgenstein came to Russell's rooms late one night and paced up and down, in a distraught mood, for hours. Russell asked him whether he was thinking about logic or his sins, and Wittgenstein answered "Both!" Russell was convinced that, although Wittgenstein was eccentric, he was a genius.

In 1913, Wittgenstein's father died and left him a huge fortune. This Wittgenstein gave away, some of it in the form of anonymous benefactions to Austrian poets and writers. Wittgenstein himself assumed a rather austere life-style, which he maintained for the rest of his life. He ate simply, dressed simply, had no family, and lived in very humble rooms.

*Life's Work*

Wittgenstein's early masterpiece, and the only philosophical book that he published during his lifetime, is best known by the title *Tractatus Logico-Philosophicus*—or, for short, the *Tractatus*. This was published in the original German in 1921 and first appeared in an English-German bilingual edition in 1922. Wittgenstein stated in the preface that the gist of the book lies in the following statement: "What can be said at all can be said clearly, and what we cannot talk about we must pass over in silence." The book is quite terse and follows a special numbering system in which each section (sometimes only a single sentence) receives a number based on its relative importance to the whole. The main statements are given the numbers one through seven. Number one says "The world is all that is the case"—that is, the world is the totality of facts or situations. One of the essential features of Wittgenstein's early philosophy, as expressed in the *Tractatus*, is that the most basic statements (or elementary propositions) of language achieve meaning by picturing facts. More complicated factual statements are built up from these. Thus, when all the true propositions have been stated, everything that can be said has been said; the rest is silence. As Wittgenstein claimed in the *Tractatus*, there are some things that are inexpressible—he spoke here of things that are mystical—and to try to express these in language will only result in nonsense.

Wittgenstein claimed that his *Tractatus* solved the problems of philosophy. So, he left philosophy and pursued various other professions. He became a village schoolteacher in the Austrian mountains, a gardener in a monastery, and a worker at sculpture and architecture. In 1929, however, Wittgenstein returned to Cambridge and to philosophy. His *Tractatus*, already acknowledged as a classic work, was accepted as his Ph.D. dissertation, and he became first a research fellow and later a professor. Until his death in 1951, Wittgenstein wrote many volumes of philosophy (almost always in German) but did not publish any of these (or have them translated into English). He taught philosophy at Cambridge, but, instead of lecturing, he used a method of discussion and thinking aloud. Most of his influence—and it was considerable—occurred through the students who attended his discussions and those who took dictation from him (in English). Wittgenstein, however, found the atmosphere of Cambridge life to be sterile. He would sometimes leave to spend weeks and months in out-of-the-way places in Norway and Ireland and would write philosophy there.

The new philosophy that Wittgenstein developed in the 1930's and 1940's retained its focus on language but gave up the monolithic idea that language always functions in merely one way, that is, via the picturing relation. He now came to emphasize the great variety of uses of language and the fact that language is intertwined with the rest of human life. His later work, best seen in his posthumously published *Philosophical Investigations* (1953), provides some explicit criticism of the views earlier taken in the *Tractatus*. Wittgenstein went on to develop his thoughts in new and positive directions.

Wittgenstein's view of the nature of philosophical problems changed. He now came to see problems as tied to individuals. Thus he said, for example, that the philosopher's treatment of a problem is like the treatment of an illness. Just as in medicine there is always a patient (and never an illness alone) who is to be cured, in philosophy there is a person who is the bearer of philosophical questions or confusions. The doctor does not treat diseases in the abstract, and the philosopher does not treat problems in the abstract.

The later philosophy of Wittgenstein has been characterized as a therapeutic approach. A philosophical problem is seen as a sort of difficulty. A person who has such a problem is lost, in a sense, and Wittgenstein's aim is to show this person how to get out of the difficulty. One image he used was that of knots. Although philosophy should be simple, he said, in order to untie the knots of our thinking it must be at least as complicated as those knots.

Wittgenstein believed that language itself was exceedingly tricky and often extremely misleading. At one point he said that philosophy is a battle against the bewitchment of intelligence by means of language. In emphasizing the variety of ways in which language is used, Wittgenstein opposed the idea that any one form of language or thought—the scientific, for example—is in some sense basic or foundational. If anything is foundational, according to Wittgenstein, it is one's practice or way of life.

Wittgenstein believed that some of the occasions on which people are most likely to be misled occur in thinking and talking about mathematical abstractions, psychological concepts, and language itself. Although he did not confine his thought and writing to these areas, he did concentrate his attention on what he regarded as the temptations that are likely to appeal to thinkers in these areas and on the means of overcoming these temptations.

### *Summary*

Ludwig Wittgenstein's influence spread rapidly from Cambridge to other areas of the English-speaking world and to Scandinavia. This influence operated largely through his students and by word of mouth. Since his death in 1951, more and more of his philosophical writings have been published, and his influence has spread, although it remains significantly stronger in English-speaking countries and in Scandinavia and weaker on the European continent, Latin America, and elsewhere.

It is not an exaggeration to say that Wittgenstein was a leader in a philosophical revolution. The revolution focuses particular attention on language and on the ways in which people can be confused or misled, especially by ordinary language.

One recent movement that takes its inspiration from Wittgenstein is known as "ordinary language" philosophy. Herein, the emphasis is on the ordinary meanings of customary terms, clarity of expression, and down-to-earth common sense rather than special philosophical or technical terminology, impressive-sounding but vague language, and high-flown metaphysical notions.

Although it is true that Wittgenstein's own views and practice in philosophy changed over time, and many scholars distinguish sharply between the earlier and the later approaches, one constant concern of his focuses on the idea that clarity of thought and expression is of the first importance and nonsense is always to be rejected, and sometimes even fought against.

*Bibliography*

Fann, K. T., ed. *Ludwig Wittgenstein: The Man and His Philosophy.* New York: Dell, 1967. A collection of articles by friends, students, and scholars of Wittgenstein. Included are articles on Wittgenstein as a person, a teacher, and a philosopher, and treatments of various aspects of Wittgenstein's philosophical work.

Janik, Allan, and Stephen Toulmin. *Wittgenstein's Vienna.* New York: Simon & Schuster, 1973. An illustrated survey showing the many connections between Wittgenstein's philosophical development and modern movements in architecture, literature, music, psychoanalysis, and other fields, in the setting of late nineteenth century Viennese culture.

McGinn, Colin. *Wittgenstein on Meaning: An Interpretation and Evaluation.* New York: Basil Blackwell, 1984. The long first chapter of this work is especially useful in providing a large-scale view of the later Wittgenstein views on meaning, understanding, and language.

McGuinness, Brian. *Wittgenstein, A Life: Young Ludwig, 1889-1921.* Berkeley: University of California Press, 1988. The first volume of a projected two-volume authorized biography, providing by far the fullest account to date of Wittgenstein's early life. This first volume concludes with a discussion of the *Tractatus.* Includes illustrations.

Malcolm, Norman. *Ludwig Wittgenstein: A Memoir.* 2d ed. New York: Oxford University Press, 1984. This book is a gem, written by Wittgenstein's most prominent American philosophical student. Malcolm allows the reader to see the force of Wittgenstein's personality as well as his particular way of practicing philosophy. The second edition includes numerous letters that Wittgenstein wrote to Malcolm.

Pears, David. *The False Prison*. 2 vols. New York: Oxford University Press, 1987 and 1988. The first volume covers Wittgenstein's early philosophy; the second covers the time from 1929 to his death. Pears focuses clearly on Wittgenstein the philosopher rather than on Wittgenstein the person. His treatment of Wittgenstein's work is scholarly and reliable.

Wittgenstein, Ludwig. *Culture and Value*. Edited by G. H. von Wright, in collaboration with Heikki Nyman. Translated by Peter Winch. 2d ed. Oxford: Basil Blackwell, 1980. A bilingual edition of sentences and paragraphs taken from all periods of Wittgenstein's life, arranged chronologically, addressing a wide range of topics in art, music, philosophy, religion, science, and the like.

*Stephen Satris*

# MAX WOLF

*Born:* June 21, 1863; Heidelberg, Baden
*Died:* October 3, 1932; Heidelberg, Germany
*Area of Achievement:* Astronomy
*Contribution:* Wolf was the first astronomer to use an astronomical camera to discover asteroids by combining the camera with a mechanical telescope. During his very full career, Wolf discovered 582 asteroids with 228 of these receiving general recognition. This figure is a personal record of discoveries in astronomy which has been difficult to surpass.

## *Early Life*

Max Wolf was the son of Franz Wolf and Elise Halwerth. He was attracted to astronomy at an early age and, while a student at Heidelberg, erected his own small observatory. Since his father was a wealthy physician, Wolf was able to afford this private facility. In 1884, he discovered the comet which bears his name. This discovery so fired his interest in astronomy that he gave up all of his other studies to pursue a career in this field, earning a Ph.D. from Heidelberg with a dissertation in celestial mechanics.

In 1891, Wolf discovered his first asteroid, using photography. For this discovery, he was awarded the Lalande Prize of the Paris Academy of Sciences. After a visit to the United States, during which he received financial support for a sixteen-inch double telescope, Wolf returned to Heidelberg to work with the Grand Duke of Baden to build a new observatory at Königstuhl. In 1893, Wolf was named director of this new observatory and, simultaneously, became extraordinary professor of astrophysics at the University of Heidelberg. In 1902, he was elected to the chair of astronomy at the same university. Wolf remained at Heidelberg for the rest of his life, discovering his last asteroid, 1219 Britta, there only a few months prior to his death.

## *Life's Work*

Wolf had two major accomplishments during his career. The first was the use of an astronomical camera in connection with a telescope to hunt for asteroids. To accomplish this search, the telescope was centered on a conveniently located bright star. The clockwork of the telescope kept track with the movement of the star so that photographs showed the star as a dot of light. Asteroids and comets moving across the field around the star would appear on the photograph as lines. Visual observation with the telescope alone would then determine whether the line was a comet or an asteroid. Because the clockwork drive for telescopes was not entirely accurate, the photographic session had to be monitored constantly to keep the star in the cross hairs of the telescope. Wolf developed the technique for this method of sky search to a high degree. His methods were adapted widely by other astronomers.

The second great accomplishment of Wolf's career was the discovery of the Trojan asteroids, a large number of asteroids outside the asteroid belt and in the orbit of Jupiter. In 1906, Wolf observed an asteroid, which he called Achilles, whose orbit seemed unusual. Mathematical computations showed that Achilles was in the orbit of Jupiter. Although this seems impossible, an eighteenth century mathematician, Joseph-Louis Lagrange, had determined that, in theory, a small object can travel in the same orbit as a large object if the two objects and the sun form an equilateral triangle. In order to do this, the small object must be about sixty degrees ahead of or behind the large one. Wolf was searching sixty degrees ahead of Jupiter when he discovered Achilles. The name "Achilles" was chosen by Wolf because other asteroids had feminine names, but this one was outside the asteroid belt.

The discovery of Achilles suggested that one should search sixty degrees behind Jupiter, and there other bodies were found. The first of these was named Patroclus. This established a pattern; all these asteroids were named for heroes of the Trojan War, and the two groups are collectively called the Trojan asteroids. All of those in the Achilles group, except one, Hector, are named for the Greeks, and, except for Patroclus, the second group are named for the defenders of Troy. Some seven hundred Trojan asteroids have been identified.

*Summary*

By combining the best technology of his time with accepted theories, Max Wolf was able to demonstrate the factuality of the Lagrange theory with respect to Jupiter. No other planets have asteroids at the Lagrange points of sixty degrees ahead or behind. By demonstrating an effective method of searching for asteroids, Wolf advanced early twentieth century knowledge of astronomy. The technology of astronomy of the late twentieth century has led to so many asteroid discoveries that one astronomer has called them "vermin of the skies." In Wolf's day, they were a new and exciting field of observation and discovery.

*Bibliography*

Freiesleben, H.-Christ. "Maximilian Franz Joseph Cornelius Wolf." In *Dictionary of Scientific Biography*, edited by Charles Coulston Gillispie, vol. 14. New York: Charles Scribner's Sons, 1976. This reference work has a biographical sketch of Wolf and includes a short bibliography of his astronomical articles, most of which are in German and are untranslated.

Gehrels, Tom. *Asteroids*. Tucson: University of Arizona Press, 1979. This textbook on asteroids has several references to Wolf and his work. It explains the significance of asteroids in the planetary scene.

Kowal, Charles T., ed. *Asteroids: Their Nature and Utilization*. New York: John Wiley & Sons, 1988. Kowal describes Wolf's discovery of the Trojan asteroids and discusses the Lagrange theory in layperson's terms.

Mitton, Simon, ed. *The Cambridge Encyclopedia of Astronomy.* New York: Crown Books, 1977. A basic reference work, this book has good articles on asteroids and the Trojan asteroids. Includes a brief biographical sketch on Wolf that focuses on his work.

Vaucouleurs, Gérard Henri de. *Astronomical Photography: From the Daguerrotype to the Electron Camera*. New York: Macmillan, 1961. A history of the photographing of asteroids. Contains numerous references to Wolf's work and several photographs and charts of asteroids.

*Michael R. Bradley*

# WILHELM WUNDT

*Born:* August 16, 1832; Neckerau, Baden
*Died:* August 31, 1920; Grossbothen, Germany
*Areas of Achievement:* Psychology and physiology
*Contribution:* Wundt did much to develop psychology as an independent discipline. Beginning in 1879, Wundt established a psychological institute at the University of Leipzig, where he directed many experiments in which subjects studied their sensations and feelings. He was an effective teacher, who trained many of the next generation's leading psychologists.

## *Early Life*

Wilhelm Wundt was born in Neckerau, Baden, on August 16, 1832. He came from a distinguished family that included two university presidents as well as theologians and other scholars. Wundt's father was a Lutheran pastor. Wundt's childhood was apparently lonely; indeed, even as an adult with a successful career, Wundt was generally shy and withdrawn. When Wundt was eight, he came under the tutelage of his father's assistant, a young vicar whose guidance supported Wundt for several years. After failing his first year at the Catholic *Gymnasium* at Neckerau, Wundt transferred to the Heidelberg *Gymnasium*, where he was more comfortable, and was graduated in 1851.

Wundt's scholastic record was mediocre, but with the help of his maternal uncle he gained admission to the premedical program at the University of Tübingen, where he stayed for only a year before transferring to the University of Heidelberg. His diligence earned for Wundt a summa cum laude in three years and a first place on the state board medical examination.

After a year of study at the University of Berlin, Wundt returned to Heidelberg in 1857 as a lecturer in physiology, but he overworked himself preparing lectures on experimental psychology and contracted a serious illness that forced him to recuperate for a year in the Swiss Alps. In 1858, Wundt took a position as assistant to the distinguished physiologist Hermann von Helmholtz, who had been appointed head of the Institute of Physiology at the University of Heidelberg. Wundt wearied of his tenure with Helmholtz and resigned in 1863, but by that time he had published his first book and launched what was to become an astonishingly prolific scholarly career.

Wundt became active in politics in the 1860's, serving as president of the Heidelberg Workingmen's Educational Association and completing two terms in the Baden parliament. In 1871, however, he returned to the University of Heidelberg for three more years; during this period, he published one of the most important books in the history of psychology, *Grundzüge der physiologischen Psychologie* (2 vols., 1873-1874; *Principles of Physiological Psychology*, vol. 1, 1904). Wundt revised this work in six more editions through 1911, and it remained the basis for his work in experimental psychology.

After three final years at Heidelberg, Wundt left there for the University of Zurich. His stay at Zurich was brief; after one year, he moved to the University of Leipzig to accept the chair in philosophy. He remained at Leipzig for the remainder of his life, establishing and lecturing in the Psychological Institute, from which he derived his fame as an educator.

### *Life's Work*

The Psychological Institute began in 1879 in makeshift quarters, and, before it was given better housing in 1897, Wundt had trained a large number of the best-known experimental psychologists of the next generation. Wundt's institute was especially influential in its nurturing of the most prominent American psychologists, among them Granville Stanley Hall and the English-born Edward Bradford Titchener. In 1881, Wundt founded a journal, *Philosophische Studien*, as the voice of the new institute. In the same decade, he published a series of philosophical tomes: *Logik*, in two volumes (1880-1883), *Ethik: Eine Untersuchung der Thatsachen und Gesetze des sittlichen Lebens* (1886; *Ethics: An Investigation of the Facts and Laws of the Moral Life*, 1897-1901), and *System der Philosophie* (1889). His scholarly output in the 1880's was prodigious. Besides the three long philosophical works, Wundt published numerous articles in *Philosophische Studien* as well as the second and third revised editions of the two-volume *Principles of Physiological Psychology.* This huge work was an attempt to explain the mind in a series of elements interrelated by the principle of association, a holdover from earlier theorizing about the mind in England. This period in Wundt's career culminated in his appointment in 1889 as rector of the University of Leipzig.

The 1890's were no less fruitful, producing a fourth edition of *Principles of Physiological Psychology* (1893), an important theory of feeling presented in *Grundriss der Psychologie* (1896; *Outlines of Psychology*, 1897), several revisions of the earlier philosophical works, and more articles. In *Outlines of Psychology*, Wundt built upon the *Principles of Physiological Psychology* and tried to demonstrate a three-part structure to explain feelings. Wundt believed that feelings can be measured in terms of their pleasantness or unpleasantness, their degree of strain or relaxation, and their components of excitement or calm. The basis for this analysis was the unverifiable record of personal experience and its effect was to enrich the theoretical understanding of the workings of the mind. Wundt's efforts to find experimental evidence for this new theory led to strenuous testing by others in Germany and the United States, and although the results were equivocal the work was important in fostering the studies of the new laboratories.

The century ended with the publication of the first volume of Wundt's

*Völkerpsychologie* (1900; cultural psychology), an immense undertaking that reached ten volumes by 1920. *Völkerpsychologie* occupies a problematic position in the huge corpus of Wundt's work. Two of its volumes treat aspects of language, two are on myth and religion, two on society, and one each on art, law, culture, and history.

The special nature of the *Völkerpsychologie* can be explained by the German differentiation between *Naturwissenschaften*, or natural science, and *Geisteswissenschaften*, the less rigorous observation that does not depend on experimental evidence. Historians of experimental psychology have understandably slighted *Völkerpsychologie*, but Wundt obviously saw the work as an integral part of his complete vision of the study of the mind's workings and not as a late interest attached as a huge footnote to his experimental work. He had indeed defined the topic as early as 1862, explaining it more fully in 1904 in a reference to "other sources of psychological knowledge, which become accessible at the very point where the experimental method fails us."

*Summary*

Wilhelm Wundt's major contribution was his establishment of the psychological institute that put psychology on a firm experimental basis, dividing it from metaphysics. The use of such instruments as tachistoscopes, pendulums, and sensory mapping apparatus put psychology into the laboratory, and it is now difficult to imagine the intensity of some of Wundt's opponents. There were those, for example, who predicted that self-conscious examination of one's mental and emotional responses would lead to insanity. Wundt's laboratory studies involved the recording by trained subjects of their mental reactions to controlled events, and from these studies Wundt isolated two elements of the mind, sensation and feeling. In *Outlines of Psychology*, Wundt went beyond the associationist theory that influenced him in *Principles of Physiological Psychology* to advance a picture of the mind's creative vitality: The mind was to be seen not as a mechanical manipulator of static elements but as an organic and dynamic synthesis of the mental and the physical.

Wundt was a teacher of great influence and authority who assigned research projects to students and directed dissertations. In the roughly four decades that he ran his laboratory, Wundt directed 186 doctoral theses, seventy in philosophy and the others in psychology. (His most famous student, however, was not a psychologist but Hugo Eckener, commander of the *Graf Zeppelin*.) The list of Wundt's students who founded their own psychology laboratories in the United States includes Frank Angell, Edward A. Pace, and Edward Scripture. Lightner Witmer started the first psychological clinic in the United States in 1896, three years after he received his degree under Wundt. Harry Kirke Wolfe founded the department of psychology at the

University of Nebraska; Charles Judd, who translated Wundt's *Outlines of Psychology* into English, founded both the department of educational psychology at the University of California at Berkeley and the psychology laboratory at New York University. Wundt's influence was so strong that, by 1900, twelve of the forty-three psychological laboratories in the United States had been started by former students of Wundt.

Wundt was not a flamboyant man, but he drew large gatherings of students to his lectures and taught more than twenty-four thousand students during his long career. He continued to be interested in politics throughout his life and spoke ardently in support of the German cause in World War I, judging France, Russia, and especially England to be coconspirators against Germany.

*Bibliography*

Blumenthal, Arthur. "A Reappraisal of Wilhelm Wundt." *American Psychologist* 30 (1975): 1081-1083. A much-praised fresh look at Wundt that takes *Völkerpsychologie* seriously and sees Wundt's work as more of a piece.

Boring, Edwin G. *A History of Experimental Psychology.* New York: Appleton-Century-Crofts, 1950. A standard history of the subject but lopsided in its treatment of Wundt in that it slights *Völkerpsychologie*.

Hilgard, Ernest R. *Psychology in America: A Historical Survey.* New York: Harcourt Brace Jovanovich, 1987. Chapter 2 gives a succinct account of Wundt as a "systematic psychologist," treating him with William James.

Hothersall, David. *History of Psychology.* Philadelphia: Temple University Press, 1984. Chapter 4, "Wilhelm Wundt and the Founding of Psychology" is divided into sections such as "Wundt the Man," "Wundt as Advisor," and "Wundt's Research" that provide an excellent overview of the man and his career.

Littman, Richard. "Social and Intellectual Origins of Experimental Psychology." In *The First Century of Experimental Psychology,* edited by Eliot Hearst. Hillsdale, N.J.: Lawrence Erlbaum, 1979. A useful look at Wundt's work from a modern perspective.

Rieber, Robert W., ed. *Wilhelm Wundt and the Making of a Scientific Psychology.* New York: Plenum, 1980. A valuable collection of eight essays on Wundt plus two selections in translation from Wundt's own work. The essays include "Personal History Before Leipzig," four articles about Wundt's influence, and three appreciations by Wundt's contemporaries.

Robinson, Daniel N. *Toward a Science of Human Nature: Essays on the Psychologies of Mill, Hegel, Wundt, and James*. New York: Columbia University Press, 1982. Superb essays in intellectual history, elaborating the approach in Wundt's time to such issues as the mind-body problem and definitions of the self. Very stimulating but not for beginners.

Wertheimer, Michael. *A Brief History of Psychology.* New York: Holt, Rinehart and Winston, 1970. The two chapters "Wilhelm Wundt" and "The Contemporary Scene in the Age of Wundt" offer a convenient introduction to the subject.

*Frank Day*

# IANNIS XENAKIS

*Born:* May 29, 1922; Brăila, Romania

*Areas of Achievement:* Music, architecture, engineering, and mathematics

*Contribution:* Xenakis is one of Europe's most prestigious avant-garde composers. His works exhibit a new and individual kind of musical thinking based on physics, mathematics, and architecture. Especially important for Xenakis has been the mathematics of probability. He introduced the term "stochastic music" for music utilizing probabilistic processes, and he has sometimes used computers to aid in the elaborate calculations demanded.

*Early Life*

Of Greek parentage, Iannis Xenakis was born on May 29, 1922, in Brăila, Romania. His father, Charcos Xenakis, was a wealthy businessman; his mother was Fantins Parlou Xenakis. Xenakis early became familiar with the rich folk music of his native region of the Lower Danube, and he was influenced considerably by the Byzantine music of the Orthodox rite. As a boy, he also demonstrated a fascination with unpitched sounds. In 1932, his family returned to Greece. There, he was reared and educated, eventually attending a Greek-English college on the island of Spetsai. Xenakis' first exposure to music from Ludwig van Beethoven to Johannes Brahms dates from this period. In 1934, he began studying composition with Aristotle Koundourov, a former pupil of Mikhail Ippolitov-Ivanov.

Deciding to divide his time and energy between the sciences and music, Xenakis successfully passed the entrance examinations for the Polytechnic Institute in Athens in 1940. His studies in Athens were prolonged by the Nazi invasion of Greece, for he spent much of his time fighting with the resistance. Xenakis became secretary of a resistance group at the Polytechnic Institute in 1941, and he was jailed and tortured several times. His face was disfigured, and he lost completely the vision in one eye when struck by a tank during street fighting in Athens on New Year's Day, 1945. He was captured, imprisoned, and sentenced to die as a terrorist but managed to escape. Completing his studies at the Polytechnic Institute in 1947, he received his degree in engineering. In September of that year, he left Greece on a forged passport, eventually entering France illegally as a political refugee and a stateless person. Xenakis would become a French citizen in 1965.

In Paris, Xenakis became interested in architecture, studying with Le Corbusier, one of France's best-known modern architects. From 1948 to 1959, he worked as Le Corbusier's assistant and closest collaborator in planning housing projects in Nantes and Marseilles and a number of ambitious structures in Europe and elsewhere, including the assembly building at Chandigarh, India, and the Baghdad Stadium. Though Xenakis earned his living from achitecture during this period, music was not put aside. Both Arthur Honegger and Nadia Boulanger turned him down as a pupil in composition in 1949, but he managed to get advice and criticism from Darius Milhaud. In 1950, he entered the Paris Conservatoire, where he studied composition under Olivier Messiaen. Messiaen was struck by the fecundity and originality of his largely self-taught pupil's musical ideas. In 1953, Xenakis married Françoise, a novelist and a former heroine in the French Resistance. Her Christian name, Françoise, is all she would take from her family, choosing to be known by her married name only. Iannis and Françoise Xenakis have one child, a daughter.

*Life's Work*

The key to Xenakis' creative awakening is an identity of approach to architecture and music; indeed, he sees no cleavage between the theories of music and architecture. In order to satisfy the unity of thought and the sense of cohesion that his intellect demanded, Xenakis located problems that were common to both architecture and music. He could develop his architectural ideas by articulating them in space, while in music he could arrange his ideas in time. Xenakis was also concerned with a major difference between architecture and music: The experience of space in the former is reversible, but time in the latter is not. In 1954, within a month of starting design work on the Couvent de St. Marie la Tourette—a Dominican monastery and the most ambitious project assigned him thus far by Le Corbusier—he jotted down ideas for *Métastasis*, the first of a major series of compositions that would challenge the existing body of contemporary music.

The remarkable parallel in method of design between *Métastasis* and the monastery is clear from the hundreds of plans and sketches drawn and signed by Xenakis and scattered with notes by Le Corbusier. Different functions were allotted to the various portions and levels of the ensemble. Extraordinary sculptural forms were designed for the different elements, severe geometric solids, arranged in a free, flowing open form around the basic square. Space was used dynamically, freeing elements such as the sharp pyramid of the oratory to soar into the sky from the hollowed square of the courtyard surrounded by flat roofs, in a vigorous display of positive and negative space. No chronological order emerges in the design work for the monastery. Xenakis worked on several parts at the same time, stopping to develop a new idea and returning months later to make modifications. He found such an approach—attacking problems from both ends, detail and general—useful in music as well as architecture.

In 1954, while working on the designs for the Couvent de St. Marie de la Tourette, Xenakis began to develop his own method of musical composition, one that he called "stochastic," from the Greek root meaning "straight aim."

In actuality, it involved controlled improvisation. As a mathematician, he evolved his method from the laws of mathematical probability, probability calculus, set theory, and symbolic and mathematical logic. Thus, his music was worked out according to the probabilities of certain notes, sonorities, and rhythms recurring in a given work. Instead of thinking in terms of harmony, which composers have done for centuries, Xenakis thinks in terms of sound entities that have the characteristics of intensity, pitch, and duration, as associated to one another by and within time.

The stochastic method is related to Jacques Bernoulli's Law of Large Numbers, which maintains that as the number of repetitions of a given chance trial (such as flipping a coin) increases, the probability that the results will tend to a determinate end approaches certainty. A stochastic process, then, is one that is probabilistic in the sense of tending toward a certain goal. Though John Cage and others who use the contingency process in music have sought to undercut the primacy of the composer by pursuing the ideal of indeterminacy, Xenakis has maintained the principle of indeterminacy and the dominance of the composer. His goal is the expression in music of the unity he sees as underlying all activity, human and nonhuman, scientific and artistic.

Xenakis' first important composition in his stochastic method was *Métastasis* (1954), for an orchestra of sixty-one instruments, each required to play its own music. Clear musical ideas occur and merge into nebulous, unidentifiable states to give birth to new phenomena in an uninterrupted chain of destruction-construction, or metastasis. The piece begins with the strings sustaining several measures of the note G; meanwhile, gliding glissandi in the rest of the orchestra and expanding dynamics help to create an eerie effect and to arrive at a dramatic climax. The possibilities of simulating electronically produced sounds with conventional instruments is explored. Textures are dense, and sonorities are overpowering.

In October of 1955, at the Donaueschingen Festival in Germany, Hans Rosbaud introduced *Métastasis*. Many in the audience were scandalized, and Xenakis had to wait another four years before his work could be performed in Paris. A second work, *Pithoprakta* (1955-1956), for an orchestra of fifty musicians and similar in nature to *Métastasis*, was first performed in Munich in March, 1957, under the direction of Herman Scherchen. Xenakis received the Geneva Prix de la Fondation Européenne pour la Culture for these two compositions in 1957; both were used by the New York City Ballet in 1968 for a ballet entitled *Métastasis and Pithoprakta*, choreographed by George Balanchine.

*Diamorphoses*, developed in the studios of the Groupe de Recherche Musicale de la Radio-Télévision Française in Paris in 1957, marks Xenakis' earliest experiment with electronic music on magnetic tape. His interest in electronic music increased after meeting Edgard Varèse in 1958 at the Brussels World Exposition. Still working in Le Corbusier's office, Xenakis designed the Philips Pavilion at the exposition, where Varèse's *Poème Électronique* on magnetic tape was regularly projected through four hundred or more speakers. Xenakis wrote *Concret PA*, a short electronic piece for magnetic tape, intended as a welcoming piece at the Philips Pavilion.

From its very inception, the Philips Pavilion raised one controversy after another: It vexed its sponsor by its extreme conceptions; it annoyed Le Corbusier, who came into conflict with Xenakis over its authorship; it outraged critics with its weirdness; yet, it delighted the public by the thousands. In conceiving the form and mathematical expression of the Philips Pavilion, Xenakis invented an architecture constructed entirely from surfaces derived from the hyperbolic paraboloid. A graph of ruled surfaces plotting the string glissandi of *Métastasis* demonstrates that the architecture of the pavilion orginated in Xenakis' composition.

Having not seen eye to eye with Le Corbusier for some time, Xenakis decided to strike out on his own in 1960. Though still intermittently active in the field of architecture, he has devoted himself almost entirely to music since that time. By the early 1960's, he had considerable support among the more radical of contemporary musicians and found himself a focal center at modern music festivals and the recipient of a number of commissions.

From magnetic tape, Xenakis went to the computer. He found the computer valuable in stochastic computations. Between 1956 and 1962, *ST/4* for string quartet, *ST/10* for ten instruments, and *ST/48* for forty-eight musicians playing forty-eight different parts were produced. "ST" represents stochastic; the adjoining number indicates the number of instrumentalists required. In these pieces, the program is basically a complex of stochastic laws by which the composer orders the electronic brain to define all the sounds, one after the other, in a previously calculated sequence. In reviewing a performance of *ST/48*, one critic noted that bowed glissandi were used so frequently that the listener soon became saturated with the device. He noted that *ST/48* has enough going on in it to hold one's attention at first hearing, but repeated exposure caused the novelty to wear off. Xenakis' *Atrées* (1956-1962), for ten instruments, was programmed and calculated on the computer.

Xenakis also experimented in the area of "games." First performed in 1971 by Radio Hilvershum in Germany, *Duel* (1959) was a competitive "game" for two orchestras and two conductors. Each orchestra played different music mathematically devised from a single theory. The audience picked the winner. *Stratégie* (1962), which was premiered in April of 1963, was similarly constructed. Awarded the Prix Manos Hadjidakis in 1962, Xenakis also came to the United States for the first time. At the invitation of Aaron Copland, he taught composition at the Berkshire Music Center at Tanglewood, Massachusetts. Later in 1962, he served as artist-in-residence in Berlin at the invitation of the West Berlin Senate and the Ford Foundation.

Xenakis' *Eonta* (1963-1964) was premiered in Paris in 1964 under the direction of Pierre Boulez. In this piece, the motor energy is provided by the piano, while the brass harnesses it. Similarly controlled power is generated by *Akrata* (1964-1965), commissioned by the Koussevitzky Music Foundation and written for fifteen wind instruments and vibraphone. *Terretektorh* (1965-1966) and *Vamos Gamma* (1967-1968) required that orchestra members be scattered among the unsuspecting audience. A variety of sonorities, including noise elements, are then unleashed on the audience.

In 1965, the first Xenakis Festival was held at the Salle Gaveau in Paris. The following year, Xenakis was invited to participate in the Musicological Congress in Manila and to attend the Japanese premiere of *Stratégie* in Tokyo. In 1960, he also founded Équipe de Mathématique et Automatique Musicales in Paris. For Montreal's Expo 67, he conceived and realized a light and sound spectacle entitled *Polytope de Montréal* for the French Pavilion. In 1967, Xenakis was appointed associate professor of music at Indiana University, where he founded and directed for five years the Center for Mathematical and Automated Studies.

In 1969, Xenakis received a commission for a ballet by the Canadian Arts Council. He wrote not only his own music but also his own story. *Kraanerg* is set in the year 2069, when the youth who now control the world decree all persons over the age of thirty must be exterminated. It is filled with architectural buildings into aural space and with strange and chilling sonorities. Xenakis commented on his own music at the Composers Showcase in New York on May 11, 1971. His *Bohor I* (1962), for magnetic tape, elicited a strong unfavorable response. One woman screamed throughout the final few minutes.

The 1970's were to be productive and glamorous years for Xenakis. Commissioned by the Gulbenkian Foundation in Lisbon, his *Cendrées* (1974), for chorus and orchestra, is a wordless chant. *Erikhthon* (1974), for piano and orchestra, *Noomena* (1975), for large orchestra, *Empreintes* (1975), for orchestra, *Phlegra* (1975), for eleven instruments, and *Retours-Windungen* (1976), for twelve cellos all received premieres in the mid-1970's. During the 1970's Xenakis was the recipient of the Bax Society Prize in London, the Maurice Ravel Gold Medal in Paris, the Grand Prix National de la Musique in Paris, and the Prix Beethoven in Bonn. He was made an honorary member of the British Computer Art Society in 1972, and, in 1975, he was made an honorary member of the American Academy and Institute of Arts and Letters. Xenakis was finally permitted to return to Greece in 1974; there, he received a hero's welcome. In 1976, the Sorbonne conferred on him an honorary doctorate in humane letters and sciences.

Works of Xenakis in the 1980's include *Shar* (1983), for large string orchestra; *Khall Perr* (1983), for brass quintet and percussion; *Tetras* (1983), for string quartet; *Naama* (1984), for harpsichord; *Lichens* (1984), for orchestra; and *Thallein* (1985), for orchestra. In 1980, Xenakis was elected a member of the European Academy of Sciences and of Arts and Letters in Paris and a member of the National Council of Hellonie Resistance in Greece. He became a member of the Académie des Beaux Arts in Paris in 1984. Xenakis has continued to compose and teach.

*Summary*

Despite a plurality of approaches, Iannis Xenakis' music is characterized by coherence and unity. The beginning point of each new phase of composition is analytic. Because his creative work is based on a strong theoretical foundation, analysis and creation are inseparable for Xenakis. In various compositions, he has attacked the hierarchic structure of the orchestra, giving each player equal responsibility; in others, he has pushed instrumentation to extremes, making nearly impossible demands on the players. It has been argued that Xenakis' influence has grown to the point that it has changed popular understanding of what is "musical" in music to include the unthinkable and unplayable within its boundaries. The results of such a change now seem so natural and even necessary that few have taken the trouble to identify the specific influences of Xenakis and his work on this process.

Xenakis was one of the first of his contemporaries to reevaluate and articulate in writing and music the force of science, mathematics, logic, and philosophy in the center of a modern conception of the arts. He succeeded in clearing new ground for music in restoring it as a serious experimental discipline, one with a substantial body of theory that has vital connections with different branches of learning. In his work, he has rendered a dynamic depiction of the universe informed by modern science. Within the bounds of the same composition, this depiction may be developed in sounds that are brutal, harsh, and jarring, yet also poetic, musical, and beautiful.

*Bibliography*

Bois, Mario. *Iannis Xenakis: The Man and His Music*. London: Boosey and Hawkes, 1967. Record of an extended conversation with Xenakis, along with a description of Xenakis' works.

Hiller, Lejaren. *The Computer and Music*. Ithaca, N.Y.: Cornell University Press, 1970. Chapter 4, on French experiments in computer composition, sets Xenakis' work in this area prior to 1970 in perspective.

Matossian, Nouritza. *Xenakis*. New York: Taplinger, 1986. The best treatment in English of Xenakis and his work to date. Includes a list of musical compositions, a catalog of architectural projects, a list of distinctions received by Xenakis, a bibliography of books and articles by and about Xenakis, and a discography.

Russcol, Herbert. *The Liberation of Sound: An Introduction to Electronic Music*. Englewood Cliffs, N.J.: Prentice-Hall, 1972. A good overview of developments in electronic music that leads to a better understanding of Xenakis' work in this medium.

Xenakis, Iannis. *Formalized Music*. Bloomington: Indiana University Press, 1971. First published in Paris in 1963 as *Musique formelles*, this is a collection of previously published essays. Now recognized as one of the most important theoretical contributions on composition to emerge from the postwar period.

*L. Moody Simms, Jr.*

# AHMAD ZAKI YAMANI

*Born:* June 30, 1930; Mecca, Saudi Arabia

*Areas of Achievement:* Diplomacy and politics
*Contribution:* Between 1962 and 1986, Yamani was the best-known spokesman for Middle Eastern oil producing countries' interests in the Organization of Petroleum Exporting Countries (OPEC). He built a considerable reputation as a moderate interested in reconciling strong nationalist demands among producers and the expectations of Western industrialist consuming countries.

## *Early Life*

Ahmad Zaki Yamani was born in Mecca, Saudi Arabia, on June 30, 1930. The Yamani family name derives from its probable origin among the tribes of southern Arabia, or the Yemen. Genealogically the family descends from the Hashemite clan within the Quraysh tribe. The Hashemite clan is especially noble in Islamic tradition, having been the clan of the Prophet Muhammad.

Yamani's father was at the time of his birth *qadi*, or chief judge, of the Islamic Supreme Court of the Hejaz district of the new Saudi kingdom. This post represented a continuation of a long family tradition: Yamani's grandfather had been a grand mufti, or jurisprudent, in the late Ottoman Turkish period (to 1914). During the early years of Yamani's childhood, his father was absent from the family home, serving as grand mufti in Indonesia. Later he filled the same prestigious post in Malaysia.

The young Yamani received his early education in Mecca. When he was seventeen, his father sent him to study law, not at the Azhar, which was the main institution of learning in Islamic subjects, but at the law faculty of the University of Cairo. Yamani was so successful in his study of law that the Saudi government awarded him a scholarship to study at the New York University Comparative Law Institute. It was during his stay in New York that Yamani met and married his first wife, Laila Faidhi, a Ph.D. student in education at New York University and daughter of a well-known Iraqi author and lawyer.

After earning his M.A. in comparative jurisprudence, Yamani and his wife spent a year at the Harvard Law School, where he focused his studies on international legal dimensions of capital investment. This led to a second American master's degree.

Yamani returned to Saudi Arabia in 1956, after nine years of study abroad. He was soon appointed to his first governmental post in the ministry of finance's newly formed department of *zakat* (religious alms tax) and income tax. Within a year, the first child of the Yamani family, their daughter

Mai, was born. A second daughter, Maha, followed in 1959. Their son, Hani, was born in 1961.

*Life's Work*

Yamani's exposure to technical questions relating to the Saudi petroleum industry began even while he was an official in the ministry of finance. In 1957, the controversial director of the Saudi Office of Petroleum and Minerals (Petromin), Abdullah Tariki, called upon the young Yamani to draft complicated oil exploration contracts, most notably the one governing Japanese offshore concessions. His skillful work attracted the attention of Crown Prince Faisal, who summoned him to his personal residence. Yamani's biographer suggested that Faisal already had an important political strategy in mind: to replace the rather brash Abdullah Tariki, who had pioneered successful Saudi renegotiation of the internationally dominant Arabian American Oil Company (ARAMCO) concession, with the calm and professional lawyer Yamani.

Following creation of the Organization of Petroleum Exporting Countries (OPEC) in 1960, Faisal's preference for Yamani took on concrete form. In March, 1962, Yamani was appointed minister for petroleum. One of the major internal development projects Yamani would support fully soon after becoming minister was Arabia's unique University of Petroleum and Minerals in the "oil capital" at Dhahran. This specialized school had been set up with the cooperation of American professors who designed a curriculum based on engineering, science, and industrial management.

Beyond these types of supportive activities, Yamani's reputation as a moderate but determined representative of Arabian oil interests came to the fore in the late 1960's. Particularly after the 1967 Arab-Israeli War, world attention focused on the Middle Eastern members of OPEC to see if an effort would be made to use oil exports as a political weapon. Following the January, 1971, Tehran meeting of OPEC—after an organization-wide call for a 55 percent tax on foreign concessionaires' production profits and a uniform price increase—Yamani's role became key. After a crisis was averted by compromising on a five-year interim tax of 35 percent, OPEC raised the ante, demanding either direct participation by each exporting country in the total operations of the companies or nationalization (Libya's solution in mid-1971). When ARAMCO tried to strike a bilateral deal with Arabia that would put other OPEC members at a disadvantage, Yamani refused to cooperate: Within a short time, 20 percent participation, based on Saudi compromises, became standard among the moderates. Arabia held the line even after Iraq's nationalization of the British-controlled Iraq Petroleum Company, offering another compromise: an immediate adjustment to 25 percent participation, to rise to 51 percent in stages by 1982.

Even then, there was clear dissatisfaction among some OPEC members, who suspected that Yamani's moderation spelled a willingness to cooperate with Western oil consumers. This view was dispelled at the time of the October, 1973, Middle East War and the Saudi-backed Arab decision to impose an oil embargo on supporters of Israel. In this matter, Yamani took the lead in condemning the West, including the United States. In an interview with *Newsweek* in December, 1973, Yamani indicated that he was not opposed to cooperation with Washington and the oil companies but expected some concrete signs of U.S. aid in making Israel compromise politically and militarily. He even went so far as to open splits in the oil consuming world by offering to deal separately with "preferred" importers, especially Japan.

On the whole, however, Yamani came out of the petroleum turmoil of the mid- to late 1970's with his moderate image intact. This was in part a result of the fact that the Saudi oil giant, under Yamani's guidance, frequently found itself offsetting (by increasing its own share of world production, thus easing supply and demand pressures) the extreme inflationary price demands of the Iranian oil giant across the Persian Gulf. In an OPEC meeting in late 1976, for example, Yamani made a special trip back to Riyadh to obtain (then) Crown Prince Fahd's agreement that, no matter what Iran's extreme increase demands might be, Arabia and the United Arab Emirates (representing 40 percent of OPEC production) would keep their price more than a dollar under other members. Experts looking back on the oil price bonanza to 1980 suggest that, had it not been for Yamani's moderating influence, the price per barrel would have been in the fifty dollar range, at least ten dollars over the peak reached before trends went in the other direction.

The period between 1976 and 1986—the year of Yamani's dismissal as oil minister—was anything but a calm and secure one for Yamani. First, he would be personally affected by the chaotic politics of the Palestine/Israel question: In December, 1975, he and a number of other oil negotiators narrowly escaped death when terrorists captured their plane following an OPEC meeting in Vienna. Even before these events, however, a less dramatic but ultimately more definitive source of turmoil in the next ten years of his career occurred: On March 25, 1975, only two days after Yamani's second marriage was concluded with Tammam al-Anbar, daughter of a former Saudi ambassador, King Faisal was assassinated. Although King Khālid occupied the throne for the next few years, the crown prince, Fahd, began already to demonstrate his opposition to Yamani's obvious dominance in making Saudi oil policy. When Khālid died in 1982, and during the first few years of Fahd's reign, the oil price boom was over, making it essential for OPEC's members to readjust. Readjustments had to do not only with relations with oil consumers but also with internal budgets that had become immensely inflated and dependent on continued high levels of revenue from oil. By October, 1986, King Fahd's disagreements with his oil minister, especially following a clash between the Iranian and Saudi delegates to an

OPEC summit in Geneva, led to Yamani's dismissal after twenty-four years in office.

*Summary*

Ahmad Zaki Yamani represents, like Egyptian President Anwar el-Sadat, a familiar face and symbol of apparent rationalism in the troubled late twentieth century scenario of Middle East politics. In part this stemmed from his relaxed technocratic style, which allowed him to engage Western diplomats and politicians in a way that did not alienate them. Lack of external signs of nationalistic fervor, however, did not mean that Yamani was willing to compromise easily on the critical issue of defending oil as the Middle East's only, or nearly only, important raw material for export. In short, during his long tenure as Saudi oil minister, he showed again and again that maintaining a political and economic balance in adjusting clashing interests between producers and consumers must be recognized as a necessity in Middle East-Western relations.

*Bibliography*

Kelly, John B. *Arabia, the Gulf and the West*. London: Weidenfeld & Nicolson, 1980. After offering two general historical chapters, this book analyzes the international politics of oil and, very important, the way petroleum fits into the economy and society of Saudi Arabia. There is very substantial coverage of Yamani's dealings with ARAMCO and his policies toward European and Japanese oil consumer interests.

Robinson, Jeffrey. *Yamani: The Inside Story*. New York: Atlantic Monthly Press, 1989. This is the only full-length biography of Yamani available in English. It is highly informative and contains all essential details, but tends to be overly journalistic in style, with uneven jumping from personal impression to personal impression.

"Working Hard for Yamani." *New Republic* 195 (September 29, 1986): 4. This is an unsympathetic account of Yamani's speech given at the time of the 350th anniversary celebration of Harvard University. The observations came at a time when oil prices were dropping rapidly, and Yamani was calling for actions to halt the slump, to safeguard both consumers' and producers' interests.

Yamani, Ahmad Zaki. "The Man Who Has What Makes the World Go Round." Interview by Wendy O'Flaherty, in *Maclean's* 91 (June 26, 1978): 46-47. This Canadian interview with Yamani covers three main questions: how long Arabia can continue its policy of keeping oil prices down by increasing its share of world production, Yamani's suggestion that Soviet oil reserves may be seriously diminishing, and views on Canada's oil producing potential in the 1980's.

___________. "Yamani on Oil—and Israel." Interview by Armand de

Borchgrave, in *Newsweek* 94 (July 9, 1979): 21. *Newsweek*'s senior editor Borchgrave spoke with Yamani following the momentous Geneva conference of OPEC, a meeting that raised oil prices per barrel from $18 to $23.50. In this interview, Yamani implies that a serious world economic catastrophe (an increase to $50) could occur if something happened in the Middle East to further exacerbate the world shortage of oil. This "something" was tied to Israel's increasingly hostile actions against Arab states and U.S. lack of reaction to the same.

*Byron D. Cannon*

# HIDEKI YUKAWA

*Born:* January 23, 1907; Tokyo, Japan
*Died:* September 8, 1981; Kyoto, Japan
*Area of Achievement:* Physics
*Contribution:* Yukawa's most important work concerned the nature of elementary particles making up the universe and the nuclear forces controlling their interactions. He formulated the theory of the short-range strong nuclear force, predicting the pion particle as an intermediate transference medium.

## *Early Life*

Hideki Yukawa was born in Tokyo, Japan, on January 23, 1907. His father, a professor of geology at Kyoto University, played an important role in developing his son's interest in science. Early ability in mathematics led him to attend Kyoto University, where he specialized in physics and theoretical mathematics, astounding his professors with his brilliant insights into interpretations of physical theories.

He was graduated in 1929 with a basic science degree. For his graduate education, he decided on Osaka University, where, because of his physics record, he was able both to teach, joining the faculty in 1933, and to study for his advanced degree. The doctorate in physics was awarded to him in 1938 from Osaka University. In 1932, he married a classical Japanese dancer, Sumi, with whom he had two sons.

In October, 1934, at the age of twenty-seven Yukawa, after giving his imagination free rein on numerous sleepless nights, read his first and most celebrated paper, "On the Interaction of Elementary Particles, I," to the Physico-Mathematical Society meeting in Osaka. Unfortunately, the article and presentation were not well received by the attending Japanese physicists. Yukawa's wife, however, encouraged him to publish it because she believed in his enthusiasm. The epoch-marking paper appeared in 1935 in the society's *Proceedings of the Physico-mathematical Society of Japan*.

## *Life's Work*

In his first original work, Yukawa had derived equations he believed would solve the contemporary problem of what held the atomic nucleus together. In his theory of nuclear forces, he postulated the existence of a new elementary particle, one possessing a mass several hundred times greater than that of the electron. Without such a particle acting, as he theorized, as an extremely strong form of nuclear glue, the positively charged protons would all immediately repel one another so fiercely that all nuclei beyond simple hydrogen nuclei would cease to exist. It had previously been thought that the neutron, discovered in 1932 by Sir James Chadwick, might be part of the solution, but Yukawa showed that an entirely different exchange force had to be present to counteract the mutual repulsion of the protons. His predictions included an unknown particle's acting as the transfer agent for this force, an effective range for the force of very short distance, a strength vastly greater than that of the electrical repulsion force between like charges, but a force whose strength decreased so quickly over space as not to have any significant effect on the inner-shell electrons. He predicted a mass for the new particle of 270 times the electron, and that it should be spontaneously radioactive, self-destructing with an extremely short life span.

Yukawa's theory of a particle that is emitted and reabsorbed too quickly to be detected showed that, in the exchange process, protons become neutrons, and neutrons change to protons, with the same phenomena occurring for antimatter particles. These changes required two charged particles, a positive meson and negative meson, the negative one for antimatter, the positive one for normal matter. Also, since exchange forces could work between proton-proton or neutron-neutron, a neutrally charged meson was necessary, one acting as its own antiparticle.

In 1936, Carl D. Anderson found in cosmic ray tracks a particle that at one time was thought to be the meson but that was soon shown not to be, weighing only 207 electronic masses, bearing only positive or negative charges, and not reacting with protons or neutrons (it is now known as a mu-meson). In 1947, Cecil Frank Powell discovered a new meson, of mass 273, which fit the description for Yukawa's predicted particle. The new meson was called a pi-meson, or pion. With the construction of high-energy cyclotrons, it became possible to produce pions in large enough numbers to study their behavior and nature. In the 1950's, Robert Hofstadter, using his 600-million-electron-volt linear accelerator, showed both the neutron and proton as consisting essentially of clouds of pions.

In 1936, Yukawa further advanced elementary-particle physics with his prediction that a nucleus could absorb one of the innermost shell electrons, a process equivalent to emitting a positron (a positively charged electron). Since those electrons were in the K-shell, the process became known as K-capture.

Yukawa became a professor of physics at Kyoto University in 1939, continuing his theoretical work there through World War II, even after the American occupation forces destroyed his small cyclotron. In 1948, as a guest of J. Robert Oppenheimer, he went to the Institute for Advanced Study at Princeton, staying for a year before going to Columbia University as a visiting professor. In 1949, he received the Nobel Prize in Physics. In 1953, he left the United States to return to Kyoto University as the first director of Japan's Research Institute of Fundamental Physics. He had donated most of his Nobel Prize money to Osaka and Kyoto universities, to thank them for their encouragement and to motivate younger students. He remained as director there until 1970.

After his first pioneering work, Yukawa contributed greatly to the detailed theory of particle physics. By his advances and his teaching ability, he built an advanced school of theoretical physicists. He had declined the invitation of Columbia University to stay there because he wanted to train new people in his field, which had few specialists in Japan. He became the editor of a new journal, *Progress of Theoretical Physics*, providing a much-needed outlet for important contributions in all areas of physics from his own school and his colleagues.

Yukawa always preferred to pursue fundamental problems, using insights based on intuitive methods found often among great geniuses such as Albert Einstein, a close acquaintance of Yukawa until Einstein's death in 1955. Yukawa did not, he maintained often, seek immediate appreciation of his work, because he believed that his work would eventually be understood and appreciated. By 1954, he had begun to stress the importance of scientists' accepting social responsibility. He became highly visible in scientific and other groups working for the cause of peace and against nuclear armaments. That year, 1954, he broke his own imposed silence to denounce atom bomb tests. He tried to establish the role of scientists from a perspective of integrity and independence. In 1962, he was vocal at the First Kyoto Conference of Scientists, noting that "physics cannot be separated from humanity. The results of physics are inevitably connected with the problems of humanity through their application to human society."

After setting out to discover the innermost secrets of nature, to explain the atom and the universe, Yukawa died at his home in Kyoto at the age of seventy-four. Many physicists grieved at his death, many publicly becoming even more fiercely determined to obtain Yukawa's objective of world peace.

*Summary*

Although he was interested in theoretical physics from all viewpoints, Hideki Yukawa was principally committed to increasing the depth of Japanese contributions to physics by the training and influencing of new physicists. His great work, of elucidating the nature of the nuclear force using a virtual particle, the meson, to cement the nucleus together, provided the step necessary to break the deadlock in understanding the atom's place in the universe. Based solely on theoretical calculations, he explained how the atom fixed its stability and why the proton and neutron were stable within the central core. Without any experimental justification, he predicted a new fundamental particle, the first of the exchange particles, mathematically determining its size, nature, and the fact that there should be three different ones, differing in charge, decay mode, and half-lives. His contributions to elementary-particle physics and quantum mechanics have revolutionized the entire nature of the field.

In addition, Yukawa helped formulate his country's viewpoints on world peace, nuclear disarmament, and the social responsibilities of scientists toward the rest of civilization. He strongly believed that physicists and others, instead of being concerned only with the technical feasibility of discoveries or advances, needed also to develop criteria for using good judgment to further the cause of humanity instead of harming it.

*Bibliography*

Alfvén, Hannes. *Worlds-Antiworlds: Antimatter in Cosmology.* San Francisco: W. H. Freeman, 1966. A delightfully written book dealing with the structure of the universe based on the interaction of regular and antimatter. Starting with what the world consists of, the nature of the fundamental particles is discussed, along with their importance in formulating a plasma, the most abundant form of matter. For beginners in physics and cosmology.

Davies, P. C. *The Forces of Nature.* New York: Cambridge University Press, 1979. A well-written description of the forces controlling the universe and their associated particle natures. Traces the works of gravity, electromagnetism, and the strong and weak nuclear forces, identifying their associated exchange particles. Mesons are discussed as they pertain to Yukawa's ideas and subsequent discoveries. For laypersons.

Dodd, James. *The Ideas of Particle Physics.* New York: Cambridge University Press, 1984. A well-written overview of the current ideas on basic particles and the forces that control them. Fundamental forces are identified, and the interactions of particles under weak and strong nuclear forces are discussed. Covers intermediate transfer particles to present ideas of quarks. Contains a good glossary and additional references.

Gueller, Sam. *Frontiers of Physics.* New York: Vantage Press, 1987. An all-encompassing work, covering the range of problems in modern physics. Extremely interesting discussions on the nature of gravity, particles, and the possibility of a unified theory of the forces of nature. For the layperson. Gives an insight into philosophical problems of modern development.

Mauldin, John H. *Particles in Nature: The Chronological Discovery of the New Physics.* Blue Ridge Summit, Pa.: Tab Books, 1986. A quantitative overview of the particle view of the universe, starting with basic physics and reaching to principles of invariance, fields, and matter waves. Identifies all the currently known particles, their interactions with one another and the nucleus. Mesons as exchange bodies are studied, and their relationship to quarks is clarified. Includes good pictures and extensive references.

Nambu, Y. *Quarks.* Philadelphia: World Scientific, 1981. Written as an introduction, this work explains what elementary particles are and how the various quarks and leptons act to control the universe. Detailed section on the birth and development of the Yukawa theory and how it gave rise to the newer models of particle construction. Discusses chromodynamics, gauge theories, and unified theories. Well written and well illustrated.

Segrè, Emilio. *From X-Rays to Quarks: Modern Physicists and Their Discoveries*. San Francisco: W. H. Freeman, 1980. Written for the layperson, this work traces the history of elementary particles in the twentieth century, from Wilhelm Röntgen's discovery of X rays to modern ideas on the quarks as fundamental building blocks. Deals with the mesons and their roles in nature, along with the other forces present in the atom. Well written with additional references.

Trefil, James S. *From Atoms to Quarks*. New York: Charles Scribner's Sons, 1980. A well-written introduction to the discovery of particles and the structure of the nucleus. Starting with the simplified physics of the atom, cosmic-ray experiments are identified, leading to the discovery of the mesons. The importance of accelerators in understanding the nature of the particle proliferation is stressed. Includes a glossary.

*Arthur L. Alt*

# SA'D ZAGHLŪL

*Born:* June 1, 1859; Ibyana, Egypt
*Died:* August 23, 1927; Cairo, Egypt
*Areas of Achievement:* Government and politics
*Contribution:* Zaghlūl was modern Egypt's outstanding politician before Gamal Abdel Nasser. He led the 1919 revolution against the British and founded the Wafd Party.

## *Early Life*

Sa'd Zaghlūl Pasha was born on June 1, 1859, at Ibyana, Egypt. His parents were Sheikh Ibrahim Zaghlūl and Miriam. Of peasant extraction, Ibrahim possessed wealth and his village's Muslim leadership. When Ibrahim died during Sa'd's early youth, Miriam and her stepson, Shanaui, arranged for Sa'd's education so he would become, like his father and grandfather, a Muslim sheikh. In 1864, Sa'd began study at Ibyana's mosque school. In 1870-1873, he studied recitation of the Koran under a famous teacher at Dusuq's main mosque.

In 1873, Zaghlūl entered al-Azhar University, exhibiting independence by lodging outside the student inhabited area. At al-Azhar Zaghlūl met Jamāl ad-Dīn al-Afghānī and Muhammad 'Abduh. The former's stress on anti-imperialism, constitutionalism, and revitalized Arabic captivated Zaghlūl. In 1880, Zaghlūl left al-Azhar without a degree. In October, 1880, Muhammad 'Abduh, chief editor of the Egyptian government's official gazette, hired Zaghlūl. They used the publication to mold public opinion. In May, 1882, Zaghlūl shifted to the ministry of the interior as an aide and then to Giza province's legal department as an overseer.

In 1881-1882, Zaghlūl vocally supported the Urabi Revolt. This caused loss of his position, deprivation of civil rights, and barring from governmental service. He now represented some of the accused in the revolt. In June, 1883, Zaghlūl was arrested as a member of the Society of Revenge, an organization pledged to end Great Britain's occupation and the khedivial regime. In October, 1883, he was freed on bond. In 1884, Zaghlūl became a lawyer in the new national court system. He rose rapidly because of his courtroom eloquence. In 1892, his reputation brought an unprecedented appointment as a deputy judge in the appellate court. His legal success also led to entrée into Egypt's Turco-Circassian aristocracy. In 1896, he married a member of this class, Safiyya, daughter of Prime Minister Mustafa Pasha Fahmī. The marriage was arranged by Princess Nazli, cousin to Khedive 'Abbās II. She was Zaghlūl's mentor in Egyptian high society and he her lawyer. Following her advice, he studied French. At Nazli's salon, Zaghlūl met the head of the British occupation in Egypt, Sir Evelyn Baring (later Lord Cromer).

*Life's Work*

In 1904, Cromer made Zaghlūl Egypt's first minister of education, the title "pasha" being awarded by the khedive. Zaghlūl checked the autocratic British adviser in his ministry, assigned to Egyptians several jobs formerly always reserved for Britons, founded the School of Qadis (judges in Islamic law courts), enlarged the Training College and added a section for training secondary school teachers, expanded the use of Arabic in schools, established free education in governmental institutes for poverty-stricken students, and disciplined a British headmistress.

In 1910, Zaghlūl became minister of justice. His efforts to make the cabinet effective in governing Egypt aroused the British, 'Abbas, and his prime minister. Zaghlūl sought vainly to render three repressive bills ineffective. In March, 1912, he resigned upon his failure to prevent prosecution of Muhammad Farid, the nationalist leader. In December, 1913, Zaghlūl was the only candidate elected to represent two constituencies in the new Legislative Assembly, winning easily. In January, 1914, by sixty-five to fourteen votes, he became the elected vice president of the Legislative Assembly, which he dominated. He helped to bring down Prime Minister Muhammad Sa'īd and sought to replace him with Fahmī. Since the latter had fallen under the influence of his son-in-law Zaghlūl, the British agent, Lord Horatio Herbert Kitchener, vetoed him. Because of World War I's outbreak, the British authorities prorogued the assembly *sine die*. The British refused three times, 1914-1918, to allow Prime Minister Husain Rushdi to take Zaghlūl into his cabinet.

On November 13, 1918, Zaghlūl and two colleagues sought permission to go to London to present their demands for Egypt's complete autonomy. When the British government refused, Zaghlūl organized the Wafd to gain Egyptian independence. He secured thousands of signatures throughout Egypt giving the Wafd power of attorney to act for the nation. The British adviser to the ministry of the interior sought to break this campaign. Zaghlūl composed a long, eloquent appeal to the president of the Paris Conference, Georges Clemenceau, protesting the British protectorate. These and other actions by Zaghlūl led the British on March 9, 1919, to deport Zaghlūl to Malta. Revolutionary fervor now gripped students, workers, lawyers, government clerks, and others throughout Egypt. The British squelched the revolt, but Special High Commissioner Edmund Allenby, sensing a dangerous undercurrent of bitterness and nationalism, on April 7, 1919, freed Zaghlūl and three associates and allowed them to travel to Europe.

Frustration plagued Zaghlūl in Europe. The Paris Peace Conference shunned him. In 1920 in London, Lord Alfred Milner met with him informally, but Zaghlūl refused terms that legalized and strengthened Great Britain's position in Egypt. Thinking he would obtain better terms through backing by the Egyptian people, Zaghlūl agreed to the Wafd's submitting

Milner's proposals to them. The public disliked the proposals, whereupon Zaghlūl demanded more from Milner, who then canceled negotiations. Zaghlūl returned to Egypt in March 1921.

Violence erupted in Egypt. Prime Minister 'Adlī Pasha Yakan rejected Zaghlūl's demand that he head the Egyptian delegation going to London to negotiate with Great Britain. Riots and demonstrations supported Zaghlūl. 'Adlī failed in negotiations in London and resigned. In December, 1921, Allenby deported Zaghlūl to Aden, then to the Seychelles, and finally to Gibraltar. In exile Zaghlūl keenly watched developments. He condemned Great Britain's 1922 declaration of Egypt's independence, claiming it was a sham. He denounced the Constitution of 1922 because of its vast royal powers and the difficulty in changing it.

In March, 1923, Allenby released Zaghlūl. The Egyptian people gave him a tumultuous reception. A dislike for other politicians led King Fu'ād I to a temporary rapprochement with Zaghlūl. In the 1923-1924 elections, Zaghlūl led the Wafd to victory, winning 90 percent of the seats in the Chamber of Deputies. On January 27, 1924, Zaghlūl became prime minister. Optimism engulfed Egypt, being best reflected in the self-confidence and deep sense of responsibility shown by the deputies under Zaghlūl's guidance. In September, 1924, Zaghlūl went to London to negotiate a treaty with Prime Minister James Ramsay MacDonald. The latter rejected Zaghlūl's demands: withdrawal of British forces, no control by the British government over Egypt and abolition of the two offices of judicial and financial advisers, no limitation on Egypt's conduct of foreign affairs, abandonment of Great Britain's claim to protect foreigners and to defend the Suez Canal, and unity of Egypt and the Sudan.

Anglo-Egyptian relations soon reached a boiling point. Zaghlūl gave cabinet positions to two noted extremists. In November, 1924, in Cairo, Sir Lee Stack, Governor-General of the Sudan and commander in chief of Egyptian forces, was assassinated. Zaghlūl expressed profound regret, and his government put a price of ten thousand pounds on the assassins' heads. High Commissioner Allenby issued an ultimatum to Egypt, asking for an apology, punishment of the assassins, prohibition of political demonstrations, payment of 500,000 Egyptian pounds, withdrawal within twenty-four hours of Egyptian troops in the Sudan, immediate removal of all restrictions on irrigation in the Sudan El-Gezira, and withdrawal of all objections to Great Britain's assumption of responsibility for foreigners in Egypt. Zaghlūl accepted only the first, second, and fourth demands. Allenby held firm and took over the Alexandria customs. Then, on November 23, 1924, Zaghlūl resigned. His successor accepted all the demands, and the king dissolved parliament. Zaghlūl temporarily left politics, discouraged by politicians' opportunism and reactionary monarchy.

Zaghlūl soon returned to public life, however, determined to preserve the constitution because it would allow his party to recover power, to avoid clashes with Great Britain for fear it would nullify the constitution, and to form a Wafd-Liberal Constitution coalition to overthrow the cabinet. In the 1926 elections, Zaghlūl led the Wafd to outstanding victory, but the high commissioner vetoed Zaghlūl's becoming prime minister. Zaghlūl headed the chamber and quieted anti-British agitation. Soon, however, on August 23, 1927, Zaghlūl died. His death deepened the cynicism in society.

*Summary*

Sa'd Zaghlūl's life became synonymous with obtaining Egypt's independence. His pre-1914 career involved a cautious course through service in the British Occupation. As minister of education and minister of justice he sought to prepare Egypt for freedom through moderate reform and Egyptianization of the administration. Thus he advanced secularism in education and law and promoted modernization of al-Azhar University.

By 1914, Zaghlūl emerged as Egypt's leading nationalist. This position he maintained in World War I, counseling loyal opposition. In 1919, Zaghlūl led Egypt's greatest revolution between that of 'Urābī Pasha and Nasser. Nothing, not two exiles, illnesses, attempts on his life, British imperial might, King Fu'ād I's machinations, or politicians' intrigues, deflected Zaghlūl from working for a truly independent Egypt. Perhaps had he lived longer he would have succeeded, because he had modified his extremism toward Great Britain as his life ebbed.

Welding peasants and townspersons together, Zaghlūl created the Wafd, Egypt's largest mass party. This legacy would bode ill for the future. As Wafd chief, Zaghlūl became, in 1924, the first prime minister of the modern Kingdom of Egypt. His administration brought direct suffrage but established a pattern of spoils system by party and continued the practice of muzzling the press. Zaghlūl gained reverence as "The Grand Old Man of Egypt." Tallness, leanness, noble mien, and quick wit characterized him. His oratory captivated audiences. His wife was called "Mother of the Egyptians." Zaghlūl's home became a national museum.

*Bibliography*

Ahmed, Jamal Mohammed. *The Intellectual Origins of Egyptian Nationalism*. London: Oxford University Press, 1960. Emphasizes Zaghlūl's many years of apprenticeship in Egypt's social and political life. Stresses that Zaghlūl's long service and association with Muhammad 'Abduh produced qualities of leadership and intellect that he used skillfully and intelligently.

Harris, Christina Phelps. *Nationalism and Revolution in Egypt*. Stanford, Calif.: Hoover Institution on War, Revolution, and Peace, 1964. Objective treatment of Zaghlūl. Contrasts Zaghlūl's conciliatory attitude toward Great Britain in 1920 with the British government's intransigent stand.

Criticizes Great Britain for the harsh ultimatum of 1924 imposed upon Egypt at the dawn of her first democratic experiment.

Hourani, Albert. *Arabic Thought in the Liberal Age, 1798-1939*. London: Oxford University Press, 1962. In his activities before 1914, Zaghlūl reflected the beliefs of Jamāl ad-Dīn al-Afghānī and Muhammad ʻAbduh. After 1914 Zaghlūl became more exacting in his dealings and more exclusive in his conception of the Egyptian nation.

McIntyre, John D., Jr. *The Boycott of the Milner Mission: A Study in Egyptian Nationalism*. New York: Peter Lang, 1985. In 1919, Egypt developed the idea of "complete independence" during the boycott campaign against the Milner Mission. Zaghlūl got Milner to include recommendations in his report that would cause the British cabinet to dismiss them.

Marlow, John. *A History of Modern Egypt and Anglo-Egyptian Relations 1800-1956*. Hamden, Conn.: Archon Books, 1965. Denies that Zaghlūl was a statesman. Asserts he had no interest in the Egyptians' welfare or any enthusiasm for reforming the Egyptian administration.

Sayyid-Marsot, Afaf Lutfi al-. *Egypt's Liberal Experiment: 1922-1936*. Berkeley: University of California Press, 1977. Holds that Zaghlūl galvanized and united the nationalist movement until he became synonymous with it. Believes that Zaghlūl sowed and nurtured the seeds of many political ills that beset political life for decades to come.

Smith, Russell Yates. *The Making of an Egyptian Nationalist*. Ann Arbor, Mich.: University Microfilms, 1973. Sympathetic doctoral dissertation on Zaghlūl's pre-1919 political career. States that Zaghlūl's outlook was based on his assumption that Great Britain was avoiding preparing Egypt for self-government.

Vatikiotis, P. J. *The Modern History of Egypt*. London: Weidenfeld & Nicolson, 1969. Notes Zaghlūl's achievements as minister of education and then as minister of justice. Clearly delineates the strengths and weaknesses in Zaghlūl's political activity.

Zayid, Mahmud Y. *Egypt's Struggle for Independence*. Beirut: Khayats, 1965. Affirms that Zaghlūl's political role before 1918 was the prelude to his later leadership. Observes that initially after World War I Zaghlūl "was ready to forget the Sudan."

*Erving E. Beauregard*

# EMILIANO ZAPATA

*Born:* August 8, 1879; Anenecuilco, Morelos, Mexico
*Died:* April 10, 1919; Hacienda Chinameca, Morelos, Mexico
*Areas of Achievement:* Social reform and the military
*Contribution:* Zapata was a notable rebel leader of peasant guerrillas in the Mexican Revolution who became a legendary folk hero among the poor Mexican farmers of Morelos because of his idealistic devotion to land reform and his brilliant guerrilla tactics during the Revolution.

## *Early Life*

Emiliano Zapata, born in the small village of Anenecuilco in the tiny Mexican state of Morelos on August 8, 1879, was the ninth of ten children, only four of whom survived, born to Cleofas and Gabriel Zapata. The Zapatas were a proud family of primarily Indian heritage. They owned a modest ranch and lived in a small adobe-and-stone house, but they were better off than many of their neighbors who, owning no land, had to work on the lands of the wealthy sugar plantation owners in a state of virtual peonage. Zapata, with little formal education, attended an inadequate school at the nearby village of Ayala. When he left school at the age of twelve, he could barely read and write.

Orphaned at the age of fifteen, Zapata and his elder brother, Eufemio, inherited the ranch although his brother soon left home as did his two sisters. Zapata worked the land and even sharecropped a few acres from the local hacienda, supplementing his earnings by buying and selling mules and occasionally horses. Zapata developed into a skilled horseman and a well-respected horse trainer. The characteristics of the native peoples were reflected in the young Zapata—he was quiet, honest, courteous, gentle, and distrustful of strangers. Zapata's own attachment to the land and village was evidenced by his people, who saw the land as belonging to the villagers since they, like their Indian ancestors, had no clear concept of private land ownership.

As a young boy, Zapata learned to hate the rich landowners in Morelos as he witnessed evictions of peasants from their huts and small plots of land. The sugar planters, who needed more land for expansion into world markets, were supported by the Mexican government, which was headed by the despotic dictator, Porfirio Díaz. Zapata was a popular young man; he was something of a dandy and often dressed on holidays in black with tight-fitting trousers completed by an enormous sombrero. His appreciation for the fine life extended to riding a black or white, silver-saddled horse. His single life would end with his marriage, at the age of thirty-two, in 1911. His wife, Josefa Espejo, was the daughter of a successful livestock dealer from Ayala.

Conflict with authority was not unusual for Zapata, as he often defended fellow villagers against the oppressive landowners or the rural police. This conflict not only hardened him and won for him respect from the villagers but also helped to prepare him for the leadership role that was thrust upon him in 1909 when he was elected, at the age of thirty, president of the village council and defense committee of Anenecuilco. He was about to participate in the cataclysmic Mexican Revolution, which would forge for him a place in Mexican history.

*Life's Work*

Zapata became immersed in regional politics in 1909, when he supported an anti-Díaz candidate for the governorship of Morelos. The corrupt Díaz, however, used his influence along with federal troops to get his own candidate "elected." Zapata continued to fight for peasant land rights and unsuccessfully sought legal assistance on behalf of the villages. In 1909, unrest in Morelos led to the formation of small, poorly armed guerrilla bands seeking redress against the oppressive policies of the government. Disappointed at the futility of legal means, Zapata urged direct action and led villagers in taking the disputed fields. Others in the area followed Zapata's example and began reclaiming disputed lands.

In 1910, the ruthless Díaz, swept aside by the tide of revolution, was replaced by Francisco Madero, who promised sweeping reforms for Mexico. Madero called for the various revolutionary leaders, including Zapata, to disband their guerrillas and support him. Zapata was willing to comply with Madero's request, but, when Madero's promised land distribution did not occur, he and other dissatisfied leaders throughout Mexico rose in rebellion against Madero. The guerrilla chieftains elected him supreme chief of the revolutionary movement in the south. He later became General Zapata, head of the Liberation Army of the South. His efficiency, honesty, and popular appeal led to large numbers of followers in the ranks of his ragtag army. He proved to be a strong leader, who inspired his troops through quiet persuasion.

Unlike Madero, who seemingly wanted only middle-class political and economic reform for Mexico, and other revolutionary leaders who supported narrow self-interest, Zapata passionately sought social justice for the mistreated landless peasants of Morelos and neighboring states in the south. This position placed him out of the mainstream of the Revolution with its emphasis on middle-class values and made him the target of Madero and later leaders such as Victoriano Huerta and Venustiano Carranza, who saw him as a troublemaker and radical. Zapata nevertheless persisted in his passion for the rural poor.

In 1913, the sadistic and brutal General Huerta seized control of the government and had Madero murdered. Zapata had hoped to lay down his arms and go home and farm his lands, but, after initially offering support to

Huerta, he soon found himself in conflict with the new president. Zapata, the "Attila of the South" as the Mexican newspapers called him, was one of four guerrilla leaders who opposed Huerta along with Carranza in the northeast, the infamous Pancho Villa in Chihuahua to the north, and Álvaro Obregón in Sonora to the northwest. Huerta was also opposed by the President of the United States, Woodrow Wilson. In the face of such opposition, Huerta fell from power in 1914.

Carranza, in an attempt to take power, invited all the revolutionary leaders to a convention in order to solicit their support, but Villa and Zapata refused to participate. Zapata was willing to quit the Revolution if Carranza would adopt his Plan of Ayala, which called for distribution of land to the landless peasants. According to the plan, a portion of land would be expropriated from each hacienda with the landowners receiving compensation. Landowners who would not cooperate would lose their entire lands. Stolen lands, furthermore, would be returned to the proper owners. Zapata had one of his chief aides, Otilio Montaño, a former schoolteacher, compose the plan, which was proclaimed by Zapata and his leading chiefs in November, 1911. Some suggested that Zapata had the plan written to counter charges from Mexico City that the Zapatistas were simply bandits who looted and pillaged in the countryside and not revolutionaries fighting for a true cause. Carranza found Zapata's demands to be too inflexible and did not agree to them.

Five years of brutal civil war ensued as General Obregón allied himself with Carranza against the recalcitrant Villa and Zapata. Mexico City, a virtual no-man's-land with generals coming and going, on one occasion was occupied by the forces of Villa and Zapata. The citizens of Mexico City expected the Zapatistas to wreak havoc in the city but were amazed at their timidness and gentleness. Later, Zapata and his followers quietly left the city to Villa.

In 1915, Obregón's forces defeated Villa, leaving Zapata in opposition to Carranza. Carranza denounced Zapata as a renegade and bandit who knew nothing about government. Zapata's followers continued to threaten the capital and in areas under their control confiscated land without using the legal procedures advocated by Carranza. Even though they were unorganized, Zapata's men were effective fighters who laid traps and ambushes, cut supply lines, took small towns while avoiding larger ones, and always avoided open formal battles unless they had a good assurance of victory. These tactics proved frustrating to the large government forces of Carranza.

For several years, Carranza attempted, without success, to defeat Zapata in Morelos. General Pablo González commanded Carranza's troops there and carried on a "scorched earth" policy against the Zapatistas by destroying those villages that he believed might give sanctuary to Zapata. The corrupt González showed little respect for Zapata and his troops, labeling them as uneducated, country hicks. In 1919, González, with the help of one of his colonels, Jesús M. Guajardo, had Zapata killed through treachery and deceit. González had Guajardo pretend to defect to Zapata in order to kill him. On April 10, Guajardo invited Zapata to dine with him at his hacienda, and, after some hesitation, Zapata accepted. When Zapata reached the door, Guajardo's men fired two volleys at point blank into him. The beloved leader of the peasants was dead. His body was strapped to a mule and taken to Cuautla, the capital of Morelos, and openly displayed. Though thousands came to see the body, many of his supporters refused to believe he was dead; they thought that it was a trick to fool the authorities and that Zapata had actually escaped. People later reported that they saw Zapata riding across the fields of Morelos on his white horse. Yet the hero who could do no wrong in the eyes of the landless peasants was gone; his ideals, however, did not die with him because the farmers of Morelos continued their cry for "land and liberty" long after 1919.

*Summary*

Emiliano Zapata occupies a controversial place in Mexican history. To his followers, he was a romantic folk hero who died for a noble cause. To his enemies, he was a savage villain, the leader of wild revolutionary bandits who committed atrocities on the Mexican populace. Being a radical revolutionary in their eyes, he also did not conform to their notion of middle-class revolution. The truth no doubt lies somewhere in between. Zapata was an honest and simple man who reluctantly became an effective leader of disorganized guerrillas who adapted his military tactics to fit the situation at hand and avoid defeat by larger and better armed forces. (Interestingly enough, these same tactics would later be used in limited wars following World War II.) He was a born leader who used his natural abilities to try to right the wrongs he saw in his native land. The provincial Zapata pales in comparison to revolutionary leaders such as Vladimir Ilich Lenin and Mao Tse-tung, who were worldly intellectuals who brought about a radical transformation in their respective societies. It is interesting to note that Zapata did not break with the Church as did other Mexican revolutionaries, who criticized the Church for doing little to ease social ills in Mexico. Nevertheless, he remains a legend and an inspiration to the downtrodden and unfortunate natives of Mexico.

*Bibliography*

Brenner, Anita. *The Wind That Swept Mexico: The History of the Mexican Revolution, 1910-1942*. Austin: University of Texas Press, 1943. This book contains one hundred concisely written pages of text, and it contains 184 historical photographs, which present the Mexican Revolution in all of its drama and poignance. The author witnessed the Revolution as a child.

Dunn, H. H. *The Crimson Jester: Zapata of Mexico*. New York: Robert M. McBride, 1933. A sensationalized account of Zapata's life written in dialogue form. The author compares Zapata to Geronimo and Julius Caesar. Contains no bibliography.

Newell, Peter E. *Zapata of Mexico*. Somerville, Mass.: Black Thorn Books, 1979. A simply written, straightforward biography of Zapata. Contains interesting photographs and illustrations. Written primarily from secondary sources.

Parkinson, Roger. *Zapata*. New York: Stein & Day, 1980. A very interesting and scholarly book that builds on Womack's biography. Contains a helpful index, a bibliography, and end notes.

Ruiz, Ramón Eduardo. *The Great Rebellion: Mexico, 1905-1924*. New York: W. W. Norton, 1980. A scholarly reinterpretation of the Mexican Revolution. The author emphasizes the middle-class nature of the Revolution. Contains an excellent chapter on Zapata.

Womack, John. *Zapata and the Mexican Revolution*. New York: Alfred A. Knopf, 1968. Probably the definitive work on Zapata. A scholarly analysis of Zapata and his role in the Revolution. Contains a very helpful bibliography, footnotes, and appendices.

*James E. Southerland*

# FERDINAND VON ZEPPELIN

*Born:* July 8, 1838; Konstanz, Baden
*Died:* March 8, 1917; Charlottenburg, Germany
*Area of Achievement:* Aeronautics
*Contribution:* Zeppelin developed the concepts and designs for the construction of the first practical airships capable of navigating over long distances. The success of Zeppelin's rigid dirigibles served to stimulate experimentation in all areas of aeronautics and paved the way for military and commercial applications of airships.

## *Early Life*

Ferdinand von Zeppelin was born into a family with a long history of military and diplomatic service. His grandfather, Ferdinand Ludwig Zeppelin, was minister of foreign affairs for the King of Württemburg; his father, Count Frederich von Zeppelin, was in the diplomatic service of a German prince. In 1834, Count Frederich married Amelie Macaire d'Hogurre, then living in her grandparents' house in Konstanz, Baden; it was there that Ferdinand, his brother Eberhard, and his sister Eugenie were born. In 1840, Count Frederich retired from his diplomatic post, purchased a large estate near Girsberg, on the shores of Lake Constance, and devoted his life to managing his estate, rearing his children, and caring for his invalid wife.

Ferdinand's mother and father were gentle, loving parents, and they provided for their children a home that was harmonious and completely free of ostentation. When Ferdinand entered a preparatory school in Stuttgart, he concentrated on studies in physics, chemistry, and mathematics, a course that was a significant departure from the one normally followed by boys intent on a military career. It was an early indication, however, that Zeppelin's career would not follow a predictable pattern.

In 1857, at age nineteen, Zeppelin was graduated from the War Academy at Ludwigsburg and joined an infantry regiment as a lieutenant. After only a year, he became disenchanted with the monotony of the army's discipline and asked for a leave of absence to continue his engineering studies at the University of Tübingen. He then elected to join an engineer corps stationed at Ulm—a post considered inappropriate for a count, but one which he believed was more suited to his interests and sense of adventure. In less than a year, he was promoted to the rank of first lieutenant and was assigned to the general staff.

With little prospect of being involved in military action on the home front, young Zeppelin turned his attention to the Civil War being fought in the United States. He conceived the idea of acting as a military observer for the German army, ostensibly to study the organization of volunteer armies that were being used extensively in the American conflict; he believed, moreover, as he prophetically noted in his request to the king: "The Americans are especially inventive in the adaptation of technical developments for military purposes. I do not have to mention the benefits such a journey promises to have for the general enlightenment."

In May of 1863, Zeppelin's leave of absence was approved and he set sail for the United States. He obtained letters of introduction from President Abraham Lincoln that enabled him to travel freely among the Union armies; he also participated in several campaigns, including the battles of Fredericksburg and Ashby's Gap in Virginia. Desiring to learn as much as possible about this new world, he then embarked on a journey westward, traveling first by train through the northeast from New York City through Buffalo, Erie, Cleveland, and Detroit. From Detroit he explored Lake Huron and Lake Superior by steamer. In Superior, Wisconsin, Zeppelin joined a small party intent on exploring the headwaters of the Mississippi River; after a journey of twenty-one days, the party arrived at Fort Snelling in St. Paul, Minnesota.

During his visit at Fort Snelling Zeppelin was able to observe the flight of a captive hot-air balloon. The Union Army had been experimenting with the use of balloons as observation posts and, at Fort Snelling, was in the process of evaluating the merits of a new design. Zeppelin seized the opportunity for a flight and purchased enough gas to ascend several hundred feet. It was there that the military advantages of an aerial reconnaissance platform became evident to him; it was there, too, that he first started thinking of ways to control the flight of a free-floating balloon.

### *Life's Work*

Ten years would pass before Zeppelin began to work seriously on his designs for a controllable balloon, although he did continue to research the literature then available on the subject. He returned to Germany with a rank of captain and served on the personal staff of King Charles I of Württemberg during the war between Austria and Prussia. He received his first decoration for bravery—the Knight's Cross—during the Battle of Aschaffenburg in 1866; he earned a second commendation—the Royal Cross, First Class—for his exploits during the war with France in 1870. During the siege of Paris, he again had the opportunity to observe the effective use of free-floating balloons during a military operation. The siege lasted for four months, but more than a hundred influential military and political leaders were able to escape from the city using a total of sixty-four hot-air balloons. Convinced that this exploit had seriously prolonged the war, Zeppelin renewed his studies of balloons and began developing some preliminary designs for a rigid dirigible.

The specifications that he chose for his airship were to remain practically unchanged over the course of his career. He envisioned an elongated, aerodynamically shaped airship with an internal, lightweight skeletal framework supported by a number of separate gas-filled cells attached to the framework. The payload and the engines would be contained in separate gondolas suspended below the main structure; the control surfaces, such as rudders, would be attached to the exterior of the airship in a position that would provide maximum control over direction and attitude. In 1887, he sent a letter to the king describing his designs and outlining the various applications that he could foresee for such an airship. Zeppelin believed that his invention would be very important in warfare, suitable for civilian transport, and beneficial for voyages of exploration and discovery.

Although his political and military career had flourished (he was promoted to the rank of brigadier general in 1888), Zeppelin decided to devote more of his time to his family; thus, in 1890 he retired from the army and returned to his home in Stuttgart. This early retirement allowed him to continue the development of his airship.

The realization of his dream of powered, controlled flight would not be fulfilled for another decade. He hired Theodore Kolb, an experienced engineer, and together they began a series of tests on engines, propellers, and construction materials. The most serious problem confronting Zeppelin—one that would continue to impede his work throughout the next fifteen years—was financing the construction of his design. He appealed to his friends in court, but the government was not interested in funding his experiments; the war ministry believed that Zeppelin's ideas were too radical. In 1896 Zeppelin sent a report on his designs and experiments to the German Association of Engineers with the request that they review his designs and perhaps support his request for funds from the government. The society reported favorably on the project; as a result, a company was formed for the construction of the airship, and solicitations were made to the public for support. Approximately 90 percent of the $250,000 required for the project was obtained through public subscriptions and the remainder came from Zeppelin's personal funds. The Daimler Motorworks was contracted to design and build a lightweight gasoline engine. The company also needed to find a supplier of the then-scarce metal aluminum.

On July 2, 1900, Zeppelin's dream became a reality: The first rigid, engine-powered airship was ready for its first flight. The floating hangar was turned into the wind and the airship was pulled out by a small steamer. To the crowd of spectators on the shore, it was an impressive sight. The LZ-1 was a cigar-shaped airship 419 feet long and thirty-eight feet in diameter, supported by seventeen gas cells containing eleven thousand cubic meters of gas. Suspended below the airship were two gondolas connected by a long gangplank; the rear gondola supported two Daimler gasoline engines turning four propellers. At 8:03 A.M., the airship was freed of its restraining ropes, and, driven by its propellers, the ship moved away at a speed of about eight miles per hour. The flight lasted about fifteen minutes and the ship landed safely near Immenstaad. Although there had been some difficulties with the directional controls, Zeppelin declared that the flight was a success. In the next four months, the LZ-1 made two more flights, during which refinements to the engines and steering mechanisms were tested. Airspeed approached eighteen miles per hour and control of the airship improved. By then, however, the funds had become depleted and the company could no longer pay for material and gas. As a result, the LZ-1 was dismantled and the hangar torn down.

During the next five years Zeppelin used his entire personal fortune to begin construction of a second ship. Through lotteries and other public appeals he was able to raise enough money to finish the LZ-2. It flew successfully in 1906 and demonstrated the increased speed and control that the new eighty-five-horsepower engines provided. Unfortunately, the ship was destroyed by fire during a storm shortly after its first flight. Completely destitute and disheartened by the disaster, Zeppelin thought that his work was at an end. Public sentiment had turned in his favor, however, and, as a result, the Parliament voted to subsidize the construction of the LZ-3. It proved to be such a success that the government authorized a sum to be included in the annual budget for the construction and testing of airships.

For the next eleven years, Zeppelin worked tirelessly on the design and testing of more than a hundred airships. He was at the helm of the LZ-4 during its flight from Lake Constance to Switzerland. The airship carried eleven passengers at the amazing speed of forty miles per hour. In 1912, he piloted the navy's first ship (LZ-12) on its historic trip of more than a thousand miles to and from Denmark. He helped to develop the airships used in the first commercial airline routes, and during World War I he supervised the construction of more than a hundred airships for the army and navy.

### *Summary*

The first decade of human flight is representative of human ingenuity in its most adventuresome and audacious form. In particular, the sight of the massive airships that appeared in the skies over Germany, Great Britain, France, and the United States seemed to symbolize the inevitable mastery of humankind over the forces of nature. It is not often remembered that three years before the flight of Orville and Wilbur Wright, Ferdinand von Zeppelin and a crew of three had piloted a four-hundred-foot-long airship on a flight over southern Germany for a distance of four miles and at an altitude of thirteen hundred feet. Furthermore, in the year 1910, when a single American pilot took forty-nine days to fly thirty-two hundred miles across the United States, Zeppelin's dirigible (LZ-6) had flown thirty-four trips carrying a total of eleven hundred passengers for a distance of thirty-one hundred miles.

The technological innovations that accompanied the development of the airship found applications in aircraft design and other areas of engineering. Zeppelin was responsible for the development of the alloy Duralumin in his search for lighter and stronger structural materials. Zeppelin was convinced that his airships would be an important asset to the army in the event of war but, ironically, it was the German navy that derived the most benefit from his Zeppelins. At the outbreak of World War I, several of Zeppelin's airships were armed with machine guns and fitted with bomb racks, but they proved to be susceptible to the vagaries of the weather and attacks by enemy aircraft; thus, they were only marginally effective as weapons. Yet the navy found that their long range made them ideally suited to scout the location of enemy warships and eventually had more than sixty airships in service during the war. In January, 1915, two army airships did succeed in crossing the English Channel to discharge their small loads of bombs on two English cities, but the damage was more psychological than real. This air raid demonstrated one important fact: Cities and civilians could no longer rely on fortifications or oceans to protect them from feeling the effects of war. The Zeppelins were perceived to be more of a threat than they actually proved to be, but their existence prompted the British to develop more effective antiaircraft weapons and stimulated the development of high-performance aircraft capable of flying to the high altitudes at which the airships operated.

On the occasion of his seventieth birthday, Zeppelin expressed the hope that one day his airships would provide the means to bring together the peoples of the world; in fact, he did live long enough to see the establishment of regular air routes between a number of cities in Europe. His airship, the *Victoria Luise*, made nearly five hundred scheduled flights carrying a total of ninety-eight hundred passengers. Unfortunately, he did not live to see the great flights of the 1920's and 1930's: the flight of the British R34 across the Atlantic Ocean in July of 1919, of the *Norge*, four thousand miles across the North Pole in 1926, and of the *Graf Zeppelin* around the world in 1929.

The culmination of Zeppelin's work was the magnificent airships—the *Hindenburg* and the *Graf Zeppelin*. From 1928 to 1937, they carried a total of forty thousand passengers on regularly scheduled flights between Germany, New York, and Buenos Aires, providing accommodations and service comparable to those of the finest ocean liners. For a time it appeared that the airship would dominate long-distance air travel, but the explosion of the *Hindenburg* at Lakehurst Naval Station in 1937 ended that possibility; thereafter, production of rigid airships ceased.

*Bibliography*

Goldsmith, Margaret. *Zeppelin: A Biography*. New York: William Morrow, 1931. A general biography containing many personal anecdotes that illustrate the unique personality of the subject.

Hoyt, Edwin P. *The Zeppelins*. New York: Lothrop, Lee & Shepard, 1969. An abbreviated account of the development of the Zeppelins with an emphasis on the use of the airship as a military weapon.

Lehman, Ernst A., and Howard L. Mingos. *The Zeppelins*. New York: Sears, 1927. An account of the wartime activities of Germany's airship squadrons by two of Zeppelin's associates.

Nitske, W. Robert. *The Zeppelin Story.* South Brunswick, N.J.: A. S. Barnes, 1977. A general history of the development of the rigid airship, beginning with the experiments with free-floating balloons and concluding with the development of successful long-range airships capable of transoceanic travel.

Ventry, Lord, and Eugène M. Koleśnik. *Airship Saga: The History of Airships Seen Through the Eyes of the Men Who Designed, Built, and Flew Them*. Poole, Dorset, England: Blandford Press, 1982. A pictorial history of the airship containing numerous personal accounts of the inventors and aviators who flew them.

*C. D. Alexander*

# CLARA ZETKIN

*Born:* July 5, 1857; Wiederau, Saxony

*Died:* June 20, 1933; Arkhangelskoye, near Moscow, U.S.S.R.

*Areas of Achievement:* Women's rights, politics, social reform, trade unionism

*Contribution:* With Friedrich Engels and August Bebel, Zetkin pioneered a Marxist analysis of women's status in a capitalist society. Her objective was to create a new social order free of political and economic oppression.

## *Early Life*

Clara Eissner, the eldest of three children, was born in Wiederau near Leipzig in Saxony, a small town of textile workers and small farmers. Her father, Gottfried Eissner, poor but educated, was the village schoolteacher and church organist. His second wife, Josephine Vitale Eissner, was the widow of a doctor in Leipzig, a believer in the French Revolutionary ideals of liberty, equality, and fraternity. Frau Eissner founded in Wiederau a *Frauenverein*, or women's educational society, to teach local women to expect and get economic equality.

Women's educational societies of this type were offshoots of the bourgeois German Women's Association and the Federation of German Women's Associations, led by feminist idealists such as Auguste Schmidt and Luise Otto. In 1872, when Herr Eissner retired, the family moved to Leipzig so that Clara could attend the Van Steyber Institute founded by Schmidt and Otto. While at the institute from 1875 to 1878, Clara read social democratic newspapers and other socialist writings and attended meetings of the Leipzig Women's Education Society and the National Association of German Women.

In 1878, Clara met some local Russian students and émigrés, who introduced her to Wilhelm Liebknecht's German Social Democratic Party (SPD), and her political education began. One of the émigrés from Odessa, Russia, Ossip Zetkin, introduced Clara to scientific socialism and the writings of Karl Marx and Friedrich Engels. He also encouraged her to live a working-class life-style and to attend lectures of the Leipzig Worker's Education Society. In 1879, she visited Russia, and during an extensive stay she developed a strong appreciation of Russian revolutionary spirit. Clara's newly raised proletarian consciousness led to a break with her family and her mentor, Schmidt.

When Ossip was expelled from Germany for illegal political activity under the government's 1878 Anti-Socialist Law, Clara left Germany. First, she went to Linz, Austria, where she tutored factory workers. In 1882, she moved to Zurich with leaders of the exiled SPD to write propaganda for

Party literature to be smuggled into Germany. In November, 1882, after five months in Zurich, Clara moved to Paris to join Zetkin. Although she did not marry him, for fear of losing her German citizenship, Clara took Ossip's name and had two sons by him, Maxim (1883) and Konstantine (1885).

*Life's Work*

During these years in Paris, Clara Zetkin began her life's work of using scientific socialism to improve the condition of the proletariat and to achieve equality for proletarian women. Ironically, the second stage in her evolution from political theorist to activist resulted from a reconciliation with her bourgeois family. In 1886, Zetkin succumbed to the harsh poverty of the Paris years and, suffering from tuberculosis, was invited by her family to return to Leipzig to convalesce. In Leipzig, she gave her first public speech to explain Bebel's ideas in his book *Die Frau und der Sozialismus* (1879; *Woman and Socialism*, 1910). Bebel's theory was that class revolution would end the oppression of both workers and women and lead to women's economic development and equality with men. This was Zetkin's view as well.

Returning to Paris, Zetkin nursed Ossip until his death in January, 1889, from spinal tuberculosis. Zetkin's grief was cut short by the need to prepare for the Second International Congress, which met in Paris on the centennial of Bastille Day (July 14, 1889). As one of only eight official woman delegates, Zetkin represented working-class women of Berlin and had clearly moved from theory to activism. Zetkin's speech, published later as *Die Arbeiterinnen und Frauenfrage der Gegenwart* (1889; *Working Women and the Contemporary Woman Question*, 1984), stated clearly that the issue of women's emancipation is a question of work. Blaming capitalism for women's oppression, Zetkin declared that women's work outside the home would not result in an improvement of the family income or independence until women's labor no longer resulted simply in profits for capitalists. Neither political equality nor access to education and the benefits of capitalism would solve the problem; only a social revolution and the end of the capitalist system would. At the congress, however, Zetkin's view that women should have no special privileges was vetoed. The delegates favored equal pay for equal work and opposed dangerous work for women.

At this Second International, Zetkin was named one of seven women to create the Berlin Agitation Committee responsible for educating and recruiting women into the SPD. This committee became the executive of a Socialist women's movement. Zetkin accepted this appointment only because women were by German law forbidden membership in political parties; she believed that women should be equal members of the party.

In 1890, the Reichstag did not renew Otto von Bismarck's Anti-Socialist

Laws, and the SPD exiles returned to Germany. In Stuttgart, Zetkin was named editor of *Die Gleichheit*, the SPD's journal for women. The first issue, in January, 1892, defined the journal's policy and purpose as educating enlightened women about Marxism and Social Democratic principles and the need for economic equality while opposing bourgeois feminist emphasis on reforms of the law.

During these years when women could not belong to the SPD, the trade union movement served as a means of recruiting women. Zetkin printed handbills, gathered strike funds, and set up international communication networks among the unions. She gave more than three hundred speeches, and, by 1896 and the SPD Congress at Gotha, her position on women had changed in response to the contemporary German political context. Although Zetkin still believed that the needs of proletarian women were different from those of bourgeois women and that only the destruction of the capitalist system would relieve women's oppression, she conceded that women needed special protections to allow them to be mothers as well as workers. Zetkin did not claim special privilege, however, and, while working for the SPD, she also reared her two sons. Zetkin also conceded that women's suffrage would make socialism stronger in the fight against capitalism.

Such concessions were the exception not the rule. As early as 1890, Zetkin was fighting the battle against Eduard Bernstein's revisionist interpretation of Marx's doctrine that approved compromise with capitalism and the abandonment of the class struggle. The years after 1900 saw the SPD and the women's movement become more concerned with protective legislation—insurance benefits, education, and suffrage. Zetkin found herself under attack as well. Revisionists complained that *Die Gleichheit* under Zetkin's leadership was too theoretical and demanded that the journal appeal to a more general audience. In 1905, as the circulation began to grow, she added supplements for housewives and for children, until by 1914, with a readership of 125,000, these features became a regular part of the paper.

Complaints against Zetkin were difficult to act upon because she had become an important leader in the SPD. Although women could not be members of the SPD until 1908, after 1890 women were elected to party congresses, and in 1895 Zetkin was the first woman elected to sit on the SPD governing body. In 1906, she was appointed one of seven members of the central committee on education at a time when the German government was trying to strengthen religious influence in the schools.

In 1908, when women were finally permitted to participate legally in political party activity, Zetkin fought hard to preserve an autonomous women's movement both to prevent decisions about women from being made by a predominantly male SPD executive committee and to preserve a radical enclave within the party. Again Zetkin's perspective had changed. She saw not only that proletarian women had different needs from those of bourgeois women but also that proletarian women had different needs from proletarian men. In 1907, the First International Women's Conference was held in Stuttgart at the same time that the International Socialist Congress was meeting there. A separate International Women's Bureau was created with Zetkin as Secretary and *Die Gleichheit* as the official organ of communication. The Second International Women's Conference met in 1910 in Copenhagen, where Zetkin led the fight to oppose socialist support for a restricted female suffrage as proposed in Great Britain and Belgium.

As Europe moved closer to war, Zetkin, along with Rosa Luxemburg and other radical socialists, found their struggle against revisionism becoming more difficult and unpopular. They had to fight not only the German government and capitalism but also a more conservative SPD that favored parliamentary methods and officially opposed the mass strike. In 1911, at the SPD Congress in Jena, Zetkin and Luxemburg fought unsuccessfully to get the party to condemn all imperialism, including that of Germany. On August 4, 1914, Zetkin, Luxemburg, Franz Mehring, and Karl Liebknecht denounced the party's decision to vote for war credits. In March, 1915, Zetkin, without party permission, organized another women's conference to protest the war. After spending a few months in protective custody for continuing to oppose the government in *Die Gleichheit* against party orders, Zetkin was finally removed as editor by the SPD in May, 1917. They claimed her views in support of the Bolshevik Revolution and against war were unpalatable to women.

By this time Zetkin had transferred her political allegiance first to the Independent Social-Democratic Party, or antiwar socialists, and then had joined Liebknecht, Luxemburg, and Mehring as a founding member of the Gruppe Internationale, or the Spartacus League, which in November, 1918, became the German Communist Party (KPD).

Zetkin's message, however, did not change. In 1919, addressing the Comintern (the Third International Congress), Zetkin reminded the party that a dictatorship of the proletariat could not work without proletarian women. She warned the Communist Party to educate women for their role in the international struggle. Elected international secretary of Communist women in 1920, Zetkin proclaimed again that the woman question was part of the worker question.

Zetkin's new postwar political duties required her to live part of the time in the Soviet Union, where she worked with Vladimir Ilich Lenin and Aleksandra Kollontai, the only Russian woman on the Comintern. Although her health was not good, Zetkin continued to write and speak out against persecution, including racist acts in the United States. In addition, she represented the German Communist Party in the Reichstag as long as Adolf Hitler allowed it to meet. In the summer of 1932, she went to Berlin to convene the Reichstag, a privilege traditionally exercised by the eldest living member.

She took the opportunity to denounce Fascism and Hitler and to appeal for the creation of a United Front of Workers to include the millions of laboring women. Within a year, she died, on June 20, 1933, in the Soviet Union.

*Summary*

Although Clara Zetkin was estranged from Soviet politics after the death of Lenin, she was buried with great ceremony in the Kremlin wall. Attending her funeral and eulogizing her were Soviet and Eastern European Communist officials, including Joseph Stalin, Nadezhda Krupskaya (Lenin's widow), Kollontai, Nikolai Ivanovich Bukharin, Andrei Marti of Czechoslovakia, Karl Radek of Germany, and Béla Kun of Hungary.

Zetkin had little personal life, but she reared her two sons and, in 1899, she married the painter Georg Friedrich Zundel, eighteen years younger. This marriage lapsed during World War I and ended in divorce in 1927, when Zetkin was seventy. Politics was the core of her being. In this political struggle, it was Zetkin's dynamic personality that allowed her to carry on simultaneously the struggle with and against socialist men, fighting with them for class and party solidarity and against them for women's autonomy and power. A staunch defender of the proletariat, from first to last, she saw women's liberation in the larger historical context of the workers' drive for socialism. Women's problems, she believed, would be solved only by socioeconomic change and through class struggle. An internationalist to the end, she opposed war as a capitalist tool against the workers. Clear-sighted and committed, Zetkin lived and died devoted to her causes.

*Bibliography*

Boxer, Marilyn J., and Jean H. Quataert, eds. *Socialist Women: European Socialist Feminism in the Nineteenth and Early Twentieth Centuries*. New York: Elsevier, 1978. A collection of articles on the relationship of women's issues and socialism linking Zetkin to the movement in several European countries.

Evans, Richard J. "Theory and Practice in German Social Democracy, 1880-1914: Clara Zetkin and the Socialist Theory of Women's Emancipation." *History of Political Thought* 3 (Summer, 1982): 285-304. Contrasts Zetkin's views about the women's movement in 1889 with those of 1896 seen in the contemporary German political context. Her new position favored a separate Socialist women's organization and women's suffrage.

Nettl, J. P. *Rosa Luxemburg*. 2 vols. London: Oxford University Press, 1966. There is also a one-volume abridged edition (London: Oxford University Press, 1969). Illuminates the significant relationship between Zetkin and Luxemburg.

Pore, Renate. *A Conflict of Interest: Women in German Social Democracy, 1919-1933*. Westport, Conn.: Greenwood Press, 1981. Attributes the character of women's involvement in the SPD to Zetkin, lauding her unswerving adherence to the twofold fight for socialism and women's rights.

Porter, Cathy. *Alexandra Kollontai: The Lonely Struggle of the Woman Who Defied Lenin*. New York: Dial Press, 1980. Contains some discussion of the relationship of Zetkin and the Soviet government after World War I.

Zetkin, Clara. *Clara Zetkin: Selected Writings*. Edited by Philip S. Foner. Translated by Kai Schoenhals. Foreword by Angela Y. Davis. New York: International Publishers, 1984. The introduction supplies the most complete analytical survey published in English of Zetkin's life and ideas. It draws substantially on an unpublished Ph.D. thesis by Karen Honeycutt.

*Loretta Turner Johnson*

# GEORGY KONSTANTINOVICH ZHUKOV

*Born:* December 2, 1896; Strelkovka, Russia

*Died:* June 18, 1974; Moscow, U.S.S.R.

*Areas of Achievement:* The military, government, and politics

*Contribution:* Zhukov was the most important Soviet staff and field commander throughout World War II and was involved in the planning and/or execution of all the primary battles and campaigns against the Germans. Zhukov was the first career military man to be selected as a member of the Presidium (Politburo) of the Communist Party, came to be feared as a rival by both Joseph Stalin and Nikita S. Khrushchev, and was decisive in preventing Khrushchev's ouster in 1957.

## *Early Life*

Georgy Konstantinovich Zhukov was born December 2, 1896, in the village of Strelkovka, Kaluga Oblast, Russia. Strelkovka is approximately one hundred miles southwest of Moscow. Zhukov was born to poor peasants, his father serving as the village shoemaker. At eleven years of age, since his parents could no longer afford to pay for his education, he was taken in to be reared by his grandfather. His grandfather lived in Moscow, where he was a laborer in a metallurgical plant. Zhukov worked at several menial jobs and then apprenticed himself to a furrier and leather dresser. He continued his schooling and became a master at his trade. Then, in 1915, the military was calling up those born in 1896, so he was inducted into the czarist army.

Zhukov was placed in the Tenth Novgorod Dragoon Regiment, which received a short training period before being ordered to the front lines. From 1915 to 1917, the regiment was almost constantly engaged in battle. He became known throughout the unit for his enthusiasm and bravery, and was promoted through the ranks until he attained the highest noncommissioned rank. He was presented twice with the Cross of St. George, the highest military award given to noncommissioned officers. Soon after the February Revolution in 1917, the soldiers of his unit elected him to be chairman of the Squadron Soviet (council) and their representative on the regimental soviet of deputies. The Soviets exerted control over the army, allowing the officers to do only what they approved, and therefore Zhukov's leadership role was significant.

After the October Revolution that same year brought the Bolsheviks to power, Zhukov helped in the organization of the Red Army, and, during the Russian Civil War (1918-1920) and Polish War (1920), he served in the Red Cavalry. He began as platoon commander and then advanced to squadron commander in the important First Cavalry Army, which was the shock force of the Red military. The commander of his brigade was Semyon K. Timoshenko, future marshal and defense minister, who became Zhukov's sponsor during the interwar period. Zhukov was wounded but recovered to fight anew, and for his many contributions he received many citations in Orders of the Day, an engraved saber from the group commander, a gold watch with an inscribed commendation from the Defense Council of the Soviet Republic, and the highest army military decoration, the Order of the Red Banner.

Zhukov chose a professional military career at the end of the wars. He had joined the Communist Party in March, 1919, and was a member the rest of his life. He was graduated from an advanced training program for cavalry officers in 1925. From 1928 to 1931, he attended the Frunze Military Academy, specializing in armored operations. He also traveled to Germany in the 1920's to study armor. In 1936 and 1937, Stalin had him and other astute observers gather information from the Spanish Civil War, including the testing of Soviet tank tactics in actual combat. He was able to survive the massive military purge in 1937, perhaps because he was out of the country. Thus, he and other junior officers were blessed subsequently with the opportunity to rise rapidly in rank and position because of the vacancies created. Zhukov already had served successively as commander of a cavalry regiment, brigade, and division, and in 1937-1938 he was commander of the Third, then the Sixth Cavalry Corps. In 1938-1939, he was designated the deputy commander of cavalry, Belorussian Military District. In 1939, he was ordered to head the Far East First Army Group with the mission of driving Japanese invaders out of the Mongolian People's Republic. His success caused the Presidium of the Supreme Soviet to bestow on him the highest military award of his country, the Golden Star with title of Hero of the Soviet Union. In January, 1940, he was appointed chief of staff of the Soviet forces fighting the Finns. In May, 1940, Zhukov was promoted to general of the army and was assigned commander of the Kiev Military District. From February to the end of July, 1941, he was given the positions of chief of the general staff of the Soviet army and deputy people's commissar of defense of the Soviet Union. Thereby, at age forty-four, Zhukov occupied the second-highest military offices of his country, with the top positions of marshall of the Soviet Union and minister of defense entrusted to his benefactor, Timoshenko. He also was designated an alternate member of the Central Committee of the Communist Party in February, 1941.

### *Life's Work*

During World War II, Zhukov personally and directly was important to the planning or the implementation, or both, of all the main battles and campaigns. Often he was in Moscow serving as a leading figure in the supreme command headquarters. At such times, his chief occupation was with overall strategy and the formulation of specific campaign plans. In several instances, he was selected by Stalin personally to represent him and supreme headquarters on field duty at the front line. When acting in such a capacity, he was endowed with virtually unlimited powers of command and decision-making. When Leningrad was threatened so quickly in 1941, Zhukov hurriedly was dispatched there in September to halt the invading forces and to organize more adequate and permanent defenses. In October, he moved quickly to Moscow to direct the frantic preparations for saving that most important city, preparations that continued on into 1942. His skillful use of reserve troops undoubtedly saved Moscow from being taken. As commander in chief of the Western Front during the winter of 1941-1942, he also took advantage of the Russian weather to direct offensive actions against the climatically unprepared enemy. When the Nazis resumed offensive operations from spring to fall of 1942, Zhukov was in charge of defensive actions and acted with particular significance in planning the defense of the Caucasus. In August, he was appointed first deputy people's commissar of defense and deputy supreme commander in chief, second only to Stalin.

The struggle for Stalingrad had already begun, and Zhukov became responsible for planning its defense and coordinating the movements of the various forces. He deserves much credit for the ultimate victory that finally came in January, 1943, in this greatest battle of World War II and its turning point in the European theater. For his achievement he was named marshal of the Soviet Union, which was the country's highest military title. He then planned and commanded the largest tank battle of the war at Kursk-Orel, was in charge of devising the strategies for the offensives of 1944 and overseeing their execution, and personally commanded the final drive on Berlin. In both 1944 and 1945, he again was designated Hero of the Soviet Union. It seemed fitting that in Berlin on May 8 of the latter year, it was Marshal Zhukov, in the name of the Soviet Union, who accepted the unconditional German surrender from Field Marshal Wilhelm Keitel.

From the end of the war until January of the following year, Zhukov stayed in Germany as the commander of the Soviet occupation forces and the Soviet representative on the Allied Control Commission. Then he was recalled to the Soviet Union to serve as deputy minister of defense and commander in chief of the Soviet ground forces. Yet his great popularity as the returning war hero apparently caused Stalin to view him as a potential threat, for soon Zhukov was relieved of both positions and given assignments outside the capital city. First he was relegated to the position of commander of the Odessa Military District. Then his appointment to command the Ural Military District was even more of a demotion. From 1946 through 1952, therefore, Zhukov was removed from significant and highly visible government activities. Even historical writings on the war years made mention of his name much less frequently, and his accomplishments were described in a fashion similar to that used to describe those of many other leaders. Almost unlimited praise and credit were given to Stalin for every important decision and activity of the war.

Zhukov's role in affairs changed immediately, however, with Stalin's death in March, 1953. When a new government was formed three days later, he was named first deputy to Minister of Defense Nikolai Bulganin, who was a Communist Party and Soviet government politician. Zhukov was listed as the highest ranking Soviet military officer, and his position was indicative of the importance that the new leaders attributed to the military establishment. The army cooperated in July in the arrest and death of Lavrenti Beria, secret police chief, and Zhukov was given full membership in the Party's Central Committee. Military leaders, particularly Zhukov, were important political activists in the power struggle that ensued between Khrushchev and Georgi M. Malenkov. Zhukov backed Khrushchev because of their long friendship and the support by Malenkov of a reduction in military expenditures. In February, 1955, following his success, Khrushchev replaced Malenkov with Bulganin as chairman of the council of ministers and gave to Zhukov the position of minister of defense.

Thereafter, Zhukov's power and influence in not only the military but also the political and governmental activities of the Soviet Union were enormous. That same year he went with Khrushchev and Bulganin to the Geneva Conference and in 1957 visited Yugoslavia and Albania. At the Twentieth Party Congress in February, 1956, he was selected for alternate membership in the Presidium. That December, on the occasion of his sixtieth birthday, he became the only man to be awarded his fourth Golden Star and designated four times Hero of the Soviet Union. The apex of his political power and influence occurred the next spring and summer as a majority of the Presidium attempted to remove Khrushchev as top leader. Zhukov stated that the armed forces would "not permit anyone to bid for power" and then provided planes for Central Committee members to come quickly to Moscow to settle the crisis by reversing the decision of the Presidium. In addition, the Central Committee elected Zhukov a full member of the Party Presidium, a position of leadership and an honor that no other career military man has attained.

Circumstances changed abruptly, however, and on October 26, 1957, Zhukov was removed as minister of defense. A week later he was dismissed from his Presidium and Central Committee positions "for violating Leninist principles concerning the administration of the armed forces." He had implemented programs to enhance military professionalism that lessened control from the Party's political advisers. This brought him into fundamental disagreement with Khrushchev and most other leading Party officials. Zhukov was accused of fostering a personality cult within the armed forces, and, along with his removal from all Party and government positions, he was publicly disgraced for allegedly questioning Party leadership of the military. He retired from active military service.

Zhukov completely disappeared from Soviet public affairs until after Khrushchev's tenure as top Party and government leader ended in the fall of

1964. In addition, few saw him in a private capacity. Official publications stated little in a positive sense about him during this time. In 1965, however, at the twentieth anniversary celebration of the victory over Germany, he made his first major public appearance. He was seen by thousands with other noted Soviet figures atop Vladimir Ilich Lenin's tomb in Red Square. On December 1 of the following year, he was awarded for the sixth time the Order of Lenin in recognition of "services to the armed forces." Three years later, his youth and military memoirs, *Vospominaniia i razmyshleniia* (1969; *The Memoirs of Marshal Zhukov*, 1971), were published in the official magazine of the ministry of defense, five years before his death.

*Summary*

Georgy Konstantinovich Zhukov's greatest achievements were in the realm of military leadership. In this area, his plans, decisions, and influence directly affected the lives of millions of combatants and the survivability of his country during its period of crisis. They impacted as well on the power levels and relationships between nations. The full significance of his impact can be appreciated even more by the fact that a leading Soviet officer wrote later that Zhukov at times even corrected Stalin, something no one else dared even to try to do. It was during the mammoth struggle of World War II that Zhukov made such a major difference. His strategical and tactical plans were often very bold and innovative. Thus, it can readily be assumed that, in his absence, other actions, even very different ones at times, would have been undertaken. He was the top military figure throughout the conflict, second in power to only Stalin himself, was involved with all the great battle areas, and was the dominant general in both defensive and offensive actions against the Nazis. As such, his achievements are difficult to overestimate.

Second only to his military contributions were those Zhukov made in the area of politics and government. After the death of Stalin, in a time of great uncertainty, the military leaders became a powerful political force. Certain of them, most especially Zhukov, were key players in the triumph of Khrushchev over Malenkov in their struggle for power. The height of Zhukov's political power and influence came in 1957, when he worked successfully with others to prevent a majority of the Presidium from ousting Khrushchev as top party leader. He became the first professional military man to become an alternate member, then a full member, of the Presidium of the Communist Party.

In addition to the awards and honors previously mentioned, a host of others were bestowed upon Zhukov in his lifetime. He became the most decorated military person in Soviet history. After his death in 1974, he was accorded the final great honor of being buried beside the Kremlin Wall in Red Square with his country's other leading heroes.

*Bibliography*

Bialer, Seweryn, ed. *Stalin and His Generals: Soviet Military Memoirs of World War II*. New York: Pegasus, 1969. This book is authored by military officers, from the top ones down to the regimental level. Zhukov is the author of three articles and is the object of much comment by his contemporaries. Contains maps, notes, and a biographical index.

Chaney, Otto Preston, Jr. *Zhukov*. Norman: University of Oklahoma Press, 1971. This is probably the best and most useful of all books on Zhukov. It is fair and judicious, researched thoroughly, and comprehensive. Contains maps, illustrations, notes, a bibliography, appendices, and an index.

Clark, Alan. *Barbarossa: The Russian-German Conflict, 1941-1945*. New York: William Morrow, 1965. This work is a detailed and balanced account done in a scholarly manner after much research. There is much about Zhukov. It is a good source to begin with to get the overall picture. Contains maps, illustrations, charts, notes, a bibliography, and an index.

Erickson, John. *The Soviet High Command: A Military-Political History, 1918-1941*. New York: St. Martin's Press, 1962. Zhukov appears a surprising amount in this exhaustive narrative. It is well researched and is a good source for Zhukov in the 1918-1941 years. Contains maps, notes, appendices, a bibliography, and an index.

Kerr, Walter. *The Russian Army: Its Men, Its Leaders, and Its Battles*. New York: Alfred A. Knopf, 1944. Kerr was a correspondent in the Soviet Union during World War II and observed much and interviewed many. He writes in a down-to-earth fashion. Zhukov appears often. Contains maps and an index.

Shtemenko, Sergei M. *The Soviet General Staff at War, 1941-1945*. Translated by Robert Daglish. Moscow: Progess, 1970. Shtemenko served on the general staff, but he was also knowledgeable about front-line activities. His book is written from the perspective of a devoted nationalist and Communist, but it contains much good inside information. Zhukov is mentioned often. Contains maps and illustrations.

Werth, Alexander. *Russia at War, 1941-1945*. New York: Dutton, 1964. Extensive treatment is given to Zhukov in this balanced account of Soviet events from 1939 to 1945. Werth experienced many of the matters he writes about, presented in an easy, flowing style. He allows the reader to see Zhukov's role within the full perspective of Soviet affairs. Contains maps, a chronological table, a bibliography, and an index.

Zhukov, Georgy. *The Memoirs of Marshal Zhukov*. New York: Delacorte Press, 1971. Zhukov writes of his childhood and youth and of his military life to April, 1946. It is a detailed account that contains much not found elsewhere. Contains maps and illustrations.

*James G. Nutsch*

# INDEXES

# BIOGRAPHICAL INDEX

## BIOGRAPHICAL INDEX

# BIOGRAPHICAL INDEX

# AREAS OF ACHIEVEMENT

## AREAS OF ACHIEVEMENT

# GEOGRAPHICAL INDEX

GEOGRAPHICAL INDEX